The Audio Programming Book

The Audio Programming Book

edited by Richard Boulanger and Victor Lazzarini

foreword by Max V. Mathews

The MIT Press
Cambridge, Massachusetts
London, England

For information about quantity discounts, email specialsales@mitpress.mit.edu.

Set in Stone Serif and Stone Sans on 3B2 by Asco Typesetters, Hong Kong. Printed and bound in the United States of America.

Library of Congress Cataloging-in-Publication Data

The audio programming book / edited by Richard Boulanger and Victor Lazzarini; foreword by Max Mathews.
    p.   cm.
Includes bibliographical references and index.
ISBN 978-0-262-01446-5 (hardcover : alk. paper) 1. Computer sound processing. 2. Signal processing—Digital techniques. 3. Music—Computer programs. I. Boulanger, Richard Charles, 1956–. II. Lazzarini, Victor, 1969–.
ML74.3.A93   2011
006.5—dc22   2010001731

10   9   8   7   6   5   4   3

This book is humbly dedicated to our teachers, mentors, and friends Max V. Mathews, F. Richard Moore, and Barry Vercoe. They paved the way and they showed the way. They were great explorers who freely and passionately shared their discoveries, their treasures—their source code. Moreover, they invited every one of us to join them on the journey, to follow their example, and to find ways to become a part of their great adventure and to build upon the solid foundation that they laid down for us. All the contributors to this book stand on the shoulders of these three giants of computer music. It is our hope that the book will help the next generation to fully appreciate the great gifts of Mathews (MUSIC V), Moore (cmusic), and Vercoe (Csound), and that it will help them find their own unique and inspiring way to take the world one step further on this extraordinary audio adventure.

Contents

Foreword by Max V. Mathews   xi

Preface   xiii

Acknowledgments   xv

Introduction   xxi

C Programming Basics

0   An Overview of the C Language with Some Elements of C++   3
Victor Lazzarini and Richard Boulanger

1   Programming in C   55
Richard Dobson

Audio Programming Basics

2   Audio Programming in C   185
Richard Dobson

3   Working with Audio Streams   329
Gabriel Maldonado

4   Introduction to Program Design   383
John ffitch

Audio Programming Essentials

5   Introduction to Digital Audio Signals   431
Victor Lazzarini

6   Time-Domain Audio Programming   463
Victor Lazzarini

Spectral Audio Programming

7   Spectral Audio Programming Basics: The DFT, the FFT, and Convolution   521
Victor Lazzarini

8   The STFT and Spectral Processing   539
Victor Lazzarini

9   Programming the Phase Vocoder   557
Victor Lazzarini

Programming Csound Opcodes

10   Understanding an Opcode in Csound   581
John ffitch

11   Spectral Opcodes   617
Victor Lazzarini

Algorithmic Synthesis and Music Programming

12   A Modular Synthesizer Simulation Program   629
Eric Lyon

13   Using C to Generate Scores   655
John ffitch

14   Modeling Orchestral Composition   677
Steven Yi

Appendixes

A   Command-Line Tools Reference   697
Jonathan Bailey

B   Debugging Software with the GNU Debugger   719
Jonathan Bailey

C   Soundfiles, Soundfile Formats, and *libsndfile*   739
Victor Lazzarini

D   An Introduction to Real-Time Audio IO with PortAudio   771
Victor Lazzarini

E   MIDI Programming with PortMIDI   783
Victor Lazzarini

F   Computer Architecture, Structures, and Languages   797
John ffitch

G   Glossary   823
John ffitch with Richard Dobson, Victor Lazzarini, and Richard Boulanger

H   An Audio Programmer's Guide to Mathematical Expressions   855
John ffitch

Contents of the DVD   869

References   873
About the Authors   879
Index   881

Foreword

This is not just a book; it is an encyclopedia of mathematical and programming techniques for audio signal processing. It is an encyclopedia focused on the future, but built upon the massive foundations of past mathematical, signal processing, and programming sciences.

It is clearly written and easy to understand, by both human readers and computers. It gives complete information, from the basic mathematics to the detailed programs needed to make sound. It is the essential library, not only for computer musicians, but also for all computer scientists, including those who work in the fields of communication and artificial intelligence.

Today the dominant language in which to write programs is C (including C++). A half-century ago, sound synthesis programs for music were written in assembly language. The resulting music had few voices and uninteresting timbres. Programs were tedious to write. Block diagram compilers, including MUSIC V, cmusic, and Csound, greatly expanded the musical possibilities by giving composers and sound designers tools with which to create their own timbres from blocks of code—oscillators, envelopes, filters, mixers, etc. These blocks performed tasks that electronic musicians were familiar with and that they could understand. Block diagram compilers were a great step forward, but they imposed limits on what the computer was allowed to do, in many ways because of their limited library of audio modules or opcodes.

These limits have now been swept away. This book makes it practical to write a new C program for each new piece of music. The composition *is* the C program. This is the great step forward.

A half-century ago, computer sound processing was limited by the speed and expense of existing hardware. Today those limits are gone. Affordable laptop computers are from 10,000 to 100,000 times as powerful as the roomful of equipment in a typical 1960s computer center. And this book sweeps away the programming limits and makes practical musical use of the great power of laptops.

Early computers could not be used to perform a piece of music in real time—they took many seconds to compute a single second of sound. But today real-time performance is possible, and practical real-time programming is a big part of this book. Thus, laptops can join with chamber groups and orchestras and thereby add rich new timbres to the already beautiful timbres of acoustic instruments.

What now is the musical challenge of the future? I believe it is our understanding of the power and limitations of the human brain, and specifically discovering which sound waves, sound patterns, timbres, and sequences humans recognize as beautiful and meaningful music—and why. This book holds the key to copiously producing the software, sounds, and music we need to truly and deeply explore these many and hidden dimensions of our musical minds.

Max V. Mathews

Preface

"But how does an oscillator really work?" My 40-year journey to *The Audio Programming Book* began with that question. Some of the answers came from Tom Piggott (my first electronic music teacher, and the one who got me started with analog synthesizers—an EML200 and an Arp2600).

More answers came from Alan R. Pearlman, founder and president of the ARP Synthesizer Company, the man who commissioned my first symphony, *Three Soundscapes for Synthesizers and Orchestra*.

Still more answers came from Dexter Morrill, who offered me a Visiting Composer's Residency at Colgate University, where I made my first computer music. It took days back then, but I rendered "Happy Birthday" in MUSIC 10 and played the rendered soundfile for my dad over the phone on his birthday.

And more answers came from Bruce Pennycook, who was also in residence at Colgate. (We would work through the night and end our sessions with breakfast at a local diner; I picked his brain every spare minute; he taught me how to do *stereo panning* and gave me his sub-bass oscillator instrument, LOW.)

I started to really answer the question in Barry Vercoe's summer workshop at the Massachusetts Institute of Technology, in which I learned *music11*. (I will never forget Barry filling whiteboard after whiteboard, and revealing, one morning, that an oscillator consisted of a phasor and a table.)

I made my way from MIT to the Center for Music Experiment at the University of California at San Diego, where I learned about cmusic from Dick Moore, Gareth Loy, and Mark Dolson. My first cmusic composition, *Two Movements in C*, featured a new trick that they taught me to do with two oscillators: FM synthesis.

Life brought me back to Boston, and Barry invited me to continue my work at MIT's new Media Lab, where I got to explore and beta-test his new language, Csound. By his side, I was able to further my understanding and to share some of the answers I had found along the way through *The Csound Book*.

Overlapping with my time at the Computer Audio Research Lab in San Diego and the MIT Media Lab, I got to know and work with Max V. Mathews. He invited me to work in his studio at Bell Labs. (He would sleep in the recording booth there so that I could compose and program.) We have worked together for more than 25 years now, touring, performing, lecturing, and sometimes sailing. It was from him that I learned the programming language C. We would spend days and days going over every single line of his *Conductor* and *Improv* programs, his *Scanned Synthesis* program, his *PhaserFilters* program, and his MUSIC V program. (Imagine my surprise upon discovering that an oscillator is also an envelope generator, and then the mind-bending fact that if you "scan" a "mechanically modeled" wavetable, an oscillator can "be" a filter.)

But still, it took John ffitch, Richard Dobson, Gabriel Maldonado, and Victor Lazzarini to teach me to actually "program" an oscillator—right here in *The Audio Programming Book*.

Yes, for me *The Audio Programming Book* answers my first question and many others. I think you will agree that ffitch, Dobson, Maldonado, and Lazzarini are wonderful teachers, and that the other contributors are their "young apprentices." I hope the book will answer all your questions and will raise new ones too.

Richard Boulanger

Acknowledgments

This book has had a long period of gestation, and while we have been at it the world has changed; some things have disappeared, and some new things have been invented. But the basic elements of what we wanted to teach are still as relevant today as they were when we started. Along the way, we have also been helped and supported by many others, and we would like to give our thanks to them here.

from Victor Lazzarini

I would like to acknowledge the support of my parents. Their support throughout my education years and beyond, both affective and financial, was essential to my developing career and life. Even though they might at some point have doubted the wisdom of embarking on a music degree instead of medical school, they have never been anything but supportive.

I would also like to give thanks to the An Foras Feasa research institute in Ireland, which provided the funds for my sabbatical at a time when I was heavily involved in finishing this book. In particular, I would like to say thanks to its director, Margaret Kelleher, and to John Keating, whose office I was able to use in that period. At the NUI Maynooth Music Department, I would like to thank all my colleagues for their friendship and support, Fiona Palmer for allowing my research leave at a busy time for the department, and Barra Boydell for his advice, guidance, and example in all things academic. I would also want to acknowledge the help and support of my research colleagues Joe Timoney and Tom Lysaght, with whom I have worked for many years and who taught me a lot *about* signal processing.

My involvement in this book would not have happened had I not made a decision one morning in 2005 to join the Csound users' discussion list. A Csounder since 1993 and an audio developer since 1996, I had always been a retiring sort of person who was not involved "in the community" (although I had contributed to Csound privately by sending things to John ffitch). But that morning, for some reason, I decided to join the list. and this whole new world suddenly appeared, almost by extension. So I would like to extend my gratitude to fellow Csounders for the years of interesting conversation and bug reports. Of these new friends, I would in particular like to acknowledge my new friends Steven Yi and Oeyvind

Brandtsegg. I would also want to thank John ffitch and Richard Dobson, who have been great mentors to me on the art of programming and making noise with it. Last, but not least, I need to thank my colleague and co-editor "Dr. B." for providing the opportunity first to contribute to this book and then to co-edit it. His support and guidance have contributed substantially to my development as a researcher and a composer.

Another group of people I would like to acknowledge and thank is the Linux Audio Developers "family," like-minded individuals who are in the business of teaching, learning, and sharing computer music code as members of the great brotherhood of free and open-source software. We would not be where we are now in our field without the efforts of countless people contributing to FOSS projects, in many guises—a practice that dates back to the beginnings of computer music.

Finally, I have to thank my three kids, Danny, Ellie, and Chris, for their love and for keeping me on firm ground at times when my mind was about to take off. Another special dedication goes to my wife Alice, who has put up with my work-related bad moods and my computer-bound "disappearances." Her love and support have helped me through a lot of bad weather, for which I am very grateful.

from Richard Boulanger

Over the years, there have been many brilliant and dedicated students who have helped me work on, work out, and work through the chapters, the code, and the ideas of the contributing authors. Not only have they worked on this project with me, but they have also been a huge part of my compositions, my concerts, my lectures, and my research. Their spirit is in the pages of this book and is channeled through all of my creative work. To date, the gifted and dedicated students who have served as my musical assistants and collaborators have included Paris Smaragdis, Eric Singer, Jacob Joaquin, Young Choi, Luigi Castelli, Greg Thompson, and Kathryn Bigbee. I am eternally grateful to them.

A number of my students wrote chapters for this book. I want to recognize and thank them for their contributions to my classes and my teaching. When you read and study their contributions here, I am sure that you too will recognize the dedication, commitment, and brilliance of Joo Won Park, Barry Threw, Tae Min Cho, Andrew Beck, Federico Saldarini, and Johannes Bochmann, and you will know how lucky I have been to work with them.

A number of undergraduate and graduate students read specific chapters and offered feedback that helped to focus the authors and significantly improve the final content of this book and the associated DVD. The student reviewers from the Berklee College of Music were Bobby Pietrusko, David Buchs, Jason McClinsey, Victor Magro, Matthew Thies, Gautam, Paul Marinaro, Danny Patterson, Brian Baughn, Nicolas Villa, Tom Owen, and Sean Meagher, those from New York University were Won Lee and Nicholas Barba, the reviewer from McGill University was Huey How, and the reviewers from the MIT Media Lab were Noah Vawter, Victor Adan, and Adam Boulanger. Thanks to all of you for making the time and making a difference.

From the very beginning, I had one student who not only worked through all the chapters but also found the time to put his talent for graphic design to work; he contributed most of the figures that appear in this book. His name is Robert Gerard Pietrusko. This talented musician, engineer, programmer, and designer was able to translate some murky code and concepts into transcendent and illuminating illustrations.

As the manuscript approached the finish line, two students offered to help me: Jonathan Bailey and Tim Lukens. The three of us put together a solid Audio Programming class at Berklee, and they helped me to write strong tutorial chapters to support that class. In addition to making the time to write some very musical code, both of these guys found the time to write significant and important chapters of their own for the book—Jonathan, in fact, wrote two. There is no possible way that I can thank Jonathan Bailey and Tim Lukens enough for all the work that they did to make this book happen, and to make our chapters what they are. Their "musical" code is at the very core of my writing and my teaching, and for that I am most grateful to them both.

Clearly, my students have been a profound and deep source of inspiration to me, but at Berklee the real support for my research and my development has come from my department chairmen, David Mash and Kurt Biederwolf, and from my deans, Don Puluse and Stephen Croes. For more than 22 years they have supported my travel, my studies, my courses, and my compositions; moreover, they have brought my collaborators to the college to work with my students and to work with me. They continue to support my growth and development, and I will be forever grateful to them for this wonderful gift.

A number of colleagues read and reviewed the preliminary chapters and code for this book. Their insights helped to focus this book on the target audience. I would like to thank Javier A. Garavaglia, Michael Rhoades, Luis Jure, Sal G. Sofia, Josep M. Comajuncosas, Mark Ballora, David L. Phillips, and Steven Yi.

Of all the comments and the constructive criticism that I received over the years, perhaps the most important "wake-up call" came from my closest colleague, collaborator, and friend, Lee Ray. About two years ago, I asked Lee to "check out" the "final" draft. He read every page—at the time, all 3,000. And after two months, Lee probably made one of the most difficult phone calls of his life. He let me know "everything" that was broken, missing, dull, out of place, out of date, redundant, inferior, and in some cases inappropriate. Time had clouded my judgment and my ability to see what was there and, more important, what I was missing. Lee's insights opened my eyes again and helped to get me back on the right track.

In the beginning, the number of contributing authors was slightly larger than the final group. They began this journey with me, but for one reason or another some contributions do not appear in the book. Still, I want to thank the contributors for helping to move the project forward and for reading, reviewing, suggesting, and inspiring. On behalf of all the contributing authors I would like to thank Michael Gogins, Javier Garavaglia, Micha Thies, IOhannes m zmoelnig, Craig Stuart Sapp, Nick Didkovsky, and Matt Ingalls. These are the most productive, prolific, and inspiring developers on the computer music scene today, and I am grateful for their help.

Clearly, I am grateful to all my contributing authors for their brilliant contributions, but there are four contributing authors who have been working with me on this project from the very beginning, almost 10 years ago. Over this period, computer technologies, compilers, processors, and platforms changed dramatically, and most times the "amazing technological breakthroughs" broke everything that we had built (and trashed everything I had tested and edited). There were so many times that we had to set out in an entirely new direction that any "normal" programmer or professor would have just given up. Still, when everything was broken, these four were determined enough and committed enough to pick up the pieces, rewrite their code, and start all over. Time and time again, they forged ahead. I learned a great deal from each of them, and I stand in awe of all the creative possibilities they have manifest through the software that they have written. A small glimpse of that dynasty is now a part of this book. Richard Dobson, Gabriel Maldonado, John ffitch, and Eric Lyon: on behalf of all of your future and current students (and I consider myself to be one among them), I thank you all for everything you have taught me over these past 10 years.

One other contributor deserves special mention: Victor Lazzarini. Victor came along when we were well into the project, and yet, with his code and his words, he raised the book up to a new level of relevance and excellence. Where there was a hole, he would fill it. Where there was a missing piece, he would find it (in his brilliant mind) and then write it up (and code it up) in what seemed like no time at all. And when all his chapters were written, and all his code was fully tested and running on all platforms, he offered to help edit and test the mountain of words and code. Before I knew it, I had a brilliant, passionate, and dedicated "partner" on this project. Together we would "tag team" around the world and around the clock, and we managed to get two years' work done in a matter of months.

I asked Doug Sery at the MIT Press if I could officially offer Victor the title of co-editor. (He was already doing the job.) I was prepared to argue that he had become indispensable, that he had spent six months making one significant contribution after another, and that he brought an essential and substantive level of expertise to the project (as was evident from the content of his chapters and his code). But I didn't need to present my case at all. Doug had noticed the difference in the quality and content of the product. He had noticed the accelerated rate of production too. In fact, in less than a minute, Doug gave me the thumbs up. Because of Victor's expert editorial contributions, this book is now in your hands. I am honored and proud to have him as a major contributing author and as my co-editor.

I can't end these acknowledgments without thanking my parents, Dick and Claire Boulanger. It's sad because I work hard to impress them, but when they look at any single page of this book they both shriek with horror and wish I would just "slow down" and "smell the roses" and spend some time enjoying life with them by the pool. Oh well. Even if there isn't a single page in here that makes one bit of sense to you, know that it's all for you and because of you, mom and dad—with respect, gratitude, and love. And now that it's done, there might be a bit more pool time.

And I can't end these acknowledgements without apologizing to my three wonderful sons, Adam, Philip, and Adrien. I hope you can forgive me for my absence over the past 10 years, and for the all-too-frequent "short-fuse verbal explosions" when I was struggling at the computer to find a word and you would have liked me to listen, for a minute or two, to some of your words.

When I started this book, Adam was graduating from high school; now he is married and graduating from MIT with a Ph.D. Where did that time go? Philip is playing classical cello professionally in Chicago and pursuing his second master's degree. When I started this project, he was practicing to get a decent chair in the Massachusetts Southeast District Orchestra. Adrien was in elementary school (second grade, I think), and we were both obsessed with Pokémon. As the text was delivered to the MIT Press, Adrien was starting college.

I hope Adrien will use this book in one of his CS classes someday. I hope Adam (Dr. B. v2.0) will teach one of his classes from this book someday, or his daughter Anaïs. And I hope Philip and I can get back to performing and touring and making new music together—working on our *Book of Dreams*.

This book is about making "new" music by discovering new ways of transforming and transfiguring sounds. I hope it will open a door to tomorrow's concert hall and online classroom for my sons and for you, your students, and your children.

Finally, I offer my deepest and most heartfelt thanks to my wife Colette. This beautiful, caring, and loving cardiac-rehab nurse put all the pieces of this quite literally broken and broken-hearted man back together. I had a heart attack along the way, and Colette brought me back to life and back to this project. Without her love, her understanding, and her sacrifice, neither the book nor I would have seen the light of this day.

But in the end, it was the faith, support, and encouragement of Doug Sery that kept this project alive, in me and at the MIT Press. Everyone interested in audio programming truly has him to thank for this fantastic book—and we sincerely do thank you, Doug.

Introduction

In chapter 0, we provide a complete overview of the C language and some essential elements of C++. Using examples written from a musician's perspective, we guide the reader through the elements of these two languages that will be used in the audio programming chapters of this book.

In chapter 1, Richard Dobson introduces readers with no prior experience to the basics of C programming. All the examples employ a music-oriented focus, from MIDI-frequency calculations to the textual breakpoint file and a tuning-fork emulation including the creation of raw binary soundfiles. It also introduces primary tools such as *Audacity* and *Gnuplot*.

In chapter 2, Richard Dobson introduces the specially written *PortSF* soundfile library. This is used to develop a number of useful programs designed to demonstrate the generation and processing of basic envelopes and waveforms (including examples of additive synthesis). In the course of introducing further important C language elements, it explores the development of the table-lookup oscillator and other basic tools.

In chapter 3, Gabriel Maldonado shows us how to send audio data to the operating system's standard output, to a raw binary file, to a RIFF-Wave file, and directly to the audio interface in real time by using different libraries: the *Tiny Audio Library*, *PortSF*, and *PortAudio*.

In chapter 4, John ffitch introduces important software engineering principles such as object-oriented design. These are articulated through the construction of a simple wave-table playback program. The description includes debugging the resulting program and some additional notes on the thought processes of program construction.

In chapter 5, Victor Lazzarini introduces more formal aspects of digital signal processing theory, including some basic mathematical concepts. Programming examples demonstrate some essential operations on audio signals. The chapter concludes with a look into the implementation of FM synthesis.

In chapter 6, Lazzarini explores several basic elements of waveform processing, including synthesis and the transformation of audio signals. These processes are presented as components implemented as C++ functions, exposing the details of their operation. The chapter concludes with an introduction to plug-in development, with the VST architecture used as an example.

In chapter 7, Lazzarini introduces the theory and implementation of basic operations in the spectral domain. The chapter takes an intuitive approach, but it still covers the very important mathematical descriptions of each operation. It concludes with a discussion of a fully functional convolution program.

In chapter 8, Lazzarini goes a step beyond chapter 7 by looking into time-varying spectral analysis and resynthesis. Here he discusses the implementation of a basic Short-Time Fourier Transform operation and a few examples of basic manipulation in the frequency domain.

Chapter 9, also by Lazzarini, complements the study of spectral processing (featured in chapters 7 and 8) by introducing a basic tool for the job: the phase vocoder. It also demonstrates how the phase vocoder can be used in time stretching, filtering, and pitch scaling. It concludes by looking at an alternative method of frequency estimation and its use in additive synthesis.

In chapter 10, ffitch studies and analyzes a number of simple Csound opcodes to reveal the mechanisms by which they are integrated into the overall system. This leads to some practical advice concerning the creation of opcodes.

Chapter 11, by Lazzarini, complements the extensive exploration of time-domain Csound opcodes in chapter 10 with a short look at the processing of spectral audio. Two examples are provided, showing the separate manipulation of amplitude and frequency aspects of input signals.

In chapter 12, Eric Lyon develops a specification language based on the model of patchable analog synthesizers. Patch descriptions written in this language are transformed into working Csound code.

In chapter 13, ffitch presents a case study of an algorithmic composition (actually an algorithmic remixer) to show how C can be used to generate Csound scores and to perform simple analytic calculations. He demonstrates that small programs are not difficult to write, and that, despite all the teaching of advanced software engineering, there are times when a "little" program can prove very powerful, musical, and beautiful.

In chapter 14, Steven Yi offers observations about the orchestra as a performance ensemble and surveys some of the techniques composers have used in writing for it. Yi derives a model for music making from these observations, and he presents a C++ class library implementing this model, and a program demonstrating how the library can be used.

Appendix A—written for those new to UNIX-compatible environments—covers basic techniques for navigating a Bash command shell, for building code using the GNU compilation tools `gcc` and `make`, and for editing files with the `emacs` text editor.

Appendix B is a debugging tutorial for beginning developers. It covers the basics of using `gdb` to debug audio programs. Techniques for preparing your programs for debugging, for slowing down and stepping through code line by line, and for viewing application state and memory are reviewed.

Appendix C, an overview of soundfile formats from the raw to the self-describing, focuses on the use of *libsndfile*.

Appendix D covers the basics of real-time audio programming using the *PortAudio* library. It demonstrates the two modes of operation supported by the library, *blocking* and *asynchronous*, with comparative programming examples.

Appendix E introduces MIDI programming using the *PortMIDI* library. It features three examples covering output, input, and the combination of these two.

Appendix F is a short introduction to how computers work and to the functioning of their main components. Further, this appendix shows how computer languages are compiled into a form that can be executed.

Appendix G is a glossary that provides support for the entire book. It includes entries that range from simple definitions, to more extended ones, with some tutorial elements. This appendix offers a concise introduction to a range of words and topics that readers may encounter in this book or in other resources. The readers are presumed to have music as their primary field of knowledge; accordingly, the glossary concentrates on subjects relating to programming, audio engineering, and computer architectures. Computing has created a very large body of jargon words. This appendix explains those you are most likely to meet as a computer musician.

Appendix H presents and explains the most important mathematical concepts for the audio programmer and computer musician, and other mathematical concepts that audio programmers and computer musicians might encounter.

The Audio Programming Book

C Programming Basics

0   An Overview of the C Language with Some Elements of C++

Victor Lazzarini and Richard Boulanger

The programming languages C and C++ are used throughout this book, and yet the details of the languages are often secondary to the more important issues of audio programming. After all, this is *The Audio Programming Book*, and programming audio is the main goal. However, it is appropriate to reserve a little space here at the beginning for a general discussion of the languages themselves. C is often described as a small language, and therefore we believe it possible to present, discuss, and review the whole of it in a very compact way.

0.1   C and C++

Most people get somewhat confused when learning about the programming languages C and C++. Sometimes the two are confused into one; sometimes C is taken to be C++ and vice versa. They are, effectively, two separate and different languages, so they should not be confused. In practice, they are very similar and share many elements, but we should be careful not to mistake one for the other. As a rule of thumb, just think of C++ as a C with extra elements. While not the complete picture, this is often all you need to know.

Sometimes C is taught with some elements of C++ that simplify the coding. While this might be reasonable for someone who knows what is C and what is C++ in the code, for beginners this is very confusing. A secondary issue here is that C++ allows a more sophisticated programming approach, known as *object-oriented programming*, which is complex to tackle for the novice. In this chapter, we will only deal with C at first; at the end, we will introduce some features of C++.

0.2   Building C Programs

0.2.1   Compiled and Interpreted Languages

C is what we call a *compiled* language. This is because programs, written with C code in a text file, are generated by a package of programs called the *compiler*. These programs transform the text code into binary codes that are understood by the machine and the operating system. The process of compilation/program building is discussed below.

Interpreted languages, such as Python, are generally higher-level languages that are dependent on an *interpreter* program, which translates the text code into machine actions directly. Their advantage is that the result of the programming can be seen immediately. On the other hand, generally speaking, the overhead of interpreting the code can make these languages very inefficient for intensive tasks (such as calculating the output of a synthesis routine, in the case of a music system).

0.2.2 Compiling

After opening your console/terminal window, you can invoke the compiler program can be called by the simple command

```
cc mysource.c
```

where `cc` is the C compiler and *mysource.c* is the name of your source file. (`gcc` is a very widespread compiler, if you are using it, just change the command for `gcc`.) The output of this command will be a binary executable file called *a.out*, which you can rename (using `mv`) if you want. This file will sit in the directory you are working on.

For more practical uses, you can output the binary executable to a different file, using '`-o . . .`' (just as in Csound '`-o`' means "output to"):

```
cc -o myprogr mysource.c
```

On Windows machines your program filename will have the extension `.exe`. On other systems no extensions are used.

0.2.3 Source Files

Source files are text (ASCII) files containing the source code written in C, which will be used to build the program. There can be just one or many of these needed to build a program.

0.2.4 Header Files

Header files (usually with extension `.h`) are files with definitions and parts of code which are included in (i.e. they will be copied to) the source files. The compiling process will use the code in these header files in the compilation process.

0.2.5 Libraries

C is a very lean language. It has a number of built-in definitions, rules, etc.; the rest is done by elements (functions, data definitions, etc.) existing in libraries. These are pre-compiled (i.e. they are already in binary) and are added to the executable at the last phase of the build of the program. In this phase, called linking, references to libraries are linked to the actual binary code.

There are libraries for virtually anything you want to do in C: math, sorting, comparing things, controlling processes, playing audio and MIDI, etc. When using different libraries, you will have to inform the compiler which one(s) you are using. This can be done with the relevant command-line options. (For more details, see appendix A.)

0.2.6   The Build Process

The "program build" has three main phases:

1. Pre-processing. This expands all include header files (by copying them into the source code) and other preprocessor statements (which usually start with the character #) found in the source file(s).
2. Compiling. This reads the source code and transforms it into binary code for the machine you are targeting (i.e. the machine for which you're building the program).
3. Linking. This links all references to binary code that is not in the source code (i.e. in libraries), as well as putting together all source binaries (if there are multiple source files).

These three stages can be done in one go, or if you like, separately. Usually, when building large pieces of software it is common to do steps one and two at one time and then leave the linkage process for later. The source files are compiled into binary files called *object files* (extension `.o`), which can later be combined (*linked*) to make the program. This is usually the case when there are many source files in the project. This procedure enables the programmer to compile the different source files only when they have been modified, saving time and resources. Utilities such as `make` or `scons` can be used to maintain a build project and will automatically call the compiler and the linker to build from sources that have been updated.

0.3   The Structure of C Programs

0.3.1   Program Format and Layout

A C executable program requires that at least one function be present in it. This is what we call the *entry point* of the program: where it starts executing and also providing the exit point, i.e. when the function ends, the program also finishes. By default this function is called `main()`, but this can be changed by a compiler flag (although we will not normally do it). This function can take two forms:

```
int main( );
```

and

```
int main(int argc, char* argv);
```

The first form does not take any arguments and, being the simplest, is the one we will use first. Both forms are supposed to return (i.e. "answer with") an integer number, which is passed as a code to the operating system (generally 0 means OK). The second form will be discussed later in section 0.15. In addition to `main()`, the program can also have other functions, although they are not absolutely required.

0.3.2　Character Set and Reserved Symbols

The C Programming Language uses the following characters:

```
A-Z   a-z   0-9   .   ,   :   ;   '   $   "   #   %   &   !   _
{}   []   ()   <   >   |   +   -   /   *   =   tab space
```

There are only 32 keywords (which are reserved symbols) in the C language. They are combined with the formal syntax to form the language proper. These symbols cannot be used for any other purpose:

```
auto      double    int       struct    break     else      long      switch
case      enum      register  typedef   char      extern    return    union
const     float     short     unsigned  continue  for       signed    void
default   goto      sizeof    volatile  do        if        static    while
```

0.4　An Example Program

Our first example is the one traditionally given in C courses:

```
#include <stdio.h> /* header file for IO */
int main()         /* main function */
{
    printf("Hello World\n"); /* print message */
    return 0; /* function returns 0 (OK) */
}
```

Here we have all the typical components of a program:

- A main function matching one of the forms given above.
- A header file, in this case for the standard input/output library.
- An executable statement, to do something (print to the screen).
- Since the function is said to return an 'int', a return statement.
- Statements are always terminated with a semicolon.
- Comments, between /* */, which will not be seen by the compiler.

If you build this program with the commands shown above and then run it, you will get `Hello World` printed to the terminal.

0.5 Data Types

The first element of C programming is based on the concept of a *variable*. Basically, variables are memory slots that are reserved for you to stored numeric values or characters in. In C, we need to declare these at the start of a function before we can use them, by stating the variable type and its name. The basic data types for variables are the following:

int—an integer (a whole number)
float—a floating-point value (with a decimal part)
double—a double-precision floating-point value
char—a single character.

In addition, we will also see the type **void**, which is used to indicate "no type" or "any type," depending on its use. As for names, all variables must begin with a letter or an underscore.

0.5.1 Integer Data Types

An int variable, in most systems, can store a value in the 32-bit range from −2,147,483,648 to 2,147,483,647, but this is system dependent. For example,

```
int a;
```

creates a memory slot for an int and calls it a. Other types of integers also exist: a short integer or short is stored as a 16-bit number (two bytes), and its range is from −32768 to 32767. Integers can be signed (the default) or unsigned. The latter are positive only and have twice the positive range of a signed integer (from 0 to 4,294,967,295). The type long can be used to mean 32-bit integers.

```
unsigned int ua; /* an unsigned integer */
unsigned long ulb; /* an unsigned long integer */

short sample; /* a 16-bit integer */
```

0.5.2 Floating-Point Data Types

Floating-point data types are so named because they store a decimal-point number in two parts: an exponent (which tracks the point position) and a mantissa (which holds the actual numbers over which the point "floats").

float: A floating-point number has about seven digits of precision and a range of about 1.E−36 to 1.E+36. A float takes four bytes to store. Example: float result;
double: A double precision number has about 13 digits of precision and a range of about 1.E−303 to 1.E+303. A double takes eight bytes to store. Example: double value;

0.5.3   Characters

The type `char` holds a single character, stored in one byte. Example:

```
char c;
```

This type is most often used to store ASCII characters (which are themselves seven-bit codes), but in fact can be used for any single-byte numerical use.

0.5.4   Assignment and Arithmetic Operations

You can store a value in a variable using

```
name = value;
```

For instance,

```
a = 10;
```

stores the value 10 in the `int` variable a. Note that '=' is the assignment operator and does not mean equality (which is '==', as we will see later). The arithmetic operators are the following:

addition: a+b
subtraction: a–b
multiplication: a*b
division: a/b

Care must be taken with situations like a = 10.0/3. If 'a' is an integral type (`int`, `char`, etc.), the result will be truncated to 3. If it is a floating-point number, it will be expanded up to the type precision (single or double), e.g., 3.3333333. This means (1) that integer division truncates the result and (2) that if a `float` is involved in the calculation, integers will be converted into `float`.

0.5.5   Casting

Data types can be converted one into another by using a `cast`:

```
int a;
float b;
. . .
a = (int) b;
b = (float) a;
```

Conversions between integral and floating-point types will cause truncation, as was discussed above. It is also important, when converting types, that the recipient have enough range to hold the data; if it doesn't, overflow may occur.

Table 0.1
Order of operations in C and C++.

Operator	Associativity
( ) [ ] -> . expr++ expr++	Left to right
! ~ ++expr --expr (*type*) * & sizeof	Right to left
* / %	Left to right
+ -	Left to right
<< >>	Left to right
< <= > >=	Left to right
== !=	Left to right
&	Left to right
^	Left to right
|	Left to right
&&	Left to right
||	Left to right
?:	Right to left
= += -= *= /= >>= <<= &= ^= |=	Right to left
,	Left to right

0.5.6 Arithmetic Ordering

Expressions are calculated using a certain precedence order, shown in table 0.1. If in doubt of the precedence of operations, use parentheses to group them.

0.5.7 Variable Declaration and Initialization

A variable has to be declared before it is used, so that the compiler can create the memory slot for it. You can also assign an initial value to a variable when you declare it. For example,

```
int a, i=1;
```

declares two variables (separated by commas) and initializes the second to 1.

0.5.8 Variable Scope

Variables declared within a program block are valid, and "in existence," only inside that block (and enclosed blocks). A program block is delimited by braces, so a function is a program block. These variables are called *local* to separate them from variables declared outside any block, which are *global* and are seen by all functions within the source-code file. It is best to avoid global variables.

0.5.9 Constants

Constants are numeric values that cannot be changed throughout a program. Integer constants are normally written in base-10 format (decimal system): 1, 2. For long integer constants an `L` is added: `2L`, `10L`. Floating-point constants will have two forms: with an `f` at the end, for floats and just with a decimal point somewhere for doubles (`2.f` is a `float`; `2.0` is a `double`).

Integer constants can also be written as either hexadecimals (base 16) or octals (base 8). An octal constant is preceded by '`0`' and a hexadecimal by '`0x`'.

The decimal 31 (`0001 1111` in binary) can be written as an octal (`037`) or as a hexadecimal: `0x1F`.

Octal units will range from 0 to 7. Hexadecimal ones will range from 0 to `F`, with `A`–`F` representing the decimals 10–15. For instance, `F` in hexadecimals represent (1-valued) set bits, so a 16-bit bitmask `0xFFFF` is a series of 16 set bits (`1111 1111 1111 1111`).

Macros can be used to give constant names. The pre-processor statement `#define` will do this for you, and so

```
#define END 10000
```

will substitute `10000` for any instances of the word `END`, so you can use `END` as a constant in your code. The preprocessor takes care of this for you.

0.6 Standard Input and Output

In order for a program to communicate with the outside world, we need some sort of data input and output. The simplest type of IO is provided by the standard C library console IO functions. Since all IO is handled by libraries, more sophisticated ways of doing this are implemented by different systems, but the standard IO is the one that is present everywhere, so it is very useful in many situations.

0.6.1 `printf` and Format Specifiers

The **printf** function is usually of the form

```
printf(format-string,...)
```

where '`...`' means a variable number of arguments (which can be zero). The format string determines how many parameters it will have. If it contains format specifiers in the form of '`%`' characters, it will call for one or more extra arguments. In the case of

```
printf("Hello World");
```

Table 0.2

The ANSI C format specifiers.

Specifier	Type	Print
%c	char	Single character
%d (%i)	int	Signed integer
%e (%E)	float or double	Exponential format
%f	float or double	Signed decimal
%g (%G)	float or double	Use %f or %e as required
%o	int	Unsigned octal value
%s	string (char array)	Sequence of characters
%u	int	Unsigned decimal
%x (%X)	int	Unsigned hex value

we only have a format string and, as this contains no % characters it results in Hello World being printed without anything extra. As an example of a format specifier, %d means *print a value as a signed decimal integer*, so

```
printf("Total = %d", total);
```

will print Total = and then the value of the variable total.

Here are some important notes on format specifiers:

1. The specifier following % indicates the type of variable to be displayed as well as the format in which that the value should be displayed.
2. If you use a specifier with the wrong type of variable, you will see some strange things on the screen, and the error often propagates to other items in the printf list.
3. You can also add '1' in front of a specifier to mean a *long* form of the variable type, and 'h' to indicate a short form. Short integers are 16-bit (two bytes) whereas long ones are 32-bit (four bytes). For example, %ld means a long integer variable (usually four bytes), and %hd means a short int. Notice that there is no distinction between a four-byte float and an eight-byte double. The reason is that a float is automatically converted to a double precision value when passed to printf, so the two can be treated in the same way.

0.6.2   More on Format Specifiers

The % specifiers that you can use in ANSI C are given in table 0.2. A modifier that will determine how the value will be printed can precede each specifier. The most general modifier is of the form

```
flag width.precision
```

Table 0.3

The ANSI C format modifiers.

Flag	Use
-	Left justify.
+	Always display sign.
space	Display space if there is no sign.
0	Pad with leading zeroes.
#	Use alternate form of specifier.

Table 0.4

Examples using the # modifier.

Specifier	Display
%#o	Adds leading 0 to octal value
%#x	Adds leading 0x to hex value
%#f or %#e	Ensures decimal point is printed
%#g	Displays trailing zeros

where `width` specifies the number of characters used in total to display the value and `precision` indicates the number of characters used after the decimal point. The format modifiers are shown in table 0.3.

For example, `%10.3f` will display a float using ten characters with three digits after the decimal point. (The "ten characters" would consist of the decimal point and a minus sign, if there were one.) The specifier `%-10d` will display an `int` left justified in a ten-character space. The specifier `%+5d` will display an `int` using the next five character locations and will add a plus sign or a minus sign to the value. The # modifier can be used as shown in table 0.4.

Finally, ASCII control codes can be used in a string as shown in table 0.5. These escape sequences are used to display non-printing or special characters. They essentially control how the text is positioned on the screen.

0.6.3 scanf

The `scanf` function works in much the same way as the `printf`, as it has the general form

```
scanf(controlstring,...)
```

In this case the control string specifies how strings of characters, usually typed on the keyboard, should be converted into values and stored in the listed variables. To store values, the `scanf` function has to have the addresses of the variables rather than just their values.

Table 0.5

Escape sequences and their results.

Escape sequence	Special character or behavior
\b	Backspace
\f	Formfeed
\n	Newline
\r	Carriage return
\t	Horizontal tab
\v	Vertical tab
\'	Single quote
\"	Double quote
\0	Null character
\a	Alert (beep)

So we will pass the *address of* the variable (&variable) instead of just the variable. In general, all of the relevant format specifiers listed in connection with printf can be used with scanf. The scanf function processes the control string from left to right, and each time it reaches a specifier it tries to interpret what has been typed as a value. If you input multiple values, then these are assumed to be separated by *white space* (i.e. blanks, newline, or tabs). For example,

```
scanf("%d %d",&i,&j);
```

will read in two integer values into i and j. The integer values can be typed on the same line or on different lines as long as there is at least one white space between them. Note, however, that in the case of the %c specifier scanf does not skip white space and it will read the next character typed, regardless of what it is.

The width modifier can be used in scanf to limit the number of characters accepted to width. For example,

```
scanf("%10d",&i)
```

would use, at most, the first ten digits typed as the new value for i.

0.6.4   A Simple Example

Here is a simple addition program to demonstrate the use of IO and arithmetic in C:

```
#include <stdio.h>
int main()
{
    int a,b,c;
```

```
      printf("\n Please enter a number: ");
      scanf("%d",&a);
      printf(" Please enter a second number: ");
      scanf("%d",&b);
      c=a+b;
      printf("%d + %d = %d \n",a,b,c);
      return 0;
}
```

This program will prompt the user for two numbers, using `printf()`, take them in with `scanf()`, then print out the resulting sum. Notice that each line is executed in sequence and that `scanf()` blocks waiting for input. Also notice that we could have saved using a third variable ('c') by performing the sum as one of the arguments to the last `printf()`, as in

```
printf("%d + %d = %d \n",a,b,a+b);
```

0.7   Control of Flow

C provides a number of ways of controlling the flow of execution of a program, so that it does not always have to proceed statement by statement as in the previous example. Before we examine the different forms of controlling the flow, we have to introduce ways of checking the truth of conditions and statements: logical expressions.

0.7.1   Logical Expressions

A logical expression is an expression used to test a certain *condition* in a flow control statement. For example, a > 0 is true if a contains a value greater than zero, and b < 0 is true if b contains a value less than zero. The concept of truth in C is very simple: 0 if not true and non-0 if true. So a logical expression generally evaluates to 0 or non-0 (say, 1). The following relational operators are used in logical expressions:

```
>    <    >=    <=    ==    !=    &&    ||
```

Note that the equality operator is == and not simply =. The last operator means "NOT equal to." Because truth conditions are zero or non-zero, a zero-valued variable can also be used to indicate falsehood, and a non-zero variable to indicate truth.

0.7.2   Conditional Execution

One of the programming devices use to control the flow of a program is called *conditional execution*. This is performed by an 'if' statement:

```
if (a > 0) printf("%d is positive", a);
```

If the condition is false, the program continues with the next instruction. In general, the if statement is of the form

```
if (condition) statement;
```

The "statement" above can be a single statement or a program block. In addition, it is also possible to select between two statements, one to be obeyed when the condition is *true* and one to be obeyed when the condition is *false*. You can do this using

```
if (condition) statement1;
else statement2;
```

This is a variation of the if statement. In this case statement1 is carried out if the condition is *true* and statement2 if the condition is *false*. Notice that both parts of the if-else statement can be blocks or single statements terminated by a semicolon:

```
if (f2 ==0) printf("division by zero !!!\n");
else printf("%f/%f = %f\n",f1, f2, f1/f2);
```

A third form of 'if' can be used for selecting several options:

```
if (condition) statement1;
else if(condition2) statement2;
. . .
else if(conditionN) statementN;
else else-statement;
```

This can be used if several conditions need to be checked, and the last else is used to catch the case where none of the above are true.

0.7.3   Conditional Operator

A condensed form of if-else can be found within the construction

```
a = b > c ? b : c;
```

which means the following: if b is bigger than c, then a = b; else a = c. The general form is

```
condition ? true-expression : false-expression;
```

The result of the expression is the *true-expression* if the condition is true; otherwise the result is the *false-expression*.

0.7.4   Switch

An alternative to select from several options is the switch statement, a multiple selection statement. A variable is successively tested against a list of integral constants. When a match is found, the program executes from the matched label onwards. The general form of the `switch` statement is

```
switch(expression)
{
    case constant1: statement sequence; break;
    case constant2: statement sequence; break;
    . . .
    case constantN: statement sequence; break;
    default: statement sequence; break;
}
```

Each case is labeled by one or more integer-valued constants. The `default` label is reached if no matches are found. The `default` is optional. If all matches fail and `default` is absent, no action takes place. When a match is found, the program switches execution to the statement sequence associated with that case. The use of 'break' is important, because the execution will continue forward within that program block, possibly executing more than one of the 'cases'. Using 'break' ensures that the program block is exited after the relevant statements have been executed. For example:

```
switch (i)
{
    case 1:
        printf("one");
        break;
    case 2:
        printf("two");
        break;
    case 3:
        printf("three");
        break;
    case 4:
        printf("four");
        break;
    default:
        printf("out of range");
}
```

This program fragment recognizes the numbers 1–4 and prints the value of a variable in English. The `switch` statement differs from `if` in that `switch` can only test for equality, whereas the `if` conditional expression can be of any type. Also, `switch` will work with only `int` and `char` types.

0.7.5   A Music Theory Example

Here we demonstrate the three forms of conditional execution introduced above. This is a little music theory program that calculates the interval between two notes and prints its semitone length and name. We ask the user to input two notes, which we take in as characters and then translate into numerical pitch classes (0–11). The reason for the dummy variable is that the user is expected to separate the two note names by a "carriage return" (or "enter") character, or even a blank space. As we are scanning characters, these have to be accounted for, so the dummy variable is used as a placeholder. (Though we could have used 'note2', for the sake of clarity we have not.)

```c
#include <stdio.h>

int main()
{
    char note1,note2, dummy; /* note names, dummy char */
    int pc1, pc2, interval; /* pitch classes, interval */
    printf("Please enter two natural notes.\nfirst note: ");
    scanf("%c%c",&note1, &dummy);
    printf("second note: ");
    scanf("%c",&note2);
    switch(note1){ /* translating from note name to pitch class */
        case 'C': case 'c':
        pc1 = 0;
        break;
        case 'D': case 'd':
        pc1 = 2;
        break;
        case 'E': case 'e':
        pc1 = 4;
        break;
        case 'F': case 'f':
        pc1 = 5;
        break;
        case 'G': case 'g':
        pc1 = 7;
        break;
        case 'A': case 'a':
        pc1 = 9;
        break;
        case 'B': case 'b':
        pc1 = 11;
        break;
```

```
        default:
        printf("error: %c is not a natural note\n",note1);return 1;
}
switch(note2){
    case 'C': case 'c':
    pc2 = 0;
    break;
    case 'D': case 'd':
    pc2 = 2;
    break;
    case 'E': case 'e':
    pc2 = 4;
    break;
    case 'F': case 'f':
    pc2 = 5;
    break;
    case 'G': case 'g':
    pc2 = 7;
    break;
    case 'A': case 'a':
    pc2 = 9;
    break;
    case 'B': case 'b':
    pc2 = 11;
    break;
    default:
    printf("error: %c is not a natural note\n",note2);return 1;
}
/* calculate the interval and keep it modulo 12 */
interval = pc2 - pc1;
if(interval < 0) interval += 12;
else if(interval > 11) interval -= 12;
/* print the number of semitones. The special case of
unison (0) has to be handled correctly, so we use the
conditional operator for this */
printf("%d semitones up or %d semitones down\n", interval,
        interval ? 12-interval : 0 );
/* now we print out the interval name */
switch(interval){
    case 1:
    printf("minor 2nd up or major 7th down\n");
    break;
    case 2:
```

```
                printf("major 2nd up or minor 7th down\n");
                break;
                case 3:
                printf("minor 3rd up or major 6th down\n");
                break;
                case 4:
                printf("major 3rd up or minor 6th down\n");
                break;
                case 5:
                printf("perfect 4th up or perfect 5th down\n");
                break;
                case 6:
                printf("augmented 4th \n");
                break;
                case 7:
                printf("perfect 5th up or perfect 4th down\n");
                break;
                case 8:
                printf("minor 6th up or major 3rd down\n");
                break;
                case 9:
                printf("major 6th up or minor 3rd down\n");
                break;
                case 10:
                printf("minor 7th up or major 2nd down\n");
                break;
                case 11:
                printf("major 7th up or minor 2nd down\n");
                break;
                default:
                printf("unison \n");
        }
        return 0;
}
```

As we will see later, this program is longer than it has to be if we use all the tools that the C language offers. However, it demonstrates what is possible with the elements introduced so far.

0.8 Loops

Until now we have been using programs that have a certain number of instructions that are read and executed, line after line depending on control flow statements (if, else, or switch). If we want some parts of the program to be repeated, we will have to use a neat programming device: the *loop*.

0.8.1   The while and do while Loops

You can repeat any statement using either the while loop:

```
while(condition) { . . . }
```

or the do while loop:

```
do { . . . } while(condition);
```

The condition is just a test to control how long you want the program block to carry on repeating. In the case of the while loop, before the code block is carried out the condition is checked, and if it is *true* the block is executed one more time. If the condition turns out to be *false*, the loop is exited. In the case of the do while loop, it will always execute the code within the loop at least once, since the condition controlling the loop is tested at the bottom of the loop.

One of the typical ways of controlling a loop is to employ a counting variable, which will be incrementing every time the loop repeats:

```
a = 0;
while(a < 10){
. . .
a = a + 1;
}
```

The increment is such a common operation that we have a special operator for it:

```
++a; or a++;
```

In this case, ++a increments a before using its value, whereas a++ means "use the value in a, then increment the value stored in a." Decrement operators (--) also work in the same way. In addition, += and -= are used to increment or decrement by more than 1.

Other ways of stopping a loop include querying the user with scanf() and examining the value of an arithmetic expression.

0.8.2   The for loop

The loop controlled by a counting variable is so common that a special form is designed to provide a compact way of doing it. This is implemented by the for loop

```
for (counter=start; counter < end; counter++) statement;
```

which is equivalent to

```
counter = start;
while (counter < end)
{
    statement;
    counter++;
}
```

Here is an example creating the classic Fahrenheit-to-Celsius conversion table:

```
for (fahr = 0 ; fahr <= 300 ; fahr = fahr + 20)
    printf("%4d %6.1f\n", fahr, (5.0/9.0)*(fahr-32));
```

0.8.3   Another Music Theory Example

Here we show the use of a loop to implement a repetitive task. In this program, we want to print the notes of a major scale in ascending steps. This involves adding two semitones to a starting note at every repetition, except after the third note, when we have just one semitone. In order to print the note names, we translate the pitch class numbers by bringing them to the range 0–11 (modulo 12, we can use the % operator since all notes are now non-negative).

```
#include <stdio.h>

int main()
{
    int note, i;
    printf("Please enter the key (in pitch-class number, 0-11): ");
    scanf("%d",&note);
    /* make sure start note is not negative */
    while (note < 0) note += 12;
    /* build the scale */
    for (i=0; i < 7; i++){
        /* translate pitch-class to note name */
        if(note%12==0) printf("C ");
        else if(note%12 == 1) printf("Db ");
        else if(note%12 == 2) printf("D ");
        else if(note%12 == 3) printf("Eb ");
        else if(note%12 == 4) printf("E ");
        else if(note%12 == 5) printf("F ");
        else if(note%12 == 6) printf("Gb ");
        else if(note%12 == 7) printf("G ");
        else if(note%12 == 8) printf("Ab ");
        else if(note%12 == 9) printf("A ");
        else if(note%12 == 10) printf("Bb ");
```

```
        else printf("B ");
        /* find the next pitch class, jump
        a semitone only after 3rd step */
        if(i != 2) note += 2;
        else note++;
    }
    printf("\n");
    return 0;
}
```

0.8.4   Break and Continue

The `break` statement allows you to exit a program block from anywhere within it (we saw how it can be used in a switch block). So it can be used to exit a loop from inside it, without using the loop conditional test. The `continue` statement is used to jump directly to the test from anywhere in the loop, skipping any remaining statements.

0.9   Bitwise Operations

C permits a set of low-level operations, known as *bitwise*, that add some useful functionality to the language. These operators, as the name implies, are defined to work at the bit level, on the individual zeroes and ones that make up the binary information. They are defined for integer use.

0.9.1   Bitwise Logic

A number of operators are defined for bitwise operations; they compare each bit of one operand with the corresponding bit of the other operand:

&   bitwise AND
| bitwise inclusive OR
^   bitwise exclusive OR
~   ones complement (unary operator).

Bitwise AND (`&`) returns a set bit (1) only when both sides of the operation have that bit set. It is often use with bitmasks to filter bytes off an integer:

```
short mask = 0xFF00, value, masked;
value = 0x0111;
masked = mask & value;
```

In the example above, the mask will only let the higher byte pass, filtering off the lower one. Thus the value of `masked` will be 0×0100:

```
   0000 0001 0001 0001
&  1111 1111 0000 0000
------------------------------
   0000 0001 0000 0000
```

The bitwise OR (|) returns a set bit when either operands have a set bit. It is used to turn bits on (and to combine bytes).

```
masked = mask | value;
```

will turn the higher-order byte to $0 \times FF$, resulting in $0 \times FF11$:

```
   0000 0001 0001 0001
   1111 1111 0000 0000
------------------------------
   1111 1111 0001 0001
```

The bitwise exclusive-OR returns a set bit when only one operand has a set bit, otherwise it will return a zero. The unary ones complement operator (~) converts each set bit into a zero and vice versa.

The bitwise logic operators can be combined in short-hand expressions with the assignment operator, for the updating of variables. For example:

```
value &= mask; // same as value = value & mask;
```

0.9.2 Bitshift Operators

Two operators can be used to shift bits in an integer:

<<   left shift
>>   right shift

They shift bits by a number of positions specified by the right-hand operand: x << 1 shifts all bits by one position to the left, and x >> 2 shifts all bits by two positions to the right.

Left-shifts fill the vacated bits with 0-bits. Right-shifts will depend on the type of the operand: for unsigned types, bits will be filled with zeroes; for signed types, the sign bit is preserved and the shifted bits will be filled with sign bits (the first bit). This is platform dependent, but in the major systems we use this is the norm. They employ a representation for signed integers called "twos complement." In it, the first bit (sign) is 1 for negative numbers and 0 for positive numbers.

Left shifts are equivalent to multiplication (a fast way of doing it):

x << n   multiplication by 2^n.

Right shifts are equivalent to division (with rounding):

x >> n   division by 2^n.

Thus, a fast way of multiplying or dividing by 2 is to left or right shift a number by one position. The division will be rounded down to an integer.

0.10   Functions

In C, functions are also known as *subroutines* or *procedures*. A function is simply a block of code grouped together and given a name. This block of code can then be invoked just by using its name in a statement. For instance a function can be declared to print a message and exit:

```
void message()
{
    printf("This is my message\n");
}
```

Now that it is defined, you can use it:

```
int main()
{
    message();
    return 0;
}
```

As the function does not return anything, it is defined with the return type `void`, meaning "nothing." It also does not take any arguments, so there is nothing inside the parentheses.

Note that any variables declared inside a function (a code block) are only valid and seen inside that block. These variables are local and they will disappear when function exits. In order to pass in values to local variables and to get the answers out of functions, we will use arguments (parameters) and return values.

0.10.1   Arguments and Return Types

Passing values to a function is done via its arguments. These are defined within the parentheses, each one with its type and separated by commas. Arguments declared like this also behave as local variables for the function. In order to pass the answer (if any) that the function provides, we use the keyword `return`:

```
int sum(int a, int b)
{
    int result;
    result=a + b;
    return result;
}
```

This defines a function (called `sum`) with two parameters, a and b, both integers, returning an integer, and can be used as

```
a = sum(2,2);
```

This is a call to the `sum` function with a set to 2 and b set to 2, and so `result` is set to 4.

You can also initialize parameters to the results of expressions such as

```
a = sum(x+y,z*w);
```

This will set a to the result of x+y and b to z*w. The values of the arguments are *copied* into them as the function is called. C passes copies of variables as arguments, not the variables themselves. In summary, a function has the general form

```
type FunctionName(arguments)
{
    statements
}
```

Notice that the function will always exit when it reaches a return statement. The rest of the code beyond it will be skipped. The return statement can return a value or (in the case of `void` return types) nothing at all.

0.10.2   Prototypes

Before a function is used, the compiler must be given the return type and any arguments for it. Thus, in order to use it, we will first have to declare it. We need not completely define (implement) it before it is used; we need only declare it. In that case, we can provide the function prototype: its type, name, and arguments. For instance,

```
int sum(int, int);
```

is the prototype for the sum function defined above. The function definition can then go elsewhere in the source code—after `main()`, or even in a different source file. By default, if a function is not declared before use, it is assumed to be an `int` function—which is not always correct.

0.10.3   A More Compact Version of the Interval Program

Now we can use functions to implement tasks that might be repeated with different inputs, so we can have a more compact program. Here we put the translation code of our first music theory example program into a function, then call it when we need pitch classes for the interval calculation:

```c
#include <stdio.h>

/* this function implements translation */
int nameToPc(char name){
    switch(name){
        case 'C': case 'c':
            return 0;
        case 'D': case 'd':
            return 2;
        case 'E': case 'e':
            return 4;
        case 'F': case 'f':
            return 5;
        case 'G': case 'g':
            return 7;
        case 'A': case 'a':
            return 9;
        case 'B': case 'b':
            return 11;
    default: /* error code */
        return 100;
    }
}

int main()
{
    char note1,note2, dummy;
    int interval;
    printf("Please enter two natural notes.\nfirst note: ");
    scanf("%c%c",&note1, &dummy);
    printf("second note: ");
    scanf("%c",&note2);
    /* to calculate the interval, we call nameToPc() to translate */
    interval = nameToPc(note2) - nameToPc(note1);
    if(interval > 20 || interval < -11) {
        printf("either %c or %c are invalid notes\n", note1, note2);
        return 1;
    }
    if(interval < 0) interval += 12;
    else if(interval > 11) interval -= 12;
    printf("%d semitones up or %d semitones down\n", interval,
            interval ? 12-interval : 0 );
    return 0;
}
```

0.10.4 The Standard Library

The Standard C Library provides a great number of functions that perform very useful tasks, including input and output, math, string and character manipulation, and memory allocation. The advantage of using this library is that it has more or less the same behavior across platforms and is generally guaranteed to work everywhere. Table 0.6 shows some of the functions in the Standard C Library.

0.11 Arrays

So far we have been able to create memory slots only for single variable types, but in many applications we will require whole blocks of memory for storing values contiguously. This can be done using arrays. For example,

```
int a[5];
```

declares an array called a with five elements. The first element is a[0] and the last a[4], so all the arrays are zero-based. In general you have

```
type array[size]
```

which declares an `array` of the specified type and with size elements. The first `array` element is array[0] and the last is array[size-1]. Arrays can be initialized as follows:

```
int a[5] = {1,2,3,4,5};
```

The `for` loop and arrays go together very well. The `for` loop can be used to generate a sequence of values to pick out and process each element in an array in turn—for instance,

```
for (i=0; i<5; i++) a[i] = i+1;
```

to fill the array with 1, 2, 3, 4, 5.

0.11.1 Two-Dimensional Arrays

In C it is possible to create arrays of two dimensions, sometimes also called two-dimensional matrices. Such an array's numbers of rows and columns define a two-dimensional matrix. Thus, a 2-D array can be declared as follows:

```
a[rows][columns]
int a[10][10]; /* a 10x10 matrix */
```

A two-dimensional array is actually an array of arrays; it can be initialized, just as any other array, by placing the columns in row order:

```
int a[3][2] = { {0, 1},
                {2, 3},
                {4, 5} };
```

Table 0.6
Some of the more popular functions from the standard C library.

stdio.h	**I/O functions**
getchar()	Returns next character typed on keyboard
putchar()	Outputs a single character to screen
printf()	Outputs to stdout
scanf()	Reads data from stdin
string.h	**String functions**
strcat()	Concatenates a copy of str2 to str1
strcmp()	Compares two strings
strcpy()	Copies contents of str2 to str1
ctype.h	**Character functions**
isdigit()	Returns non-0 if arg is digit from 0 to 9
isalpha()	Returns non-0 if arg is a letter of alphabet
isalnum()	Returns non-0 if arg is a letter or digit
islower()	Returns non-0 if arg is a lowercase letter
isupper()	Returns non-0 if arg is an uppercase letter
math.h	**Mathematics functions**
acos()	Returns arc cosine of arg
asin()	Returns arc sine of arg
atan()	Returns arc tangent of arg
cos()	Returns cosine of arg
sin()	Returns sine of arg
exp()	Returns natural logarithm e
fabs()	Returns absolute value of num
sqrt()	Returns square root of num
time.h	**Time and date functions**
time()	Returns current calendar time of system
difftime()	Returns difference in secs between two times
clock()	Returns number of system clock cycles since program execution
stdlib.h	**Miscellaneous functions**
malloc()	Provides dynamic memory allocation
rand()	Returns a pseudo-random number
srand()	Used to set starting point for rand()

0.11.2   Strings: Arrays of Characters

Strings are arrays of characters, and the C programming language uses the convention that the end of a string of characters is marked by a `null` character (ASCII code 0). To store the `null` character in a character variable, you can use the notation `\0`. However the compiler will automatically add a `null` character and store each character in a separate element when you use a string constant. A string constant is indicated by double quotation marks, a character constant by single quotation marks): `"A"` is a string constant and `'A'` is a character constant. It is important to realize and remember that strings are always arrays and so cannot be assigned directly, as in

```
char string[40];
string="name"
```

However, you can print strings using `printf` and read them into character arrays using `scanf`. You can also initialize a string with a string constant:

```
char name[40] = "hello";
```

But to manipulate strings we will need functions that deal with the fact that they are arrays (and that they are terminated with a null character). Standard library string functions, such as `strcmp()` and `strcat()`, are designed to operate on such arrays of characters.

0.11.3   A More Elegant Version of the Scale Program

We can now make our scale program more elegant by using an array of strings as a translation table. First, we get the key as a string, use a loop to look it up on the table, and obtain the index to it, which is our pitch class (from 0 to 11). Then we can use the table again to print out the note name. We use the `strcmp()` library function to match the strings. It returns 0 if the strings are the same.

```
#include <stdio.h>
#include <string.h>
int main()
{
    int note, i;
    char key[3];
    char* scale[12]={"C","Db","D","Eb",
                "E","F","Gb","G",
                "Ab","A","Bb","B"};
    printf("Please enter the key(capitals only, "
           "use b for flats,     eg. Eb):");
    scanf("%s",key);
    /* use table to translate note name to pitch class */
```

```
        for(i=0; i < 12; i++)
            if(strcmp(scale[i],key)==0){/* found the note */
                note = i; /* pitch-class is array index */
                printf("== %s major scale ==\n", key);
                break;
            }
            else note = -1; /* note not found */
        if(note >= 0){
            for (i=0; i < 7; i++){
            /* use table to translate pitch-class to note name */
            printf("%s ", scale[note%12]);
            if(i != 2) note += 2;
                else note++;
            }
            printf("\n");
            return 0;
        }
        else{
        printf("%s: invalid key\n", key);
        return 1;
        }
    }
```

0.12   Pointers

As we mentioned earlier, a *variable* is a memory slot that has been given a name. For example, int x; is an area of memory that has been given the name x, and x=10; stores the data constant 10 in memory slot x. The computer accesses its own memory by using a memory map with each location of memory uniquely defined by a number called an *address*. A *pointer* is a variable that holds this location of memory, the *address* of a variable. We declare it just like any other variable, but we use an asterisk to mark it. For example,

int *pa;

is a pointer to an integer. To use a pointer, we will employ two special operators: & and *. We have already seen that the & operator returns the address of a variable. For example,

int *pa, a;

declares pa, a pointer to int, and an int, and the instruction

pa=&a;

stores the address of a in pa. We say that pa is *pointing* at a.

The operator '*' is the *indirection* operator. A '*' in front of a pointer variable gives the value stored in the variable pointed at. That is, `pa` stores the *address* of a variable, and `*pa` is the *value* stored in that variable.

```
a = 10;
b = *pa; /* b is now also 10 */
*pa = 12; /* a is now 12 */
```

In summary:

- A pointer is declared by a '*' in front of its name.
- The address of a variable is given by a '&' in front of its name.
- To obtain or store the value of a variable (pointed at), use '*' in front of a pointer.

0.12.1 Pointers and Arrays

Pointers and arrays are closely connected. If you declare an array as

```
int a[10];
```

you are also declaring a pointer `a` to the first element in the array. Here, `a` is equivalent to `&a[0]`. The only difference between `a` and *a pointer variable* is that the array name is a constant pointer and cannot be used as a variable. In this sense, `a[i]` and `*(a+i)` are equivalent, which makes possible what is called *pointer arithmetic*, adding integers to pointers to step through a memory block. The compiler will know how many bytes to move forward when you add a certain number of memory slots to it. If it is an `int`, it will jump four bytes (system-dependent of course) each step, if it is a `double`, then it will jump eight bytes. This is one of the reasons why the compiler needs to know the type of a variable when you declare it.

Finally, when you pass an entire `array` to a `function` then by default a pointer is passed. This allows you to write functions that process entire arrays without having to pass every single value stored in the array, just a pointer to the first element:

```
int randarray(int *pa, int n)
{
    int i;
    for (i=0; i < n; i++)
    {
        *pa = rand()%n + 1;
        pa++;
    }
}
```

The loop can in fact be reduced to

```
for(i=0; i<n; i++) *(pa+i)=rand()%n+1;
```

or

```
for(i=0; i<n; i++) pa[i]=rand()%n+1;
```

If you define pa as a pointer, you can use array indexing notation with it as well as pointer arithmetic.

0.12.2   Strings, Arrays, and Pointers

We now see that a *string* is just a *character array* with the end of the valid data marked by an ASCII *null* character '\0'. Manipulation of strings is based on pointers and special string functions. For example, the strlen(str) function returns the number of characters in the string str. It counts the number of characters up to the first null in the character array, so it is important to use a null-terminated string.

We need a function to copy strings, because simple assignment between string variables does not work. For example,

```
char a[10],b[10];
b = a;
```

does not copy characters. It just makes pointer b set point to the same set of characters that a points to, but a second copy of the string is not created (in fact, this code will not even compile). What we need is strcopy(a,b), which copies every character in a into the array b up to the first null character. Similarly, strcat(a,b) adds the characters in b to the end of the string stored in a, and strcmp(a,b) compares the two strings, character by character, and returns 0 if the results are equal.

Notice that, to assign a character array to a string, you cannot use

```
a = "hello";
```

because a is a pointer and "hello" is a string constant. However, you can use

```
strcopy(a,"hello");
```

because a string constant is passed in exactly the same way as a string variable, i.e. as a pointer. And remember, a string can always be initialized. For example:

```
char a[6]="hello";
```

0.12.3   A Transposition Program Using Pointer Arithmetic

As an example of the use of pointer arithmetic (i.e. incrementing and decrementing memory addresses), we present a program that calculates the result of transposing a note by any number of semitones (positive or negative). This program uses an array that is a table of note names. We set a pointer to the start address of that array and then increment it until we find the base note. We then add to this pointer the interval in semitones (after bringing this to the range 0–11), then make sure the address is in the correct range (otherwise we wrap it around). This will result in the pointer being set to the address in the table where the correct note name is:

```c
#include <stdio.h>
#include <string.h>

int mod12(int note){
    while(note < 0) note += 12;
    while(note >= 12) note -=12;
    return note;
}

int main() {
    char note[3], **p1, **p2,
        *table[12] = {"C","C#","D","D#",
                      "E","F","F#","G",
                      "G#","A","A#","B"};
    int interval;
    printf("Enter base note (capitals, use # for sharps, eg. A#): ");
    scanf("%s", note);
    printf("Enter interval in semitones: ");
    scanf("%d", &interval);
    /* point p1 to the beginning of the array and p2 to its end */
    p1 = table;
    p2 = table+11;
    /* now find the base note position,
    incrementing the pointer until we find it */
    while(strcmp(*p1,note)){
        p1++;
        if(p1 > p2) { /* if we're past the end */
        printf("could not find %s\n", note);
        return 1;
        }
    }
    /* add the interval to the address of the base note */
    p1 += mod12(interval);
    /* if beyond the end of the table, wrap it around */
    if(p1 > p2) p1 -= 12;
    /* print result */
    printf("%s transposed by %d semitones is %s\n",
            note, interval, *p1);
    return 0;
}
```

0.12.4   Pointers to Functions

In C it is possible not only to have pointers to built-in data types, but also to have pointers to functions. With this facility, we will be able to manipulate functions as pointers, pass them to other functions, put them in arrays, and so on. It is quite an advanced principle, but very useful. For instance,

```
void (*pf)();
```

is a pointer to a function that takes no parameters and does not return anything. In that case, we can assign

```
void message(){ printf("my message\n"); }
pf = message;
```

and call the function using a pointer:

```
(*pf)(); /* will call message() */
```

or, even simpler,

```
pf();
```

This is because `(*pf)()` and `pf()` are equivalent, both being the function that is pointed at. In general, we have this form for function pointer declarations:

```
return-type (*pointer-name) (arguments);
```

Why do we need something like this? Well, function pointers are useful for *callbacks*, i.e. functions not invoked directly by you but by existing code. For instance, suppose we have the function

```
void message_printer(int times, void (*callback)(char *msg),
                     char *user_mess){
     int i;
     for(i=0; i < times; i++) callback(user_mess);
}
```

This invokes a user-defined function to print out a user-supplied message, a callback. The user would then supply a callback for `message-printer()` to call it, as in the following example:

```
void my_important_message(char *mess){
     printf("VERY IMPORTANT: %s \n", mess);
}

void my_warning_message(char* mess) {
     printf("WARNING: %s\n", mess);
}
```

```
int main() {
message-printer(10, my_important_message, "functions can be pointers");
message-printer(1, my_warning_message, "but be careful");
return 0;
}
```

This advanced concept can be much more useful than the trivial example above, but this gives you an idea of what a callback is. These types of programming constructs are often seen in audio systems, where the programmer supplies a callback that will be used by the system to perform a particular task (such as sending audio samples to the soundcard).

0.13   Structures

The array is an example of a data structure made up of a single data type. If you need something that holds a variety of types together in a single block, you will need a *single data structure* using a single name, provided in the C language by `struct`.

0.13.1   User-Defined Data Types

With C structures we have a new, user-defined, data type. To use them, first we need to define what the new type looks like, using `struct`:

```
struct note
{
    char name[3];
    int duration;
    char intensity[5];
};
```

Then we can declare a variable of that type, to be used in the program:

```
struct note first;
```

Notice that the new variable is called `first` and is of the type `note`. This can be considered as valid a data type as any of the built-in types, such as `float` or `int`. In general, you can define a structure using

```
struct name
{
    list of member variables
};
```

and you can have as many member variables as you need. Once defined you can declare as many examples of the new type as you like, using

```
struct name list of variables;
```

For example,

```
struct note first, second, third;
```

and so on. If you want to avoid using `struct` for variable declaration, you can use `typedef`. For instance,

```
typedef struct _note
{
    char name[3];
    int duration;
    char intensity[5];
} note;
```

```
note first;
```

defines the structure, and a new type based on it called `note`, then uses the newly created data type directly. To use the data type, you can access each member by name, using a period to link the variable name and the requested structure member:

```
first.name
first.duration
```

Once you have used a qualified name to get down to the level of a member variable, it behaves like a normal variable of the type defined in the structure. For example,

```
first.duration = 120;
```

is a valid assignment to an `int`, and

```
strcpy(first.name, "C");
```

is a valid statement. Notice that to access the member we use the structure variable name and not the structure type name. You can also define a structure that includes another structure as a component and of course that structure can contain another structure and so on. Structures can be initialized using syntax that is similar to array initialization:

```
note first = { "Ab", 80, "mf" };
```

As another example of the use of structures, we would like to define a type to hold complex numbers. A complex number is composed of two parts—a real part and an imaginary part—that can be implemented as single or double precision values. This suggests defining a new `struct` type:

```
typedef struct comp
{
    float real;
    float imag;
} complex;
```

After this, you can declare new complex variables using

```
complex a,b;
```

The new complex variables cannot be used as if they were simple variables. C does allow you to assign structures as in

```
a = b;
```

Being able to assign structures and operate on them is even more useful when they are bigger. What we can do is to define a function to operate on a structure. You can pass entire structures as parameters and return entire structures. As with all C parameters, structures are passed by value; thus, if you want to allow a function to alter a parameter you have to remember to pass a *pointer* to a `struct`. For instance, multiplication of complex numbers can be defined as follows:

```
complex mult(complex a, complex b)
{
    complex c;
    c.real=a.real*b.real-a.imag*b.imag;
    c.imag=a.real*b.imag + a.imag*b.real;
    return c;
}
```

You can then write a complex multiplication as

```
x=mult(y,z)
```

The following program example demonstrates the use of structures and how to operate on them:

```
#include <stdio.h>

typedef struct comp
{
    float real;
    float imag;
} complex;

complex mult(complex a, complex b)
{
    complex c;
    c.real=a.real*b.real - a.imag*b.imag;
    c.imag=a.real*b.imag + a.imag*b.real;
    return c;
}

int main()
```

```
{
    float re, im;
    complex a, b;
     get two complex numbers as inputs */
    printf("Please enter the first complex number (re, im): ");
    scanf("%f %f", &re, &im);
    a.real = re; a.imag = im;
    printf("Please enter the second complex number (re, im): ");
    scanf("%f %f", &re, &im);
    b.real = re; b.imag = im;
    /* multiply them */
    a = mult(a,b);
    printf("Their product is %f + %fi \n", a.real, a.imag);
    return 0;
}
```

Finally, notice that passing a `struct` by value (to a function) can use up a lot of memory in the case of large data structures (which is not the case in the example above). This is because a copy of the structure is made for the function argument. To avoid this, you can use pointers to structures.

0.13.2   Pointers to Structures

You can declare a pointer to a structure in the same way as any pointer. For example,

`person *ptr`

defines a pointer to a `person`. You can use a pointer to a `struct` in the same way as any pointer, but the typical means of structure access makes it look rather awkward. For example,

`(*ptr).age`

is the age component of the `person` structure that `ptr` points at—i.e. an `int`. You need the brackets because a period has a higher priority than an asterisk. The use of a pointer to a `struct` is so common that you can use

`prt->age`

to mean the same thing as `(*ptr).age`. The notation gives a better idea of what is happening: `prt` points (`->`) to the structure and `age` selects which component of the structure we want.

0.13.3   Structures and Functions

Structures can only contain built-in data types, so a function cannot be directly defined inside a structure. However, as we can declare pointers to functions, we could use them to hold functions, which in some cases might be useful. For instance, it would be nice to be able to have an increment function for the complex data type. First, we could declare a structure containing a function pointer

```
typedef struct comp {
    double real, imag;
    void (*incr)(struct comp *p);
} complex;
```

Then we could define a function to operate on the data (we'll use a pointer, as it is more efficient):

```
void incr1(complex *p){ p->real++; p->imag++; }
```

To use this structure and its associated function, we can write the following code:

```
complex a = { 0, 0, incr1 };
a.incr(&a);
```

0.13.4   Structures and C++

Defining functions to work on data structures is very useful. In C++, there will be an easier way to do it. Structures with functions associated with them are in fact a point of connection between C and C++, as they become *classes* in C++. In simple terms, a C++ class is a structure in which you can define members that are functions (not only function pointers). You will also be able to control access to the data members of a class. Moreover, the same '.' access system applies to the *class* and the use of pointers and the '->' operator. These elements will be further discussed in later sections of this chapter.

0.14   Dynamic Memory Allocation

So far we have not bothered with how memory is set aside for data you use in a program. In the usual variable declaration, the compiler works out how to allocate storage. For example, when you declare

```
int a;
```

the compiler sorts out how to allocate memory to store the integer, and with `int a[256];` it allocates space for 256 `int`s and sets the name a to point to the first element. This is static, automatic storage—storage that is allocated at "compile time." But another way to do this is to use dynamic allocation, with the `malloc` function:

```
pa = malloc(size);
```

Here `malloc` allocates a certain number of bytes (`size`) and returns the address of that location. Since we can retrieve the size of any data type with the `sizeof(...)` function, we can allocate storage using

```
pa = malloc(sizeof(int)*N);
```

where `N` is the number of `int`s you want to create. But because `malloc` is used to allocate an arbitrary memory block, it returns a `void` pointer, which must then be cast to the right type:

```
pa = (int *) malloc(sizeof(int)*N);
```

This makes the value returned by `malloc` a pointer to `int`. After this definition, you can use `ptr` as normal. For example,

```
pa[n]
```

is the nth element of the array. When you are finished with the memory, you'll have to use `free(pa);` to free it.

0.15   Command-Line Arguments

Now let us look at how to get arguments off a command line. This uses the second form of `main()` shown at the beginning of the chapter. Command-line arguments are passed to a program through two arguments to the `main()` function. The parameters, are called `argc` and `argv`, are seen in the following main prototype:

```
int main(int argc, char **argv)
```

The `argc` parameter holds the number of arguments on the command-line and is an integer. It will always be at least one because the name of the program is the first argument. The `argv` parameter is an array of string pointers. All command-line arguments are passed to `main()` as strings. For example:

```
#include <stdio.h>

int main(int argc, char *argv[])
{
    int i;
    for (i=1; i<argc; i++) printf("%s", argv[i]);
    return 0;
}
```

This program will print out all of its arguments, starting with the program name.

0.15.1   A Program for Analyzing Serial Music

We will now use many of the C language tools learned in this chapter to create a fully functional program for analyzing serial music. Suppose we want to apply the rules of twelve-tone music to create a matrix with all the serial forms that derive from a single tone row. The first row of the matrix will receive the original twelve notes, from left to right. The inversion of the series will fill the first column of the matrix, from top to bottom. To complete the matrix, the other rows will receive transposed versions of the original series, each one starting with the note in the first column. When the matrix is complete, we will be able to read all the transposition forms of the original series in the rows from left to right, the retrograde forms in the same rows from right to left, the inversions in the columns from top to bottom, and the retrograde of inversion forms in the opposite sense. Here are the steps that we will have to take to achieve this:

1. As in previous examples, we will take pitch classes from 0 to 11, which form the original series, from the command-line arguments, and place this series in the first row of the matrix.
2. We will use two arithmetic formulae for the inversion and transposition of the original series. The inverse form, appearing in the first column, is given by

$$P_{m,1} = [(P_{m-1,1} + (P_{1,m-1} - P_{1,m})] \bmod 12 \tag{1}$$

and, the subsequent transpositions are given by

$$P_{m,n} = [(P_{1,n} + (P_{m,1} - P_{1,1})] \bmod 12. \tag{2}$$

3. We will then use a translation table to print the serial matrix.

Using many of the principles introduced earlier in the chapter, we can create a very compact program. Note that we will not check for correct inputs (in the range of 0–11, but we will apply mod12 to all input pitch classes) or repetition of notes (required by certain types of serial music). Here is the program:

```c
#include <stdio.h>
#include <stdlib.h>

int mod12(int note) {
    while(note >= 12) note -= 12;
    while(note < 0) note += 12;
    return note;
}

int
main(int argc, char** argv)
{
    int series[12][12], offset;
    int n, m, i;
    char* table[12]={"C","Db","D","Eb",
                     "E","F","Gb","G",
                     "Ab","A","Bb","B"};

    if(argc != 13) {
        printf("usage: %s note1 note2 ... note12\n", argv[0]);
        return -1;
```

```
    }
    /* loop until all available notes are entered*/
    for(n = 0; n < 12; n++)
        series[0][n] = mod12(atoi(argv[n+1]));

    /* create inversion in column 1 */
    for(m = 1; m < 12; m++)
        series[m][0] = mod12(series[m-1][0] + series[0][m-1]
                                - series[0][m]) ;

    /* create all transpositions */
    for(m = 1; m < 12; m++)
        for(n = 1; n < 12; n++)
            series[m][n] = mod12(series[0][n] + series[m][0]
                                    - series[0][0]);

    for(m = 0; m < 12; m++){
        /* print the pitch classes, row by row, using the
            translation table */
        for(n = 0; n < 12; n++) printf(" %s ", table[series[m][n]]);
        printf("\n");
    }

    return 0;
}
```

This concludes our tour of C, which demonstrates how compact yet expressive and efficient it can be. As a complement, let us look briefly at some elements of C++.

0.16   Moving to C++

The C++ programming language is a super-set of C. As such, it supports and allows all the C coding we have done so far, but it introduces new elements and additional resources, which hopefully make life easier for the programmer. There are many new features in C++ (in fact, C++ is anything but a small language), only a few of which we will introduce here. We must remember that if strict C is required, then we cannot use any C++ features in a program. When writing pure C code, we should use the file extension .c; when writing C++ code, we should use .cpp. This will avoid confusion and make sure that the building tools call the right compiler (for C or for C++).

0.16.1   Variable Declaration Anywhere in the Code

The C programming language allows variables to be declared only at the start of a code block ({ }), whereas C++ allows variables to be declared anywhere. For instance:

```
/* C example */
void func(){
int a,b,c;
    a = g();
    b = f();
    c = a+b;
}
// C++ example
void func(){
    int a;
    a = g();

    int b;
    b = f();

    int c = a + b;
}
```

0.16.2   Default Value for Arguments in Functions

In C++ it is possible to declare functions with default arguments:

```
float func(int a=0, int b=1, float f=0.5f);
```

```
float func(int a, int b, float f){
    return a+b*f;
}
```

When called as in

```
a = func();
```

this function will return `0.5`.

In order to use this facility, in the declaration, we define which arguments are to have default values by initializing them. In the function definition, we just implement the code as before.

0.16.3   Memory Management: new and delete

C++ provides a simpler mechanism for memory allocation, which is perhaps less awkward than `malloc()` and friends. This mechanism is implemented with two C++ operators: `new` and `delete`.

The former is used to allocate memory for any built-in or user-defined variable type, as in

```
// memory allocation for float pointer variable a
```

```
float *a = new float;
// ditto for int pointer variable b
int *b = new int;
// ditto for struct Mystruct pointer variable s
MyStruct *s = new MyStruct;
```

Memory can be allocated for arrays, as in

```
int size = 512;
float *array = new float[size]; // 512 floats.
```

As this is a dynamic memory allocation, a variable can be used to determine how much memory will be allocated. Only one dimension of a multi-dimensional array can be allocated at a time. To free the memory, we use `delete`:

```
delete a;
```

For arrays, we use a slightly different form:

```
delete[] array;
```

0.16.4   Structures and Data Types

In C++, when defining a structure, we are also creating a new data type, so we do not need the `typedef` keyword to define it. In fact, a `struct` is a special case of a programming structure called a *class*, which can also contain *constructors* and *methods* (functions that are members of a class). For the moment, it is sufficient to know that we can write

```
struct MyStruct {
    int a, b;
    float f;
};           // no need for typedef...

MyStruct obj;
obj.a = 1; // etc...
```

0.16.5   Line Comments

C++ also supports a single-line comment, using '`//`' as the first characters in a line of code. We have been using this type of comments in the examples above. This turns all the text on the rest of the line into a comment (until a new line character is seen).

0.17   Data Abstraction

Data abstraction is another important element of programming that is enabled in a more consistent way by C++ than by C. It consists of defining new data types that would model something—perhaps signal-processing components or unit generators. We will define a data type by deciding what it is made of (its *member variables*) and what it can do (its *operations*). C++ structures provide good support for this type of programming. For example, we can define a structure to hold an oscillator's data (the *dataspace*) and functions or methods (the *methodspace*) as follows:

```
struct Osc {
    // dataspace
    float *table; // ftable
    float phase; // phase offset
    float ndx; // ndx
    int length; // ftable length
    int vecsize; // vector size
    float rate; // sampling rate
    float *output; // output audio block

    // methodspace
    Osc(float *tab, float ph=0.f, int len=def_len,
            int vsize=def_vsize, int sr=def_sr);
    ~Osc() { delete[] output; }
    float *Proc(float amp, float freq);

};
```

The structure holds all the data members that make up the oscillator, the data that needs to be persistent (i.e. present in memory) between invocations of the process function. The methodspace is made up of the bare minimum necessary: an initializing function (the *constructor*), the deallocating function (the *destructor*), and the oscillator function proper. The constructor will always have the same name as the structure, and the destructor will have a '~' before the structure name. This is called automatically when the instance of the structure is deallocated. In order to use this data type, all we need do is create one (using all the default parameters):

```
Osc bing(table);
```

and the process function will generate audio, as in

```
output(fp_out, bing.Proc(0.5f, 440.f));
```

Since `Proc()` is a member of `osc`, it is accessed means of a '.'. Notice that in the present design the function returns the audio block, which has been allocated inside the data type by the constructor. Member functions such as those declared above can be defined inside the `struct` definition (as in ~osc()) or externally. The syntax for the latter is

```
struct_name::member_func()
```

For example, the constructor will be defined as

```
Osc::Osc(float *tab, float ph, int len, int vsize, int sr){
    table = tab;
    phase = ph;
    length = len;
    vecsize = vsize;
    ndx = 0.f;
    rate = sr;
    output = new float[vecsize];
}
```

and the processing function will be

```
float *Osc::Proc(float amp, float freq) {
    float incr = freq*length/rate;
    for(int i=0; i < vecsize; i++){
        output[i] = amp*table[(int)ndx];
        ndx += incr;
        while(ndx >= length) ndx -= length;
        while(ndx < 0) ndx += length;
    }
    return output;
}
```

The above code demonstrates that functions belonging to a `struct` have access to their local variables and to the member variables of the structure they belong to. This is very useful because table indexes and wave tables can be kept outside the function and separate from the rest of the program. In addition, each instance of the `Osc` data type will have its own individual member variables, and the user need not supply them to the processing function.

0.17.1   Function Overloading

Function overloading is another feature of C++. It is possible to have functions with same name in a class, as long as their arguments differ in type or in number. Function selection, then, depends on argument types at the function call. It is possible to supply more than one processing method to the structure, say to take in audio vectors for the amplitude and/ or frequency arguments (for audio rate modulation of these parameters). Because of overloading, it is possible to use the same name (`Proc()`) for these functions:

```
struct Osc {

    // dataspace
    float amp; // amplitude
    float freq; // frequency
    float *table; // ftable
    float phase; // phase offset
    float ndx; // ndx
    int length; // ftable length
    int vecsize; // vector size
    float rate; // sampling rate
    float *output; // output audio block

    // methodspace

    Osc(float amp, float freq, float *tab, float ph=0.f,
        int len=def_len,int vsize=def_vsize, int sr=def_sr);
    ~Osc() { delete[] output; }
    // fixed amp & freq
    float *Proc();
    // variable control-rate amp & freq
    float *Proc(float amp,float freq);
    // audio-rate amp
    float *Proc(float *amp,float freq);
    // audio-rate freq
    float *Proc(float amp,float *freq);
    // audio-rate amp & freq
    float *Proc(float *amp,float *freq);

};
```

0.17.2 Usage Examples

fixed parameters

```
Osc zing(0.5f,440.f,wtable);

for(...) {
    sig = zing.Osc(); // 440 Hz -6dB sound
}
```

FM synthesis

```
Osc mod(ind*fm, fm, sintab);
Osc car(amp, fc, sintab);
```

0.18   Data Hiding and Encapsulation

Another feature of C++ that can be useful for systems design is the support for data hiding and encapsulation. This allows us to make certain bits of the data structure available only for member functions, and not for functions that are external to the data structure. One reason this might be useful is that we can keep things in a structure completely separate from the rest of the program. We can then provide an interface for accessing only certain elements of our data types, the ones we want to grant access to. This will provide a more robust data type, which will be able to behave only in ways defined by us.

In a structure, all members are accessible from the outside: they are public by default. If we use the keyword 'private', we can keep them from being accessed by external code:

```
struct Osc {

    // dataspace is now private
    private:

    float *table; // ftable
    float phase; // phase offset
    float ndx; // ndx
    int length; // ftable length
    int vecsize; // vector size
    float rate; // sampling rate
    float *output; // output audio block

    // methodspace needs to be accessible
    public:

    Osc(float *tab, float ph=0.f, int len=def_len,
        int vsize=def_vsize, int sr=def_sr);
    ~Osc() { delete[] output; }
    float *Proc(float amp,float freq);

};
```

We can still create an instance of our data type, because the constructor is public:

```
Osc ping(table);
```

But we cannot read or write to the member variables:

```
ping.ndx = 1; // not allowed, ndx is private
```

0.18.1   Classes

In C++, a version of `struct` exists in which all members are private by default. It is called a `class`:

```
class Osc {
    // dataspace is private by default
    float *table; // ftable
    (...)
    // methodspace needs to be accessible
    public:
    Osc(float *tab, float ph=0.f, int len=def_len,
        int vsize=def_vsize, int sr=def_sr);
    (...)
};
```

Classes and structures are basically the same thing, although the former is more commonly used. They provide the support for a programming style called *object-oriented programming* (OOP), in which the ideas discussed above in relation to data abstraction and data hiding play an important part. In OOP parlance, we call the instances of a data type *objects*.

0.18.2   A C++ Program for Analyzing Serial Music

In this subsection, we will present a version of our serial analysis program using the concept of data hiding and encapsulation. We will start by modeling the concept of a twelve-tone series and the basic operations that we can apply to it:

```
class Dodecaphonic {
    protected:
    int series[12]; /* the tone row, hidden from outside */
    int mod12(int note) { /* the modulus as an internal method */
        while(note >= 12) note -= 12;
        while(note < 0) note += 12;
        return note;
    }
    public:
    Dodecaphonic() { /* default constructor */
        for(int i=0; i < 12; i++) series[i] = 0;
    }
    Dodecaphonic(int *notes) { /* constructor from an array */
        for(int i=0; i < 12; i++) series[i] = mod12(notes[i]);
    }
    int get(int index){ return series[mod12(index)]; /* get & set
                                                        notes */
    void set(int note, int index) {
            series[mod12(index)] = mod12(note); }
```

```
    Dodecaphonic transpose(int interval); /* the three basic
                                              operations */
    Dodecaphonic invert();
    Dodecaphonic retrograde();

};

/* defining the operations. All of them return a Dodecaphonic object */
Dodecaphonic Dodecaphonic::transpose(int interval){
    Dodecaphonic transp;
    for(int i=0; i < 12; i++)
        transp.set(mod12(series[i]+interval), i);
    return transp;
}

Dodecaphonic Dodecaphonic::invert(){
    Dodecaphonic inv;
    inv.set(series[0],0);
    for(int i=1; i < 12; i++)
        inv.set(mod12(inv.get(i-1) + series[i-1] - series[i]), i);
    return inv;
}

Dodecaphonic Dodecaphonic::retrograde(){
    Dodecaphonic retr;
    for(int i=0; i < 12; i++) retr.set(series[i], 11-i);
    return retr;
}
```

Notice that in this simple class we did not have to allocate new memory or do any extensive initialization. Because of that, we do not have to define a destructor (the compiler will provide a default one), and assignment (=) will work by default. In more complicated cases, a "copy constructor" and an "assignment operator" would have to be defined for this to work correctly. These issues, however, are beyond the scope of this chapter. Also, `transpose()` and other manipulation methods do not modify the state of the object, but return a new object with the desired state (this is a design decision; state-modifying methods could also have been implemented).

    With this class in hand, it is very simple to create a little program that will give us one of the four versions of an original series (transposed, inverted, retrograde, inverted retrograde). Because each operation returns a dodecaphonic object, we can operate directly on the returned value, without the need to use a variable to hold it. For example,

```
b = a.invert(); c = b.transpose(1);
```

can be written as

```
b = a.invert().transpose(1);
```

Here is a program that uses this class (the ellipsis is a placeholder for the class code defined above):

```
#include <stdio.h>
#include <stdlib.h>
. . .

int main(int argc, char** argv)
{
    Dodecaphonic row, res;
    int interval, n;
    if(argc != 14 || argv[1][0] != '-'){
        printf("usage: %s [-oN | -rN | -iN | -irN] "
               "note1 note2 ... note12\n",
               argv[0]);
        return -1;
    }
    for(n = 0; n < 12; n++) /* initialize the row object */
        row.set(atoi(argv[n+2]), n);
    switch(argv[1][1]){
    case 'o': /* original transposed */
        interval = atoi(argv[1]+2);
        res = row.transpose(interval);
        break;
    case 'r': /* retrograde */
        interval = atoi(argv[1]+2);
        res = row.retrograde().transpose(interval);
        break;
    case 'i': /* inverted */
        if(argv[1][3] != 'r'){
            interval = atoi(argv[1]+2);
            res = row.invert().transpose(interval);
        }
        else { /* inverted retrograde */
            interval = atoi(argv[1]+3);
            res = row.invert().retrograde().transpose(interval);
        }
        break;
    default:
        printf("unrecognized option \n");
        return -1;
    }
```

```
for(n = 0; n < 12; n++)
    printf("%d ", res.get(n));
printf("\n");
return 0;
}
```

0.18.3   Inheritance

Classes (and structures) can also be created from other classes by inheritance. This allows the re-use of code (rather than rewriting it) and the definition of a common interface for various interrelated objects (all derived classes will share some code, especially functions). The syntax for deriving a class from an existing one looks like this:

```
class Osci : public Osc {

(...)
};
```

This makes Osci a derived class from Osc. All public members in Osc are also made public in Osci. Thus Osci can access all the public members in Osc, but not the private ones. In order to make private members accessible to derived classes, we must use the keyword protected, which means private to the class and all its subclasses.

0.18.4   Virtual Functions

C++ has also a mechanism that allows functions to be specialized in subclasses. These are called *virtual functions*. By using the keyword virtual for a function on the *superclass*, we can make these functions overridable; that is, we can supply new code for their implementation:

```
class Osc {

    (...)
    virtual float *Proc(float amp,float freq);
};
```

The Proc() function can be then re-declared and re-implemented in a derived class (Osci, say) to implement an interpolated lookup (instead of truncation):

```
class Osci : public Osc {

    (...)
    virtual float *Proc(float amp,float freq);
};
```

This allows a system to provide an interface for processing functions, which can be implemented by derived classes. The OOP term for this is *polymorphism*. An example of the use of such a mechanism is found in the application programming interface for VST plug-ins, which is written in C++ and is based on the derivation of classes from a *base class*.

0.18.5 Overloaded Operators

Similarly to overloaded functions, it is possible to define overloaded forms of specific operators for a certain class definition. The operators =, +, –, *, /, <<, and >> can be overloaded. For instance, we could set up the overloading of operator + for our `Osc` class as follows:

```
class Osc {

    (...)
    float *operator+(float val) {
        // adds val to every sample in the output block
        for(int i=0; i < vecsize; i++) output[i] += val;
        // returns the audio block
        return output;
    }

};
```

Now using '+' with an `Osc` object and a `float` has a definite meaning: add that number to every sample in the output audio block of the `Osc` object (and return a block of samples). Here is an example of how it can be used:

```
Osc oscil(...);
float a = 1000.f;
float *buffer;
(...)

for(...) {
    (...)
    buffer = oscil + a;
    (...)
}
```

0.19 Final Words

In this chapter we have focused on the aspects of C++ that should be useful for audio programming, and on almost the whole of the C language. We hope the chapter has served as a quick refresher course if you are an experienced programmer and as an inspiring appetizer if you are a beginner.

Clearly, C++ is much more extensive than C. C++ has its own powerful and robust standard library, the C++ Standard Template Library, which is beyond the scope of this chapter but is well worth exploring.

In the chapters that follow, you will find both "slow-cooked" and "fast-food" audio recipes in C and C++ that will sustain, nourish, and inspire the development of your own unique audio and musical applications regardless of your level of expertise. Along the way, you will learn to program in both C and C++; at the same time, you will learn the fundamentals and secrets of digital signal processing, software synthesis, computer music, algorithmic composition, and digital audio.

1 Programming in C

Richard Dobson

1.1 Why C?

This section concentrates, as any first section on programming must, on the essential features of the language used. However, unlike general books on programming, this book has a specific focus, from the outset, on music and audio applications. A useful advantage of this is that it gives an opportunity to address in very practical ways the question of *why* you need to know this, or do that. We have all seen instruction manuals with statements such as "to decouple the bifurcated sprocket flange, use the long-handled dingbat"—without explaining why, and in what circumstances, you would want or need to do it.

In each of the examples of C code that follow, some audio or music aspect is incorporated or developed. This gives a clear focus, and I hope it will give at least partial answers to the "why" question, but a "pure" presentation of the language runs the risk of concealing issues that a more thorough theoretical approach might consider important. So the approach here is based on the desire to get results, rather than on a foundation of theory; theoretical principles will arise rather as an emergent feature, on which a stronger emphasis is placed in later sections. Nevertheless, the question "Why C?" is worth addressing at the outset.

The most obvious problem we face in programming audio processes is speed of computation. Many techniques, such as spectral transformation, have been known about for decades, but only with computer processing speeds at the level they have reached in the last few years has it been possible to use them in real time. Even now, ensuring that the code is as efficient as possible is still of great importance, especially for real-time performance. It translates into more of everything (more oscillators, more filters, more channels) and higher quality (better filters, better reverbs, and so on). Fortunately for the purposes of this book, computers are fast enough now that we can in many cases afford the luxury of code that is arguably inefficient to a degree, but demonstrates a process clearly. Nevertheless, throughout the book, hints and tips on "optimizing" working code for maximum performance will be given; and as your understanding develops, these techniques will gradually become part of your stock in trade. They are typically based on knowledge of how compilers work, or how computers work (e.g. how data is moved around in memory), or both. C programming does tend to demand that, sooner or later, this knowledge will be essential.

The C language has often been described as "close to the hardware." Expressions in the language can be compiled to very efficient machine code, exploiting the facilities of each processor. Some idioms in C, such as the auto-increment and decrement operators and the address-of and pointer operators, match machine-level instructions exactly. As a result, C programs may run as fast as programs written in low-level assembler code. The complexity of modern processors, coupled with a powerful code optimizer (an essential component of any C compiler), can even mean that a compiled C program may be more efficient than a skilled programmer can achieve working in assembler. However, these idioms presuppose an understanding of how the processor handles instructions and data, and even of exactly how that data is stored in memory. C does little to hide such things from the programmer, and does even less to prevent you from writing code that can crash the program (and maybe even the computer). Thus, C is a "permissive" language—it allows you to do things that it would be a very good idea *not* to do.

One aspect of C that facilitates closeness to the hardware is, curiously enough, the complete absence, within the language itself, of anything to do with input and output. Text input from a keyboard and output to a screen or printer depend on hardware, and usually on the facilities of a supporting operating system. However, an embedded processor may have neither—perhaps it is connected to transducers and a set of LEDs. All such facilities are external to the language and have to be supplied by libraries, which now are highly standardized and which a complete compiler package will always include.

This closeness to the hardware also has made the C language pre-eminent for the writing of operating systems. C is associated primarily with UNIX and its variants. Many people today maintain that the ideal platform for the development of audio applications is one or other flavors of UNIX (including Linux and now Macintosh OS X) and its native C compiler. That compiler will include a set of libraries supporting all aspects of the operating system, including support for input and output devices of all kinds.

In view of the importance of speed for audio programming (and the need to be able to talk directly to hardware such as A to D and D to A converters, MIDI ports, and so on), it is easy to understand why C has become popular. As a result of its widespread use, a lot of expertise and a lot of help are available, and there is a great mass of published source code (covering the range from simple tools to advanced large-scale applications) to draw upon.

Despite being close to the hardware, C also has the characteristics of a "high-level language." ("High-level" means close to the user; "low-level" means close to the hardware.) It provides a variety of powerful and flexible facilities for creating and managing large applications, while making it easy to write simple yet useful tools. Much that is very useful can be done without the need for "advanced" programming skills. This power comes only partly from the language itself, which supports a "building-block" approach to programming. The rest comes from the development environment supporting the compiler itself—copious messages from the compiler to help track down errors, and a powerful text pre-processor that, though in principle external to the language, is in practice inseparable from it.

The popularity of C has stimulated the development of very sophisticated development environments supporting many "visual" tools. Perhaps the most important tool is the "source-level debugger," which makes it possible to run a program a line at a time, watching how the data changes. The debugger will run a program for you, and if the program crashes it will automatically show you the line of code that triggered the crash, and give some indication of what the cause is (such as reading from non-existent memory). It is also possible to make a program stop at a particular place in the code ("setting a breakpoint"), where again you can inspect the state of all relevant data, and even change it before resuming execution.

But the compiler cannot tell you what to do to fix a bug. Thus, knowing how to fix problems ("debugging") and, better, knowing how to avoid them in the first place ("defensive programming") soon become central skills for the programmer to master. Audio programs that depend on running at full speed for correct operation (e.g. because a process has to respond to signals from the hardware) offer special challenges in this respect.

Other "why" questions arise from specific aspects of the language, or from the chosen application domains of music and audio. These will be addressed within the context of each topic or each code example. The reasons for coding one way rather than another may arise not only from the requirement for speed, but also from the desire for audio quality, or simply from the need for clarity of design, so that the code can be read six months later and still be understood. Programmers rarely like to "reinvent the wheel," so whenever they come up with some code that might be of general use they may put a bit of extra work into it to make it as reusable as possible. At other times, code is written a particular way to facilitate testing and debugging. One may also encounter discussions about "ugly code" and "beautiful code"—there is a strong aesthetic element to programming, as is true of most technical disciplines.

In short, we want to write code that works well, that makes sense when we read it, that is easy to modify and extend, and that we may be able to use again in other projects. You will find that documenting your code becomes at least as important as writing it. Even excellent code is of little use if you don't know how to use it.

The main point to carry with you as you read this chapter concerns the use of libraries. For writing audio applications, we cannot avoid the use of libraries; indeed, we will be very grateful for their existence, as they remove from us a great deal of hard work, and make possible what would otherwise be impossible. This will become very much clearer as you work through the chapters in this book. The question "What is a library, exactly?" has not been answered yet, but it will be answered soon. Indeed, you will find, almost by accident, that as you work through the book you are in a real sense creating your own library; and all it takes to complete that process is use of the standard "library-maker" tool (not a technical term) that is part of the compiler. All you need know at this stage is that a library stores sections of code (those building blocks mentioned above) that you expect not to change and you expect to use frequently. As you will soon discover, a modern C compiler includes a large number of standard libraries, and in order to use them to the full you will have to be able to read and understand the documentation.

1.1.1 Your First C Program

Before proceeding, it is worth looking at appendix A (which deals with the compiler and command-line tools) so that you have an idea of the programming environment we will be using. These early examples assume a traditional command-line environment. While all the example programs presented here are available on the DVD as complete projects, it is preferable that you practice typing in the code by hand, especially if you are unpracticed at typing. The text editor, used to write and edit programs, is of supreme importance, so the sooner you get familiar with it the better.

Listing 1.1 is a faintly musical version of the classic "Hello World" program that everyone traditionally writes first when learning a new language. Although it is extremely short, it illustrates many of the fundamental aspects of C described above. Listing 1.1 includes line numbers (starting from 1) in the left margin for convenience. These are not actually part of the program code—all text editors used for writing programs will display, somewhere on the screen, the line containing the typing cursor.

Listing 1.1

```
1   /* wonder.c:displays "What a Wonderful World!" in the terminal */
2   #include <stdio.h>
3
4
5   int main()
6   {
7       printf("What a Wonderful World!\n");
8       return 0;
9   }
10
```

The first thing to notice about this example is that there is a lot of what is called "white space": there are empty lines, and some lines are indented. As far as a C program is concerned, all this white space is almost always unimportant. There are situations where the presence or absence of white space is meaningful ("syntactically significant"), but a lot of the time we can use it freely, to lay out the code as we wish.

Line 1 comprises a text comment. You could delete this whole line and the program would still compile. Comments are ignored by the compiler; they are there purely for the benefit of the human reader. This comment simply identifies the name of the file and its purpose. A comment in C is anything placed between the /* and */ character pairs (there must be no space between the * and the /). These are characters that cannot legally occur together as C code. There is no requirement for the comment to fit on a single line. The lines below equally form a legal comment:

```
/* This is a comment,
   running over
   several lines.
*/
```

Apart from their primary use to add annotations to source code, comments are often used to prevent lines of code from being compiled, without having to delete them. There are other, arguably better ways of doing this, but the practice is widespread. Depending on your text editor, text inside a comment may be drawn in a special color, to make it easy to see where the comment starts and ends. If this is the case, try deleting the closing */ and see what happens.

Some programmers like to write elaborate titles and descriptions at the head of a source file, as in the following example:

```
/******************** WONDER.C     **************/
/*
 *
 * Version 1.0 RWD 10/1/2002.

 ********* DESCRIPTION *********
 *
 *This program writes a friendly and affirmative message to the user.
 * TODO: Add more lines from the song.
 */

/**** BUGS AND LIMITATIONS *****
 * No bugs found.
 * It would be good to have the computer sing the text.
 *
 */
```

There is no need to type this in (hardly necessary for a program as simple as this); but make sure you can see how many separate comments there are, by looking for the matching /* */ pairs. Note that you are not allowed to nest comments (putting one /* */ pair inside another one). Such descriptive blocks are often used to carry copyright or licensing information. The rest of the text comprises C code to be compiled—this is where we have to get everything right.

Skipping line 2 for a moment, we see a block of code extending from line 5 to line 9. This block defines a *function*. The function is the primary building block used in computer programs. Here we have just one function, called main. This is the one function a C program must contain in order to be compiled as an executable program. You are not allowed to have duplicate functions (i.e. with the same name) in C. The term 'function' comes from mathematics and is used to describe some procedure that takes an input (consisting of one or more numbers) and produces an output (also consisting of one or more numbers). The definition of a function must allow for the possibility of either or both input and output. In this case, the `main` function outputs a single integer number, indicated by the type specifier word `int` in line 5.

In the code, `int` is an example of a C *keyword*, a word that belongs to the language, and is therefore *reserved* (you can't use it as the name for anything else). It is one of a collection of keywords that define basic numeric types (see section 1.2). Another keyword in this program is `return`, used in line 8.

After the function name `main` there is a pair of parentheses. These provide a space for any input data. In this case there is no input, so we can just write the parentheses by themselves. Later, we will see alternative ways of defining the `main` function to enable it to receive input from the user.

So far, the `main` function looks as follows:

```
int main()
```

But this is incomplete—it does not define what the function does. This is the job of the function's *body*. The body of a function is defined by code placed between braces, as in this example:

```
{
    return 0;
}
```

Now the complete structure of the `main` function looks as follows:

```
int main()
{
    return 0;
}
```

You can, in fact, replace all of lines 5–9 with the above, and the program will compile. It just won't appear to do anything. However, it is actually performing one task. The `main` function is defined as producing an integer result; and the one line of code shown above does this: it causes `main` to output the value 0. To do this we are using the C keyword `return`, followed by the required value. In the jargon of C programming, the return value of `main()` is 0. Overall, this line of code forms a C "statement." As was shown above, a C statement is terminated by a semicolon. Where to put a semicolon is one of the aspects that most often confuse beginning C programmers. As you study the code examples in this book, take careful note of where a semicolon is required and where it is not. You will see that the code inside the `main` function comprises one or more statements, each ending in a semicolon (look back at listing 1.1), but the function body (defined by braces) is *not* followed by a semicolon.

What happens to the value returned by `main()`? In the majority of cases it is just ignored; however, where programs are run remotely, from a UNIX shell script or from a DOS batch file, it is possible to read the return value, and to take action accordingly. Typically, a return value of 0 means that "the program terminated without errors," and anything else means that some error occurred. For example, if a program requires a file to be opened, but the name given is incorrect (e.g. the file doesn't exist), you can trap this in the program and have `main()` return some other value, such as 1. You will see as you work through later sections of this chapter that this principle is entirely general—the return value from a function may be something you use elsewhere, or it may be an indication of success or failure.

The substance of listing 1.1 is found in line 7:

```
printf("What a Wonderful World!\n");
```

This is the line of code (a single C statement, ending in a semicolon) that does something useful: it writes a message to the console. The presence of a matching pair of parentheses looks very like the format of the `main()` function just described—and indeed this statement does contain a function, whose name is `printf`, which is shorthand for "print with formatting." Inside the parentheses is the text to be displayed (referred to by programmers as a *string*, or sometimes a *character string*), within double quotation marks. In the jargon of programming, this string is the *argument* to the function `printf`, and overall the statement constitutes a *function call*.

The final two characters in the message string may be unfamiliar. They relate to the "formatting" aspect of the `printf` function. The first of the two characters is a backslash. In the context of a character string, this is called the *escape character*. It signifies that the following character is not to be written literally to the console, but is instead a control instruction to arrange the text in a particular way. In this case the control character is n, which signifies "new line" (sometimes also called "carriage return and line feed"). To see how this works, you can delete these two characters, re-compile and run the program, and see what happens.

In line 7, the control characters are at the end of the line. However, they could be placed anywhere in the string. You can even write a string that contains only the control characters, and you can write them as many times as you like. For example:

```
printf("\nThe Hills are alive,\nWith the Sound of Music!");
printf("\n");
```

We will see in later sections that `printf` is even more versatile than this. It can print numbers too, and control characters are available to organize numbers with respect to spacing, number of digits, and even to write them in technical formats such as hexadecimal.

1.1.2 Library Functions and the `#include` Directive

Two questions remain unanswered. Previously, it was stated that the C language does not contain a "print" command, yet here we are using one, called `printf`. Where does it come from? And what is the meaning of line 2, which we so casually skipped over earlier?

The `printf` function is an important example of a C library function, in this case supporting text output to the console. Most important, it is a "standard library" function that you can expect any C compiler to include. But it is not part of the C language itself. The compiler has to be given information about it—its name, its inputs, and its outputs. This information takes the form of a "declaration." We will discover how a declaration is written in a later section. The important thing to grasp at this stage is that the declaration of `printf` is contained in a text file called `stdio.h` (the file extension `.h` is used by convention to show that the file is a C "header file"), and is incorporated into your program by a *preprocessor* command ("directive"). This is the purpose of line 2 in listing 1.1. Your code file is passed to this preprocessor before being passed to the compiler itself. The preprocessor strips out all the comments, and can also be asked to perform text substitutions, or to add text from another file, using the preprocessor directive `include`. All preprocessor directives are indicated by the initial `#`, followed by the name of the command—e.g. `#include`. The whole directive is then followed by the name of the required file, enclosed in angle brackets:

```
#include <stdio.h>
```

Although by convention the command immediately follows the character `#` without an intervening space, this is not mandatory. The spacing

```
# include <stdio.h>
```

is legal.

When the compiler is installed on your system, a large number of header files are stored in a special "include" directory. The compiler thus "knows about" this directory, and will automatically search it to find the requested file. The use of the angle brackets, as shown above, ensures that this directory is searched first for files. An alternative notation using double quotation marks asks the preprocessor to search the directory containing the current file, before searching further:

```
#include "myfuncs.h"
```

This would be used typically for "local" include files that are specific, and usually private, to a project. You will see plenty of examples of this in later sections, especially in projects involving multiple source files.

When your program is compiled, the compiler also looks for the code for `printf` in a library file in a `lib` directory, and links that code with yours to create the final executable. In subsequent sections, you will be introduced to many more "standard" C functions that are required to be supported by all C compilers.

1.1.3 Exercises

Exercise 1.1.1

Create a new program, perhaps called `music.c` (if you are using an IDE, you will also have to create a project for it called `music`), and write a new message of your choice. Add some informative text inside a comment block at the top of the file.

Exercise 1.1.2

Find out what happens (i.e. what messages the compiler reports) if you

(a) leave out `#include <stdio.h>` (you can do this without deleting text, by commenting out the line using `/*` and `*/`)
(b) leave out the angle brackets
(c) swap the braces and the parentheses
(d) leave out one or both of the semicolons
(e) replace the first semicolon with a comma
(f) leave out the return statement
(g) leave out the final brace.

1.2 Adding Something of Your Own—An Introduction to Variables and Types

1.2.1 Basic Arithmetic in C

In this section we will see how to perform basic arithmetical calculations in C. To do this, we need a means of representing numerical values, an idea of how the computer stores them, and a means of performing arithmetical operations on them. This may already sound complicated, but fortunately the way arithmetical expressions are written in C is very similar to how they might be written down on paper. Whether using paper and pencil or writing a computer program, in order to work anything out we need to be able to represent numbers by name. For example, you probably will recognize this simple calculation for finding the area of a rectangle:

```
area = width * height
```

By convention, an asterisk is used to signify "multiplied by" or "times." We replace `width` and `height` with numbers and perform the calculation, the result of which is `area`. The line above is a simple arithmetical statement. To make it a complete C statement, we must add a semicolon:

```
area = width * height;
```

Note the use of appropriate words, rather than arbitrary letters or symbols. The names make it completely clear what the task is, and thus the code is "self-documenting."

1.2.2 Expressions and Statements

It is very important to understand the difference between expressions and statements. An expression in C is anything that can be "evaluated" (i.e. that has a numerical result)—for

Table 1.1

Binary operators.

Operator		Example	Description
Assignment	=	c = b	Assign the value of b to c.
Addition	+	c = b + a	Add a to b and assign this value to c.
Subtraction	–	c = b – a	Subtract a from b and assign this value to c.
Multiplication	*	c = b * a	Multiply a and b and assign this value to c.
Division	/	c = b / a	Divide b by a and assign this value to c.
Modulo	%	c = 12%11	Result after integral division. The value of c is 1.

example, the right-hand side of the calculation above, here enclosed in parentheses to make the point clearer:

```
(width * height)
```

Expressions can contain expressions, for example

```
(100 + (width * height))
```

Ultimately, even a single number is an expression, evaluating to itself. A statement is any legal expression, or combination of expressions, possibly combined with one or more C keywords, and terminated by a semicolon. Indeed, the semicolon by itself is a legal C statement, and this fact commonly gives rise to errors when a semicolon is used by mistake. Normally, a statement changes something; typically, a variable acquires a new value, or the flow of control through the program is changed.

An expression can also be a statement—for example,

```
width * height;
```

This is, however, useless, as the value of the expression is ignored.

1.2.3 Operators

As was noted above, an asterisk is used to indicate multiplication. In C terminology, it is an *operator*. More specifically, it is a binary operator, as it operates on two numbers (or expressions). C possesses a large number of operators, including ones for the basic arithmetic operations, identical to the usual algebraic symbols (see table 1.1).

Both + and – can also be use as "unary" operators, though in practice only – has to be used explicitly:

```
val = -64; /* unary negation */
```

Subsection 1.2.10 describes the way C decides in what order these operations are carried out when an expression incorporates several of them.

1.2.4 Numeric Types

We are already remarkably close to performing a calculation in C, but some information the compiler needs is missing. It needs to know what sorts of numbers we are using so it can store them correctly and so it can perform the correct kind of processing on them. The two most important classes of numbers are integers ($-1, 0, 1, 2, 3, \ldots$) and floating-point numbers (e.g., 3.14159, -0.707, 1.414).

C includes a wide range of integer types (described in subsection 1.2.5), but the most frequently used has the keyword `int`. There are two floating-point types: a `float` occupies four bytes and is described as a *single-precision* number, and a `double` usually occupies eight bytes and, as its name suggests, is a *double-precision* number.

To complete the statement above in C code, we must define each of our variables in terms of a numeric type:

```
double area;
double width;
double height;
```

These declarations tell the compiler to set aside some memory to hold each variable, and define what type each one is. In the next line, we put some numbers into the variables:

```
width = 10.0;
height = 21.5;
```

The semicolon is ubiquitous: a variable declaration is a statement, as is an "assignment"—a statement using the operator =, properly called the *assignment operator*. In programming jargon, we would say that the value 10.0 is assigned to the variable width. It is also common to refer to the "right-hand side" of an assignment statement (the right-hand side has to be an expression, therefore) signifying a possibly elaborate calculation that produces a result that can be stored on the left-hand side.

Why call `area`, `width`, `height`, and so on "variables"? We can assign a value as often as we like to a variable, like so:

```
width = 10.0;
width = 0.0;
width = 1000.3;
```

However, all that is remembered is the last assignment. So literally, the contents of the variable `width` can vary over time. We can also assign the value of one variable to another:

```
height = 21.5;
width = height;   /* a square! */
```

Most important, we can perform the full calculation, which is where we started[1]:

```
area = width * height;
```

1.2.5   Integers—A Special Case

The examples above used "double" variables, which ensure a precise result for our calculation. It would also be possible to define all three variables above as integers instead, by using the type keyword `int`:

```
int area;
int width;
int height;
```

However, we cannot store fractional (floating-point) numbers in such variables, only whole numbers:

```
width = 20;
height = 7;
area = 21.5;     /* compiler will issue a warning here! */
```

The particular quality of integer calculations emerges when we try to perform division:

```
area = 26;
height = 10;
width = area / height;
```

Here `width` receives the value 2, whereas the use of floating-point variables would result in a more accurate fractional value of 2.6.

Historically, the integer is the oldest computer data type, and floating-point calculations had to be performed by means of much arcane code and were therefore extremely slow. Even today, many digital signal processors used for audio use integer calculations, which can be performed very rapidly and which offer the highest precision for a given storage size.

1.2.6   Sizes of C Numeric Types

One other important aspect of integers that the programmer has to consider is that there is a limit to the size of the number that can be represented, depending on the number of bits used. A 16-bit integer can store numbers from 0 to 65,535 (65,536 numbers in all). Therefore, no negative numbers can be represented at all. However, a long-established system called "twos complement" enables "signed" numbers to be stored by treating the most significant (leftmost) bit as a "sign" bit. In the case of a 16-bit integer, the "signed" range is from −32,768 to +32,767; this is how 16-bit audio samples are stored.

A 32-bit integer can similarly be "signed" or "unsigned." The numbers are, of course, much larger: the signed 32-bit range is from −2,147,483,648 to +2,147,483,647.

So important are integers that a C compiler supports several types (shown in table 1.2, which assumes a typical 32-bit platform). Note that both "signed" and "unsigned" forms

Table 1.2

Integer types in C. *The `int` type is dependent on the CPU integer size.

Integer type	Size	Number of values		Minimum	Maximum
`char`	1 byte	2^8	Signed	−128	127
			Unsigned	0	256
`short`	2 bytes	2^{16}	Signed	−32,768	32,767
			Unsigned	0	65,536
`long`	4 bytes	2^{32}	Signed	−2,147,483,648	2,147,483,647
			Unsigned	0	4,294,967,265
`int`	*	*	Signed	*	*
			Unsigned	0	*

are explicitly supported. "Signed" is the default for all numeric types, so it is only necessary to use the "unsigned" qualifier when such a form is required. For 16-bit DOS and Windows (8086 CPU family), an `int` is 2 bytes (equivalent to `short`), whereas on 32-bit architecture (MC68000, PPC, Pentium) an `int` is 4 bytes (equivalent to `long`). Thus, using the `int` type is unsafe if a specific numeric range is required. In this case `long` or `short` should be used. On 64-bit platforms, `int` will similarly be 64 bits, and the same caveat applies. Use of the name `long long` is already widely established to indicate a 64-bit integer type, though not yet standard. Strictly speaking, the C standard allows considerable latitude in defining the sizes of numeric types (as they will have to reflect the nature of the hardware). For example, C only mandates that a `short` will not be larger than an `int` and that a `long` will not be smaller than an `int`. Thus, it is theoretically possible (though very unlikely these days) for a `short`, an `int`, and a `long` all to be the same size.

1.2.7   The `sizeof()` Operator

Sometimes it is important to be able to find the size of a type, such as a numeric type, programmatically. This is especially important where code is intended to run on multiple platforms. C provides the `sizeof()` operator for this purpose. It has the appearance of a function call (where the name of the type is the argument), but in fact it is a C keyword. It returns the size of the type in bytes:

```
int intsize = sizeof(int);
/* may return 2 or 4, depending on the machine */
```

We will introduce an important use of the `sizeof()` operator in section 1.5, in connection to user-defined data types.[2]

1.2.8   A Musical Computation

The task here is fairly simple but useful, and just complicated enough to justify a computer program: to convert a MIDI Note number to the equal-tempered frequency in hertz. We will develop the task on paper first, so to speak, and then see how it would appear as a C program.

First we need some background information. MIDI Note data values use an unsigned seven-bit integer range, i.e. from 0 to 127 inclusive. These numbers have to embrace key numbers, various controllers (including Pitchbend and Modulation), Key Velocity and Pressure, and so on. So converting MIDI values into other things is going to be a very common operation.

Middle C on the piano keyboard is defined to be MIDI Note 60. Given the international tuning standard, in which Concert A = 440, and assuming equal temperament (E.T.), middle C has a frequency of approximately 261.626 Hz. An octave contains 12 semitones, so that C an octave below middle C would correspond to MIDI Note 48. The full theoretical MIDI range 0–127 (not known to be covered by any keyboard yet made) extends five octaves below middle C (to MIDI Note 0) and almost six octaves above it.

An octave jump corresponds to a frequency change by a factor (or ratio) of 2: doubled for an octave rise, and halved for an octave fall. So an octave below Concert A would have the frequency 220 Hz. A further octave fall halves the frequency again, to 110 Hz. A single semi-tone rise corresponds to the (approximate) value 1.0594631, which is (approximately) the twelfth root of 2 (a semi-tone "only" in E.T. 12 tuning). That is to say, multiply 1.0594631 by itself twelve times and you should get the value 2.0. This operation, known as raising to a power, is notated mathematically as 1.0594631^{12}.

To ensure the best possibly accuracy, we can use the computer to calculate the semitone ratio itself. Recall the rules of indices, according to which a power of 1/2 corresponds to the square root and a power of 1/12 corresponds to the twelfth root. So we might notate this as

$$semitone\_ratio = \sqrt[12]{2}. \tag{1}$$

The two numbers 2.0 and 1.0594631 (or better, its computed value *semitone_ratio*) are all we really need to calculate any equal-tempered 12-tone interval, given a starting base frequency[3].

For example, calculate the frequency of the C sharp above Concert A in Equal Temperament. Concert A is 440, and by definition C sharp is four semitones above A (major third), so the calculation is simply

$$Csharp = 440 \times (1.0594631^4) \approx 554.365.$$

The one other piece of numerical information we need is the frequency of the lowest note, MIDI Note 0. This is five octaves below middle C—well below the audible range. An octave drop is a factor of 0.5, so a five-octave drop requires the value 0.5 to be multiplied by itself five times: 0.5^5. This gives 0.03125. Multiply this by the frequency of middle C and we get the frequency of the MIDI Note 0, or C0. As shown above, each rise of a semitone involves a multiplication by 1.0594631. So to find the interval between MIDI Note 0 and MIDI note 73 (which happens to be the Csharp calculated above), we first multiply 1.0594631 by itself 73 times: 1.0594632^{73}. We then have to multiply the base frequency C0 by the result of this calculation to obtain the required result. It is now time to look at listing 1.2, where the full computation is performed, and the result printed to the console. If you type this in and compile it, you could call it "*midi2freq.c*," and the program itself as 'midi2freq'.

Listing 1.2
Calculate the frequency of a MIDI note:

```
1    /* listing 1.2. Calculate frequency of a MIDI Note number */
2    #include <stdio.h>
3    #include <math.h>
4
5    int main()
6    {
7        double semitone_ratio;
8        double c0; /* for frequency of MIDI Note 0 */
9        double c5; /* for frequency of Middle C */
10       double frequency; /* . . . which we want to find, */
11       int    midinote;    /* . . . given this note.    */
12
13       /* calculate required numbers */
14
15       semitone_ratio = pow(2, 1/12.0); /* approx. 1.0594631 */
16       /* find Middle C, three semitones above low A = 220 */
17       c5 = 220.0 * pow(semitone_ratio, 3);
18       /* MIDI Note 0 is C, 5 octaves below Middle C */
19       c0 = c5 * pow(0.5, 5);
20
21       /* calculate a frequency for a given MIDI Note Number */
22       midinote = 73;    /* C# above A = 440 */
23       frequency = c0 * pow(semitone_ratio, midinote);
24
25       printf("MIDI Note %d has frequency %f\n", midinote, frequency);
26
27       return 0;
28   }
```

You can test this program by changing the number assigned to "midinote," re-compiling, and running it. (Sections 1.3 and 1.4 explain how to avoid this tiresome process.)

As expected, there is more code here than in listing 1.1. Nevertheless, the layout of the program follows the same structure. First, in line 3, a new header file, <math.h>, is included. This is required to supply the definition of the C library function pow( ) that is used in the program. This is the function that raises a number to a power. While you study the details of the code, notice the comments (inside the /* */ pairs), which describe both the purpose of the program and what the various lines of code do.

Lines 7–11 contain declarations of variables, using names that help describe what the code is doing. Two numeric types are used: the `double` and the `int`. These declarations must appear before any other lines of C code appear.[4] The compiler reads the code from the top down, and needs to know about all these variables, and set aside storage for them, before it can process code that uses them. You will find that C++ is more flexible, and that it allows you to declare a variable anywhere, but in C they must all be declared first, as here.[5] Notice that each declaration is terminated, as usual, with a semicolon.

Because the variables are declared inside the `main()` function, they are described as "local" to that function, or simply as "local variables." The alternative is to declare variables outside `main()`, after the preprocessor `#include` statements. Such variables are then "global"— accessible anywhere in a program. This is generally regarded as a bad idea, as it can be very difficult to control how they are modified. (For more on this, see section 1.3.)

Each variable is identified by a unique name. There is a lot of flexibility allowed in creating names. Essentially any printable character can be used, as long as it is not otherwise used by C. This excludes characters such as *, /, -, %, &, and ? (in fact most of the pictorial characters), but it does include the underscore, which is very useful for creating multi-word names, given that a name cannot incorporate any white space. Also, numeric characters are allowed, but not as the first character of a name. So the name `5c` would be illegal. It is also illegal to use a C keyword as a variable name:

```
int return; /* illegal name! */
```

You might experiment by deliberately writing illegal names and re-compiling to see what error messages the compiler gives you. Sometimes error messages are a bit obscure, and it is very useful to know what they most likely refer to.

Some programmers like to create extremely long names more akin to descriptive comments—for example,

```
int an_extremely_long_variable_name_representing_a_MIDI_note;
```

This can get out of hand very quickly, however, and a good rule of thumb is to try to avoid names longer than 32 characters or so. It should still be practicable to use a range of expressive names.

Lines 15–19 perform the essential intermediate calculation steps described above. They demonstrate three slightly different ways of using ("calling") the `pow()` function, and in so doing they reveal a lot about how expressions are handled in C. Inside the parentheses, this function requires two floating-point numbers: the "base" number and the number to which it is to be raised. In the header file `<math.h>` this function would be declared as follows:

```
double pow(double base, double power);
```

This shows that the function takes two arguments (defined inside the parentheses, and separated by commas) of type `double`, and returns a value also of type `double`. The names shown above ("base" and "power") are optional (and ignored by the compiler), but are clearly useful for documenting what the function does. The minimum version of this declaration would therefore be

```
double pow(double, double);
```

You can add this line to the list of variable declarations (say into line 11), and then remove line 3, where `<math.h>` is included, and the program will compile as before. It is worth looking at the use of this function in listing 1.2 in more detail. Line 15 calls the `pow()` function in almost the simplest way possible:

```
semitone_ratio = pow(2, 1/12.0);
```

The result or output from the function is assigned to the variable `semitone_ratio` using the assignment operator. As we know, everything on the right-hand side of the "equals" sign must be an expression that evaluates to a value. That value must be in the form of one of the legal C types (here, a `double`). It follows that the type on the left-hand side of the "equals" sign must be the same, as it is here. Thus the statement

```
semitone_ratio = "twelve";
```

would be illegal, because it tries to make a `double` equal to a character string, which is obviously impossible. It would be flagged as an error by the compiler, probably using the term "type mismatch."

Inside the function call, the first argument is a simple number, 2. To C this is actually an integer (`int` type), but as the required argument is a `double`, which is another number type, C is happy to make a conversion automatically. (For more about converting numeric types, see subsection 1.2.10.) This conversion does take a little time to do, and to eliminate that you could add a decimal point and a zero to 2:

```
semitone_ratio = pow(2.0, 1.0/12.0);
```

C will recognize "2.0" as a floating-point number, and will automatically treat it as a `double`. The second argument in this call to `pow()` is not a simple number but a simple arithmetic expression, 1/12.0. Because no variables are used, only explicit numbers, the compiler will usually make this calculation itself, rather than creating code for it. The use of at least one decimal point ensures that the calculation is performed in floating-point fashion. Writing "1.0/12" would be just as good. However, if you had typed the line as

```
semitone_ratio = pow(2.0, 1/12);
```

the numbers 1 and 12 would be treated as integers, and the expression 1/12 would evaluate to 0 (the result of integer division of 1 by 12), which is clearly not going to work as intended. However, it is legal code, and the compiler probably will not warn you about it. All the compiler can assume is that that is what you meant in the first place. You will not be aware that something is wrong until you run the program.

In line 17 the first argument is not an explicit number, but a variable to which we have previously assigned a value:

```
c5 = 220.0 * pow(semitone_ratio, 3);
```

In this case, the call to pow() is itself part of a more lengthy expression, the value of which is assigned to the variable c5. Line 19 shows pow() called with two numeric arguments (the second integer again converted by C into a double), and line 23 shows it called with two variables.

Line 25 is the same printf function introduced in listing 1.1, but here demonstrating one of its primary uses: to write "formatted" numeric data to the console. "Formatting" means many things; in this context it simply means embedding numbers of various types inside a text string, the numbers being obtained from variables within the program.

In addition to the message string, two further arguments are given: midinote and frequency. Inside the message string, you will see two occurrences of %. This has the special meaning for printf of signifying the start of a "formatted conversion." For each argument following the message string, we insert % into the message at the required position, followed in each case by a letter indicating the type of the argument. A d or an i indicates an integer (d stands for 'decimal' or 'denary'), and an f indicates a floating-point number. There are many other possibilities. The first % conversion uses the first argument (following the initial message string), the second conversion uses the second argument, and so on:

```
printf("%d o'clock %d o'clock %d o'clock rock,\n," 1, 2, 3);
```

1.2.9 Initializing Variables and Reducing the Line Count

In listing 1.2 each variable is declared on a separate line. For just four variables this does not really matter, but a larger program may involve dozens or even hundreds of variables, making the code very long. C allows variables of the same type to be listed together, separated by commas:

```
double semitone_ratio,c0,c5,frequency;
```

You lose the scope for adding comments about each variable doing this; the use of expressive names can compensate to some extent, but most programmers tend to mix multiple declaration lines like the above with individual lines where comments are needed.

It is also possible to give a variable an initial value when it is declared:

```
int midinote = 73;
```

Not surprisingly, this is called *initialization*. It can be applied to some or all variables in a multiple declaration statement:

```
double semitone_ratio = 1.0594631, c0 ,c5, frequency = 440.0;
```

Moreover, in an initialization, the right-hand side can even be an expression:

```
double semitone_ratio = pow(2, 1/12.0);
```

Note that this requires that the pow() function has already been declared, as it would be if the library header file math.h is #included, as shown in line 3. Try rewriting listing 1.2 to make these changes.

A numeric expression can be used anywhere a simple number can be used. This means, taken to the extreme, that the whole calculation of listing 1.2 can be compressed into a single expression, eliminating at a stroke three variables:

```
frequency = (220.0*pow(pow(2,1.0/12),3)*pow(0.5,5))
             *pow(pow(2,1.0/12), midinote);
```

This has reduced the code to almost the theoretical minimum, but at high cost—it is far less understandable and much more difficult to modify, it is more likely to lead to errors, and it is less efficient—the expression pow(2, 1/12.0) is calculated twice. There is no virtue in trying to make the code as compact as possible if it merely increases the chances of making mistakes, or if it makes the code harder to understand. The goals of writing code are not only to be correct and to be efficient, but also to be *clear*—you need the code to be as self-explanatory as possible. You may understand it now, having just written it, but not when you go back to it six months later.

1.2.10 Operator Precedence in Numeric Expressions

As a C expression can combine several calculation steps, C defines strict rules for deciding in what order to carry them out. These rules are based on the principle of operator precedence. Operations with high precedence are performed before operations with lower precedence. Multiplication and division have higher precedence than addition and subtraction and thus will be performed before addition and subtraction. The statement

```
float val = 15 + 440 * 2.5;
```

will evaluate to 1115.0, as if the expression on the right-hand side were written as

```
float val = 15 + (440 * 2.5);
```

Where two operations have equal precedence level, C has to have a rule to decide which to perform first. This rule is that operations are performed from left to right. In programming terminology, the operation "associates left to right." In the statement

```
frequency = 210.0 / 3 * 4.0;
```

the result will be 280, not 17.5, as the division is performed first.

In the case of addition, the order of evaluation will not matter: 200 + (10 + 20) is the same as (200 + 10) + 20. But this is not the case for subtraction:

```
midinote = 200 - 10 - 20;
```

Depending on which subtraction is performed first, `midinote` will equal 170 or 210. Again, the operations are performed in order from left to right. The statement above will accordingly evaluate to 170, as if written as

```
midinote = (200 - 10) - 20;
```

If in doubt, use parentheses to make it clear in what order you want the operations carried out. Parentheses effectively have the highest precedence of all. Many expert programmers routinely write complex expressions of this kind, without parentheses, as they know what the evaluation order will be. On the one hand this is entirely reasonable, especially for simple expressions, but on the other hand adding parentheses even where technically they are not necessary can help to document the code (e.g. to indicate that certain groups of numbers or expressions relate to each other) and to prevent mistakes.

While all the arithmetic operators associate left to right, the "equals" ("assignment") operator associates right to left. This makes it possible to write statements such as

```
int a,b,c;
a = 0;
b = 1;
c = 10;
a = b = c;
```

The statement a = b = c; is equivalent to the following two lines:

```
b = c; /* b now has the value 10 */
a = b; /* a now has the value 10 */
```

1.2.11   More on Type Conversion—the Cast Operator

In listing 1.2 and in the description that followed it, we have seen two examples in which a number of one type (e.g. an `int`) was automatically converted to another (e.g. to a `double`). The most explicit example occurs in line 23:

```
frequency = c0 * pow(semitone_ratio, midinote);
```

How do we know a type conversion is happening here? First, the function `pow()` is defined as having two arguments of type `double`. However, in the function call above, the second parameter is in fact `midinote`, declared as an `int`. In this case the compiler is automatically inserting a conversion process known as a *cast*. It is also possible to specify the cast explicitly in the code:

```
frequency = c0 * pow(semitone_ratio, (double) midinote);
```

Thus the cast operator consists of a type specifier enclosed in parentheses, placed directly in front of the number or expression to be converted. It has a higher precedence than the operators `*`, `/`, and `%`. Note that the `cast` embodies a hidden copy; the type of the object being cast does not change.

Casting an `int` to a `double` is a no-loss change, as this data type can hold much larger numbers than any of the standard C integer types. This process is often described as "promoting" the number. Casting a `double` to an `int` is a far more drastic change:

```
int ival;
double dval = 21.5;
ival = (int) dval;
```

The cast to an `int` has the effect of removing the fractional part of the `double`, so that `ival` receives the `int` value 21 in the above example. Also, the 64-bit `double` can represent numbers outside the range of a 32-bit `int`. As a result, any conversion from a floating-point value to an integer, if performed without an explicit cast (and, more generally, any conversion from any numeric type to a smaller one—a "demotion"), will trigger a warning message from most compilers. In the context of audio programming, the most common use of the cast is in converting floating-point samples into integer ones, not least the ubiquitous 16-bit sample:

```
double fracsamp;
short samp;
fracsamp = 0.5;
samp = (short) (fracsamp * 32767);
```

As a revision exercise, you might like to make sure you understand why the following version of the line above will not produce the intended result:

```
samp = (short) fracsamp * 32767;
```

1.2.12 Going the Other Way: Converting a Frequency to the Nearest MIDI Note

The code fragment below illustrates the use of the cast operator to obtain a required integer result; it also introduces another important function from the standard C math library. The fragment can directly replace lines 21–25 of listing 1.2. You also need to add a new variable `fracmidi` of type `double` to the variable list. If you do this, you may want to change to program name, for example to freq2midi. This example uses the C math library function

```
double log(double arg);
```

which finds the natural logarithm (to base *e*) of the argument:

```
/* find nearest MIDI note to a given frequency in Hz */
/* uses the log rule:
    log_a(N) = log_b(N) / log_b(a)
         to find the log of a value to base 'semitone_ratio'.
*/

 frequency = 400.0;
 fracmidi = log(frequency / c0) / log(semitone_ratio);
 /* round fracmidi to the nearest whole number */
 midinote = (int) (fracmidi + 0.5);
 printf("The nearest MIDI note to the frequency %f is %d\n,"
    frequency,
    midinote);
```

You may be wondering why `midinote` is declared as an `int` rather than a `char`. In terms of the calculation, it could be, so you could make the change and the program would run as expected. However, in doing this you would be relying on the internal "promotion" of the char to an `int`, in the call to `printf()`, where the format specifier `%d` is used. There is a format specifier for chars: `%c`. But that assumes, reasonably, that the char is an ASCII character and the value 69, for example, would be written as "E." Needless to say, to a musician that would be doubly confusing.

Note the use in the example above of a simple method for rounding numbers: adding 0.5 to the floating-point value before applying the cast. For audio purposes we often require more sophisticated rounding methods, so that negative and positive values are rounded symmetrically, but this simple method works very well for simple rounding of positive numbers.

Use of the `int` type also facilitates the detection of errors caused by a user supplying a number outside the allowed range. The detection and handling of errors (whether your own or the user's) is an essential aspect of programming, as will be seen in the next section.

1.2.13   Exercises

Exercise 1.2.1
Using the `sizeof()` operator and `printf` statements, write a small program to report the size in bytes of each of the following:

int   char   short   long   float   double

This will be of particular interest and importance if you happen to be using a 64-bit machine.

Exercise 1.2.2
The statement

```
samp = (short) fracsamp * 32767;
```

is intended to convert a floating-point sample (± 1.0) to the 16-bit integer range. However, the output is not as expected. Why?

Exercise 1.2.3

Replace the calls to `pow()` with literal values, in order to simplify the all-in-one statement shown in subsection 1.2.9. Make sure the computed result is correct. What might you lose as a programmer by making such a change?

Exercise 1.2.4

As was suggested in the text, modify listing 1.2 to avoid reliance on the compiler's automatic type promotion from `int` to `double`. Use a cast where appropriate. For example, change 1/12.0 to 1.0/12.0.

Exercise 1.2.5

(a) The sounding length of a string sounding C4 ("middle C") is given as 660 cm. Modify listing 1.2 to print out the lengths of string required for each semitone up to the next octave (C5, 330 cm).
(b) What further language facilities would make this task easier?

Exercise 1.2.6

(a) Implement the program *freq2midi* as suggested in subsection 1.2.12.
(b) We define pitchbend as a percentage deviation half a semitone above or below a MIDI note. Maximum deviation is therefore ± 50 percent. For example, given a frequency of 430 Hz, the nearest notes are 69 (f = 440) and 68 (f = 415.3). The deviation is therefore $10/24.7 = -0.405 = -40$ percent (approximately). Extend *freq2midi* to report the frequency deviation above or below the calculated MIDI note, as a percentage. (To print a percentage symbol using `printf`, precede it with the same symbol.)

```
int bend = 45;
printf("pitchbend = %d%%\n",bend);
```

(There is an important follow-up to this exercise in the next section.)

1.3   Introduction to Pointers, Arrays, and the Problem of User Input

It will probably not have escaped your notice, if you have run the programs presented in the previous sections, that having to re-compile every time you change the number for `midinote` or `frequency` is very tiresome. This section introduces changes to listing 1.1 to make it function interactively—it asks the user for some data, which is then processed.

What is involved in receiving input from the user? In the context of a command-line program, the user will be typing something at the keyboard, which the program reads and presumably processes in some way. The challenge here is a basic one—we don't know in advance, and we have fairly limited means for controlling just what, or how much, the user is going to type. The user may not even type anything at all. Therefore, some of the code we write deals not with the core task, but with handling user input—making sure we read all of it, and checking for the unexpected.

Thus an interactive program has to do two things: provide some space (memory), which we hope is sufficient for anything the user will likely type, and test that data to make sure it is what we need.

1.3.1   Strings and the C Pointer Type

In the previous programs, we relied on the `printf()` function to print variables to the console. We now have the opposite task—the user will (we trust) type numbers as a string of numeric characters, and the program will have to convert that into a C variable. It is time to understand a little more about exactly how a string is represented in the computer. Consider the string

```
"one two three four"
```

This string is stored in memory one character at a time in successive ascending memory locations. It is the task of the compiler to decide exactly where it is stored. The above string will occupy eighteen successive bytes of memory (remember, the space is also a character), starting at some location N determined by the compiler.

However, an additional "null" byte (the character \0) is added at the end, so the string occupies nineteen bytes. Thus, any function that is required to access the string need only know where the first character is, and it can completely trust that all following bytes also belong to this string, as far as that final null byte. The location in memory of this first byte is its "address," and that address is accordingly the address of the whole string. The full technical term for this is a *null-terminated string*; this is the way all strings are implemented in C.[6] Thus, in the statement

```
printf("one two three four");
```

the `printf()` function is given the address of the start of the string.

So the address is itself an object, a variable that can be passed around. As it is a variable, it has to have a type—in this case, it is a *pointer type*, because it "points to" a location in memory. As it points to a row of characters (which may of course be just one character long), its full type definition is 'pointer to `char`'. It declared as

```
char* message;
```

which could also incorporate an initialization to a string:

```
char* message = "one two three four";
```

Here the asterisk is not a multiplier; it is the indicator of a "pointer" type. In this statement, 'message' is assigned the address of the start of the given string, in effect the memory location of the first character. It is now possible to replace the `printf()` statement above with

```
printf(message);
```

The list of format specifiers for `printf()` includes one for strings: `%s`. This leads to yet another way of creating messages for `printf()`:

```
char* two = "two";
char* four = "four";
char* six = "six";
printf("%s %s %s eight," two, four, six);
```

or even[7]

```
char* message = "%s %s %s eight";
printf(message, two, four, six);
```

1.3.2   The Array

To receive text input from the user, we have to set aside some memory to hold the text. This requires a character "array." An array is simply a row of objects of a single type. This requires a different notation, one that incorporates information on how much space we want:

```
char message[256];            /* array of 256 chars */
```

The brackets ("subscript notation") indicate the definition of an array, and the number inside the brackets indicates how many items of the stated type to provide space for. The result of the statement above is that a fixed block of 256 bytes of memory is set aside (since a `char` is one byte in size), and the address of the start of it is stored in the variable 'message'.
    The forms

```
char message[]; /* unspecified size */
```

and

```
char message[0];
```

are illegal. Either of them will trigger an error message from the compiler. Needless to say, negative sizes will also be rejected. Subscript notation is also used to read and write individual elements of an array:

```
char Beatle[5] = "John";
char letter;
letter = Beatle[0];  /*       letter = 'J' */
Beatle[2] = 'a';                /* Beatle now = "Joan" */
```

Here the number in brackets is termed the array 'index' or 'subscript' and, as can be seen, counts from 0, not (as one might intuitively expect) from 1. In binary arithmetic, a single bit holds two values, 0 and 1, and so can be used to count two items. 0 therefore has to signify the first item, and 1 the second.

The power of the subscript notation becomes more apparent when we realize that an integer variable (of any integral type) can be used for the index:

```
int position;
position = 3;
Beatle[position] = 'l';
position = 0;
Beatle[position] = 'P';
position = 2;
Beatle[position] = 'u';
position = 1;
Beatle[position] = 'a';
/* Beatle now contains "Paul" */
```

As well as enabling programmatic changing of the index value, this also supports self-documenting code, as the index name can become descriptive.

Arrays can be formed using any type. Of course, the string initialization system can be applied only to arrays of char. In declaring the size of an array to contain a string, it is essential to count the terminating null byte as part of the string. C provides a generic notation using braces (note the final semicolon here), which enables arrays of any type to be initialized in a single statement:

```
int FullChord[4] = {60,64,67,72};       /* MIDI notes for C Major */
int root = 0, third = 1, rootnote;
FullChord[third] = 63;    /* change chord to C minor */
rootnote = FullChord[root];     /* Middle C */
```

Figure 1.1 shows the construction of a string array element by element using this notation, including the all-important terminating null character.

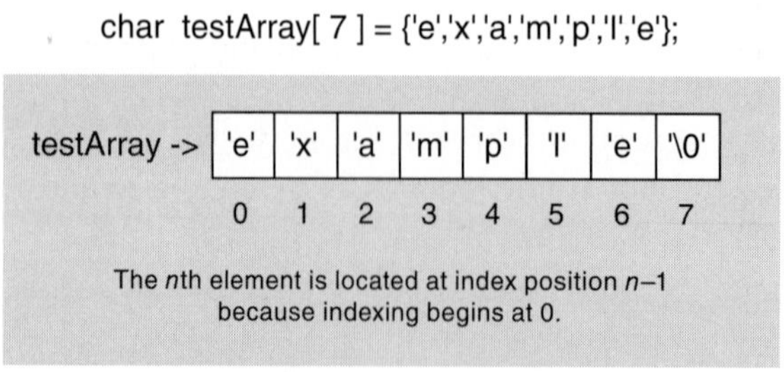

char testArray[7] = {'e','x','a','m','p','l','e'};

testArray ->	'e'	'x'	'a'	'm'	'p'	'l'	'e'	'\0'
	0	1	2	3	4	5	6	7

The nth element is located at index position $n-1$ because indexing begins at 0.

Figure 1.1
A string as a null-terminated array of characters.

If there are too many elements in the initialization block, the compiler will flag an error. However, if there are too few, the remaining elements in the array will be initialized to 0:

```
int LargeChord[32] = {60}; /* first element = 60, all others set to
zero */
```

In section 1.5 we will learn how C enables the programmer to step through arrays programmatically, so that possibly very large arrays or other data structures can be initialized and modified using a small amount of code.

1.3.3 NULL

In addition to the initializations described above, it is possible, and often a very good idea, to initialize a pointer (of any type) to the special value NULL (defined in stdlib.h). It is always written in upper case. Exactly how this is defined is discussed in a later section; suffice it to say here that it is a form of zero for pointers. Many functions that return pointers will use NULL to indicate errors.

1.3.4 Array Index Errors

It is probable that more bugs in C programs are caused by misuse of pointers and arrays than by any other single programming error. There are two bad things one can do with an array index. One is the following:

```
double buffer[32];
buffer[-2] = 1.0594631; /* ERROR! Index below start of array */
buffer[33] = 2.0; /* ERROR! Index beyond end of array */
```

The problem here is that the compiler will very likely not warn you about these errors, and if the index is in fact a variable, it will in any case have no way of knowing. C does very little "hand-holding" of programmers, and if you over-run the bounds of an array it will do nothing to stop you. Sometimes the program will seem to run correctly, but it may suddenly crash on some machines and not on others, and the point of the crash may be in some seemingly unrelated part of the program.

Indexing errors of the kind discussed above are especially damaging when you are modifying data in memory, because in most compilers the memory spaces below and above an array may belong to the system, holding information on other data used elsewhere. Maybe you will be affecting other variables in your program, so it will appear that those variables are causing the crash.

There are nevertheless good reasons why even an explicit negative index is not automatically treated as an error by the compiler. We will see in later sections that a pointer can be assigned the address of any element, e.g. one in the middle of an array. In this case, a negative index relative to that new pointer is perfectly valid. The danger arises only if the bounds of the overall array itself are exceeded.

A subtle problem arises using indexing on strings used to initialize pointers:

```
char* name = "John";
name[2] = 'a';          /* DANGER: may crash! */
```

This will compile, but the program may crash with an access violation, because an attempt is being made to modify a string that is "constant" and which the compiler has stored in a protected area of memory. This may be to stop programmers trying to rename Windows "Windoze," which would never do. However, if you declare 'name' as an array, all will be well:

```
char name[] = "John";      /* NB: sizeof(name) = 5 */
name[2] = 'a';             /* safe: name now = "Joan" */
```

This demonstrates probably the easiest way to initialize a char array—it is not necessary in such cases to supply a size for the array inside the brackets as that is now available from the initialization string. Usefully, with this form of initialization, the `sizeof` operator can also be used to find the size of the string programmatically.

As you work through the chapters of this book, you will discover a range of techniques that programmers use to keep such coding errors to a minimum. Together these form a repertoire of techniques for "defensive programming." We have already met some of these techniques: the use of informative variable names, explanatory comments, and the robust testing of user input. As our programs grow in complexity, we will need to pay ever greater attention to defensive programming. We hope we will "get it right first time," but the more our programs depend on input from outside, and the larger our programs become, the more we must be on the lookout for code with unintended side effects.

1.3.5 Converting Number Strings to Variables: The `const` Keyword

We have used the `printf()` function to write a numeric variable to the console in text form. In order to get a number interactively from the user, we need to be able to do the reverse. The standard C library offers three conversion functions: `atof()`, `atoi()`, and `atol()`, which convert into `double`, `int`, and `long`, respectively. They are declared in the header file `stdlib.h`, which therefore must be `#included` in any source file that uses them. They all have the same format, differing only by return type:

```
double atof(const char*);
int atoi(const char*);
long atol(const char*);
```

Their use is straightforward:

```
double dval;
int ival;
long lval;

dval = atof("1.0594631"); /* dval = 1.0594631 */
ival = atoi("440"); /* ival = 440 */
lval = atol("65536"); /* lval = 65536 */
```

The const keyword is often used in such declarations. It indicates that the supplied argument is treated as "constant" or "read only"; it will not be modified. That is to say, the pointer is a "pointer to a constant char." When a plain (non-pointer) type is used as a function argument, it is copied into the function's private memory space, so that the variable is not modified. When the argument is a pointer, the pointer is copied, but the memory it points to could be modified. Some functions are expressly designed to do this, and would be declared without the const keyword. An important example is the function gets(), which obtains text typed at the console:

```
char* gets( char *buffer );
```

Here the buffer argument receives the string from the user, and must therefore be a pointer to a char array of adequate size, while the return value will duplicate the buffer or will be NULL to indicate an error.

Conversely, the presence of const in a function declaration is a guarantee that the function will not modify your data. It therefore becomes another element in our repertoire of defensive programming techniques. It is also a signal to the compiler that some sorts of optimizations can be performed.

The use of these functions is easy:

```
double frequency;
char* message = "1.0594631";

frequency = atof(message);
/* frequency now has the value 1.0594631 */
```

The only issue to remember is what happens if the message string does not in fact contain the expected numeric characters—in this case, these functions return 0, in the appropriate type:

```
message = "one thousand";
frequency = atof(message);
/* frequency now has the value 0.0 */
```

However, this will produce a plausible result:

```
message = "1000pointfive";
frequency = atof(message);  /* frequency = 1000.0 */
```

as atof() simply stops reading at the first non-numeric character.

Thus you cannot know with certainty whether the user has actually typed a 0 or whether it has typed some other incorrect text. Of course, this is an issue only if 0 is a reasonable number for the user to give. The standard C library offers more elaborate functions, such as `strtod()`, that both trap incorrect text, and identify it for you by returning any offending text via a pointer to a `char` array, that you provide.

The `const` keyword can be used to trap the problem mentioned at the end of the previous section. By declaring the pointer as a pointer to `const char`:

```
const char *name = "John";
name[2] = 'a';
```

The second line will now trigger a warning from the compiler that an attempt is being made to modify `const` or read-only memory.

1.3.6   Testing, Comparison, and Decision Making: The `if` Keyword

Listing 1.2 does very little that cannot be handled by a pocket calculator. In order to write a reasonably practical interactive program, we need to be able to check user input for correctness, and be able to quit the program if input is incorrect. The ability to make simple "yes-no" or "true-false" decisions (very quickly) lies at the heart of computing. Such a decision is, of course, binary—there are only two possible answers. At the level of binary logic, "yes" corresponds to "true" and is associated with the value 1, while "no" equates to "false" and has the value 0. We will see later that literally every C expression can be evaluated in terms of "true" or "false." At this stage, all we need is the ability to make a comparison between two expressions (e.g. two numbers) and to take alternative actions based on the result.

A frequent programming requirement is to find out if two variables are equal. This is one of many comparison tests for which C provides special operators. These are listed in table 1.3. As they are binary operators (like the arithmetic operators), they are placed between the two values being compared. For example, the "equality" operator is used to find if two variables are equal. The expression

Table 1.3
The C comparison operators.

Operator		Example	Description
Equal to	==	a == b	a is equal to b
Not equal to	!=	a != b	a is not equal to b
Bigger than	>	a > b	a is bigger than b
Smaller than	<	a < b	a is smaller than b
Bigger than or equal to	>=	a >= b	a is bigger than or equal to b
Smaller than or equal to	<=	a <= c	a is smaller than or equal to b

```
(width == height)
```

(an example of a C "conditional expression" or "conditional test") will evaluate to 1 if the values are identical, or to 0 otherwise.

The C language includes the keyword `if`, which is placed in front of the expression to be tested:

```
if(width == height)
```

As it stands, this is incomplete—it is not yet either an expression or a statement. To form a complete "if statement," it must be immediately followed by a C statement, to be executed if the test is successful (i.e. if the expression evaluates to 'true'):

```
if(width == height)
printf("it's a square!");
```

By convention, the body of the statement is indented if it appears in the next line, showing that it depends on the outcome of the preceding `if` expression. If you need to write more than one statement depending on the same `if` expression, the statements must be enclosed by braces, which serve to indicate a single "code block":

```
if(width==height)
{
    found_square = 1;
        printf("it's a square!");
}
```

One of the traps for the unwary with `if` statements is adding a final semicolon. This can easily occur by accident in the process of editing code, and it is often difficult to spot:

```
if(width == height);
```

This is in fact legal C, because the semicolon by itself is a legal statement that does nothing (a "null statement"). The true meaning is clearer when we use appropriate layout:

```
if(width == height)
    ;   /* do nothing! */
```

C is fairly flexible with respect to comparisons between different numeric types. However, comparisons between plain variables and pointers will be flagged as errors by the compiler, as will be comparisons between pointers to different types (e.g. a `float` pointer with an `int` pointer). The one important exception is `NULL`, which can be compared with any pointer type. One of the more idiosyncratic styles I have come across is

```
if(a == b)
    {
        do_something();
    }
```

This works perfectly well so long as braces are always used (as is often recommended). However, in

```
if(a == b)
    do_something();
if(c == d)
    {
        do_something_else();
    }
```

the dependent statements have different degrees of indentation but are in fact at the same "level."

The amount of indentation also attracts different opinions. Indents of two, four, and eight spaces are common. A subtler issue is whether to use hard spaces or a tab. (Most text editors can be set to use a requested tab size.) So long as one approach or the other is used consistently throughout, there should be few problems with layout if the text is transferred between platforms. If in doubt, remember that the use of hard spaces will always be portable.[8]

1.3.7   An Interactive Version of Listing 1.2

Each time the program is run, it asks the user to type in a MIDI Note number. If it is recognized as a reasonable number, the corresponding frequency is displayed. Otherwise, an error message is displayed and the program finishes. You can either create a new file (or project) for this or just edit listing 1.2, keeping the same program name. Apart from the fact that this version is a little more useable, the latter approach reflects more closely how programs are usually developed—incrementally, adding features step by step. The program uses the function `gets()`, described above, to read a line of text typed by the user in response to a prompt.

When `gets()` is called, it waits for user input from the console (which must include a final 'return' keypress), then places whatever was typed in the `char` array supplied as the function argument. That array must be large enough to accommodate whatever we suspect the user might try to type. The return value, also a `char` pointer, is simply a copy of the input argument. The function can also signal an error in special circumstances, by returning `NULL`. While those circumstances are not likely to apply here, this possibility is nevertheless tested for in the program. Comparing pointers with `NULL` is a very common programming procedure, and is very important, as trying to read from or write to memory pointed to by `NULL` can be guaranteed to crash the program. To detect errors, listing 1.3 uses four `if` statements with three different comparison operators. In each case, the `return` keyword is used to exit the program if an error is detected, with 1 as the error value.

Listing 1.3

```c
#include <stdio.h>
#include <stdlib.h>
#include <math.h>

int main()
{
    double c5,c0,semitone_ratio,frequency;
    int midinote;
    char message[256];
    char* result;

    semitone_ratio = pow(2, 1.0/12);
    c5 = 220.0 * pow(semitone_ratio, 3);
    c0 = c5 * pow(0.5, 5);

    printf("Enter MIDI note (0 - 127): ");
    result = gets(message);
    if(result == NULL){
        printf("There was an error reading the input.\n");
        return 1;
    }
    if(message[0] == '\0') {
        printf("Have a nice day!\n");
        return 1;
    }
    midinote = atoi(message);
    if(midinote < 0){
        printf("Sorry - %s is a bad MIDI note number\n",message);
        return 1;
    }
    if(midinote > 127){
        printf("Sorry - %s is beyond the MIDI range!\n",message);
        return 1;
    }
    frequency = c0 * pow(semitone_ratio, midinote);
    printf("frequency of MIDI note %d = %f\n", midinote, frequency);

    return 0;
}
```

The use of compound expressions was demonstrated in subsection 1.2.8. As any C expression can be evaluated to a value, it follows that one or both sides of a comparison operator could also be a compound expression; for example, incorporating a function returning a value. In listing 1.3, the return value from `gets()` is tested only once, so the code could reasonably be compacted as follows, eliminating a variable:

```
printf("Enter MIDI note (0 - 127): ");
if(gets(message) == NULL){
    printf("There was an error reading the input.\n");
    return 1;
}
```

The compiler will make sure that the function call is executed first (it has the highest precedence), and the result then passed to the conditional test.

1.3.8   Exercises

Exercise 1.3.1
Listing 1.3 has no comments. How "self-documenting" is the code? Add some comments wherever you think they would be useful.

Exercise 1.3.2

(a) Make a new interactive version of *"freq2midi"* from the previous section.
(b) Implement rounding of the printed pitch deviation percentage value, so that positive and negative values are symmetrically rounded. For example, 38.7 should be rounded to 38, and −38.7 should be rounded to −39.

Exercise 1.3.3

(a) Add a further test on the number supplied from the user in listing 1.3, to detect and reject floating-point values (since MIDI notes are integers).
(b) Try to detect whatever erroneous input the user might make, and respond with an appropriate error message.

Exercise 1.3.4
What messages does the compiler write if

(a) you omit the final double quotation marks in a printf statement?
(b) you omit the variable name associated with a format specifier in printf?

1.4   The Command Line—Getting Data from the User

1.4.1   What Is the Command Line?

As its name suggests, the command line is a means of communicating with a computer using text commands typed from the keyboard, and using the medium of a "command shell" or a "console program"—for example, the Bash shell in UNIX, the DOS console in Windows, or the Terminal in Macintosh OS X. While it is not the oldest way of sending commands to a computer, it is by far the longest established, and despite the inexorable progress of WIMP-based systems (Window Icon Menu Pointer), usually referred to simply as a GUI (Graphic User Interface), it refuses to go away. Significantly, the Apple Macintosh, having eliminated the command-line interface as both unnecessary and "user-unfriendly," has recently re-acquired it with the introduction of OS X, which is based on the UNIX-like BSD kernel. Thus the three most widely used operating systems all now support a console-based command-line interface, which is ideal for developing and running simple programs such as those presented in this section. Indeed, for many advanced users (and especially on Linux and other UNIX-like platforms) it remains the ideal environment in which to work, even on complex projects.

A typical text command consists of a program name (e.g. 'copy'), followed by one or more 'arguments'—words separated by spaces. Let us suppose there is a program `sfmix` that takes two or more soundfiles and adds them together (i.e. mixes them) to create a new soundfile. The documentation for the program tells us that the first argument should be the name of the new output file, and all following arguments should be the names of input soundfiles to add together. The command line might look like this:

```
sfmix backing.wav drums.wav guitars.wav
```

This runs the program `sfmix`, creating the output file *backing.wav* from the input files *drums.wav* and *guitars.wav*. This works because the operating system supports a standard method for both running a command-line program and giving it the arguments from the user. The operating system has no idea what these arguments mean—they are nothing more than text strings separated by spaces. It does one very useful thing, however: it separates each string into a list, and gives that list to the program to use as it wishes. Thus, rather than having to ask the user interactively for each filename, the program is given all the names automatically from the command line.

The command-line environment is most strongly associated with the UNIX operating system and its variants, including Linux and OS X. However, the principles are much the same on Windows using the DOS console. Programs can be run just as illustrated above. The only immediately relevant difference from a classic UNIX-style environment is that the command to list the contents of a directory is `ls` on UNIX-style systems, whereas it is `dir` in DOS. By using command-line arguments, a program can be designed to handle a range of inputs from the user. The usual environment for command lines is a shell application or terminal window such as the Windows DOS Console, **Terminal** in OS X, or an **Xterm** in Linux. Table 1.6 shows some typical shell commands. (N.B: To run a program in the current directory—e.g. in which the program has been built—in a UNIX-like environment (Linux, OS X Terminal), the program name must be prefixed by the "current directory" shorthand `./` as follows:

```
> ./cpsmidi 72
```

Other commands, such as cd to change directory, are the same.

   If you have not already done so, you may want to try out some of the pre-compiled command-line programs supplied on the DVD as a way to develop fluency in using such tools. Most of them are projects from later chapters in this book. Although they involve much more elaborate C programming than we can do at the moment, there is no reason not to use them as prefabricated tools with which useful creative work can be done. The chances are high that you will very soon think of some new facility that is not provided by a given program. There can be no better incentive to develop your programming skills than the prospect of crafting exactly the tools you want for the work you want to do.

1.4.2   The Extended main() Function: Receiving Command-Line Arguments

In the programs demonstrated so far, we have used the main() function with no arguments. There is an alternative extended form, which is required whenever we want information from the user at the beginning of the program:

```
int main(int argc, char* argv[]);
```

The first argument, argc, is simple enough. It is an int, and the name means "argument count," the number of space-separated strings supplied in the command line. This number will always be at least 1, as the first argument (counting from 0, as is always the case in C) is the name of the program itself. The second argument is a little more complicated and needs some detailed explanation. You have already seen declarations of pointers (such as char* name;) and of arrays (such as char name[32];), but argv combines both the pointer and array notations. The name argv is shorthand for 'argument vector', and 'vector' here is a synonym for 'array'. So we have an array argv[ ]of 'pointer to char': char*.

   The key aspect to remember here is that a pointer to char can itself signify an array, in the sense of a character string (i.e. null-terminated), which indeed is the case here. Thus, taking the example above as our example command line, this array of strings would be laid out as follows:

```
argv[0]points to "sfmix"
argv[1]points to "backing.wav"
argv[2]points to "drums.wav"
argv[3]points to "guitars.wav"
```

This is shown graphically in figure 1.2.

   An array can also be understood as a *container*, so instead of "points to" you could say "contains."[9] There is also a final implicit argv[4] which contains NULL. However, this is not counted in argc, so for this example argc would have the value 4. This final NULL element can in principle be used in code that steps through the argv array until the NULL is

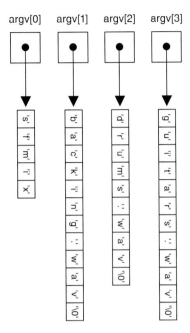

Figure 1.2

Command-line arguments as pointers to strings.

found. However, as `argc` is always available (and a more convenient basis for a loop), such usage is rare. Note that the first argument (`argv[0]`) contains the name of the program. This may seem superfluous (after all, we have written the code, so we know what we have called the program), but it can be surprisingly useful. If nothing else, we will not be caught out if the user decides to rename the program.

In a program, you might use `argv` to print a message to the users, perhaps about some error:

```
printf("Cannot find the file %s\n," argv[2]);
```

Since the expression `argv[2]` evaluates to a `char*`, it can be used as the associated variable for the string format specifier `%s`. Similarly, it can be passed as the parameter to any function expecting a `char*` :

```
/* read number of oscillators requested */
int num_oscs = atoi(argv[3]);
if(num_oscs > 100)
    printf("too many oscillators!\n");
```

Just as in the previous program examples, we will have to check each argument for reasonableness. The simplest and most important test, however, is the one applied to `argc`. We know how many arguments we need, and we must check for this before trying to read any of them:

```
if(argc < 4){
    printf("insufficient arguments.\n") ;
    printf("usage: sfmix outfile infile1 \
              infile2 [infile3 . . ..]\n");
    return 1;               /* exit the program */
 }
```

For command-line programs, this "usage message" is a very common procedure, which users come to expect and rely on. If they type just the name of the program, they should be given a full usage message listing the purpose of the program and the name and purpose of each argument. You will see this incorporated in all the programs that follow.[10]

1.4.3   The `**` Notation for `argv`

The `main` function supports an alternative definition of `argv`:

```
int main(int argc, char** argv)
```

where `**` means that `argv` is a "pointer to a pointer." In principle, pointer variables can incorporate any amount of "indirection." I have seen the following in programs:

```
char**** very_indirect_variable;
```

This might perhaps be a pointer to an array of string arrays, or it might not. The `**` notation is, however, very common in programs that deal with lists of strings. It is arguably less appropriate than the explicit array notation, for `main()`—a variable that is a "pointer to a pointer to char"—may, in the end, be pointing only to a single character. Opinions on this differ, however, and you will find many `main` functions defined this way—perhaps merely because it is marginally quicker to type.

Listing 1.4 shows a revision to listing 1.3 to obtain input from a command-line argument. This is the first program in the present chapter that can be considered "useful," as the user can run it with any MIDI note as input—one need not compile the program each time. Exercise 1.4.1 invites you to incorporate this change into the complementary program outlined in subsection 1.2.11 (converting frequency into MIDI). Listing 1.4 could be made even more useful by allowing the user to enter any number of MIDI notes.

Listing 1.4

```
/* cpsmidi.c : convert MIDI note to frequency, using command line
             argument */
#include <stdio.h>
#include <stdlib.h>
#include <math.h>
```

```
int main(int argc, char* argv[])
{
    double c5,c0,semitoneratio;
    double frequency;
    int midinote;                          /* could be a char */

    semitoneratio = pow(2,1.0/12);
    c5 = 220.0 * pow(semitoneratio,3);
    c0 = c5 * pow(0.5,5);

    /* if the program is not called cpsmidi,
        either change the lines below,
            or use the argv[0] system, shown commented out below */
    if(argc != 2){
        printf("cpsmidi : converts MIDI note to frequency.\n"
                /*,argv[0]*/);
        printf("usage: cpsmidi MIDInote\n" /* ,argv[0]*/);
        printf(" range: 0 <= MIDInote <= 127 \n");
        return 1;
    }
    midinote = atoi(argv[1]);
    /* use argv[1] to echo a bad argument string to the user */
    if(midinote < 0){
        printf("Bad MIDI note value: %s\n",argv[1]);
        return 1;
    }
    if(midinote > 127){
        printf("%s is beyond the MIDI range!\n",argv[1]);
        return 1;
    }

    frequency = c0 * pow(semitoneratio,midinote);
    printf("frequency of MIDI note %d = %f\n",midinote,frequency);
    return 0;
}
```

Finally, if you think that command-line arguments exist only for command-line programs, think again: a Windows GUI program also reads command-line arguments, as will any UNIX (or Linux or Apple OS X) program. In Windows, for example, it is possible to invoke the Notepad application from the DOS console, giving it the name of a file to edit:

```
notepad freq2midi.c
```

The procedure on Apple OS X is only slightly different. To run the soundfile editor *Audacity* from the Terminal, you can type

```
open -a Audacity.app myfile.aiff
```

The command-line handling skills you develop here will stand you in good stead when developing more advanced GUI applications.

1.4.4   Exercises

Exercise 1.4.1

Convert all the programs developed so far to use `argc` and `argv`. Don't forget to incorporate the extensions suggested in previous exercises.

Exercise 1.4.2

Add a usage message to each program.

Exercise 1.4.3 (experimental)

(a) Extend the program with a further command-line argument that defines the "root A" tuning. For example, "Baroque" pitch defines A = 415 Hz. In fact, A = 440 Hz is itself a relatively recent "standard"—especially in the United States, where the pitch of A = 435 Hz was recently in widespread use.

(b) (experimental) Add a further argument that defines the division of the octave. For example, a popular alternative temperament uses a 19-note equal-temperament division. A value of 24 would define a quarter-tone ET scale. In each case, trap inappropriate user input with suitable error messages.

1.5   Controlling Repetition: Looping and Counting

So far, with one exception, every one of the example programs has dealt with a single piece of data—a single MIDI note, or a single frequency value. The exception is the character string, which takes the form of an array of single characters. It is possible to make arrays of any type (e.g. a block of floating-point audio samples), and it becomes essential to have the means for processing the array as a whole, while addressing individual elements within it, in a structured and systematic manner, regardless of how large the array is. The image of a production line is a very natural one with respect to dealing with arrays. Given that they contain multiple instances of only one type of object (`char`, or `float`, for example), we can imagine a process that more or less automatically repeats itself for each element. We would like to be able to press a button, so to speak, to start this process, and be able to press another button to stop it again.

As audio programmers, we will be creating and processing such arrays (and other data structures) all the time, and the sheer number of elements is far too great for anyone to contemplate writing code that processes each one in a written list. Fortunately, the need to address an individual element of such arrays directly is rare; most of the time we want to apply the same process to each element just as described above—for example, to change the *amplitude* of an array of audio samples. We can use the power of the C language to make such tasks easy. With a few lines of code, we will be able to read and process every element of an array of any size. The tools for this are two cornerstones of all programming: *iteration* (counting) and *looping* (repeating instructions). These are especially important tasks in audio programming, as we will be working all the time with blocks of samples, such as tables containing waveforms, memory buffers containing delay lines or audio streamed from a disk or from a soundcard, or tables of frequencies and amplitudes for oscillators. In a typical application we have to step through the block, making a change to each sample as we go. On a larger scale, when we need to read a soundfile, we usually need to read it in blocks (the whole file may be far too large to fit in memory all at once), so we have to use iteration and looping to read each block and process it. This is, then, a process of "mass production." We can use the power of the language to repeat steps automatically, at very high speed, on blocks of data of any size. In this section we move from writing calculations to writing *algorithms*—methods for performing a concretely defined task, usually involving many repeated steps. In a sense, this is the first section in which we embark on true computer programming. We will learn about how to create *loops*, and also more about the use of C's *auto-increment* and *auto-decrement* operators, which are designed to support the highly efficient mass production we need. Finally, we will apply all this new knowledge to build on the programs we have already built, and to produce perhaps the first truly useful program so far.

1.5.1 The `while` Loop

As its name suggests, a loop is a block of code (it need not be a single instruction) that repeats over and over. However, a code block that simply repeated forever—an "endless loop"—would not be very useful. If you have used a sampler, you will be familiar with the way a sound is looped (to maintain a sustaining sound) while a key is held down. This is a form of endless loop—it is broken out of only when you release they key. Should it fail to do that, you have a real problem.

So, the most important aspect of using loops is *control*—making sure that they stop when we want them to. The simplest way to do this is to count the number of times the loop repeats, and stop when a limit is reached.

The simplest loop construct in C is the `while` loop. Listing 1.5.1 shows an example of its use.

Listing 1.5.1

```
1    #include <stdio.h>
2    int main(){
3          int i;
4
```

```
5          i = 0;
6          while(i < 10) {
7                  printf("%d ,"i);
8                  i = i + 1;
9          }
10         return 0;
11     }
```

The output from this program is simply

```
0 1 2 3 4 5 6 7 8 9
```

Instead of writing the `printf()` statement ten times, we have written it just once, and used the while loop to generate the repeats. In this program we have decided to write ten numbers, so could in principle write each one explicitly. But suppose this was a program called 'count' and had a command-line argument that set the number to count to. We cannot know in advance what this number will be, and of course it may be different each time we run the program. We can only implement this task using a loop, where the input from the user is used to control the loop.

The `while` statement is similar to the `if` statement in that it comprises a conditional test (inside the parentheses, followed by a "dependent" statement or code block (in braces). The main difference is that, whereas an `if` statement may execute the dependent code once and move on, the `while` statement will repeat the dependent code forever, so long as the conditional expression is true. (See figure 1.3.)

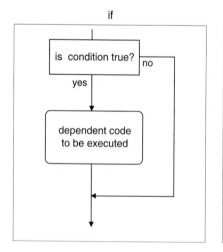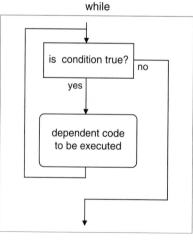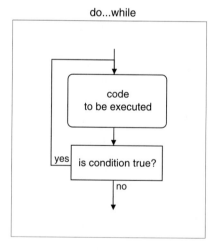

Figure 1.3
Comparing if . . . while and do . . . while.

There are three essential elements of loop control illustrated in this example:

1. Line 6 is the conditional test, associated with the `while` keyword itself,: (i < 10). At the end of each iteration, program control will automatically return to the conditional test, and evaluate it again. So long as the expression evaluates to 'true', the code inside the dependent block { }will execute repeatedly.

2. Line 8 is the update of the control expression, i = i + 1; In the control expression (i < 10), i is a variable which is declared outside the block, and modified at each repeat ("iteration"). The effect is simply that at each repeat i is increased by 1, as shown by the output of `printf()`.

3. Line 5 is the initializer statement, i = 0 ;This sets the starting value of the controlling variable. This is placed before, and outside, the `while` statement. In this case it is set to 0, but it could be anything. For example, in this variation the numbers count downward from 9 to 0[11]:

```
i = 9;
while(i >= 0){
    printf("%d," i);
    i = i - 1;
}
```

1.5.2 The ++ and -- Operators

In listing 1.5.1, the update expression increases the variable i by 1:

```
i = i + 1;
```

This algebraically impossible expression, commonplace in programming, means "let i have the value it currently has, plus 1." The process of adding 1 to something is termed an *increment*, and similarly, subtracting 1 is called a *decrement*. So common is this form of counting that special automatic increment (++) and decrement (--) operators were added to C, reflecting in many cases identical machine-level instructions.

Auto-increment increases a variable by 1:

```
i++;    /* equivalent to i = i +1; */
```

Auto-decrement decreases a variable by 1:

```
i--;    /* equivalent to i = i - 1; */
```

Since this form can be used as part of a more complex expression, it enables a loop to be expressed in a very concise form. The example below is exactly equivalent to the code in listing 1.5.1 (note that we now can omit the braces):

```
i = 0; /* initializer */
while(i < 10) /* conditional expression */
```

```
printf("%d ,"i++); /* update in the dependent code */
```

The comments indicate the three loop elements required.

There is a subtle aspect to these increment and decrement operators. In the `printf()` statement above, i is auto-incremented *after* its value has been used by `printf()`—this is the "post-increment" operator. It is also possible to place the ++ characters before the variable name, forming a pre-increment operator:

```
printf("%d," ++i);
```

In this case, i is incremented first, and the new value is passed to `printf()`. The result will be that each number printed would be one larger (i.e. 1 to 10 instead of 0 to 9).

The auto-decrement operator functions in the same way:

```
printf("%d ",i--); /* print the i, then reduce it by one */
printf("%d ",--i); /* reduce i by one, then print the value */
```

These last examples illustrate the idiomatic way to use the auto-increment and decrement operators in the context of a larger expression, and especially in the context of loops. They can be used on their own (sometimes merely to save typing), but they were born for use as part of larger expressions, in which they are usually the most efficient method of increment.

1.5.3 General Update Operators

While the increment and decrement operators are intended for use with integer variables (and also with pointers, as we'll see later), they will also work with floating-point variables:

```
double var = 1.5;
var++; /* var now = 2.5 */
```

This is not idiomatic C programming, however, and it is not recommended[12]—any C programmer reading the expression var++ will assume that var is an integer variable. A more general update expression that can be used with floating-point types uses one of the arithmetic operators (+, -, *, /) together with the = sign:

```
float a = 1.0;
a += 2.5; /* equivalent to a = a + 2.5; a has the value 3.5 */
a -= 0.5; /* a now = 3.0 */
a /= 2.0; /* a now = 1.5 */
a *= 3.0; /* a now = 4.5 */
```

The % (modulus) operator can also be used in this way, but only for integral types:

```
int a = 10;
a %= 3;              /* a now = 1 */
```

Note that it is illegal to have a space between the arithmetic operator and the = sign:

```
a + = 5;      /* syntax error */
```

In the example below, update notation is used inside a loop to calculate the intervals of the equal-tempered scale, and write them to an array. Post-increment is also used, applied to the counter i in the array index expression:

```
double ratio = 1.0, semitone_ratio = pow(2,1/12.0);
double intervals[12];
int i;
i = 0;
while(i < 12){
    intervals[i++] = ratio;  /* uses auto-increment*/
    ratio *= semitone_ratio; /* uses update operator */
}
```

The examples in this subsection demonstrate the use of the primary arithmetic conditional tests—for equality (=), "less than" (<), and "greater than" (>), together with their inverses, "not equal to" (!=), "greater or equal" (>=), and "less or equal" (<=). As we shall see, these already offer the programmer considerable flexibility in designing conditional tests associated with loops. C also supports a group of "logical" operators that make it practicable to test multiple conditions together.

1.5.4 The for loop

As was shown above, a complete looping construct involves three control elements: an initializer statement, a conditional expression, and an update statement (e.g. a counter) that usually updates a parameter in that expression. C offers a compact looping construct based on the keyword for that places all three elements together; it is by far the most popular and widely used of all the looping constructs in C. It is best demonstrated by example:

```
int i;
for(i = 0; i < 12; i++){
    intervals[i] = ratio;
    ratio *= semitoneratio;
}
```

This functions identically to the while example in the previous section. The for statement has the structure

for(initializer_statement; conditional_expression; update_expression)

This must be followed, as in the case of the while construct, by either a single statement or a block of statements enclosed by braces, as shown above. The three elements are demarcated

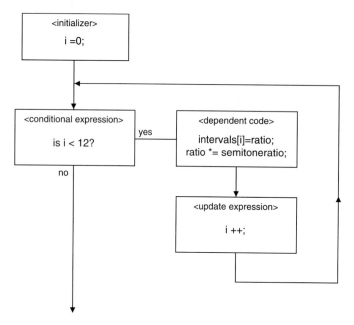

Figure 1.4
The for loop.

by the two required semicolons—a semicolon should not be used to terminate the update expression.

The for loop runs as follows (see figure 1.4), assuming that the conditional test evaluates to **true**:

(1) The initializer statement is executed: i = 0;
(2) The conditional expression is evaluated: i < 12;
(3) The result is true, so . . .
(4) The dependent code inside the braces is executed.
(5) Control returns to the top, and the update expression is executed: i++
(6) The loop continues from step (2) until the condition evaluates to false.
(7) When the condition evaluates to false, control passes to the statements after the for block.[13]

1.5.5 The do { } while ( ) Loop

There is an argument (among computer scientists, at least) that says that any programming language requires only one loop construct; anything further is "syntactic sugar." In that case, C is very sweet indeed, as in addition to the while and for loops it also offers a variation on the `while` loop that places the dependent block at the top and the conditional test at the bottom:

```
int i;
i = 0;
do {
    printf("%d ,"i++);
}
while(i < 10);
```

Note that the `while` expression is terminated by a semicolon, to complete the `do - while` statement. The special aspect of this form of loop is that the dependent block will always be executed at least once, as the conditional test is placed after it. In the example above it makes no significant difference, but there are common situations in which this would be the most appropriate form of loop. One typical situation is reading data from a file (a soundfile, for example); in such a situation, we usually make at least one read attempt before finding out if we have read everything, or if we have suffered an error. Real code to do this is usually lengthy, so this example uses some fictitious functions (it is sometimes called "pseudo-code" for this reason)[14]:

```
int sampsread;
do {
    sampsread = readsamps("tubularbells.wav");
    if(sampsread > 0){
        process_samps(sampsread);
        write_samps("plasticbells.wav," sampsread);
    }
}
while (sampsread > 0);
```

1.5.6   Breaking Out of Loops Early: The `break` Keyword

The do loop example above has one unsatisfying aspect: the expression

```
(sampsread > 0)
```

is used twice: inside the dependent code block (do), and in the conditional test (`while`). This is generally regarded by programmers as tautologous and wasteful. We would prefer not to have to duplicate code in this way if it can be avoided.

Consider what happens if the test inside the do block fails—if the function `readsamps()` returns 0. This means that no more soundfile data is available (we assume we have reached the end of the file). There is also the ever-present danger of a system error whenever disks are accessed—a fault could arise at any time, and a robust program has to be able to handle that situation.

In short, we often want to be able to break out of a loop early—either when there is no more data, or if there is a system error. Recalling the comparison with the production line; if there is a problem, we need to be able to stop the machinery immediately. Happily, C provides the break keyword that does just that. Using break, we can rewrite that example a little more elegantly, and at the same time more expressively:

```
int sampsread;
do {
    sampsread = readsamps("tubularbells.wav");
    if(sampsread == 0)
        break; /* end of file, or error */
    process_samps(sampsread);
    write_samps("plasticbells.wav," sampsread);
}
while (sampsread > 0);
```

If the break instruction is reached, control jumps right out of the do block and past the while expression, to whatever the next instruction is.

Given the reasonable assumption that sampsread is in fact guaranteed to become 0 eventually, even if the conditional while part of the statement is really redundant, we can rely entirely on the sampsread test to exit the loop. This is a surprisingly frequent situation, and you will often encounter loops constructed this way, with a dummy conditional test that always evaluates to true, and relying on break instead. So, instead of running an explicit count to manage the loop, we set the loop to run forever, but watch for a condition or event that we know will occur eventually.

In the for() initialization expression, all three elements are optional, leaving just the two semicolons:

```
for(;;){
    sampsread = readsamps("tubularbells.wav");
    if(sampsread == 0)
        break;                  /* end of file */
    process_samps(sampsread);
    write_samps("plasticbells.wav," sampsread);
}
```

and any non-zero integer evaluates to true:

```
while(1){
    sampsread = readsamps("tubularbells.wav");
    if(sampsread == 0)
        break;                  /* end of file */
    process_samps(sampsread);
    write_samps("plasticbells.wav," sampsread);
}
```

These are common constructs in real programs, but they are safe only if break can be *guaranteed* to be called at some point.

So where are the three elements that all loops are supposed to have? They are now embedded in the looped code: the assignment to sampsread is both the initializer and the update, and the conditional test is clearly the if statement.

Assuming that in a real program the function write_samps() will also return a value (below zero) that can indicate an error, we would have to check that too:

```
if(write_samps("plasticbells.wav," sampsread) < 0)
    break;
```

In this case it is purely a check for an exceptional situation—normally one hopes that a write to a file will always succeed.

1.5.7 Writing a Program to Create Unusual Musical Scales

We have learned quite a few C programming skills already—we know how to use the extended form of the main() function to get command-line arguments from the user, we know how to program simple loops, using auto-increment and update operators, and we also know something about calculating equal-tempered intervals. The program developed in this subsection combines all these elements into a useful program that can create scales with any number of notes to the octave (not just 12 semitones), up to some reasonable limit, and starting at any MIDI note requested by the user. There is a great interest in the use of such scales among composers, and one of the much-lauded virtues of experimental computer music is that one need not be limited by conventions such as the classical 12-note chromatic scale.

Since this is arguably our first real program, the process of designing and writing it is presented from scratch, with the full program listing presented at the end. Try to resist the temptation just to look ahead to the listing. Instead, follow the process all the way through, starting with a new empty project. There is not very much typing involved, and we will reuse some code from section 1.2. You might assume that the first thing to do is (somehow) to start writing code. But it isn't—the first thing to do is to sit down and think carefully about what the program is going to do, and in particular how the user is going to use it.

The goal of this program is to display the frequencies of equal-tempered intervals for N notes per octave. If N is 12, we will get the notes of the standard chromatic scale. Another popular octave division is 19 notes. If N is 24, we will get a quarter-tone scale. If we write each frequency on a separate line, 24 lines seems a reasonable limit for this program.

We need to set a limit, because we are going to define an array to hold the interval data, and we can only define an array with an explicit constant size. (We will see how to get around this limitation in section 1.7.) So we need the size to be that of the largest number N we intend to support.

We know that one command-line argument will be *N*, the number of notes in the octave. We also need a MIDI note, so that will be the second argument. Our program (which will be called *"nscale"*) will therefore have the following usage:

```
nscale notes midinote
```

where `notes` is the number of notes per octave and `midinote` is the base note on which to build the scale. Therefore, there will be a total of three command-line arguments, including the program's name.

We can now create a source file (*"nscale.c"*) in a new project, and write a skeleton `main()` function. We are printing to the console, so we will need `<stdio.h>`. As we are using mathematical functions such as `pow()`, we will also need `<math.h>`. We should also put in a small comment line, to say what the program is.

Listing 1.5.2 shows the skeleton program so far. This will compile and run; if you run it with no arguments (or indeed with anything more than two arguments), the usage message will be written to the screen.

Listing 1.5.2

```c
/* nscale.c. Display E.T frequencies for an N-note octave, from a
           given MIDI note */
#include <stdio.h>
#include <math.h>

int main(int argc, char* argv[])
{
    /* declare variables here. . .*/

    if(argc != 3){
        printf("usage: nscale notes midinote\n");
        return 1;
    }

    /* program code goes here */

    return 0;
}
```

We now need to add some functionality to this skeleton, where the comment indicates. We can start by reading our required arguments into variables and testing them for acceptability. If they are not acceptable, we must inform the user helpfully and quit the program. Both `notes` and `midinote` are integer numbers, so they can both be `int`. We must declare all our variables at top level, after the opening brace of `main()`:

```c
int main(int argc, char* argv[])
{
    int notes, midinote;
```

First, we read notes from argv[1], and make sure it is between 1 and 24:

```
notes = atoi(argv[1]);
if(notes < 1){
    printf("Error: notes must be positive\n");
    return 1;
}
if(notes > 24){
    printf("Error: maximum value for notes is 24\n");
    return 1;
}
```

Then we do the same for midinote, from argv[2]. The legal MIDI range is from 0 to 127:

```
midinote = atoi(argv[2]);
if(midinote < 0){
    printf("Error: cannot have negative MIDI notes!\n");
    return 1;
}
if(midinote > 127){
    printf("Error: maximum MIDInote is 127\n");
    return 1;
}
```

Again, at this point you can compile the program, and test it first by giving it a correct pair of arguments (10 and 69, say), and then by various combinations of out-of-range values, to make sure the error messages appear as intended.

We can now deal with the core functionality of the program. This is to calculate the frequency of the requested MIDI note, and use that to create a table of notes frequencies spanning one octave from that base note. We can reuse the core arithmetic code from listing 1.2, remembering to add all the variables used in that code, immediately below the variables we have already declared. If possible, use the copy and paste facilities of your editor to do this:

```
int notes, midinote;
double frequency,ratio;
double c0,c5;
```

Note that what was called semitone_ratio is now just called ratio—we are no longer calculating just semitones, so a more general variable name is appropriate here. Now, we can copy the calculation code from listing 1.2, complete with comments, into our source file, after all the argument checking code:

```
ratio = pow(2.0,1.0 / 12.0);
/* find Middle C, three semitones above low A = 220 */
c5 = 220.0 * pow(ratio,3);
```

```
/* MIDI note 0 is C, 5 octaves below Middle C */
c0 = c5 * pow(0.5,5);
frequency = c0 * pow(ratio,midinote);
```

Note that the hard-coded assignment to midinote in the original program is deleted, as we are now getting that from a command-line argument.

All we have to do now is to generate the list of frequencies, and print them to the console. There are two ways of doing this, but either way, we need a loop to generate the numbers, as they may be from 1 to 24 in number.

The first way is simply to calculate each note, and print it to the console, all inside the loop. However, at the back of our minds we are thinking that this data may be useful in other programs (or maybe even within an extended version of this program), so that it is worth using an array to contain these notes. We will therefore use two loops—one to create the frequencies, and the other to print them out.

We decided that the maximum for notes is 24, so we can define an array that size, of double. This is the standard type to use for arithmetic calculations, giving maximum precision. Add the following line immediately below the other variable declarations:

```
double intervals[24];
```

To calculate intervals for N notes per octave, we use the same calculation we have already used for 12 semitones, but replacing 12 with notes:

```
ratio = pow(2.0, 1.0 / notes);
```

To generate the complete scale, we just multiply each frequency by this ratio, to get the next frequency. This is a clear description of an "iterative process"—a loop. All C programmers turn to the for loop as their first instinct, so we shall be no different:

```
for(i = 0; i < notes; i++){
    intervals[i] = frequency;
    frequency *= ratio;
}
```

We can use the for loop again to print the frequencies to the console:

```
for(i = 0; i < notes; i++){
    printf("%f\n", i, intervals[i]);
}
```

We are now ready to compile and test the completed program. But it fails to compile. We have had a compilation error reported. The exact wording will depend on the compiler, but we will get something like this:

```
error C2065: 'i' : undeclared identifier
```

The correct response to this error is "Oops!" We forgot to declare the variable i we have used in the for loops (in C, all variable names are "identifiers"). This is probably one of the most common everyday slips for C programmers. Everyone uses i as the counter in a for loop—typing it is almost an automatic process—and it is very easy indeed to forget to add it to the variables list.

So add that variable (an int) to the int list at the top of main(), and this time hope that the program will compile cleanly. Now we can test it, perhaps with numbers from which we can predict the results. For example, to print a standard chromatic scale from A = 220, use arguments 12 and 57. The complete program is shown in listing 1.5.3.

Listing 1.5.3

```
/* nscale.c: Display E.T frequencies for an N-note octave, from a
            given MIDI note */
#include <stdio.h>
#include <stdlib.h>
#include <math.h>

int main(int argc, char* argv[])
{
    int notes,i,midinote;
    double frequency,ratio;
    double c0,c5;
    double intervals[24];

    if(argc != 3){
        printf("Usage: nscale notes miditnote\n");
        return 1;
    }

    notes = atoi(argv[1]);
    if(notes < 1){
        printf("Error: notes must be positive\n");
        return 1;
    }
    if(notes > 24){
        printf("Error: maximum value for notes is 24\n");
        return 1;
    }

    midinote = atoi(argv[2]);
    if(midinote < 0){
        printf("Error: cannot have negative MIDI notes!\n");
        return 1;
    }
```

```
    if(midinote > 127){
        printf("Error: maximum midinote is 127\n");
        return 1;
    }

    /*** find the frequency of the MIDI note ***/

    /* calc standard E.T semitone ratio */
    ratio = pow(2.0,1.0 / 12.0);
    /* find Middle C, three semitones above low A = 220 */
    c5 = 220.0 * pow(ratio,3);
    /* MIDI note 0 is C, 5 octaves below Middle C */
    c0 = c5 * pow(0.5,5);
    frequency = c0 * pow(ratio,midinote);

    /* calc ratio from notes, and fill the frequency array */
    ratio = pow(2.0,1.0/notes);
    for(i = 0; i < notes; i++){
        intervals[i] = frequency;
        frequency *= ratio;
    }

    /* finally, read array, write to screen */
    for(i = 0; i < notes; i++){
        printf("%f\n", intervals[i]);
    }

    return 0;
}
```

1.5.8   Exercises

Exercise 1.5.1

Write a short page of user documentation for the program *"nscale"* in listing 1.5.3. Assume the user knows what a chromatic scale is but is not familiar with the mathematical basis of equal temperament.

Exercise 1.5.2

Rewrite the loops in listing 1.5.3 to use (a) the while loop and (b) the do loop. What are you relying on in the latter case? Be sure to test both changes by running the program.

Exercise 1.5.3

The output of the program as shown does not include the final octave pitch, printing only N notes. Modify listing 1.5.3 to add the extra value. The program will then write one more number than the value given for `notes`. For example, if `notes = 24`, the program will print 25 numbers.

Exercise 1.5.4

Modify the final `printf()` statement to add a counter to the beginning of each line, that would have the following form:

```
1: 220.000000
2: 233.081881
. . .
```

Exercise 1.5.5

(This requires some mathematical acuity.) You have decided that you want to be able to use an interval other than the octave as the basis for the frequency calculations. Add another argument to "*nscale*," defining this interval (2.0 = one octave, 4.0 = two octaves, 1.5 = half an octave, etc.), and modify the program accordingly. Ensure that the new argument is tested for reasonableness. Update the documentation you wrote in exercise 1.5.1.

Exercise 1.5.6

If you are familiar with Csound, modify the final `printf()` statement to write the list of frequencies as a single Csound "f1" statement in the score, using "GEN 2." It would be worth giving this program a different name. The first value "p-field" should give the number of frequencies in the list. For example, the 12-note chromatic scale staring at 220 (MIDI note 57) would be written as

```
f1 0 16 -2 12 220.000 233.081881 . . . 415.304698
```

Remember that Csound f-tables must have a size that is a power of two, or power-of-2 plus 1. (Practical note: Most operating systems support redirection of text output to a file: `nscale 12 57 > ftable.txt`. Thus, the text from your program could be copied from the `ftable.txt` file into a Csound score.)

Exercise 1.5.7

If you forget to declare a variable ("identifier") that you are using, the compiler will report an error. What does your compiler report if you declare a variable but don't use it? What does it report if you declare it twice?

Exercise 1.5.8

(a) From listing 1.5.3, arbitrarily remove one of the following characters: ( ) { } [ ]. Then run the compiler. What errors does the compiler report? How accurate and helpful are they?
(b) Do as in (a), but instead replace the removed character with one of the others.

(c) Ask a non-programming friend to make some subtle arbitrary edit. If the compiler reports an error, use the information to discover and fix the change.

1.6 Using Pointer Arithmetic and Adding Options to a Program

1.6.1 Introduction

C is unusual among high-level languages in giving the programmer direct access (under the supervision of the operating system) to memory addresses, via the pointer type. A machine address, you will recall, is a number identifying the place in memory where some item of data is stored. As it is just an integer, it can be used with the basic addition and subtraction operators. This also includes the use of the ++ and -- operators. Programmers generally refer to this as "pointer arithmetic." All C programmers have to become adept at pointer arithmetic, but it is especially important for audio programmers, who routinely have to step through arrays of audio samples, or other data, efficiently.

In this section you will learn more about how to read from, and write to, a variable via a pointer to it. This will enable you to read and write to blocks of memory (for example, lines of text, or wavetables containing synthetic waveforms or sampled sounds, or lines of text) and, more generally, to manipulate blocks of data in a way that is both efficient and flexible. Much of the time, we will be dealing with "lots of something"—lots of MIDI notes, lots of audio samples, lots of wavetables, lots of envelopes, and so on (in other words, collections of all the same type of data). In this situation, since the compiler knows which memory space a single item occupies, we can use pointer arithmetic to move this data around, and to move it around efficiently, even when we may not know in advance how much data there is.

This section demonstrates the use of pointer arithmetic to step through command-line arguments in a way that enables us to support the use of optional arguments to a program, and, generally, a variable number of arguments. Thus, we begin to see the potential power of command-line tools wherever a single highly configurable task is to be performed. As usual, the program presented here builds further on previously presented code examples. In particular, this program shows just how easy it is to create a file in C, and to write text to it.

1.6.2 Indirection and the "contents-of" and "address-of" Operators

As we learned in section 1.3, the declaration below defines ptr as a "pointer to a double":

```
double* ptr;
```

This is a variable, then, that contains the machine address of another variable (figure 1.5). We cannot do anything with this, however, until it has something proper to point to (as it stands, the address it contains is random—whatever the memory happens to contain—and

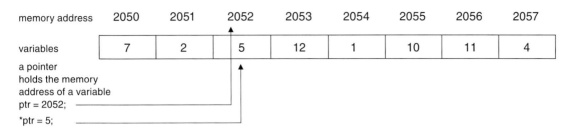

Figure 1.5
Pointers and memory addresses.

something we should not use). We have to give it something to point to—to *initialize* the pointer:

```
double buffer[1024];
ptr = buffer;
```

In C, the name of an array is in effect a pointer to the first element of it (`buffer[0]`). So this assignment sets `ptr` to point to the beginning of `buffer`. We can now both read and write to `buffer` by the means of a pointer. The technical term for this is *indirection*. Instead of writing

```
buffer[0] = 1.0594631;
```

we can now assign this value indirectly, via the pointer:

```
*ptr = 1.0594631;
```

We would typically read this as "set the contents of `ptr` to 1.0594631." So here ∗ is not a multiplication (which would be meaningless here, of course), but a "contents-of" operator. This notation can be used on both the left-hand and the right-hand side of an assignment:

```
double* ptr; /* pointer; currently uninitialized */
double val;/* a simple number variable */
ptr = buffer; /* now it has something to point to:
                the first element of buffer, i.e. buffer[0] */
*ptr = 1.0594631; /* buffer[0] now contains 1.0594631 */
/* read the contents of ptr: */
val = *ptr;    /* val now = 1.0594631 */
```

This works because the name of the array is equivalent to the "address of" the first element of it. C provides an "address-of" operator, &, to enable us to write such a thing explicitly:

```
double* ptr;
double val;
ptr = &val; /* find the address of val, and assign it to ptr */
```

Any time we declare a variable such as val, the compiler has to find a place in memory to store it. It is this address that we assign to the pointer ptr. So in reading the last line of the above example, we would say "set ptr to the address of val." With this done, we can initialize val *indirectly*, via the pointer:

```
*ptr = 1.0594631;
printf("%f", val);
```

This will print the number 1.0594631. So we can replace the assignment

```
ptr = buffer;
```

with the exactly equivalent (if rather more awkward-looking) statement

```
ptr = &buffer[0];
```

which would be read as "set ptr to the address of element 0 of buffer."

By itself, this notation does not really seem to do very much except make things look confusing. After all, why not just say

```
val = 1.0594631;
```

and be done with it?

As will be discussed in the next section (and indeed throughout the book), one of the most powerful uses of pointers is in conjunction with loops. They enable all sorts of "mass-production" techniques to be used, at high efficiency—exactly what we need for writing audio applications, which can easily demand more CPU power than we have. Often we can avoid a great deal of costly copying of data by manipulating pointers and addresses. The key principle to understand is *that addresses can themselves be treated as variables*. The compiler is in fact doing just this, behind the scenes—a special aspect of C is that it gives a lot of this power to the programmer too.

1.6.3   Moving Pointers Around

Because a pointer is an integral type (a memory address), whatever the type of the object it points to, it is possible to apply the increment operator to them as an alternative way of stepping along an array. It is in tasks such as this that the power and the expressiveness of pointer arithmetic become most apparent.

The fragment below sets each element of the array buffer to zero:

```
double buffer[1024];
double* ptr = buffer; /* set ptr to point to the start of table */
int i;
for(i = 0; i < 1024; i++) {
   *ptr = 0.0;
   ptr++; /* move pointer to next element of the array */
}
```

At the end of the `for` loop above, the pointer `ptr` is pointing to the position `table[1024]`, i.e. one step beyond the end of the array. Audio programmers are especially fond of this technique, as very often it results in faster code than the array index notation. Note that you must always make sure that you know what such a pointer is pointing to. If you follow that loop with another indirect write,

```
*ptr = 1.0594631;
```

you could cause a crash, as that memory address is outside the array, and belongs to something else. The same problem arises if the loop test is stated incorrectly:

```
for(i = 0; i <= 1024; i++) {
    *ptr = 0.0;
    ptr++;/* move pointer to next element of the array */
}
```

But few C programmers write this code this way. The most effective use of the ++ operator is in conjunction with some other operation (again, because such combinations are often available as single machine instructions). Instead, the `for` loop would be written as follows:

```
for(i = 0; i < 1024; i++)
    *ptr++ = 0.0;
```

This would be read as "set the contents of `ptr` to `0.0`, then increment `ptr`." This is an example where it is important to understand C *precedence rules*. (See subsection 1.2.10.) In this case, the `*ptr` combination is applied first, followed by the increment operation, applied to the pointer. Note also that, by condensing the loop code to a single statement, this notation has also enabled us to dispense with braces. You will find some form of the above two lines liberally scattered throughout programs in this book.[15]

More generally, C supports the use of the addition, subtraction, and comparison operations on pointers. This is perhaps the most striking demonstration of how C can be "close to the hardware"—machine code depends a great deal on pointer arithmetic. Pointer arithmetic is both one of the most widely exploited features of C, and also one of the most criticized. A major selling point of the language Java, for example, was that it did not permit either pointers or pointer arithmetic.

The code in listing 1.6.1 demonstrates a way of finding the value and position of the maximum positive sample in an array, stepping backward one sample at a time. In this way, it will find the maximum sample nearest the start of the buffer. It assumes the same `buffer` of `1024 floats`, but now filled with audio samples:

Listing 1.6.1

```
1   double* ptr = buffer + 1024; /* point to last element */
2   double maxval = 0.0;
```

```
3    unsigned long pos = 0;
4
5    while(--ptr >= buffer) {
6        if(*ptr >= maxval){
7            maxval = *ptr;
8            pos = ptr - buffer;
9        }
10  }
11  printf("the maximum sample is %f, at position %d\n",
12       maxval, pos);
```

There are several details to observe in this example:

(1) In the conditional test in line 5, the pre-decrement operator is applied to the pointer ptr. This steps the pointer back one element before the comparison with buffer is made. Thus ptr has had to be initialized in line 1, using the addition of a constant integer to a pointer, to point at the element immediately beyond the array (buffer + 1024). As it happens, this is exactly the position it ended up at in the previous code example.

(2) The >= operator is used to compare ptr with the address of the start of the array. The comparison ensures that the first value (*buffer, or buffer[0]) is inspected. As pointers are integral numbers, such comparisons can be relied upon to be exact, and as we are stepping back one element at a time, toward the beginning of the array, we cannot fail to find it eventually.

(3) To find the maximum value nearest the start of the buffer, the >= operator is used in line 6. If only the > operator were used, this would fail to find the nearest maximum sample where several samples have the same value (e.g. in a square wave).

(4) The position of the maximum sample is found by the calculation in line 8, subtracting one pointer from another. This exploits the fact that the name of an array (buffer) is equivalently the address of the first element. The difference between that and the value of ptr gives the distance from the start of the buffer to the maximum sample.

Automatic pointer increments are commonly used in processing blocks of audio samples. In such cases, the size of the block is often fixed, and can be guaranteed to not be zero. This is the case, for example, in all the audio processing code in Csound, which uses buffers of samples that are always ksmps in size. As a result, Csound uses the do loop in an especially interesting way, in conjunction with pointer increments. Listing 1.6.1 shows a typical example from code that implements a simple filter to block DC in a signal. The variable nsmps is initialized to ksmps, and the arrays pointed to by samp and ar are both nsmps in size.

Listing 1.6.2

```
1    nsmps = ksmps;
2    do {
```

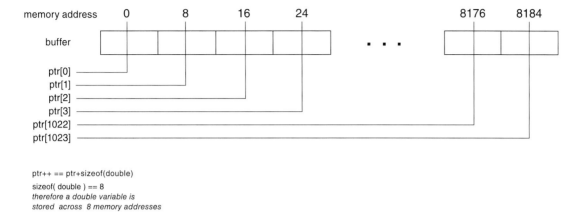

ptr++ == ptr+sizeof(double)

sizeof(double) == 8
*therefore a double variable is
stored across 8 memory addresses*

Figure 1.6
The compiler's view of an array.

```
3       float sample = *samp++;
4       output = sample - input + (gain * output);
5       input = sample;
6       *ar++ = output;
7     } while (--nsmps);
```

Note the use of pointer increments (line 3, line 6) to step forward through the blocks of samples, while the loop counter `nsmps` is pre-decremented inside the `while` test (line 7). The loop will terminate when `nsmps` no longer evaluates to "true," which will be the case when it reaches zero. At that point, the loop has counted down from 30 to 1, as required.

In the expression `sample = *samp++`, the operator `++` has a higher *precedence* than the dereference operator `*`. This means that the pointer is incremented, not the value pointed at. Because the postfix `++` increments after the variable is used, the dereferencing (i.e. the value pointed at is assigned to `sample`) occurs *before* the pointer increment. The counter variable is not used inside the processing block.

This example demonstrates a very common practice in C programming—increments tend to be post, while decrements tend to be pre. Why this back-to-front way of stepping through a block? It is often the case that auto-decrement is faster than auto-increment, and similarly that a comparison against zero is faster than comparison with some non-zero value. As this loop repeats at the audio sample rate, even small gains (maybe just one CPU instruction) can accumulate to give a big gain.

Figure 1.6 illustrates how array indexing works at the compiler level—the compiler knows how large each element is, and automatically calculates the distance from the start of the array.

Don't worry if pointer arithmetic looks daunting—you don't have to use it. The code in listing 1.6.1 can just as well be written stepping forward and using index notation, as in listing 1.6.3.

Listing 1.6.3

```
1   double maxval = 0.0;
2   unsigned long pos = 0;
3   int i;
4   for(i=0; i < 1024; i++){
5       if(buffer[i] > maxval){
6           maxval = buffer[i];
7           pos = i;
8       }
9   }
10  printf("the maximum sample is %f, at position %d\n", maxval,
12           pos);
```

Note that as we are now stepping forward, the >= operator is now replaced by the > operator. Many programmers tend to code loops this way to begin with, aiming initially for as much clarity as possible, and look for ways to optimize it for speed after it has been tested.

It can be argued that a good modern compiler will optimize this code better anyway, and there is a good case for leaving well alone, unless the speed gain is really significant. In the end it is often far more important that you write code you understand, and feel comfortable with—especially if you are likely to want to change it or add to it later.

1.6.4   Extending the Command Line with Optional Arguments

One way of measuring the "power" of a computer program is to look at the amount of control it offers the user. A program that does just one thing may be useful, but a program that offers the user choices may be both useful and powerful. In this subsection the task is to add to the usefulness of the program presented in the previous section (listing 1.5.3) by adding some optional controls to change the content of the output, and to add the possibility of writing the output to a text file. So far, the command line for a program has been completely fixed—either it is correct or it is not. In this section you will learn how to create a command line that incorporates optional elements. Parsing it will therefore involve not only reading and testing required arguments, but also detecting and testing optional ones.

Optional arguments are a standard feature of UNIX-style command-line programs, and some conventions are established which are reflected in the approach presented here. To keep things manageable, all required arguments are kept together, and all optional arguments are placed either before or after these.

The program developed in the previous section (listing 1.5.3) printed a list of frequencies to the screen. The first refinement added in this section is an option to print the plain frequency ratios as well. This will add a second column of values to those generated previously. Secondly, the option is provided to specify the base frequency as a MIDI note value, instead of a raw hertz value. Finally, an option is provided to write the generated information to a text file. The first two of these options are simple switches, to turn a facility on, or to change format to a single alternative; the third requires a filename to be provided by the user.

For the new program `iscale`, the command line will be defined by the usage message below (which would be printed to the command line):

```
iscale [-m] [-i] N startval [outfile.txt]
```

```
where:
-m means: interpret startval as a MIDI note
(default: interpret as frequency in hertz)
-i means: print interval ratios as well as frequency values
(default: print just frequency values)
outfile.txt: name of (optional) file to write output to
```

The purposes of the conventions illustrated here are (1) to indicate optional arguments (in the usage message) by enclosing them within brackets (not typed by the user) and (2) to indicate optional arguments placed before required ones by a required prefix character: -. Such arguments are often referred to as "switches" or "flags," especially if, as here, they serve to turn on a special facility, or to change behavior. This means that the code required to parse the command line can be very simple. There are two required arguments; there may be a fourth argument after these; and all optional arguments preceding them use the character - as a prefix. To parse this command line, therefore, is a simple three-stage procedure: (a) Handle any flag arguments, stepping along the argument list. (b) Check that we have at least two remaining arguments, and process them. (c) If we have a third argument, process that too.

The first stage (a) is of course essential. We cannot assume that any of the optional flags are used, so when we parse the `argv[]` array of the `main()` function we cannot rely on N being `argv[1]`, for example.

We can use pointer arithmetic to solve this problem. Recall from section 1.4 that the various arguments supplied by the user are delivered to the `main()` function as an array of character strings, together with an argument count (which includes the name of the program):

```
int main(int argc, char *argv[])
```

Suppose that the supplied command line is as follows:

```
iscale -m 19 57
```

This would be contained in `argv` as

```
argv[0] = "iscale"
argv[1] = "-m"
argv[2] = "19"
argv[3] = "57"
```

and `argc` would be set to 4. We can equivalently say that `argv` is "pointing to" the beginning of the array of arguments, and we know there are four arguments.

Each element of `argv` is simply a `char` pointer (an address), and the compiler knows how big this is, just as it does in the case of the `buffer[]` array in listing 1.6.1. So, as in that example, we can use the `++` operator to move `argv` along the array, eliminating each argument as it does so. At the same time, we must decrement `argc` so that it tells us how many arguments are left, counting from `argv`'s current position. The following sequence demonstrates how the argument list changes as this procedure is performed.

Step 1

```
argv++;
argc--; /* argc now = 3 */
```

This steps over the name of the program, leaving us with the user's argument list:

```
argv[0] = "-m"
argv[1] = "19"
argv[2] = "57"
```

Step 2

```
argv++;
argc--; /* argc now = 2 */
```

Steps 1 and 2 are shown graphically in figure 1.7, from which we can see that `argv` now contains the two required arguments:

```
argv[0] = "19"
argv[1] = "57"
```

Figure 1.7 illustrates what is clearly an iterative (repeating) process, for which a loop is appropriate. In this case, the loop test will be for the presence of the prefix character -. Since we have established the convention that the first argument not using this character is the first *required* argument, the loop must break as soon as this condition is found.

In section 1.3 we learned how to access individual characters of a char array. The same principle applies to an array of char arrays (strings). Suppose `argv[1]` contains the address of the string -m—we can read the individual characters using brackets, but as this is an array of arrays, we need two pairs (see figure 1.8):

```
argv[1][0] contains '-'
argv[1][1] contains 'm'
```

argv[]	"-m"	"19"	"57"

| (1) | argv++;
argc--; | argc now = 3 | argv[0] | argv[1] | argv[2] |
| (2) | argv++;
argc--; | argc now = 2 | | argv[0] | argv[1] |

Figure 1.7
Stepping through `argv[ ]`.

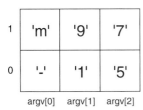

argv [0] [0] == '-'
argv [0] [1] == 'm'
argv [1] [0] == '1'
argv [1] [1] == '9'
argv [2] [0] == '5'
argv [2] [1] == '7'

Figure 1.8
`argv[ ]` as an array of arrays.

If this looks messy to you, you can create a variable to represent an individual argument:

```
char* arg = argv[1];
arg[0] contains '-'
arg[1] contains 'm'
```

Programmers sometimes do this, especially if there is heavy use of brackets or if the code is being repeated many times (the compiler may have to generate more code to translate the brackets). This technique reduces the level of indirection with respect to each string.

1.6.5 Dealing with Alternatives: `if . . . else`

In the `iscale` program we have introduced two possible flag options: –m and –i. Any other character following the – will be an error. In English pseudo-code, we would say

if there is a flag
    if the flag is 'm'
        set MIDI option
    otherwise
        if the flag is 'i'
        set interval option

> otherwise
>> report an "incorrect flag" error

In C, the keyword `else` is used for "otherwise"; it is an optional extension to the `if` keyword, and it must be followed by a complete C statement or statement block. It always belongs to the immediately preceding `if`. The example below demonstrates a series of `if. . .else` tests; it also shows how the individual characters of an argument are accessed to parse the argument (see section 1.3).

Listing 1.6.4

```
if(argv[1][0] == '-'){/* is it an optional flag ? */
    if(argv[1][1] == 'm')
        ismidi = 1;
    else if(argv[1][1] == 'i')
        write_interval = 1;
    else {
        printf("error: incorrect flag option %s\n", argv[1]);
        return 1;
    }
}
```

The `else` keyword is used with both `if`s to ensure the error message is reported only if the flag is neither `'m'` nor `'i'`. Note the code layout in the above example, with `else if` run together on a single line. This is the usual convention for this type of code sequence, even though this is, strictly speaking, a series of "nested" `if. . .else` statements. Braces make the true relationships of the options explicit:

Listing 1.6.5

```
if(argv[1][0] == '-'){   /* is it an optional flag ? */
    if(argv[1][1] == 'm')
        ismidi = 1;
    else {
        if(argv[1][1] == 'i')
            write_interval = 1;
        else {
            printf("error: incorrect flag option %s\n", argv[1]);
            return 1;
        }
    }
}
```

You may want to work through the versions on listings 1.6.4 and 1.6.5 to assure yourself that the logic is the same in each case for any given flag option. One reason the layout of listing 1.6.4 is preferable is that it shows that each alternative lies at the same logical "level" (and should thus be indented identically).

This also gives a very practical advantage: should you want to add another flag option, all that is required is the insertion of another `if. . .else` combination; or rather, an `else. . .if` combination. For example, if you had code that could play the calculated scale through the audio output, you might define a new command-line flag "-p," with an associated variable:

```
int playit = 0;
```

This would be detected using a new `else. . .if` combination inserted into the code above:

Listing 1.6.6

```
if(argv[1][0] == '-'){
    if(argv[1][1] == 'm')
        ismidi = 1;
    else if(argv[1][1] == 'i')
        write_interval = 1;
    else if(argv[1][1] == 'p')
        playit = 1;
    else {
        printf("error: incorrect flag option %s\n", argv[1]);
        return 1;
    }
}
```

This conveniently minimizes the amount of code indentation, while enabling rapid additions (and removals) without affecting code elsewhere.

1.6.6   Using Local Variables—the Scope of a Variable

In the above example, the expression `argv[1][1]` is used three times. It would be good to simplify this (and maybe even make the code more efficient) by removing this duplication. This can be done by declaring a new `char` variable to contain the flag character:

Listing 1.6.7

```
char flag;
if(argv[1][0] == '-'){
    flag = argv[1][1];
```

```
    if(flag == 'm')
        ismidi = 1;
    else if(flag == 'i')
        write_interval = 1;
    else if(flag == 'p')
        playit = 1;
    else {
        printf("error: incorrect flag option %s\n", argv[1]);
        return 1;
    }
}
```

C requires that all variables be declared at the top of `main()`, before any other C statements. However, C also supports the use of variables local to a statement block (enclosed by braces); these are, naturally enough, termed *local variables*. As the `if` test above is followed by a statement block enclosed by braces, we can place the declaration of `flag` at the top of the block.

Listing 1.6.8

```
if(argv[1][0] == '-'){
    char flag;
    flag = argv[1][1];
    if(flag == 'm')
        ismidi = 1;
    else if(flag == 'i')
        write_interval = 1;
    else if(flag == 'p')
        playit = 1;
    else {
        printf("error: incorrect flag option %s\n", argv[1]);
        return 1;
    }
}
```

Used this way, the variable `char` exists only within the block; it cannot be accessed from outside. The variable is therefore a temporary one, used a few times and then discarded. The technical term for this behavior is *scope*—the variable has "local scope" within the block in which it is declared. The basic principle of scope is that a variable exists at a given statement block level, and at any lower level. Thus the variables declared at the top of `main` have scope within `main`, and also within any statement blocks inside `main`.

Because a local variable exists only within the block in which it is declared, there is no reason not to use the same name in other blocks at the same level.

Listing 1.6.9

```c
float buffer[1024];
float* bufptr = buffer;
int ascending = 0;

/* create ascending or descending ramp */
if(ascending){
   int i;
   for(i = 0; i < 1024; i++)
      *bufptr++ = (float) i;
 }
 else {
   int i;
   for(i = 1024; i; i--)
      *bufptr++ = (float) i;
 }
```

If the variable i declared in the else block is omitted, the compiler will report an error because the previous i is not accessible outside its block.

1.6.7   Creating a Text File—the Special FILE Type

In addition to optional flag arguments preceding our required command-line arguments, we have also specified an optional extra final argument giving a filename to which to write the output of the program (which we will in any case be writing to the screen as usual). Detecting this argument is easy—if we have used the procedure of the previous section to step past any flag arguments, we know that our required arguments are in argv[0] and argv[1], and that argc must be at least 2. If it is in fact 3, we know that argv[2] contains the filename. Of course, if argc is more than 3, the user has typed something superfluous. In this case, it is purely a matter of courtesy to point this out to the user, if we so choose.

To create and write to a text file, we will need the three functions (declared in stdio.h) listed in table 1.4. These all use a pointer to a strange object called FILE. As well as the

Table 1.4
Standard C functions to create, write, and close a text file.

Function	Description
FILE *fopen(const char* name, const char* mode);	Open a file for reading or writing.
int fprintf(FILE *fp, const char* format, ...);	Write formatted text to FILE.
int fclose(FILE *fp);	Close an open FILE.

simple types used so far, such as int, double, and char, C allows the programmer to invent any arbitrary types. The FILE type is also defined in stdio.h, and we need know nothing about it at all except that it is used by these functions to represent an instance of a file, that it must always be typed in upper case, and that it is always referred to indirectly via a pointer.

These functions are far from the full extent of the facilities the C library provides for dealing with files (to say nothing of those specific to a particular operating system), but for the simple requirements of this program (writing lines of text to a file) they are all we need. The function fprintf() is perhaps the most interesting, as it is almost identical to the printf() function we have been using since section 1.2, the only difference being the initial FILE pointer argument. The text formatting options are, however, identical, which means that we can use the same format string for fprintf() that we use for printf().[16]

Perhaps unexpectedly, the single function fopen() can be used both for reading and writing a file. It is worth considering briefly what sorts of tasks we may want to perform on a file. Here are some candidates:

- Create a new file (for writing).
- Read an existing file.
- Append data (writing) to an existing file.
- Overwrite some or all of a file.

The second mode argument to fopen() enables us to specify what we want, in a simple way. It is a pointer to a const char string (the const qualifier meaning, as you will recall, that the function guarantees not to modify the string in any way). The basic options are: "w" for writing, "r" for reading and "a" for appending.

In the program as specified, all we need do is create a file and write lines of text to it, so the "w" mode is as much as we need. Note that this will overwrite an existing file of the same name.

1.6.8   Putting It All Together

The full program iscale is shown in listing 1.6.10. It falls into distinct blocks, indicated by an empty line. The first stage (lines 1–40), after the declarations of top-level variables, looks for any optional flag arguments, setting the flag variables ismidi and write_interval if required. Note that these are both initialized, in their declarations, to the required "default" values. Note also how the flag checking code illustrated in subsection 1.6.6 is embedded in a loop stepping through the argument list, with pointer arithmetic used to move argv along the array. Because the code reads argv[1], it is necessary to check that argc is at least 2 (line 24), otherwise the code would be reading outside the argv array. The loop breaks if the test in line 25 fails, indicating that all optional flags, if any, have been read.

The required arguments are processed in the next section (lines 42–72). Note that this code depends on the variable ismidi, in order to interpret the startval argument correctly. The comments in the code show how these arguments are tested for reasonableness. The error messages are useful not only for the user but also for the person reading the code.

The next stage (lines 74–82) checks for the optional file argument by checking the value of argc. At the very end of the program, we must close this file (line 126), if it has been created. We will know whether it has been created because the FILE* pointer fp is initialized to NULL (line 75); if it is still NULL at the end, we know it is unused, and there is nothing to close. One user-friendly aspect of this code is that if for some reason the file cannot be created (fopen() returns NULL in this case) the program does not terminate (it can still write information to the screen) but merely prints a warning message. A C library function perror() is used—this prints a message describing the cause of the most recent system error. A file may fail to be created for many reasons; for example, it may be already open in another application, so access is denied, the disk may be full, the filename may be incorrectly formed, or there may be a hardware fault. Similarly, any attempt to write to a file (indeed, any attempted access at all) may result in an error, so it is equally important to test the return value of fprintf()—this will be the number of bytes written, or a negative value in the case of an error. In all such situations, perror() can be used to display the cause of the error.

One habitual exception to this rule is fclose(); while this does return a value indicating success or failure, there is not much that can be done, especially when the program is terminating anyway, so this value is often ignored by programs, as here. In other situations, for example where multiple files are being used, it may be more important to advise the user if an error arises.

The next stage (lines 84–103) comprises the heart of the program, in which the array of frequencies is calculated. In line 88 the variables c0 and c5, which have no other use, are declared *local variables*. If you tried exercise 3 in the previous section, you may notice that this program implements one solution to that problem. The array intervals[] is declared to be one larger than the maximum accepted value for notes, and the loop tests (line 100, 107) use the <= operator, rather than the < operator normally used in such loops.

The final section of the program (lines 105–121) prints the results to the screen, using printf(), and also to the file if requested, using fprintf with the same format strings. The program offer the possibility to write out the raw interval values as well as specific frequency values, so the if and else keywords are used several times to deal with each pair of options, all inside a single loop running through the intervals array. Note that the calls to fprintf() read the return value into the variable err, and if non-zero break out of the loop. That variable is then tested (line 123), and perror() used with an optional custom message (line 124), to report the cause of the error. In line 18 err is initialized to 0. By ensuring that it is not used in any other context, we can simply test this for a negative value (line 123), which is then sufficient to indicate both that the optional file facility was used, and that there was an error.

Listing 1.6.10

```
1    /* iscale.c */
2    /* generate E.T tables for N-notes to the octave (N <= 24) */
3    #include <stdio.h>
4    #include <stdlib.h>
5    #include <math.h>
6
7    /* usage iscale [-m][-i] N startval [outfile.txt]
8        -m : sets format of startval as MIDI note
9        -i : prints the calculated interval as well as the abs freq
10       outfile: optional text filename for output data
11   */
12
13   int main(int argc, char* argv[])
14   {
15       int notes,i;
16       int ismidi = 0;
17       int write_interval = 0;
18       int err = 0;
19       double startval,basefreq,ratio;
20       FILE* fp;
21       double intervals[25];
22
23       /* check first arg for flag option: argc at least 2 */
24       while(argc > 1){
25           if(argv[1][0]=='-'){
26               if(argv[1][1]== 'm')
27                   ismidi = 1;
28               else if(argv[1][1]== 'i')
29                   write_interval = 1;
30               else {
31                   printf("error: unrecognized option %s\n",argv[1]);
32                   return 1;
33               }
34               /* step up to next arg */
35               argc--;
36               argv++;
37           }
38       else
39           break;
40       }
41
42       if(argc < 3){
```

```
43      printf("insufficient arguments\n");
44      printf("Usage: iscale [-m][-i] N startval [outfile.txt]\n");
45      return 1;
46      }
47 /* now read and check all arguments */
48 /* we now expect argv[1] to hold N and argv[2] startval */
49      notes = atoi(argv[1]);
50      if(notes < 1 || notes > 24){
51      printf("error: N out of range. Must be between 1 and 24.\n");
52      return 1;
53      }
54      startval = atof(argv[2]);
55      if(ismidi){
56          if(startval > 127.0){
57          printf("error: MIDI startval must be <= 127.\n");
58          return 1;
59          }
60      /* for MIDI, startval = 0 is legal */
61          if(startval < 0.0){
62          printf("error: MIDI startval must be >= 0.\n");
63          return 1;
64          }
65      }
66      else { /* it's freq: must be positive number */
67      /* check low limit */
68          if(startval <= 0.0){
69          printf("error: frequency startval must be positive.\n");
70          return 1;
71          }
72      }
73
74      /* check for optional filename */
75      fp = NULL;
76      if(argc==4){
77          fp = fopen(argv[3],"w");
78          if(fp==NULL){
79          printf("WARNING: unable to create file %s\n",argv[3]);
80          perror("");
81          }
82      }
83
84 /* all params ready - fill array and write to file if created */
85
```

```
86      /* find basefreq, if val is MIDI */
87      if(ismidi){
88          double c0,c5;
89          /* find base MIDI note */
90          ratio = pow(2.0,1.0 / 12.0);
91          c5 = 220.0 * pow(ratio,3);
92          c0 = c5 * pow(0.5,5);
93          basefreq = c0 * pow(ratio,startval);
94      }
95      else
96          basefreq = startval;
97
98      /* calc ratio from notes, and fill the array */
99      ratio = pow(2.0,1.0/notes);
100     for(i=0;i <= notes;i++){
101         intervals[i] = basefreq;
102         basefreq *= ratio;
103     }
104
105 /* finally, read array, write to screen, and optionally to file */
106
107     for(i=0; i <= notes; i++){
108         if(write_interval)
109         printf("%d:\t%f\t%f\n", i, pow(ratio,i), intervals[i]);
110         else
111         printf("%d:\t%f\n", i, intervals[i]);
112         if(fp){
113             if(write_interval)
114                 err = fprintf(fp,"%d:\t%f\t%f\n",
115                     i, pow(ratio,i), intervals[i]);
116             else
117                 err = fprintf(fp,"%d:\t%f\n", i, intervals[i]);
118             if(err < 0)
119                 break;
120         }
121     }
122
123     if(err < 0)
124         perror("There was an error writing the file.\n");
125     if(fp)
126         fclose(fp);
127     return 0;
128 }
```

1.6.9   Testing the Program

This program is clearly more complex than previous ones (shown not least by its length), and the use of optional command-line arguments gives greatly increased importance to the process of testing it. Once you have compiled it, be sure to test all combinations of optional and required arguments, and also make sure that incorrect command lines (e.g. use of a non-existent flag) are tested. Try your best to make the program crash. What you miss, someone else (perhaps a paying customer) will be sure to find, sooner or later. Some specific suggestions for tests are given in the exercises. Before doing this, study the code carefully, while thinking about all the errors a user might make. Can you anticipate user errors that the code does not deal with? Don't forget to check the contents of the optional text file, to make sure it corresponds to the information written to the screen.

1.6.10   Exercises

Exercise 1.6.1
Add the description of all arguments to the usage message in line 44 (see subsection 1.6.4).

Exercise 1.6.2
Without running the program (i.e. by reading the code), decide how the following command lines will be handled:

(a) `iscale -m -i -m 19 60`
(b) `iscale -i - 19 60`
(c) `iscale m 19 60`
(d) `iscale 19 data.txt`

Test your conclusions by running the program with these command lines. If you have found problems, explain their causes and suggest possible solutions. (Hint: the library documentation for your compiler is your friend.).

Exercise 1.6.3
In lines 107–121, the expression `pow(ratio,i)` is used twice, and the expression `intervals[i]` is used four times. Eliminate this repetition by using two variables local to the `for` block.

Exercise 1.6.4
Extend `iscale` with an optional flag that appends data to the output text file, if it already exists. Thus successive runs of the program will add another set of tables to the file. Using `fprintf()`, ensure that these tables are clearly separated, and add a line of text giving a descriptive name for each set. Remember to update the usage message.

Table 1.5
A simple envelope breakpoint file.

x	y
0.00	0.00
0.05	0.10
0.75	1.00
0.85	0.25
1.50	0.25
1.95	0.10
2.00	0.00

Exercise 1.6.5
Adding to the above exercise, before each set of data, print to the file the full command line used.

Exercise 1.6.6
In lines 107–121, if `fprintf()` returns an error, the loop is broken, with the result that output to the screen is also stopped. Is this a serious problem? If so, rewrite the code so as to separate writing to the screen from writing to the file.

1.7   Creating Types, Functions, and Memory

1.7.1   The Time/Value Breakpoint File

After devoting so much attention to calculating musical scales, it may come as something of a relief to move onto a different area of musical processing. The object that is the focus of this section is the standard time/value breakpoint file. If you have explored the compiled versions of the programs included on the DVD, you will have found several that use such files, for making time-varying changes to a sound. Some example breakpoint files (with the file extension ".brk") are also provided. You will use the knowledge gained in this chapter to create some of these programs yourself. You may like to devote a little time to trying out those programs, before proceeding further with this chapter.

As its name suggests, a breakpoint file is a text file comprising at least two lines containing pairs of numbers—time and value—defining how some parameter (e.g. amplitude) varies over time. A simple breakpoint file describing an amplitude envelope is shown in table 1.5. The same data is represented graphically in figure 1.9. If you think that this looks like the "automation" tracks often used in audio editors, you would be right—that is exactly what it is. Depending on the product, such automation tracks can be more or less sophisticated (e.g.

Table 1.6
Some common shell commands.

Action	DOS	UNIX
Directory separator	\	/
Change directory	cd	cd
Copy file	copy	cp
List directory	dir	ls
Move file	move	mv
Delete file	del	rm
Create directory	mkdir	mkdir
Remove directory	rmdir	rmdir
Current directory	.\	./
Parent directory	..\	../

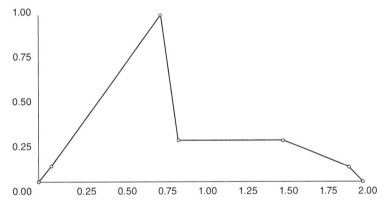

Figure 1.9
A simple envelope.

some may allow the definition of curves between points, as well as simple linear ramps), but the principle is the same.

In order to use a breakpoint file reliably, with multiple applications, we must rely on the data having certain properties and boundaries. A breakpoint file must comply with a number of rules, if it is to be portable, and of long-term use. Even from studying the one example in table 1.5 we can deduce a number of these:

- The file lists one breakpoint per line.
- A breakpoint comprises two floating-point numbers separated by white-space (spaces and/ or tabs).

- The first number gives the time for the breakpoint, the second number gives the value at that time.
- The times must be increasing.
- The first point must have a time of 0.0.
- There can be any (finite) number of breakpoints.

Additional rules might include the following:

- Two breakpoints cannot have the same time (i.e. the difference between points must be > 0).
- No empty lines are allowed, except (perhaps) at the end.
- Only one breakpoint set allowed per file.
- A breakpoint file must contain at least two points.

A breakpoint file has certain properties:

- The time difference between adjacent points can vary.
- A given breakpoint set will have a duration (time of final point), and minimum + maximum values.

Some breakpoint files will have properties specific to an audio process:

- Breakpoint files with values between 0.0 and 1.0 inclusive can be used as amplitude envelopes.
- Breakpoint files with values between −1.0 and 1.0 inclusive can be used as (stereo) pan trajectories, where −1 defines "full Left," 0 defines "Center (mono)" and 1 defines "full Right."

This information is sufficient to enable a programmer, even without seeing an example of a breakpoint file, to write a program that can read a file, decide if it is legal, and determine its properties. The same code can also be used as part of a larger application that uses the breakpoint data to perform audio processing. The use of the word 'object' is no accident. In this section, you will embark on some elementary "object-oriented" programming. The time/value breakpoint is the "object" in question, and we will learn how to represent it as an object in C. We will also learn how to define functions that use or create this object—in Object-Oriented Programming these would be called "methods," though we would need to move into C++ programming to realize that concept fully.

The remaining challenge presented by the breakpoint file arises from the fact that it can be of any size. As we cannot know in advance how many breakpoints a given file contains, we cannot define an array in advance, in which to store them (as an array can only be defined with a fixed size). So we need to be able both to obtain memory of some arbitrary size from the operating system, but also, if required, we will need to be able to expand the size. In learning how this is done, we will also, at last, discover exactly how NULL is defined.

1.7.2 Defining Custom Objects in C using the `struct` Keyword

So far, we have learned about the "simple" variable types supported by C (`int`, `float`, `char`, etc.), and about the array, which is a collection of a single type. We can also use arbitrary combinations of these types to define new ones. We have to be able to do two things—define a type, and define a variable of that type. The first task is fulfilled by the C keyword `struct` (short for "structure"). The code below uses this to define a breakpoint as two doubles:

```
struct breakpoint {
    double time;
    double value;
};
```

Note the use of braces to enclose the elements comprising the structure, and the terminating semicolon. The name following `struct` ('breakpoint') is formally termed the `struct` "tag." This structure would be identical to an array of two doubles, except for the crucial difference that each element has a name. Although not as useful for the program developed in this section, it is also possible, and very common, to define `struct`s containing different types. Suppose that it was convenient to define a breakpoint where time is measured not in seconds, but in discrete "ticks" (perhaps, samples). The `struct` could be defined as

```
struct tickpoint {
    unsigned long ticks;
    double value;
};
```

The `struct` demands more work from the compiler than does the array, as in the former the type and size of each element has to be recorded, and used whenever that `struct` is referenced.

For example, an instance of the breakpoint structure defined above could be declared simply as

```
struct breakpoint point;
```

Note that the keyword `struct` must be used as well as the struct name; "point" is the name of the variable we have defined. We can combine structure definition and variable declaration into one statement:

```
struct breakpoint {
    double time;
    double value;
} point;
```

We can now fill in the elements of the new variable by name. To do this, the element name is appended to the variable name separated by a stop character:

```
point.time = 0.0;
point.value = 0.5;
```

It is also possible to use an initializer list (see subsection 1.3.2):

```
struct breakpoint point = {0.0,0.5};
```

An important operation allowed for `structs` is assignment or copy:

```
struct breakpoint point1,point2 = {0.0,0.5};
point1 = point2; /* point1 now contains {0.0,0.5} */
```

No other operators are allowed with `structs`—for example, you cannot write arithmetic expressions with them:

```
struct breakpoint point3;
point3 = point1 + point2;/*error: + not allowed with structs*/
```

To be able to do such things, we will have to progress to C++, which among many other things allows such operators to be "overloaded"—that is, defined for any custom object. In C, we will have to define our own functions to do these things[17].

1.7.3   Defining Custom Types using the `typedef` Keyword

It is probably already apparent that typing the `struct` keyword plus the tag is a somewhat tiresome amount of typing. We really want to use a single name to specify the object, so that we can write

```
breakpoint point;
```

instead. The magic C keyword that enables us to do exactly that is `typedef`. The format for `typedef` is simple (note the final semicolon):

```
typedef <existing type> <typename> ;
```

A common use for `typedef` is to define shorthand names for unsigned integer variables. The example below is familiar to all Windows programmers:

```
typedef unsigned short WORD;
typedef unsigned long DWORD;
```

Though it can seem that `typedef` simply performs some form of text substitution, it really does define a new C type that can, for example, be given to `sizeof`:

```
long size = sizeof(DWORD);
```

As soon as an object has been `typedef`ed in this way, it can be used in `struct` definitions, and even as part of a further `typedef`:

```
/* define an object describing a soundfile */

typedef struct soundfile_info {
    DWORD nSamples;
    DWORD samplerate;
    WORD nChannels;
    char* name;
} SFINFO;

/* create an instance of the SFINFO object, and initialize it */
SFINFO info;
info.nSamples = 1234567;
info.samplerate = 96000;
info.name = "main title";
info.nChannels = 6;
```

You may reasonably ask at this point why we now seem to need two names for this structure —"soundfile_info" and "SFINFO," the first of which is not used. As it happens, when we use `typedef` the structure tag (`soundfile_info`) is optional.[18] Thanks to `typedef`, the declaration can be simplified:

```
typedef struct {
    DWORD nSamples;
    DWORD samplerate;
    WORD nChannels;
    char* name;
} SFINFO;
```

The two forms are about equally likely in modern C programs.

Returning to the task at hand, we can now use `typedef` to create the breakpoint type in the form we wanted:

```
typedef struct breakpoint {
    double time;
    double value;
} BREAKPOINT;
```

By convention, such names are usually written in upper case, as demonstrated above, to make them distinctive. This is not a hard and fast rule (as you read more code from various sources you will find many examples where lower-case type is used), but it is a good convention to adhere to for such type definitions. You can correctly deduce, for example, that FILE is a type created using `typedef`—as you can easily discover if you study the code in the `stdio.h` header file.

We can also declare an array of BREAKPOINTs:

```
BREAKPOINT points[64];
```

Should we so choose, we can initialize the first breakpoint using array index notation (brackets) and the dot notation for accessing elements of a structure :

```
point[0].time = 0.0;
point[0].value = 1.0;
```

1.7.4 Text Substitution: Introducing the `#define` Preprocessor Directive

While `typedef` is a C keyword to define possibly complex types, it is also possible in simple cases to use text substitution via the C preprocessor directive `#define`. A simple text substitution would be to replace an explicit constant value with a symbol:

```
#define BUFFERSIZE 1024
```

Note that there is no semicolon terminating the line—this is not C code as such, but instructions to the preprocessor. This symbol can then be used in an array declaration:

```
short sampbuf[BUFFERSIZE];
```

Similarly,

```
#define SAMPLE float
```

This might be used to facilitate experimentation with alternative sample types in a program:

```
SAMPLE sampbuf[BUFFERSIZE];
```

This now declares an array of floats. The symbol `SAMPLE` will probably be used everywhere a numeric type would be: if late in the design you decide you want to use doubles instead, you merely have to change the definition and re-compile:

```
#define SAMPLE double
```

Thus the preprocessor supports a form of global search and replace—anywhere the same value is used, with the same meaning, it is better to use a `#defined` symbol for it, both to enable to value to be changed globally without tedious editing and to contribute to the documentation of the program, than to use numeric constants directly.

The `#define` directive, used widely in C programming, can be employed to substitute complex sequences of frequently used code text with simpler ones.[19] The difference between `#define` and `typedef` is that the former is literally text substitution—before the compiler itself is invoked, whereas `typedef` is a language keyword, understood by the compiler itself, and thus can create true abstract types in ways that are beyond the scope of the preprocessor. The main hazard at this stage is getting the order right. With `#define`, the synonym or alias name (e.g. `SAMPLE`) is written first, followed by the text to be substituted, whereas with `typedef`, the order is opposite, and the type description must be a correct C type declaration:

```
typedef float SAMPLE;
```

1.7.5   Working with Types: User-Defined Functions

Given an array of breakpoints (e.g. read from a file), one of the important pieces of informa-tion we may require is the maximum breakpoint value contained in the data. It is easy to see that any application dealing with breakpoints is likely to want this information. This is a pri-mary reason for wanting to create a set of functions specific to the BREAKPOINT type, which can be used repeated, in any application.

Creating a function in C is not at all difficult (you do it every time you write a program involving main()), but there are a few rules to observe, demanded by ANSI C. From what you have learned already, you know that a function is defined by a name, followed by paren-theses that may contain arguments supplied to the function:

```
float larger(float first, float second);
```

In this case, the function called larger takes two float arguments and returns a float result. As its name suggests, it returns the value of the larger of the two arguments. However, this is not a function buried in some standard C library; we have to implement it in full our-selves. The line above is in fact the "declaration" of the function—its *prototype*, to use the correct terminology. ANSI C requires that every function used in a file must be provided with a prototype declaration such as this, ahead of the first use of the function. Normally, the function prototype is placed at the top of the source file, or is stored in a header file which is #included in the usual way.

To complete the definition of the function, we have to write the function body:

```
float larger(float first, float second)
{
    if(first < second)
        return second;
    else
        return first;
}
```

The only difference between this user-defined function and main() is that as well as writing the function, we have to provide a prototype declaration, which replaces the function body (enclosed in braces) with a semicolon. It could hardly be simpler, could it? Given the proto-type declaration at the top of the file (or supplied in a header file), we can place this function definition anywhere we like in a source file, other than inside another function. The proto-type ensures that wherever the function is used, the compiler knows exactly what to do. It also protects the programmer from what can be easy mistakes:

```
result = larger(0.5);      /* error: function requires two arguments */
result = larger(0.5,0.4,0.1);   /* error: too many arguments */
larger("one",2.5);    /* error: incorrect argument type */
```

One possible error (which as far as C is concerned is not an error at all) that will not be reported by most compilers is discarding the return value:

```
larger(0.5,0.2);        /* no warning message! */
```

Listing 1.7.1 shows the prototype and definition of a function that reads an array of BREAKPOINTs and returns a BREAKPOINT containing the maximum value, and the time. Note the pointer argument—as BREAKPOINT is a type, it can be used like any other C type, including the definition of pointers. Also note that the function returns a BREAKPOINT, which is not a single value but a struct. This is something that the original version of C (known as Kernighan and Ritchie C after its authors) did not allow, but was introduced with ANSI C.

Listing 1.7.1: The User-defined Function—maxpoint

```
/* The prototype*/

BREAKPOINT maxpoint(const BREAKPOINT* points, long npoints);

/* input: points = array of BREAKPOINTS,
npoints gives the length of the array */
/* output: copy of the BREAKPOINT containing largest value */

/* the function definition */

BREAKPOINT maxpoint(const BREAKPOINT* points, long npoints)
{
    int i;
    BREAKPOINT point;

    point.time = points[0].time;/* initialize from first point */
    point.value = points[0].value;

    for(i=0; i < npoints; i++){
        if(point.value < points[i].value){
            point.value = points[i].value;
            point.time = points[i].time;
        }
    }
    return point;
}
```

Note also from this example that a user-defined function can have its own private ("local") variables, not visible outside the function. In the return statement, a copy of the internal variable point is made, so that though that variable will not exist after the function is called, the output is valid.

1.7.6   The `void` and `size_t` Types: Creating Memory and Dealing with Variable Quantities

Before we can use the new function, we need to obtain some breakpoints. The problem is, as stated earlier, that when we are reading them from a file, we do not know how many there are, in advance, so we cannot simply declare an array, and trust that it will be enough. Instead, we need to request some memory directly from the operating system, and if need be, request some more later. When we are finished with it, we must release it back to the system. The technical term for this procedure is "dynamic memory allocation." The standard C library supports four functions to enable us to do this, declared in `stdlib.h`:

```
void* malloc(size_t size);
void* calloc(size_t nobj, size_t size);
void* realloc(void *p, size_t size);
void free(void *p);
```

These functions introduce two new C types:

(1) `size_t`: This is a symbol #defined by the compiler (in <stdio.h>) according to the target machine architecture. It will typically be defined as an `unsigned int` (which is itself defined according to the platform—see subsection 1.2.6). It is rare for programmers to need to pay attention to this. Most requests for memory will use an int or a long (which on 32-bit systems are the same size anyway), and the compiler will take care of any type conversion without fuss. However, pedantic programmers will ensure that all arithmetic destined for use with `malloc` is performed using the type `size_t`, or at least is cast to that type beforehand.

(2) `void*`: Of the two types, this is by far the more important. As a C programmer you will be working with the `void` keyword a great deal of the time. A memory request to the system is simply for a block of bytes, and all the system can do is return a generic or type-agnostic pointer to this block. The name chosen for this is 'void' in the sense of "void of meaning." The one thing the system will guarantee to do is to supply a pointer that is suitable for the largest single C type (usually a double)—e.g. aligned to a memory address that is a multiple of eight bytes. This will then equally be suitable for any other type. The programmer simply casts this pointer (see subsection 1.2.10) to the required pointer type. For the same reason, the amount of memory requested (in bytes) has to be calculated with respect to the type using the `sizeof` keyword. Listing 1.7.2 shows an attempt to allocate a block of 4 megabytes to hold a large sound sample.

Listing 1.7.2

```
1 /* request enough memory to hold a lot of samples */
2 #define SAMPLELEN 1048576
3
4 float* sampbuf;
```

```
5
6   sampbuf = (float*) malloc(SAMPLELEN * sizeof(float));
7   if(sampbuf == NULL){
8       puts("Sorry - not that much memory available!\n");
9       exit(1);
10  }
11  /* do something useful with all this memory. . ...*/
12  process_sample(sampbuf);
13  /* and remember to return it at the end */
14  free(sampbuf);
```

Note that the return value from `malloc` will be NULL if the system is unable to meet the request.[20] We can now understand how NULL is defined in <stdio.h>:

```
#define NULL ((void*) 0)
```

This defines NULL to be integer 0, cast to a "pointer to void." The special aspect of the `void*` exploited here is that is can be compared to any pointer type, without need for a cast. There is no need, for example, for a test such as

```
if(sampbuf == (float*) NULL)
```

The code in lines 8 and 9 warrants some comment. If the memory request is rejected, we cannot assume that there is any memory available at all.[21] A problem with the library function `printf()` is that it may itself request some memory internally, while generating the string to be output. This may likely also fail in this situation, so that `printf()` is not a safe function to use to report memory allocation errors. Instead, the simpler library function `puts()` is used.

1.7.7 Expanding Allocated Memory on Demand: Reading Breakpoints from a File

Reading data from a text file presents many challenges, the primary one being, as already noted, that we do not know in advance how much storage to provide for the data. We also have to allow for the possibility, since this is a plain text file, very possibly written by hand, that the contents may be incorrect in some way. Fortunately, the format of a breakpoint file is very simple, and we can survive with a simple method to read it.

From the list of memory functions above, you will have noted the function `realloc()`. This offers exactly what we need—it will take an existing allocated block and change its size, returning a pointer to the modified block (or NULL on failure). That pointer may or may not be the same as the original one. If `realloc` fails, the original block is still valid, with all its data, and we have the choice whether to keep that, even though incomplete, or abandon the task altogether. The solution presented here takes the latter course, confident that for the data quantities involved, memory failure is not likely.

The logical design of this function (for that is what we will write) is worth setting out in pseudo-code before coding in C. The procedure is, in essence, to start with a small block of memory obtained using `malloc`, and commence reading breakpoints from the file, one line at a time. If we fill that block, we have to expand it by some amount, then continue. When reading the line, we will do some basic format checking, to ensure we find two numbers per line, and we can also check that the first value (time) is always greater than the previous one, by keeping track of the current time value. In pseudo-code, this could be written as follows:

blocksize = 64
count = 0
allocate initial block of blocksize breakpoints

while(we have read a line from the file){
    if(line is incorrect) break
    if(block is full)
        expand block by blocksize; break on realloc error
            copy breakpoint to next place in array, increment count
    }

return the block and count to user

Since we are designing a function, the information on the input and output specifics is essential, in order to create the function prototype. The output is a list of BREAKPOINTs—this is simply a pointer to a BREAKPOINT, or NULL if there was an error. A second output is the size of the array, and as a function can only return a single object, we will have to use a function argument for this, using a pointer to an external variable. The other input is a pointer to an open FILE. This leads to the following prototype:

```
BREAKPOINT* get_breakpoints(FILE* fp, long* psize);
```

We expect this function to be used this way, given an input file *envelope.brk* (ignoring error checks for now):

```
FILE* fp;
long size = 0;
BREAKPOINT* points;

fp = fopen("envelope.brk","r");
points = get_breakpoints(fp,&size);
```

As a block of allocated memory is created by our function, and returned to the caller, it will be the caller's responsibility to `free()` the block at the end of the program.

To read and parse a line of text from a file, we will use two functions from the standard C library. These functions are declared in `<stdio.h>`:

```
char *fgets(char *line, int maxline, FILE *fp);
int *sscanf(char *string, const char* format, ...);
```

The function `sscanf()` has a clear relationship to the now familiar `printf()`; indeed the conversion specifiers are almost identical. To extract two floating-point numbers from a string, sscanf would be used as follows:

```
char* string = "0.0 0.5\n");
double time;
double value;
if(sscanf(string,"%lf%lf",&time,&value) != 2)
    printf("There was an error\n");
```

Note that the addresses of the target variables are passed to the function (their types must of course correspond to the type specifiers), and that it returns the number of conversions that were successfully made. sscanf returns the special value EOF (usually −1) if the string is empty. Note especially that whereas `printf()` uses the specifier `%f` regardless of whether the supplied variable is a `float` or a `double`, sscanf needs to make the distinction explicit—you must use `%f` when you supply the address of a `float`, and `%lf` ("long float") if you supply the address of a `double`.

There is one aspect of sscanf about which we can do nothing without making things very much more complicated: as soon as the required number of conversions is made, the function will return. This means that a string such as the following will be scanned successfully, using the above code, with no error reported:

```
"0.0 0.5 this is the first line of a breakpoint file\n"
```

Therefore, our parsing of the breakpoint file will not be utterly unforgiving. Any text following the two required numbers will be ignored. It is entirely up to you whether you regard this as a bug or as a feature.

1.7.8 Skipping Parts of a Loop: The `continue` Keyword

One facility that sscanf allows us to implement easily is to accept empty lines. Handwritten text files can easily contain these at the end (from repeated pressing of Enter), and it will seem silly to report an error in such cases. In this situation there is no other work to do, except to read the next line. The keyword `continue` enables us to do just this:

```
while(fgets(line,size,fp)){
    if(sscanf(line,"%lf%lf",&time,&value) < 0)
        continue; /* go read the next line */
 /* we got data - do other processing from here*/
}
```

Of course we don't want an endless loop—so how is the loop broken? The function `fgets()` will return NULL when it has reached the end of the file, and as far as `while` (or any conditional test) is concerned, that counts as a zero value, which will terminate the loop.

1.7.9 Putting All the Components Together

Listing 1.7.3 shows a complete implementation of get_breakpoints(), incorporating all the elements discussed. It presumes a command-line environment, and prints some error and warning messages. The starting size for the breakpoint array is set internally at 64 (line 4), and the size of the string to hold a line is set at 80 (line 7), which should be ample. The variable lasttime (line 5) is used to track the time of each new breakpoint (lines 29–34), and break if there is an error. Much of the code is devoted to testing the various possible return values from sscanf, to detect essential errors (lines 16–28). Note that sscanf writes directly into the appropriate element of a private BREAKPOINT. The precedence of the various C operators works in our favor here—simply by prefixing the address-of operator to the array expression

&points[npoints].value

the expression evaluates to the address of the required element of the selected BREAKPOINT. It is worth analyzing this step by step:

(1) points[npoints] evaluates to a BREAKPOINT object at position npoints in the array.
(2) points[npoints].value evaluates to the value element of that breakpoint.
(3) &points[npoints].value evaluates to the address of that element (type double*).

Finally, the auto-incremented count is tested against size, and if they are equal, realloc is called to expand the memory (lines 35–47). The code allows for the possibility of the expanded block having a different address, using a temporary pointer private to the if block (line 36). If realloc fails, it is essential to set the pointer points to NULL, as this will be checked by the calling function, and if it is not NULL, the caller will expect to free() it after processing. Freeing a block of memory twice is an error that in the worst case will cause a program to crash.

Listing 1.7.3: The Function get_breakpoints()

```
1 BREAKPOINT* get_breakpoints(FILE* fp, long* psize)
2 {
3   int got;
4   long npoints = 0, size = 64;
5   double lasttime = 0.0;
6   BREAKPOINT* points = NULL;
7   char line[80];
8
9   if(fp==NULL)
10      return NULL;
11  points = (BREAKPOINT*) malloc(sizeof(BREAKPOINT) * size);
12      if(points==NULL)
```

```
13            return NULL;
14
15        while(fgets(line,80,fp)){
16            got = sscanf(line, "%lf%lf",
17                &points[npoints].time,&points[npoints].value);
18            if(got <0)
19                continue;              /* empty line */
20            if(got==0){
21                printf("Line %d has non-numeric data\n",npoints+1);
22                break;
23            }
24            if(got==1){
25                printf("Incomplete breakpoint found at point %d\n",
26                npoints+1);
27                break;
28            }
29            if(points[npoints].time < lasttime){
30            printf("data error at point %d: time not increasing\n",
31                npoints+1);
32            break;
33        }
34        lasttime = points[npoints].time;
35        if(++npoints == size){
36            BREAKPOINT* tmp;
37            size += NPOINTS;
38            tmp=(BREAKPOINT*)realloc(points,sizeof(BREAKPOINT) *size);
39            if(tmp == NULL)   {  /* too bad! */
40            /* have to release the memory, and return NULL to caller */
41                npoints = 0;
42                free(points);
43                points = NULL;
44                break;
45            }
46            points = tmp;
47            }
48        }
49        if(npoints)
50        *psize = npoints;
51        return points;
52        }
```

Now we can write a full program to read breakpoints and report the maximum value, using these two functions, get_breakpoints() and maxpoint(). First, the definition of BREAK-

POINT must be written, followed by the prototypes of the two functions, followed in turn by the full definition of those functions, as shown in listings 1.7.1 and 1.7.3. The main program is responsible for parsing the command line as usual, opening the file, and after processing, releasing the array of breakpoints obtained from get_breakpoints(). The main() function is shown in listing 1.7.4, and the full program file (*"breakdur.c"*) is available on the DVD. No further comment will be made about this program here—you should now be able to understand how it works just by reading the code.

Listing 1.7.4: The *"breakdur"* main Function

```c
int main(int argc, char* argv[])
{
    long      size;
    double    dur;
    BREAKPOINT point, *points;
    FILE* fp;

    printf("breakdur: find duration of breakpoint file\n");
    if(argc < 2){
        printf("usage: breakdur infile.txt \n");
        return 0;
    }
    fp = fopen(argv[1],"r");
    if(fp == NULL){
        return 0;
    }
    size = 0;
    points = get_breakpoints(fp, &size);
    if(points==NULL){
        printf("No breakpoints read.\n");
        fclose(fp);
        return 1;
    }
    if(size < 2){
        printf("Error: at least two breakpoints required\n");
        free(points);
        fclose(fp);
        return 1;
    }
    /* we require breakpoints to start from 0 */
    if(points[0].time != 0.0){
        printf("Error in breakpoint data: first time must be 0.0\n");
        free(points);
```

```
        fclose(fp);
        return 1;
    }
    printf("read %d breakpoints\n", size);
    dur = points[size-1].time;
    printf("duration: %f seconds\n", dur);
    point = maxpoint(points,size);
    printf("maximum value: %f at %f secs\n", point.value,point.time);
    free(points);
    fclose(fp);
    return 0;
}
```

1.7.10 Exercises

Exercise 1.7.1
Listing 1.7.1 can be improved. The local variable `point` is initialized to the first point in the supplied list. The loop then makes a redundant comparison with that same point. Modify the code to skip this first test. Include tests to validate the input `points` argument accordingly. (Hint: the function should not rely on the caller (`main`) validating supplied arguments.)

Exercise 1.7.2
Defensive programming: The number of points in a list cannot be negative. Change the breakpoint code to use `unsigned long` rather than `long`. Hint: To write an `unsigned long` using `printf`, use the format specifier `%lu`.

Exercise 1.7.3
Test *breakdur* by supplying a variety of non-breakpoint files—a C source file, even a soundfile.

Exercise 1.7.4
Make some functions that apply simple processing to a BREAKPOINT array. These might include

(a) stretch/shrink times
(b) normalize values relative to some maximum value
(c) shift values up or down
(d) scale values by some arbitrary factor
(e) truncate or extend to a given duration
(f) insert or delete a point.
(g) something of your own devising.

Which tasks can be performed "in place" rather than by creating a new array? What does this exercise demonstrate about the advantages and disadvantages of arrays?

1.8   Generating and Displaying Breakpoints

1.8.1   Introduction

If you have worked through the code and exercises in the previous section, you may already have discovered that reading breakpoints as columns of numbers is less than ideal, the more so when evaluating possibly subtle changes. Almost by definition an envelope (being what a breakpoint file typically represents) is a shape. The most intuitive way to inspect such data it is therefore graphically, as seen in figure 1.9. Fortunately, tools are available that enable such data to be displayed with very little work from the user. Such displays are of special importance to audio programmers, who deal as a matter of routine both with breakpoints in general and amplitude envelopes in particular. We may be able to inspect breakpoint files numerically when they consist of only a few lines, but for anything more extended a graphical display is essential. This is even more the case with regard to audio data itself, which we will study in subsequent chapters.

This section introduces the widely used free package Gnuplot, available for all platforms. See the software section of the DVD for instructions on installation for your platform (note that on OS X you also need to install AquaTerm). It can be used to display any data represented as numeric text files. This may be in the form of a breakpoint file, or of audio data presented as text. Advanced uses enable multiple data files to be plotted on the same display for comparison purposes, together with a wide range of formatting and annotation facilities.

In this section, however, we will need only the simplest plotting facilities. It extends the work done in the previous section by looking at the programmatic creation of simple attack and decay shapes, where the number of data points generated can easily exceed what can be meaningfully inspected in text form. The creation of such data may be the goal of a whole programming project. However, it is at least as important to understand graphical display as part of the development process for a project; for example to verify that some block of data is being created or processed correctly. Tools such as Gnuplot thus become part of the testing and debugging techniques employed by all programmers.

1.8.2   The Basic Gnuplot Plot Command

Gnuplot is an interactive text-based program (a form of *interpreter*). On launching, it presents an internal command prompt at which various plotting or other commands are typed. Note the difference between usage on Windows, compared to OS X and other UNIX-based platforms. On Windows, when launched (the Windows version is called "wgnuplot") a self-contained command window is created, leaving your DOS window free for other work. For UNIX-like systems such as OS X and Linux, you will want to use two command windows—one for Gnuplot itself, one for running the programs that generate the data to be plotted. In typical usage, a program may be run multiple times with different parameters to generate the data, which can then be plotted by reusing the same command within Gnuplot. The description that follows is based on the use of Terminal in OS X.

The first step is to create a breakpoint file, such as the one shown in table 1.5. Create the text file exactly as shown, and call it *envelope.txt*. Open a Terminal session and change to the directory in which you have stored the file (here assumed to be called `datafiles`). Launch Gnuplot (without any arguments) by typing its name. Some announcement text is printed, followed by the Gnuplot prompt:

```
    G  N  U  P  L  O  T
Version 4.0 patchlevel 0
last modified Thu Apr 15 14:44:22 CEST 2004
System: Darwin 8.11.0

Copyright (C) 1986-1993, 1998, 2004
Thomas Williams, Colin Kelley and many others

This is gnuplot version 4.0. Please refer to the documentation for
command syntax changes. The old syntax will be accepted throughout the
4.0 series, but all save files use the new syntax.

Type 'help' to access the on-line reference manual.
The gnuplot FAQ is available from http://www.gnuplot.info/faq/

Send comments and requests for help to
<gnuplotinfo@lists.sourceforge.net>
Send bugs, suggestions and mods to
<gnuplot-bugs@lists.sourceforge.net>

Terminal type set to 'aqua'
gnuplot>
```

Now type the following command exactly and press Enter:

```
plot "envelope.txt" with lines
```

Gnuplot will launch an AquaTerm window and display the data, with a simple annotation giving the name of the file (figure 1.10). Note in particular that Gnuplot automatically scales and marks the axes of the plot to match the range of the data. Later we will use a small enhancement to this plot command, but for 99 percent of the time the above basic command is all you will need. You are nevertheless encouraged to study the Gnuplot documentation (e.g. type "help plot" at the Gnuplot prompt) to see a description of all the plotting commands and options. Gnuplot is widely used to create figures for technical papers and books—the various formatting, titling, and annotation commands are well worth getting to know, as is the facility for outputting to graphic file formats as an alternative to the screen.

Having displayed *envelope.txt* for the first time, experiment with changing the data and reissuing the plot command. You can do this manually using a text editor, but if you worked

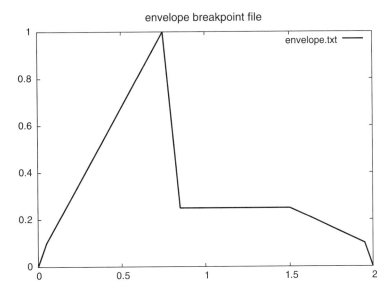

Figure 1.10
An example of Gnuplot output.

exercises 1.7.4 and 1.7.5 you should have at least one program that applies a transformation and outputs the new data. Explore changes to both the time and value columns, to see how they are reflected in the display. Note that Gnuplot uses a command history facility, so that to repeat a command you do not have to retype it. Use the up-arrow key to select any previous command, and press Enter. Changes can be made and observed very quickly this way.

1.8.3   Generating Breakpoint Data: The Exponential Decay

The principle of the basic time/value breakpoint file is that (as we see in the output of Gnuplot) values at intermediate times lie on a straight line between adjacent points. The values can mean whatever the user chooses. However, where the data represents amplitude (as in the case of the amplitude envelope) straight lines do not result in a musically natural sound. A "natural decay" (as heard in a plucked string, or in reverberation) follows a curved amplitude trajectory. Thus, instead of the simple linear decays in *envelope.txt* between 1.0 and 0.25, or between 0.1 and 0.0; we need a curved line—specifically, we need an *exponential decay*. Expressed at its simplest, this says that the decay starts quickly, then slowly (almost) levels off over time, as in this simple series of reducing amplitude values:

1.0, 0.5, 0.25, 0.125, 0.0625, 0.03125, 0.015625, ...

We recognize this as a geometric series, with a constant ratio of 0.5—each value is half the preceding one. Clearly, the numbers become unmanageable very quickly, the more so when we consider how long we may want a natural decay to last, suggesting both a lot of numbers, and a lot of very small numbers. The answer, of course, is to use the power of the C language to generate all these numbers for us, and to verify the correctness of the code by displaying the output via Gnuplot. It is hardly important to a program these days whether it is processing 10 numbers or 10,000, but it is clearly important to us, if the only alternative is to attempt to write them manually.

One general formula for an exponential decay is

$$x = ae^{-k/T}, \tag{2}$$

where a and k are constants and T represents the *time constant*—the rate of decay.[22] For our purposes, a always equals 1, for the starting value of the decay envelope. We can implement this directly in C using the math library function `exp()`. The great merit of this calculation is that we need to use `exp` only once, to obtain the value for the constant ratio (which we know will be a value less than 1). To generate the decay, we simply multiply the previous output by the constant ratio the required number of times. This is illustrated in the program *expdecay* (listing 1.8.1), which for brevity omits the argument error checking a full program would have to employ.

Listing 1.8.1

```
/* expdecay.c */
/* implement formula x[t] = a* exp(-k/T) */
#include <stdio.h>
#include <stdlib.h>
#include <math.h>

int main(int argc, char**argv)
{
    int i,nsteps;
    double step,x,a,T,k;
    double dur;

    if(argc != ARG_NARGS){
        printf("usage: expdecay dur T steps\n");
        return 1;
    }

    dur = atof(argv[1]);
    T = atof(argv[2]);
    nsteps = atoi(argv[3]);

    k = dur/nsteps; /* the constant time increment */
    a = exp(-k/T); /* calc the constant ratio value */
    x = 1.0; /* starting value for the decay */
```

```
        step = 0.0;
        for(i=0; i < nsteps; i++){
            printf("%.4lf\t%.8lf\n",step,x);
            x = a * x;
            step += k;
        }
     return 0;
}
```

One further reason the code is so short is that no attempt is made to write the data to a file. We can instead use output redirection at the command line to send the output text to a file, for example using the command

```
expdecay 1 0.5 200 > expdecay.txt
```

Then plot the data using the Gnuplot plot command, as shown above.

This example demonstrates a particularly compact way to add data output to a program temporarily, for the purposes of testing and debugging. Such small programs are also commonly written by C programmers to test something such as a mathematical function or process, prior to incorporation in a more complex application.

Even this small program offers useful scope for exploration. This is especially important for any readers less familiar with the mathematics. Experiment first with the value for T (the time constant). Small values such as 0.5 and lower create a very steep decay, while higher ones (perhaps above 1.0) create shallow decays. The shallower the decay, the longer it takes for the values to reach a low level that we might call silent (perhaps down to 0.0001). The more points that are used, the smoother the displayed curve will be, and the closer the values will approach 0 without ever reaching that value.

Note that the format specifier for the breakpoint value in the printf statement asks for eight decimal places. One clear disadvantage of text output is that the precision of the numbers is determined by that of the output text. Even apparently small values of amplitude matter in audio. The use of eight decimal places ensures that the behavior of the decay calculation can be observed to a sufficiently low level to cover all reasonable audio requirements.

1.8.4 The Exponential Attack and the stdout and stderr Output Streams

The fact that the exponential decay never reaches zero presents the audio programmer with a problem. Just as the most musical shape for the decay stage of an envelope for a musical note is the exponential, we find that we really want a similar shape for the attack stage of a note (e.g. the first breakpoint pair in *envelope.txt*). The intuitively obvious solution is simply to generate the decay envelope in reverse. However, we have to ask ourselves, at what point can we say the decay envelope has terminated? Naturally for musical purposes it must do so, but mathematically the decay continues forever. The numbers become ever smaller but, like

Zeno's hare, never reach their target.[23] Furthermore, we have to remember that any number multiplied by zero remains zero. If we are to retain the loop that creates the data, some small but non-zero start value has to be provided. While the program above represents in some sense a "pure" implementation using the exp function directly, it does not necessarily give us the control we need for practical and general envelope generation. We need first to be able to create both attack and decay curves, and second to be able to create them over a variety of numerical ranges.

We encountered a very similar problem in section 1.2, where we used the pow function to calculate the frequencies of MIDI notes. These ideas lead to the solution shown in listing 1.8.2, which can be used to create exponential attack and decay breakpoint data over an arbitrary range. Mathematically, the functions exp, pow, and log are members of a family expressing the same underlying concepts in different ways, and the audio programmer will seek to use whichever combination is best suited to the task at hand.

Listing 1.8.2: General Exponential Attack and Decay

```
1  /* expbrk.c generate exponential attack or decay breakpoint data */
2  #include <stdio.h>
3  #include <stdlib.h>
4  #include <math.h>
5
6
7  int main(int argc, char** argv)
8  {
9      int i,npoints;
10     double startval,endval;
11     double dur,step,start,end,thisstep;
12     double fac,valrange,offset;
13     const double verysmall = 1.0e-4;/*~-80dB */
14     if(argc != 5){
15         fprintf(stderr,
16             "Usage: expbrk duration npoints startval endval\n");
17         return 1;
18     }
19     dur = atof(argv[1]);
20     if(dur <=0.0){
21         fprintf(stderr,"Error: duration must be positive.\n");
22         return 1;
23     }
24     npoints = atoi(argv[2]);
25     if(npoints <= 0){
26         fprintf(stderr,"Error: npoints must be positive!\n");
```

```
27          return 1;
28      }
29      step = dur/npoints;
30
31      startval = atof(argv[3]);
32      endval = atof(argv[4]);
33      valrange = endval - startval;
34      if(valrange == 0.0){
35          fprintf(stderr,
36              "warning: start and end values are the same!\n");}
37      /* initialize normalized exponential as attack or decay */
38      if(startval > endval){
39          start = 1.0;
40          end = verysmall;
41      valrange = -valrange;
42      offset = endval;
43      }
44  else{
45          start = verysmall;
46          end = 1.0;
47          offset = startval;
48      }
49
50      thisstep = 0.0;
51  /* make normalized curve, scale output to input values, range */
52      fac = pow(end/start,1.0/npoints);
53      for(i = 0; i < npoints; i++){
54          fprintf(stdout,"%.4lf\t%.8lf\n",thisstep,
55                          offset + (start * valrange));
56          start *= fac;
57          thisstep += step;
58      }
59      /* print final value */
60      fprintf(stdout,"%.4lf\t%.8lf\n",
61              thisstep,offset + (start * valrange));
62
63      fprintf(stderr,"done\n");
64      return 0;
65  }
```

As a somewhat more complete program than *expdecay.c, expbrk.c* incorporates basic error
checking of input arguments. These necessarily involve printing messages to the user;
additionally, a simple message is printed at the end to confirm the program has run to

completion. However, this does not interfere with the primary task, inherited from *expdecay.c*, of printing the breakpoint output in such a way that it can be redirected to a file for display by Gnuplot. It achieves this by making use of the fact that C (in conjunction with the operating system) defines not one but two standard output text streams, `stdout` and `stderr`. The former is automatically used by the plain `printf` function, but in this case both are used via the `fprintf` function to make the difference explicit. When text output is redirected, only text written to `stdout` is redirected to a file; anything written to the `stderr` stream remains directed to the screen. Thus, a program can generate both primary output and secondary error, or informative, output, and the two can be clearly separated when that is required.

The very small starting value for the attack curve is defined internally in line 13; this is nevertheless something to be experimented with. As the comment indicates, this value affects the steepness of the attack. As before, the program should be tested and explored using Gnuplot to display the data. Note that the program arguments now include start and end values—it is possible to create exponential decays descending from 2 to 1, from 4 to −3, and so on.

1.8.5   Not All Curves Are Exponentials: The log10 Gnuplot Test

It has already been noted that the tail of an exponential decay comprises very small numbers. We discover early on that displaying such numbers graphically, in the context of the data as a whole, is difficult, as eventually they are too small to be drawn even by a one-pixel line. A solution is to use a logarithmic vertical scale. A standard scale for amplitude values is the Decibel, defined by the formula

$$P(dB) = 20.0 \log_{10}(x). \tag{3}$$

This is discussed further in later chapters. Suffice it to say here that this calculation can be performed within Gnuplot as an extension of the basic plot command, so that there is no need to add it to the programs themselves. Using this calculation on an exponential decay (within the range 1 to 0) is especially illuminating. Example:

```
plot "longdecay.txt" using (20.0 * log10($2)) with lines
```

Here the notation $2 picks out values in the second column in the file. An exponential curve plotted this way appears as a straight line, covering the full range of the data. Other non-exponential curves will typically convert to some form of curve when using the `log` transformation. The slope of the line correlates directly with the time constant of the exponential. Audio amplitude values in the range 0 to 1.0 are said to be in the "normalized range." If your data includes any zero values,[24] the above command has to be extended further by adding a small constant, since a value of zero is illegal for logs:

```
plot "longdecay.txt" using (20.0*log10($2+0.00001)) with lines
```

This example gives but a hint of the very extensive support within Gnuplot for mathematical computation—you can apply a wide range of arithmetical modifications to your data before displaying it.

1.8.6 Exercises

Exercise 1.8.1
The code archive of the *musicdsp* mailing list (www.musicdsp.org) includes an example under the Synthesis category of an exponential decay generator ("Fast Exponential Envelope Generator"). Make a program to implement and test this code, using Gnuplot to display the output.

Exercise 1.8.2
The simplest possible envelope generator for sound synthesis comprises a two-segment attack-decay shape, where the peak value is user-controllable, as is the duration of each segment. Write a program to generate such an AD envelope as standard breakpoints. Use two duration arguments and a single-level argument, together with an argument to set the overall number of points. Use Gnuplot to verify correctness.

Exercise 1.8.3

(a) The following program generates either an attack or decay curve using the exp function. How does the attack curve differ from the example of *expdecay.c*? Where might such an attack curve be found?

(b) Modify the code that computes `thisval` within the `for` loop, to eliminate duplicate calculations. Here is the original program:

```
/* expad.c generate exponential attack or decay breakpoint data */

#include <stdio.h>
#include <stdlib.h>
#include <math.h>

int main(int argc, char** argv)
{
    int i,npoints;
    double T,k,a;
    double ystart,yend;
    double dur,thisval,thisstep;

    if(argc != 6){
        fprintf(stderr,"insufficient arguments.\n");fprintf(stderr,
            "Usage: expad duration npoints startval endval T\n");
```

```
            return 1;
    }
    dur = atof(argv[1]);
    if(dur <=0.0){
        fprintf(stderr,"Error: duration must be positive.\n");
        return 1;
    }
    npoints = atoi(argv[2]);
    if(npoints <= 0){
        fprintf(stderr,"Error: npoints must be positive!\n");
        return 1;
    }
    ystart = atof(argv[3]);
    yend = atof(argv[4]);
    if(yend == ystart){
        fprintf(stderr, "Warning: start and end values are the
                            same!\n");
    }

    T = atof(argv[5]);
    k = dur/npoints; /* npoints = "sample rate" */
    a = exp(-k/T); /* T = time constant */

    thisstep = 0.0;
    thisval = ystart;
    fprintf(stderr,"a = %.6lf\n",a);
    /* make normalized curve, scale output to
    input values and range */
    for(i=0;i < npoints;i++){
        printf("%.4lf\t%.8lf\n",thisstep,thisval);
        thisval = a * thisval + (1.0-a) * yend;
        thisstep += k;
    }
    /* print final value */
    printf("%.4lf\t%.8lf\n",thisstep,thisval);

    fprintf(stderr,"done\n");
    return 0;
}
```

Exercise 1.8.4

(a) Revisit the exercises in the previous section, and develop the transformation functions into programs that output a breakpoint file to the screen so that it can be displayed by Gnuplot.

(b) Read the documentation for the Gnuplot `plot` function; then create a single plot that reads two breakpoint files, to compare breakpoint data before and after transformation.

Exercise 1.8.5

In the example programs, the precision for the times and values is set at 4 and 8 decimal places respectively (`%.4lf`, `%.8lf`). Is this enough? Test with (a) a large number of points (e.g. 44,100 per second) and (b) very long steep decays. What is the maximum meaningful precision for writing doubles in text form using `printf`?

1.9   Toward the Soundfile: From Text to Binary

1.9.1   Introduction

In this section we take a significant step on our journey toward the goal of working directly with sound. So far, our programs have generated output in the form of text, either to the screen or to a text file. We have seen how general-purpose tools such as Gnuplot can be used to present such data graphically. This will continue to be an important activity, but without some audio data to work with, breakpoint files remain inert, in some sense meaningless until we can hear their effect. Visualization remains an important tool in the programmer's armory; this section extends that work to include the generation of audio data first in text form, and secondly in the form of a ''raw'' binary file. The soundfile editor Audacity (available on the DVD) is introduced here as a freely available tool that can be used to display and audition raw binary soundfiles.

The introduction of the raw binary soundfile inevitably raises the subject of how such data is represented in the computer and on disk. Indeed, it immediately exposes programmers not only to relatively familiar issues such as sample formats, but also to some very low-level aspects of number representation in the computer, such as byte ordering. As we delve further into the programming of audio processes, and into the use of soundfiles and other data formats, we need to become progressively conversant with these subjects. Readers for whom this aspect is very new may find it useful to study the appendixes in this book on computer architecture, number representations, and mathematics. While these topics are referenced as necessary within individual sections, there is much to be said for a concerted independent or at least parallel study of them. By their nature these topics lie in the background of the business of designing creative audio software. However, as we progress in our knowledge of C and of computer audio processing, we will find that that background becomes increasingly prominent; indeed it soon becomes indispensable for success as audio and music programmers. With this in mind, the material presented in this section may be taken as a foretaste of things to come.

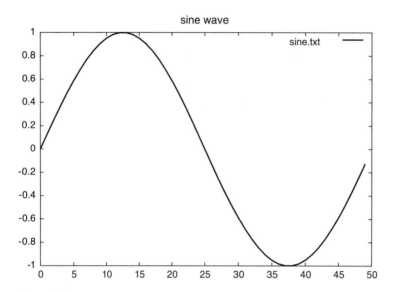

Figure 1.11
The sine wave.

1.9.2 The `sin` Function: Creating a Sine Wave

The sine wave (figure 1.11) is arguably the most important signal both in audio and in audio processing. We will learn more about its significance in later sections, where we will use it for (among other things) additive synthesis. Mathematically it describes the motion of a swinging pendulum (a classic example of "simple harmonic motion"), and similarly the motion of vibrating strings. It is a particular form of the more general waveform called a *sinusoid*, which defines the shape of the waveform without consideration of the starting value. By itself it is an extremely simple vibration and musically relatively uninteresting as a sound—the great majority of sounds in which musicians are interested are much more complex.

There is one familiar musical tool that is conventionally regarded as producing a sound almost as "pure" as a sine wave: the tuning fork. In this section we will combine our knowledge of the exponential decay with a sine wave to create a simple software tuning fork. Our focus is here not so much on the theory or the mathematics of the sine wave but on the creation of a data file or a sound file containing a tuning fork tone that we can both display graphically and listen to. This in turn will lead us first to a consideration of the information we need to associate with such files in order to represent or audition them as intended, and second to a consideration of the issues we have to bear in mind concerning the representation of numeric data in the computer and on disk. We will also need to consider, even at this preliminary stage, what we might want in such a program to make it usable, whether musically or for study and experimentation.

Listing 1.9.1 presents the minimal code used to create the plot in figure 1.11. It is indeed more minimal that most of the previous code examples in that it uses no command-line arguments. It uses the method introduced in section 1.8, writing a list of numbers to `stdout` that can be redirected to a text file:

```
./sinetext >sine.txt
```

Listing 1.9.1: Generate Single-Cycle Sine Wave

```
1   /* sinetext.c */
2   /* write sinewave as text */
3   #include <stdio.h>
4   #include <stdlib.h>
5   #include <math.h>
6   /* conditional compilation - is M_PI defined? */
7   #ifndef M_PI
8   #define M_PI (3.141592654)
9   #endif
10
11  int main(int argc, char** argv)
12  {
13      int i,nsamps;
14      double samp;
15      double twopi = 2.0 * M_PI;
16      double angleincr;
17      /* set number of points to create */
18      nsamps = 50;
19      /* make one complete cycle */
20      angleincr = twopi / nsamps;
21      for(i=0; i < nsamps; i++){
22          samp = sin(angleincr *i);
23          fprintf(stdout,"%.8lf\n",samp);
24      }
25      fprintf(stderr,"done\n");
26      return 0;
27  }
```

In section 1.7 we encountered the C preprocessor directive `#define`. In line 7 of listing 1.9.1 we encounter `#ifndef`, one of the two complementary directives for *conditional compilation* used to detect if some symbol has not been defined. The positive form is `#ifdef`. Each of the two forms requires a terminating `#endif` directive (line 9). Any legal C code can be placed between `ifndef` and `endif`—either a simple definition or extensive blocks of code. In this case we are looking for `M_PI`, which is defined in the header file `<math.h>` in all standard UNIX C compilers, including gcc in OS X and Linux. As its name indicates, it supplies the value of the fundamentally important mathematical number (.This is, however, not a definition mandated by ANSI C. And Microsoft compilers do not provide such a definition, so users of those compilers have to define it themselves. The term *conditional compilation* is exact—if the test expressed by the directive fails, the associated code is removed before the file is delivered to the compiler itself. Indeed, the #ifdef/#endif combination is a handy way of excluding a block of code from compilation—or even a whole file of code if that is necessary. This might be done to select between alternatives, or (as here) to modify code differences between compilers or platforms. It is also often used (especially in C++ programs) to prevent the duplication of code in header files that may otherwise be included more than once.

Lines 15 and 20 of listing 1.9.1 represent the mathematics involved. We will learn more about the mathematics in future sections. At this stage, the essential aspect to bear in mind is that a single cycle of a sine wave has a length defined mathematically as 2π radians. Because the C sin function (line 22) takes an argument in radians, the only number we need is 2π, which we have defined in line 15 as a variable. The output is a double, with values ranging between -1.0 and $+1.0$. We must then sample this cycle over a number of points to generate the list of numbers to supply to Gnuplot. We met this principle of sampling in section 1.8 when we generated an exponential decay as a breakpoint file. While handwritten breakpoint data can define points at arbitrary times, we also defined a special form of breakpoint data with equally spaced points. This therefore becomes an example of sampling. The exponential decay drawn with ten points is not very smooth—it is in effect a coarsely sampled approximation of the smoothly curved decay shape. When Gnuplot is given a single column of numbers, it automatically treats then as equally spaced in this way. In this example the sine wave is generated using a modest 50 points. The calculation in line 20 defines the distance (expressed as a small angle increment) between each two points, here 1/50 of the complete cycle. This angle increment is multiplied by the loop index to calculate each successive value (line 22).

Although only 50 points were used, the curve in figure 1.11 looks very smooth. We can see the underlying sampled nature of the data by using a slightly different plot command in Gnuplot:

```
plot "sine.txt" with impulses
```

or

```
plot "sine.txt" with steps
```

The latter illustrates the output of a digital-to-analog converter (DAC) when supplied with a sampled sine wave—it requires a special filter to remove the steps and reconstruct the waveform as intended.

1.9.3   Toward the Tuning Fork: Frequency Generation and the Keyword enum

To develop *sinetext.c* into a full tuning-fork simulation, we need first to elaborate the arithmetic to incorporate a *sample rate*. As it stands, with our fixed 50-point sine wave we can only generate different pitches by defining a different sample rate. At the standard CD sample rate of 44,100 Hz, our 50-point sine wave will have a frequency of 882 Hz. To obtain the international tuning standard frequency for "Concert A" (440 Hz), we would have to use a sample rate of 22,000 Hz. Clearly, this is impractical—we need to scale the number of points instead.

Listing 1.9.2 expands *sinetext.c* into a more complete program with arguments. Line 27 employs the revised arithmetic to incorporate both a sample rate and a requested frequency. This formulation is worth bearing in mind, as it will be used frequently in nearly every program concerned with audio synthesis or processing.

Listing 1.9.2: Expanded Version of sinetext.c with Arguments

```
1    /* sinetext2.c */
2    #include <stdio.h>
3    #include <stdlib.h>
4    #include <math.h>
5
6    #ifndef M_PI
7    #define M_PI (3.141592654)
8    #endif
9
10   /* define our program argument list */
11   enum {ARG_NAME,ARG_NSAMPS,ARG_FREQ,ARG_SR,ARG_NARGS};
12
13   int main(int argc, char** argv)
14   {
15       int i,nsamps;
16       double samp,freq,srate;
17       double twopi = 2.0 * M_PI;
18       double angleincr;
19
20       if(argc != ARG_NARGS){
21           fprintf(stderr,"Usage: sinetext2 nsamps freq srate\n");
22           return 1;
23       }
24       nsamps    = atoi(argv[ARG_NSAMPS]);
25       freq      = atof(argv[ARG_FREQ]);
26       srate     = atof(argv[ARG_SR]);
```

```
27      angleincr = twopi*freq/srate;
28
29      for(i=0;i < nsamps; i++){
30          samp = sin(angleincr*i);
31          fprintf(stdout,"%.8lf\n",samp);
32      }
33
34      fprintf(stderr,"done.\n");
35      return 0;
36  }
```

This program introduces a new method for managing program arguments. Hitherto we have simply used numeric indices into the argv array to pick up arguments. Here we use the C keyword enum to define a meaningful name for each value. The great value of enum lies in its automatic assignment of ascending numbers (simple integers) to the symbol list (enclosed in braces on line 11), starting with zero. (Remember, argv[0] is always the name of the compiled program.) We can then use those names to select the required argv entry (lines 24–26). This technique offers two benefits to the programmer. First, it is self-documenting —a name is always more meaningful than a raw number. This is therefore a simple example of *defensive programming*, as it helps to reduce the possibilities for errors. Second, this is a program under development, and it we may add, remove, or reorder program arguments as development proceeds. In the present case we can arbitrarily reorder the arguments, and use of the enum list ensures that the correct value is always obtained from a given argv entry. Note that for the sake of brevity (with the exception of the test associated with the usage message in line 20) input arguments are not checked for correctness. This is reasonable in a small intermediate test program such as this; should it be found useful as a general-purpose program among many others, those error checks will have to be added.

1.9.4   The Utility Program *text2sf*: Converting Text to a Soundfile

The program in *sinetext.c* can be used as before, directing the output to a text file for inspection using Gnuplot. However, since the data clearly represents a sound, we want to hear it, and we want to confirm that we are indeed generating the frequency we requested. In future sections we will be writing fully practical programs that output standard soundfiles. However the principle introduced in the previous section is still relevant—that in testing and debugging code it is convenient to add simple text output of audio data to programs under development, in just this way, using a bare minimum of code. All we need is a tool that enable us to audition the output as well as inspect it visually.

The utility program *text2sf* supplied on the DVD (in both executable and source form) is provided to perform this task. It is written using the small-scale cross-platform soundfile library *portsf* which is introduced in the next section, and which is fully amenable to editing and modification. As supplied, its command line is

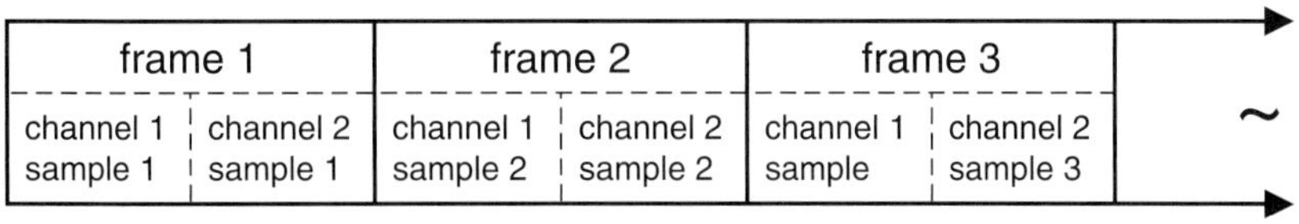

Figure 1.12
Interleaving samples in a file.

```
text2sf infile outfile srate chans gain
```

where `infile` = input text data file, `outfile` = output soundfile (.wav or .aiff formats), `srate` = sample rate of the data, `chans` = number of interleaved audio channels in `infile`, and `gain` = amplitude factor applied to input data (1.0 = no change)

The outfile format is set by the filename extension—use .wav for a WAVE file and .aiff (or .aif) for an AIFF format file. One argument that may be conspicuous by its absence is a selector for the output soundfile sample type. As supplied, this is set internally to create a plain 16-bit soundfile; it is left as an exercise for the reader to modify this in the manner of their choice to offer some or all of the choices offered by the portsf library.

The `chans` argument indicates that a data file can contain more than one audio channel. In a soundfile, samples are interleaved, leading to the notion of the multi-channel sample frame (figure 1.12). In effect, sample for each frame are delivered to the soundcard in order, followed by the samples for the next frame, and so on.

Once the output soundfile has been created, we can play the it using the player or editor of our choice, and we can verify that the frequency is as specified. (You may want to seek out a real tuning fork for purposes of comparison.) The equivalent for a text file is very simple: each line corresponds to a multi-channel frame, so a stereo file would appear as a text file with two columns of data. We can explore this aspect by making a small modification to line 23 of listing 1.9.1:

```
fprintf(stdout,"%.8lf\t%.8lf\n",samp,samp *samp);
```

This creates a two-channel data file in which the second channel is the square of the first.[25] After re-compiling, run the program to create a file named *stereo.txt*.

To display the sound data in Gnuplot requires us to know how to interpret multiple columns in a file. When presented with a single column, these columns are treated as data for the y axis, and the lines are counted internally to provide equally spaced values for the x axis. However, a two-column data file is interpreted as data for the x and y axes respectively (in other words, a breakpoint file), which is not what we want here. To overrule this, we have to ask Gnuplot to plot both columns on the y axis, specifying each column explicitly:

```
plot "stereo.txt" using($1) with lines, "stereo.txt" using($2) with
lines
```

The using directive defines an expression inside the brackets to be used to create the data. This could be an arbitrary arithmetic expression, but here the prefix $ is used by itself to select a particular column from the file (counting from 1). Note that the filename must be specified for each column. It is equally possible to plot data from two or more different files, using the same syntax.

1.9.5   Our First Tuning Fork Emulation

From section 1.8 we have two alternative forms of the exponential decay. One might be called a "purist" solution, insofar as it is close to the textbook definition of the function. The second is more pragmatic from the musician's point of view, addressing the very musical issue of ensuring that the decay always reaches silence whatever the overall length. We need to explore both solutions. The procedure is, however, broadly the same in the two cases—we want to apply the exponential decay to our sine-wave generator. We have developed and tested each component separately, so all that should be required now is to combine them into one program.

Listing 1.9.3 shows a solution based on *expdecay.c*. As befits a slightly more user-oriented program, it incorporates output to a named text file. The all-important code that transforms the basic sine wave into a decaying tone is simplicity itself—a simple multiplication (line 45). The raw argument "T" from *expdecay.c* is changed into the slightly more expressive name "slope" (line 22).

Listing 1.9.3: Tuning Fork Program Version 1

```
1   /* tfork.c virtual tuning fork combining sinetext.c and expdecay.c */
2   #include <stdio.h>
3   #include <stdlib.h>
4   #include <math.h>
5
6   #ifndef M_PI
7   #define M_PI (3.141592654)
8   #endif
9
10  enum {ARG_NAME,ARG_OUTFILE,ARG_DUR,ARG_HZ,
            ARG_SR,ARG_SLOPE,ARG_NARGS};
11
12  int main(int argc, char** argv)
13  {
14          int i,sr,nsamps;
15          double samp,dur,freq,srate,k,a,x,slope;
16          double twopi = 2.0 * M_PI;
17          double angleincr;
```

```
18          double maxsamp = 0.0;
19          FILE* fp = NULL;
20
21          if(argc != ARG_NARGS){
22              printf("Usage: tfork outfile.txt dur freq srate
                    slope\n");
23              return 1;
24          }
25      fp = fopen(argv[ARG_OUTFILE],"w");
26      if(fp==NULL){
27          fprintf(stderr,"Error creating output file %s\n",
                    argv[ARG_OUTFILE]);
28          return 1;
29      }
30
31      dur = atof(argv[ARG_DUR]);
32      freq = atof(argv[ARG_HZ]);
33      srate = atof(argv[ARG_SR]);
34      slope = atof(argv[ARG_SLOPE]);
35      nsamps = (int)(dur * srate);
36      angleincr = twopi * freq / srate;
37      k = dur/nsamps;
38      a = exp(-k/slope);
39      x = 1.0;
40
41      for(i=0;i < nsamps; i++){
42          samp = sin(angleincr*i);
43          /* apply exp decay */
44          x *= a;
45          samp *= x;
46          fprintf(fp,"%.8lf\n",samp);
47      }
48      fclose(fp);
49      printf("done\n");
50      return 0;
51  }
```

Apart from that, there is essentially nothing new in this program beyond the fact that it merges two previous programs—except perhaps that, because the functional aspects have already been developed and tested, we can reasonably expect such a merge to work correctly first time. We cannot really call this a modular program, but in a sense its development has been modular. We can expect our programs to increase ever more in complexity (certainly in length), such that it will become more and more important to test sections of such code in isolation as much as possible, making full use of tools such as Gnuplot and *text2sf* and any other such tools that we may discover or develop along the way.

1.9.6   Tuning Fork Program Version 2

Following the same principles, listing 1.9.4 demonstrates a tuning fork emulator based on *expbrk.c*. However, this example does feature a couple of changes to enhance the overall utility of the program, again in the spirit of looking ahead. The first of these is the new command-line argument amp. So far, all the programs have generated exponential decays starting from the normalized maximum value of 1.0. Any music-oriented program will have to offer control of amplitude, so this argument is added in case it comes in handy. The exponential decay itself is formally defined always covering the full normalized range, shown explicitly in lines 38–39, while the amplitude parameter is applied to the output of the sine-wave generator (line 44).

Listing 1.9.4: Tuning fork v2 with `maxsamp` **report**

```
1    /* tfork2.c alternate tuning fork generator based on expbrk.c
2     * - decay is always to ~silence regardless of duration. */
3    #include <stdio.h>
4    include <stdlib.h>
5    #include <math.h>
6
7    #ifndef M_PI
8    #define M_PI (3.141592654)
9    #endif
10
11   enum {ARG_NAME,ARG_OUTFILE,ARG_DUR,
          ARG_HZ,ARG_SR,ARG_AMP,ARG_NARGS};
12
13   int main(int argc, char** argv)
14   {
15       int i,sr,nsamps;
16       double samp,dur,freq,srate,amp,maxsamp;
17       double start,end,fac,angleincr;
18       double twopi = 2.0 * M_PI;
19       FILE* fp = NULL;
20
21       if(argc != ARG_NARGS){
22           printf("Usage: tfork2 outfile.txt dur freq srate amp\n");
23           return 1;
24       }
```

```
25      fp = fopen(argv[ARG_OUTFILE],"w");
26      if(fp==NULL){
27          printf("Error creating output file %s\n",
                      argv[ARG_OUTFILE]);
28          return 1;
29      }
30
31      dur = atof(argv[ARG_DUR]);
32      freq = atof(argv[ARG_HZ]);
33      srate = atof(argv[ARG_SR]);
34      amp = atof(argv[ARG_AMP]);
35      nsamps = (int)(dur * srate);
36      angleincr = twopi*freq/ srate;
37
38      start = 1.0;
39      end = 1.0e-4; /* = -80dB */
40      maxsamp = 0.0;
41      fac = pow(end/start,1.0/nsamps);
42
43      for(i=0;i < nsamps; i++){
44          samp = amp * sin(angleincr*i);
45          samp *= start;
46          start *= fac;
47          fprintf(fp,"%.8lf\n",samp);
48          if(fabs(samp) > maxsamp) {
49              maxsamp = fabs(samp);
50          }
51      }
52
53      fclose(fp);
54      printf("done. Maximum sample value = %.8lf\n",maxsamp);
55      return 0;
56  }
```

The second addition, following the same philosophy, is the tracking of the maximum sample in the file (lines 40 and 48–49). This is such a useful facility in general that it is incorporated as an automatic facility into the *portsf* library, introduced in chapter 2—and indeed optionally into the header of the soundfiles themselves. In the context of a simple exponential decay it is almost redundant as the maximum sample would be expected to be the starting value of the exponential; however, we are generating a sine wave (whose values start from zero), so that the peak value will not be the first value in the audio data but at the first peak of the waveform. Later in chapter 2 we will be applying envelopes and all manner of other transformations to soundfiles, and the automatic reporting of the peak amplitude will be of considerable value in generally monitoring results and in identifying any gross errors.

1.9.7   The Raw Binary Soundfile

An alternative to writing audio streams as text data is to write them directly in binary form. The difference in code is minimal, but it offers some significant advantages. The most obvious of these is the size of the generated file. In the examples presented so far, each sample has been written as floating-point numbers with some eight decimal digits of precision. With the additional leading zero and decimal point, this requires ten bytes of storage per sample, plus further bytes representing white space and end of line. In contrast, a 32-bit floating-point sample by definition requires only four bytes of storage, with no further overhead. A 32-bit file may well be one-third the size of the equivalent text file, and a 16-bit file further reduces that by half while still offering CD-quality precision. It is thus a more tractable format for general storage and distribution, especially where the need is more to display the data graphically or to audition it than to inspect individual sample values. It is also significantly more resistant to casual and error-prone editing than a text file.

Starting from listing 1.9.4, the changes required to generate a raw binary file are slight indeed. The simplest change is to the format specified for `fopen` (line 25) to indicate '*binary*' mode:

```
fp = fopen(argv[ARG_OUTFILE],"wb");
```

This change is not strictly necessary on UNIX-based platforms, but it is required by Visual C++ and some other Windows compilers.

A slightly more involved change must be made to the code that writes the data to disk. Instead of using `fprintf`, which by definition writes formatted text, we must use the function `fwrite`, which writes arbitrary blocks of memory to disk:

```
size_t fwrite(const void * ptr,size_t size,size_t count, FILE* fp);
```

In this declaration, we have the following:

- `size_t` is defined by the compiler as an integer type appropriate to the platform. It can be assumed to be at least a 32-bit unsigned type, but it may be larger (e.g. 64 bits on a 64-bit platform).
- `ptr` is a pointer to the memory block to be written; being a pointer-to-`void` the address can be that of any object, whether a single local variable or a large block of memory.
- Together, `size` and `count` define the size of the memory block to be written. Typically, `size` will refer to the size of any standard or user-defined type such as `char` or `int` (i.e. where its size can be found using the `sizeof()` operator), while `count` defines the number of such elements to be written. This is also the value returned by the function.
- `fp` is the pointer-to-`FILE` to be written, as created by `fopen`.

For example, to write a single 32-bit `float` to the file, line 47 has to be modified to

```
float fsamp; /* declared at the top of the code block */ . . .
fsamp = (float) samp;
if(fwrite(&fsamp,sizeof(float),1,fp) != 1){
    printf("error writing data to disk\n");
    return 1;
}
```

1.9.8 Platform Particulars: The Endianness Issue

Being written in English, the words in this book are read from left to right across the page. There are other languages, most familiarly Arabic and Hebrew, that are written from right to left. For reasons too arcane and ancient to discuss here (mainly concerned with very low-level implementation of some arithmetic operations), a similar situation exists for the ordering of multi-byte numeric data (such as a 4-byte `float`) in memory and on disk. Instead of right and left, we have lower and higher memory addresses. In a big-endian system, the most significant byte (MSB) lies at the lower memory address. This corresponds in general terms to the left-to-right reading order. The alternative is a little-endian architecture, in which the MSB lies at the higher memory address.

Figure 1.13 shows how a given 32-bit integer is represented in big-endian and little-endian architectures. The main thing about the little-endian representation is that, while the ordering of the bytes is reversed, the ordering of individual bits within each byte is not. The consequence of this is that when we write a multi-byte numeric value to a file, it is written with the endianness native to the platform. On Intel-based platforms, data will be written in little-endian form; on machines based on the PowerPC as used in older Macintoshes, it will be written in big-endian form. Applications that offer the facility to read soundfiles in raw binary format have to be told when endianness to use in reading the file. If we want to read a big-endian file on a little-endian machine, or vice versa, we must reverse the bytes of each number. As with text files, we must inform the receiving application of the sample

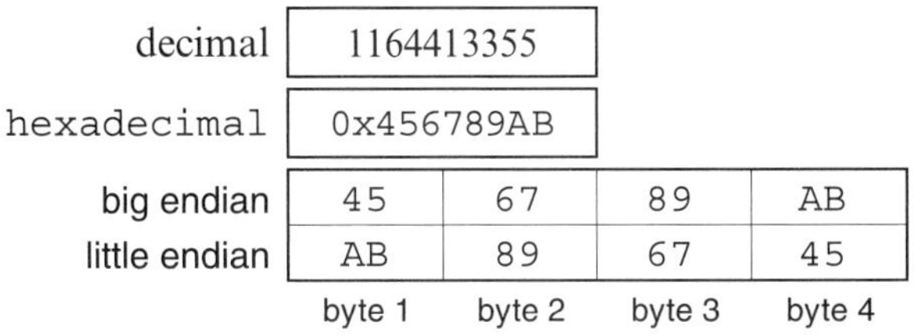

decimal	1164413355			
hexadecimal	0x456789AB			
big endian	45	67	89	AB
little endian	AB	89	67	45
	byte 1	byte 2	byte 3	byte 4

Figure 1.13
Big-endian and little-endian storage.

rate and number of channels. For raw binary files, we also must tell the application what types and sizes of numbers the file contains, and the endianness.

1.9.9 A Raw Binary Version of *tfork2.c*

Listing 1.9.5 shows the revised version of *tfork2.c* that is to write output as a raw binary soundfile. Only minor changes are required. However, the main loop that generates the data has been expanded to offer a choice between two sample types: 16-bit shorts and 32-bit floats (lines 76–108). It also uses a small utility function (lines 17–25) to report the platform endianness that I came across many years ago when looking at the code of an audio analysis tool called SNDAN.[26] This origin is acknowledged in the code, which uses a simple pointer-based technique to detect endianness in order to report that information to the user as a reminder.

Listing 1.9.5: `tforkraw.c`

```
1   /* tforkraw.c gen raw sfile with native endianness */
2   /* based on tfork2.c */
3   #include <stdio.h>
4   #include <stdlib.h>
5   #include <math.h>
6
7   #ifndef M_PI
8   #define M_PI (3.141592654)
9   #endif
10
11  enum
12  {ARG_NAME,ARG_OUTFILE,ARG_DUR,ARG_HZ,ARG_SR,
13                  ARG_AMP,ARG_TYPE,ARG_NARGS
14  };
15  enum samptype {RAWSAMP_SHORT,RAWSAMP_FLOAT};
16
17  /* thanks to the SNDAN programmers for this */
18  /* return 0 for big-endian machine, 1 for little-endian machine*/
19  /* so we can tell user what order the data is */
20  int byte_order()
21  {
22      int one = 1;
23      char* endptr = (char *) &one;
24      return (*endptr);
25  }
26
```

```c
27  const char* endianness[2] = {"big_endian","little_endian"};
28
29  int main(int argc, char** argv)
30  {
31      unsigned int i,nsamps;
32      unsigned int maxframe = 0;
33      unsigned int samptype, endian, bitreverse;
34      double samp,dur,freq,srate,amp,step;
35      double start,end,fac,maxsamp;
36      double twopi = 2.0 * M_PI;
37      double angleincr;
38      FILE* fp = NULL;
39      float fsamp;
40      short ssamp;
41
42      if(argc != ARG_NARGS){
43          printf("Usage: tforkraw outsfile.raw dur"
44              "freq srate amp isfloat\n");
45          return 1;
46      }
47
48      dur = atof(argv[ARG_DUR]);
49      freq = atof(argv[ARG_HZ]);
50      srate = atof(argv[ARG_SR]);
51      amp = atof(argv[ARG_AMP]);
52      samptype = (unsigned int) atoi(argv[ARG_TYPE]);
53      if(samptype > 1){
54          printf("error: sampletype can be only 0 or 1\n");
55          return 1;
56      }
57      /* create binary file: not all systems require the 'b' */
58      fp = fopen(argv[ARG_OUTFILE],"wb");
59      if(fp==NULL){
60          fprintf(stderr,"Error creating output file %s\n",
61              argv[ARG_OUTFILE]);
62          return 1;
63      }
64
65      nsamps = (int)(dur * srate);
66      angleincr = twopi * freq / srate;
67      step = dur / nsamps;
68      /* normalized range always - just scale by amp */
69      start =1.0;
```

```
70      end = 1.0e-4;
71      maxsamp = 0.0;
72      fac = pow(end/start,1.0/nsamps);
73      endian = byte_order();
74      printf("Writing %d %s samples\n",nsamps,endianness[endian]);
75      /* run the loop for this samptype */
76      if(samptype==RAWSAMP_SHORT){
77          for(i=0;i < nsamps; i++){
78              samp = amp * sin(angleincr*i);
79              samp *= start;
80              start *= fac;
81              /* use 32767 to avoid overflow problem */
82              ssamp = (short) (samp * 32767.0);
83              if(fwrite(&ssamp,sizeof(short),1,fp) != 1){
84                  printf("Error writing data to file\n");
85                  return 1;
86                  }
87              if(fabs(samp) > maxsamp) {
88                  maxsamp = fabs(samp);
89                  maxframe = i;
90              }
91          }
92      }
93      else {
94          for(i=0;i < nsamps; i++){
95              samp = amp * sin(angleincr*i);
96              samp *= start;
97              start *= fac;
98              fsamp = (float) samp;
99              if(fwrite(&fsamp,sizeof(float),1,fp) != 1) {
100                 printf("Error writing data to file\n");
101                 return 1;
102             }
103             if(fabs(samp) > maxsamp) {
104                 maxsamp = fabs(samp);
105                 maxframe = i;
106             }
107         }
108     }
109     fclose(fp);
110     printf("done. Maximum sample value = %.8lf at frame %d\n",
111             maxsamp,maxframe);
112     return 0;
113 }
```

Lines 81 and 82 demonstrate a simple if not necessarily purist solution to the problem of generating 16-bit audio. Audio signals are bipolar—in terms of normalized values, samples range between −1.0 and +1.0. However, all signed integers present a problem: the maximum 16-bit positive value (32,767) does not exactly match the maximum negative value (−32,768). If we scale our floating-point values by 32,768, both +1.0 and −1.0 will translate to −32,768, which is enough to introduce severe clicking in the output. In *tforkraw.c* this danger is avoided by scaling by 32,767 instead. However, by no means do all audio programmers approve of this approach. When a conversion is performed in the opposite direction, receiving 16-bit samples and converting to the normalized range, the natural (and safe) approach is to divide by 32,768. Only when the same factor is employed in both directions will the conversion be bit-accurate—an important criterion for many professional audio users. This remains a subject for debate among programmers (especially those implementing file format support). A simple answer is to avoid generating signals close to digital peak in the first place—but Murphy's Law dictates that when users can do something, they will do it.

1.9.10 Auditioning Raw Soundfiles: the Audacity Soundfile Editor

Audacity is an open-source cross-platform soundfile editor that is in wide use throughout the audio and music community. (Versions for all major platforms can be found on the DVD.) Among its many facilities is the loading of raw binary soundfiles. From the File menu select "Import" ("Raw Data." After you select a file, a small dialog window is displayed in which you can set the required properties of the file (figure 1.14).

A wide range of sample type options is supported in the first drop-down list. The Macintosh version has one oddity: by default, the "Start offset" entry box (the byte position at which conversion should start) is pre-filled with the value 1. Expect to set this value to zero for the plain raw soundfiles considered here. The main purpose of that box is to allow

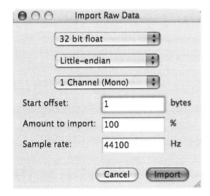

Figure 1.14
Opening raw soundfiles in Audacity.

soundfiles with unrecognized or damaged headers to be opened. This requires knowing how large that header is, which may require some detective work with a binary file editor; or some guesswork. Any header data translated into samples will almost invariably appear as rubbish audio, easy to see and easy to eliminate on a second attempt. Select sample type, endianness, and channel count according to your knowledge of the file, or make a guess. If in any doubt, when you have opened a file, set your playback volume to low before playing. Files imported with the wrong format will almost always be both loud and grossly distorted, though often audio is recognizable even in this extreme situation.

1.9.11   Exercises

Exercise 1.9.1
Add all necessary error checking to the programs in this section, including testing the return value from `fprintf`.

Exercise 1.9.2
A quick revision question: what does `const` signify for the first argument to `fwrite`?

Exercise 1.9.3
Replace the `freq` argument in the program of your choice with a MIDI note argument.

Exercise 1.9.4
In the waveform generation code of any of the tuning fork programs, change the call to the `sin` function with a call to the `cos` function. View and audition the output in both text and binary forms.

Exercise 1.9.5
Modify *sinetext.c* to write both `sin` and `cos` outputs in that order (i.e. per line) to a two-channel text file. Use Gnuplot to display the data using its default x/y mode (i.e. do not use a "using" directive). Before doing this, predict what the display will show. What does this demonstrate about the relationship between the `sin` and `cos` functions?

Exercise 1.9.6
Look on the DVD for a raw file called "`mystery.raw`." Use Audacity to display and audition this file, by discovering the properties of the file—sample type, number of channels, byte order, and sample rate.

Exercise 1.9.7
Modify *sinetext.c* to output sample values as full-scale 16-bit integers (written as a text file). Confirm the change by displaying the data in Gnuplot. Ensure that the data is represented correctly.

Conclusion

The nine sections of this chapter formed a more or less complete course on the C language with a particular music and audio direction. If you have followed the examples carefully and completed some of the exercises, you should be able to start doing some proper audio programming, dealing with digital signals and embarking on an interesting journey through the field of musical signal processing. The following chapters will guide you in this exploration, so please proceed to chapter 2, where the focus will start to shift from programming in general to the specific goal of manipulating sound.

Notes

1. However, this is not quite the whole story. Programmers use the term *'variable'* to describe *all* data elements defined in a program, whether they are literally variable or not. As we will see in the next section, we can even have a "constant variable." To the programmer, a variable is anything that can exist on the left-hand side of an assignment—something that has a symbolic name.

2. Readers will occasionally find the integer type name `size_t` employed in programs. This relatively esoteric name attempts to avoid the problems of guessing what the "native" integer size is on a particular platform. It is used by some functions in the C standard library and is described in section 1.7.

3. It is illuminating to compare these intervals with those of "pure" or "Just intonation" tuning. For example, the perfect fifth in mean tone has the ratio $3/2 = 1.5$, very slightly wider than in E.T. The major third has the ratio $5/4 = 1.25$; the E.T equivalent is much wider, and really out of tune. These pure ratios derive directly from the natural harmonic series: the major third is the distance from the fourth harmonic to the fifth harmonic.

4. According to the C89 standard, used in this book and generally the most commonly implemented. Later standards have changed this.

5. This may be too arcane, but actually you can declare variables in C code at the start of blocks anywhere in your program. The following is legal C code:

```
main(int argc, char **argv)
{
    int i;
    for(i = 0; i < 5; i++){
        float x; /* check this out! */
        x = i * 2.5;
        printf("%f\n", x);
    }
}
```

6. However, this is not the only way to implement a string. In the language Pascal, for instance, the length of a string is stored as the first element, followed by the characters that make up the string. Pascal was the original programming language for the Macintosh, and Mac developers still need to know about "Pascal strings."

7. In some cases, white space (spaces and tabs) is important to C; in other cases, it is not. A pointer declaration can be made in any of these styles:

```
char* message;
char *message;
char * message;
char*message;
```

They all mean the same thing to the compiler. The first two forms are about equally popular; the last is legal but very uncomfortable to the eye, and is not recommended.

8. Regarding the placement of braces in `if` statements, there are a number of layout styles in common use. The two most common styles are as follows:

```
if(a == b)
{
    do_something();
}
```

and

```
if(a == b) {
    do_something();
}
```

Both of these styles clearly show where the end of the block is in relation to the controlling `if` expression. The degree of indentation is the same whether or not braces are used. The second style is probably the most common, not least because is the more economical of space.

9. We will encounter the concept of a container again in DVD chapters 3–5.

10. This runs somewhat counter to the traditional UNIX command-line tool, which is designed to work as part of a chain or sequence of programs, the output of one becoming the input to another. The system as a whole is called a *pipe*, and the format of the data piped from one process to another is almost always plain text. For this reason, a usage message can only be invoked by using a special command argument such as `-help`; otherwise the program simply starts, and it may run forever waiting for text input.

11. Warning: A variant of the above code that programmers can be tempted to use changes the conditional expression to use the `!=` ("not equal to") operator:

```
while(i != 0){
        printf("%d",i);
        i = i - 1;
}
```

This form of test expression can be simplified further to

```
while(i){
...
```

The logic of this is reasonable enough: as the integer variable is reduced by one each time, it must reach the value 0 eventually, and the test will evaluate to *true*. However, unlike the first example using the `>=`

operator, this loop is vulnerable to a bug. If `i` is initialized to a negative value (which might be caused by a typing error), the dependent code will make it more negative each time, and the loop will continue to iterate with the variable becoming increasingly negative "forever"—or, rather, until the number overflows the numeric range of the integer type and "wraps around" from negative to positive. If this variable is being used to access an array, a crash is inevitable. The safe use of loops depends on the programmer being absolutely sure that the loop tests can deal with all eventualities. It can also be argued that the use of the `>=` operator is more self-documenting, as it expressly indicates that the variable `i` cannot be negative.

12. If the destination variable is declared as `float`, and the expression uses a constant:

```
float x = 1.0;
x += 2.1;
```

The compiler may issue a warning about loss of precision, as the constant is treated as a `double`, forcing the whole calculation to be performed at double precision, which has to be converted back into a `float`. To avoid this warning, the constant can be declared as a float by using the 'f' suffix:

```
x += 2.1f;
```

13. Programming reminder: In any `for` loop that reads or writes to an array using an increasing index, as in the example above, the conditional test is always of the form `i < arraysize`. This is because C array indices always counts from zero, so that in an array of 12 elements the highest element is at index = 11. The conditional test above ensures that at the final increment, when i = 12, the test evaluates to false and control passes to the instruction after the `for` block. Even after many years of experience, programmers can still get caught by indexing errors that point outside the array, so this warning is likely to appear several times in this book. As a result, techniques to trap such errors are very important.

14. Style note: Consistent with other C idioms, braces are not required when the dependent code is a single statement:

```
do
    printf("%d ",i++);
while(i < 10);
```

Many programmers prefer to use braces anyway, especially while developing a program—what starts out as a single statement can very often become several. Others will go in the other direction and reduce the code to two lines:

```
do printf("%d ",i++);
while(i < 10);
```

Both forms make the `do` loop look rather strange, and the use of braces at all times is strongly recommended.

15. Indirect auto-increment: What would be the meaning of applying `++` to the expression `*ptr`? This would be read as "increment the variable pointed to by `ptr`," and it is a common procedure. You must use parentheses to force the compiler to do it the way you want:

```
double count = 0;
double* ptr = &count;
(*ptr)++; /* count now = 1.0, ptr still points to it */
```

Using ++ this way, on a floating-point variable, is legal, and has the expected result. You may occasionally see this in code, but it is rare, and is not recommended, as it is not really idiomatic for floating-point variables (there are no corresponding machine instructions to exploit). The increment/decrement operators are best used with integral variables, such as counters, as illustrated by all the other examples in this section.

16. File streams: The use of a computer screen display is taken so much for granted these days that it is easy to forget that there was a time before such devices were available. Output devices on early computing systems included such things as punched cards and tape, and the classic "teletype" printer/typewriter. What these devices had in common was that they received (or sent) a stream of data, one character at a time. Thus the screen, the keyboard, and a disk file are all examples of a "stream device." In C, three standard input/output ("i/o") streams are defined:

```
stdout /* primary output stream */
stderr /* stream to receive error messages */
stdin /* stream from which input is received e.g. teletype keyboard */
```

A data file on disk is merely a further instance of a stream device. The difference between printf and fprintf is that printf outputs only to stdout, whereas the more general fprintf can write to any named stream. It is often used, for example, to write to stderr:

```
fprintf(stderr,"there was an error\n");
```

Note that printf and fprintf can be used with the same set of formatting options.

In UNIX-based systems, stdin and stdout have a further stream-related significance, in that the stdout stream from one program can be piped to the stdin of another. Many of the arcane programs found in classic UNIX systems (including Gnu/Linux and OS X) are designed with this piping technique in mind—by default they read from stdin and write to stdout, and only to/from a disk file if expressly commanded to do so by means of the UNIX *redirection* command >. This example uses the UNIX command ls to redirect a detailed directory listing to a text file: ls -l >directory.txt. The UNIX pipe symbol | connects the output of one process to the input of another: ls | grep sine > sinefiles.txt. This writes the names of all files containing "sine" to the file *sinefiles.txt*.

17. What would it mean to add two breakpoints together? Think about it. It seems obvious enough to add the value elements, but what about the times? The compiler has no idea what the variables signify. A struct can contain any defined C type, including pointers. In many, perhaps most cases, even a human programmer would find it impossible to define a meaningful arithmetic operation on a struct, so it is hardly surprising that the compiler cannot do it.

18. We just need a name somewhere. We can name the struct:

```
struct mystruct {
    int var1;
    int var2;
};     /* we can now declare a variable of type struct mysruct */
```

or we can declare a variable using an "anonymous struct":

```
struct{
    int var1;
    int var2;
} mystructvar;/* mystructvar is a variable: */
mystructvar.var1 = 440;
```

or we can use typedef as shown in the text.

19. Note the use of an outer pair of brackets in the definition of NULL. This is done to avoid any mis-interpretations that might arise through C precedence rules. Here is a simple example of the need for such brackets:

```
#define SQUARE(n) n * n
```

This is a small macro definition, replacing any instance of the text represented by the symbol n (which is not a variable but a placeholder for whatever text the programmer supplies) with the given substitute text. The idea is that to square a number of any type, the one macro can be used:

```
int w, x = 5;
double y,z = 10.0;
w = SQUARE(x);
y = SQUARE(z);
```

These initializations of x and z will result in the expected values: 25 in w and 100.0 in y. Upper-case letters for the macro symbol are used here to show, by convention, that this is a macro and not a function call. But suppose the innocent programmer uses an expression instead of a single variable:

```
w = SQUARE(x+1);
```

After text substitution ("macro expansion") by the preprocessor, the expression will become

```
w = x + 1 * x + 1;
```

Since the C precedence rules require that the multiplication be performed first, the result will be not 36 but 11. By enclosing both the target of the macro in brackets, and the placeholder symbol each time it is used,

```
#define SQUARE(n) ((n) * (n))
```

the problem is avoided. The macro will now expand to

```
w = ((x+1) * (x+1));
```

which will give 36, as required. Note that the presence of many levels of brackets is a burden only to the compiler—it will not result in any extra machine code. So if in any doubt, use brackets freely.

20. In line 9, the library function exit() is used, rather than return. As its name suggests, exit() immediately quits the program, releasing all resources (memory, open files) in the process. The argument value given to exit is the same as the value that would be used with a call to return. You will see that exit is very commonly used in command-line programs, especially in response to allocation failures. The advantage to the programmer is obvious (no cleanup code has to be written), but if this function were to be incorporated into a GUI-based application (where an internal process may be run and rerun many

times) calls to exit() must be eschewed in favor of a more controlled recovery to a higher level of the application, with a warning message presented to the user. This does demand much more planning by the programmer, as it may be that the allocation failure occurs low down in some function, and the error return has to be rippled back through many parent functions before it can be presented to the user. For the same reason, calls to functions such as printf or puts may need to be removed or changed, as they do not generally have a place in a GUI application. In a VST plug-in, for example, if the plug-in initialization function cannot obtain memory, or has any other problem, it has to return an error value, and the host application will notify the user accordingly.

21. Can malloc() fail these days? The problem is that it is increasingly rare for memory requests to fail, unless for a truly huge amount. Even here, the machine will try to use virtual memory using space on a hard disk, and it is more likely that the operating system itself will start to warn that virtual memory is low, before rejecting a memory request. Thus code written to deal with allocation failures may never get executed, and therefore may never get tested. Tools do exist (sometimes supplied by compiler vendors) that deliberately "stress" memory, to enable such code to be tested. A comparatively simple solution, if hardly rigorous, is to create a "wrapper function" for functions such as malloc, in which you can add code to deliberately reject a request, say if it exceeds some arbitrary limit:

```
void* stress_malloc(size_t size)
{
    size_t limit = 1024 * 1024 * 2; /* limit to 2MB */
    if(size < limit)
        return malloc(size);
    else
        return NULL;
}
```

You can then use #define to make all calls to malloc become calls to your wrapper function:

```
#define stress_malloc malloc
```

Note that this memory is all "virtual memory." Many operating systems have special function calls that request memory that must be in hardware RAM. Audio programmers often rely on this to create buffers used to record or play back audio. These requests are much more likely to fail, and it is especially important to ensure that code to deal with such allocation failures is fully tested.

22. There is also the highly important number e, the base of the natural logarithms, one of several numbers named and studied by the great 18th-century mathematician Leonhard Euler—who among a multitude of mathematical accomplishments wrote a substantial treatise on harmony. The value of e is approximately 2.718, but like its close companion π it is a transcendental number with no finite numerical representation. The exponential function is its own derivative. That is, if you measure the slope of the curve at each point, the result is another exponential curve. The genius of Euler is something to be celebrated by both musicians and mathematicians.

23. Until of course they fall below the smallest number that the hardware can represent. For doubles this is a very small number indeed, but even this will be reached eventually, such numbers become "denormalized," and this can create problems, especially on Intel-based machines (where it is know as "the denormal problem"), which work inconveniently hard to maintain precision, resulting in processing suddenly slowing to a crawl.

24. This can happen if the precision with which values are written to a text file is too low; small values will be misleadingly written as zero.

25. We are relying on the very useful fact that the square of a number between 0 and 1.0 is a smaller number within that range; and we remember also that the square of a negative number is a positive number. Readers are invited to predict what the square of a sine wave will look like, and then to *confirm* that prediction with Gnuplot.

26. It is nevertheless a widely documented and employed "hacker" technique, so it has probably been reinvented multiple times.

Audio Programming Basics

2 Audio Programming in C

Richard Dobson

In the previous chapter we learned how to play and display "raw" binary soundfiles using Audacity. In order to play such a soundfile, we needed to tell the program, not only the sample rate, sample type and channel count; but also the endianness of the samples themselves. The purpose of a dedicated soundfile format such as WAVE and AIFF is to encapsulate this information in a header section prefixed to the audio data itself, which an application can read to determine the format of the file. Such a file format can thus be described as "self-describing." Writing code to read and write such soundfiles is a complicated job, not least because of the many alternative formats a soundfile can have. There is a clear trade-off for the audio programmer. It is easy to write a raw soundfile, as we have seen, but such files are only portable with the greatest difficulty, and more cumbersome to play. The possibility of forgetting what format a given file has is very great. Conversely, writing the code to write (and more particularly, to read) a self-describing file format is a non-trivial task, especially where that format is very complex with many variations and options.[1]

Fortunately, several C libraries have been created that deal with all the arcane details of writing modern soundfile formats, so that reading and writing such files need be no more difficult than reading or writing a text file. The formats define all the above information, and often much more, including optional information that while not essential to play a file, is nevertheless useful.

This chapter demonstrates how to generate simple waveforms, such as a triangle wave and a sine wave, and write them to a soundfile, and also how to modify or combine sounds. In the process we are introduced to further elements of the C language, and to further techniques of code design. As you may suspect, these programs will be longer, and more complex than before, as many more tasks are being performed. This complexity includes the use of multiple source files, and the use of external libraries that need to be linked to our program. This is, however, such a common task that many tools have been developed over the years to streamline the process as much as possible. One such tool is the *makefile*, a text file that defines all the elements and actions needed to build a program, together with any *dependencies* such as external libraries.

Behind the details of new C keywords, the arithmetic of sine waves, and the definition of new functions lie deeper and increasingly important issues of robustness, flexibility, extensibility, and, embracing all these, comprehensibility. As our programs develop in sophistication, so will our ambitions as programmers rise, and it becomes more and more likely that in writing any one program we will anticipate many further possibilities.

In particular, just as the programs in this section make use of a pre-written code library, you will yourself be writing many functions that are likely to be required for many different projects, and which could therefore also form components of your own library. So in reading the following sections, consider not only the immediate task at hand, but also how general a block of code or a function is, and whether you might find uses for it in other projects.

This chapter therefore assumes and expects that you will now be contemplating, at least, writing your own programs, above and beyond the examples given here. You will be creating building blocks of code; and it almost goes without saying that building blocks can be used to make many very different edifices. The challenge is in designing those blocks for maximum re-usability, while ensuring that they are also as easy to use as possible. It remains one of the most interesting and intriguing exercises for the programmer, to anticipate the future use of something. Often, new ideas demand that a function be rewritten *a posteriori*. Yet in writing a program the programmer's first thought is understandably, to "get it working," and worry about other possibilities later. As a result, it can often happen that a program is written twice. The first is a "proof of concept" version that works; the second version learns from the first and implements enhancements, alternative approaches to design, increases modularity and robustness, and identifies blocks of code worth generalizing into a library for use elsewhere. Once this is done, the program may even be rewritten a third time. This is normal.

2.1   A Simple Soundfile Library: *portsf*

2.1.1   The *Portsf* Header Files—Public and Private Files

The *portsf* soundfile library, developed especially for this book, was designed to be as simple as possible to use. It is not intended in any way to be an alternative to "industrial-strength" libraries such as *libsndfile*. It comprises only two source files, each with an associated header file:

```
ieee80.c
ieee80.h
portsf.c
portsf.h
```

This relatively small size reflects the fact that only the two most common soundfile formats are supported, AIFF and WAVE, though this includes 24-bit and 32-bit formats (both integer and float), and multi-channel files, including the new WAVE_FORMAT_EXTENSIBLE format introduced by Microsoft to support surround sound and high-precision audio (e.g. 24-bit and beyond). Libraries such as *libsndfile* (demonstrated elsewhere in this book) support a very wide range of formats (including compressed formats such as ADPCM), and are highly efficient, but are also very much larger, using a large number of source files, with code that is very much less accessible to beginning programmers.

The two files *ieee80.c* and *ieee80.h* are very small (the header file especially so), and are made distinct as a courtesy to the author, Bill Gardner of MIT and Wave Arts (you can read the details in the header file). Both are "private" files required by *portsf.c* (specifically, to deal with the sample-rate field in AIFF headers). There is no technical reason why these files could not be concatenated into one; you might like to try this as an exercise. However, in the form shown, they conveniently illustrate an important distinction between private and public header files.

To use the library, the only header file the user needs to #include is *portsf.h*—this defines all the structures and functions in the library. We will be making frequent reference to this file in the following sections. As this is a public header file, we will use the angle brackets with #include:

```
#include <portsf.h>
```

This header file defines all we need to know about the *portsf* library—various custom types and structures, and the specialized functions for handling soundfiles. The main implementation file *portsf.c* on the other hand is large and complex, making use of several C language idioms not so far presented. It will nevertheless repay study. You will for example notice immediately the use of *conditional compilation* (as introduced in the previous chapter) using #ifdef and #ifndef. With long headers such as this, any technique that can be used to avoid duplication of effort is very welcome. In this case, the conditional compilation is used to detect if *portsf.h* has already been included by another source file. If so, the whole body of the file is skipped. As it happens, this also enables the file to be read by C++ programs, C++ being especially disapproving of duplicated type definitions. If at this stage you are alarmed by *portsf.c* and feel you do not understand it, the answer is that it doesn't matter (much). Often, code for a general-purpose library is very complex, not least *because* it seeks to be general-purpose; but all we need to know about are the various definitions and declarations in the header file.

Unlike *portsf.h*, the header file *ieee80.h* is, conversely, a *private* file used internally by the two C files, and if you inspect these, you will notice that the other form of the #include directive is used there:

```
#include "ieee80.h"
```

This, you will recall from chapter 1, asks the compiler to search first in the directory that contains the current source file (i.e. the file containing the #include directive).

When *portsf* is created as a true library module, the files *ieee80.h* and *ieee80.c*, together with *portsf.c*, will in effect disappear; the main header file *portsf.h* will be your only means of access to the library. Thus the ieee80-related functions are private to the library, not accessible to the programmer, and in some future implementation may be redefined, or maybe even eliminated completely. This is a form of code *encapsulation*. If the user depended directly on the existence and exact form of these functions they could not be removed or modified without breaking user projects. In the following sections you will discover further mechanisms in C for supporting such encapsulation (you may also encounter the expression "data hiding" in this context); the language C++ develops this much further into a core principle of software design.

2.1.2   The Makefile

For the first time, we require a special (non-system) header file stored not in our project directory but elsewhere. As a result we will need to tell the compiler where to find it, by adding the directory containing required header files (their *path*) to the list to be searched by the compiler. The procedure for doing this is compiler-specific, but whichever one you use will give you an option to set this "search path" for header files. The recommended approach in this book is to use the UNIX-style development system based on the use of a "makefile." This includes Linux, OS X and the MinGW environment on Windows. On the DVD, a makefile is provided for all example programs in each chapter.

A makefile defines all the stages of compiling a program—or indeed of several programs; It is read by a special command-line program called *make*, standard on all UNIX-based systems (including OS X). You will find that a single makefile supports building all the programs in a chapter. Typing make will automatically build all of them (building *portsf* as well if necessary). For projects involving a number of source files, external libraries, and other special build options (such as whether to make a "debug build," or a "release build" optimized for speed), such a makefile is essential. The proprietary project files used by compilers such as Visual Studio or Xcode are themselves in essence makefiles, albeit typically somewhat extended and verbose. One important task handled by *make*, in conjunction with the makefile, is tracking whether source files need to be rebuilt or not—i.e. by noting the creation date of object files and other dependencies. If a project comprises dozens (or hundreds) of source files, this speeds up development considerably by avoiding unnecessary recompilation.[2]

The supplied makefiles are written specifically for the directory structure as found on the DVD—the paths are *relative* to the examples directory, for example using the "`../`" notation to indicate the parent directory. Later on, you may feel confident enough to create your own project directory structure, and create or modify makefiles accordingly. You will use *make* in conjunction with your makefile to ensure that common files and libraries exist in only one place, but can be used in any project by setting their paths in the makefile. You will see that all the makefiles have much in common, with file and program names being the main differences. Eventually you will become confident enough to write your own makefile, by modifying one of these examples.

Despite the observations above, try to resist the temptation to copy all of the examples from the DVD together, or to build all the programs at once. A key element of learning to program lies in physically *writing* code—creating new files, maybe new directories, even modifying a makefile to support a new program. In some cases, the text presents a preliminary version of a program that is not provided as such on the DVD. It is especially important to follow the detailed step-by-step descriptions of the process, adding and changing code as you go. It is only through this direct hands-on experience that you will gain the confidence to work independently on your own projects.

2.1.3 Soundfile Formats—enum and typedef

We have already encountered the enum keyword for defining a list of symbols, associating them in order with ascending integer values. This offers a convenient alternative to a possibly long list of individual definitions using the preprocessor directive #define. It is also possible to apply the typedef keyword to the enum statement, so that, in principle, each symbol in the enum list is no longer the default int, but has the new custom type. This results in a more expressive form of self-documentation than if, for example, a plain int were to be used, or a list of #defines. The new type can then be employed both for function arguments and return values. For example, *portsf.h* defines an enum type for a number of soundfile channel properties:

```
typedef enum { STDWAVE, MC_STD, MC_MONO, MC_STEREO, MC_QUAD,
               MC_LCRS, MC_BFMT, MC_DOLBY_5_1, MC_WAVE_EX }
    psf_channelformat;
```

This defines the possible speaker formats supported by *portsf*. It includes support for the most common WAVEFORMATEXTENSIBLE speaker position definitions (meaningful only for the WAVE format). The symbol STD_WAVE serves as a "default" value, representing any "standard" soundfile with no special speaker positions—any soundfile format can be represented this way. Additionally, the symbol MC_WAVE_EX acts as a category for any other speaker-feed combinations not otherwise supported explicitly.

Similarly, *portsf.h* defines enum types for the available file formats and the all-important sample type:

```
typedef enum {
    PSF_FMT_UNKNOWN = 0,
    PSF_STDWAVE,
    PSF_WAVE_EX,
    PSF_AIFF,
    PSF_AIFC
} psf_format;
```

```
typedef enum {
    PSF_SAMP_UNKNOWN = 0,
    PSF_SAMP_8,    /* not yet supported! */
    PSF_SAMP_16,
    PSF_SAMP_24,
    PSF_SAMP_32,
    PSF_SAMP_IEEE_FLOAT
} psf_stype;
```

The significance of distinguishing PSF_STDWAVE and PSF_WAVE_EX in psf_format is that files in these formats have the same file extension, .wav, so it is not sufficient to deduce the file format solely from the file name. Similarly, it is not uncommon for a file with the extension .aif or .aiff to be in the newer AIFF-C format, despite the fact that Apple advocate a distinct extension—.afc or .aifc.

These custom types are then used in the main structure defined in *portsf.h* to contain the essential properties of a soundfile, again using typedef:

```
typedef struct psf_props
{
    long                srate;
    long                chans;
    psf_stype           samptype;
    psf_format          format;
    psf_channelformat   chformat;
} PSF_PROPS;
```

This custom type is used variously as argument and return value in a number of functions in *portsf*. When a soundfile is opened for reading, a PSF_PROPS structure is automatically filled in; when a file is written, the programmer must likewise ensure that all fields contain valid values. Taken together, the custom types and the *portsf* functions define an *application programming interface* (API). An API is intended to hide all the low-level implementation details (e.g. byte-swapping), while providing sufficient flexibility and power to support a range of projects. We will see how all the elements of the *portsf* API work together in the following sections, which begin with a demonstration program using the library to convert a soundfile from one format to another. For more details, see appendix C.

There is a limit to the amount of documentation a developer can supply with a library—some degree of prior knowledge has to be assumed. In the case of *portsf*, it is assumed the user is familiar with the use of soundfiles, and with the use of WAVE and AIFF soundfiles in particular. The structure PSF_PROPS introduced in the previous section collects this essential knowledge into one object; the fact that it contains only five elements demonstrates that one need not know very much about a soundfile in order to be able to use it. This knowledge can be summarized as follows:

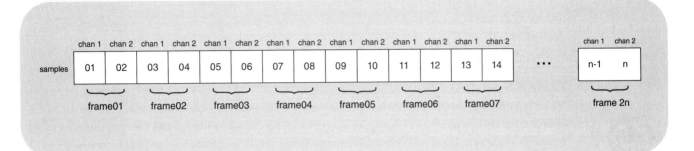

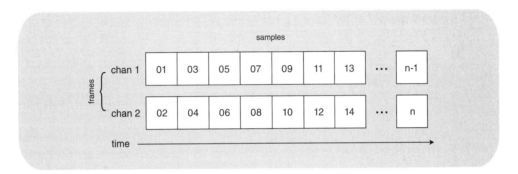

Figure 2.1
Interleaved sample frames.

▪ A soundfile contains audio data at a particular *sample rate* (number of samples per second). Most audio systems support a range of standard sample rates—22,050, 44,100, 48,000, 96,000 and even 192,000 hertz for DVD audio. We can store this parameter in

PSF_PROPS structure element: `srate`

▪ A soundfile can contain several channels of audio—one for mono, two for stereo, six for Dolby 5.1, and so on. In a multi-channel file, the sample rate defines the *frame rate*, where one frame contains one sample for each channel. As a soundfile represents audio that has either been recorded through, or is intended to be played back through, a soundcard, these samples are necessarily *interleaved*, see figure 1.12 in chapter 1. An alternative view of interleaved samples is shown in figure 2.1. This is represented by the following structure element:

PSF_PROPS element: `chans`

▪ A soundfile can contain audio samples in a range of data formats. By far the most common format is 16-bit, represented by the C `short` data type. Other formats in widespread use include 24-bit "packed" (stored in three bytes), and 32-bit floats, represented by the C `float` data type. Less common, but possible, is the 32-bit integer format, represented (at least in a 32-bit platform) by the C `long` (and, usually, `int`) data type. Other formats are possible: the older 8-bit sample type is still in use here and there, but is not currently supported in *portsf*, though provision has been made for its support at some future date. A 64-bit floating-point sample is possible in both the AIFF and WAVE formats, but this is currently not supported by *portsf*. A more exotic sample format is supported by the `WAVEFORMATEXTENSIBLE` file format. This distinguishes between the actual sample size and the "container size." A typical example of this would be a 24-bit "unpacked" format in which the three bytes of the sample are contained in a 32-bit word. Such formats (which will be very rare in a soundfile) are not currently supported in *portsf*, which records only the overall container size. Note the first symbol `PSF_SAMP_UNKNOWN`, which is used to indicate that a soundfile has some unrecognized sample type.

`PSF_PROPS` element: `samptype`

• A soundfile can be written in a number of file formats. One reason for this variety is the different storage formats on different platforms (see note 1). The WAVE and AIFF formats are the most familiar, but there are many others, only two of which are currently supported by portsf. The new `WAVEFORMATEXTENSIBLE` format from Microsoft has already been mentioned—this is intended to replace WAVE, and includes support for multi-channel audio with defined speaker positions, and support for high-resolution sample formats including the concept of a container size, as described above. It also supports user-defined custom formats (new versions of WAVE had to be registered with Microsoft; the new format enables anyone to define a new custom format without this requirement). You can find full technical documentation on this format at http://www.microsoft.com/hwdev/tech/audio/multichaud .asp. Additionally, the new AIFF-C format is supported. This was originally designed by Apple to support a range of compressed sample types, but a recent extension added support for a 32-bit floating-point format, which the original AIFF format could not support. The portsf library does not support compressed audio types in any of the file formats. Again, it is possible that a user may seek to open or create a file in an unsupported format; accordingly, this is provided for in the custom format entry `PSF_FMT_UNKNOWN`.
• A soundfile can contain audio channels associated with specific speaker positions. This property is relatively new, but has greatly increased in importance thanks to the popularity of surround sound. With a stereo signal, it is established largely by convention that channel 1 is front left, and channel 2 is front right. Beyond that, speaker positions were undefined inthe standard WAVE format, and it was primarily for this reason that the `WAVEFORMAT-EXTENSIBLE` format was introduced by Microsoft. Apple had, in the initial specification for the AIFF format, proposed standard speaker positions for several surround formats, but in so doing highlighted the difficulties in doing so. Two four-channel configurations were defined, for quad surround and LCRS Surround, but there was no means of indicating which of these was contained in a given soundfile—a four-channel AIFF file is therefore ambiguous, accord-

ing to its own specification. At the time of writing, the only soundfile formats unambigu-ously supporting defined speaker positions are WAVEFORMATEXTENSIBLE, and the new CAF file format introduced by Apple (not supported by *portsf*, but supported by *libsndfile*). The *portsf* library supports only the primary subset of many possible channel configurations, as defined for psf_chformat. One symbol in that list, MC_BFMT, requires further explanation. This refers to a custom version of WAVEFORMATEXTENSIBLE designed to hold an Ambisonic B-Format signal. This is an advanced form of surround encoding, representing the specially processed outputs of three coincident figure-eight microphones (oriented to the three spatial axes), which together can record a complete spherical "soundfield"—this includes informa-tion about the height of a sound, as well as its distance and position in the horizontal plane. This format therefore contrasts with the other channel formats in that the channels repre-sent not speaker feeds, but a compact encoding of a full three-dimensional soundfield, which has to be decoded before being passed to loudspeakers. It is possible to decode to speaker lay-outs containing a large number of speakers; a minimum of four speakers would be required to decode the signals for horizontal surround sound, and a minimum of eight speakers in a cube layout, to decode with height.

PSF_PROPS element: chformat

This it is currently only relevant when the file format is PSF_WAVE_EX; it is ignored for all other formats (STDWAVE is assumed).

Finally, one important property of all the file formats supported by *portsf* is that the file header (which stores the properties of the file such as sample rate, sample type and number of channels) can also contain further optional information contained in special "chunks"—collectively, the AIFF and WAVE formats store all information in distinct chunks, each of which has a unique name (both "WAVE" and "AIFF" are examples of chunk names). We will see in the next section how *portsf* includes support for one very useful optional chunk.

2.1.4   Initializing the *portsf* Library

Somewhat unusually for a soundfile library (and unlike any of the file i/o functions in the C standard library), *portsf* includes an initialization function, to be called before any other functions in the library are called:

```
int psf_init(void);
```

Currently this function does very little, but it is expected that future versions of the library will be more dependent on it. *Portsf* maintains an internal block of information on all active soundfiles, up to an internal fixed limit, currently set at 64. The function psf_init ensures that this block is in a clean state at startup. There is a corresponding function that should be called at the end of a program, as part of final "cleaning up":

```
int psf_finish(void);
```

This closes any soundfiles that have been left open and returns the library to the same clean state. In command-line programs, such things do not matter (as the operating system will close any open files anyway when the program terminates); but in GUI-based programs that can in effect restart multiple times (they are "re-entrant"), these functions will ensure that the library is always in a stable state.

Both functions return the value 0 to indicate success. Currently, `psf_init()` cannot in fact fail, so no harm is done in ignoring the return value. The function `psf_finish()` will return a non-zero value if there is an error closing a file. In future versions of the library, both these functions may increase in importance.

2.1.5 Basic Soundfile Handling in *portsf*—the `switch...case` Keywords

A soundfile API of any usefulness must support the basic tasks associated with all file handling—opening and creating files, reading and writing data, and closing them again. Error reporting is also essential—for example, in the case that a user tries to open a file that doesn't exist, or tries to write to a file that is not open, and also in the case of a system error such as a disk failure. The API may also offer other useful secondary facilities.

Opening a Soundfile for Reading

The function to open an existing soundfile is shown in *portsf.h* as

```
int psf_sndOpen(const char *path, PSF_PROPS *props, int rescale);
```

The comments in the header file indicate how this function is to be used:

```
/* open existing soundfile. Receive format info in props.
   Supports auto rescale from PEAK data, with floats files.
   Only RDONLY access supported.
   Return sf descriptor >= 0, or some PSF_E_ + on error.
*/
```

Though somewhat terse, these comments provide quite a lot of information:

(1) "`open existing soundfile`" tells the programmer that this function cannot be used to create a new file.

(2) "`only RDONLY access supported`" tells the programmer that you can read from the opened file but cannot write to it. "RDONLY" is standard C shorthand for "ReaD ONLY" (echoing the standard C file i/o API). Thus, *portsf* enforces "non-destructive" processing—you cannot modify an existing soundfile.

(3) "`Return sf descriptor >= 0`" tells the programmer that the int value returned from the function will be a value that identifies the file (for future use with other functions). Any value below zero will signify an error. The *portsf.h* header file defines a long list of possible error values (needless to say, as an `enum` list). Most programmers will just test the value against zero, and if negative, will simply tell the user "there was an error," but ideally the

specific error value can be used to give the user a more informative message, such as "that is not a soundfile."

The comments also describe the input arguments to the function. The first of these should be fairly obvious—the name of the file. The second is almost as obvious—a pointer to the `PSF_PROPS` structure described in subsection 2.1.3; the comments indicate that if the function succeeds, the structure will then be filled with information describing the file.

The third argument is, however, very strange-sounding, and is an example of a non-essential but sometimes useful facility. The comments refer to "PEAK data." This is a reference to an optional header chunk that a WAVE or AIFF file can contain, which records the value and position of the loudest sample, for each channel in the file. We encountered a prototype for this facility at the end of chapter 1 (see listing 1.9.4). In *portsf* this is encapsulated as an automatic facility. It is especially useful with floating-point soundfiles. While the "normal" range of a floating-point sample is ± 1.0, it is also possible to have numbers larger than that—"over-range samples." You would expect that playing such a soundfile would result in unpleasant clipping and distortion. However, if the file contains the PEAK chunk, the information about the largest sample can be used to rescale the audio data automatically, to bring it within the normal range. This facility is represented by the rescale argument to `psf_sndOpen`. If rescale is non-zero (one would usually just use the value 1), rescaling is applied, otherwise samples will be read unaltered. Of course, if the file does not contain a PEAK chunk, the rescale argument is simply ignored. This facility is provided primarily for use in soundfile playback applications, where over-range samples will necessarily be clipped. By reading the PEAK data from the header when the file is opened, *portsf* can automatically rescale the audio data so that such soundfiles can be rendered without clipping. In most other situations, we want to read in the data unchanged, so that the rescale argument to `psf_sndOpen` would be set to zero.

To open an existing soundfile, therefore, we need an instance of the `PSF_PROPS` structure, to receive format information about the file, and an `int` variable ("soundfile descriptor"), to receive the return value from `psf_sndOpen`. Given, for example, a 16-bit stereo WAVE file at 44,100 Hz, called *"sample.wav,"* we can open it as follows, and give the user some information about it:

```
PSF_PROPS props;
int sf;

sf = psf_sndOpen("sample.wav",&props,0);

if(sf < 0){
    printf("Error: unable to open soundfile\n"):
    return 1;
}
printf("Sample rate = %d\n", props.srate);
printf("number of channels = %d\n", props.chans);
```

However, the use of custom types in `PSF_PROPS` leads to a difficulty. The function `printf()` cannot know anything about this type—were we to try to display it using the method above, it would merely write whatever number `PSF_SAMP_16` happened to have been given by the compiler—not very informative to the user. Instead, we need to write code to test for each possible value, and print an appropriate message:

```
if(props.stype == PSF_SAMP_8)
    printf("sample type: 8bit\n");
else if(props.stype == PSF_SAMP_16)
    printf("sample type: 16bit\n");
. . .
```

We encountered this potentially long sequence of `if...else` tests in chapter 1. To handle such situations a little more elegantly, C provides the keywords `switch` and `case`, which together provide a flexible system for selecting among alternatives, where the variable being tested is of an integral type, such as `char`, `short` or `int` (recall that C treats all `enum` types as being equivalent to `int`). It is demonstrated in listing 2.1.2 in the form of a function

```
int check_sampletype(psf_stype type);
```

that will display the sample type of the file and will return a value indicating whether we can accept it or not. The function can be used to replace the code suggested above:

```
if(!check_sampletype(props.stype)){
    printf("file has unsupported sample type\n")1
    return 1;
}
```

Listing 2.1.2: Selecting Among Alternatives—the `switch. . .case` Keywords

```
1    int check_sampletype(psf_stype type)
2    {
3        int accept = 1;
4
5        printf("sample type: ");
6        switch(type){
7        case(PSF_SAMP_8):
8            printf("8 bit\n");
9            accept = 0;    /* No 8bit files! */
10           break;
11       case(PSF_SAMP_16):
12           printf("16 bit\n");
13           break;
14       case(PSF_SAMP_24):
15           printf("24 bit\n"):
```

```
16          break;
17      case(PSF_SAMP_32):
18          printf("32bit (integer)\n");
19          break;
20      case(PSF_SAMP_IEEE_FLOAT):
21          printf("32bit floating point\n"):
22          break;
23      default:
24          printf("unknown\n");
25          accept = 0;
26      }
27
28      return accept;
29  }
```

There are several things to note about the use of switch and case:

(1) The keyword switch takes a single argument of any integral type (enclosed in curved brackets), followed by a code block enclosed by braces (lines 1, 2, 29).

(2) The code block can contain one or more "selection statements," using either the case (e.g. line 7) or default (line 23) keywords. Only one default statement can be used, but any number of case statements can be used.

(3) The case keyword takes a single argument, signifying a specific value of the variable used as the argument to switch, followed by a colon, and then by any number of statements to be executed (e.g. lines 7–10). Execution then passes to the following selection statement, or reaches the end of the switch block. The default keyword (also followed by a colon) takes no argument—it applies to all values not matched by the provided case statements.

(4) To stop execution "falling through" from one selection statement to the next, the break keyword can be used to jump out of the switch block (e.g. line 10).

(5) Selection statements can be in any order. For example, the default statement can be placed first.

(6) As the code belonging to each selection statement is deemed to be just one level below the switch expression, the switch and case expressions are usually given the same indentation. The programmer is free to change this, however.

(7) The case keyword can only be used inside a switch statement block.

Opening a Soundfile for Writing

To create a new soundfile, we would expect a similarly named function, and in *portsf* this function is somewhat more elaborate than psf_sndOpen:

```
int psf_sndCreate(const char *path, const PSF_PROPS *props,
                  int clip_floats, int minheader, int mode);
```

(1) The first two arguments are the same as those for `psf_sndOpen`, except that the second is also declared as const, indicating that the `PSF_PROPS` data is now an input, and will not be modified. We will have to fill this structure with the required format data for the file, before passing it to `psf_sndCreate`.

(2) The argument `int clip_floats` is used to set the way in which floating-point data is written to the file. As was noted above, the unique aspect of floating-point soundfiles is that the samples can contain over-range values. Depending on the application, you may or many not want these to be clipped to the normal maxima, −1.0 and +1.0. Use of this facility depends on whether you have requested that the soundfile include the PEAK chunk, which records the maximum values in the file. As not all applications will even know about the PEAK chunk (and will simply ignore it when reading), the safe approach is to set this argument to 1; but for experimental purposes you may want, for example, to offer the user the choice. Needless to say, this parameter is ignored for all other sample formats.

(3) `int minheader`: it is an unfortunate fact of life that many applications fail to deal with WAVE formats that contain optional chunks before the audio data—many older UNIX-originated programs suffer from this. By setting `minheader` to 1, the soundfile is created with a "minimum header" containing just the required format and data chunks—this therefore means that no PEAK data will be written to the file. Ideally, of course, `minheader` should be set to 0 always, and will be in all the examples presented here.

(4) `int mode`: this final argument is provided to offer some control over read-write access to the file. The possible modes are defined by the custom enum type `psf_create_mode` defined in *portsf.h*:

```
/* second two are speculative at present! */
typedef enum {PSF_CREATE_RDWR, PSF_CREATE_TEMPORARY,
              PSF_CREATE_WRONLY } psf_create_mode;
```

The comment indicates that in fact only the first option is supported, to create a 'normal' file with public read/write access. The other options seek to create 'private' soundfiles, in one form or another, and may be implemented in future versions of *portsf*.

To create a soundfile, we need, as for `psf_sndOpen()`, to define a `PSF_PROPS` variable, with the essential difference that this time we have to fill in the format properties explicitly —if we have not already obtained format information from another file:

```
int ofd;
PSF_PROPS props;

/* define a hi-res 5.1 surround WAVE-EX file, with PEAK chunk
support */
props.srate = 96000;
props.chans = 6;
props.samptype = PSF_SAMP_24;
props.format = PSF_WAVE_EX;
props.chformat = MC_DOLBY_5_1;
```

```
ofd = psf_sndCreate("soundtrack.wav",&props,1,0, PSF_CREATE_RDWR);
if(ofd < 0){
    printf("Error: unable to create output file\n");
    return 1;
}
```

Setting a File Format from the Name

A common requirement among users who have to move soundfiles between platforms (e.g. from a Macintosh to a PC) is to convert from one format to another—for example, from WAVE to AIFF. But how does the user indicate this? In command-line applications (and, arguably, in general), the simplest and best method is for the user to specify the format by using a filename with the appropriate file extension; .wav, .aiff, .aifc, etc. With this approach, there is no danger of a user specifying, for example, the WAVE format but giving a filename with the .aiff extension.[3] The *portsf* API supports this system by means of a function that returns the file format from the given filename:

```
psf_format format;
format = psf_getFormatExt("soundtrack.wav");
```

This returns a value of type `psf_format`, which can therefore be assigned directly to the appropriate element of the `PSF_PROPS` structure:

```
props.format = format;
```

Note that this function will return the value `PSF_FMT_UNKNOWN` if an unsupported file extension (or no extension at all) is used.[4]

Closing Soundfiles (and Recording Peak Sample Values with the PEAK Chunk)

Having opened a soundfile, we will have to close it again at some point. We would expect to find a function to do this in the library; one that takes as an argument the descriptor obtained from `psf_sndOpen`. Indeed, on examining *portsf.h* we find just such a function:

```
int psf_sndClose(int sfd);
```

The return value is used to indicate any error arising from closing the file. Occasionally, it is important to tell the user that the function has failed, and why, as it may indicate a problem with the system. In a command-line program, this is generally not considered so important, especially right at the end of a program, so the return value is ignored. One interesting aspect of this function is indicated by the following comment:

```
/* . . . Updates PEAK data if used. */
```

As sample frames are written to disk, the maximum value per channel is automatically tracked, so that when the file is closed, the PEAK data can be written to the header. For this to happen, of course, `minheader` in `psf_sndCreate` must be set to 0, as shown above. To support access to this information, *portsf.h* includes a very simple structure (defined again as a custom type using `typedef`) to hold the peak data for one channel. The structure contains the sample value itself, and the position (in sample frames) in the file of the first such sample:

```
typedef struct psf_chpeak {
    float val;
    unsigned long pos;
} PSF_CHPEAK;
```

The library necessarily includes a function to read the current PEAK data from the file:

```
long psf_sndReadPeaks(int sfd, PSF_CHPEAK peakdata[], long *peaktime);
```

This function takes a soundfile descriptor (as returned from `psf_sndCreate`), and a pointer to an array of `PSF_CHPEAK` structures. It is the responsibility of the user to ensure that the array is at least large enough to contain the data for each channel in the file (e.g. as given in `props.chans`):

```
PSF_CHPEAK peaks[6];
long peaks_valid, peaktime;
peaks_valid = psf_sndReadPeaks(ofd, peaks, &peaktime);
```

In most cases, the number of channels in a file will have been chosen by the user, so that you will have to allocate space for the peaks array using `malloc`:

```
PSF_CHPEAK* peaks;
peaks = (PSF_CHPEAK*) malloc(props.chans * sizeof(PSF_CHPEAK));
```

The `peaktime` value is rarely needed and can generally be ignored. It corresponds to a field in the PEAK chunk itself, which indicates the time when the PEAK data was written to the file. This time can be checked (a task that is often system dependent, and which is beyond the scope of the present chapter), and if it is clearly different from the modification time of the file as a whole (i.e. substantially older), it indicates that an attempt to modify the audio data in place may have been made (i.e. using "destructive editing"), and therefore that the PEAK data may be unreliable. If you do not need the peaktime information, it is safe to supply NULL as the third argument to `psf_sndReadPeaks`:

```
peaks_valid = psf_sndReadPeaks(ofd, peaks, NULL);
```

2.1.6 Reading and Writing—The Sample Frame

The working unit in *portsf* is the multi-channel sample frame. This means that it is not possible, for example, to read just the first (left-channel) sample of a stereo file. This would in all but the most abnormal circumstances be an error, and *portsf* prevents the user from making such errors.

More importantly, the library automatically performs all the low-level calculations and conversions required to read sample frames (of any supported type) from a soundfile into the user's working sample buffer. For this, the recommended sample format is the 32-bit float, into which 24-bit samples can be converted without loss of precision:

```
long psf_sndReadFloatFrames(int sfd, float *buf, DWORD nFrames);
long psf_sndWriteFloatFrames(int sfd, const float *buf, DWORD nFrames);
```

It is the user's responsibility to supply a buffer of at least nFrames * props.chans * sizeof(float) bytes.

The functions both return the value −1 for an error. The function psf_sndWriteFloat-Frames will not return a positive value less than nFrames. In the case of psf_sndRead-FloatFrames, a return value less than nFrames will indicate that the end of the file has been reached. For the same reason, a return value of 0 does not signify an error. Programs should expect this and always use the return value in future calculations. Note that the nFrames argument is defined as a custom DWORD type. This name is borrowed from Windows usage, and signifies (on a 32-bit platform) an unsigned long. Clearly, a negative value for nFrames has no meaning—it is best to prevent such usage altogether.

We can now implement a simple copy procedure with very few lines of code:

```
float* frame = (float*) malloc(props.chans * sizeof(float));
/* copy file one (multi-channel) frame at a time */
framesread = psf_sndReadFloatFrames(ifd,frame,1);
while (framesread == 1){
/* <---- do any processing here! ------> */
    psf_sndWriteFloatFrames(ofd,frame,1);
    framesread = psf_sndReadFloatFrames(ifd,frame,1);
}
```

This will copy a soundfile having any number of channels, and in any of the supported sample formats, while also tracking the PEAK value and position for each channel. As the comment indicates, in a program that performs any processing, this compact loop probably will expand to accommodate code to apply filtering or other signal processing. To change the file and sample format from that of the input file, all that is required is to modify the PSF_PROPS structure as desired; *portsf* will take care of all the details.

2.1.7 Streamlining Error Handling—The goto Keyword

The code shown above excludes necessary checks for read and write errors, which a practical program must always contain. Even a basic soundfile copy program requests at least three resources from the system—two files and some memory via a call to malloc. Any or all of these requests can fail, and to be fully responsible we must release all acquired resources when we encounter such an error before quitting the program. We have already seen some examples of this in previous programs, where a call to `fclose` or to `free` may appear several times, in code that detects different errors.

While being responsible, programmers also want to be economical, and such duplicated code seems wasteful. It can also become somewhat complicated—depending on the error, different combinations of resources need to be released. Ideally, we want to place all error recovery at one point (e.g. at the end of the program), and simply jump to that point on detection of an error, at which point we release all resources still active. The keyword `goto` does just this, jumping unconditionally to a statement marked by a label:

```
if(sndWriteFloatFrames(ofd,frame,1) != 1)
    goto cleanup;

/* lots of code. . .. */
cleanup:
if(frame)
    free(frame);
```

The label is also referred to as a "jump target," and takes the form of a unique name followed by a colon. It can be placed anywhere, but by convention, and not least to promote readability, it is always placed at the start of a line.

The one important restriction with `goto` is that the jump target must be in the same function as the `goto` itself—typically this will be the `main` function. Thus you cannot jump out of one function into another—which is probably just as well.[5]

2.1.8   Using `portsf` for Soundfile Conversion with PEAK Support

The conversion program shown in listing 2.1.3 requires the *portsf* library, either by compiling with all the *portsf* source files or by accessing it as a pre-built library. The latter approach is implemented in the examples folder on the DVD. This build procedure is outlined below, which should be read in conjunction with the *02BOOKexamples-guide.doc* programmer's guide found in the chapter 2 "examples" folder on the DVD.

Listing 2.1.3 can be regarded as a simple template or skeleton program for any application that applies a process to a sound, non-destructively. As was noted in the comments (line 92), such processing would be placed inside the main loop copying sample frames. It is worth taking careful note not only of the details of the C language idioms employed, but also of the overall structure. We are already moving to the situation where we are quite comfortable with the C language itself, and pay more and more attention to the strategic and design aspects of programming.

As we have come to expect, the bulk of the code deals with error checking, and messages to the user—`goto` is used to direct all error situations to the cleanup code at the end of the file (lines 113–124). The secret to this approach is to ensure that all relevant variables (soundfile descriptors, pointers to allocated memory) are initialized to default states (lines 13–17); the cleanup code can then easily discover which resources are active and need to be released. Note that not all errors result in a call to goto: this is only used once a resource such as the first open file has been acquired (line 41). One small detail is the variable error that is incremented when an error is detected. This is only used to ensure that the main function returns the value 0 for success, or 1 for an error.

The code demonstrates a useful aspect of the printf function—it is possible to write several strings in sequence (e.g. lines 22–26), inside one printf call. Note that the strings are not separated by commas or other characters, but only by (optional) white space.

In line 57, the function psf_sndCreate is called with the clip_floats argument set to zero. Coupled with the fact that psf_sndOpen is called with rescale also set to zero, any floating-point input file will be copied to the *outfile* with any over-range samples copied unaltered. It is of course simple to change this behavior (see exercises, below). The program reports the PEAK values at the end (lines 103–111).[6]

Listing 2.1.3: sf2float.c

```
1    /* sf2float.c : convert soundfile to floats */
2    #include <stdio.h>
3    #include <stdlib.h>
4    #include <portsf.h>
5
6    enum {ARG_PROGNAME, ARG_INFILE, ARG_OUTFILE,ARG_NARGS};
7
8    int main(int argc, char* argv[])
9    {
10       PSF_PROPS props;
11       long framesread, totalread;
12       /* init all resource vars to default states */
13       int ifd = -1,ofd = -1;
14       int error = 0;
15       psf_format outformat = PSF_FMT_UNKNOWN;
16       PSF_CHPEAK* peaks = NULL;
17       float* frame = NULL;
18
19
20       printf("SF2FLOAT: convert soundfile to floats format\n");
21
22       if(argc < ARG_NARGS) {
23           printf("insufficient arguments.\n"
24                     "usage:\n\tsf2float infile outfile\n");
25           return 1;
```

```
26      }
27      /* be good, and startup portsf */
28      if(psf_init()){
29          printf("unable to start portsf\n");
30          return 1;
31      }
32
33      ifd = psf_sndOpen(argv[ARG_INFILE],&props,0);
34      if(ifd < 0){
35          printf("Error: unable to open infile %s\n",
36              argv[ARG_INFILE]);
37          return 1;
38      }
39      /* we now have a resource, so we use goto hereafter
40      on hitting any error */
41      /* tell user if source file is already floats */
42      if(props.samptype == PSF_SAMP_IEEE_FLOAT){
43          printf("Info: infile is already in floats format.\n");
44      }
45      props.samptype = PSF_SAMP_IEEE_FLOAT;
46      /* check outfile extension is one we know about */
47      outformat = psf_getFormatExt(argv[ARG_OUTFILE]);
48      if(outformat == PSF_FMT_UNKNOWN){
49          printf("outfile name %s has unknown format.\n"
50              "Use any of .wav, .aiff, .aif, .afc,.aifc\n",
51                  argv[ARG_OUTFILE]);
52          error++;
53          goto exit;
54      }
55      props.format = outformat;
56
57      ofd = psf_sndCreate(argv[2],&props,0,0,PSF_CREATE_RDWR);
58      if(ofd < 0){
59          printf("Error: unable to create outfile %s\n",
60              argv[ARG_OUTFILE]);
61          error++;
62          goto exit;
63      }
64
65      /* allocate space for one sample frame */
66      frame = (float*) malloc(props.chans * sizeof(float));
67      if(frame==NULL){
68          puts("No memory!\n");
```

```
69          error++;
70          goto exit;
71      }
72      /* and allocate space for PEAK info */
73      peaks = (PSF_CHPEAK*) malloc(props.chans *
74          sizeof(PSF_CHPEAK));
75      if(peaks == NULL){
76          puts("No memory!\n");
77          error++;
78          goto exit;
79      }
80      printf("copying....\n");
81
82      /* single-frame loop to do copy, report any errors */
83      framesread = psf_sndReadFloatFrames(ifd,frame,1);
84      totalread = 0; /* running count of sample frames */
85      while (framesread == 1){
86          totalread++;
87          if(psf_sndWriteFloatFrames(ofd,frame,1) != 1){
88              printf("Error writing to outfile\n");
89              error++;
90              break;
91          }
92          /* <---- do any processing here! ------> */
93          framesread = psf_sndReadFloatFrames(ifd,frame,1);
94      }
95      if(framesread < 0) {
96          printf("Error reading infile. Outfile is incomplete.\n");
97          error++;
98      }
99      else
100     printf("Done. %d sample frames copied to %s\n",
101             totalread,argv[ARG_OUTFILE]);
102     /* report PEAK values to user */
103     if(psf_sndReadPeaks(ofd,peaks,NULL) > 0){
104         long i;
105         double peaktime;
106         printf("PEAK information:\n");
107         for(i=0;i < props.chans;i++){
108             peaktime = (double) peaks[i].pos / props.srate;
109             printf("CH %d:\t%.4f at %.4f secs\n",
110                     i+1, peaks[i].val, peaktime);
111         }
```

```
112     }
113     /* do all cleanup */
114     exit:
115     if(ifd >= 0)
116         psf_sndClose(ifd);
117     if(ofd >= 0)
118         psf_sndClose(ofd);
119     if(frame)
120         free(frame);
121     if(peaks)
122         free(peaks);
123     psf_finish();
124     return error;
125 }
```

2.1.9 Building Programs with *portsf*

There are two approaches readers can take in building *sf2float* and later programs using *portsf*. Both are command-line based. The first, very simple approach, is to copy the chapter 2 examples directory (complete with its sub-directories) from the DVD to any convenient location, cd to the chapter 2 examples directory and run make on the selected program:

```
$ make sf2float
```

This will first build *portsf* (if not already built) and install the library file *libportsf.a* in the directory *lib*. It will then build *sf2flloat*. This is covered in more detail in the accompanying guide document. Note that, as required for all such development, you will have at least three basic directories—*include* for your header files, *lib* for your libraries, and one or more working directories for your projects. As described above, relative paths are used—so long as the whole examples directory is moved as a unit, the programs will build as described.

The alternative approach is more demanding, but offers a much deeper insight into the build process, including a first step at editing a makefile (see exercise 2.1.7). The goal is to create a standard working environment supporting all your programming projects, whether based on *portsf* or otherwise.[7]

Test the program first by running it without arguments, to confirm that the usage message is displayed:

```
./sf2float
```

Then test using any suitable soundfile. This would primarily be a 16-bit WAVE or AIFF file. Use Audacity to confirm that the new file is correct. However it is as important to test the error handling, e.g. by supplying a soundfile in an unsupported format such as a raw binary file, or using an *outfile* name with an unsupported extension.

2.1.10   Exercises

Many of these exercises invite you to discover things on your own. If you find that you are stuck, consider the possibility that other programs presented in this book may well demonstrate solutions to these exercises.

Exercise 2.1.1
In the program *sf2float*, the main loop to copy samples does so one frame at a time. This is not very efficient. Modify the code to use a larger multi-frame buffer, so that the loop cycles per block rather than per frame. Remember to pay attention to the return value from `psf_sndReadFloatFrames`.

Exercise 2.1.2
The program *sf2float* does not report the progress of the copy to the screen. For a long file, the program may appear to have frozen. Remedy this by adding a variable to count the number of samples copied, and display a progress message at some regular interval. Hint: Use the format specifier "\r" (carriage return) within `printf` to overwrite the same line with the updating message string.

Exercise 2.1.3
Study the description of the function `psf_sndSize` in *portsf.h*. Modify the program to copy up to some limit (which must be less than or equal to the length of the file) defined by the user on the command line.

Exercise 2.1.4

(a) Based on the examples shown in this section, add a function to give a complete display of the infile properties at the start of the program. Include the size of the file in this information. Use the `switch...case` keywords to print information on the file format and sample type.
(b) Adapt this into a new program *sfprop* that just reports the format information of a soundfile. Report the PEAK information if present. You may find this useful as a utility to verify output soundfiles are as intended.

Exercise 2.1.5
Sound level is often better expressed in decibels (dB), than as simple amplitude. Full-scale (1.0) is equivalent to 0 dB, and half-amplitude (0.5) is equal to approximately −6 dB. The calculation to convert a normalized amplitude (within ± 1.0) to dB is

```
loudness (dB) = 20.0 * log10(amp);
```

Refer to your compiler documentation regarding the math library function (defined in `<math.h>`):

```
double log10(double x) ;
```

Use this function to modify the display of the PEAK data at the end of *sf2float.c* (lines 106 and 107) to display the PEAK value for each channel in dB, as well as raw amplitude. If you have built *sfprop* (Ex 4(b) above), modify that in the same way.

Exercise 2.1.6 (difficult)

Study the description of the function `psf_sndSeek` in *portsf.h*. Modify *sf2float* to copy the infile N times (N specified by the user), without a break, to the *outfile*, i.e. to perform simple looping. Use `psf_sndSeek` to 'rewind' the infile back to the beginning each time. (Hint: Study the compiler documentation for the C library function `fseek`. This is used internally by `psf_sndSeek`.)

Exercise 2.1.7

This exercise involves a makefile. In the "example" directories on the DVD for each chapter, the *portsf* directory is replicated for each chapter. Move the whole *portsf* library to a separate location on your system, and modify the makefile to put *libportsf.a* in a personal *lib* directory that you create. Do the same for the *include* directory. This is to have just one copy of both on your system. Then modify the supplied *makefiles* to use the new locations, and confirm that all the programs build without errors.

2.2   Processing Audio

The key to this and the following sections is line 92 of *sf2float.c*:

```
/* <---- do any processing here! ------> */
```

The focus of most of the work in this chapter will be on inventing code to replace this comment. The simplest possible replacement is proposed in this section. There may be a temptation to go directly to the "examples" directory and build the program as supplied. You already know how to build programs; the core of the process is to practice writing and modifying code. In the next section no final program listing is given; instead, full details are given for how to modify *sf2float.c*. Dive in.

2.2.1   The First Audio Process: Changing Level

The program shown in listing 2.1.3 was described as a template that can be used as the basis for a number of simple audio utilities working on a soundfile. There are however a few lines that will need to be removed, to make this a truly neutral template program: delete lines 39–

45, which we used to set the output file format to floats. With audio processing tools, users will generally expect the output file to have the same format as the input file.

We will begin with one of the simplest yet most fundamental procedures we need to perform on a sound: changing level (amplitude), as done by the ubiquitous volume control. Again you have the choice either to build a new project from scratch, or use the files supplied on the DVD. Writing and building from scratch is much more likely to give you the feeling of being a real C programmer, however impatient you may be to build and test the program. The new program is called *sfgain*. We can describe the basic structure of this program very simply as a series of stages (which we will be able to refer to and expand in the course of this chapter):

Stage 1: Define variables.
Stage 2: Obtain and validate arguments from user.
Stage 3: Allocate memory, open *infile* and *outfile*.
Stage 4: Perform main processing loop.
Stage 5: Report to the user.
Stage 6: Close files, free memory.

You might find it useful to add some comments to *sfgain.c* indicating each of these stages. As you develop new programs, you will typically be moving upward and downward between these stages as you add functionality, by creating a function or process for stage 4, which requires variables defined in stage 1, some memory allocated in stage 3, a revised command line, and maybe some extra files (stage 3). Any new resources will need to be returned to the system (stage 6). And at any point, you may need to add or modify messages to the user (e.g. stage 5). Infiltrating all these stages is the constant attention to error detection and recovery.

Intuition would suggest that we should be able to change the amplitude of a soundfile just by multiplying each sample value by the required scale factor—say by 0.5 to reduce amplitude by a half, or by 2.0 to double the amplitude. As it happens, intuition is completely correct here.

All we need is a variable to hold a loop counter, and another to hold the amplitude factor from the user (stage 1):

```
int i;
float ampfac;
```

and a simple loop to step through each channel of the frame, placed in the frame loop as indicated by the comment (stage 4, lines 81–90 of listing 2.1.3):

```
while (framesread == 1){
    totalread++;
    for(i=0; i < props.chans; i++ )
        frame[i] *= ampfac;
```

```
    if(psf_sndWriteFloatFrames(ofd, frame, 1) != 1){
        printf("Error writing to outfile\n");
        error++;
        break;
    }
    framesread = psf_sndReadFloatFrames(ifd,frame,1);
}
```

To make a complete program, all that remains to do is to ensure that we have an appropriate title message (line 18)

```
printf("SFGAIN: change level of soundfile\n");
```

update the usage message to indicate the new argument (stage 2, lines 20–25)

```
if(argc < 4){
    printf("insufficient arguments.\n"
            "usage:\n\t"
            "sfgain infile outfile ampfac\n"
            "\twhere ampfac must be > 0\n");
        return 1;
}
```

and add the code to pick up and check the value:

```
ampfac = (float) atof(argv[3]);
if(ampfac <= 0.0){
    printf("Error: ampfac must be positive.\n");
    return 1;
}
```

You are now ready to build and test the program.

2.2.2 Amplitude vs. Loudness—the Decibel

Exercise 2.1.5 introduced the calculation for converting an amplitude value into decibels (dB):

$$\text{loudness}_{dB} = 20 \times \log_{10} amp \tag{1}$$

where *amp* is in the range 0 to 1.0. We also need the complementary formula for converting dB to amplitude:

$$amp = 10^{\text{loudness}_{db}/20}. \tag{2}$$

There is a very simple reason why the decibel is so important to audio engineers (and indeed to anyone working with audio): the decibel scale (being logarithmic in nature, as the

Table 2.1
Amplitude and dB scales.

Floating-point PCM amplitude	16-bit PCM amplitude	dB
1.0	32,768	0
0.75	24,576	−2.4987
0.5	16,384	−6.0206
0.25	8,192	−12.0412
0.1	3,277	−20.0
0.05	1,638	−26.0206
0.01	328	−40.0
0.001	33	−60.0

formula shows) reflects how the human ear perceives changes in sound level much more closely than linear amplitudes. However, a value in decibels does not necessarily correspond to a specific amplitude value. An amplitude value (e.g. the value of a single audio sample) corresponds to a voltage in an analog system, and thus in a sense represents an "absolute" value—for example, 0.25 volts. A decibel value is, strictly speaking, a *ratio*—a comparison between two values. It can tell us that the difference between 0.25 and 1, or between 8,192 and 32,768, is the same—in this case, a difference of about 12 dB. One would say "0.25 is 12 dB below 1.0," and equally that "8,192 is 12 dB below 32,768." Thus the decibel enables us to refer to level changes independently of the actual range used. However, to use the decibel to refer directly to levels, we have to have an agreed "reference level" to compare it with, just as we have to relate the sample value to maximum to appreciate the level it represents.

In the case of a digital waveform, the reference level is digital peak—e.g. 1.0 in the case of floating-point samples, or 32,768 in the case of 16-bit samples.[8] For a combination of historical and industrial reasons, this reference level is defined in decibels as 0, so that all levels below it are expressed as negative numbers. Table 2.1 illustrates the relationship between sample values and dB values, for floats and 16-bit sample types, using 0 dB to signify digital peak. Thus, a reduction by 0.5, which intuitively we might think of as a "half as loud," is *perceived* as a much smaller reduction—perhaps as little as one "notch" of a volume control. A typical listener who sets the volume control to make a sound "half as loud" may be reducing the level by as much as 40 dB.

We can now understand why it is said that the theoretical maximum "dynamic range" (difference between loudest and quietest sounds) is stated as 96 dB for a 16-bit system. Each bit (representing a factor of 2) represents a difference of approximately 6 dB.[9] More to the point, the sorts of level changes that the listener will perceive correspond to much larger raw amplitude changes than we might expect. Reducing amplitude by a factor of 0.25 sounds like a lot, but it is only a drop of 12 dB, and a sound at that level is still pretty loud.

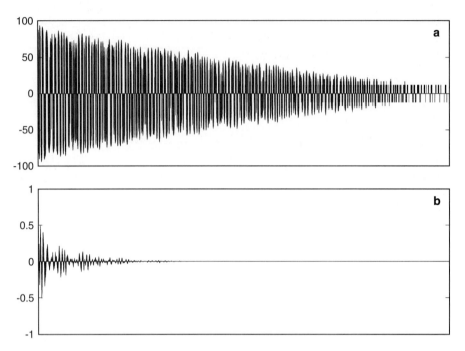

Figure 2.2
Reverb decay on (a) dB and (b) amplitude vertical scales.

Thus it can be much more meaningful to the user to be able to express both level differences, and absolute levels, in dB. Apart from anything else, this means that simple numbers such as −6, −12, and −18 can be used, rather than obscure decimal amplitudes with lots of leading zeroes.

A vivid example of the difference between the linear amplitude scale and the logarithmic decibel scale is the envelope shape of a reverberant decay. As we saw at the end of chapter 1, viewed on a waveform display using the usual amplitude scale, the decay (such as one can see of it) has the characteristic exponential curve (figure 2.2b). Viewed on a logarithmic (loudness) scale, the envelope becomes a straight line (figure 2.2a). You will also have noticed that in the linear display, much of the signal is not even visible, though the loudest sample is only some 3.5 dB below peak. As a general rule of thumb, in the typical waveform display on a digital audio workstation (DAW), a signal more than 30 dB below peak will be hidden by the zero line.

2.2.3 Extending *sfgain*—Normalization

Sometimes the requirement is not to change level *by* a certain amount, but to change it *to* a certain level. A common practice in audio production is to "normalize" a sound, or a whole track, to a standard level, the argument being that it is important to make as much use of the available dynamic range as possible—especially in a 16-bit medium such as a CD. It is, however, generally a bad idea to normalize a soundfile right up to digital peak—most real signals will in fact *clip* at the DAC, quite badly. Even in a 16-bit system, where every bit is felt to be precious, a little headroom is advisable, say about 3 dB. With the increasing use of 24-bit audio, this headroom can afford to be much larger—it is not unusual for the normalization point (the point that may be marked as "0 dB" on a VU meter) to be as much as 24 dB below digital peak. Thus, a program that will normalize a soundfile to a specified dB level will be very useful. With only a little work, the program *sfgain* can itself be used as a template for a normalization tool. We will call this new program *sfnorm*, and the new source file *sfnorm.c*.

We already have the procedure that changes level. The two extra tasks are to obtain the required output level value from a user parameter expressed in decibels, and to obtain the maximum amplitude of the input file, from which we can then calculate the required scale factor. If we are lucky, the input file will already have the PEAK information in the header, but as this header chunk is not yet universally adopted, we must be prepared to scan the *infile* to find the value the hard way. Thus, in this stage of the program, we will have to use some conditional code using `if...else`.

To create our new normalization program, we have to augment the basic program structure shown in section 2.1 as follows:

Stage 1: Set up variables.
Stage 2: Obtain and validate arguments from user.
Stage 3: Allocate memory, open the *infile*.
Stage 4a: Read PEAK amplitude of the *infile*; if not found,
Stage 4b: Scan the whole *infile* to obtain peak value; rewind file ready for processing stage.
Stage 4c: If peak > 0, open *outfile*; otherwise, quit.
Stage 5: Perform main processing loop.
Stage 6: Report to the user.
Stage 7: Close files, free memory.

Note that stage 4c deals with the possibility that the infile may be silent (`peakval = 0`). By deferring the opening of the *outfile*, not only can we avoid a possible division-by-zero error; we can also avoid leaving a spurious output file on the user's system. The bulk of our attention will be on stage 4, from which we will obtain the amplitude scale factor used in stage 5, which will remain virtually unchanged from before.

We need a few extra variables to hold the decibel value, the peak amplitude of the infile, and the calculated scale factor (stage 1):

```
double dbval, inpeak = 0.0;
float ampfac, scalefac;
```

The command line is essentially unchanged, except that we must tell the user that the third argument must be a dB value not above zero (stage 2):

```
if(argc < 4){
   printf("insufficient arguments.\n"
           "usage:\n\t"
           "sfnorm infile outfile dBval\n"
           "\twhere dBval <= 0.0\n");
   return 1;
}
```

We can then read and validate the dbval from the user:

```
dbval = (atof(argv[3]));
if(dbval > 0.0){
   printf("Error: dBval cannot be positive.\n");
   return 1;
}
ampfac = (float) pow(10.0,dbval/20.0);
```

Stage 3: So far, we have no reason to change any of the code to open soundfiles, and allocate memory.

Stage 4: Notice where this stage is so far in the program, just before the main processing loop of stage 5. It requires that all memory is allocated, and that at least the input file has been opened. In fact, because of the test in stage 4c, we need to place this stage 4 code before the code that opens the *outfile*, so that if the input file proves to be silent, we can avoid creating an output file we can't use.

While developing a program such as this, we recall that any code of general usefulness might be most conveniently written as a function, for possible incorporation into a library. In this case, the significant added element of this program is step 3b—scanning a soundfile to find the maximum sample value. This could even prove useful as a program by itself. In fact, you have already seen an example of this procedure, applied to a buffer of data (chapter 1, listing 1.6.3).

There is one essential detail to add to this basic buffer-scanning loop. Audio samples are both positive and negative, and we want the "absolute value" of the largest sample. If, for example, the maximum positive sample in the file is 0.5, but the maximum negative sample is −0.7, the maximum amplitude value we need is 0.7.

The C math library (<math.h>) offers two functions for finding the absolute value of a sample, covering integer and floating-point types:

```
int abs(int val);
double fabs(double val);
```

As we are using buffers of floats, we will need to use fabs. We can then modify the code of listing 1.6.3 to create a function that returns the maximum absolute value of a sample buffer:

```
double maxsamp(float* buf, unsigned long blocksize)
{
    double absval, peak = 0.0;
    unsigned long i;

    for(i=0; i < blocksize; i++) {
        absval = fabs(buf[i]);
        if(absval > peak)
            peak = absval;
    }
    return peak;
}
```

This function receives a buffer of samples, together with a "blocksize" value that gives the full size of the buffer. Thus this function is completely general—it can be used to find the absolute maximum value of any buffer of samples. You can place this function anywhere in *sfnorm.c*, so long as it is outside `main`. Some programmers prefer to place such functions after `main`, others before. Either way, you will have to add the declaration of the function:

```
double maxsamp(float* buf, unsigned long blocksize);
```

below the list of `#included` files—which must now also `#include <math.h>`.

To scan the infile, we can employ the same loop used to process the outfile, removing the calls to `psf_sndWriteFloatFrames`, changing `ofd` to `ifd`, and inserting our required processing code, which checks the return value from `maxsamp` against our running value of `inpeak` (stage 4b):

```
framesread = psf_sndReadFloatFrames(ifd,frame,1);

while (framesread == 1){
    double thispeak;
    blocksize = props.chans;
    thispeak = maxsamp(frame,blocksize);
    if(thispeak > inpeak)
        inpeak = thispeak;
    framesread = psf_sndReadFloatFrames(ifd,frame,1);
}
```

However, as was suggested in exercise 1 of the last section, it is inefficient to loop over a single sample or frame. By way of a solution to that exercise, you can `#define` a buffer size in frames, near the top of the file:

```
#define NFRAMES (1024)
```

You can then add a variable `nframes` that is initialized as

```
unsigned long nframes = NFRAMES;
```

and modify the code above accordingly. Using this, you can change the size of the buffer simply by changing the defined value. As warned by that exercise, we can no longer compare `framesread` against the value 1, but must simply check that it is positive—the final block read from the file may be smaller than `NFRAMES`. Also, note our custom function `maxsamp` expects the plain size of the buffer in samples. This is fine, as in this program we are not concerned about which channel contains the maximum sample, so we can simply multiply `framesread` by the number of channels:

```
framesread = psf_sndReadFloatFrames(ifd,frame,nframes);

while (framesread > 0){
    double thispeak;
    blocksize = framesread * props.chans;
    . . .

    framesread = psf_sndReadFloatFrames(ifd,frame,nframes);
}
```

For this to work, we must also modify the preceding memory allocation to `frame` by specifying the correct size:

```
frame = (float*) malloc(NFRAMES * props.chans * sizeof(float));
```

We can then modify the final processing loop in exactly the same way so that that also benefits from the optimization.

We are not quite done with stage 4: as indicated by the conditional test in stage 4a, we don't want to do all this work if the *infile* contains PEAK data already. We already have code to do this, used at the end of the program to report the final peak values of the *outfile*. We can copy this code almost verbatim for stage 4a, simply by changing `ofd` to `ifd`, and removing the messages we don't need. The PEAK data gives the absolute maximum sample value for each channel, and we simply want the largest of these (stage 4a):

```
/* get peak info: scan file if required */
/* inpeak has been initialized to 0 */
if(psf_sndReadPeaks(ifd,peaks,NULL) > 0){

    long i;
    for(i=0; i < props.chans; i++){
        if(peaks[i].val > inpeak)
            inpeak = peaks[i].val;
    }
}
else {
    /* scan the file, and rewind */
}
```

As the comment indicates, after scanning the file, we must rewind the file (seek back to the beginning), so that it can be read again in the main processing loop. *Portsf* supplies the function `psf_sndSeek` with which to do this. We need to use the symbol `PSF_SEEK_SET`, which asks *portsf* to jump to the position in the file given in the second argument. By setting this to 0, we effectively rewind the file back to the beginning:

```
if((psf_sndSeek(ifd, 0, PSF_SEEK_SET)) < 0){
    printf("Error: unable to rewind infile.\n");
    error++;
    goto exit;
}
```

Note that this must be placed at the end of the `else { }` block above, as it is relevant only if we have in fact scanned the file. In theory, it should not matter, but any disk access has the potential for errors, and it is a good principle to avoid doing anything unnecessary.

Stage 4c requires us to check that the *infile* is not silent. This code will be placed immediately following the `if...else` block above, before the code that creates the *outfile*:

```
if(inpeak==0.0){
    printf("infile is silent! Outfile not created.\n");
    goto exit;
}
```

We have but one final piece of code to add to the original template code before we can calculate the scaling factor from the user's requested level (converted from dB) and the peak level of the *infile*. This can be placed immediately above the final processing loop, which is unchanged except for the use of `nframes`:

```
scalefac = (float)(ampfac / inpeak);
```

This calculation is one of the reasons we checked for a non-zero peak value from the *infile*. If `inpeak` is zero, the statement above will cause a division-by-zero error,[10] which can often crash a program. Even if it doesn't crash, you can be sure the *outfile* will contain garbage.

All code from stage 5 onward can be retained without changes—so you are done, and ready to compile and test. Make sure all the messages to the user are appropriate to the new program—in copying code it is easy to overlook this sort of detail. If you are choosing to write or edit a makefile, check that you have the correct names for source files and for the program name itself. As with *sfgain*, a complete version of *sfnorm* is on the DVD in the examples directory, but try to resist looking at this unless you are badly stuck over a compilation problem.

2.2.4 Exercises

Exercise 2.2.1

In subsection 2.2.3, it is suggested that the process of finding the peak amplitude of a sound-file would be a useful program in its own right. Of course, not every file has a PEAK chunk. Using *sfnorm.c* as a starting point, and linking with the *portsf* library, write and document this program, calling it *sfpeak*. Alternatively, modify *sfnorm* so that it can also be used *just* to find the peak of the infile.

Exercise 2.2.2

In *sfgain*, a value for `ampfac` of 1.0 would result in an *outfile* identical to the *infile*—a needless operation. Trap this situation, advise the user, and terminate the program without creating a file.

Exercise 2.2.3

Write documentation for *sfnorm* and include suggestions about what target values to use for `dbval`.

Exercise 2.2.4

(a) The program *sfgain* expects a linear amplitude factor from the user. Modify the program to take a dB factor instead. Remember to change the usage message accordingly.

(b) Using an optional command-line flag, modify *sfgain* to enable to user to specify a scale factor in either linear or dB forms.

Exercise 2.2.5 (advanced)

In *sfnorm.c*, the task of finding the larger of two values is applied in several places. This is a very common operation, and the C language supports a special construct to code it very concisely. The compiler can often find extra optimizations for it:

```
val = val_2 > val_1 ? val_2 : val_1;
```

The construct is formed by a conditional test, here a comparison:

```
val_2 > val_1
```

followed by a question mark followed by two expressions (here, simple numeric values) separated by a colon:

```
val_2 : val_1
```

If the conditional test evaluates to 'true', the result of the whole expression is the left-hand value (here, `val_2`); otherwise it is the right-hand value (here, `val_1`). Thus, if `val_2` = 0.5 and `val_1` = 0.7, the statement

```
val = val_2 > val_1 ? val_2 : val_1;
```

says "if val_2 is greater than val_1, set val = val_2, otherwise set val = val_1." Thus `val` will be set to the value of `val_1` in this case. So common is this procedure that a macro definition is in very general use:

```
#define max(x,y) ((x) > (y) ? (x) : (y))
```

With this macro, code such as

```
absval = fabs(buf[i]);
if(absval > peak)
        peak = absval;
```

can be rewritten more concisely, but also more expressively:

```
absval = fabs(buf[i]);
peak = max(absval,peak);
```

Although the macro looks like a function call, it is *inline* code where the text is expanded by the preprocessor. The advantage of the macro is that it can be used with any type, whereas different functions would have to be defined for each distinct combination of types. This is also a disadvantage—we must always take care to supply reasonable arguments to such a macro, or the results will be "undefined." Add the macro definition to the top of *sfnorm.c*, identify all the instances where the maximum of two values is sought (one is illustrated in the example above), and replace them with code using the macro.

2.3   Stereo Panning

2.3.1   Introduction

So far, in our handling of soundfiles, we have not had much interest in the "width" of the file—how many channels there are. The programs *sfgain* and *sfnorm* can accept soundfiles with any number of channels—you can as easily normalize a six-channel file as a mono file. In this section we will be paying particular attention to the number of channels. If you have ever used either a mixing desk or a software mixer in a DAW application, you will be familiar with the process of panning a mono sound between two stereo speakers. It is a very routine, almost mundane process, and you might well imagine that there is not very much to it for a programmer. However, even for a simple process such as panning, there are better and worse ways of doing things. Less surprising perhaps is that the better way ("constant power panning") involves a little more mathematics than the worse way.

While there is clear utility in a program that will pan a whole soundfile into a single stereo position, we will make things a little more creative by mimicking what happens in an interactive application, where the pan position is moving—e.g. to move a sound from far left to far right. To do this within a plain command-line program, we can make use of a breakpoint file, as introduced in chapter 1 (subsection 1.1.7), in which the values represent the pan position ranging from $-1 =$ full left, to $+1.0 =$ full right. In doing so, you will learn about one of the cornerstones of audio programming: linear interpolation.

In this section, the task at hand is to create some functions—design *algorithms*—so as to do some serious audio processing. In doing this, we will have an opportunity to practice further all the skills learned so far, such as using multiple source files and creating functions. We are starting to think less about the C language and more about how to design and implement musical and useful audio tools. Increasingly, we will be developing functions, and families of functions, that are of general usefulness, and a major concern now is to establish a tidy and practical system for storing general-purpose source files. In due course, these may be used to create new custom libraries, just as we have already done for *portsf*. While all the programs presented in this chapter can be built using the directory structure copied from the DVD, we need to consider how we may make those examples the basis for a permanent and expanding repertoire of tools, and thus to look beyond that directory structure to one of our own devising.

As we move into serious audio processing, issues that so far have been almost peripheral to the language topics introduced in each section now are presented to us head-on—issues of efficiency, robustness, and generality. These issues are so important that they cannot possibly be encompassed even in a full chapter of text, and questions may be raised that do not have straightforward right/wrong answers. Such questions are not merely philosophical or conceptual—they have direct and immediate effects on the code we write. It becomes even more important, therefore, that you study and seek to follow through the exercises at the end of each section. Some are in the form of revision questions, but others enter more deeply into these issues and demand that you think, form opinions, and make decisions, though neither the opinions nor the decisions are likely to be conclusive.

2.3.2 Refinements to the Template Code

In section 2.2, the program *sfgain* was presented as a simple general-purpose or template program, which can be used as the basis for a large number of audio programs operating on soundfiles. In the DVD's examples directory you will find a file called *main.c* that consolidates this approach, including an implementation of the more efficient buffer processing described in subsection 2.2.2.

The code in *main.c* incorporates "wizard"-like comments, using the text "TODO: ..." to indicate where you may have to add new code specific to your program. For example:

```
if(ifd < 0){
    printf("Error: unable to open infile
            %s\n",argv[ARG_INFILE]);
    error++;
```

```
        goto exit;
}
/* TODO: verify infile format for this application */
```

This example reminds you to add code to check, for example, that the file has the expected number of channels.

Finally, the code documents the program structure described in the last section in the context of the program *sfnorm*:

```
printf("processing....\n");              /* STAGE 4 */
```

However, in *main.c* this structure is expanded to a seven-stage plan by augmenting the original stage 4:

Stage 3: Allocate memory, open infile.
Stage 4a: Perform any special data pre-processing, opening of extra data files, etc.
Stage 4b: Open outfile, once all required resources are obtained.
Stage 5: Perform main processing loop.
Stage 6: Report to the user.
Stage 7: Close files, free memory.

Note that errors can in principle arise at any of these stages (except, one hopes, stage 1): *main.c* routes any detected errors to the final "cleanup" stage, using the `goto` keyword.

2.3.3   A Simple Formula for Stereo Panning

We need a function that, given a position parameter (in the range $-1 \ldots +1$), returns two values, representing the amplitude scaling factors (range $0 \ldots 1$) for the left and right output channels. Ordinarily, a function can return only one object, but, as was demonstrated in chapter 1 (subsection 1.7.5), we know that ANSI C permits functions to return a structure. We can exploit this by defining a simple structure with two fields:

```
typedef struct panpos
    double left;
    double right;
} PANPOS;
```

and we can then define a panning function that returns a `PANPOS` object:

```
PANPOS simplepan(double position);
```

Intuitively, stereo panning is a simple procedure—a variable proportion of the signal is fed to each channel, such that for a pan from full left to full right, and, assuming maximum amplitude $= 1.0$, the level in the left channel fades from maximum to zero, while that of the right channel increases from zero to maximum. This could then be implemented using a plain linear fade (see figure 2.3). The arithmetic for a linear fade is simplicity itself, made

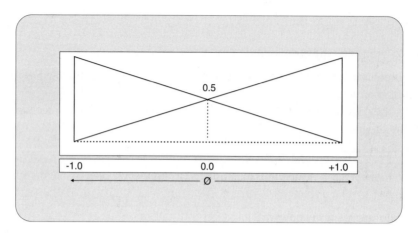

Figure 2.3
Linear panning.

only marginally more complicated by the input range between -1.0 and $+1.0$, which must be mapped to the required amplitude range for each channel:

```
PANPOS simplepan(double position)
{
    PANPOS pos;

    position *= 0.5;
    pos.left = position - 0.5;
    pos.right = position + 0.5;

    return pos;
}
```

2.3.4   Multiple Conditional Tests—The Logical || and && Operators

Having defined a panning function and a type, we need somewhere to put them. We are ready to embark on the creation of the first version of the panning program, which will be called *sfpan*. Again, rather than simply copying the file from the DVD (which represents where we finish, not where we start), follow the procedures here to create it from scratch. Our program will progress through a preliminary version to a final version; along the way, some important new C idioms will be introduced. Copy the template file *main.c* as a new source file, *sfpan.c*. Add the definition of PANPOS, and add the function prototype and definition of simplepan to *main.c*, above the main function. Later, if we decide this code is generally useful, we may transfer it to dedicated source and header files, as we have previously done with the BREAKPOINT code.

To convert the new file into a pan program, two basic processing steps are required: one to deal with the change of channels and one to create storage for the new stereo samples that will be written to the *outfile*. We will also have to define any required variables, to define the command line, and to check arguments from the user.

Although the plan is to support time-varying panning using a breakpoint file, we will keep things simple at this early stage by defining a numeric argument to contain a fixed pan position inside the defined range. This will enable us to verify the correctness of the program, running it with different panpos values, before adding breakpoint-file support, which we can reasonably expect to involve greater complexity. This system of *incremental development* will become increasingly important as projects increase in ambition and complexity. To begin with, the command line will be

```
sfpan infile outfile panpos
```

Change the usage message accordingly, adding a description of the correct range for panpos. Add a variable called panpos (type double) to the end of the variables list at the top of main.

It will be necessary to modify the enum list for arguments by adding a symbol for the new argument:

```
enum
{ARG_PROGNAME,ARG_INFILE,ARG_OUTFILE,ARG_PANPOS,ARG_NARGS};
```

Before the call to psf_sndOpen, we need to add code to read and check the panpos argument for correctness. The interesting aspect of this is that we need to check that the value lies within the legal range, so we need to compare it to two values:

```
pos = atof(argv[ARG_PANPOS]);
if(pos < -1.0) {
    printf("Error: panpos value out of range -1 to +1\n");
    error++;
    goto exit;
}
if(pos > 1.0){
    printf("Error: panpos value out of range -1 to +1\n");
    error++;
    goto exit;
}
```

This seems an unnecessary duplication of code. Indeed it is, and C offers a means to avoid it by means of a pair of "logical" operators that enable the programmer to combine any number of conditional tests into a single expression. In English, we want to say "If panpos is less than −1 OR is greater than 1.0, report an error."

The || operator is the C operator for the word OR, called "logical OR":

```
if( (pos < 1.0) || (pos > 1.0) ){
    printf("Error: panpos value out of range -1 to +1\n");
    error++;
    goto exit;
}
```

Here parentheses enclosing each conditional expression have been added to make the structure clear; in fact they are not needed, as the logical-OR operator has a lower *precedence* than the conditional expressions on either side of it, so the form below will work as intended:

```
if( pos < 1.0 || pos > 1.0 )
```

C also includes a complementary "logical-AND" operator, notated as two adjacent ampersands, which might be used as follows:

```
if(panpos >= -1 && panpos <= 1.0)
    printf("position is between the speakers");
```

One much-exploited feature of the use of logical operators is the fact that the first 'false' result is taken as the result of the whole expression, so that subsequent tests (listed from left to right) are not computed. This is often used to combine a pointer check with an operation using it:

```
int i = 1;
while( argv[i] != NULL && (argv[i++][0] == '-') ){
    argv++; /* skip over any optional flag arguments */

}
```

As soon as `argv[i]` evaluates to `NULL`, the loop is broken, so that second test, which would now cause an access violation, is not executed.

2.3.5 Changing Format from Input to Output—Mono to Stereo

As was noted above, *main.c* is channel-agnostic—it simply copies the `infile` properties to the `outfile`. For a pan program we require the `infile` to be mono, so we must add the test to *sfpan.c* accordingly, after the file is opened:

```
if(inprops.chans != 1){
    printf("Error: infile must be mono.\n");
    error++;
    goto exit;
}
```

Further down, just before creating the outfile, the copy is made:

```
outprops = inprops;
```

Remember, this is a copy of a struct—each member of the structure is copied. All we have to do to create a stereo outfile is to change one field:

```
outprops.chans = 2;
```

As the output data will be twice the size of the input, we will need to create an output frame buffer that is also twice the size of the input buffer. Add the new variable after all the others:

```
float*outframe = NULL;          /* STAGE 1 */
```

Allocate the memory for it immediately before opening the outfile:

```
/* create stereo output buffer */
outframe = (float *) malloc(nframes *
    outprops.chans * sizeof(float));
if(outframe == NULL){
    puts("No memory!\n");
    error++;
    goto exit;
}
```

Don't forget to release the resource at the end:

```
exit:
    if(outframe) free (outframe);
```

We can now add the processing code itself, to the main loop. As the function `simplepan` returns a PANPOS, we need a variable to receive it:

```
PANPOS thispos;            /*STAGE 1 */
```

Just before the main processing loop, we call `simplepan()` with the `position` received from the user, and use the `left` and `right` fields of `thispos` inside the loop to generate the output samples. For each input sample we will be calculating two output samples (i.e. the samples are *interleaved*), so we need a new counter `out_i` for the latter. The whole block is shown in listing 2.3.1, with the required changes in boldface.

Listing 2.3.1: A Processing Loop to Do Linear Panning:

```
thispos = simplepan(position);
while ((framesread =
               psf_sndReadFloatFrames(ifd,inframe,nframes)) > 0)
    {
```

```
int i, out_i;
for(i=0, out_i = 0; i < framesread; i++){
    outframe[out_i++] =
        (float)(inframe[i]*thispos.left);
    outframe[out_i++] =
        (float)(inframe[i]*thispos.right);
}
if(psf_sndWriteFloatFrames(ofd,outframe,framesread)
        != framesread){
    printf("Error writing to outfile\n");
    error++;
    break;
}
}
```

Note that here it is possible to initialize more than one variable in the for statement.[11]

The initial version of *sfpan* is now finished, and it is time to build and test it. To build it, we must write the rules for *sfpan* into the makefile (see the guide document for full details). Each rule comprises a pair of lines (the second indented with a tab, not a space). The first line gives the *target* (here the program name) and its dependencies; the second gives the instruction (that is, calls the compiler):

```
sfpan: sfpan.c ./lib/libportsf.a
        $(CC) -o sfpan sfpan.c $(INCLUDES) $(LIBS)
```

For each program maintained by this makefile, a similar rule will be written.

To test this program, first check the three fundamental values for panpos: −1 for full left, 0 for center (mono: equal level in both channels), and +1.0 for full right. You can use any mono soundfile as input, but as well as a musical source, consider using a test signal such as a full-amplitude sine wave (we saw how to create such a signal in the previous chapter) that will enable you to observe the levels in the output file precisely and to confirm that they are as expected. For example, when panpos is set to zero, the level in each channel should be exactly half that of the source.

These basic tests of correct behavior are important, but performing critical *listening* tests on a program that can only place a sound in a fixed position is difficult. To be able to evaluate this pan algorithm properly, we need to be able to hear how the sound moves across the stereo field. For this, we must use a breakpoint file.

2.3.6   Extending *sfpan* with Breakpoint-File Support

Thanks to the work we did in chapter 1, we already have a complete function to read a text-file containing time/value breakpoints. Rather than simply import that function into *sfpan.c*, we can anticipate that we may develop several functions handling such files (and the

BREAKPOINT type), so that it would be much better to create a source file dedicated to them. Looking ahead, we can expect these functions will probably become a library in their own right. The main point to appreciate is that while each specialization of *main.c* belongs to the particular application, and must therefore exist in the application project directory, breakpoint functions are general, suitable for use by any program that needs them. Though we are not yet quite ready to create a library, we can make a start by creating a new file *breakpoints.c* , to begin with in our project directory. Later we may move it to a new dedicated directory, along with other general-purpose source files. (This will require a change to the makefile.) Similarly, we need to create a header file *breakpoints.h*. We can place this in the *include* directory that also contains *portsf.h*.

Before we can start writing new code, we must copy to these files everything we already have relating to the BREAKPOINT type. Add an #include directive for *breakpoints.h* at the top of *breakpoints.c*, using angle brackets (as this is a public header file):

```
#include <breakpoints.h>
```

The header file will contain the definition of the BREAKPOINT type and prototypes for the BREAKPOINT-related functions get_breakpoints and maxpoint. As one of the arguments to get_breakpoints uses the FILE type, add #include <stdio.h> to the top of *breakpoints.h*. Similarly, copy the code of the two BREAKPOINT-related functions from *breakdur.c* (see chapter 1) into *breakpoints.c*.

Note that get_breakpoints uses several C library functions (malloc, realloc, and free), so that *breakpoints.c* also needs #include <stdlib.h>. Finally, add *breakpoints.c* to the makefile. The file becomes a new *dependency* for *sfpan*:

```
sfpan: sfpan.c breakpoints.c ./lib/libportsf.a
        $(CC) -o sfpan sfpan.c breakpoints.c $(INCLUDES) $(LIBS)
```

We are now ready to design the program. This entails identifying what may be needed at each stage of the program. Some materials we already have; others will have to be implemented from scratch.

In stage 1 (define variables), some elements are obvious. We are reading a text file opened with fopen, so we need a FILE* variable, and we need other variables to hold the size of the breakpoint file, and also a pointer to the breakpoint data itself (see *breakdur.c* in chapter 1):

```
FILE* fp = NULL;
unsigned long size;
BREAKPOINT* points = NULL;
```

We can expect to return to this stage as other stages get developed. We also need to update the usage message to reflect the new facility:

```
if(argc < ARG_NARGS){
    printf("insufficient arguments.\n"
```

```
    "usage:\n\t"
    "sfgain infile outfile posfile.brk\n"
    "\tposfile.brk is breakpoint file"
    "with values in range -1.0 <= pos <= 1.0\n"
    "where -1.0 = full Left, 0 = Centre, +1.0 = full Right"
    );
    return 1;
 }
```

In stage 2 (obtain and validate arguments from user), there are two tasks. The first is simply to open the named breakpoint file. We already have code do this from chapter 1 (subsection 1.1.7). It includes some important basic error checking on the file:

```
/* read breakpoint file and verify it */
fp = fopen(argv[ARG_BRKFILE],"r");
if(fp == NULL){
    printf("Error: unable to open"
            "breakpoint file %s\n",argv[ARG_BRKFILE]);
    error++;
    goto exit;
}
points = get_breakpoints(fp, &size);
if(points==NULL){
    printf("No breakpoints read.\n");
    error++;
    goto exit;
}
if(size < 2){
    printf("Error: at least two breakpoints required\n");
    free(points);
    fclose(fp);
    return 1;
}
/* we require breakpoints to start from 0 */
if(points[0].time != 0.0){
    printf("Error in breakpoint data: "
                    "first time must be 0.0\n");
    error++;
    goto exit;
}
```

We also need to check that the breakpoints in the file are all within the allowed range. The function get_maxpoint employed in *breakdur* does half the job, and we could create a matching function `get_minpoint` to do the other half, but using both functions would mean scanning the data twice. This would be trivial for a short handwritten breakpoint file, but if it has been extracted from a soundfile (as we will be doing later in this chapter), and contains potentially thousands of points, this is an overhead that is worth avoiding. Instead, we can modify the code demonstrated in subsection 2.3.4 above into a general-purpose function that is given the desired range and scans the array of breakpoints, returning 0 if an out-of-range value is found and returning 1 if all is well:

```
int inrange(const BREAKPOINT* points,
        double minval,
        double maxval,
        unsigned long npoints)
{
    unsigned long i;
    int range_OK = 1;

    for(i=0; i < npoints; i++){
        if(points[i].value < minval || points[i].value > maxval){
            range_OK = 0;
            break;
        }
    }
    return range_OK;
}
```

Add the declaration of this new function to *breakpoints.h*, and copy the whole function body into *breakpoints.c*. You can then call this function after the other validation tests shown above:

```
if(!inrange(points,-1,1.0,size)){
    printf("Error in breakpoint file: "
            "values out of range -1 to +1 \n");
    error++;
    goto exit;
}
```

Note that this uses the operator ! (logical-NOT or "negation"), so that the test asks

```
"if breakpoint data NOT in range, report error"
```

The NOT operator will return 'true' if applied to the value zero, and 'false' otherwise, which is why `inrange` returns 0 if an out-of-range value is found. If we have an acceptable breakpoint file, all we need do is apply it to the soundfile, in the main processing loop. It is at this stage that we need to be able to describe *exactly* what we are trying to do.

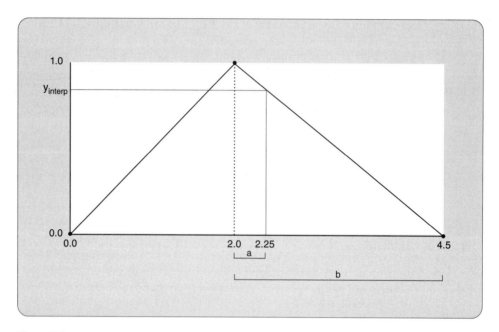

Figure 2.4
Linear interpolation of breakpoint data.

2.3.7   Basic Breakpoint Processing—Using Linear Interpolation

The task at hand is, given a series of time/value breakpoints at arbitrary (non-decreasing) times, to find a value at a time between adjacent points. This is illustrated in figure 2.4 for the case of a breakpoint file containing the data

0.0   0.0
2.0   1.0
4.5   0.0

where we want to know the value at time $= 2.25$. It is useful in following this procedure to consider not an individual breakpoint, but a pair of adjacent points, which we will call a *span*. In the above file there are two such spans, the first 2 seconds long and the second 2.5 seconds long. We want to know the value at time $= 2.25$, indicated by the upward arrow under the horizontal axis.

Given that the target time cannot be negative, that the time of the first point must be zero, and that successive times cannot decrease, it is a simple matter to step along the array until we find a breakpoint whose right-hand time is above or equal to the target time—in this case, the second span. We need to know how far along this span the requested time is, expressed as a simple fraction of the whole span—that is, the ratio between the distance from the left time to the target time (marked *a* in figure 2.4) and the width of the whole span (marked *b* in figure 2.4):

$$a = time - time_{left} = 0.25$$

$$b = time_{right} - time_{left} = 2.5$$

$$fraction = \frac{a}{b} = 0.1.$$

As the breakpoint file defines a simple line connecting the values of a span, we can apply this fraction to the span values to find the required value:

$$c = value_{right} - value_{left} = -1.0,$$

$$target\_distance = c \times fraction = -0.1,$$

$$target\_value = value_{left} + target\_distance = 1.0 - 0.1 = 0.9.$$

There are two special cases to consider:

(1) Two spans happen to have the same time. In this case, *b* will be zero, and we would encounter a division-by-zero error, when calculating *fraction*. There can be situations in which an instant jump from one value to another is reasonable, and in any case decisions on whether this is acceptable should not be left to a low-level function, so the general solution is to return the right-hand span value in this situation.

(2) The requested time is after the final breakpoint time, as may easily be the case if, say, a 5-second breakpoint file is applied to a 10-second soundfile. We return the final value, which thus becomes a constant value applied *ad finitum*.

Listing 2.3.2 shows a complete function for finding values for a given time in a supplied BREAKPOINT array. Copy this into *breakpoints.c* and add the declaration to *breakpoints.h*. Note how the comments identify each of the tasks described: scanning the file, dealing with a time beyond the end of the data, avoiding the division by zero, and finally calculating the required value.

Listing 2.3.2: Function `val_at_brktime`

```
1    double val_at_brktime(const BREAKPOINT* points,
2            unsigned long npoints, double time)
3    {
4        unsigned long i;
5        BREAKPOINT left,right;
6        double frac, val, width;
7
8        /* scan until we find a span containing our time */
9        for(i=1; i < npoints; i++){
```

```
10          if(time <= points[i].time)
11              break;
12      }
13      /* maintain final value if time beyond end of data */
14      if(i == npoints){
15          return points[i-1].value;
16      }
17      left = points[i-1];
18      right = points[i];
19
20      /* check for instant jump - two points with same time */
21      width = right.time - left.time;
22      if(width==0.0)
23          return right.value;
24      /* get value from this span using linear interpolation */
25      frac = (time - left.time) / width;
26      val = left.value + (( right.value - left.value) * frac);
27
28      return val;
29  }
```

For some important questions relating to this function, see the exercises at the end of this section.

2.3.8 Completing and Testing the New *sfpan*

There remains just one task to do in order to add the new panning function to *sfpan*: obtain the time values to supply to the function. In the pursuit of ultimate quality, we want to do this per sample. Thus, we need to calculate the time of each sample. This is not as costly as it might sound. The distance between samples is constant, and it is equal to the reciprocal of the sample rate:

```
double timeincr = 1.0 / inprops.srate;
```

Thus, all we need do is initialize a time variable to zero outside the processing loop:

```
double sampletime = 0.0;
```

and increment this by timeincr for each sample. The variables must be declared at the top of main (stage 1), but perhaps they are best initialized immediately above the start of the processing loop (and of course timeincr cannot be initialized until the soundfile is opened), to make it clear to anyone reading the code that the initializations are closely associated with that loop. Finally, our original call to simplepan before the loop must be moved inside the loop, receiving the incrementing sampletime value. This leads to the final code for the processing loop:

```
/* init time position counter for reading envelope */
timeincr = 1.0 / inprops.srate;
sampletime = 0.0;

while ((framesread = psf_sndReadFloatFrames(ifd,inframe,nframes)) > 0)
{
    int i, out_i;
    double stereopos;

    for(i=0, out_i = 0; i < framesread; i++){
        sstereopos = val_at_brktime(points, size,sampletime);
        pos = simplepan(stereopos);
        outframe[out_i++] = (float)(inframe[i]*pos.left);
        outframe[out_i++] = (float)(inframe[i]*pos.right);
        sampletime += timeincr;
    }

    if(psf_sndWriteFloatFrames(ofd,outframe,framesread)
            != framesread){
        printf("Error writing to outfile\n");
        error++;
        break;
    }
}
```

It is now time to build and test the complete program. If you get compilation errors, remember to study the first message especially carefully; most errors at this stage will be simple typing mistakes.

Testing involves selecting a suitable input file and creating a breakpoint file containing a panning trajectory that fits the duration of the file (or is perhaps shorter—test the final-value behavior here). Don't try to do anything "imaginative" yet. A simple three-point breakpoint file is all you need to check performance in both directions:

```
0.0    -1.0
2.0     1.0
4.0    -1.0
```

This pans the sound steadily from full left to full right and back again slowly enough that the motion can be heard clearly. Remember that, as an audio/music programmer, you are evaluating not only whether a program works without crashing, but also the sonic and musical quality of the results. So use test sources that enable that evaluation to be conducted easily. For evaluating a panning function, a sound that is reasonably constant in level is required. You can use a sine wave (especially useful for testing graphically with Audacity), but it is generally thought that impulsive sounds are easier to locate in the stereo field, so a plain drum loop can also be effective. You need a reasonably good audio setup in a space without disruptive reflections. Headphones are often useful, but only as an adjunct—for evaluating a panning process, you need to listen over properly spaced stereo loudspeakers.[12]

Don't forget to test the program's basic functionality. Check that it correctly opens a mono file while rejecting others, and that it generates a stereo output file without crashing or printing inappropriate error messages. Conversely, also test that the correct messages are displayed if, for example, you pass the name of a non-existent file.

It is also important to define in advance (whenever you can) what you are *expecting* to hear. If you have a program (perhaps a DAW) that can also pan sounds dynamically using automation, use that to create a sound to compare against the output of *sfpan*. Sometimes it can be very difficult to evaluate a new effect without precedent, and it helps to have something to relate it to. Suffice it to say that the normative requirement for a stereo panner is for the sound to be heard to move smoothly across the stereo field, maintaining a sense of constant distance from the listener, and therefore a constant sound level.[13]

2.3.9   A Better Panner—The Constant-Power Function

If you have followed all the procedures described above, and have listened to the output from *sfpan*, you may have formed one or more of the following impressions:

- The sound tends to be pulled into the left or the right speaker.
- The sound seems to recede (move away from the listener) when the input file is panned centrally.
- The level seems to fall slightly when the sound is panned centrally.

The reason for this is that the amplitude and the perceived intensity (or loudness) of a sound are not equivalent. The ear is more sensitive to intensity than to amplitude (which is why the decibel scale is so important to audio engineers), and intensity (which relates to the *power* of the signal) is measured by reading not the amplitude but the *square of* the amplitude. If we want to find the overall intensity of a pair of sound sources, we need to square the amplitude of each signal to get the power, add these values together, then take the square root of the result to get back to an amplitude:

$$P = \sqrt{amp_1{}^2 + amp_2{}^2}. \tag{3}$$

If we apply this formula to the signal level in each speaker when `simplepan` is used to place a sound centrally, we discover that the result does not sum to 1:

$$P = \sqrt{0.5^2 + 0.5^2} = \sqrt{0.5} = 0.707. \tag{4}$$

This is equal to a decrease in level of 3 dB. Intuitively we can grasp this if we note that two equally loud singers are not twice as loud as one (which is just as well; otherwise an average-size choir would exceed the threshold of pain). Therefore, instead of the simple linear function, we need a function that, when subjected to the above formula, evaluates to 1 over the

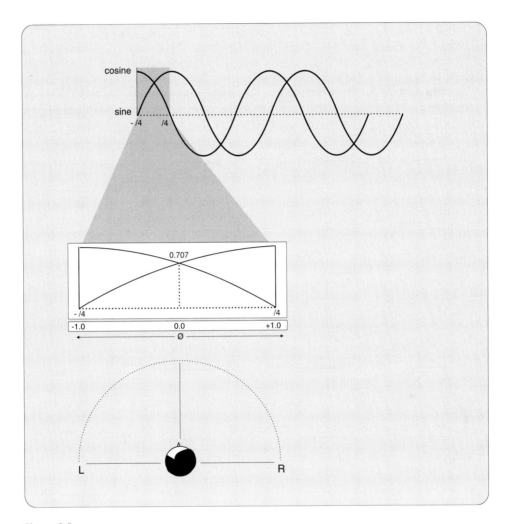

Figure 2.5
Constant-power panning.

required range. Such a function will ensure *constant power* wherever the sound is placed within the stereo field. Mathematicians can devise any number of functions that meet this requirement. The functions most widely used for a constant-power panner are those corner-stones of "audible mathematics," the sine and cosine functions (figure 2.5).

The formulae for a constant-power pan function are

$$A_{left} = \frac{\sqrt{2}}{2}[\cos(\theta) + \sin(\theta)] \tag{5}$$

and

$$A_{right} = \frac{\sqrt{2}}{2}[\cos(\theta) - \sin(\theta)], \tag{6}$$

where θ is the angle of the panned signal. All trigonometric calculations are performed on angles measured in radians, rather than degrees, so a single cycle of a sinusoid has a range of 2π radians. Thus a quarter-sector has a length of $\pi/2$. As the panning range we are using (between -1 and $+1$) has a width of 2, we have to scale the pan function by the inverse of 2 to arrive at the required amplitude value for each channel. The full constant-power function, shown in listing 2.3.3, is a direct replacement for simplepan.

Listing 2.3.3: A Constant-Power Panning Function

```
1    PANPOS constpower(double position)
2    {
3        PANPOS pos;
4        /* pi/2: 1/4 cycle of a sinusoid */
5        const double piovr2 = 4.0 * atan(1.0) * 0.5;
6        const double root2ovr2 = sqrt(2.0) * 0.5;
7        /* scale position to fit the pi/2 range */
8        double thispos = position * piovr2;
9        /* each channel uses a 1/4 of a cycle */
10       double angle = thispos * 0.5;
11
12       pos.left       = root2ovr2 * (cos(angle) - sin(angle));
13       pos.right      = root2ovr2 * (cos(angle) + sin(angle));
14       return pos;
15   }
```

Several things are worth noting about this function.

Lines 5 and 6: Constant values are declared using the const keyword. This is both "defensive programming" and good documentation, and often it leads to extra efficiency in the code generated by the compiler.

Line 5: To obtain the numeric value of PI, we can write out the number explicitly, as we did in the final examples of chapter 1:

```
#define PI = 3.1592654
```

As we saw in chapter 1, UNIX-based compilers offer a more precise definition, providing the symbol M_PI. A popular alternative is to get the compiler to compute it for us:

```
double PI = 4.0 * atan(1.0);
```

The function atan is the standard arctan function, and like cos and sin it is defined in <math.h>.

Lines 5–10: The calculations are written out step by step, following the description of the formula, with each calculation commented accordingly. An obvious optimization is to condense the code by merging all calculations involving constants; for example, `piovr2` can be defined directly as `2 * atan(1.0)`. The full optimization procedure is left as an exercise.

Add `constpower` to the top of *main.c* as a complete replacement for `simplepan`. Then recompile and repeat the listening tests using the same test breakpoint file. You should hear that the pan is much more even in level as the sound traverses the stereo field.

2.3.10   Objections to *sfpan*

We have done quite a lot in this chapter. We have written a program to do constant-power panning that includes support for dynamic panning using a breakpoint file. In the process, we have learned the principles of linear interpolation. The program has been tested, and it works. Satisfying as that is, there is a major criticism that can be made of *sfpan*: it is extremely inefficient.

The primary culprit is the function `val_at_brktime`. This is called every sample (itself something we want to avoid, as every function call incurs some code overhead), and each time it is called it scans the breakpoint array from the beginning. And much of the time it will be scanning to the same breakpoint span. For an array of just a few elements, one can argue that this does not matter. However, it is not only possible but likely that some breakpoint files will be much larger, running to 1,000 points or more (for example, an envelope extracted from a large soundfile, with 100 points per second stored in the file).

The problem is that `val_at_brktime` "does not scale well." An algorithm that may be acceptable for a small data set may be very unacceptable for a large one. The larger the breakpoint file, the slower the program will run—and the program will run progressively slower as it approaches the end of the breakpoint data. Much of the time, `val_at_brktime` does redundant processing. Once the required span has been found, it is absurd, as well as wasteful, to go all the way back to the beginning just to find that same span all over again. Users also dislike software that runs faster or slower depending on the input. Our ideal solution is a method that runs at a single efficient speed, regardless of the size of the data.

There are many possible solutions, all, perhaps inevitably, more complicated than the simple approach presented here. A few require knowledge of aspects of C yet to be described, but many can be written without further knowledge of the language, by thoughtful design that analyzes the problem, perhaps engaging in a little lateral thinking in the process. (One solution is presented in the next chapter, where amplitude envelopes take center stage, and where the issue of large breakpoint files has to be addressed at the outset.)

A second objection to `val_at_brktime` is that it is not robust, in that it doesn't check the validity of input arguments. There is much to check—the pointer to the array of breakpoints must not be `NULL`, `npoints` must be at least 2, breakpoint times must not go backward, and the time value itself cannot be negative. All these checks could be added, and the format of the function could be revised so that it returns an error value. The required breakpoint value could then be returned via a pointer supplied from the calling function, which also must not be NULL.

However, all these procedures take time, an audio programmer's most precious resource. Instead, when the function is implemented, we trust that it will be used correctly—the breakpoint data is validated for reasonableness when it is loaded, for example. Again for reasons of efficiency, it is very undesirable to have to check a return value every sample, and all those validation checks add to the overhead of the function. In the chapters that follow, we will meet both alternative implementation strategies and further C language idioms, all of which will help to increase both the efficiency and the robustness of our code.

2.3.11 Exercises

Exercise 2.3.1

The function val_at_brktime has this code in lines 14–15:

```
if(i == npoints){
    return points[i-1].value;
```

Explain why the array index is i-1 rather than i. What assumption about the array is being relied on here?

Exercise 2.3.2

(a) Optimize the function constpower: reduce all calculations involving constant values to one, and eliminate the double calls to cos and sin on the same argument.
(b) Write documentation for the program *sfpan* (using constpower) for a musically literate but non-mathematical reader.

Exercise 2.3.3

(a) In the text it is suggested that a function minpoint could be written, to complement the existing function maxpoint. Write this function. Test it using a variety of handwritten breakpoint files. For example, test it with files containing values that are all positive or all negative.
(b) Suggest at least two alternative ways of defining a single function that can find and return both the minimum and maximum values in a breakpoint file (scanning the array only once), together with the line(s) containing each. Discuss the advantages and disadvantages of each method, and implement and test your preferred solution. Assume that the function will be called with legal arguments.

Exercise 2.3.4

(a) Write a test program for the `simplepan` and `constpower` functions (not involving any soundfiles) that checks the calculated overall intensity of a sound (amplitude 1) when panned from full left to full right over 128 steps. Use this program to confirm that the two pan functions behave as described.

(b) (optional) Adapt the program to create a textfile of breakpoints that can be displayed graphically, e.g. using Gnuplot. Modify the program to generate a file that demonstrates the change in intensity in one channel. (This will, in effect, display the pan function under test.)

Exercise 2.3.5 (advanced)

As was noted in the text, the function `val_at_brktime` is very inefficient. Modify *sfpan* to solve this problem, by implementing the method of `val_at_brktime` directly in the `main` function, so that the code steps through the breakpoint file only once, as the soundfile is processed. Preserve the sample-by-sample behavior, e.g. by ensuring that successive breakpoints at identical times are handled correctly.

2.4   Envelopes as Signals—Amplitude Processing

2.4.1   Introduction

The previous section introduced breakpoint-file processing as an enhancement to a basic pan program. From this it became clear that breakpoint files correspond pretty closely to what is often termed "automation data," in audio workstations, or even simply as "envelopes" (figure 2.6). In this chapter we will embrace breakpoint-file handling from the outset. Here the term "envelope" will be particularly appropriate, as we implement two complementary tasks—extracting an amplitude envelope from a soundfile, and applying an amplitude envelope to a soundfile.

We will develop two programs: *envx* and *sfenv*. Both will follow the structure of the *main.c* template. At the end of chapter 1 we explored the distinctive nature of the two kinds of data: the soundfile and the breakpoint file. The former is a regularly timed stream of audio samples, whereas the latter is an arbitrary time-ordered list of time/value points, which may be irregularly sampled—the breakpoints maybe unevenly spaced in time. In exploring the exponential decay, we saw how the breakpoint file can ultimately become as regularly and densely sampled as the sound data, culminating in the generation of a decaying sine wave. In this instance, the envelope's shape was computed every sample.

In *envx*, our task is to extract the amplitude envelope from an existing soundfile, to become a breakpoint file. As we shall see, this leads to a fairly simple program. For *sfenv*, we have to process a regular stream of samples while reading from a source that is possibly sampled irregularly. We may be presented with a few breakpoints widely separated in time,

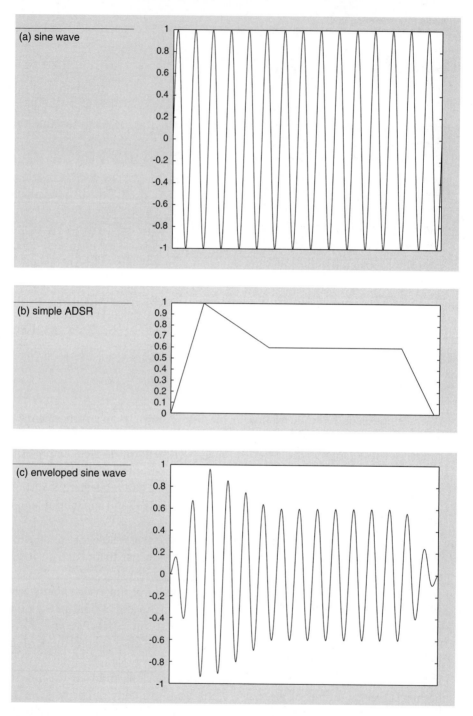

Figure 2.6
Enveloping an audio signal.

or, at the other extreme, we may even been given two points with the same time. The underlying task is, in effect, to convert the breakpoint data into a regular sample *stream*, which is then applied to the input sound. The method we will use is called *linear interpolation*. In chapter 1 we saw how a plotting program such as Gnuplot can be used to draw breakpoint data—the lines connecting the points are themselves created using linear interpolation.

We saw an example of linear interpolation in the previous section, where it was noted that the process employed is very inefficient and wasteful. In this section, a solution is presented that addresses that issue. While *sfenv* is a little more complicated than either *envx* or *sfpan*, the programming principle employed is the simple and fundamental one of counting.

The evolution of these programs demonstrates a principle that is easily overlooked by programmers. In the majority of cases (and almost invariably for code of any complexity) the required approach is to implement the same program several times. The first version must work (it may be called the "proof of concept" version); later versions seek to improve the overall design (i.e. by learning from the mistakes or other defects of the original version) and the details of the code so as to meet as many of these other objectives as is possible. The extent to which this is so can be seen from the fact that later chapters will demonstrate yet more alternative methods for generating and processing audio streams, as further criteria arise from musical and/or technical requirements. Indeed, we are already conscious of the need to approach the current task thinking of future needs; what works here, with *this* method, may yet not be ideal for use with *that* task. Conversely, if the method developed here does to be general enough, and broad enough in scope, we are also conscious of the need to package or generalize the method to make its use elsewhere as straightforward as is possible.

By definition, a soundfile represents a digital audio signal. The numbers we generate from a breakpoint file using linear interpolation are not an *audio* signal in the same way (no negative values, for example), yet they still represent a signal of a special kind, complete with a sample rate. Our task in this section is therefore to perform *signal processing* where one signal, the breakpoint stream, is, in effect, being synthesized and applied to the other. With *envx* we are extracting a signal from an existing one. Our preoccupation with the digital processing and generation of signals will only increase as we continue the journey.

2.4.2   The *envx* Program—Describing the Task

An envelope describes some relatively slowly time-varying property of a sound. The amplitude envelope is probably the most familiar example, as the creation and control of amplitude envelopes is an essential synthesis tool.

To extract the envelope from a soundfile such as an instrument sample, we must perform the reverse process—we must track the overall amplitude trend of the signal, which by definition changes far more slowly than the oscillations of the underlying waveform. Although

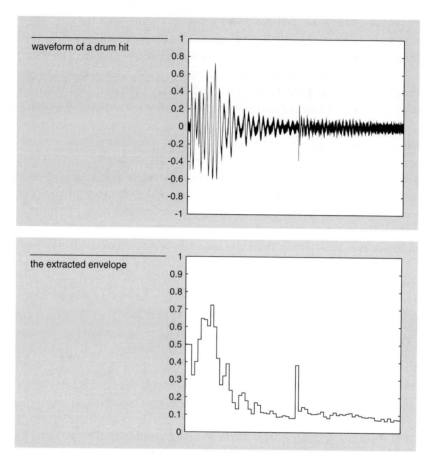

waveform of a drum hit

the extracted envelope

Figure 2.7
Extracting an amplitude envelope.

this description does suggest that the process is a form of low-pass filtering, we do not want to discard or ignore audio information; rather, we want to find the maximum absolute sample over successive small blocks of samples (figure 2.7). The extracted envelope data lies within the positive "normalized" range from 0 to 1.0. It can be applied to some other sound-file (e.g. one containing some simple synthetic waveform) to reproduce the dynamic character of the source. We use linear interpolation to generate a stream of amplitude values, which are multiplied with the audio samples, thus "enveloping" the source. In the context of real-time audio processing, the combination of these two procedures is usually termed *envelope following*.

2.4.3   Extracting Envelope Data from a Soundfile

We begin, as before, by copying *main.c* to a new file *envx.c*. As should now be routine, we make some preliminary changes to the template code. We already know that the output will not be a soundfile, but a *textfile*, so all the code that deals with an output soundfile (including the code to report PEAK information) must be removed. In its place, we will be adding code to write to an output textfile. The enum list of `argv` symbols can remain unchanged (it already covers a basic `infile` and `outfile` command line), as can the code that checks for optional flag arguments (at this stage, we may or may not know whether we need this code).

One aspect we want to change early on is the comment string at the very top of the file that describes the program (stage 2):

```
/* envx.c :
extract amplitude envelope from mono soundfile*/
```

Similarly, we can change the announcement string near the top of `main`:

```
/*STAGE 2 */
printf("ENVX: extract amplitude envelope"
        "from mono soundfile\n");
```

We can also complete an initial version of the usage message:

```
/* check rest of commandline */
if(argc < ARG_NARGS){
    printf("insufficient arguments.\n"
    /* TODO: add required usage message */
        "usage: envx insndfile outfile.brk\n"
    );
    return 1;
}
```

We must also look at the code for opening the input soundfile (stage 3), and consider what changes we may need. In this case a very pertinent instruction in the template code is

```
/* TODO: verify infile format for this application */
```

It is only practical to extract an envelope (at the level of precision we are interested in) from a mono soundfile, so we must ensure that we reject any multi-channel files:

```
/* verify infile format is acceptable */
if(inprops.chans > 1){
    printf("Soundfile contains %d channels: "
            "must be mono.\n",inprops.chans);
```

```
        error++;
        goto exit;
    }
```

The other change we need to add to the template code is to add code to open the output text file (stage 4). (We have encountered this task before, at the end of chapter 1.) We use the function fopen with the mode for writing, "w":

```
/* create output breakpoint file */
fp = fopen(argv[ARG_OUTFILE],"w");
if(fp == NULL){
    printf("envx: unable to create breakpoint file %s\n",
            argv[ARG_OUTFILE]);
    error++;
    goto exit;
}
```

Accordingly, we add the declaration for the FILE *fp variable to the list at the top of main, initializing it to NULL at the same time. Having added code to open a file, this is also a good time to add code to close it again, at the bottom of main, after the exit label (stage 7):

```
/*TODO: cleanup any other resources */
if(fp)
    if(fclose(fp))
        printf("envx: failed to close output file %s\n",
                argv[ARG_OUTFILE]);
```

2.4.4   Implementation of Envelope Extraction

For extracting amplitude envelopes, we can re-use the function maxsamp introduced in section 2.2 for the program *sfnorm* to find the largest absolute sample value of successive short blocks (we will call them "windows") of samples. The window must be short enough to capture transient information, such as a percussive attack, but not so short that it ends up reproducing the waveform itself. A secondary possibly conflicting consideration is to minimize the amount of data produced. Add this function unchanged to the top of the source file, not forgetting to add its declaration too.

As a rule of thumb, a 15-millisecond window is sufficient to capture the envelope of most sounds—this gives around 66 envelope points per second. Nevertheless, as there will always be a reason to set either a shorter or a longer window, we will want to provide the user with the means to do so. From the description above, it is clear that the best approach is to implement 15 msec as a "default" setting—this simply means that in the absence of instructions from the user, that is what the program will use. Therefore, rather than add a new required command-line argument, we can add an optional flag argument (e.g. *iscale*, used in chapter

1). As the object being modified is a "window," the flag character can appropriately be 'w', and this has to be followed by a number representing milliseconds. This will lead us to extend the usage message (stage 2):

```
printf("insufficient arguments.\n"
    "usage: envx [-wN] insndfile outfile.brk\n"
    "           -wN: set extraction window size to N msecs\n"
    "                (default: 15)\n"
);
```

This requires a variable to hold the value received from the user, such as

```
double windur;    /* duration of the window in msecs */
```

Additionally, we need to set up a default value for windur (expressed in milliseconds). Add this line under the #include statements at the top of the file:

```
#define DEFAULT_WINDOW_MSECS (15)
```

We can then incorporate this into the declaration of windur:

```
double windur = DEFAULT_WINDOW_MSECS;
```

Having defined windur, we can insert the required code to detect and read any command-line flags (stage 2). This simply involves adding a new case statement to the switch block included in the template code. The complete block is shown in listing 2.4.1, with the added code shown in boldface.

Listing 2.4.1: Implementation of the -wN Flag

```
if(argc > 1){
    char flag;
    while(argv[1][0] == '-'){
        flag = argv[1][1];
        switch(flag){
        /*TODO: handle any flag arguments here */
        case('\0'):
            printf("Error: missing flag name\n");
            return 1;
        case('w'):
            windur = atof(&argv[1][2]);
            if(windur<=0.0){
                printf("bad value for Window Duration."
                    "Must be positive.\n");
                return 1;
            }
            break;
```

```
        default:
            break;
        }
        argc--;
        argv++;
    }
}
```

We can now turn our attention to the code that implements the processing task of this program (stage 5). A simple procedure for envelope extraction uses the window size (in samples) as the size of each block read from the disk:

```
unsigned long winsize;
```

This value is calculated from `windur` (converted to seconds) using the sample rate of the infile. This is therefore a stage 3 task:

```
/* set buffersize to the required envelope window size */
    windur /= 1000.0;                           /* convert to secs */
    winsize = (unsigned long)(windur * inprops.srate);

    inframe = (float*) malloc(winsize * sizeof(float));
    if(inframe==NULL){
        puts("No memory!\n");
        error++;
        goto exit;
    }
```

In this way, inside the main processing loop, we can use the function `maxsamp` unmodified, passing it the sample block just read:

```
while ((framesread = psf_sndReadFloatFrames(ifd, inframe,
        winsize)) > 0){
    double amp;
    amp = maxsamp(inframe, framesread);
    ...
}
```

We want to write each new amplitude value, together with its time, to the output text file in the standard time/value format. We therefore require a counter to track the time of each block as it is read:

```
double brktime; /* holds the time for the current breakpoint time */
```

Having already converted `windur` to seconds, all we need do is increment the counter with this value, inside the loop. (See listing 2.4.2.)

Listing 2.4.2

```
brktime = 0.0;
while ((framesread = psf_sndReadFloatFrames(ifd, inframe,
        winsize)) > 0){
   double amp;
   amp = maxsamp(inframe, framesread);
       /* store brktime and amp as a breakpoint */
       ...
   brktime += windur;
}
```

Note that the order of the statements ensures that the first breakpoint time written to the file is always zero, as we require. To this end, brktime is initialized immediately before the processing loop. It is equally reasonable to initialize such variables in the declaration; doing it here helps to document the code by placing initializations as close as is possible to the code that depends on them.

The final task is to write each breakpoint line to the text file as it is calculated, as indicated by the comment line in listing 4.2. For this, we can use fprintf, not forgetting to check for any errors:

```
if(fprintf(fp,"%f\t%f\n",brktime,amp) < 2){
   printf("Failed to write to breakpoint file
           %s\n",argv[ARG_OUTFILE]);
   error++;
   break;
}
```

Note the use of the TAB control character \t in the fprintf format string to ensure that the numbers are nicely aligned in columns in the text file. As a help to the user, we can add a further counter variable to count the number of breakpoints generated:

```
unsigned long npoints;
```

This is used in the same way as brktime, except that it can simply be updated using the ++ increment operator. This counter can be used in a simple information message at the end of processing (stage 6), replacing the PEAK code in the template file:

```
if(framesread < 0)    {
   printf("Error reading infile. Outfile is incomplete.\n");
   error++;
}
   else
       printf("Done: %d errors\n",error);
   printf("%d breakpoints written to %s\n",
           npoints,argv[ARGV_OUTFILE]);
```

The complete processing loop is shown in listing 2.4.3. All the work we have done so far we have done to prepare for and support these 14 lines of code.

Listing 2.4.3

```
npoints = 0;
brktime = 0.0;
while ((framesread =
            psf_sndReadFloatFrames(ifd,inframe,winsize)) > 0){
    double amp;
    /* find peak sample of this block */
    amp = maxsamp(inframe,framesread);
    if(fprintf(fp,"%f\t%f\n",brktime,amp) < 2){
        printf("Failed to write to breakpoint file %s\n",
               argv[ARG_OUTFILE]);
        error++;
        break;
    }
    npoints++;
    brktime += windur;
}
```

You are now ready to build the program (remembering to update the makefile) and to test it on a range of input soundfiles. If you get compilation errors, the recommendation is, as usual, to refer to the example included on the DVD only as a last resort. Explore in particular the effect of different window sizes, not just on the amount of data generated but also on the shape of the extracted envelope as displayed in Gnuplot. See the exercises at the end of this section for further suggestions.

2.4.5   Efficient Envelope Processing—The Program `sfenv`

This program has a format very similar to that of *sfpan*; it takes a soundfile and a breakpoint file as inputs, and it produces a soundfile as output. Thus, although you can create a project from scratch, it is also reasonable to copy "sfpan" itself to a new file, *sfenv.c*, making the usual initial changes reflecting the new name and purpose. Note that this program requires the file *breakpoints.c* as well as the *portsf* library. Change the primary source filename to *sfenv.c* and make the usual initial code changes. Update the makefile too.

As was indicated in the introduction to this chapter, this program will be a little more complex than *envx*. The stated goal is to apply an amplitude envelope defined in a breakpoint file to a source soundfile, avoiding the inefficiencies identified in the previous section with respect to *sfpan*. This therefore demands an initial code analysis stage, to identify the code responsible for the inefficiency, while retaining any code that we may be able to keep for the improved version. As was noted, the troublesome code is in the function `val_at_brktime`—in *breakpoints.c*, the function is given a pointer to what is presumed to be the beginning of the breakpoint array.

The code can be broken down into four steps, using the idea of the "span" between adjacent breakpoints ("left" and "right"), where the "required span" is one spanning the target time, inclusive of the end points:

1. Step through the array from the beginning until the required breakpoint span is found.
2. If the target time is after last available span, return the final value of the final span.
3. If the span times are the same (in other words, we have a vertical jump in value), use the right-hand value.
4. If the span times are not the same, calculate the required value using linear interpolation.

The inefficiency clearly lies in the first of these stages. Recall that this function is called every sample, so that in the vast majority of cases step 1 (which amounts to a crude "search algorithm") will repeatedly find the same span. To avoid this unnecessary overhead, we need code that is able to keep track of where we are in the array, moving from one position to the next only when it is time to do so. In other words, whereas the function as implemented supports the use of arbitrary time values (and is thus a form of random access), we want to optimize the process for the important special case of non-random, forward *sequential* access by eliminating the costly search stage. It should not come as any surprise that to achieve this the top-level code must employ counter variables to keep track of the current breakpoint span inside the processing loop. The counting process must ensure that, within the process loop, the required span is available without the need for a search—including moving to the next span when required. Because breakpoint times are arbitrary (though guaranteed not to be decreasing), the process of moving from one span to the next may occur at any sample (spans may be smaller, larger or even exactly the same size as the sample block size) and is independent of the process loop.

In `val_at_brktime`, the counting process is revealed in the code that accesses a span:

```
left = points[i-1];
right = points[i];
```

From this we can determine that two counters are needed (representing the left and right indexes into the array), and that two `BREAKPOINT` variables are required:

```
BREAKPOINT leftpoint, rightpoint;
unsigned long ileft, iright;
```

We also need the `curpos` and `incr` variables as used in *envx*. The span index counters `ileft` and `iright` must be initialized to 0 and 1 respectively. When the time comes to move to the next span, both counters will be incremented, and the variables required for the interpolation will have to be recalculated. In `val_at_brktime` one variable is used:

width (frac is of course able to be a local variable inside the processing loop, as in *envx*). We can identify a complementary variable "height" represented by the expression

```
(right.value - left.value)
```

In val_at_brktime this expression is reasonable enough, but in the context of repeated processing it will evidently have the same value for any given span, so calculating it for each sample is wasteful. Here are the variables we will use to hold these values:

```
double frac, height, width;
```

We now have a complete initialization stage (beginning of stage 5), shown in listing 2.4.4. Whereas frac can, as before, be a variable local to the processing loop, width and height must be declared at top level, as they need to be initialized outside the loop.

Listing 2.4.4

```
1   /* init time position counter for reading envelope */
2   incr = 1.0 / inprops.srate;
3   /* setup counters to track through the breakpoint data */
4   curpos = 0.0;
5   ileft = 0;
6   iright = 1;
7   /* setup first span */
8   leftpoint = points[ileft];
9   rightpoint = points[iright];
10  width = rightpoint.time - leftpoint.time;
11  height = rightpoint.value - leftpoint.value;
```

The span code will be repeated inside the loop when the time comes to move to the next span. The first part of the complete processing loop can be taken almost verbatim from the code of val_at_brktime; this covers the check for a vertical jump and the interpolation inside a span. The second part deals with the check for end of span. This check can arise on any sample. If it finds a new span, it can simply repeat lines 8–11 of listing 2.4.4. Note that it does this by checking for the end of the available breakpoint data—see listing 2.4.5.

Listing 2.4.5

```
1   for(i=0; i < framesread;i++){
2       if(width == 0.0)
3           thisamp = rightpoint.value;
4       else {
5           /* not vertical: get interp value from this span */
6           frac = (curpos - leftpoint.time) / width;
7           thisamp = leftpoint.value + (height * frac);
8       }
```

```
9      /* move up ready for next sample */
10     curpos += incr;
11     /* if end of this span, step to next one if available*/
12     if(curpos > rightpoint.time){
13         ileft++; iright++;
14         if(iright < npoints){/*we have another span, move up */
15             leftpoint = points[ileft];
16             rightpoint = points[iright];
17             width = rightpoint.time - leftpoint.time;
18             height = rightpoint.value - leftpoint.value;
19         }
20         /* otherwise, we have reached the end of the data */
21     }
22     inframe[i] = (float)(inframe[i] * thisamp);
23 }
```

Before compiling and running the program, it is a good idea to check the completed code mentally for the various specific situations it has to be able to deal with by following the instructions step by step, assuming a particular input. It is especially important to check all the conditional tests that are used—for example, to check that the code will produce a valid value for `thisamp` in each of the cases listed below:

(1) the first audio sample
(2) inside a span (the interpolation code)
(3) the end of the current span, moving to the next
(4) when a vertical span is detected
(5) after the end of the breakpoint data—beyond the final span.

If you tried the last test in this list, you found that even after the end of the breakpoint data all the code as far as line 14 is still executed, which clearly is unnecessary and wasteful and which clearly requires optimization. The clue to the problem is in the comment in line 20. (Of course a comment is not executable code.) We could do with a variable that registered the fact that the end of the data has been reached, which we could then test within the loop. Such a variable would have only two values, corresponding to the two possible situations, and is often termed a "flag" variable. The usual choice for these variables would be 0 and 1, where 0 is, as we know, equivalent to the 'false' result of a conditional test.[14] The choice of name is also important. Apart from the general requirement of readability, it helps if the name makes it clear that it is a flag variable and not a counter:

```
int more_points;
```

This must be initialized to 1 (= "true") before the processing loop, and it is set to 0 if the test in line 14 evaluates to 'false'. We can then wrap all the calculation code inside the loop in a test for the new variable. The final version of the processing loop is shown in listing 2.4.6.

Listing 2.4.6

```
1   for(i=0; i < framesread;i++){
2       if(more_points){
3           if(width == 0.0)
4               thisamp = rightpoint.value;
5           else {
6               /* not vertical: get interp value from this span */
7                   frac = (curpos - leftpoint.time) / width;
8                   thisamp = leftpoint.value + ( height * frac);
9           }
10          /* move up ready for next sample */
11          curpos += incr;
12          if(curpos > rightpoint.time){/*go to next span? */
13              ileft++; iright++;
14              if(iright < npoints){/* have another span, go */
15                  leftpoint = points[ileft];
16                  rightpoint = points[iright];
17                  width = rightpoint.time - leftpoint.time;
18                  height = rightpoint.value - leftpoint.value;
19              }
20              else
21                  more_points = 0;
22          }
23      }
24      inframe[i] = (float)(inframe[i] * thisamp);
25  }
```

You should now be ready to compile and test the program. Use the program with a variety of breakpoint files—ones longer or shorter than the source (make sure the last value of the shorter one persists through the remainder of the output file), and ones with vertical jumps. (For a simple example of the latter, see table 2.2.)

Table 2.2
An envelope with a vertical jump.

x	y
0.0	0.0
2.0	0.5
2.0	1.0
3.5	0.85
3.5	0.25
4.5	0.1

You can then move onto more musical explorations, using *envx* and *sfenv* in combination. Create an envelope from a soundfile using *envx*, and apply that breakpoint file to another soundfile (or even to the original one—that often gives interesting results). The program *sfenv* can now be regarded not only as a musical tool in its own right, but also as a way to test *envx*. Suitable test soundfiles for applying envelopes include basic constant-amplitude waveforms such as sine waves and triangle waves—by loading the output files in a soundfile viewer such as Audacity, you can see immediately if the envelope has been applied as required. Similarly, Gnuplot is your workhorse tool for viewing breakpoint files.

2.4.6 Exercises

Exercise 2.4.1
By studying the code (including *breakpoints.c*), discover how it deals with the following breakpoint-file input:

(a) Only two breakpoints are supplied, but with the same time.
(b) Three or more breakpoints have the same time.

Adjacent breakpoints are not vertical, but are extremely close together, i.e. closer than two successive samples at the source sample rate. In each case, identify solutions that do not require processing to be aborted. Where appropriate, advise the user.

Exercise 2.4.2
Add an optional facility to *sfenv* to normalize the breakpoint amplitude data before processing.

Exercise 2.4.3
When a soundfile is enveloped twice (or more) by the same envelope, what would you expect the result to be? Test your prediction using a simple Attack, Decay, Sustain, Release (ADSR) envelope on a constant-amplitude source file. What is the special significance of this experiment with respect to amplitude envelopes? Make suitable modifications to *sfenv* to enable you to explore this further.

Exercise 2.4.4

(a) Test the error handling of both programs by attempting to write to insufficient disk space (e.g. to a floppy disk or a flash disk).
(b) The C library function `remove` defined in `<stdio.h>` can be used to delete a file from the disk (which must not be open):

```
int remove( const char *path );
```

Modify *envx* to delete the breakpoint file in the event of an error during processing, which would cause the file to be either empty or incomplete. Include a message to inform the user that the file has been deleted. Do the same to *sfenv* with respect to the output soundfile.

Exercise 2.4.5

(a) Modify *envx* to trap the case in which the –w flag is used to define a window size smaller than the distance between two samples in the source soundfile. Decide on a smallest reasonable size, implement your decision, and augment the usage message accordingly.
(b) Is there a largest reasonable size for the window size in *envx*? If there is, modify the program accordingly.

Exercise 2.4.6 (advanced)
Modify *envx* to normalize all the breakpoint data (i.e. scaled so that the peak amplitude value is 1) before it is written to the file. Add an optional flag to the command line to control this. (Hint: It is possible to calculate exactly how many breakpoints a given source file will require, given the window size.)

2.5   Waveform Synthesis

So far, we have used only existing soundfiles in our programs. The time has come to create our own sounds. In a way, this is the culminating task of all the programming studies so far. The primary interest for many readers will doubtless be the synthesis of complex, beautiful, arresting, surprising, powerful, original sounds, and there are many techniques for making such sounds—techniques that often match the sounds themselves in complexity. However, we have also discovered, most recently in the last section, that there is a need to use soundfiles consisting of simple waveforms for testing other programs and processes. We found that, to verify the correct operation of a program that applies an amplitude envelope to a soundfile, it helps if we have a soundfile containing a simple and pure signal such as a sine wave with constant amplitude throughout. In fact, audio and electronic engineers use a variety of dedicated test equipment, such as signal or "function" generators, to provide test signals with well-defined properties. Often such tools are designed and built by the engineers themselves to meet some specific requirement. That is to say, they are designed to enable the user to perform a particular task, such as generating a sine wave, as easily as possible. As an audio programmer, you will not only be designing synthesis and processing tools, you will also be designing the tools with which to design and test them.

For the programmer building a set of tools, an important consideration is to make their use as seamless as possible. You want to be able to select the tool, "plug it in," and use it. Even if working code models are available, you do not want to have to write them out from scratch each time. Thus an important aspect of designing synthesis tools is *encapsulation*—creating self-contained objects (functions, data types, etc.) that can be simply plugged into the framework code. This was the reason for the original function to convert breakpoint data into a sample stream, `val_at_brktime`. This function "hid" all the low-level code to scan through the breakpoint data; all the programmer had to do was call the function. However, this came at a price: the function was very inefficient and wasteful for this particular task. This inefficiency was overcome at the cost of re-exposing all the low-level code inside `main`. For a single program using one such object, this doesn't matter very much. However, it does not demand a great leap of the imagination to realize that we may want to use many of these objects, and for that reason adding large amounts of low-level code directly into `main` is not an attractive prospect. The classic demonstration of this is seen in additive synthesis, which uses a bank of oscillators (generating sine waves), each controlled by an amplitude envelope. Such an oscillator bank may require several hundred oscillators, and therefore may also require several hundred amplitude envelopes. Many other techniques can be expected to demand the use of several such objects. The programmer wants to create an oscillator with, ideally, one line of code, and to extract the signal from it with another line of code.

In this section, this requirement for encapsulation is tackled at the outset, as a program to generate some standard waveforms is developed. This approach is then applied to the envelope streaming code of the previous section, to realize the combined virtues of efficiency and encapsulation. This will enable the synthesis program to offer breakpoint-file control of both amplitude and frequency, without requiring `main` to be overfilled with low-level code. The result will be a set of basic synthesis and envelope-generation tools that can be expected to find wide use in future projects.

Some words of caution are required here. Space precludes more than an overview of the fundamental principles and techniques of sound synthesis. The focus here is not so much on learning about these as on learning how to use C (and later C++) to implement them. The variety of approaches to sound synthesis is matched by a similar variety in the ways of implementing them. In this section and in the following sections, this issue takes center stage. Far from demonstrating *the* way to implement something, the message emerges that there are many ways of implementing it, depending not only on the character of the target synthesis technique but also on the present and future requirements of the programmer. Sometimes efficiency of design may defer to convenience of coding, or to the requirements of greater flexibility in usage. Design decisions may derive not only from technical issues but also from musical and artistic requirements. Therefore, despite all the discussions about generality of design and modularity of the code, it is very much a moot point just how possible it is to achieve "complete" generality, given the composer's aptitude for both using and misusing the tools provided. A tool is designed for a use and cannot be expected automatically to be appropriate for hitherto unimagined uses.

2.5.1   Periodicity, Phase Increments, and the Trigonometric Functions

The `sin` function was first introduced in chapter 1 (as a virtual tuning fork) and subsequently in section 2.3 (in the context of the constant-power panning process). But despite the occasional hint, we have yet to consider the theory behind the sine wave in general and the `sin` and `cos` functions in particular. In taking on the task of sound synthesis, this exercise cannot be postponed any longer. In this subsection we engage with the theory head-on and discover something of why the `sin` and `cos` functions are so important to audio programmers and to musicians.

The full prototype of the `sin` function is

```
double sin(double angle);
```

The challenge in this subsection is to somehow convert this into an oscillator function such as

```
double oscil(double frequency);
```

where successive calls to `oscil` generate the required stream of samples forming a sine-wave signal. To do this, we need to understand a little more about sine waves and a great deal more about "angle."

2.5.1.1 Sine and Cosine—Going Round in Circles

In figure 2.5, sine and cosine waves are shown superimposed. To the casual eye, these two signals appear to be just two instances of the same signal, one shifted in time (i.e. horizontally). That understanding is correct—they are both examples of what mathematicians call a *sinusoid*. The difference between the two signals truly is the temporal distance between them. In the case of the sine and the cosine, this difference is both exact and fundamental. It arises from the two-dimensional view of a circle, and specifically of an object rotating at constant speed on the circumference of this circle, such as the second hand of a clock. Imagine that this represents an object in a two-dimensional world in which one cannot view a clock face directly, but only on edge, e.g. from below or from the side (figure 2.8). The problem here is that, viewed from any one point, the position of the hand is ambiguous. Viewed from below, 10 seconds is indistinguishable from 20, and 0 is indistinguishable from 30. Unless one already knows both the starting point and the direction of rotation, this ambiguity cannot be resolved. To provide this essential information, a second viewpoint must be introduced, at 90° to the first—e.g. a view from the right side[15] (figure 2.9). This will immediately show if the seconds hand stands at 0 or 30. Recording the positions from both viewpoints, as the hand rotates, leads to a sine wave (viewed from the left or right) and a cosine wave (viewed from above or below). As can be seen from the figure, the difference between sine and cosine is that the sine wave starts from a value of 0, whereas the cosine wave starts from 1.

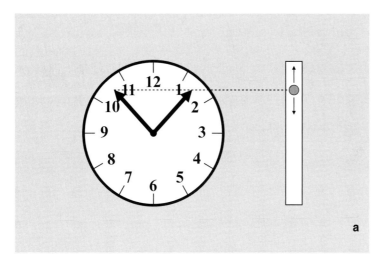

Figure 2.8
Reading a clock in the plane.

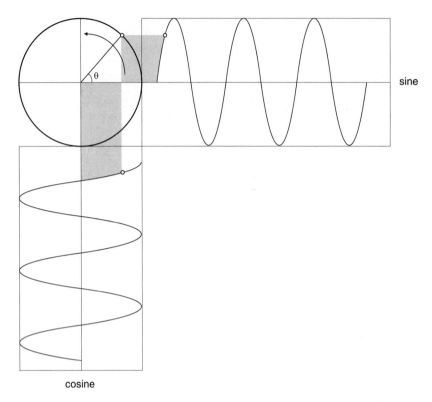

sine

cosine

Figure 2.9
Resolving the ambiguity—sine and cosine views of a revolving point.

Hence, to represent the position of the minute hand completely, two numbers are needed—either the direct horizontal and vertical coordinates, or a reference position and an angle. Indeed, where the reference position is defined in advance, just the angle value is required. We can now see that the sine and cosine functions define the reference position, and the required angle is the argument passed to the function. To complete the picture, we also need to know the direction of rotation, in order to know the position given by the angle. As it happens, the sine and cosine functions presume counterclockwise rotation, and the starting point is at "15 seconds" in terms of a clock, or at 1.0 on the horizontal axis, where cos(angle) = 1 and sin(angle) = 0. We can now see that this is exactly what is shown in figure 2.5.

2.5.1.2 Moving in Steps—The Sampled Phase Increment
To create a sine-wave oscillator in the computer, all we have to do is store, in successive samples, either the horizontal (cos) or vertical (sin) viewpoint as the angle changes in equal-

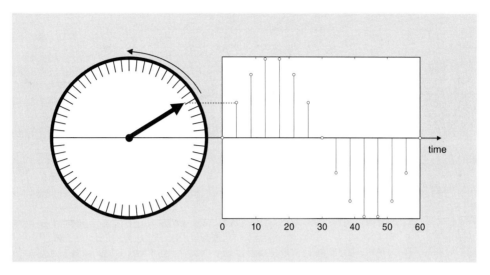

Figure 2.10
A sampled clock.

size steps around the circle. The speed of these steps is the *sample rate*, and the size of the step is the *phase increment*. For example, if we divide the circle into clock seconds, record one complete revolution second by second, and read the view of the second hand from the *x* axis, we will create a single-cycle sine wave comprising 60 samples (figure 2.10). So the sample rate is 1 sample per second, and the phase increment is 1/60 of the complete circle. If we continue with further revolutions, we obtain further cycles of this sine wave, ad infinitum—a "periodic signal," an oscillator. "Periodic" thus refers to any signal that can be described in terms of going around in a circle. To raise the frequency by an octave, we simply double the increment, so that in 60 samples we go around the circle twice. However, we still have to produce some specific numbers: a number representing amplitude (which corresponds to the radius of the rotating point), a number representing the size of a complete revolution, and then a number representing each angle increment. The amplitude is easy—we define it to be 1. The solution to the angle question draws not on clocks, longitude or latitude, but on the pure mathematics of circles.

2.5.1.3 π and the Radian

The number π is so famous that whole books have been devoted to it. It signifies the ratio of the circumference C of a circle to its diameter D (figure 2.11). In practice, as previous figures have shown, the radius R of the circle is more important to our purposes, so π is more conveniently expressed in terms of the radius. Among the many striking properties of this ratio, arguably the most extraordinary is that it cannot be represented exactly by a fraction (a ratio

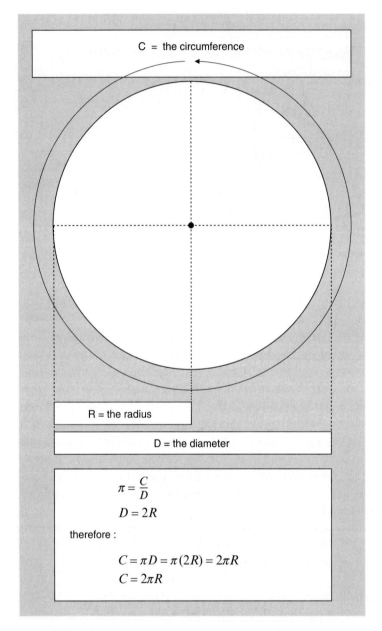

Figure 2.11
Geometry of the circle.

of integers) (and thus it is "irrational") or even by a finite series of fractional expressions (thus it is also "transcendental"). The digits of π go on forever. Therefore, any computer-based numerical representation inevitably involves approximations,[16] and the use of π is itself essential for a vast range of calculations. In short, for audio programmers π is the foundation of everything. Common C definitions for π and 2π are shown (with a little more precision than was used in chapter 1) in listing 2.5.1. We will be needing both π and 2π very frequently from now on.

Listing 2.5.1: C Definitions of π and 2π

```
#ifndef M_PI
#define M_PI (3.1415926535897932)
#endif
#define TWOPI (2.0 * M_PI)
```

In our terms, the circumference is equivalent to one full cycle of a sinusoid, so we can say that this same "unit cycle" has a *length* of $2\pi R$. The trick now is to recognize that an angle is equivalent to the length of the arc it subtends (relative to the circumference), so that, as well as signifying the radius, R can also signify the angle created by an arc the same length as the radius (figure 2.12). This "unit angle" is the *radian*, and the complete rotation around the circle can now be described, following the formula above, as a rotation by "two π radians." This is the basis both of formal mathematical computations involving circles and angles and of the C library trigonometric functions, including, of course, `sin` and `cos`. From table 2.3 we can see clearly that the values of `cos` repeat those of `sin` offset by one quadrant (quarter of a circle), or $\pi/2$. This offset constitutes the *phase difference* between the two sinusoids. Consider any start position in this circle—a starting phase. Each quarter-step around the circle is equivalent to the addition of $\pi/2$ to this position, that is, a *phase increment* of $\pi/2$ each time.

2.5.1.4   The Aliasing Problem

We can see from the figures and from table 2.3 what is meant by *aliasing* in a digitally sampled system. It is the result of trying to represent a frequency that is above half the sample rate (the Nyquist limit). In terms of the "unit cycle," this means any angle increment that is equal to or greater than π (exactly half the circle). In table 2.3 we see that both `sin` and `cos` can find within the circle two points equal to zero. These points are thus ambiguous. Given the fact that we are seeing only snapshots of the rotating phase, we have in this case no idea in which direction the phase is rotating—either direction would give the same answer. This is a graphical representation of the Nyquist limit. Given a sinusoid exactly at that frequency, and depending on the exact sampling times, we may "see" either opposite peaks of the cycle or the two zero crossings. So in this case we see either a DC signal (0 Hz) or a signal at the Nyquist limit of some amplitude.

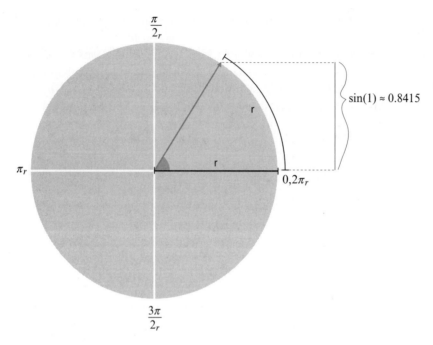

Figure 2.12
The radian.

Table 2.3
Values of sin( ) and cos( ) for fractions of π.

sin	cos
$\sin(0) = \sin(2\pi) = 0.0$	$\cos(0) = \cos(2\pi) = 1.0$
$\sin(\pi/2) = 1.0$	$\cos(\pi/2) = 0$
$\sin(p) = 0$	$\cos(\pi) = -1$
$\sin(3\pi/2) = -1$	$\cos(3\pi/2) = 0$

Similarly, if the angle increment is larger than π radians (for example, three quarters of the circle, or $3\pi/2$), the snapshots will look identical to a rotation of $\pi/2$ in the opposite direction. (This is why in films rotating wagon wheels or airplane propellers can appear to be turning backward.) The consequence is that any attempt to generate a frequency above the Nyquist limit will in fact generate a frequency symmetrically below it, in opposite phase. Seen in terms of the stream of digital samples, we need a minimum of two samples (of opposite sign) to define a sinusoid, and that minimum itself is the Nyquist limit. We really need to keep frequencies just *below* the Nyquist limit to be sure not to incur aliasing.

2.5.2 A Sine-Wave Oscillator in C—Calculating Sample Increments

We know that the C library function sin takes an argument in radians, and we know that a full cycle of a sinusoid covers an angle (which we can also consider as a length) of 2π radians. The one arithmetic task we must perform in order to write a sine-wave oscillator is to reconcile these values with an audio sample rate. For a given sample rate SR, we have

```
incr = 2 * M_PI / SR ;
```

Rendered as a sample stream, stepping around the circle by this value of incr, will generate one cycle in 44,100 samples—a 1-hertz signal. It is now a simple matter to define an increment for any frequency:

```
incr = freq * 2 * M_PI / SR ;
```

To complete our sinusoid oscillator, therefore, given a sample rate and a required frequency, we merely have to define a starting phase and convert the frequency into a phase increment, passing the accumulating phase to the sin function for as many samples as we require. Prototype code starting at zero phase, and writing to a hypothetical array of floats, is shown in listing 2.5.2.

Listing 2.5.2: A Basic Sine-Wave Oscillator

```
1    double startphase = 0.0;
2    double srate       = 44100.0;
3    double freq        = 440.0;
4    double curphase    = 0.0; /* use M_PI/2 for cosine */
5    double incr        = freq * TWOPI / srate;
6
7    for(i=0; i < outsamps; i++) {
8        output[i] = (float) sin(curphase);
9        curphase += incr;
10       if(curphase >= TWOPI)
11           curphase -= TWOPI;
12   }
```

Note the code (lines 10 and 11) to "wrap" the increasing phase by 2π. It is quite common for programmers to omit this step, relying on the ability of the sin function (as defined by the ANSI standard) to accept a phase of any size (typically up to $\pm 2^{63}$ before loss of accuracy), and perform the required wrapping internally. The code as shown is clearly more self-documenting, which is arguably more important at this stage; and, as will be seen later, there are waveforms not involving sin or cos that do require direct wrapping in this way, so adding this code is a good habit to get into. It has also to be said that not all compilers are the same, and some have been found to degrade very quickly when large "unwrapped" values are given to the sin and cos functions.

We can also see from this code what the meaning of a negative frequency is: it will lead to a negative value for incr, which therefore rotates the phase around the circle in the opposite direction, or, so to speak, backward through the wave cycle. For plain synthesis of a signal, we have no need for a negative frequency, and we can argue the case for not supporting it. However, should we want to implement FM (frequency modulation) synthesis, negative frequency values are not only possible but likely, so we will have to add code to wrap curphase upward:

```
if(curphase < 0.0)
    curphase += TWOPI;
```

There is scope for a subtle error here, an error that all audio programmers should watch for. If both the maximum test and the minimum test use a plain < or > operator, neither the maximum phase value nor the minimum phase value is included, posing the danger of a slight numerical error (and in even worse cases, an infinite loop). In the above example, the maximum value TWOPI is compared to using >= (line 10), while the minimum value is checked with >.

2.5.3   Creation of Oscillator Objects—Code Encapsulation

At the most fundamental level, an *object* is defined by two things: (1) it has internal "state," and (2) it has associated functions, or "methods," which depend on or modify that state, and which may receive inputs and generate outputs. In the case of the oscillator, the variables associated with internal state are plain to see—the phase itself and the phase increment. The sample rate and frequency (where we will want the latter to be time-variable) are inputs, and the generated sample stream is the output.

We have already seen an example of an object with internal state: the original version of the breakpoint stream object, epitomized by the now much discussed function val_at_brktime. The problem with this function, as we saw in section 2.4, was that the state was in effect re-computed each time the function was called, and similarly that state was destroyed each time the function returned.

To avoid this repeated creation and destruction of internal state, we need to define a data structure to contain it, together with functions that use it. To do this, we need a struct containing the variables declared in listing 2.5.2. To emphasize the fact that we are trying to define an object, and to make it as easy to use as is possible, we can declare this struct an *abstract type* using typedef. Note that this is a definition of a type and not the declaration of a variable. This code belongs in a header file, which you are now ready to create—call it *wave.h* (listing 2.5.3). We will add more material to this header file as we proceed, not least the prototypes of functions that use the new type. Start by adding the definitions for M_PI and TWOPI in listing 5.1. Similarly, create the implementation file *wave.c* (which will of course #include "wave.h") to contain the definition of the functions that apply to this structure. Through all the following descriptions, keep in mind the principle that is at work:

a fully worked "object" comprises a tightly coupled combination of structure and functions. In a very real sense, the functions *belong* to the structure.

Listing 2.5.3 Definition of the OSCIL Abstract Type

```
/* wave.h ; definition of OSCIL type */
typedef struct t_oscil
{
    double twopiovrsr; /* to hold a constant value 2PI/sr */
    double curfreq;
    double curphase;
    double incr;
} OSCIL;
```

Note that OSCIL includes a variable, twopiovrsr, to contain the value of a frequently required constant (which is dependent on the input parameter srate). Always conscious of the need to avoid unnecessary duplication or recalculation of code, we will want to look for any opportunity to use such variables (which are really *constants* for a given sample rate) when implementing code that must run very frequently. This enables us to use variables of the new type just as we do any standard C type:

```
OSCIL sine_oscil;
```

Now we need to turn our attention to the implementation file *wave.c*. We require, as a minimum, two functions that take a pointer to an OSCIL object as an argument: an initialization function (which will have to define the required sample rate) and a function that generates samples. Pointer arguments are required, as we need to be able to modify the internal state contained within the oscillator. Listing 2.5.4 shows a simple initialization function, with the frequency-related variables initialized to zero. Note the use of the *pointer indirection* notation -> to access the variables inside the OSCIL structure. The code uses the defined symbol TWOPI we previously added to *wave.h*.

Listing 2.5.4 Simple Initialization Function for an OSCIL Object

```
void oscil_init(OSCIL* osc, unsigned long srate)
{
    osc->twopiovrsr = TWOPI / (double) srate;
    osc->curfreq = 0.0;
    osc->curphase = 0.0;
    osc->incr = 0.0;
}
```

This requires that a complete object of type OSCIL has been declared, and that the pointer to it has been passed to oscil_init. We may, for example, use a simple creation function that does nothing more than allocate storage and return the pointer:

```
OSCIL* oscil(void)
{
    OSCIL* osc = (OSCIL*) malloc(sizeof(OSCIL));
    if(osc == NULL)
        return NULL;
    return osc;
}
```

This separation of creation and initialization is often necessary in interactive real-time applications (including audio plug-ins) where the sample rate may not be available at the time the object is created. This also makes it possible to re-initialize an object—for example, to restart an envelope, or to set a new sample rate. However, this dual-function approach is not always ideal for self-contained programs, being more vulnerable to errors, especially by those still at the early stages of learning programming. For example, if by mistake only a pointer to OSCIL is declared and passed to the function, or if the pointer is NULL, oscil_init will crash with an access violation error. To prevent that, and to encapsulate the object even further, it is possible to design a function that will both create and initialize the object at once (listing 2.5.5). Add that function to *wave.c*. Instead of void, the function returns either NULL (in the event of a memory failure) or a pointer to a fully created and initialized object.

The main aspect of this approach is the use of malloc to create external storage for an OSCIL, which will persist after the function returns.[17] The documentation for this function should tell the user to free this object when it is no longer required.

Note that it is entirely reasonable to define alternative creation or initialization functions for a particular object type. The only requirement imposed by the C language is that the names of functions must be unique.

When we come to explore C++, we will discover a valuable new facility known as "function overloading," which allows multiple functions of the same name to be defined so long as the argument lists and/or the return types are different. For now, however, we can manage very well with our compact all-in-one approach.

Listing 2.5.5: A Combined OSCIL Creation and Initialization Function

```
OSCIL* new_oscil(unsigned long srate)
{
    OSCIL* p_osc;

    p_osc = (OSCIL*) malloc(sizeof(OSCIL));
    if(p_osc == NULL)
        return NULL;
    p_osc->twopiovrsr = TWOPI / (double) srate;
    p_osc->curfreq = 0.0;
    p_osc->curphase = 0.0;
    p_osc->incr = 0.0;
```

```
        return p_osc;
}

/* used like this: */
OSCIL *osc = new_oscil(44100);
```

We can now define the sample-generation function[18] (listing 2.5.6), which is modeled on the example in listing 2.5.2. It must be called for each required sample. It incorporates the required support for a changing value for frequency, and for negative frequencies. It is important to check its behavior on the first call. The first thing this function does after generating the initial sample (dependent only on curphase) is check for a change of freq, which updates the value of incr if necessary—a standard "read and update" approach. Note that incr is recalculated only when curfreq changes, so that in the case of an unchanging frequency redundant processing is kept to a minimum. Note also that no error checking is performed on the input pointer—this is for reasons of efficiency, as this function will be called *very* frequently.

Listing 2.5.6 Sample Generation Function for the OSCIL Type

```
double sinetick(OSCIL* p_osc, double freq)
{
    double val;

    val = sin(p_osc->curphase);
    if(p_osc->curfreq != freq){
        p_osc->curfreq = freq;
        p_osc->incr = p_osc->twopiovrsr * freq;
    }
    p_osc->curphase += p_osc->incr;
    if(p_osc->curphase >= TWOPI)
        p_osc->curphase -= TWOPI;
    if(p_osc->curphase < 0.0)
        p_osc->curphase += TWOPI;
    return val;
}

/* used like this: */
for(i=0;i < nframes;i++)
    outframe[i] = sinetick(osc,freq); /* modify freq ad lib.*/
```

With this, we have succeeded almost completely in creating the function we sought at the beginning of subsection 2.5.1, the difference being the added need to pass a pointer to an OSCIL variable used to preserve the internal state of the oscillator between calls. This is a highly idiomatic approach in C. We will be making much use of it.

2.5.4   Create a Plain Test Program

Before moving on to more elaborate features, it is reasonable to implement the code developed so far in an initial "proof of concept" program that simply produces, as a mono sound-file, a sine wave at a requested duration, amplitude, and frequency. You have indeed done this before, back in chapter 1; the differences here are the design of the code and the use of the *portsf* library. You now have two possibilities: copy *main.c* to a new file and develop the new program from that, or copy and adapt one of the programs previously presented. As this is a synthesis program, there is no `infile`. Call the program *siggen* (for "signal generation"), and call the main source file *siggen.c*. As usual, the program requires linking with *portsf*; and of course we are also using the new source file *wave.c*. This also is a program that will become more complex—the version of *siggen.c* on the DVD represents the final version, not this preliminary stage. It is most important that you follow through all the details of writing this program from first principles.

The first task is to complete the source files implementing the oscillator code itself. The header file *wave.h* should now contain the definition of `OSCIL`, together with the definitions of `M_PI` and `TWOPI`, and the prototypes of the functions `new_oscil` and `sinetick` as defined in listings 2.5.4 and 2.5.5. For synthesis we need a command line with, at least, arguments for duration, amplitude, and frequency as inputs; but a sample-rate argument will be useful too:

```
sinetest outfile dur srate amp freq
```

This leads to a revised enumeration:

```
enum {ARG_PROGNAME,ARG_OUTFILE,ARG_DUR,ARG_SRATE,
      ARG_AMP,ARG_FREQ,ARG_NARGS};
```

You will have to define corresponding variables `srate`, `dur`, `amp`, and `freq` for each of these parameters in the usual way and write the code to obtain them from the command line, with the required error checking. Reject values at or below zero for each argument.

The most obvious difference from previous programs is that, as this is a synthesis program, there is no `infile`. This requires not only that all template code associated with the `infile` be removed, but also that the processing loop itself be adapted, since it will only be writing to an outfile, not reading from an infile. Here it is important to initialize the `outprops` data for `psf_sndCreate`. In the absence of an infile defining these properties, we have to set them directly:

```
/* define outfile format - this sets mono 16bit format */
srate = atof[ARG_SRATE];
...
outprops.srate = srate;
outprops.chans = 1;
```

```
outprops.samptype = PSF_SAMP_16; /* or whatever is required */
outprops.chformat = STDWAVE;
```

(In a fully developed program, all these settings might be obtained from the command line.)

From `srate` and `dur` we can derive the number of samples required (rounded to the nearest sample); this can then be used to find the required number of blocks of size `NFRAMES`, plus a remainder if there is one (here we use integer division and the number of whole blocks may be zero for a very small value of `outframes`):

```
unsigned long nbufs, outframes, remainder;
. . .
dur = atof(argv[ARG_DUR]);
. . .
outframes = (unsigned long) (dur * outprops.srate + 0.5);
nbufs = outframes / nframes;
remainder = outframes - nbufs * nframes;
if(remainder > 0)
        nbufs++;
```

Note that this uses integer division, and `nbufs` could be zero. The final conditional increment for `nbufs` ensure that the processing loop will run at least once. The preceding code will need to ensure that a zero value for `dur` is rejected.

Listing 2.5.7 shows the required modifications to the standard processing loop. Note that two index counters are now required, one for `nbufs` and one for `nframes`; the latter is set to the value of `remainder` for the final block.

Listing 2.5.7: Processing Loop for Synthesis

```
for(i=0; i < nbufs; i++){
   if(i == nbufs-1)
      nframes = remainder;
   for(j=0; j < nframes; j++)
      outframe[j] = (float) (amp * sinetick(p_osc, freq));
      if(psf_sndWriteFloatFrames(ofd,
         outframe, nframes)!=nframes){
         printf("Error writing to outfile\n");
         error++;
         break;
      }
   }
```

This completes the requirements for a basic monophonic test program for the sine-wave oscillator. Build the program, and generate some sine waves at various frequencies. Don't forget that the fact that the program runs to completion is not a sufficient guarantee that the program is working properly. The PEAK information is a first confirmation—the reported amplitude should match the requested value given to the program. Audio programmers soon discover that it is wise to inspect the output of such programs with a soundfile editor, for a visual confirmation that the results are as expected, before risking direct playback. Errors in soundfiles (such as heavy clipping or noise) may be decidedly nasty to listen to, and at worst may damage your speakers or your ears if auditioned at high levels.

With the program working correctly, you now have a means of generating source files with which to test programs such as *sfenv*. A sine-wave source offers the cleanest signal with which to audition amplitude envelopes. But this is just the beginning.

2.5.5   Generating Other Standard Waveforms

Anyone who has used a traditional analog synthesizer is aware that, in addition to the sinusoids, there are several other important geometric waveforms: the triangle, square, and sawtooth waves, which in idealized form contain an infinite number of harmonics in precisely defined amounts (figure 2.13). These waveforms are the primary building blocks of synthesizers employing subtractive synthesis, partly because they are easily generated by analog circuitry. Unfortunately, they present substantial challenges for a high-quality digital implementation, as such ideal "straight-line" waveforms are not band-limited—the sharp corners in the waveform introduce substantial amounts of aliasing, which are easily audible for even middle-range fundamental frequencies, and which no amount of filtering will properly remove. However, such signals still have a role to play—they are useful for control signals, such as low-frequency oscillators, and as test signals. Therefore, it is appropriate to add support for them to our "function generator" program, not least because these simple shapes are very easy to generate, and we can make use of much of the code already developed for OSCIL. Just how easy it is to generate these shapes can been seen in listing 2.5.8. The phase calculations already worked out for OSCIL will serve us equally well for these other waveforms, and all that is required is a custom "tick" function for each one, using the sample OSCIL structure. Note just how much code is duplicated in each function.[19] Also note the frequent use of the constant numeric expression 1.0/TWOPI. It would be reasonable to simplify this to avoid the division, perhaps by defining yet another symbol such as ONEOVERTWOPI. This is indeed possible, but it should not be necessary for optimization. As was noted earlier, a good compiler will calculate the value of such a constant expression at compile time, so that no code optimization is required; here, as it contributes to the self-documenting of the code, we may make the choice to preserve the formal expression of the calculation.

Listing 2.5.8: Tick Functions for Triangle, Square, and Sawtooth Waveforms

(a) square

```
double sqtick(OSCIL* p_osc, double freq)
{
```

time domain   frequency domain

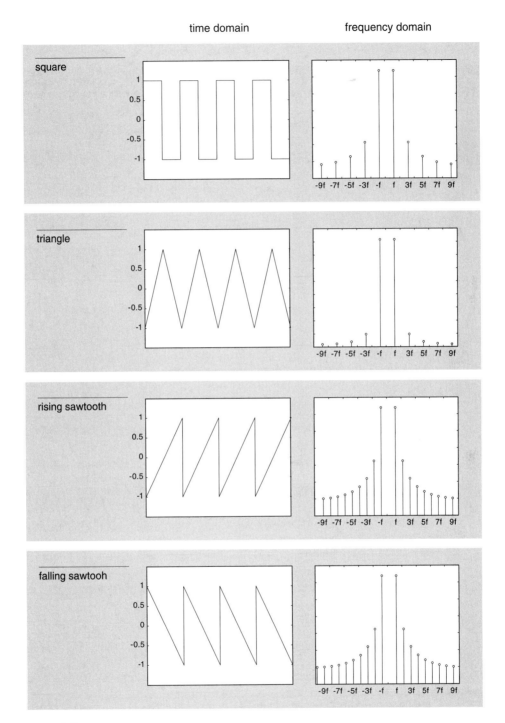

Figure 2.13
Standard geometric waveforms.

```
        double val;

        if(p_osc->curfreq != freq){
            p_osc->curfreq = freq;
            p_osc->incr = p_osc->twopiovrsr * freq;
        }
        if(p_osc->curphase <= M_PI)
            val = 1.0;
        else
            val = -1;
        p_osc->curphase += p_osc->incr;
        if(p_osc->curphase >= TWOPI)
            p_osc->curphase -= TWOPI;
        if(p_osc->curphase < 0.0)
            p_osc->curphase += TWOPI;
        return val;
}
```

(b) downward sawtooth

```
double sawdtick(OSCIL* p_osc, double freq)
{
        double val;

        if(p_osc->curfreq != freq){
            p_osc->curfreq = freq;
            p_osc->incr = p_osc->twopiovrsr * freq;
         }
         val = 1.0 - 2.0 * (p_osc->curphase * (1.0 / TWOPI) );
        p_osc->curphase += p_osc->incr;
        if(p_osc->curphase >= TWOPI)
            p_osc->curphase -= TWOPI;
        if(p_osc->curphase < 0.0)
            p_osc->curphase += TWOPI;
        return val;
}
```

(c) upward sawtooth

```
double sawutick(OSCIL* p_osc, double freq)
{
        double val;

        if(p_osc->curfreq != freq){
            p_osc->curfreq = freq;
            p_osc->incr = p_osc->twopiovrsr * freq;
        }
```

```
        val = (2.0 * (p_osc->curphase * (1.0 / TWOPI) )) - 1.0;
            p_osc->curphase += p_osc->incr;
        if(p_osc->curphase >= TWOPI)
            p_osc->curphase -= TWOPI;
        if(p_osc->curphase < 0.0)
            p_osc->curphase += TWOPI;
        return val;
}
```

(d) triangle

```
double tritick(OSCIL* p_osc, double freq)
{
    double val;

    if(p_osc->curfreq != freq){
        p_osc->curfreq = freq;
        p_osc->incr = p_osc->twopiovrsr * freq;
    }
    /* rectified sawtooth */
    val = (2.0 * (p_osc->curphase * (1.0 / TWOPI) )) - 1.0;
    if(val < 0.0)
        val = -val;
    val = 2.0 * (val - 0.5);
    p_osc->curphase += p_osc->incr;
    if(p_osc->curphase >= TWOPI)
        p_osc->curphase -= TWOPI;
    if(p_osc->curphase < 0.0)
        p_osc->curphase += TWOPI;
    return val;
}
```

Add these function definitions to *wave.c*, and their prototypes to *wave.h*. To enable the user to select any one of the available wave types, together with arguments for amplitude and frequency, you will have to add new command-line arguments to the list. The use of the enum list enables you to add these in any position without having to rewrite the existing code:

```
enum{ARG_PROGNAME,ARG_OUTFILE,ARG_TYPE,
     ARG_DUR,ARG_SRATE,ARG_AMP,ARG_FREQ,
     ARG_NARGS};
```

We also need an enum list for the waveform types themselves, not least because we may anticipate adding further choices to the list later:

```
enum {WAVE_SINE,WAVE_TRIANGLE,WAVE_SQUARE,
      WAVE_SAWUP,WAVE_SAWDOWN, WAVE_NTYPES};
```

This leads to an extended usage message:

```
printf(
    "usage: siggen outfile wavetype dur srate nchans amp freq\n"
                "where wavetype =:\n"
                "0 = sine\n"
                "1 = triangle\n"
                "2 = square\n"
                "3 = sawtooth up\n"
                "4 = sawtooth down\n"
                "dur = duration of outfile (seconds)\n"
                "srate = required sample rate of outfile\n"
                "amp = amplitude (0 < amp <= 1.0)\n"
                "freq = frequency (freq > 0)\n"
        );
```

We can receive the new information into a variable:

```
int wavetype;
. . .
wavetype = atoi(argv[ARG_TYPE]);
if(wavetype < WAVE_SINE || wavetype > WAVE_NTYPES){
    printf("Error: bad value for wave type\n");
    return 1;
}
```

To select the required oscillator function, the natural C idiom to use is the switch. . . case statement. However, we now have reached the tricky part—where in the code do we use it?

2.5.6   Pointers to Functions

The least efficient place to select the oscillator function is inside the inner processing loop:

```
for(j=0; j < nframes; j++){
    switch(wavetype){
    case WAVE_SINE:
        outframe[j] = amp * sinetick(p_osc, freq);
        break;
    ...
```

This would run the switch statement on each sample, and consume needless CPU cycles— we know that the same function will be selected each time. A less expensive solution, though at the cost of increased code size, is to apply the switch statement at top level and duplicate the complete processing loop code for each alternative:

```
switch(wavetype){
case(WAVE_SINE):
    for(i=0; i < nbufs;i++){
        if(i == nbufs-1)
            nframes = remainder;
        for(j=0; j < nframes; j++){
            outframe[j] = (float) (amp * sinetick(p_osc, freq));
        ...
    }
```

In many cases, this would prove a reasonable solution. There is, however, an even more powerful way to solve the problem. It exploits the important fact that all the tick functions are of exactly the same form:

```
double tickfunc(OSCIL* p_psc, double freq);
```

Inside the computer, functions are not so different from variables, structures, or other data—they exist in some position in memory, and therefore have a memory address associated with them. We can understand the function name as a pointer to where the function is represented in memory. Just as it is possible in C to define a pointer to any type (i.e. a variable that is a pointer—"a variable is an instance of a type"), it is also possible to define a type, and thus a variable, that is a pointer to a function. Just as the function has to be fully defined, so the pointer to it is specific to a given prototype. It is a somewhat convoluted notation, thanks to the fact that, whereas C has names for all built-in types (`float`, `int`, `double`, `char`, etc.), it does not have a general name for "a function" (not least because there is an infinite number of ways of defining functions, whereas a `float` is just a `float`). Instead, the function pointer is indicated by a special use of parentheses:

```
double (*tickfunc)(OSCIL* osc, double);
```

This declares a variable called `tickfunc` that is a pointer to a function returning a `double` and taking the two arguments enclosed in parentheses. There are two parts to this declaration: the type definition and the name. The type of the object is a "pointer to function," indicated by the asterisk enclosed in parentheses followed by another pair of parentheses containing any function arguments:

```
double (*)(OSCIL*, double)
```

while `tickfunc`, placed immediately following the lone asterisk, is the name of a variable of that type.

The parentheses around `*tickfunc` are vital. Without them, the asterisk would, following C's *associativity* rules, associate to the keyword `double`, and the definition would become that of a concrete function that returns a pointer to a double, which is not what we want (we could not assign the name of another function to it). The final trick in achieving our goal is to use `typedef` to create a name for the specific function-pointer type we want:

```
typedef double (*tickfunc)(OSCIL* osc, double);
```

This is the line we want to put somewhere in *"wave.h,"* after the definition of OSCIL itself. Given the typedef, instead of writing the long-winded definition above to declare a function-pointer variable, we can simply write

```
tickfunc tick;
```

We can then freely assign to this variable the name of any function sharing the same prototype:

```
tick = sinetick;
tick = tritick;
/* and so on */
```

This solves our problem in *siggen.c* with no code bloat and no loss of efficiency: we can run our switch statement as soon as we have read the command-line argument into wavetype, assigning the required function name to the variable tick, and inside the processing loop we can call tick rather than a specific function. (See listing 2.5.9.)

Listing 2.5.9: Using a Function Pointer to Select a Tick Function

(a) switch statement

```
switch(wavetype){
case(WAVE_SINE):
    tick = sinetick;
    break;
case(WAVE_TRIANGLE):
    tick = tritick;
    break;
case(WAVE_SQUARE):
    tick = sqtick;
    break;
case(WAVE_SAWUP):
    tick = sawutick;
    break;
case(WAVE_SAWDOWN):
    tick = sawdtick;
}
```

(b) processing loop: inner loop

```
for(j=0; j < nframes; j++)
    outframe[j] = amp * tick(p_osc, freq);
```

The ability to define pointers to functions is one of the most important features of C. They can be used anywhere any other type of pointer can be—for example, as a member of a struct, as an element of an array, or passed as arguments to other functions, or returned from functions. When the time comes to explore the fundamentals of C++, it will become evident that much of the language depends on the use of function pointers.

The example presented here depends on the fact that all the tick functions share the same prototype. As soon as we find we have to define a tick function with, say, two arguments, this simple system starts to break down. Thus the programmer must be constantly on the lookout not only for solutions to problems but also for the problems caused by the solutions. The function pointer is far from being a solution to every problem that may arise, but it is useful enough that it can strongly influence the design of functions and of whole applications.

This is a good time to rebuild *siggen*.c with the new waveform facilities and test it to find out how the new waveform shapes sound at high frequencies, where aliasing can be expected to be the most easily apparent. However, to hear aliasing in its full glory we need to be able to move the frequency around. Therefore, before considering the program complete, we should add support for at least breakpoint control of frequency. We will do this by emulating the efficiency and encapsulation of the oscillator code. We not only want to retain the efficiency developed in section 2.4, but also the encapsulation achieved in the oscillator code. In short, we will create a "breakpoint streaming engine" that performs the task described at the outset of section 2.4, to convert a breakpoint file into a stream of values at the required sample rate.

2.5.7   An Encapsulated and Efficient Breakpoint Stream Object

It will be useful here to review the elements of our oscillator design:

• a structure, containing variables that represent the internal "state," and defined as an abstract type
• a creation function—defined with arguments required for construction, such as the sample rate—that allocates a new object using malloc, initializes it, and returns a pointer to the new object
• a signal-generation function that returns values for successive sample "ticks," taking as an argument at least a pointer to an object of the defined type that preserves the running state of the object.

In implementing a streaming object for breakpoint data, we already have some resources available, defined in *breakpoints.h* and *breakpoints.c*, for instance the core BREAKPOINT type, and the function get_breakpoints, which reads the data from a file, applies some basic validation tests, and fills an array of BREAKPOINTs.

Using the example of the processing code presented in section 2.4, the structure that defines our new object requires counters to give giving the current position in the array, variables holding some information about the breakpoint data as a whole, and variables holding information about the current span. These variables should be recalculated only at the point of moving to the next span. All these ideas lead to a possible structure as shown in listing 2.5.10. You may find it useful to check these fields against the code presented in listing 2.4.6. The code will of course have to be added to *breakpoints.h*, together with the prototypes for the functions defined below.

Listing 2.5.10: Definition of the BRKSTREAM Type

```
typedef struct breakpoint_stream {
    BREAKPOINT* points;
    BREAKPOINT leftpoint,rightpoint;
    unsigned long npoints;
    double curpos;
    double incr;
    double width;
    double height;
    unsigned long ileft,iright;
    int more_points;
} BRKSTREAM;
```

We can now proceed to define the creation and initialization function for the new type. We will want to control the opening and closing of the source file externally, so the appropriate variable to pass to the creation function is an open FILE*. Note that once the breakpoint data has been copied into the array, the FILE pointer is of no more interest—there is no need to store it in the BRKSTREAM structure. As with the oscillators, the function will also require the sample rate. As a final convenience for the user, we can use a third pointer argument to receive, optionally, the size of the breakpoint data. This leads to a creation function as shown in listing 2.5.11. Note that the initialization code completely prepares the first span (as done in listing 2.4.4), and that, where errors are detected, any allocated memory is freed before the function returns.

Listing 2.5.11: The Function bps_newstream

```
BRKSTREAM* bps_newstream(FILE *fp, unsigned long srate, unsigned long
*size)
{
    BRKSTREAM* stream;
    BREAKPOINT *points;
    unsigned long npoints;

    if(srate == 0){
        printf("Error creating stream - srate cannot be zero\n");
        return NULL;
    }
```

```
stream = (BRKSTREAM*) malloc(sizeof(BRKSTREAM));
if(stream == NULL)
    return NULL;
/* load breakpoint file and setup stream info */
points = get_breakpoints(fp, &npoints);
if(points == NULL){
    free(stream);
return NULL;
}

if(stream->npoints < 2){
    printf("breakpoint file is too small - "
            "at least two points required\n");
free(stream);
return NULL;
}
/* init the stream object */
stream->points = points;
stream->npoints = npoints;
/* counters */
stream->curpos = 0.0;
stream->ileft = 0;
stream->iright = 1;
stream->incr = 1.0 / srate;
/* first span */
stream->leftpoint = stream->points[stream->ileft];
stream->rightpoint   = stream->points[stream->iright];
stream->width  = stream->rightpoint.time
                            - stream->leftpoint.time;
stream->height = stream->rightpoint.value
                            - stream->leftpoint.value;
stream->more_points = 1;
if(size)
    *size = stream->npoints;
return stream;
}
```

There is one very important point to note about this function. As well as allocating the main
BRKSTREAM object itself, which the user will know to free after use, the function also calls
get_breakpoints, which itself allocates memory. This will also have to be freed if there is
not to be a memory leak. As the contents of the BRKSTREAM structure are visible in the
header file, and thus are public, it is of course possible for the user to do this at top level:

```
free(stream->points);
```

However, one principle of encapsulation (a principle that has special importance for C++ programmers) is that the user should not have to deal with the internal management of an object, but instead should perform all processing of BRKSTREAM objects via a library of functions supplied for the purpose (an API, in other words)—functions that serve to hide the internals of the object from the user. Therefore, to complement bps_newstream, we define a simple function bps_freepoints that frees any internal memory (listing 2.5.12). The function must of course verify both the supplied stream pointer and the presence of data (in case the function is called by mistake multiple times on the same object), but it is harmless enough here to fail silently in those cases, so that no return value is needed. The following should be noted:

• A non-NULL pointer evaluates to logical "true," so it is sufficient to write if(stream) rather than if(stream != NULL).
• The if test uses the fact that evaluation of a logical expression stops on the first "false" result (see subsection 2.3.4).
• The code sets stream->npoints to NULL after calling free. This ensures that should the function be called repeatedly by mistake, it will not crash.

Listing 2.5.12: The Function bps_freepoints

```
void bps_freepoints(BRKSTREAM* stream)
{
    if(stream && stream->points){
        free(stream->points);
        stream->points = NULL;
    }
}
```

The tick function itself is shown in listing 2.5.13. There is nothing new in this except for minor reordering. The fact that this is a self-contained function enables us to return as soon as more_points is set to 0.

Listing 2.5.13: The Function bps_tick

```
double bps_tick(BRKSTREAM* stream)
{
    double thisval,frac;

    /* beyond end of brkdata? */
    if(stream->more_points == 0)
        return stream->rightpoint.value;
    if(stream->width == 0.0)
        thisval = stream->rightpoint.value;
    else {
```

```
        /* get value from this span using linear interpolation */
        frac=(stream->curpos-stream->leftpoint.time)/stream->width;
        hisval=stream->leftpoint.value+(stream->height*frac);
    }
    /* move up ready for next sample */
    stream->curpos += stream->incr;
    if(stream->curpos > stream->rightpoint.time){
        /* need to go to next span? */
        stream->ileft++; stream->iright++;
        if(stream->iright < stream->npoints) {
            stream->leftpoint = stream->points[stream->ileft];
            stream->rightpoint = stream->points[stream->iright];
            stream->width = stream->rightpoint.time
                            - stream->leftpoint.time;
            stream->height = stream->rightpoint.value
                            - stream->leftpoint.value;
    }
    else
        stream->more_points = 0;
    }
    return thisval;
}
```

2.5.8 Putting It All Together

If you have not already done so, check that you have put the new breakpoint function definitions into *breakpoints.c* and the function prototypes and the BRKSTREAM structure definition into *breakpoints.h*.

With the streaming breakpoint functions presented above, adding support for breakpoint files is a straightforward five-stage process. For example, to support an amplitude breakpoint file, do the following.

1. Declare some variables:

```
BRKSTREAM* ampstream = NULL;
FILE *fpamp = NULL;
unsigned long brkampSize = 0;
double minval,maxval;
```

2. Open the breakpoint file:

```
fpamp = fopen(argv[ARG_AMP],"r");
/* after error-checking fpamp: */
ampstream = bps_newstream(fpamp,outprops.srate,& brkampSize);
```

3. Check breakpoint data for reasonableness:

```
if(bps_getminmax(ampstream,&minval,&maxval)){
    printf("Error reading range of breakpoint file%s\n",
            argv[ARG_AMP]);
    error++;
    goto exit;
}
if(minval < 0.0 || minval > 1.0
    || maxval < 0.0 || maxval > 1.0){
    printf("Error: amplitude values out of range in file %s: "
        "0.0 < amp <= 1.0\n",
        argv[ARG_AMP]);
    error++;
    goto exit;
}
```

4. Provide an inner processing loop:

```
for(j=0;j < nframes; j++){
    amp = bps_tick(ampstream);
    outframe[j] = (float) (amp * tick(osc,freq));
    }
```

5. Clean-ups:

```
if(ampstream){
    bps_freepoints(ampstream);
    free(ampstream);
}
if(fpamp)
    if(fclose(fpamp))
        printf("Error closing breakpoint file %s\n",
            argv[ARG_AMP]);
```

However, there is one outstanding issue having to do with the processing loop. Hitherto, our programs have supported either a value or a filename, but not the choice to use either. Such a choice, to supply either a number or a breakpoint file name for amp, would be very convenient for users—indeed, it seems essential if the program is to offer sufficient functionality to be generally useful. There are several ways of doing this, of varying degrees of complexity, and whichever solution is found will have to be documented. A complex solution would involve some special sign in the command line to indicate "this is a file name" (curiously, modern operating systems allow the use of numbers as file names), but this would introduce some extra complexity for the user.

A simple solution that requires no special notation in the command line, and little extra code, is to start by *assuming* the string is a filename and attempting to open the file. If that fails (one presumes because the file doesn't exist), the string is read as a plain number. Thus step 2 will become

```
/* open breakpoint file, or set constant */
fpamp = fopen(argv[ARG_AMP],"r");
if(fpamp == NULL){
    amp = atof(argv[ARG_AMP]);
    if(amp <= 0.0 || amp > 1.0){
        printf("Error: amplitude value out of range: "
                "0.0 < amp <= 1.0\n");
        error++;
        goto exit;
    }
}
else {
    ampstream =
        bps_newstream(fpamp,outprops.srate,&brkampSize);
    ...
}
```

The inner processing loop then becomes (with both breakpoint options supported)

```
for(j=0;j < nframes; j++){
    if(ampstream)
        amp = bps_tick(ampstream);
    if(freqstream)
        freq = bps_tick(freqstream);
    outframe[j] =(float) (amp * tick(osc,freq));
}
```

Finally, modify the usage message to add the breakpoint information:

```
"amp = amplitude value or breakpoint file (0 < amp <= 1.0\n"
"freq = frequency value (freq > 0) or breakpoint file.\n"
```

The basic waveform generation has not been altered, so this should behave as previously. This completes our *siggen.c* program, which features all the elements discussed in section 2.5. When you test it, be sure to test *everything*.

2.5.9   Exercises

Exercise 2.5.1
Modify the program *sfenv* to use the new breakpoint functions. Verify that the output is identical to that of the original version.

Exercise 2.5.2

Create a frequency breakpoint file that generates a sequence of pitches fitting a standard A major arpeggio (i.e. notes A, C#, E, A, ...), ascending and descending over three octaves, starting on A = 220 Hz (C# is a major third above A, with the ratio 5/4; E is a perfect fifth above A with the ratio 3/2). Each note should last one second before changing instantly to the next. Test the file with the square, sawtooth, and triangle waveform types, using *siggen*. At which notes does the aliasing become easily audible for each waveform type?

Exercise 2.5.3

Extend *siggen* to support multi-channel outputs, adding a `chans` argument to the command line.

Exercise 2.5.4

Extend *siggen* to enable the user to select the format of the output file (16-bit, 24-bit, or 32-bit float), using an optional flag argument $-sN$ in the command line, where N = 1, 2, or 3 respectively. The default should be 16-bit.

2.5.10   More Advanced Exercises

Exercise 2.5.5

Rewrite the following code as a code macro:

```
if(p_osc->curfreq != freq){
    p_osc->curfreq = freq;
    p_osc->incr = p_osc->twopiovrsr * freq;
}
```

The macro should require termination with a semicolon:

```
UPDATE_FREQ;
```

(Hints: See the description of the ? operator in exercise 2.2.5, and see note 11 about the comma operator.)

Exercise 2.5.6

The method for deciding if a string is a number or a file name is not ideal, in that if an incorrect file name is given (i.e. a file that does not exist), it will be read as a number using the function `atof`, and the program will proceed with that assumption, possibly giving a misleading error message. Demonstrate this problem using a random non-numeric file name (that does not exist as a real file) for the `amp` argument to *siggen*.

Exercise 2.5.7

(a) Using the C library function `strtod` to replace `atof`, modify the code for reading `amp` and `freq`, where `fopen` has returned `NULL`, to determine whether the argument string is numeric. If it is not numeric (and thus must be an incorrect file name or some other incorrect string), give an error message indicating that the file name is invalid.

(b) Encapsulate the solution to (a) as a utility function. Use this prototype:

```
int isnum(const char* arg, double* val);
```

where `arg` is the string to be tested, and `val` is a pointer to the double returned from `strtod`, if successful. The function will return 0 for "false" and 1 for "true." Typical usage would be

```
char* arg = "1000.1";
double val = 0.0;

if(isnum(arg, &val))
    printf("arg = %f\n", val);
else
    printf("%s is not a valid number\n", arg);
```

Change the code written in (a) to use the new function.

(c) Decide in which source file to store the new function.

Exercise 2.5.8

(a) Create a new oscillator for *siggen* that adds dynamic pulse-width modulation to the basic square wave, with a modulation range between 1% and 99%, where the normal square wave = 50%. Retain the use of function pointers for the existing oscillators. Any modulation values outside the allowed range should be clipped to the minimum or maximum, as appropriate. The new oscillator's tick function should have the following prototype:

```
double pwmtick(OSCIL* p_osc, double freq, double pwmod);
```

(b) Add support for breakpoint-file control for the pwm waveform. Pay careful attention to the permitted range. What command-line issues are raised by this exercise?

Exercise 2.5.9

Create a second sine-wave oscillator in *siggen* to apply tremolo (amplitude modulation) to the main oscillator. Use an optional command-line flag `-tF` to set the frequency, where the default value of `F` is 0 (i.e. no modulation). Decide on a reasonable modulation depth, and fix it internally. Aim to make the code as efficient as possible, especially in the default case.

Exercise 2.5.10

(a) Revise the oscillator creation function `new_oscil` to add a second argument setting the initial phase of all oscillators, controlled from the command line via an optional flag argument. Define phase here as a fraction between 0 and 1, where giving a phase of 0.25 to the sine-wave oscillator will result in a cosine wave.

(b) Modify the starting phase of the triangle and sawtooth oscillators so that by default they match the direction of the sine wave (i.e. starting at zero, going positive) before any modifications by the user are applied.

2.6   Additive Synthesis and the Table Lookup Oscillator

2.6.1   Introduction

If you have fully explored the program developed in the previous section, especially with the sawtooth and square waveforms, it will have become almost painfully clear that the degree of alias distortion is unacceptable, except at low frequencies. The problem, in a nutshell, is that the implementation considers only the literal shape of the waveform, whereas for a usable digital implementation we need to consider the *spectrum* of the sound. Ideally, we want to avoid generating any frequency components outside the available range for a given sampling rate, i.e. at or above the Nyquist limit. This is a further problem added to those with which we have already become preoccupied, as this section also demonstrates: problems of robustness, flexibility of use, and efficiency. Solutions to these problems are often in conflict, especially where functions may be of use beyond a particular program and may eventually be included in a general library. This section develops the principle of "public" and "private" functions, introducing the important C keyword `static`.

  This section discusses two major topics, each leading to the creation of a program. Both programs generate the "classic" square, triangle, and sawtooth waveforms, using additive synthesis in order to obtain band-limited (i.e. alias-free) tones. The first topic introduces the concept of the spectrum by means of a further exploration of the analog waveforms, and develops the program *oscgen*, which implements a sinusoidal oscillator bank. We will discover more of the properties of sine and cosine waves; and we will also find, perhaps counter-intuitively, that the choice of one over the other has a very obvious impact on the results. In the process, the issue of efficiency will arise so prominently that we will need to provide a means to compare the cost of alternative methods, by measuring program execution time. The second topic introduces a classic technique for generating multi-harmonic periodic waveforms using just one oscillator, based on the principle of *table lookup*. We will demonstrate the two principal methods of table lookup, *truncation* and, yet again, *linear interpolation*. The program developed at the end of section 2.6, *tabgen*, is intended primarily as a test bed for comparing the performance (in terms of both speed and audio quality) of these two methods. Both programs are also intended as starting points for free exploration and experimentation by the reader, who is now asked to implement programs based only on an outline design, rather then on a presentation of a complete program listing. Instead, the emphasis moves more and more toward the development of a library of functions (ever-expanding) that can serve as building blocks for a wide range of applications, according to the interests of the programmer.

2.6.2 The Spectrum of the Classic Geometric Waveforms

A periodic waveform has at least one sinusoidal frequency component. By adding further components with frequencies that are integer multiples of the lowest or *fundamental* frequency, a wide range of periodic waveforms can be created. Thanks to their simple and geometric shape, it is possible to calculate the spectrum of the square, triangle, and sawtooth waveforms exactly. The spectrum is usually expressed as a sum of sinusoids, each at a given amplitude. The spectra of the three principal waveforms are illustrated in figure 2.14, together with the underlying formulae describing the relative strengths of each harmonic component.

2.6.3 A Basic Oscillator Bank for Additive Synthesis

The program developed in this section, *oscgen*, is structurally very similar to *siggen* of the previous section, which may itself be considered a convenient alternative to *main.c* as a template for synthesis programs. As usual, you can either create a new project from scratch or copy the *siggen* project into a new directory and make the usual changes—use the name *oscgen.c* for the main program source file. We require only the function `sinetick`, so the `switch` block code, which selects alternative function pointers, can be removed. The command line and usage message will need modifying—apart from the new name, we need a new argument that sets the number of oscillators to use. Where only one oscillator is requested, the output will be a sine wave, so that the old sine option 0 can itself be removed and the remainder renumbered:

```
"usage: oscgen outfile dur srate nchans amp freq wavetype noscs\n"
" wavetype:      0 = square\n"
"                1 = triangle\n"
"                2 = saw up\n"
"                3 = saw down\n"
```

From figure 2.14 we can see that synthesizing these waveforms requires an array of oscillators (an *oscillator bank*), one for each successive harmonic, where the output of each is scaled by the required amplitude factor. As usual, we will provide for modulation of both fundamental frequency and overall amplitude via breakpoint files. This requires three arrays—one for the oscillators themselves (or, rather, to contain pointers to each oscillator, as returned

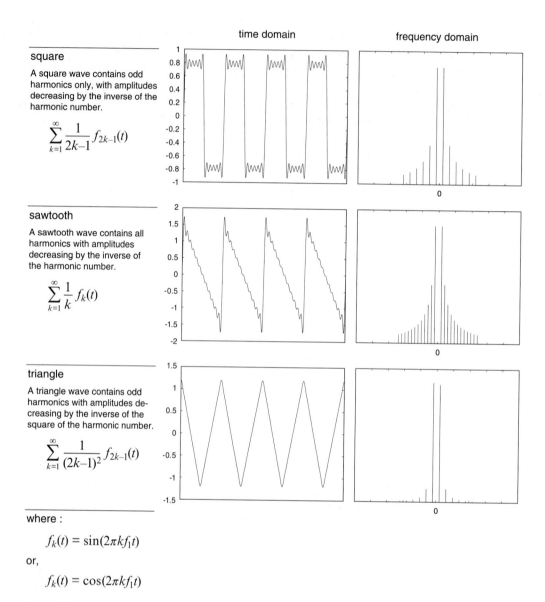

square

A square wave contains odd harmonics only, with amplitudes decreasing by the inverse of the harmonic number.

$$\sum_{k=1}^{\infty} \frac{1}{2k-1} f_{2k-1}(t)$$

sawtooth

A sawtooth wave contains all harmonics with amplitudes decreasing by the inverse of the harmonic number.

$$\sum_{k=1}^{\infty} \frac{1}{k} f_k(t)$$

triangle

A triangle wave contains odd harmonics with amplitudes decreasing by the inverse of the square of the harmonic number.

$$\sum_{k=1}^{\infty} \frac{1}{(2k-1)^2} f_{2k-1}(t)$$

where :

$$f_k(t) = \sin(2\pi k f_1 t)$$

or,

$$f_k(t) = \cos(2\pi k f_1 t)$$

Figure 2.14
Spectra of square, triangle, and sawtooth waveforms.

from the function new_oscil introduced in section 2.5); one to contain the relative amplitude values; and another to contain the relative frequencies. As some waveforms require all harmonics, and others require only odd-numbered harmonics, and we want to avoid repeated identical conditional tests inside the processing loop, the contents of the frequency array must vary according to the selected waveform.

The original osc pointer (here renamed oscs) is now required to be the name of the array of oscillator pointers, and is therefore declared a "pointer to a pointer." (We have to use a pair of asterisks, rather than OSCIL* oscs[], as the latter form requires an explicit array size to be defined in the declaration.) Also note here the use of a comma-separated list of variable declarations for the two double pointers. When code is written in this form, an asterisk must be put adjacent to each variable name.

```
OSCIL **oscs = NULL; /* will be an array of OSCIL pointers */
double *oscamps = NULL, *oscfreqs = NULL; /* for oscbank amp
                                     and freq data */
unsigned long noscs; /* from argv[ARG_NOSCS] using atoi() */
```

Allocation of these arrays takes the value of noscs as the required size (see listing 2.6.1). Note that no upper limit is set on the size of noscs—the program is deliberately casual here.

Listing 2.6.1: Constructing an Oscillator Bank

```
1   /* create amp and freq arrays */
2   oscamps = (double*) malloc(noscs * sizeof(double));
3   if(oscamps==NULL){
4       puts("no memory!\n");
5       error++;
6       goto exit;
7   }
8   oscfreqs = (double*) malloc(noscs * sizeof(double));
9   if(oscfreqs==NULL){
10      puts("no memory!\n");
11      error++;
12      goto exit;
13  }
14  /* create array of pointers to OSCILs */
15  oscs = (OSCIL**) malloc(noscs * sizeof(OSCIL *));
16  if(oscs== NULL){
17      puts("no memory!\n");
18      error++;
19      goto exit;
20  }
21  /*** initialize arrays. . . */
```

```
22  /* and then create each OSCIL */
23  for(i=0;i < noscs;i++){
24      oscs[i] = new_oscil(outprops.srate);
25      if(oscs[i] == NULL){
26          puts("no memory for oscillators\n");
27          error++;
28          goto exit;
29      }
30  }
```

When creating the program, don't forget to free these arrays at the end. In the processing loop, we will iterate over noscs, producing each sample, so we need a further local counter variable. The loop uses the method of the accumulating sum (using the += operator) to add each harmonic to the table. An accumulating sum works by adding the new value to the current value. This requires that, before the loop starts, the value be initialized to zero (we should never rely on the compiler to do this for us).

```
for(j=0; j < nframes; j++){
    long k;
    if(freqstream)
        freq = bps_tick(freqstream);
    if(ampstream)
        amp = bps_tick(ampstream);
    val = 0.0;
    for(k = 0; k < noscs; k++) {
        val += oscamps[k] *
            sinetick(oscs[k],freq * oscfreqs[k]);
    }
    outframe[j] = (float)(val * amp);
}
```

We are not quite ready to compile yet. First we must fill the arrays with the required values according to the required waveform type, as indicated in the comment in line 21 of listing 2.6.1. We are also conscious of the fact that when signals are added together, amplitudes simply add, so that, for example, when ten signals at amplitude 1 are added together, the total amplitude will be 10. In such a case, the adjustment is easy to see—we simply scale the final amplitude by 1/10 to obtain the nominal ± 1.0 amplitude. This will be further scaled by the requested amplitude value from the user, which may be time-varying. However, in using the formulas shown in figure 2.14 we are not adding signals of equal amplitude. For example, the first four harmonics (frequencies 1, 3, 5, and 7 times the fundamental) of a triangle wave require the sum

$$totalamp = 1 + \frac{1}{9} + \frac{1}{25} + \frac{1}{49} = 1.172. \tag{7}$$

The general rule is thus

$$totalamp = \sum_{n=0}^{N} \frac{1}{(2n-1)^2},$$ (8)

where $N = number\ of\ oscillators.$

Because we cannot know in advance how many oscillators the user requires, we cannot use an explicit constant rescale factor in the code. We have to calculate it cumulatively. We can do this as a variant of the familiar maxamp function, as we enter each amplitude value into the array. This requires some new variables:

```
double ampfac,freqfac,ampadjust;

    /* fill arrays for triangle wave */
    ampfac = 1.0; /* values for fundamental always the same */
    freqfac = 1.0;
    ampadjust = 0.0;
    for(i=0;i< noscs;i++){
        ampfac = 1.0 /(freqfac*freqfac);
        oscamps[i] = ampfac;
        oscfreqs[i] = freqfac;
        freqfac += 2.0;         /* odd harmonics only */
        ampadjust += ampfac;

    }
/* rescale amplitudes so they add to 1.0 */
for(i=0; i < noscs;i++)
    oscamps[i] /= ampadjust;
```

The code for the four basic waveforms is shown in listing 2.6.2. It uses the switch. . .case statement to select appropriate code for each waveform type. It also illustrates the use of the "fall-through" technique, in which two or more options can use the same code. In this example, the code exploits the fact that the downward sawtooth is merely an inversion of the upward sawtooth, which is achieved simply by multiplying all amplitudes by −1. Because there is no break statement associated with the WAVE_SAWUP option, execution falls through to the next option, so that the same code is used in both cases. A simple two-line test for WAVE_SAWUP can then be used to set the sign of ampadjust. This exploits the mathematical rule that if either the numerator or the denominator of a fraction is negative, the overall value is also negative.

Listing 2.6.2: Amplitudes and Frequencies for Four Principal Waveforms

```
freqfac = 1.0;
ampadjust = 0.0;
switch(wavetype){
```

```
case(WAVE_SQUARE):
    for(i=0;i< noscs;i++){
        ampfac = 1.0 /freqfac;
        oscamps[i] = ampfac;
        oscfreqs[i] = freqfac;
        freqfac += 2.0;
        ampadjust += ampfac;
    }
    break;
case(WAVE_TRIANGLE):
        for(i=0;i< noscs;i++){
        ampfac = 1.0 /(freqfac*freqfac);
        oscamps[i] = ampfac;
        oscfreqs[i] = freqfac;
        freqfac += 2.0;
        ampadjust += ampfac;
    }
    break;
case(WAVE_SAWUP):
case(WAVE_SAWDOWN):
    for(i=0; i< noscs; i++){
        ampfac = 1.0 /(freqfac);
        oscamps[i] = ampfac;
        oscfreqs[i] = freqfac;
        freqfac += 1.0;
        ampadjust += ampfac;
    }
    if(wavetype == WAVE_SAWUP)
        ampadjust = -ampadjust; /* inverts the waveform */
    break;
}
for(i=0; i < noscs;i++)
    oscamps[i] /= ampadjust;
```

Build and test *oscgen* in the usual way: try each of the possible waveforms, with varying numbers of oscillators, and listen to the results. In particular, use frequency breakpoint files defining pitch sweeps—these will prove the most vivid means to hear the effects of aliasing, since the alias frequencies will seem to have a life of their own, typically moving in the opposite direction to the requested pitch. As can be expected from the shape of its spectrum, the triangle wave is the least afflicted by aliasing, as the upper harmonics are so much weaker compared to those of the other waveforms. Nevertheless, when the pitch is swept continuously, even low-level aliasing can be heard, especially once you have become used to the sound of it. Programs such as *oscgen* thus become valuable tools for training the ear, whose attention is much more easily attracted by moving sounds than by static sounds.

2.6.4   Sines, Cosines, and the Amplitude vs. Shape Problem

While testing *oscgen* you may have observed that in every case the reported output amplitude was significantly below what you asked for. Moreover, as the number of oscillators increases the final amplitude decreases. When we ask for the amplitude of 0.5, say, we expect the program to deliver exactly that, but clearly it failed to do so here. It would be very reasonable to suspect that there is something wrong with the code, an incorrect piece of arithmetic somewhere. In fact the problem lies in the difference between adding sine harmonics and adding cosine harmonics. This difference is demonstrated graphically in figure 2.15. We can see clearly where the problem lies. When sines are being added, the cycles all start from zero, and the peaks of the waveforms rarely coincide. This has the overall effect of lowering the amplitude, as signals cancel each other out to varying degrees. When adding cosines are being added, the cycles all start from the peak value of 1.0, ensuring that the sum achieves the expected peak amplitude. To the listener, however, there is no perceptible difference except, cumulatively, the slight drop in amplitude.

And there is a further problem. It will not be revealed by listening, but it will be immediately apparent when one is viewing the output in a soundfile editor: whereas the square wave at least looks like a square wave, albeit at reduced amplitude, the triangle wave looks nothing like a triangle. Figure 2.16 compares the resulting shapes when summing the first four harmonics of each waveform, using either sines or cosines. In the case of sines, the expected amplitudes are all below the theoretical ones. However, a square wave generated with cosines looks nothing like a square wave (though it will still sound like one). Clearly, using such an oscillator to provide a control signal for a low-frequency oscillator will not produce the expected behavior. To solve this problem, we need to be able to tell oscillators to start with either sine or cosine phase. For audio-rate signals, arguably the priority is to ensure delivery of the required amplitude, and the exact shape of the waveform is a secondary concern. The solution suggested in exercise 9 of section 2.5 was to modify `new_oscil` with the addition of a phase argument:

```
OSCIL* new_oscil(unsigned long srate, double phase)
{
    OSCIL* p_osc;
    . . .
    p_osc->curphase = TWOPI * phase;
    . . .
}
```

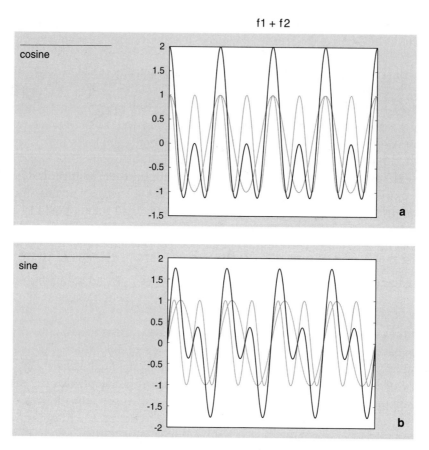

Figure 2.15
Addition of sines and cosines.

Modifying functions in this way is a natural feature of project development, but if the function happens to be contained in a library file (and is therefore used by other programs) it may be essential to preserve the original definition and behavior. An alternative solution relies on the fact that the object is still an OSCIL—so long as we use a different name, there is nothing to stop us from defining alternative creation functions for the same object, retaining the original new_oscil unchanged:

```
OSCIL* new_oscilp(unsigned long srate, double phase);
```

At this stage of development, it is appropriate to add this function, together with its prototype, to the main program file *oscgen.c*. Later you may decide that it is useful enough to transfer to the library file *wave.c*. All that is now required in *oscgen.c* is a variable to contain

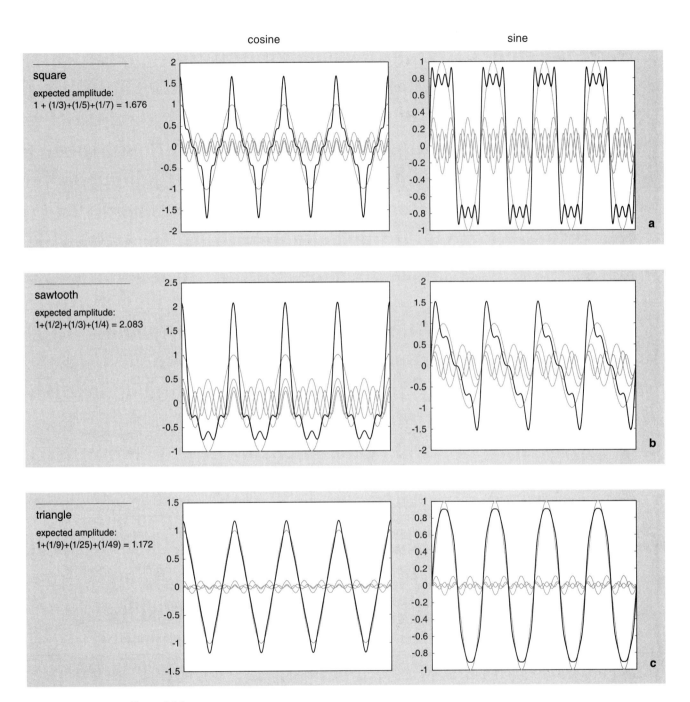

Figure 2.16
Additive waveform generation using sines or cosines.

the phase value. Where a cosine phase is required, as in the case of the triangle wave, it is initialized to 0.25:

```
double phase = 0.0;   /* default to sine phase */
...
switch(wavetype){
...
case(WAVE_TRIANGLE):
    for(i=0;i< noscs;i++){
        ...
    }
    ...
    phase = 0.25; /* set cos phase for true triangle shape */
    break;
...
```

Finally, we must modify line 24 of listing 2.6.1 to use the new creation function:

```
oscs[i] = new_oscilp(outprops.srate,phase);
```

On building and running the revised program, you should find that the triangle wave looks as it should and has the exact amplitude requested. However, the fact remains that we cannot obtain both the required waveform shape and the required amplitude using this method. The underlying problem is that we cannot rescale the amplitude of the output in real time—until the whole signal is generated, we cannot know the final amplitude, which we require in order to find the correct adjustment factor. Ideally, we would like one technique that can serve for both audio-rate and low-frequency oscillators, and guarantee exact amplitude and shape in both cases, without any requirement for post-processing. The trick, as we will shortly discover, is to adjust the amplitude when the oscillator is created, rather than during or after synthesis. But before we get to that stage we must address the important matter of measuring processing time.

2.6.5   Measuring Processing Time—The `clock` Library Function

As soon as we run the program introduced in the previous subsections using more than a few oscillators, we discover the problem: to obtain harmonic-rich tones (e.g. for low-pitched tones), many oscillators are required, which considerably increases processing time. The question of efficiency has arisen very frequently already, but so far little attention has been given to detailed comparisons. The program *oscgen* is the first so far in this book to pose any significant demands on the CPU, such that finding ways to generate tones more efficiently is a very real priority. To judge our success, we need to be able to measure the processing time of a program—specifically, the difference between the end time and the start time of the main processing loop. However, we will need something more reliable (and more automatic) than just starting the program and using a stopwatch.

While each operating system may offer its own non-portable timing facilities, the ANSI C standard library also defines a simple timing function, clock, that can be expected to be available on all systems. It is defined in the library header file <time.h>:

```
clock_t clock(void);
```

Here clock_t is an integer type internally defined by the compiler for each platform (typically as a long). The function returns the time elapsed since the start of a process (here 'process' can be understood as synonymous with "'program'), counted in "ticks." In theory (though certainly not on any systems of interest to the audio programmer), timing functions may not be available, in which case clock returns the value −1. Associated with the library timing functions is the compiler-defined symbol CLOCKS_PER_SEC, which is typically defined as 1,000, so that the nominal timer resolution is 1 millisecond.[20] It is now easy to add timing to each program that runs a processing loop:

```
clock_t starttime, endtime;
...
printf("processing....\n");
starttime = clock();
for(i=0; i < nbufs; i++) {
...
}
endtime = clock();
printf("Elapsed time = %f secs\n",
(endtime-starttime)/(double)CLOCKS_PER_SEC);
```

With this code added to *oscgen*, you will be able to measure with reasonable accuracy the cost of, say, 40 oscillators compared to 20, or to 1. This can, among other things, enable you to determine the proportion of CPU time devoted to file read/write processing. More importantly, as we will find in the next section, we can use clock to compare the differences in efficiency between competing implementations of the same technique.

2.6.6   The "Classic" Table Lookup Oscillator—Guard Point

It may come as a surprise to many readers that the method of generating sinusoids by using the C library sin and cos functions has only fairly recently become at all reasonable. This is thanks to the fact that most modern CPUs incorporate fast floating-point units in which these functions are implemented in hardware. Until that crucial development, these functions had to be implemented in software, using mathematical techniques such as the Taylor series. Before that, even the core floating-point arithmetic operations themselves depended on *emulation* using CPUs that natively supported only integer operations. CPU register sizes were also too small to contain the larger types, such as the double, so high-precision floating-point manipulation also involved use of off-chip memory, which in itself can

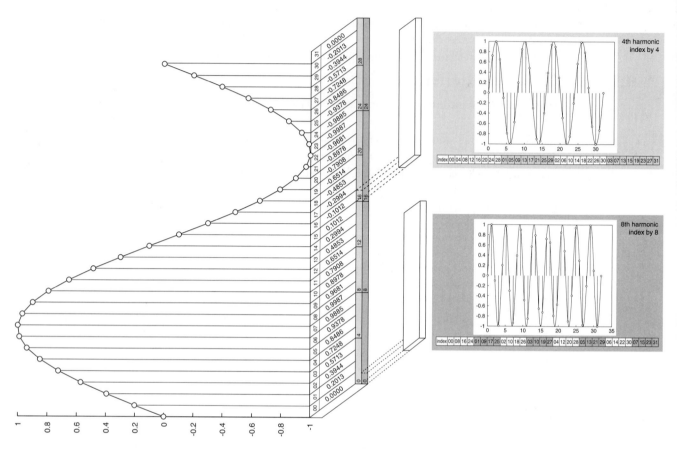

Figure 2.17
Table lookup oscillator.

increase processing time. On such machines, the calculation of any of the trigonometric or higher-level mathematical functions was extremely expensive, and unacceptable given the thousands of repeated calculations per second required for synthesis. This issue persists even today in the era of GHz clock speeds and multi-core processors.

The solution that became the most important technique in computer music was to pre-calculate one cycle of a periodic waveform such as the sine wave, stored in an array, which could then be shared by multiple oscillators (see figure 2.17). The phase increment that we give to the sin function becomes an index increment through the table—the value required for each successive audio sample is obtained by reading the value stored at the required position (index) in the table, then updating the index with the required increment. Every time this reaches the end of the table, or beyond, the index value is "wrapped around" to the equivalent within the table, reflecting the periodic (repeating) nature of the waveform. The great power of this technique becomes apparent with the realization that, when used for an oscillator, this table can contain *any* periodic waveform—for example, containing the sum of several harmonics.

The general principle of the lookup table is that it represents a single cycle of some periodic waveform—a waveform comprising a number of harmonics, following the established principles of additive synthesis. By cycling through the table at different speeds, a steady signal of a particular pitch is generated. One aspect of the table lookup method that has to be born in mind when creating multi-harmonic waveforms of this kind is that, in contrast to the freedom we allowed ourselves in *oscgen*, we must now accept a hard limit on the highest frequency that can be represented. As a lookup table is, of itself, undefined with respect to sample rate, we can only think in terms of *relative* frequency, and here the definition of the Nyquist limit as that frequency represented by the minimum of two samples comes into play. In a table lookup oscillator, the relative frequency value corresponds directly to the phase increment used to step through the table. The increment that would find just two samples per cycle would have a size of half the length of the table. Thus we can define the Nyquist limit for a table of size N as being a table increment of size $N/2$. As it would be all too easy for the user to get this wrong (e.g. simply through a typing error, or incorrect ordering of function arguments, itself an everyday hazard for programmers), it is important that this limit be tested for in any table generation function. Even this limit is a little generous—only when using the `cos` function will we get non-zero values for the Nyquist frequency (figure 2.18).

Of course, should you try to create a wavetable with the maximum possible number of harmonics, any oscillator that tries to generate a pitch higher than the "root" pitch of the table (in which each sample is used) will generate aliasing. Practical considerations therefore dictate that wavetables be created that offer a useful amount of headroom for high pitches. It will suffice to say at this stage that to cover the whole continuous frequency range with a complex waveform and avoid aliasing is a non-trivial task, e.g. involving the carefully controlled mixing of a large number of wavetables, ranging from a harmonic-rich table for low notes, to a plain sinusoid for very high frequencies close to the Nyquist limit. At least for "conventional" musical purposes, the scale of this task is mediated a little by the fact that the highest reasonable musical pitch, such as the top note of the piano, is around 4,000 Hz, which still offers scope for up to four harmonics, at the 44,100-Hz sampling rate.

The processing time is simply that required to scan the table, and is therefore independent of its contents (see figure 2.17).

Listing 2.6.3(a) shows typical code to create a table containing one cycle of a sine wave. The tricky aspect is how to obtain the required sample value. The input to this procedure is a required frequency and, of course, the sample rate. Referring to our original oscillator implemented in *wave.c*, the calculation of the phase increment for a given frequency is stated as

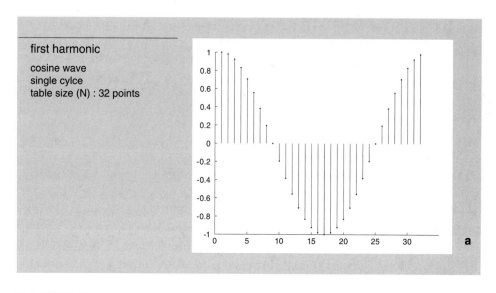

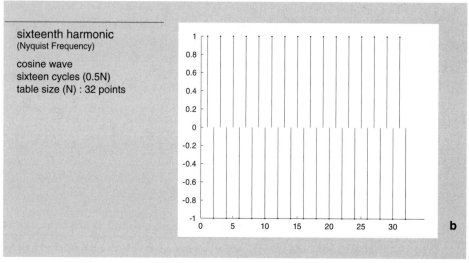

Figure 2.18
A 32-point table containing (a) a single-cycle cosine and (b) the Nyquist frequency.

```
phaseincr = TWOPI * freq / srate
```

With the use of table lookup, the table length ("TABLEN") is equivalent to the "unit cycle" length of TWOPI. The required increment relative to a given table size is then

```
phaseincr = TABLEN * freq / srate
```

As usual, we will want to store the constant value TABLEN/srate so that it is not recalculated each time. The name used in OSCIL was twopiovrsr, but for the sake of better self-documenting things it is helpful to choose a more accurate name[21]:

```
double sizeovrsr = (double) TABLEN / srate;
```

The next step is to generate the incrementing phase for each sample, with the required wrap-around. Again, we can see how this relates to the wrap-around illustrated for our original oscillator—everything that was expressed in terms of TWOPI is now expressed in terms of table length. For example, to avoid aliasing, the phase increment must be less than half the table size. The basic code for this is shown in listing 2.6.3(b). This implements a "truncated lookup" in which the nearest lower table value is used. (Recall that the int cast discards the fractional part of any floating-point value, and the value is thus "truncated.") The wrap-around code in lines 9–12 uses while tests rather than the slightly cheaper if test—this ensures that even extreme phase increments (i.e. larger than the table size) are safely wrapped within the table.

Listing 2.6.3: Table Lookup

(a) sine-wave table of 1,024 points

```
#define TABLEN (1024)    /* or some other default size. . . */
unsigned long i, len = TABLEN;
double step;
double table[TABLEN];

step = TWOPI / len;
/* fill table: contains one cycle,
    length is equivalent to TWOPI */
for(i=0; i < len; i++) {
    table[i] = sin(step * i);
}
```

(b) basic truncating lookup

```
1    /*init: */
2    double curphase = 0.0;
3    double tablen = (double) TABLEN;
4    /* generate samples */
5    for(i=0;i < nsamps;i++){
```

```
6        int index = (int) curphase; /* truncated phase index */
7        outframe[i] = (float) table[index]; /* read the table */
8        curphase += incr;  /* update phase */
9        while(curphase >= tablen)     /* wrap around phase w*/
10           curphase -= tablen;
11       while(curphase < tablen   /* support negative freqs */
12           curphase += tablen;
13  }
```

2.6.7   Table Lookup by Linear Interpolation

The truncating lookup is about as fast as a table lookup oscillator can be, but with anything but large table lengths the sound quality is very poor (see figure 2.19). The difference between the required value and the truncated value can be considerable, leading to significant distortion of the sound, referred to as *truncation noise*. To obtain acceptable quality, a table size of 8,192 points or greater is usually required, depending on the sampling rate. Though memory is plentiful on modern systems, it can still be advantageous (and can lead to faster processing) to keep memory requirements as small as possible. The standard and widely used alternative is *linear interpolation*, which we have already encountered in the context of processing breakpoint files.[22] A typical interpolating lookup oscillator is illustrated in listing 2.6.4. With this technique, table sizes as small as 128 points can still give acceptable sound quality, and a table size of 1,024 points is sufficient for all but the most stringent quality-critical requirements. Note that the upper integer index inext must be wrapped around (lines 7 and 8) as well as the underlying floating-point phase (in lines 15–18) from which the ibase index is derived via a cast to int (line 4). This is because of the situation that can and will arise when ibase is at the final point of the table and inext then needs to be at the beginning of it. The interpolation itself is performed in lines 9–12.

Listing 2.6.4: Standard Interpolating Table Lookup

```
    /* generate samples */
1   for(i=0;i < nsamps; i++){
2       int ibase, inext;
3       double frac,val,slope;
4       ibase = (int)phase;
5       inext = ibase + 1;
6       /* adjacent samples may cross table boundaries */
7       if(inext >= tablen)
8           inext -= tablen;
9       frac = phase - ibase;
10      val = p_osc->table[ibase];
11      slope = p_osc->table[inext] - val;
```

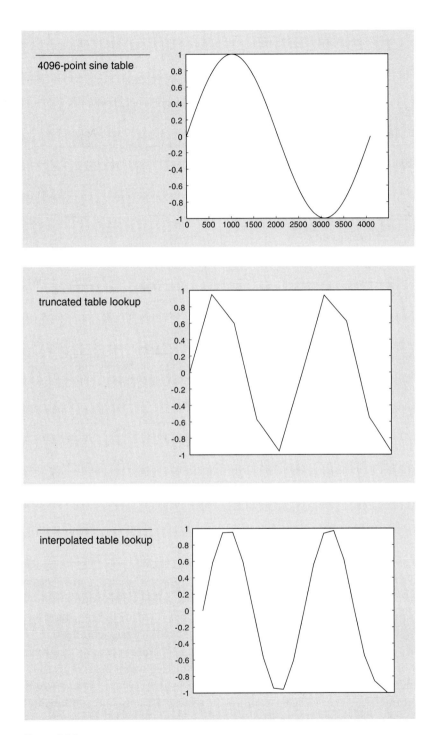

Figure 2.19
Comparison of truncated and interpolated lookup.

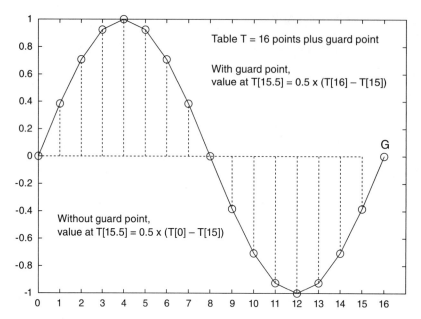

Figure 2.20
Table with guard point.

```
12      val += (frac * slope);
13      outframe[i] = (float)val;
14         phase += incr;
15      while(phase >= tablen)
16         phase -= tablen;
17      while(phase < 0.0)
18         phase += tablen;
19 }
```

This example demonstrates the extent to which the code dealing with phase wrap-around dominates the process. If we are to achieve any economies, this is the first area to look at. The overall phase wraparound cannot be avoided, but the code in lines 7 and 8 is very irritating. However, by exercising a little lateral thinking we can easily eliminate it. The trick is to use what is referred to in Csound as a *guard point*. The table is extended to the right by one element, in which is stored a copy of the first point (see figure 2.20). This then enables the upper integer index to remain always one above the lower one, which we know will always be within the table. Lines 7 and 8 can now be removed, saving a conditional test. Although this saves only two lines, all conditional tests incur some CPU load. Not only is this block of code run for every sample; it may be used for 100 oscillators or more. Thus, two saved instructions amount to several hundred saved instructions per sample. The revised skeleton code to create the table is shown in listing 2.6.5.

Listing 2.6.5: Table Creation with Guard Point

```
#define TABLEN (1024)      /* or some other default size. . . */
unsigned long i, len = TABLEN;
double step;
double table[TABLEN + 1]; /* provide a guard point at end of table */

step = TWOPI / len ;
/* fill table: contains one cycle, length is equivalent to TWOPI */
for(i=0; i < len; i++) {
    table[i] = sin(step * i);
}
table[i] = table[0];       /* guard point is copy of first */
```

2.6.8 Developments of OSCIL—A Practical Table Lookup Oscillator

In this subsection we develop *tabgen*, a new synthesis program that will generate the same signals as *oscgen* using a single table lookup oscillator. It will also enable us to train the ear to recognize the particular sonic character of truncation noise, and, more generally, to compare the quality of both truncating and interpolating oscillators for a given table size. The new project can, as usual, be created from scratch or copied from *oscgen*. In addition to the main source file *tabgen.c*, we will need a new pair of source files, *gtable.h* and *gtable.c*, to contain the code for everything to do with table lookup oscillators.

To implement a practical table lookup oscillator, we will want to apply the principles of object creation and encapsulation introduced in the previous section. We could do this from first principles, by defining a structure for the new oscillator and then a creation function that allocates an instance of the object and initializes it. However, we must be careful here—we know we may want to use possibly a large number of oscillators, and we neither need nor want to allocate memory for an identical lookup table inside each oscillator. As this table is only read from, never written to, we can create just one table, and have all the oscillators share it. Also, the whole point of this approach is to be able to define alternative tables, containing custom waveforms.

We can also take the view that the guard-point lookup table is more than simply an array —it shows all the hallmarks of an *object*. Its *public* size is different from its *private*, internal size. The guard-point table is a *special case* of a lookup table—it is considered to have a length of N, but internally, known only to itself, so to speak, it has a length of $N + 1$, because of the guard point. Similarly, functions that use lookup tables need to know that *this* table has a special character (the guard point) that makes it different from *that* table that has no guard point. This difference between the public and private views of the table, coupled with the requirement for functions that know about its special properties, is sufficient to justify defining a structure for the table as a new type, here called GTABLE.

To implement a table lookup oscillator, therefore, we need to both define GTABLE and the oscillator object that will use it. A complete example definition of GTABLE, with a self-contained creation function for a sine wave, is shown in listing 2.6.6. Note that GTABLE contains a pointer to allocated memory. This means that it will not be sufficient to simply call free on the GTABLE object itself; we will also have to free the internal memory. This is made much more convenient (especially when dealing with a large number of tables) by defining a *destruction function*. A suitable destruction function is shown in listing 2.6.7. It enables the whole object to be destroyed using one function call.

```
GTABLE* table = new_sine(1024);
/* . . .use it. . . */
gtable_free(&table); /* and destroy it when finished */
/* table now = NULL */
```

This admittedly somewhat contrived function demonstrates the sort of pointer manipulation for which C programmers are famous or notorious. However, if you have to write code to free 100 oscillators or more, each with a unique table (yes, it is possible), you will be grateful to be able to use one function call to do it.

Listing 2.6.6: Definition of Lookup Table Type GTABLE with Guard Point

(a) type definition (*gtable.h*)

```
typedef struct t_gtable
{
 double* table; /* ptr to array containing the waveform */
 unsigned long length;  /* excluding guard point */
} GTABLE;
```

(b) GTABLE creation function for sine wave (*gtable.c*)

```
1   GTABLE* new_sine(unsigned long length)
2   {
3       unsigned long i;
4       double step;
5       GTABLE* gtable = NULL;
6
7       if(len == 0)
8           return NULL;
9       gtable = (GTABLE* ) malloc(sizeof(GTABLE));
10      if(gtable == NULL)
11          return NULL;
12      gtable->table = (double*) malloc((length + 1) *
        sizeof(double));
13      if(gtable->table== NULL){
14          free(gtable);
15          return NULL;
16      }
```

```
17  gtable->length = length;
18  step = TWOPI / length ; /* make sine wave */
19  for(i=0; i < length; i++)
20    gtable->table[i] = sin(step * i);
21  gtable->table[i] = gtable->table[0];/* guard point */
22  return gtable;
23 }
```

Listing 2.6.7: The GTABLE **Destruction Function**

```
1  void gtable_free(GTABLE** gtable)
2  {
3      if(gtable && *gtable && (*gtable)->table){
4          free((*gtable)->table);
5          free(*gtable);
6          *gtable = NULL;
7      }
8  }
```

This somewhat complicated-looking function receives the address of a "pointer to GTABLE," or equivalently "a pointer to a pointer to a GTABLE." It frees the internal table memory, then the memory for the object itself, and finally sets the GTABLE pointer itself to NULL. The parentheses around (*gtable) are required because of C's precedence rules (-> has higher precedence than *). You may want to try removing them and observe the error messages from the compiler. Note the use of the logical AND operator && to check all the pointers, in order from left to right, from the supplied pointer gtable through to the internal table pointer. Only if all three pointers are valid will the function do anything. This is probably as convoluted as many C programmers want to get with pointers. Unfortunately perhaps, it is all too easy to write even more convoluted code than this.

In a similar way, we can consider the table lookup oscillator to be a special case of the "plain" oscillator implemented in OSCIL. Indeed, from inspection of listing 2.6.4 we can see that many of the elements of OSCIL appear there, such as curphase and incr. As we will want to support modulation of frequency, we will also need a curfreq element. Add to this the fact that we can define two types of table lookup oscillator—the truncating type and the interpolating type—and we have a clear picture of a family of oscillators, all based on OSCIL. In the terminology of object-oriented programming, we can say that the table lookup oscillator *derives* from OSCIL, and even that, following the metaphor of a family, they *inherit* certain aspects of behavior (such as the all-important tick function) from it. In practice, this means that the structure that defines the new oscillator will incorporate the OSCIL structure internally (listing 2.6.8). This requires that the header file *gtable.h* must include *wave.h*, to bring in the definition of OSCIL. In addition to the all-important pointer to a GTABLE, a variable is provided to contain the table length as a double, to avoid continual casting in the tick function. And, as was suggested in subsection 2.6.3, a helpfully named alternative to the twopiovrsr of OSCIL is provided.

Listing 2.6.8: Definition of OSCILT Type, Derived from OSCIL (gtable.h)

```
#include <wave.h>
typedef struct t_tab_oscil
{
    OSCIL osc;
    const GTABLE* gtable;
    double dtablen;
    double sizeovrsr;
} OSCILT;
```

The corresponding creation function is shown in listing 2.6.9. This is given the name of a GTABLE object containing some waveform. As a basic precaution against errors, such as supplying a GTABLE that has not been properly created or initialized, the input gtable is tested to make sure it is legitimate. Note the use of both forms of structure element access required here:

```
p_osc->osc.curfreq = 0.0;
```

The variable p_osc is a pointer to a GTABLE, so to access the elements of the structure the indirection operator -> is required: p_osc->osc. One of those elements, osc, is itself a complete structure (but not itself a pointer), and to access the elements of that—osc.curfreq—the plain dot operator is used.

The tick functions for both truncating and interpolating forms are shown in listing 2.6.10. Note that to be able to select between tick functions we must define a function pointer, using a different name from that defined for the OSCIL:

```
typedef double (*oscilt_tickfunc)(OSCILT* osc,double freq);
```

Listing 2.6.9: Creation Function for OSCILT (gtable.c)

```
OSCILT* new_oscilt(double srate, const GTABLE* gtable, double phase)
{
    OSCILT* p_osc;
    /* do we have a good GTABLE?*/
    if(gtable == NULL || gtable->table == NULL || gtable->length == 0)
        return NULL;
    p_osc = (OSCILT *) malloc(sizeof(OSCILT));
    if(p_osc == NULL)
        return NULL;
    /* init the osc: */
    p_osc->osc.curfreq = 0.0;
```

```
    p_osc->osc.curphase = gtable->length * phase;
    p_osc->osc.incr = 0.0;
    /* then the GTABLE-specific things */
    p_osc->gtable = gtable;
    p_osc->dtablen = (double) gtable->length;
    p_osc->sizeovrsr = p_osc->dtablen / (double) srate;
    return p_osc;
}
```

Listing 2.6.10: Truncating and Interpolating GTABLE Tick Functions

```
double tabtick(OSCILT* p_osc, double freq)
{
    int index = (int) (p_osc->osc.curphase);
    double val;
    double dtablen = p_osc->dtablen, curphase = p_osc->osc.curphase;
    double* table = p_osc->gtable->table;
    if(p_osc->osc.curfreq != freq){
        p_osc->osc.curfreq = freq;
        p_osc->osc.incr = p_osc->sizeovrsr * p_osc->osc.curfreq;
     }
     curphase += p_osc->osc.incr;
     while(curphase >= dtablen)
        curphase -= dtablen;
     while(curphase < 0.0)
        curphase += dtablen;
     p_osc->osc.curphase = curphase;
     return table[index];
}

double tabitick(OSCILT* p_osc, double freq)
{
    int base_index = (int) p_osc->osc.curphase;
    unsigned long next_index = base_index + 1;
    double frac,slope,val;
    double dtablen = p_osc->dtablen, curphase = p_osc->osc.curphase;
    double* table = p_osc->gtable->table;
    if(p_osc->osc.curfreq != freq){
        p_osc->osc.curfreq = freq;
        p_osc->osc.incr = p_osc->sizeovrsr *
        p_osc->osc.curfreq;
    }
    frac = curphase - base_index;
    val = table[base_index];
```

```
slope = table[next_index] - val;
val += (frac * slope);
curphase += p_osc->osc.incr;
    while(curphase >= dtablen)
curphase -= dtablen;
    while(curphase < 0.0)
curphase += dtablen;
p_osc->osc.curphase = curphase;
    return val;
}
```

2.6.9 Making Waves

To complete the code required for our synthesis program based on table lookup, we need some tables containing waveforms. The procedures for the basic square, sawtooth, and triangle waveforms necessarily have much in common with those shown in listing 2.6.2, as far as creating the correct mix of harmonics is concerned. The primary difference lies in the amplitude calculation, which will use the same technique of normalization demonstrated in section 2.2, in the program *sfnorm*, to rescale the data in the table to a maximum amplitude of 1.0. This is the means by which we can then guarantee that all signals will have the exact amplitude requested by the user, while also having the expected shape.

Based on the earlier example of new_sine, we require a set of functions, one for each waveform type, incorporating new code to implement normalization (of course, new_sine itself does not need this stage as it generates a single sine wave already at full amplitude). Listing 2.6.11 illustrates such a function for the triangle wave, incorporating all necessary tests for the input arguments length and nharms (line 9). The loop in lines 19 and 20 is required to ensure that the array is initialized to all zeroes. This is because the generation loop *accumulates* sample values (i.e. adds to what is already there) as each harmonic is calculated, using the += operator. Clearly, with this method it is essential that the table contain random values.

Listing 2.6.11: A Self-Contained Generation Function for the Triangle Wave

```
1   GTABLE* new_triangle(unsigned long length, unsigned longnharms)
2   {
3       unsigned long i,j;
4       double step,amp,maxamp;
5       double* table;
6       unsigned long harmonic = 1;
7       GTABLE* gtable = NULL;
8
9       if(length == 0 || nharms == 0 || nharms >= length/2)
```

```
10        return NULL;
11    gtable = (GTABLE* ) malloc(sizeof(GTABLE));
12    if(gtable == NULL)
13        return NULL;
14    table = (double*) malloc((length + 1) * sizeof(double));
15    if(table == NULL){
16        free(gtable);
17        return NULL;
18    }
19    for(i=0; i < length; i++)
20        table[i] = 0.0;
21    step = TWOPI / length;
22    /* generate triangle wave */
23    for(i=0;i < nharms; i++){
24        amp = 1.0 / (harmonic*harmonic);
25        for(j=0; j < length; j++)
26            table[j] += amp * cos(step * harmonic * j);
27        harmonic += 2;
28    }
29    /* normalize table */
30    for(i=0; i < length; i++){
31        amp = fabs(table[i]);
32        if(maxamp < amp)
33            maxamp = amp;
34    }
35    maxamp = 1.0 / maxamp;
36    for(i=0; i < length; i++)
37        table[i] *= maxamp;
38    table[i] = table[0];   /* guard point*/
39    gtable->length = length;
40    gtable->table = table;
41    return gtable;
42 }
```

This function is robust (e.g. it checks that both length and nharms arguments are valid), self-contained, and easy to use. If successful, it delivers from one function call a valid GTABLE containing a triangle wave at full amplitude. However, we can see that the code that allocates memory for the GTABLE is entirely generic and will be common to all waveform functions we write. Similarly, the normalization process is also common code, adding up to a significant proportion of the whole. It may not seem such an issue for just three or four waveforms, but we can easily imagine creating dozens, even hundreds, of waveforms, for one reason or another. On this sort of scale, economy of code becomes a major concern.

We have seen the use of functions to encapsulate a task. Here we have a task that in fact comprises distinct subtasks—and writing multiple functions that perform the same task is a sure and easy way to generate "code bloat." To avoid this, we need to split the process up, using a function for each of the common elements. As demonstrated by `new_triangle`, we can identify three tasks:

(1) generic GTABLE creation (lines 11–20)
(2) waveform generation, unique for each waveform (lines 21–28)
(3) generic table normalization (lines 30–37), which also sets guard point (line 38).

Of course we are most interested in the second of these. So our final implementation will be a compact version of `new_triangle` that will use the other two internally. This leads to the following prototypes for the functions we will need:

```
/* creates a fully allocate but empty table */
GTABLE* new_gtable(unsigned long length);
/* fills table with triangle wave */
GTABLE* new_triangle(unsigned long length, unsigned long nharms);
/* normalizes the table, and sets guard point */
void norm_gtable(GTABLE* gtable);
```

Example implementations of `new_gtable` and `norm_gtable` are shown in listing 2.6.12.

Listing 2.6.12: Waveform Generation—Common Functions (gtable.c)

(a) The GTABLE creation function. It creates storage for a table of size `length` plus a guard point. The array is cleared to zero. Note that this includes the guard point (the final loop uses <= rather than <- the guard point at the position `table[length]`).

```
GTABLE* new_gtable(unsigned long length)
{
    unsigned long i;
    GTABLE* gtable = NULL;
    if(length == 0)
        return NULL;
    gtable = (GTABLE* ) malloc(sizeof(GTABLE));
    if(gtable == NULL)
        return NULL;
    gtable->table = (double*) malloc((length + 1 * sizeof(double));
    if(gtable->table == NULL){
        free(gtable);
        return NULL;
    }
    gtable->length = length;
    for(i=0; i <= length; i++)
        gtable->table[i] = 0.0;
    return gtable;
}
```

(b) The GTABLE amplitude normalization. It sets the guard point. The input argument must be a pointer to a fully created GTABLE.

```
void norm_gtable(GTABLE* gtable)
{
    unsigned long i;
    double val, maxamp = 0.0;

    for(i=0; i < gtable->length; i++){
        val = fabs(table[i]);
        if(maxamp < val)
            maxamp = val;
    }
    maxamp = 1.0 / maxamp;
    for(i=0; i < gtable->length; i++)
        gtable->table[i] *= maxamp;
    gtable->table[i] = gtable->table[0];
}
```

Note that new_gtable is safe, though not very useful, if accidentally passed straight to a tick function—the output will merely be silent. These functions represent only the first stage in what could become a substantial library of functions to create and (perhaps more important), modify tables.

2.6.10 Public vs. Private Functions—The static Keyword

The function new_gtable is very straightforward, returning NULL if any aspect of the creation process (including a bad value for length) fails, but the function norm_gtable presents us with a problem. As shown, it performs no error checking at all (indicated also by the fact that it returns void)—it depends on the input argument gtable being a valid pointer to a fully created GTABLE. If it were to be included in a public library, it would be a somewhat risky function without error checking. At the very least, it would have to be documented thoroughly. However, much depends on how it is intended to be used. In this context, it is really a private helper function for new_triangle and its kin. To emphasize its private nature, and enforce it in code, we can use the important C keyword static, which effectively hides the function from other source files (technically speaking, the function is not identified by the linker, which links together compiled code from each source file to create the final executable—only other functions in the same source file will know about it):

```
static void norm_gtable(GTABLE* gtable);
```

Note that the static keyword is placed first in the declaration, which we can now refer to as a static function. In contrast to the declaration of public functions, static functions are declared and defined together directly in the implementation file, and not in a public or shared header file. Thus we put the declaration above at the top of *gtable.c*, with the function definition itself elsewhere in the same file. With this degree of control, we merely have to make sure that we are using the function safely, in *gtable.c*, without worrying about how it may be used or misused in other situations.

We can now define our complete set of compact waveform generation functions, including new_triangle (listing 2.6.12). Each of these functions receives a pointer to a fully created GTABLE and an argument that sets the number of partials. As usual, the sawtooth function supports both upward and downward forms.

Listing 2.6.12: Waveform Generation Functions (gtable.c)

```c
GTABLE* new_triangle(unsigned long length, unsigned long nharms)
{
    unsigned long i,j;
    double step,amp;
    GTABLE* gtable;
    int harmonic = 1;

    if(length == 0 || nharms == 0 || nharms >= length/2)
        return NULL;
    gtable = new_gtable(length);
    if(gtable == NULL)
        return NULL;
    step = TWOPI / length ;
    for(i=0;i < nharms; i++){
        amp = 1.0 / (harmonic*harmonic);
        for(j=0;j < length;j++)
            gtable->table[j] += amp * cos(step*harmonic * j);
        harmonic += 2;
    }
    norm_gtable(gtable);
    return gtable;
}

GTABLE* new_square(unsigned long length,unsigned long nharms)
{
    unsigned long i,j;
    double step,amp;
    GTABLE* gtable;
    int harmonic = 1;

    if(length == 0 || nharms == 0 || nharms >= length/2)
     return NULL;
    gtable = new_gtable(length);
```

```
    if(gtable == NULL)
        return NULL;
    step = TWOPI / length ;
    for(i=0; i < nharms; i++){
        amp = 1.0 / harmonic;
        for(j=0;j < gtable->length;j++)
            gtable->table[j] += amp * sin(step*harmonic * j);
        harmonic+=2;
    }
 norm_gtable(gtable);
 return gtable;
}

GTABLE* new_saw(unsigned long length,unsigned long nharms, int up)
{
    unsigned long i,j;
    double step,val,amp = 1.0;
    GTABLE* gtable;
    int harmonic = 1;

    if(length == 0 || nharms == 0 || nharms >= length/2)
        return NULL;
    gtable = new_gtable(length);
    if(gtable == NULL)
        return NULL;
    step = TWOPI / length ;
    if(up)
        amp = -1;
    for(i=0; i < nharms; i++){
        val = amp / harmonic;
        for(j=0;j < gtable->length;j++)
            gtable->table[j] += val * sin(step*harmonic * j);
        harmonic++;
    }
    norm_gtable(gtable);
    return gtable;
}
```

Note that the sawtooth function uses an extra argument to set the direction. This inevitably takes the appearance of a Boolean variable, but the requirements of the command line are such that in any case an enum is required (placed in *gtable.h*, it is specific to the new_saw function). This enum happens to act as a mimic of Boolean *true* and *false*:

```
enum { SAW_DOWN,SAW_UP };
```

Table 2.4
Objects required for *tabgen*.

	Functions	Purpose
GTABLE	new_triangle	Creates GTABLE containing triangle wave
	new_square	Creates GTABLE containing square wave
	new_saw	Creates GTABLE containing sawtooth wave (up/down)
	free_gtable	Destroys a GTABLE by freeing all memory
OSCILT	new_oscilt	Creates an OSCILT object; requires a GTABLE
	tabtick	OSCILT tick function performing truncated lookup
	tabitick	OSCILT tick function performing interpolated lookup

These constants enable us to call new_saw in a very self-documenting way:

```
case(WAVE_SAWDOWN):
    gtable = new_saw(tabsize, nharms, SAW_DOWN);
    break;
case(WAVE_SAWUP):
    gtable = new_saw(tabsize, nharms, SAW_UP);
    break;
```

Were the raw numbers 0 and 1 used instead, on reading the code one would always have a slight question in one's mind about which value means what.

2.6.11   Putting It All Together

It is now time to complete the design of the program *tabgen*. It is important, as always, not to leap into coding, but to start by forming a clear design that reflects the purpose of the program and is, in turn, reflected in the structure of the command line that the program will present to the user.

The preceding subsections of section 2.6 presented several families of functions, associated with a number of custom objects. Some of the functions are private or internal to others. The *tabgen* program will be concerned with only the public functions. Table 2.4 lists the main objects required, together with the functions associated with them. We will need two groups of these:

(1) Wavetable object GTABLE: lookup table using a guard point. Has internal memory. Any non-zero table size is supported.
(2) Table lookup object OSCILT: uses a GTABLE. No internal memory.

The program is required to support comparisons of both lookup methods, with respect to speed and table size. Like *oscgen*, *tabgen* should support the use of amplitude and frequency breakpoint files.

For a program such as this, rather than require a lengthy command line (and especially where so many of the arguments are numeric), a common practice is to define a default configuration, which can be changed by means of "flag" options. The main argument list can then be identical to that of *oscgen*, which is appropriate, since *tabgen* is required to produce the same output. It is reasonable to rename the final `noscs` argument of *oscgen* to `nharms` (for number of harmonics), which more accurately reflects the different implementation. This leads to the following command line:

```
tabgen [-wN][-t] outfile dur srate nchans amp freq type nharms
    -wN : set width of lookup table to N points (default: 1024)
    -t  : use truncating lookup (default: interpolating lookup)
```

You are now ready to study *tabgen*, run and test it, and compare the output with that of *oscgen*, not only to confirm the considerable increase in speed but also to confirm that the outputs are the same, save for the now consistent and precise amplitude control. A version of *tabgen* is presented on the DVD; refer to it only if you are having difficulties.

Some suggestions for testing are given in the exercises at the end of this section. Note that testing a program is not quite the same as "trying it out." Testing often requires making a prediction and confirming that the output accords with that prediction. Therefore, be systematic, for example by varying one setting at a time. Of particular interest here is the difference between the quality and performance of the truncating and interpolating lookup algorithms.

You should now feel confident enough to design and implement your own variations on the additive theme. Possible avenues for exploration include, but are not limited to, the following:

• Adapt *oscgen* to use OSCILT, to make an oscillator bank using table lookup oscillators. This could then include the use of different waveforms that are added in various ways under user control.

• Modify *oscgen* to support an "inharmonicity" or stretch factor for the frequencies of the harmonics. For example, in listing 2.6.2, the `freqfac` variable is either 1.0 or 2.0, according to the waveform. When this is changed to a fractional value, such as 1.4 or 2.23, the partials become relatively inharmonic (the distances between them are shrunk or stretched). By combining these harmonics with a suitable amplitude envelope, you can easily create metallic and bell-like timbres.

• Devise a program that accepts a list of harmonic amplitude data from the user to create arbitrary timbres.

Explore frequency modulation techniques, for example by applying vibrato to the output signal. The vibrato signal is simply an oscillator whose output is scaled to a discreet amount, such as 0.05 (so the output swings between −0.05 and +0.05 at the vibrato frequency). To apply the vibrato to the main oscillator, you scale the frequency using the vibrato signal, and then add the result to the original frequency value:

```
output = tick(osc, freq + (freq * vibsig));
```

This will ensure that the pitch deviation up and down is balanced (e.g. one semitone above and below the nominal pitch). Both sine and triangle waves are suitable for use as vibrato signals. Of course, using table lookup, you can also invent your own vibrato shapes. For the full "Pavarotti effect," the vibrato modulation may have to be increased to around 0.1.

2.6.12   Exercises

Exercise 2.6.1
Re-implement `new_oscilp` using separated creation and init functions, and test the phase variable for correct range.

Exercise 2.6.2
A pulse wave is defined as a waveform in which all the harmonics are of equal amplitude. A pulse wave containing 20 harmonics is shown in figure 2.21. Create the required generation function `new_pulse` and add it to the program *tabgen*. Update the usage message accordingly.

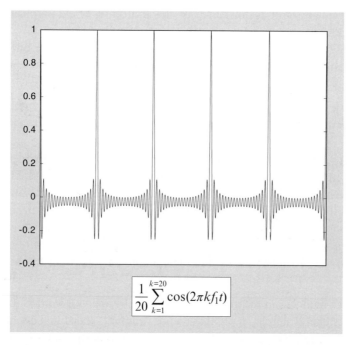

$$\frac{1}{20} \sum_{k=1}^{k=20} \cos(2\pi k f_1 t)$$

Figure 2.21
Pulse wave with 20 harmonics.

Exercise 2.6.3

One limitation of the implementation of GTABLE (and similarly with the OSCIL types) is that the example creation functions do not support declaring an instance as a local variable (i.e. on the *stack*), and initializing it with a filled table (other than by creating the code explicitly). Remedy this by implementing a further creation function int create_gtable(GTABLE* table) so that the code below is possible:

```
GTABLE table;
if(create_gtable(&table)){
    puts("no memory!\n");
    error++;
    goto exit;
}
```

The function should return 0 for success, −1 for an error. It should return an error if table already contains an allocated table.

Exercise 2.6.4

A programmer friend suggests that "all the wrap-around code (based on a while loop) could be eliminated by using the C math library function fmod, which takes the modulus (remainder after division) of a floating-point number"—for example,

```
curphase = fmod(curphase, dtablen);
```

Make this change. Compare the performance with the original code as modified above, using the program's timing facility based on clock. What conclusion(s) can you draw from this experiment?

Exercise 2.6.5

At a sampling rate of 44,100 Hz, a lookup table of 128 samples has a "root" pitch of 344.53 Hz (around "Middle F" on the piano, or MIDI note 65).

(a) Using a truncating lookup oscillator of that size to generate a triangle wave (set nharms to 20), predict the shape and sound of the output waveform when generating a fixed frequency of one-fourth the root frequency—i.e. 86.133, then when generating a frequency sweep between 50 Hz and 172 Hz over 10 seconds. Check your predictions by running *tabgen* with these parameters.
(b) Repeat (a) while increasing the table size by factors of 2 (128, 256, 512, 1,024, ...) each time. With what table size does the output sound free of distortion?

Exercise 2.6.6

On a certain computers, *tabgen* was run twice (with the default interpolating lookup) to generate a fixed frequency of 440 Hz (srate 44100) using table sizes of (a) 128 samples, and

(b) 2,048 samples. The processing time was found to be respectively 1.86 seconds and 1.77 seconds. Explain this result.

Exercise 2.6.7

Why can't we use a table lookup oscillator to synthesize inharmonic sounds?

Conclusion

This chapter introduced a number of important concepts of audio programming. Starting with self-describing soundfile formats and their attributes, we were able to proceed through basic signal processing algorithms to elements of sound synthesis. In particular, we have been able to explore a workhorse of computer music, the wavetable oscillator, in some detail. In addition to these specific elements of audio processing, we were able to complement the C language topics seen in the previous chapter with some more advanced principles. This chapter should serve as a springboard to the exploration of other aspects of audio programming found elsewhere in the book.

Notes

1. The WAVE format was designed for computers based on the Intel CPU series (IBM PC), while the AIFF format was designed for computers using the Motorola CPU family (PPC Apple Macintosh). Consequently, WAVE files are little-endian, while AIFF files are big-endian. Thus, to read a WAVE format soundfile on a big-endian machine, all numeric values (not only the samples, but also most of the file header) have to have the low and high bytes reversed, in a process known as "byte-swapping." Similarly, byte-swapping must be performed when reading an AIFF format file on a PC. For 32-bit floats, all four bytes have to be reversed. This naturally consumes some CPU time, and it is understandable that AIFF files are rarely preferred on the PC, and WAVE files are rarely preferred on the PPC Macintosh. It is one of the main tasks of any portable soundfile library to perform all the required byte-swapping, so that users do not have to worry about it.

2. The usefulness of a makefile is by no means confined to compiling programs. It can be used as a general-purpose scripting system for any project that may involve dependencies. For example, a musical project may involve the generation of new soundfiles based on old ones, which in turn may be based on yet older ones. Such soundfiles may be long, and the processes time-consuming. Thus the creation of one soundfile is dependent on that of another—the latter is then a dependency of the former. *Make* can detect whether a dependency is up to date, and only if it is not will it run the process to recreate it. This is very different from the operation of a shell script or batch file, which will blindly perform all the listed tasks, even if nothing has changed since the previous run.

3. This is not unusual. Csound, for example, uses a flag argument to indicate the file format (e.g. -W for WAVE and -A for AIFF), while the user is free to employ the opposite file extension to the one intended. It is as easy to use a file extension but forget the format flag. Many programs read the format not from the file extension but from the file header.

4. Macintosh users will be familiar with the idiomatic practice of avoiding all file extensions (considered at that time by Apple as old-fashioned), relying instead on a "File Type" property maintained by the OS. This is especially unfortunate for a general-purpose file format that is intended to be cross-platform. Significantly, with the release of OS X (which is based on a UNIX kernel), Apple now (re)asserts the importance of using and reading file extensions.

5. The use of `goto` is probably the most hotly debated aspect of C programming. Technically speaking, it is always possible to eliminate the use of `goto`; and many programmers (we can call them purists, as opposed to pragmatists) abhor its use. Nevertheless, it is a C keyword, and no tutorial would be complete without giving it at least some degree of attention. The realities are that with care, it can be used quite safely, and over time, certain "rules of thumb" have emerged that serve to ensure it is not abused. The nightmare scenario is "spaghetti code" in which control jumps all over the place and reading the flow of control (and debugging) becomes impossible. The program presented in this chapter demonstrates two such rules: that the jump target is always below the `goto` (on the page) and that there is only one label in the function, to which all `goto`s jump. Another situation in which a `goto` is sometimes favored is in escaping from a deeply nested loop, to a point beyond the topmost loop:

```
for(...) {
    for(...) {
        for(...){
            if(power_cut)
                goto dressing_room;
        }
    }
}
dressing_room:
    drink_beer();
    go_home();
```

The pragmatist will use a `goto` in this way, confident that it will not create trouble later. The purist will avoid the `goto` by, for example, introducing extra tests in each loop, so that a more respectable keyword such as `break` can be used, to step out of the nested loop level by level. Both the purist and the pragmatist will argue about which approach is the more readable.

6. Programming tip: Don't sabotage the preprocessor. Never write an explicit numeric value in a program, instead of the symbol `#define`d for it. Indeed, it is a good policy in general to seek out wherever such explicit constants are used, and consider whether a preprocessor symbol, if not a defined variable, would not manage and document things better. For example, should you decide to allocate some space for a waveform table, you might also decide to allocate some extra space for safety and debugging. This can be done in just one line:

```
buffer = (float*) malloc(520 * sizeof(float));
```

However, six months later you may not recall exactly why you did this. Using the preprocessor and a few extra lines, the intention becomes clear:

```
#define TAB_SIZE 512
#define TAB_SAFETY 8
...
buffer = (float*) malloc((TAB_SIZE + TAB_SAFETY) *sizeof(float));
```

Additionally, this enables you to redefine `TAB_SIZE` and `TAB_SAFETY` in one place in the code, and have code elsewhere change as required (you might be allocating 64 such tables, across several source files). The latter might even be wrapped inside a debug test:

```
#ifdef _DEBUG
#define TAB_SAFETY 8
#else
#define TAB_SAFETY 0
#endif
```

7. There is a yet more advanced procedure that is standard for experienced UNIX developers: to install frequently used header files and libraries in what are termed "the standard locations" (e.g. header files are placed in `/usr/local/include`, and built library files are installed in `/usr/local/lib`). This requires the user to have "`admin`" or "`root`" privileges, which may not be the case where a machine supports multiple user accounts under the management of a system administrator. No equivalent convention is established for Windows development—developers simply create whatever development environment and directory structure suits them. This might even include creating a custom `/usr` directory to mimic the UNIX architecture, and updating the user's PATH accordingly.

8. We will leave to other authorities the thorny question of whether this should be 32,768 or 32,767.

9. 16 * 6 = 96; but note that in 16 bits anything below −96dB isn't "extremely quiet"; it is silent. Or rather, it is buried in quantization noise, which will decide if the sample is silent (= 0) or not (= +1 or −1).

10. Programmer's tip: Any time you write an expression involving division, take the greatest possible care to ensure that division by zero *cannot* happen.

11. Listing 2.3.1 shows that it is possible to use multiple initializer statements in a `for` statement, each statement separated by a comma. In fact this is a general facility, and it is common to find multiple update statements too. For example, the `for` loop in listing 2.3.1 could also be implemented as follows:

```
for(i=0, out_i = 0; i < framesread; i++, out_i *= 2){
    outframe[out_i] = (float)(inframe[i] * pos.left);
    outframe[out_i+1] = (float)(inframe[i] * pos.right);
}
```

The use of multiple update statements is debatable. A good rule of thumb here is that the initializer and update statements must match, and that there should not be a lot of them. You may well find, for example, that the code in listing 2.3.1 is more readable and expressive than the alternative above, and that as an algorithm it would also scale better to an *N*-channel process (such as a surround-sound panner). Another (perhaps more "purist") argument says that only variables involved in the conditional test should be used in the initializer and update statements. It is tempting to think of the comma simply as a sort of separator between expressions, or between items in a list, but technically it is an operator, and a statement comprising comma-separated expressions has a value, which is that of the rightmost expression:

```
int j , k;
    j = k = 1;
if(j) j = 2, k = 3;
```

Here both assignments are applied: the line `j = 2,k = 3` comprises a single statement thanks to the comma, so that braces are not required after the `if` test. In practice, the comma operator should be used sparingly. It is more likely to arise by accident, as a result of a typing error. It has a natural place in `for` loops, as shown, and is sometimes useful in defining complex macros. However, one consequence of the behavior of the comma operator is that you cannot reasonably have multiple comma-separated conditional tests in a `for` loop. The result of whichever is the last test in the list is the result of the over-all test, so that preceding tests (even if false) would be ignored. This is a good example of C allowing you to do things you really should not do.

12. In a conventionally correct stereo setup, the two speakers and the listener should form an equilateral triangle, so that the speakers subtend angles of ± 30 degrees, left and right of the listening position. Ensure that speakers are not close to walls or corners (unless specifically designed to operate under those conditions), and that the room is as acoustically neutral as possible.

13. When panning a sound between speakers, and especially when composing a moving trajectory, it is often presumed that the sound pursues a straight-line path between the speakers. However, a little consideration of the geometry of this will show that this cannot be achieved without artefacts. Specifically, for a sound to follow this path, the distance of the sound from the listener will not be constant—the sound is nearer the listener at the central position, than when located right or left. Thus, it should sound louder. Also, any real sound moving in this way relative to a listener will undergo Doppler shift—that change of apparent frequency of a moving object familiar to anyone standing next to a busy road. This therefore is the difference between simple "pair-wise intensity panning" and true "spatialization," which takes into account all these and other issues, to create a truer impression of a sound located or moving in a space, including the position of the listener. Conventional pair-wise stereo panning can only assume the 'correct' stereo speaker arrangement, and similarly can only implement constant-distance panning, given that for most music applications nether Doppler shift, nor a level change at the centre, is desirable. On the other hand, for listeners sitting too far away from the speakers, the illusion of a straight-line path will be more convincing.

14. Some popular programming languages, such as C++ and Pascal, define a special quasi-arithmetical type to be used for true/false values. In Pascal the type name is "Boolean," and in C++ it is `bool`. The collective name for such variables is thus "Boolean variables," and is taken from the name of the English mathematician George Boole (1815–1864), who devised a notation and system, known as Boolean Algebra, for applying mathematical operations to logic, including symbols for TRUE and FALSE. This work subsequently became the foundation for the whole modern science of computing. Each "bit" making up a binary number is an instance of a Boolean value. The core logical operations defined by Boolean Algebra are AND, OR, and NOT. These are represented in C by the operators `&&`, `||`, and `!`. However, a continuing source of annoyance to C programmers is the fact that the fundamental values TRUE and FALSE are not represented by an explicit symbol or type—you have to use one of the integer types, such as `char` or `int`. The complication in C is that whereas FALSE is defined implicitly, but uniquely, as 0, corresponding to the value of a conditional expression such as `(1 == 0)`, TRUE is defined equally implicitly, but non-uniquely, as "any non-zero value." Thus the tests `if(-1)` and `if(1)` both succeed: both −1 and 1 evaluate to TRUE in a C conditional test. This is not of itself a problem—C is entirely consistent in its behavior, and programmers soon become familiar with the idiomatic way of doing

things. The problem arises when one attempts to overcome the absence of a Boolean type in C by defining custom symbols. The most common way of doing this is to use the preprocessor, or `typedef`:

```
#define TRUE 1
#define FALSE 0
typedef int BOOL;
```

leading to

```
BOOL more_points = TRUE;
```

There are several possible objections to this, however: in C, any non-zero value is also TRUE, so some expressions that evaluate to non-zero values cannot be safely used with TRUE as defined above. These methods do nothing to help avoid syntactically correct but semantically incorrect constructions. For example, the statements below will not trigger as much as a warning from the compiler:

```
more_points = 10;
more_points--;
```

You may not be the only programmer who has thought of name collisions. Try to find a programmer who has *not* used the names TRUE and FALSE. Indeed, the developers of Microsoft Windows thought of this a long time ago, and use both the definitions and the `typedef` shown above throughout the WIN32 API. If you need to combine Windows code with code from some other third-party source, that happens to have defined them differently, you can expect problems. Someone somewhere is bound to have done it this way:

```
#define TRUE 0
#define FALSE -1
```

In short, creating definitions for `TRUE` and `FALSE` (or in general for any two-valued type) in C is fine so long as the limitations are understood. Never use such symbols to define function arguments or return values, for example. In any case, avoid using lower-case symbols for these; `true`, `false`, and `bool` are all keywords in C++, and it has to be assumed that sooner or later code written in ANSI C will be copied into a C++ source file.

15. What is so special about viewpoints separated by a right angle? Imagine that the second hand of this imaginary clock is extremely thin, and that you do not have the benefit of stereoscopic vision. Viewed exactly on-end, this line appears as a mere point, whereas from the other viewpoint, it is visible as a line at its maximum length. Should the line change length at this position, the view of the point would be unchanged. This is a special property of sines and cosines, termed by mathematicians "orthogonality." For example, the three physical dimensions of length, width, and height are orthogonal to each other. This is not just an esoteric property of interest only to theorists; it is of fundamental practical importance. All of audio synthesis and processing depends upon this property of sines and cosines—additive (Fourier) synthesis being but one example.

16. Despite the impossibility of representing π exactly, we have no choice but to approximate is as closely as possible, for practical audio calculations. The math library functions employ `double` precision, which is comfortably accurate enough for even high-resolution audio. Many programmers simply define π as a number, and are even generous with the number of decimal places they specify:

```
#define PI (3.14159265358979323846264338327950288419716939937510)
```

But this is in fact a little optimistic for a C double. If we use C to calculate π directly (a solution often preferred over use of the preprocessor):

```
#include <math.h>
```

```
const double pi = 4.0 * atan(1);
printf("PI = %.20f,"pi); /*write out PI to 20 decimal places*/
```

the output is in fact merely

```
PI = 3.14159265358979310000
```

A standard 64-bit `double` can resolve to only 17 decimal digits (wherever the decimal point is), and as we see, the number above is accurate to only 15 decimal places. For audio this is still plenty; and even the lower precision of a `float` (no more than 8 decimal digits, but broadly comparable to the precision of a 24-bit integer) is sufficient for a dynamic range of more than 140 dB. In defining such symbols, care must be taken however to avoid name collisions. The symbol `M_PI` is supplied by some compilers, and is widely used by programmers (as is `PI`) so, whichever symbol name is used, it is important to avoid re-defining it. Given the importance of the value 2π, it is common to define this too. Note that we cannot use the symbol name `2PI` because preprocessor symbols, like C variable names, cannot begin with a number. Any serious compiler will automatically recalculate the value of `TWOPI` as a single number in the course of preprocessing the code. Technically, there can be advantages to defining `PI` and its relatives as a literal number rather than as a variable. The number can be embedded explicitly in the machine code, whereas accessing a variable from memory may prove to be a slower operation.

17. Were `OSCIL` to be declared as a local variable,

```
OSCIL* new_oscil(unsigned long srate)
{
    OSCIL osc;
    ...
    return &osc;
}
```

this would lead to a crash with an access violation as soon as one attempted to use the returned pointer. A variable declared locally like this is destroyed when the function returns. The object is created on the system stack, a temporary scratch-pad area of memory created for local variables at the beginning of a function call, and recovered afterward. Thus the returned pointer no longer points to an `OSCIL`, but to whatever has replaced it in that part of memory, almost certainly something it has no business pointing to. By creating the object with `malloc`, memory is allocated for it on the global memory *heap*. Now the returned pointer points to a genuine instance of `OSCIL`. The allocated memory must eventually be returned to the system using `free`. Allocating memory inside a function is an important and idiomatic technique. As noted in the text, documentation is essential, to tell the programmer to free the object later. Note, however, that it is reasonable to declare an instance of an object at the top level of `main` with the other variable declarations, i.e. on the top-level stack, and pass its address to `oscil_init`, as now the lifetime of the object extends beyond that of the function call:

```
OSCIL osc;
oscil_init(&osc, outprops.srate);
```

18. The name of this function is chosen in conscious tribute to the freely available "Synthesis Toolkit," written by Perry Cook in C++. Here, the functions that generate or process individual samples are called "tick." Many alternative names have been used by programmers, such as "get_sample"; but none improves on this simple, short, yet self-documenting name.

19. Listing 2.5.8 illustrates an often-encountered situation for C programmers, where lines of code are repeated identically in several places. Apart from the tedium of typing the same code multiple times (eased somewhat by the availability of cut-and-paste editing tools), the presence of the repeated code can sometimes obscure what is different in the various instances. The programmer's first thought might well be to define a function to replace the inline code:

```
double wrap_phase(double curphase)
{
    if(curphase > TWOPI)
        return curphase - TWOPI;
    if(curphase < 0.0)
        return curphase + TWOPI;
        return curphase;
}
```

For audio programmers, however, this has a major disadvantage in that it adds the overhead of a function-call in code that needs to run as fast as possible. The alternative is to define a preprocessor *macro*. In such cases the text being substituted is often lengthy, and may need to extend over several lines. The backslash has the special meaning of "line continuation" in a macro, to enable such multi-line macros to be written. The line continuation character *must* be the last character on the line (i.e. followed immediately by `<newline>`). In this example there is no parameter associated with the macro—it performs plain text substitution:

```
#define OSC_WRAPPHASE if(p_osc->curphase >= TWOPI) \
                    p_osc->curphase -= TWOPI; \
    if(p_osc->curphase < 0.0) p_osc->curphase += TWOPI
```

Note that the final semicolon is excluded from the text. While not practicable in all cases, this possibility is always welcome as it enables the macro usage to look a little more like properly formed C code:

```
p_osc->curphase += p_osc->incr;
OSC_WRAPPHASE;
```

The preprocessor will replace the symbol `OSC_WRAPPHASE` with the substitute text, so that the code passed to the compiler is identical to the original fully written out form. In such cases it is especially important that the macro name is written in upper case, to indicate to the reader that a macro is being used. As these macros are specific to the code in *wave.c* (they reference the name `p_osc`), they are best placed at the top of that file, rather than in *wave.h*.

   The warnings given in chapter 1 about possible bugs arising from the use of macros apply even more strongly here. Unless you are confident that the code will not need debugging in any way (e.g. using the source-code single-step debugging facilities of modern compilers), it is better to resist the temptation to use a macro, and keep to the fully written-out code. Don't forget that the use of extra levels of brackets (whether curved or curly) is often the key to preventing bugs in macros.

20. In practice, such standard timers are not reliably accurate to 1 msec; there can be a significant degree of timing "jitter," depending on the design of the operating system, and the time taken by the OS to switch between processes. Measured differences of the order of a few milliseconds should therefore be disregarded.

21. The use of a new structure variable `sizeovrsr` for the `OSCILT` type illustrates a common problem for C programmers. As the corresponding variable in `OSCIL`, `twopiovrsr`, is available but unused in the `OSCILT` functions, there is a good reason to use it, to avoid using what is ostensibly an unnecessary extra variable in the `OSCILT` structure (economizing on memory consumption, especially for objects that may exist in large numbers, is an important and often prime concern). However, the meaning of these variables is different in each case (one expresses a relationship to `TWOPI`, the other to a table size), and as has been emphasized frequently in this book, choosing appropriate names for variables and functions is an important aspect of securing readability and the self-documentation of your code. Conversely, programmers also like generality and economy. An alternative approach, given that we have created both `OSCIL` and `OSCILT` and are therefore able to modify both at will, is to use a generic name such as "`incrfac`" for `OSCIL`, which is neutral enough to cover any likely usage. This however makes the code for each specific oscillator less expressive and self-documenting. We are thus confronted with a choice between economy (arising from the preference for generality), and readability, that may favor the use of multiple alternative variables. The approach taken in these introductory sections is, as this example demonstrates, biased toward the latter approach. This is an issue that will not go away, however, and for C++ programmers it becomes even more taxing, as the urge, almost a moral imperative, intensifies to identify common behavior among a host of objects—leading ultimately to the creation of objects so general that they end up being called OBJECT.

22. It has to be said, however, that for the highest audio quality, linear interpolation itself performs poorly. Extended interpolation techniques are widely employed. One common technique is so-called cubic interpolation, which seeks to interpolate a curve between sample points rather than a simple line. Examples can be found in a number of Csound opcodes. A major objective of these more advanced interpolation methods is to minimize the filtering effect that can reduce the high-frequency of a sound to an unacceptable degree.

3 Working with Audio Streams

Gabriel Maldonado

3.1 Introduction

In the computer, a "stream" is a sequential flow of data that moves from one point to another. These two "points" can be two different hardware devices, such as the random-access memory (RAM) to the hard drive, or, as in the case of audio streams, the flow might move an audio signal that results from some signal processing algorithm to the digital-to-analog converter (DAC) and then out of the computer to your loudspeakers.

As you are probably well aware, digital computers only deal with numbers ('digital' derives from the word 'digit', a synonym for 'numeric'). Thus, the only kind of stream allowed by a computer is a numeric stream—a flow of binary numbers, zeroes and ones, which are combined to represent different numeric types. To generate such streams, we can *sample* analog signals[1] to *digitize* audio (as well as any sort of varying physical quantity).

A *digital audio signal* is a sequence of numbers that precisely represents the variation of air pressure that, when it stimulates our ear, produces the phenomenon we call *sound*.[2] In this section we will deal with audio streams. In particular, we will learn how to generate an audio signal in the C/C++ language and to store that signal in a file or send this signal directly to a digital-to-analog converter (DAC, the computer soundcard) in order to listen at it. Since the code that I present can be applied to both C and C++, I will refer to the language used as "C/C++." Actually C++ is a complete superset of the C programming language. Most of what is valid and true for C is also valid and true for C++. We will avoid code that is only compatible with C++ in this text. Some understanding of these languages is expected from the reader, but this text will also provide some further support for the study of programming in general.

3.2 Synthesizing Audio Streams to an Output

In this section, I will introduce a simple synthesis program *hellosine.c*,[3] and compare it with the famous *helloworld.c*[4] code. Our program will generate a sequence of *samples*[5] from a sine wave, and then stream the signal to the *standard output*.[6] There are several ways to generate such signals, and in this chapter we will use the following two:

- Using a standard C library function that calculates the sine of a number.
- Calculating a single cycle of the wave, storing it in an area of the computer's memory called a table,[7] and using the so-called table-lookup method or wave-table synthesis technique to generate the signal. In this case, any waveform stored in the table could be played—not only a sine wave, but a wave of any shape.

3.2.1   HelloWorld and HelloSine: A Comparison

This section introduces our simple audio-stream example, written in analogy to famous *helloworld.c* program that simply prints a string of text to the console and terminates:

```
/* helloworld.c */
#include <stdio.h>
main()
{
    printf("Hello, world!\n");
}
```

This program (a single *C function* called `main()`) does nothing more than *stream* a simple string to the *standard output*. In the UNIX operating system (and in DOS, the Windows console, and Linux) almost all devices, such as the screen, the keyboard, the printer, a file, etc., are considered to be a stream or a file (meaning a set of sequential data). By default, the *standard output* is associated with the console (and consequently the output is directed to the screen). But it is possible to *redirect* the standard output to another device, for example to a file, by simply calling the executable with the *redirection* character followed by the device name (in the case of a file, the name of the file itself). The redirection character is >. If we execute the program with the console line,

```
$ helloworld > pluto.txt
```

the program will not print anything to the screen, but rather, to a file named *pluto.txt*, which is created with the output from the program.

Our program *HelloSine* will do exactly the same thing, but instead of streaming a sequence of characters, it will stream a sequence of samples (as text):

```
/* hellosine.c */
#include <stdio.h>
#include <math.h>

#define SAMPLING_RATE 44100
#define NUM_SECONDS 3
#define NUM_SAMPLES (NUM_SECONDS * SAMPLING_RATE)
#define PI 3.14159265
#define FREQUENCY 440
```

```
main()
{
    int j;
    for(j = 0; j < NUM_SAMPLES; j++) {
    float sample;
            sample = sin(2 * PI * FREQUENCY * j / SAMPLING_RATE);
            printf("%f\n", sample);
    }
 }
```

By running our program, we can produce an audio stream (which in this case will be text containing a sequence of numbers) to a file. Example:

```
$ hellosine > sound.txt
```

3.2.2   A Functional Analysis of *hellosine.c*

In this section I will discuss what *HelloSine* does and see how it accomplishes its task. My goal is to provide you with some insights that will make your approach to software design more effective. When you are writing a program, it is important to begin with a clear list of ideas on what it will have to do. Therefore, I encourage you to begin their own programs by writing a set of assertions regarding the task(s) of each program. At the beginning, these assertions need not consider the peculiarities of the particular programming language that will be used to develop the program. Rather, they should be quite generic. In the case of *HelloSine* the first assertion is *Develop a program that writes the samples of a sine wave to the standard output*. When a programmer attempts to realize this sentence in the C language, he or she quickly discovers that the idea is quite clear, but that the information provided by the sentence is far from complete. "How many samples should it write, or, how many seconds?" If you have some notion about digital audio, you would ask yourself "Will the sine wave be heard? If so, what will be its frequency and amplitude? What will it have to be its sampling frequency?" All these questions must have concrete answers, because the computer only does what the programmer asks, it is unable to make a decision by itself. Such information can be provided in two ways:

- in a fixed way, i.e. embedded in the program itself
- in a parameterized way, i.e. it can be set by the user each time the program is run.

In order to be as simple as possible, our program adopts the first way (fixed).

Now the assertions can be completed:

Develop a program that will
- *write a stream of samples of a sinusoidal wave to the standard output*
- *write 3 seconds of audio samples in text format*

- *be sampled at the same sampling frequency of a commercial audio CD (44,100 Hz)*
- *correspond to the pitch of the orchestral tuning note—middle A (440 Hz)*
- *have a monophonic output (one channel).*

The specification is now complete. But I am able to use the word 'complete' only because I know that there is an existing C language library that contains a function able to calculate the sine of a number (i.e. the sin() function). Had I not been aware of this function, I would have had to figure out how to implement a sine function and add these steps to my previous outline. This set of assertions is often called the "specifications" ("specs") of a program.

Previous assertions correspond only to the first pass of the design phase, i.e. **what** the program should do. The second pass is: figure out *how* to do it. And then, only after answering the second question(s) is it possible to proceed with the third pass: *implement* it.

Here are my three phases of software development:

1. Outline what your program is supposed to do.
2. Figure out how to do it.
3. Do it.

How do we proceed to the "do" phase? Well, old programming books often suggest that we should devise a graphic scheme called a *flow chart* before beginning to write the code. Sometimes this kind of approach can be useful for beginners or for small programs, but personally, I think that in most cases it is a waste of time, especially for programs written by a single person, because a complete flow chart can turn out to be longer and complex than the code itself. Furthermore, flow charts force people to think in a particular programming paradigm, that is "structured programming," but they don't apply so well to the newer paradigms such as "object-oriented" or "declarative programming." At best, I feel that flow charts are quite useful for work-groups. Here it makes sense that everyone should literally be "on the same page," i.e. reading from the same "flow chart."

However, I don't intend to say that a flow chart is useless. I simply want to recommend that programmer not get too attached to a particular development style, such as traditional flow-charting style. Rather than using a flow-charting approach, I prefer visualizing a program as a series of input-output blocks connected by cables. This is a particularly appropriate model for audio programming, in which we are quite used to connecting audio devices like microphones to mixers to recorders to amplifiers to loudspeakers. Actually, this approach is embodied in the very user interface of a number of visual programming applications that deal primarily with audio—Max/MSP, PD, Reaktor, etc.

This kind of visualization is suited for any process dealing with signals (not only audio signals, but also control signals). These diagrams deal with the interconnection of modules or blocks, but hide the internal mechanism of each block from the programmer. Each of these signal modifying, signal processing, or signal generating blocks can be considered a "black box." And in a black box paradigm such as this, the programmer only knows the input(s), the output(s) and the behavior of the box, but knows nothing of the algorithm that is employed to make it work. This way of thinking is sometimes called "encapsulation" or "implementation hiding." These are two of the basic principles of an *object-oriented* paradigm. The most basic means for information hiding in C and C++ is the function. But normally a single function is not powerful or rich enough to speak of it as a form of object-orienting. For now, we are dealing with the "structured programming" or "imperative programming" paradigm. Figures 3.1 and 3.2 show a comparison between the flow chart and a block (black box) scheme.

Clearly the flow chart is closer to describing what actually happens in *hellosine.c*, whereas the block diagram gives us a better overview of the structure of the system and all of its connections while hiding what happens internally (in this case, there is only a block made up of the sine-wave generation mechanism). For the graphic representation, one could easily substitute a verbal description of what the program will do to accomplish its task:

1. Fill in all the `external` information that the program needs to run.
2. Based on the total duration (in seconds) and the sampling rate (in hertz), calculate how many samples the program will generate.
3. Initialize the time to zero.
4. Calculate the first sample by using the formula

$$\sin(2\pi f t), \tag{1}$$

where f is the frequency in Hz and t is the instantaneous time in seconds.
5. Output the signal to the standard output.
6. Increment instantaneous time t by a sample period (i.e. 1/samplingRate) in order to advance to the next sample.
7. Repeat steps 4–6 until all samples have been computed and sent to the standard output.
8. Exit the program.

Now that I have described what and how the program should proceed to do its task, we can move on to the implementation stage. Let's continue with our analysis. As was stated previously, the inputs of our program are embedded, and so, they can't be considered as true inputs from the actual point of view. If the programmer has to change any of these inputs, they would have to recompile the program before running it. They are implemented by means of C macros and are SAMPLING_RATE, NUM_SECONDS, and FREQUENCY (at the top of the program code). There are two further macros: NUM_SAMPLES (the number of samples to be sent to the standard output), that is obtained by using two previous arguments (i.e. NUM_SECONDS multiplied by the SAMPLING_RATE), and PI (which is nothing more than the famous constant π—the ratio between the circumference and the diameter of a circle) used in the formula, that was previously defined by the programmer.

In order to calculate and output all the samples, we need a loop iterating/repeating NUM_SAMPLES times. In the body of this loop, the temporary variable "sample" is filled each time with a new value, that is obtained by incrementing the index of the loop (the variable `j`) each cycle.

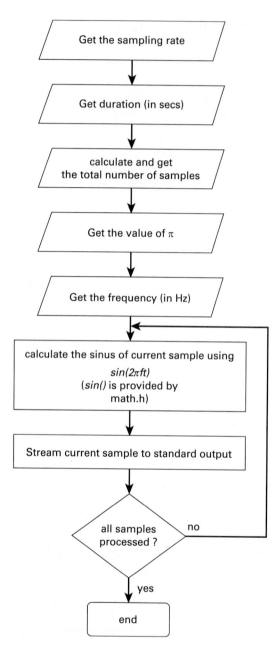

Figure 3.1
A flow chart of *hellosine.c.*

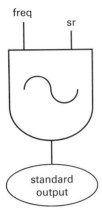

freq

sr

standard
output

Figure 3.2
A block diagram of *hellosine.c*.

Using the input macro constants, notice that the math formula: $\sin(2\pi ft)$ is translated into

```
sin(2 * PI * FREQUENCY * j / SAMPLING_RATE)
```

In particular, the instantaneous time t is incremented by a sample period by means of the `j/SAMPLING_RATE` expression, in which the `j` variable expresses both the index of the loop and current sample number.

3.2.3   Table-Lookup Oscillators

In this section we will continue to work with audio streams and we will be introduce the *table-lookup method* for generating waveforms. This method is also called *wavetable synthesis* and it can be used for both artificial sounds, generated entirely by computer calculations, and for acoustic sounds, recorded with a microphone.

Wavetable synthesis is a technique based on reading data that has been stored in blocks of *contiguous computer-memory locations*, called *tables*. This sound-synthesis technique was one of the very first software synthesis methods introduced in the MUSIC I–MUSIC V languages developed by Max Mathews at Bell Labs in the late 1950s and the early 1960s. Back then, computers were slow and reading pre-computed samples from memory was much faster than calculating each sample from scratch (as in the case of previous *hellosine.c*, in which the sin() function was called for each sample of the synthesized sound).

With table-lookup synthesis, it is sufficient to calculate only a single cycle of a waveform, and then store this small set of samples in the table where it serves as a template. In order to playback the actual sound, this stored single cycle of the waveform must be re-read in a loop at the desired frequency. Among other things, this method provided a huge advantage over the analog oscillators used in radio and electronic music studios of early 1960s because analog oscillators were capable of producing but a limited set of wave shapes (sinusoid, trian-gle, sawtooth, and square), whereas with the table-lookup method virtually any wave shape could be synthesized.

Three methods were devised to allow for the specification of arbitrary frequencies:

1. varying the reading speed (such as in the case of a tape recorder)
2. reading samples at a fixed rate, but varying the table length for each frequency (using a bigger table for lower frequencies and a smaller for higher frequencies)
3. reading samples at a fixed rate from a fixed length table, but varying the increment of the indexes of the samples to be read from the table.

The method actually used for wavetable synthesis (and the most convenient) is the third one. In order to understand it, let's suppose that, given a fixed reading rate (called the *sampling rate*), the "natural' frequency of a waveform is 100 Hz, when all subsequent samples (or elements) of the table are read, one a time. Each subsequent element of the table is num-bered by an *index*, starting from 0 up to the length of the table (−1). The first sample of the table has index 0, the second has index 1, and so on, up the last sample that is table length −1. So, in a table made up of 1,000 samples, the last sample has an index of 999.

We begin by reading the first element, and sending its value to the output, then the second, then the third, etc. After last element (having index 999) is read, the cycle restarts again from index 0 and so on.

To have a "natural" frequency of 100 Hz with a table of, suppose, 1,000 elements, all 1,000 samples must be read in a hundredth of second, so each sample must be read in $1/100/1,000 = 1/100,000$ second. This slice of time is called the *sampling period*. The sam-pling rate (actually the reading speed) is the inverse of the sampling period, so in our case it is 100,000 Hz. In most digital audio applications, the sampling rate is fixed.

If you wanted the waveform to "oscillate" at twice the frequency (200 Hz), it would be suf-ficient to read only samples with even indices, skipping the odd ones and reading one value from every other location in the table (i.e. index 0, 2, 4, ...). Again, to have a frequency of 300 Hz it is sufficient to read one sample every three indices, skipping two contiguous indexes each time (i.e. index 0, 3, 6, 9, ...).

How to obtain frequencies less than 100 Hz? Simply by reading the same sample more than once. For example, to play the waveform at a frequency of 50 Hz, it is sufficient to read the value from each sample twice and then read the next (i.e. index 1, 1, 2, 2, 3, 3, 4, 4, ...) and to listen to that waveform at 1/3 the "natural frequency" (33.33... Hz), it is sufficient to read the same sample 3 times before moving along to the next value in the table (i.e. index 1, 1, 1, 2, 2, 2, 3, 3, 3, ...).

You might be wondering at this point whether this method is capable of obtaining any frequency. The answer is no. Given the technique as explain thus far, the only frequencies that can be obtained from our table-lookup oscillator are those that are integer multiples or integer fractions of the "natural" frequency of the table. But there is a method that would allow us to obtain any frequency. In order to understand it, we have to introduce the concept of *phase* (which for table-lookup oscillators has an extended meaning), and the concept of a *sampling increment*.

In wavetable synthesis, the phase is a variable that acts as a pointer to the index of a current table element (note: this not to be confused with a *C-language pointer*, we will cover this topic in depth later). The specific phase value is advanced by the amount of the sampling increment for each sampling period, in order to point to the appropriate table-index at each subsequent reading. In the first of previous examples, a frequency of 100 Hz was obtained by incrementing the phase value by 1 for each sampling period; 200 Hz was obtained with a sampling increment of 2; 300 Hz with a sampling increment of 3 and so on. But, in order to obtain a frequency of 50 Hz, you needed a sampling increment lower than 1, actually 1/2 or 0.5; to obtain a frequency of 33.33... Hz, you needed a sampling increment equal to 1/3 or 0.333 and so on.

Actually, the value of the sampling increment determines, and is proportional to, the frequency of the wave. In most cases, the sampling increment is a *fractional number*, not an integer. The phase value is also a real number. So, if the instantaneous value of the phase is, for instance, 10.92843, the actual table element that is extracted has an index of 10 because the integer part of the phase is taken as a pointer to an index of table elements. And obviously, the possible range of values of our phase pointer can only be from 0 up to the table-length minus 1 (a 100-element table goes from 0 to 99). And when the phase value reaches or surpasses the table length, it needs to wrap back around to the beginning in order to restore the phase pointer to a useful range, and this is done by subtracting the length of the table from the calculated sampling increment (if our table is 100 samples long, and our sampling increment is 105, then our phase is set to a value of 5 and points to a table-index back at the beginning of the table). The method described here, is the "raw," un-interpolated method and this obviously introduces some error and some "noise" in the signal. To obtain a better sound quality (a more accurate representation of the data/curve stored in the table) one of several *interpolation* methods are usually employed with the most common being the *linear interpolation* method.

3.2.4   A Wavetable Example: HelloTable

In this example, named *hellotable.c*, we will send a stream of samples to an output, just as we did in *hellosine.c*, but in this case, the output will be to a location other than our standard output because sending samples to the standard output is useless if we want to actually hear the sound. In order to listen to the generated sound, we will have to send the samples to a *device* (either a binary file in one of a number of audio file formats, such as *.wav* or *.aiff*, or a physical device such as the computer's DAC) that allow us to hear it directly, in *real time* or in *deferred time* (in the latter case, deferring our listening until "after" the .aiff or .wav file containing the output samples has been written to the hard drive). As we learned previously, we'll start with a simple verbal description of the requirements of our program:

Write a program that
- will output a stream of samples to a destination (device) that can be chosen by the user, at compile time, from the following: the standard output (like previous hellosine.c); a raw binary file made up of 16-bit integer samples; a Windows standard wav-format file; or the DAC of our computer or on an audio card in real-time
- will use the wavetable-synthesis method to generate the samples
- will store a single cycle of a waveform in a table
- will allow the user to set the following parameters at run time: the frequency of the waveform in hertz; the duration of the waveform in seconds (during which the program will reiterate the single wave-cycle stored in the table the corresponding number of times); and the waveshape, chosen from: sinusoid, sawtooth, triangle or square.

Here is the (partial) source code of *hellotable.c*:

```c
#include <stdio.h>
#include <math.h>

#define SAMPLING_RATE 44100
#define PI 3.14159265

#define TABLE_LEN 512
#define SINE 0 /* macros to make array index to mean something */
#define SQUARE 1
#define SAW 2
#define TRIANGLE 3

float table[TABLE_LEN ]; /* array (table) to be filled with a
 waveform */

/* . . . OTHER CODE HERE (containing functions that
fill the table with a waveform le, initialization-cleanup, and
appropriate
 output
according to the chosen out-tination),
 see later . . . */

void main()
{
 int waveform;
 const float frequency, duration;

 printf("Type the frequency of the wave to output in Hz,
 and press ENTER: ");
 scanf("%f", &frequency);

 printf("\nType the duration of tone in seconds, and
 press ENTER: ");
 scanf("%f", &duration);
```

```
wrong_waveform:
printf("\nType a number from 0 to 3 corresponding to the "
"waveform you intend to choose\n");
printf("(0 = sine, 1 = square, 2 = sawtooth , 3 = triangle), "
"and press ENTER: ");
scanf("%d", &waveform);
if ( waveform < 0 || waveform > 3) {
   printf("\nwrong number for waveform, try again!\n");
   goto wrong_waveform;
}

   /*------ FILL THE TABLE -----------*/
switch (waveform) {
  case SINE:
  printf("\nYou've chosen a SINE wave\n");
  fill_sine();
  break;
  case SQUARE:
  printf("\nYou've chosen a SQUARE wave\n");
  fill_square();
  break;
  case SAW:
  printf("\nYou've chosen a SAW wave\n");
  fill_saw();
  break;
  case TRIANGLE:
  printf("\nYou've chosen a TRIANGLE wave\n");
  fill_triangle();
  break;
  default: /* impossible! */
  printf("\nWrong wave!! Ending program.\n");
  return;
}

init();
/*------ SYNTHESIS ENGINE START ---------*/
{
   int j;
   double sample_increment = frequency * TABLE_LEN / SAMPLING_RATE;
   double phase = 0;
   float sample;

   for (j = 0; j < duration * SAMPLING_RATE; j++) {
       sample = table[(long) phase];
       outSample(sample);
```

```
    phase += sample_increment;
        if (phase > TABLE_LEN) phase -= TABLE_LEN;
    }
}
/*------ SYNTHESIS ENGINE END -----------*/
cleanup();
printf("End of process\n");
}
```

This is only a part of the code of file *hellotable.c*; the other parts (indicated by the comment OTHER CODE HERE) will be viewed later. Here are the steps that the program has to follow in order to accomplish its task:

1. Provide default settings and "built-in" information (for example, sampling rate, symbolic tags representing the various wave shapes, etc.) in the form of *#define* constants.

2. Define a *table* in the form of a *global array* of floats, that will contain the waveform samples.

3. Provide a set of four user-defined *functions* that can fill the table with one of the possible waveshapes (not shown in previous code).

4. Provide user-defined functions that initialize and cleanup the output device (not shown in previous code).

5. Provide a user-defined function that sends each sample to the output device chosen at compile time.

6. Ask the user to provide the run-time information (frequency, duration and wave shape) by typing some numbers to the console.

7. Store the information typed by the user into numeric variables (floating-point for frequency and duration, integer for the waveshape).

8. If the user makes a mistake when typing the waveshape number, repeat the operation again (this is called "defensive programming").

9. Based on the user's choice, fill the table with a waveform cycle by selecting one of previous user-defined functions.

10. Initialize the output device by calling a user-defined function initialize the processing variables and calculate the sample-increment by using the expression

$$frequency \times \frac{table\_length}{sampling\_rate}. \tag{2}$$

12. Start cycling the wavetable-synthesis engine loop by using the following steps:

(a) Initialize the sample index to zero.

(b) Read a sample from the table according to current phase.

(c) Output the sample to the device chosen at compile time by calling a user-defined function.

(d) Increment the phase by a sample step.

(e) If the new phase value is greater than table length, subtract the table length from the phase value itself (to wrap around to the beginning).

(f) Increment the sample index by a unit.

(g) If the sample index is less than the value corresponding to the overall duration, continue looping by jumping again to step b.

13. Clean up the output device and exit the program.

(In order to make *hellotable.c* a little more readable at this point, I have omitted the definitions of the functions `fill_sine()`, `fill_square()`, `fill_saw()`, `fill_triangle()`, `init()`, `cleanup()`, and `outSample()`. These will be discussed in more detail later in this chapter.)

Let's look at the `main()` function. The integer variable waveform serves to contain a symbolic identifier, whose value is chosen by the user among those defined by previous macros—SINE, SQUARE, SAW, and TRIANGLE. The float variables frequency and duration will be used to hold the other user-supplied parameters. These variable are filled by the `scanf()` function (from the *stdio.h* library). To fill a variable (or a set of variables), this function is passed the addresses of target variables as function arguments, by means of the & operator. Syntactically, the address of a variable is equivalent to a pointer, and such pointer is passed as an argument to the `scanf()` function. After this call, the pointed target of such address is filled with an item coming from the *standard input* (by default, the computer keyboard). Thus, the program pauses at the different `scanf()` lines and waits for the user to type a number corresponding to the frequency, duration or waveform, respectively, and carries on when the *enter* key is hit.

Notice that this part of the program contains a *label*, `wrong_waveform`. A label marks a point in the source code. It is made up of a text identifier followed by a colon. Labels are used with two C/C++ statements, `goto` and `case`. The `goto` statement is used to jump to the point where a corresponding label is located, inside a function. Good programming style suggests that `goto` statements should be avoided, or at least reduced to a minimum, because they make the program difficult to read and messy. However, there are situations in which `goto` is very useful, such as in our *hellotable.c*, in which some lines are repeated until the user provides a value in the range 0–3 (i.e., it avoids wrong user inputs that could cause the program to crash.)

The other statement that works with labels is `switch()`. . .`case`, which appears next in the program:

```
switch(waveform) {
    case SINE:
        . . .something here. . .
        break;
    case SQUARE:
        . . .something here. . .
        break;
```

```
     case SAW:
        . . .something here. . .
        break;
     case TRIANGLE:
        . . .something here. . .
        break;
     default:
        . . .something here. . .
  }
```

The `switch()`. . .`case` statement allows a selection among multiple sections of code, depending on the value of an expression, in this case the content of the waveform variable. The expression enclosed in parentheses, is the "controlling expression," and must be an integer variable or constant. The switch statement causes an unconditional jump to a label belonging to a set of labels, called *case labels* enclosed in s. Such labels are different from `goto` labels, because they express an integer value, while `goto` labels are only a text literal. Depending on the value of the controlling expression, the jump goes to the corresponding matching label. The values of the case labels must be integer constants. The statements in the switch body are labeled with `case` labels or with the `default:` label, which will be used if nothing matches.

In our case, the labels are macros defined at the top of *hellotable.c*, serving as identifiers of our waveshapes. So if our variable waveform has been filled, for instance, with 1, after the `switch()` controlling expression, program flow will jump to `case SQUARE:` and will execute the two following lines. After that, the `break` statement will exit the switch block, continuing the execution.

In the `switch()` block of *hellotable.c* there are four cases (plus one default case), each contains a call to a user-defined function whose purpose is to fill the array `table[]` with a single cycle of a wave. The functions are `fill_sine()`, `fill_square()`, `fill_saw()`, and `fill_triangle()`. These functions will be examined later (together with the initialization and clean-up functions `init()` and `cleanup()`).

The synthesis engine is enclosed in a brace-delimited instruction block. The reason for this enclosure is to be able to declare some local variables placed inside the engine zone itself. The integer variable `j` is a looping index. The variable `sample_increment` (declared as a *double* in order to increase its precision), contains the sampling increment, which depends on the frequency:

```
double sample_increment = frequency * TABLE_LEN / SAMPLING_RATE;
```

The `phase` variable is also a double; it is initialized to zero, and it will be used as a storage space for the temporary phase value during the performance of the synthesis engine. The sample variable is declared as a `float` and will contain the instantaneous value of the audio wave.

The part of the code that makes up the synthesis engine begins with a `for()` loop whose body is reiterated for all samples of the output. The actual number of samples is calculated with the expression `duration * SAMPLING_RATE`, where `SAMPLING_RATE` is the number of samples per second. During each cycle of the loop, the sample variable is filled with a table element whose index is determined by the integer truncation of the phase. Since an array accepts only integer numbers as indexes, this truncation is done by converting the `phase` variable, which is a `double`, into a `long`, by means of the *cast* operator.

The current value of the sample variable is sent to the (previously chosen) output device by calling the user-defined `outSample()` function. (We'll examine this function shortly.) The current phase value is then incremented by the sampling increment, in order to allow the index of the table to point to the appropriate array element at the next cycle. When the value of the `phase` variable exceeds `TABLE_LEN`, a new cycle is starting, and the phase variable must be decremented by that amount. This pass is done by the `if()` conditional at the end of the code block.

After the loop block has generated the appropriate number of samples, the program calls the user-defined `cleanup()` function and ends. Here is the listing of the remaining code of *hellotable.c* (which was omitted from the previous listing for clarity's sake):

```
void fill_sine()/*fills the table with a single cycle
                        of a sine wave */
{
    int j;
    for(j = 0; j < TABLE_LEN; j++)
       table[j] = (float) sin(2 * PI * j/TABLE_LEN);
}

void fill_square()
{
    int j;
    for( j = 0; j < TABLE_LEN/2; j++)
       table[j] = 1;
    for( j = TABLE_LEN/2; j < TABLE_LEN; j++)
       table[j] = -1;
}

void fill_saw() /* descending ramp */
{
    int j;
    for( j = 0; j < TABLE_LEN; j++)
       table[j] = 1 - (2 * (float) j / (float) TABLE_LEN) ;
}

void fill_triangle()
{
```

```
    int j;
    for( j = 0; j < TABLE_LEN/2; j++)
        table[j] = 2 * (float) j/ (float) (TABLE_LEN/2) - 1;
    for( j = TABLE_LEN/2; j < TABLE_LEN; j++)
        table[j] = 1 -
        (2 * (float) (j-TABLE_LEN/2) / (float) (TABLE_LEN/2));
}

#ifdef REALTIME /* uses Tiny Audio Library */
#include "tinyAudioLib.h"
#elif defined(BINARY_RAW_FILE)
FILE* file;
#elif defined(WAVE_FILE) /* uses portsf library */
#include "portsf.h"
PSF_PROPS props;
int ofd;
#endif

void outSample(float sample)
{
#ifdef REALTIME /* uses Tiny Audio Library */
outSampleMono(sample);
#elif defined(BINARY_RAW_FILE)
short isample = (short) (sample * 32000);
fwrite(&isample,sizeof(short),1,file);
#elif defined(WAVE_FILE) /* uses portsf library */
psf_sndWriteFloatFrames(ofd,&sample,1);
#else /* standard output */
printf("%f\n", sample);
#endif
}

void init()
{
#ifdef REALTIME /* uses Tiny Audio Library */
    tinyInit();
#elif defined(BINARY_RAW_FILE)
    file = fopen("hellotable.raw","wb");
#elif defined(WAVE_FILE) /* uses portsf library */
    props.srate = 44100;
    props.chans = 1;
    props.samptype = PSF_SAMP_16;
    props.format = PSF_STDWAVE;
    props.chformat = STDWAVE;
```

```
    psf_init();
    ofd = psf_sndCreate("hellotable.wav", &props, 0, 0,
                        PSF_CREATE_RDWR);
#else /* standard output */
    printf("\n. . .Nothing to initialize. . .\n");
#endif
}

void cleanup()
{
    printf("cleaning up. . . ");
#ifdef REALTIME /* uses Tiny Audio Library */
    tinyExit();
#elif defined(BINARY_RAW_FILE)
    fclose(file);
#elif defined(WAVE_FILE) /* uses portsf library */
    {
     int err1, err2;
     err1 = psf_sndClose(ofd);
     err2 = psf_finish();
     if(err1 || err2)
     printf("\nWarning! An error occurred"
            "writing WAVE_FILE file.\n");
    }
#else /* standard output */
    printf("nothing to clean up. . . ");
#endif
}
```

The user functions `fill_square()`, `fill_saw`, and `fill_triangle()` simply fill the `table[]` array with the corresponding single-cycle (non-band-limited) waveshapes square, sawtooth, and triangle. Notice that, in these cases, the `for()` loop is used without braces because the statement is the assignment of the calculated sample to each element of the table. In C, braces are optional if the `for()` loop contains a single C statement. This time, the *cast* operator is used to convert an `int` variable to a `float`.

In programs made up of a single source file, the `main()` function is typically placed after all the other user-defined functions, as in *hellotable.c*. The reason for this practice is that the compiler needs to know the types of the function arguments, and the types of function return values before the lines in which such functions are called from the `main()`. Alternatively, it is typical to precede the function calls with *function prototypes*. These typically appear in the `#include` (or header) files of libraries. In this case, the bodies of such functions are usually pre-compiled into the library binary file.

Next in the code we see these lines:

```
#ifdef REALTIME /* uses Tiny Audio Library */
#include "tinyAudioLib.h"
#elif defined(BINARY_RAW_FILE)
FILE* file;
#elif defined(WAVE_FILE) /* uses portsf library */
#include "portsf.h"
PSF_PROPS props;
int ofd;
#endif
```

Here we see some C pre-processor statements, followed by lines of normal code (global variable declarations). The #ifdef, #elif defined(), #else, and #endif statements relate to *conditional compilation*. They are used to check to see if a certain macro has been defined. Depending on this, the pre-processor tells the compiler to compile or not the different chunks of code between #ifdef or #elif up to next #elif or #else statement.

In our case, the C pre-processor checks if the REALTIME macro has been defined somewhere (either in a header or as an option to the compiler). If it has been defined, the pre-processor tells the compiler to compile the line

```
#include "tinyAudioLib.h"
```

ignoring the rest. Otherwise it checks if the BINARY_RAW_FILE macro has been defined, and skips the other conditions. Thanks to conditional compilation, the *hellotable* program allows the programmer to choose, from a set of different devices, an output device at *compilation time* (not at *runtime*). The compilation options are as follows.

Realtime: the program sends the output directly to the DAC in order to play the sound while the processing stage is happening. This choice uses the *Tiny Audio Library* (a simple library that is a wraps the **Portaudio pablio** library in a way that makes it much easier to use by beginners).

Binary Raw File: the output is written to a raw audio file (16-bit mono) that can be played later with any wave players or editors that supports the specification of information about the format of the data in the raw audio file, such as the sampling rate, the number of channels (stereo or mono), and the sample resolution (8-bit, 16-bit, 24-bit, or even 32-bit floats). The advantage of using a Raw Audio File is that in this case hellosine.c doesn't require us to link in any special libraries. We can write the file by simply using the *stdio* library.

Wave File: the output is written to a standard Windows .wav file (based on Richard Dobson's *portsf* library). This format is automatically recognized by most wave players. Thus, it might prove easier to use than raw files, because the user doesn't have to remember the special format of the audio file.

Standard Output: the default choice. Sends each output sample to the *standard output* and provides numeric text strings expressing the fractional values of each sample (like *hellosine.c*).

This choice is valid if the `REALTIME`, `BINARY_RAW_FILE`, or `WAVE_FILE` macros have not been defined.

The programmer need only provide the libraries corresponding to the compilation choice, and can ignore all other libraries. Conditional compilation can help to successfully build a program that might be missing some libraries are those that might have included libraries that were platforms or operating system specific. In fact, in the second and fourth cases of conditional compilation of *hellotable.c* (i.e. Binary Raw File and Standard Output), the programmer doesn't have to provide any special library because **stdio** is available on all platforms.

Next in the source code, there is the definition of the `outSample()` function. This function accepts a `float` as an input and sends the number, from the `sample` argument variable, to an output device chosen by the user at compilation time.

Again, there are some conditional compilation statements:

1. Given the `REALTIME` choice, the input argument is simply fed as an argument to the `outSampleMono()` function (line 63) that belongs to the *Tiny Audio Library*. This function sends the *float* to the DAC in real time, in order to listen at it.

2. Given the `BINARY_RAW_FILE` choice, the *short* variable `isample` (a 16-bit integer) is filled with the `sample` input argument value, after rescaling it between the ranges of −32,000 and +32,000 (the original range was between −1 and 1). Also, in order to truncate eventual fractional values, a type conversion is done by the `cast` operator. In the following line, there is a call to the `fwrite()` function from the *stdio* standard library that writes a chunk of contiguous binary data to a previously opened file. The three input arguments required by this function are: the initial address of the data chunk operator (in our case this is simply the address of the `isample` variable), the size of one of the data elements to be written (in our case this is a *short* and its size is obtained by means of the sizeof( ) operator), the total number of data elements to be written, and finally, a pointer to a previously opened file (in our case the file is opened in the `init()` user-defined function, but its pointer was previously declared as a global variable).

3. Given the `WAVE_FILE` choice, the input argument is simply fed as an argument to the `psf_sndWriteFloatFrames()` function that belongs to the *portsf* library.

4. Given the default case, a simple `printf()` function call feeds the sample argument to the *standard output*.

The next definition seen in the code is of `init()`. At compilation time, it serves to initialize the chosen output device in the appropriate way. Here again, there are some conditional compilation statements:

1. In the case of the `REALTIME` (i.e. *Tiny Audio Library*) choice, a `tinyInit()`[function call is provided. (This is not necessary, because the *Tiny Audio Library* automatically initializes itself on the first call to an input or output function).

2. In the case of the BINARY_RAW_FILE choice, a file is opened by calling the fopen() function (belonging to *stdio* standard library) that gets, as its input arguments, a string containing the name and path of the file to be opened, and a string containing some specifiers that set the mode and operations to be applied to the corresponding file (in our case, the string wb stands for 'write' and 'binary'). The fopen() function returns a FILE pointer that fills the file global variable.

3. In the case of the WAVE_FILE choice, the fields of the global props structure belonging to the user-defined type PSF_PROPS (defined inside the *portsf.h* header file belonging to the *portsf* library), are filled, one at a time. Then a call to the psf_init() function initializes some of the hidden stuff in the *portsf* library. Finally, a call to the psf_sndCreate() function fills the ofd file descriptor.

4. In the default case, nothing has to be done in this pass.

Finally, we have the definition of the cleanup(). In an appropriate way, it serves to close the output device and terminate all pending actions. In this case, the conditional compilation statements are the following.

1. REALTIME: Calls the tinyExit() function of *Tiny Audio Library,* that closes opened devices (Note: not really necessary because the *Tiny Audio Library* automatically calls this function at exit if it is not called explicitly).

2. BINARY_RAW_FILE: Calls the fclose() function of the *stdio* standard library, which closes the corresponding file. It accepts a pointer to a previously opened file as an argument.

3. WAVE_FILE: Calls two functions: the psf_sndClose() that takes the osf file descriptor as an argument and the psf_finish() function. Return values are provided that express some information that indicates the presence or absence of errors. Such return values, used to show specific warnings, are stored in the err1 and err2 variables.

4. Default (standard output): No operation is needed to clean up.

3.3   Playing an Audio File

In this section we will write a set of *waveplayer* programs using the *Tiny Audio Library* and the *portsf* library, for playing .wav and .aif files. This application will perform two basic actions with a *streaming* read and play operation: read a block of samples from an audio file stored in the hard disk, and send samples to the DAC. This means that it is not necessary to load the entire file in memory to play it. Rather, we read a small amount of it while playing a previously read chunk. This kind of operation involves the concept of buffering. However, in these programs, most of buffering mechanism is hidden from the programmer by library functions, so that user need not worry about them. In more complex applications, the programmer will have to deal with the buffering mechanism directly.

3.3.1   A Simple Command-Line Audio File Player

The first example, *player.c*, is a program that can play a mono or stereo audio file from the command line. The command-line syntax is

```
$ player       filename
```

where `player` is the executable name and `filename` is the name of a .wav or .aif file.

Here is a verbal description of the steps that the program will cover to accomplish its task:

- Include the needed libraries.[8]
- Make declarations: Declare and define an array of floats that will act as the sample streaming buffer (see later); declare the file handle (actually a descriptor in **portsf** library) and a structure containing some information about the opened audio file; declare a long variable that will contain the number of read sample frames.
- Check the command-line syntax.
- Initialize the libraries and open the audio file; check if it has been opened correctly; exit with an error if the number of channels of the audio file is greater than 2 (only mono and stereo files are allowed).
- Perform the loop in which a block of samples is read into a buffer from the file, then such block is played by sending the buffer to the real-time output.
- Repeat the loop body until all samples of the file are played.
- Close the file, finish library operations, and exit the program.

And here is the source code of *player.c*:

```c
#include <stdio.h>
#include "tinyAudioLib.h"
#include "portsf.h"

#define FRAME_BLOCK_LEN 512
void main(int argc, char **argv)
{
  float buf[FRAME_BLOCK_LEN * 2]; /* buffer space for stereo (and
                                     mono) */
  int sfd; /* audio file descriptor */
  PSF_PROPS props; /* struct filled by psf_sndOpen(), containing
                      audio file info */
  long nread; /* number of frames actually read */

  if ( argc != 2 ) { /* needs a command line argument */
    printf("Error: Bad command line. Syntax is:\n\n");
    printf(" player filename\n");
    return;
  }
```

```
psf_init(); /* initialize portsf library*/
sfd = psf_sndOpen(argv[1], &props, 0); /* open an audio file
                                          using portsf lib */
if (sfd < 0) { /* error condition */
  printf("An error occurred opening audio file\n");
  goto end;
}
if (props.chans > 2) {
  printf("Invalid number of channels in audio file\n");
  goto end;
}

/*========= ENGINE =========*/
do {
  nread = psf_sndReadFloatFrames(sfd, buf, FRAME_BLOCK_LEN);
  if (props.chans == 2) /* stereo */
     outBlockInterleaved(buf, FRAME_BLOCK_LEN);
  else /* mono */
     outBlockMono(buf, FRAME_BLOCK_LEN);
} while (nread == FRAME_BLOCK_LEN);
  /*======== ENGINE END ======*/
end:
printf("finished!\n");
psf_sndClose(sfd);
psf_finish();
}
```

We start the program by including the necessary header files[9] for the libraries used in this code. The macro FRAME_BLOCK_LEN defines the length of the buffer block, used for the temporary storage of samples, expressed in *frames*. A *frame* is similar in concept to the *sample*, and is actually the same thing in the case of *mono* audio files. For multi-channel files, a *frame* is the set of samples for all channels, belonging to a determinate sample period. For example, in the case of a stereo file, each frame contains two samples, the first sample representing the left channel, the second one representing the right channel. In the case of a quad file a frame will contain four samples, and so on.

Next, we have the main() function head. This time the main() function takes two arguments:

```
void main(int argc, char **argv)
```

These two arguments serve the main() function to handle the command-line arguments typed by the user at the operating system shell in order to run the program. The argv argument is a pointer to char (an 8-bit integer, often used to express a character) that points to an array of strings (remember that a string in the C language is nothing more than an array of char). So, the argv pointer is used to handle the command-line arguments provided by the user when starting a program from the text-based console shell. Command-line argument access can be accomplished in the following way:

- argv[0] returns the address of a string containing the name of program executable
- argv[1] returns the address of a string containing the first command-line argument
- argv[2] returns the address of a string containing the eventual second argument
- and so on

The argc argument is an int (integer) containing the number of arguments that the user typed at the console to run the program (this number must also include the program executable name which is also considered to be an argument). From the console, each argument must be separated from others by means of blank spaces or tabs. In our case, the user has to type two arguments (the program name and the name of the audio file to be played), so argc has to contain 2. If it doesn't, an error message will be displayed and the program will stop.

Next, an array of 1,024 float elements (FRAME_BLOCK_LEN * 2) is declared and defined:

```
float buf[FRAME_BLOCK_LEN * 2];
```

This array is the buffer that will contain the block of 512 frames read from the audio file. It is dimensioned to 1,024, in order to fit 512 stereo frames. In the case of mono frames the exceeding space will not be used, but this will not affect the correct functioning of the program.

Following this section of code we declare the file identifier sfd and the props variable, which is a structure PSF_PROPS, defined in *portsf.h*. This structure contains information about an audio file opened with *portsf* lib, and has the following fields:

```
typedef struct psf_props {
    long        srate;
    long        chans;
    psf_stype   samptype;
    psf_format  format;
    psf_channelformat chformat;
} PSF_PROPS;
```

where the srate member variable contains the sample rate of the audio file, the chans variable contains the number of channels, the samptype variable (an *enum* type declared in *portsf.h*) contains the format of samples (16-bit integers, 8-bit integers, 24-bit integers, 32-bit floating-point values, and so on), the format variable contains the format of the audio file (for example .wav or .aiff), and the chformat variable contains information about channel displacement (not particularly useful in our current case). The last variable to be declared is nread, a long that will contain the number of frames read from the file by the loop engine.

The program goes on to initialize *portsf* lib and open an audio file:

```
psf_init();
sfd = psf_sndOpen(argv[1], &props, 0);
```

This function attempts to open the audio file whose name is contained in the string pointed to by `argv[1]`, and returns a file descriptor in the `sfd` variable, if that file has been correctly opened. In the case of the `psf_sndOpen()` function, a valid file descriptor is a positive integer value. It will be used by further functions that access the corresponding file as a unique identifier. If the file doesn't exist, or any other error occurs, the `sfd` variable will be filled with a negative value.

Normally, C language functions are able to return only a single argument, but there is a trick to make it possible to return any number of arguments. We use this trick with the second input argument of the `psf_sndOpen()` function. It behaves as an output argument, or better, as eight output arguments, given that eight is the actual number of member variables belonging to the `props` structure. Having an input argument behave as an output argument is done by passing the *address* of the corresponding variable (that will be filled with the return value), instead of passing the variable itself to the called function. To enable this, the address of the `props` is passed as an input argument (even if it will contain a return value), and this structure is filled by the `psf_sndOpen()` function internally (with the return value itself, i.e. the filled `props` structure). The third argument is a *rescaling* flag that is not set in our case (because we don't want to rescale the samples), so it is set to zero.

We then test if the audio file has been correctly opened, by evaluating the sign of the `sfd` variable. If it is negative, an error message is printed to the console; and in this case, the program is ended by the `goto` statement, which forces program flow to the `end:` label at the bottom of the `main()` function. We will also test the member `chans` of `props`. If the opened file has more than two channels, the program prints an error message and exits , because such types of files are not supported by the program.

The next section is the synthesis engine loop. Because the conditional has to be placed after at least one iteration has been done, a `do. . .while()` statement block is used. Look at line 32:

```
nread = psf_sndReadFloatFrames(sfd, buf, FRAME_BLOCK_LEN);
```

This function reads a block of frames and places them in the `buf` array. The input arguments are, in order, the file descriptor (`sfd`), the buffer address (`buf`), and the number of frames to be read into the buffer itself (`FRAME_BLOCK_LEN`). It returns the number of samples actually read, equal to `FRAME_BLOCK_LEN`, unless the end of the audio file has been reached.

Inside the loop, there is a conditional that switches two different lines, depending on whether the audio file is stereo or mono. Actually, the Tiny Audio Lib offers support to various buffer formats, i.e. mono or stereo, separate channels or interleaved frames, and so on.

The `outBlockInterleaved()` function accepts a buffer made up of multi-channel inter-leaved frames, whereas `outBlockMono()` accepts only mono buffers.

Finally, we have the loop conditional. When `nread` contains a value different from `FRAME_BLOCK_LEN`, it means that the end of file has been reached, and so the loop stops. The program then closes the audio file and terminates the *portsf* library operations.

3.3.2   A Command-Line Player with Some Options

A new, slightly different player is presented in this subsection. This player will allow us to specify both the starting point and the duration of the file to play. It also provides an opportunity to see how to handle the positions of a block of audio data. The command-line shell syntax of this player will be

```
$ player2 [-tTIME] [-dDUR] filename
```

where `player2` is the name of the executable; `-t` is an optional flag that must be followed by an integer or fractional number (without inserting blank spaces) denoting the starting `TIME` point expressed in seconds (note: brackets indicate that the corresponding item is optional and does not have to be typed in command line), `-d` is another optional flag followed by a number denoting the `DUR`ation in seconds of the chunk of sound actually played, and `filename` is the name of the .wav or .aiff audio file to play.

Here is our usual verbal description of the steps the program has to do to accomplish its task:

1. Include the necessary library headers.
2. Define a tiny function that displays the command-line syntax of the program in several error-condition points
3. Define the length of the array containing the streaming buffer.
4. In the `main()` function, declare (and eventually define) most local variables used in the program.
5. Check if the optional command-line flags are present, and evaluate corresponding arguments.
6. Check if the syntax is correct, otherwise display an error message and exit the program.
7. Initialize everything and open the audio file.
8. Display some audio file information.
9. Calculate play-start and play-stop points in frames.
10. Seek the calculated play-start point in the opened file.
11. Start the playing engine loop.
12. Read a block of frames and output it to the DAC.
13. Repeat step 12 until the play-stop point is reached.
14. Close the audio file, clean up the library, and end the program.

Here is the listing of the *player2.c* file:

```c
#include <stdio.h>
#include <math.h>
#include "tinyAudioLib.h"
#include "portsf.h"

void SYNTAX(){
    printf ("Syntax is:\n player2 [-tTIME] [-dDUR] filename\n");
}

#define FRAME_BLOCK_LEN 512
void main(int argc, char **argv)
{
    float buf[FRAME_BLOCK_LEN * 2]; /* buffer space for stereo (and
                                        mono) */
    int sfd; /* audio file descriptor */
    int opened = 0; /* flag telling if audio file has been opened */
    PSF_PROPS props; /* struct filled by psf_sndOpen(),
                        containing audio file info */
    long counter; /* counter of frames read */
    long length;  /* length of file in frames */
    long endpoint; /* end point of playing */
    extern int arg_index; /* from crack.c */
    extern char *arg_option; /* from crack.c */
    extern int crack(int argc, char **argv, char *flags, int ign);
    int flag, timflag=0, durflag=0; /* flags */
    long nread; /* number of frames actually read */
    double startime, dur;

    while (flag = crack(argc, argv, "t|d|T|D|", 0)) {
    switch (flag) {
        case 't':
        case 'T':
        if (*arg_option) {
            timflag=1;
            startime = atof(arg_option);
        }
        else {
    printf ("Error: -t flag set without
            specifying a start time in seconds.\n");
    SYNTAX();
    return;
        }
        break;
```

```
        case 'd':
        case 'D':
        if (*arg_option) {
            durflag=1;
         dur = atof(arg_option);
        }
        else {
            printf ("Error: -d flag set without"
                    "specifying a duration in seconds\n");
            SYNTAX();
            return;
        }
        break;
        case EOF:
        return;
        }
    }

    if ( argc < 2 ) { /* needs a command line argument */
        printf("Error: Bad command line arguments\n");
        SYNTAX();
        return ;
    }

    psf_init(); /* initialize portsf library */
    sfd = psf_sndOpen(argv[arg_index], &props, 0); /* open an audio
                                                file using portsf lib */
    if (sfd < 0) { /* error condition */
        printf("An error occurred opening audio file\n");
        goto end;
    }

    printf("file \'%s\' opened. . .\n", argv[arg_index]);
    printf("sampling rate: %d\n", props.srate);
    printf("number of chans: %d\n", props.chans);
    length = psf_sndSize(sfd);
    printf("duration: %f\n", (float) length / (float) props.srate);

    if (timflag)
        counter = (long) (startime * props.srate); /* length in frames */
    else
        counter = 0; /* beginning of file */

    if (durflag) {
        endpoint = (long) (dur * props.srate + counter);
        endpoint = (endpoint < length) ? endpoint : length;
```

```
}
else {
endpoint = length;
dur = (double) (endpoint-counter) / (double) props.srate;
}

if (props.chans > 2) {
printf("Invalid number of channels in audio file, "
       "max 2chans allowed\n");
goto end;
}

psf_sndSeek(sfd, counter, PSF_SEEK_SET); /* begin position at the
appropriate point */

printf("Playing the file from time position %0.3lf for %0.3lf
seconds. . .\n", startime, dur);

/*========= ENGINE =========*/
do {
nread = psf_sndReadFloatFrames(sfd, buf, FRAME_BLOCK_LEN);
if (props.chans == 2) /* stereo */
    outBlockInterleaved(buf, FRAME_BLOCK_LEN);
else /* mono */
    outBlockMono(buf, FRAME_BLOCK_LEN);
counter+=FRAME_BLOCK_LEN;
} while (counter < endpoint);
/*======== ENGINE END ======*/
end:
printf("finished!\n");
psf_sndClose(sfd);
psf_finish();
}
```

Since most of the code of this new file has been taken from previous examples, all lines will not be explained; only new concepts will be clarified. In the main() function, a flag opened is declared. In a program source, a flag is a variable (normally an int variable) that can contain a limited number of *states* that affect the program's behavior during execution. (Don't confuse flag variables, in the source code, with the option flags, provided at the command line. Even if they could sometimes be related, they are two very different concepts.) The states of a flag are expressed by means of the value of the variable itself. Each possible state is determined by a unique integer number which is assigned to the flag variable. And these numbers are actually symbols of some strictly non-numeric concept, and so, they will not be used as true numbers (for example, arithmetic operations on flags are senseless).

Often, as in our case here, a flag is *boolean.* This means that its possible states are either *true* or *false.* Boolean flag values are *non-zero* to indicate the *true* state and *zero* to indicate the *false* state. The flag is initially set to zero (false) to indicate that the file is not opened.

We also declare a *long* variable named *counter*, to contain the count of read frames. It is declared as *long*, not as `int`, because in some platforms `int` might express a 16-bit integer that would not be sufficient for most file lengths. The Variable `length` (a `long`) will contain the file length, and `endpoint` will hold the end point of playback, both expressed in frames.

There are three `extern` declarations: the variable `arg_index` (an index to the command-line arguments), the string pointer `arg_option` (which will point at the currently parsed command-line argument), and the function prototype of `crack()` (a function defined in another source file—actually a library function, even if in this case the library contains only this function—located in the file *crack.c*, so is compiled together with *player2.c*). Being a library function, `crack()` will be used as a black box—that is, we have only to know what it does, not how it functions internally.

Finally, we have the declarations of three flags: the `flag` variable (used as temporary storage of starting option flags provided by the user when starting the program at the command-line shell), the `timflag` variable (which signals if the –t option has been provided), and the `durflag` variable (which signals if the –d option has been provided). These two variables are linked to `startime` and `dur`, respectively, which will contain the start time and the duration optionally provided by the user from the command line.

The program execution contains a loop that checks the command-line options by evaluating the `crack()` function. This function (authored by Piet van Oostrum and provided with his `mf2t` open-source program), receives the command line by means of its arguments:

```
flag = crack(argc, argv, "t|d|T|D|", 0)
```

We can see that this function has one output argument and four input arguments. The first two input arguments, `argc` and `argv` (coming from the `main()` function), pass the command line to the `crack()` function, in order to evaluate the command line itself and see if some option flags are present. According to a UNIX-style convention, every option flag must be preceded by a hyphen. In *player2.c*, valid flags are –t and –d; in fact, the third input argument of `crack()` is a string containing the letters allowed for option flags, which in this case must be followed by a numeric datum indicating the starting point (for –t flag) and the duration (for –d flag) in seconds. In the string provided in the third argument of `crack()`, the flags we define are –t, –d, –T, and –D (upper-case letters meaning the same thing as lower-case letters). The | character indicates that other data must follow the corresponding flag letter, without spaces between the flag letter and the datum in the command line.

The last input argument of `crack()` is a boolean flag indicating whether `crack()` should raise an error message in case of unknown flags (when set to 0) or simply ignore them (when set to 1). In this case, the action of raising the error message when an unknown flag is found is enabled.

Each time `crack()` is called, it puts a found flag character in the `flag` return variable. It also fills the global variables `arg_index` and `arg_option`. The `arg_index` variable is incremented each time a new flag is found, in subsequent calls to the `crack()` function. If some data follows a found flag, such data is contained in a string pointed to by the `arg_option` pointer. The `arg_option` pointer is updated with corresponding string at each subsequent call. More information about using `crack()` is available in the file *crack.c*.[10]

The `crack()` function is called repeatedly until the last command-line flag has been read. The `switch()` block at line 28 offers two choices: if the return value of `crack()` contains the flag −t (or −T), then `timflag` is set to 1 (i.e. *true*, meaning that user has provided a custom play-start time) and the `startime` variable is filled with the corresponding value in seconds (line 33). Notice that the standard library function `atof()` has been used to convert the play-start datum from the original representation (i.e. a character string set by `arg_option` variable) into a double floating-point value. If the −t flag was specified without providing a corresponding datum, an error message will arise. In this case, the command-line syntax will be displayed by means of a call to the user function `SYNTAX()` (defined at the start of the program) and the program will be stopped. If the return value of `crack()` contains the flag −d (or −D), then the `durflag` is set to 1 (*true*) and the `dur` variable is filled with the corresponding playing duration in seconds. Again, if the user forgot to provide the datum, the corresponding messages will be displayed and the program will end. If the return value of *crack()* contains a special value defined by the `EOF` macro constant, the program will terminate (after `crack()` itself displays an error message). This will happen if the user provides a flag other than −t or −d.

If the user has not provided an audio file name, an error message is displayed (the command-line syntax) and the program terminates. Otherwise the *portsf* library is initialized and we open the file, as in *player.c*. Once this is done, the program prints some information about the opened file to the console, such as its name and sampling rate. The `length` variable is filled with the length of the file in frames by the *portsf* library function `psf_sndSize()`, and this is converted to seconds and printed to the console.

Next the program sets the counter to the appropriate initial value. (Notice how the state of `timflag` determines the conditional flow.) The endpoint is also assigned the appropriate value, with the state of `durflag` determining the conditional flow. The play-stop point (i.e. the `endpoint` variable) is calculated by adding starting time (the value of counter variable) to the duration, whose unit is converted from seconds to frames by multiplying it by sampling rate. We then need to check whether this variable exceeds the length of the file, using a conditional assignment:

```
endpoint = (endpoint < length) ? endpoint : length;
```

The right member of the assignment is a conditional that evaluates the expression inside the round braces. If the result is true, we assign the value immediately after the question mark; otherwise we assign the value after the colon. Such expressions are used quite often in C.

In case the user did not provide the -d option flag, `endpoint` is assigned the total length of the file and `dur` is set to the corresponding duration in seconds. Notice that the two members of this division are previously converted to `double` in order to produce a reliable result.

As in the previous example, if the opened file has a number of channels greater than two, the program is ended because it only supports mono and stereo files. The *portsf* library function call

```
psf_sndSeek(sfd, counter, PSF_SEEK_SET);
```

moves the current file pointer to the location corresponding to the second input argument (the counter variable). The `PSF_SEEK_SET` argument is a macro that indicates that the file pointer has to be moved by counting from the beginning of the file. (Other option macros are `PSF_SEEK_CUR`, which moves the pointer starting from current position, and `PSF_SEEK_END`, which counts backward from the end of file.) The `psf_seek()` function is similar to the `fseek()` function from the `stdio` library.

Complementing the program, we have the performance engine loop of *player2.c*. It is very similar to that of *player.c*, but in this case the exit-loop conditional compares the current counter value with the play-end point of the file (from the `endpoint` variable). At each loop cycle, `counter` is incremented by the block length.

3.4 Critical Real-Time Issues

In this section a number of special techniques will be explained that are used for streaming audio or MIDI data in real time either from an input or to an output. So far, our audio data has been simply output by means of a single C library function (***Tiny Audio Lib***). We have treated this library as a black box without being aware of what is really happening inside.

The audio engine of some of the previous applications (*player.c,* `player2.c,` *playerGUIsimple.cpp*, and *playerGUI.cpp*) was realized by means of a simple loop, something like this:

```
do {
      buf = get_new_data();
      outBlock(buf, FRAME_BLOCK_LEN);
} while (buf != NULL);
```

In this hypothetical function,[11] which gets sample data from an eventual input and returns a pointer to each data block, `buf` is a pointer to a block of samples returned by `get_new_data()`. The `buf` pointer is then used as an argument of the `outBlock()` function.

The concept of buffering is inherent in this *do-while* loop. A buffering technique is encapsulated inside the function `outBlock()`, so the user doesn't have to worry about it. The user need only fill the buffer with the proper data items (in musical cases these items are sample frames, MIDI messages, or control signal frames) and provide the address of the buffer. The `outBlock()` function call doesn't return until the block of sample frames has been sent to the target device. If this device is an audio interface, the call to outBlock() freezes the program until the block of samples is actually played by the DAC. Each time a streaming operation has successfully finished, outBlock() returns, the program is unfrozen and it continues to fill another block with the new items. Finally, the stream terminates when a NULL pointer is returned by get_new_data(). (Obviously the outBlock() function should be able to interpret a NULL pointer correctly by performing an appropriate action. This can be as simple as doing nothing or it can involve cleaning up the relevant device.)

3.4.1 FIFO Buffers

If the previous example were used for real-time audio streaming, and if the block of samples were completely played, there would be a time lag during which the program would calculate the new block of samples. If this time lag were to exceed the duration of a sample period, the audio interface would remain, for some moments, without samples to send to the output. This situation would cause a drop-out[12] in the sound, which would be perceived by the listener as an annoying click. To avoid drop-outs such as this, the solution is to use more than a single block of samples. In this case, the block passed to the function *outBlock()* would be copied to another internal block (often hidden to the user) before the samples were played by the DAC, and the program would be free to calculate another block while the audio interface was converting the samples stored in the previously copied block. This technique is often called "double buffering." If necessary, more than one block can be filled before the audio converter stage. Thus, we can have "triple buffering," "quadruple buffering," and so on. In these cases, the items of such buffering techniques would be the block of samples.[13]

Buffering is an important technique for real-time streaming, and the buffering scheme used for streaming is referred to as a FIFO (first-in first-out) *queue* or a *circular buffer*.[14] Real-time streaming buffers can be synchronous or asynchronous. When the rate of the items is constant (for example, in the case of audio or video streams), we deal with a synchronous stream; if the rate is not constant (for example, in MIDI), we deal with an asynchronous stream. There are two types of FIFO buffers: *input buffers* and *output buffers*. Input buffers receive data from an input device and feed the program such data. The data is then processed by the program, and eventually send to an output FIFO buffer, which sends such data to an output device. An input FIFO buffer is made up of a memory block and a routine that inserts the items coming from the input source into the head of the buffer (this action is normally called "push"), continuing to do such operation until there is no more buffer space available. An input-buffer-full situation can happen if the average processing speed of the program is not fast enough[15] to extract and process the incoming data. In fact, each item should remain in the buffer only for a limited amount of time, then it must be extracted and removed from the tail of the buffer by the program itself, in order to process it (this action is normally called "pop"). If the input buffer is empty, the program temporarily stops processing and waits for more data to be available.

In the case of output buffers, the data items are generated by the program and pushed to the head of the buffer. The output device receives the data items from the tail of this buffer and sends them to the output when they are needed. The processed data is popped from the buffer by the output device. In case the buffer is completely full (this is a normal case), the program waits until the buffer is able to receive more data. Be aware that, in the case of output buffers, if the program provides the processed data items more slowly than they are sent to the output the buffer can become empty. And in the case of synchronous real-time processes, a situation of an empty output buffer is an abnormal, pathologic situation in which the items (for example, samples in the case of an audio DAC, or in the case of recording, a CD in your CD burner) must maintain a strictly regular period when transferred. This situation is also called "buffer underrun."

In short, there are two kinds of FIFO buffers: input and output buffers. With an input buffer, data items are received from the outside, and pushed into the buffer by the input device. The program has the task to pop such data items from the buffer in order to process them. In real-time processes, the program has to maintain this buffer empty, or, at least, not full. If the program is not fast enough at popping data, the buffer could became full and some incoming data items could be lost. With an output buffer, data items are generated by the program, and pushed into the output buffer. In real-time synchronous streaming, the output device pops such data items from the buffer at a strictly constant rate. It is a duty of the program to maintain a full buffer, or, at least, not empty. If the program is not fast enough in pushing data, the buffer could became empty and drop-outs could occur, breaking the regularity of the streaming operation.

The larger that the buffer is,[16] the greater the security that "buffer underruns" can be avoided. Although there can never be absolute certainty that such a pathological situation will not occur, you can trust that, at a reasonable buffer size, buffer underruns cannot occur in normal situations.

Why don't we just use a huge buffer for streaming audio in real time for total security? There is a drawback in using large buffers for real-time processing, and such drawback is directly proportional to the buffer size: it is the so-called latency. The theoretical latency[17] is the average time lag that passes between a push action of a data item in the FIFO buffer and the subsequent pop action of that particular data item. Such latency is directly proportional to the buffer size and inversely proportional to the sampling rate, in the case of audio streams. Normally the latency is calculated in milliseconds, so the maximum latency can be calculated by the formula

$$maxlatency = 1,000 \times bufferSize \times \frac{blockSize}{sampleRate}, \tag{3}$$

where *bufferSize* is the size of the FIFO buffer (for example, in the case of triple buffering it is equal to 3), *blockSize* is the number of sample frames of each block (for example, 512 stereo frames), and *sampleRate* is the sampling rate (for example, 44,100 Hz). In this case the maximum latency is

$$maxlatency = 1,000 \times 3 \times \frac{512}{44,100} \approx 34.83 \text{ ms} \tag{4}$$

—that is, 34.83 ms (maximum latency delay). Now we have to calculate the minimum latency with the following formula:

$$minlatency = 1,000 \times (bufferSize - 1) \times \frac{blockSize}{sampleRate} \tag{5}$$

—that is,

$$minlatency = 1,000 \times 2 \times \frac{512}{44,100} \approx 23.22 \text{ ms}. \tag{6}$$

The theoretical average latency is obtained by the mean value between maximum and minimum latency:

$$averageLatency = \frac{minlatency + maxlatency}{2} \tag{7}$$

—that is,

$$averageLatency = \frac{34.83 + 23.22}{2} = 29.02 \text{ ms}. \tag{8}$$

Remember that this is a theoretical value, and that the real latency delay is always bigger than the theoretical one. Furthermore, in the case of simultaneous input and output data transfer (full-duplex, sometimes required for digital effects such as guitar fuzz boxes) the theoretical latency is the sum of the latencies obtained by the input and output buffers and block sizes.

The choice of the appropriate buffer size and block size is a compromise between latency and security from buffer underruns. So, most commercial audio programs, leave it up to the user to customize the optimal buffer size, and this can only be achieved by means of trail and error tests.

To sum up: Instead of sending data items directly to the output, there are at least three reasons for using FIFO buffers:

• In synchronous streaming operations, the physical output (or input) device has to guarantee a perfectly constant rate and precise timing, but a computer tends to process data at irregular speeds, so by filling the buffer with a certain number of data items, there will always be at least an item ready to be sent out.

• In both synchronous and asynchronous streaming operations, the data items could be fed faster than the output device is able to handle them, so some items could be lost. By storing the "overfed" items in the buffer, we guarantee that all items will be recognized, in turn by the output device.

• Processing and transferring blocks of data is often faster than processing single data elements one a time.

By accumulating data into the buffer, the processing engine is able to process blocks of data at the maximum speed, without the necessity of waiting for the output port to be ready to receive the datum.

3.4.2 Host-Driven and Callback Mechanisms

Since a device driver most often hides the buffering mechanism from the user, the implementation is rarely an issue. Still, a basic knowledge of these techniques is necessary in order to use the device driver's audio or MIDI API. For example, when we used the functions `outBlockInterleaved()` and `outBlockMono()` in the programs *player.c, player2.c, playerGUIsimple.cpp*, and *playerGUI.cpp*, there was actually a buffering mechanism hidden in these functions (belonging to the *Tiny Audio Library*), that was invisible to the final application programmer. However, the programmer had to provide a routine that generated each block of samples and allocated the array that would host such block.

The kind of mechanism provided by the *Tiny Audio Library* is a *blocking* mechanism[18]— it blocks the program processing each time the output buffer is full (or the input buffer is empty), waiting until new data items are ready to be processed. An API for data in/out with a blocking mechanism is easy to use, because the program is automatically blocked when there is not enough room in the audio buffer for more data items. In this case the write function will just block the program until more room is available, in a transparent way for the user. But this mechanism, even if it is simple to use, is not the most efficient, since its waiting can waste many CPU cycles that could be applied to other jobs in the meanwhile.

There are much more efficient mechanisms than blocking. Among them are multi-threading, host-driven, and callback mechanisms. Often these methods are combined in the same application. We have seen a simple way of using multi-threading in the *playerGUIsimple.cpp* and *PlayerGUI.cpp* programs. In these cases, the creation of a new execution thread has been done to separate the GUI part of the application from the audio engine. A new engine thread was created each time the "play" button was clicked, and such thread was terminated (or destroyed) each time the "stop" button was pushed. Actually the engine itself was made up of a single thread, so it was not really an example of a multi-threading engine in these cases. In fact, a multi-threading engine would take advantage of buffer-full streaming stops for calculating new samples. Such an engine is quite complicated to develop, because any non-trivial multi-threading technique is quite tricky and advanced to develop

A callback mechanism is based on the concept of *callback function*. A callback function is a function automatically called by the operating system (not by the main flow of the program) at a moment that is appropriate for its own purpose. There are several way to make the operating system calls a callback function, for example, in the Win32 operating system API there are timer objects that, when activated, are able to call a function written by the user at regular intervals of time. The user can set the duration of such time intervals. Other kinds of callback functions can be associated with computer hardware interrupts, or simply called in response to messages generated by a GUI event. We have already seen this sort of callback functions in the *playerGUIsimple.cpp* and *playerGUI.cpp* programs. Often, the best way to learn a new concept is to see it applied to a practical example. This is what we will do now, in order to learn to use the callback mechanism provided by the *Portaudio* library. In the next section we will deal with an example of callback mechanism applied to full-duplex audio streaming, based on *Portaudio*.

3.4.3   Using the Portaudio Library

The *Portaudio* library[19] is a standard, open-source, multi-platform library that is able to support real-time audio streaming very efficiently, thanks to its integrated callback mechanism. Portaudio wraps most hardware-dependent implementation code into a common API available for several operating systems, such as Windows, Linux, Solaris, FreeBSD, Mac OS, and Mac OS-X. Since version v.19, *Portaudio* provides multiple *host-API* support in the same binary. This means that, for example, under Windows it can provide *MME*, *DirectX*, and *ASIO* support in a single binary build of an application. The final application user can choose, at run time, between the different host-APIs. Portaudio provides both a *blocking* API[20] and a *callback-mechanism* API. The programmer is free to choose whichever of these is more appropriate to the specific application, but the callback mechanism is by far the most efficient (although also a bit more difficult to program than the blocking mechanism).

Up until this point, we have used the blocking mechanism in our programs; but there are two main advantages in using a callback mechanism instead of a blocking mechanism:

• It frees the CPU from dead-cycles, when the output buffer is full or the input buffer is empty, thereby optimizing the overall machine performance and allowing the main thread of execution to continue processing while the i/o buffers are flushing (i.e. the main thread is not blocked by the buffer status).

• It helps to reduce latency to a minimum, especially when using low-latency-oriented host APIs such as ASIO or ALSA.

3.4.4   The Callback Mechanism in Practice: HelloRing

The application shown in this section is a console program that implements a real-time *ring modulator*[21] in which the user sets the modulation frequency. Since ring modulation is such an extremely simple synthesis technique, it frees us to concentrate on the callback mechanism provided by Portaudio.

In this subsection we will focus will on the following:

• how to write a full-duplex audio callback function (containing the audio engine) specially suited for Portaudio

• how to get and display all the available audio devices of the Portaudio-supported host-APIs

- how to choose a specific device for input and output
- how to set the parameters of an audio stream (for example, number of channels, sampling rate, block size, and so on)
- how to initialize Portaudio and start the audio callback mechanism
- how to stop the callback mechanism and clean up Portaudio.

The user selects the audio input and audio output ports when the program starts, by choosing them from a list of available ports. Since the v19 version of Portaudio, the user can choose from all the host APIs available on the target machine. This allows the user to chose *MME*, *DirectX* or *ASIO* under Windows, *OSS* or *ALSA* under Linux, and so on.

The program ***HelloRing*** will accept a stereo input: both channels will be modulated by a sinusoidal signal (whose frequency is chosen by the user), and the two modulated channels will be sent to a stereo output.

Here is a descriptive summary of the requirements of the program *helloRing.c*:

Write a console program where
- A stereo audio signal is accepted as input, and the processed signal is streamed to a stereo output in real time, using the callback mechanism provided by the Portaudio v19 library.
- The input signal is processed in real time by means of the ring-modulation technique, i.e. each channel of the input signal is multiplied by a sinusoidal signal that acts as a modulator. This signal is calculated by means of the sine function provided by the standard C library *math.h*.
- The user is allowed to choose (1) the frequency of the modulating sinusoid, in hertz, and (2) the input and output audio device among the several host-APIs present in the target machine.

And here is a description outline of the steps that we will cover to accomplish the task:

1. Include the needed library headers.
2. Make the external declarations:
a. Define the macro constants of the frame block length, the sampling rate, and the 2π value (needed for the modulator frequency calculation).
b. Declare the portaudio stream pointer as global.
c. Declare the sampling increment as global.
3. Define the callback function that contains the ring modulation engine (that is, a loop that multiplies each channel by a sinusoid and outputs the result).
4. Define all the initialization stuff inside a function. The initialization function has to
a. ask the user the modulator frequency and get it
b. calculate the sampling increment and store it in the corresponding global variable
c. initialize *Portaudio* for operation
d. show all the available audio output devices for each host-API, and ask the user to choose one of them

e. fill the corresponding parameter structure. Such structure will contain information about the output stream, such as the chosen port, number of channels, sample format, etc. that will be used for opening the audio stream

f. show all the available audio input devices for each host-API, and ask the user to choose one of them

g. fill corresponding parameter structure

h. open the Portaudio stream

i. start the stream.

5. Define all the terminate stuff inside a function. The termination function has to

a. stop the stream

b. close the stream

c. terminate Portaudio (this cleans up all internal stuff initiated by Portaudio).

6. Define the `main()` function. The main function has to

a. call the init function at start

b. begin a dummy loop that stops only when a key is pressed by the user

c. call the termination function.

Here are the contents of *helloRing.c*:

```c
#include <stdio.h>
#include <math.h>

#include "portaudio.h"

#define FRAME_BLOCK_LEN 256
#define SAMPLING_RATE 44100
#define TWO_PI (3.14159265f * 2.0f)

PaStream *audioStream;
double si = 0;

int audio_callback( const void *inputBuffer, void *outputBuffer,
                    unsigned long framesPerBuffer,
                    const PaStreamCallbackTimeInfo* timeInfo,
                    PaStreamCallbackFlags statusFlags,
                    void *userData
                    )
{
    float *in = (float*) inputBuffer, *out = (float*)outputBuffer;
    static double phase = 0;
    unsigned long i;
    for( i=0; i < framesPerBuffer; i++ ) {
    float sine = sin(phase);
    *out++ = *in++ * sine; /* left channel */
    *out++ = *in++ * sine; /* right channel */
```

```
    phase += si;
 }
 return paContinue;
}

void init_stuff()
{
    float frequency;
    int i,id;
    const PaDeviceInfo *info;
    const PaHostApiInfo *hostapi;
    PaStreamParameters outputParameters, inputParameters;

    printf("Type the modulator frequency in Hertz: ");
    scanf("%f", &frequency); /* get the modulator frequency */

    si = TWO_PI * frequency / SAMPLING_RATE; /* calculate sampling
                                                increment */

    printf("Initializing Portaudio. Please wait. . .\n");
    Pa_Initialize(); /* initialize portaudio */

    for (i=0;i < Pa_GetDeviceCount(); i++) {
        info = Pa_GetDeviceInfo(i); /* get information from
                                        current device */
        hostapi = Pa_GetHostApiInfo(info->hostApi); /*get info from
                                                      curr. host API */
    if (info->maxOutputChannels > 0)/* if curr device supports
                                        output */
        printf("%d: [%s] %s (output)\n",i, hostapi->name, info->name );
    }
    printf("\nType AUDIO output device number: ");
    scanf("%d", &id); /* get the output device id from the user */
    info = Pa_GetDeviceInfo(id); /* get chosen device
                                    informationstructure */
    hostapi = Pa_GetHostApiInfo(info->hostApi);/*get host API struct */
    printf("Opening AUDIO output device [%s] %s\n",
            hostapi->name, info->name);
    outputParameters.device = id; /* chosen device id */
    outputParameters.channelCount = 2; /* stereo output */
    outputParameters.sampleFormat = paFloat32; /* 32 bit float
                                                    output */
    outputParameters.suggestedLatency =
            info->defaultLowOutputLatency; /*set default*/
    outputParameters.hostApiSpecificStreamInfo = NULL; /*no
                                                specific info*/
```

```
    for (i=0;i < Pa_GetDeviceCount(); i++) {
        info = Pa_GetDeviceInfo(i); /* get information from
                                       current device */
        hostapi = Pa_GetHostApiInfo(info->hostApi); /*info from
                                                       host API */
    if (info->maxInputChannels > 0) /* if curr device supports input */
        printf("%d: [%s] %s (input)\n",i, hostapi->name, info->name );
    }

    printf("\nType AUDIO input device number: ");
    scanf("%d", &id); /* get the input device id from the user */
    info = Pa_GetDeviceInfo(id); /* get chosen device information
                                    struct */
    hostapi = Pa_GetHostApiInfo(info->hostApi); /* get host API
                                                   struct */
    printf("Opening AUDIO input device [%s] %s\n",
        hostapi->name, info->name);

    inputParameters.device = id; /* chosen device id */
    inputParameters.channelCount = 2; /* stereo input */
    inputParameters.sampleFormat = paFloat32; /* 32 bit float input */
    inputParameters.suggestedLatency = info->defaultLowInputLatency;
    inputParameters.hostApiSpecificStreamInfo = NULL;

    Pa_OpenStream(/* open the PaStream object */
        &audioStream,/* portaudio stream object */
        &inputParameters, /* provide output parameters */
        &outputParameters /* provide input parameters */
        SAMPLING_RATE,    /* set sampling rate */
        FRAME_BLOCK_LEN,  /* set frames per buffer */
        paClipOff         /* set no clip */
        audio_callback,   /* callback function address */
        NULL );           /* provide no data for the callback *
    Pa_StartStream(audioStream); /* start the callback mechanism */
    printf("running. . . press space bar and enter to exit\n");
}

void terminate_stuff()
{
    Pa_StopStream( audioStream );  /* stop the callback mechanism */
    Pa_CloseStream( audioStream ); /* destroy the audio stream
                                      object */
    Pa_Terminate();                /* terminate portaudio */
}
```

```
int main()
{
   init_stuff();
   while(getchar() != ' ') Pa_Sleep(100);
   terminate_stuff();
   return 0;
}
```

At the top, we have the headers and constants used in the code. Particularly important is FRAME_BLOCK_LEN, the length, in frames, of the frame block[22] used by the Portaudio callback function. We need to be aware of the fact that the larger the block size, the higher the latency.[23] The audioStream pointer (to a Portaudio stream object[24]) is declared global:

```
PaStream *audioStream;
```

This is a handle that encapsulates a relevant number of inner gears, most of which are completely transparent to the API user. Also made global is si, which will hold the sampling increment of the modulator.

Next the audio stream callback[25] is defined, which contains the most important code: the engine of the ring modulator. This user-supplied function can have any name but must always have the same number, type, and order of arguments as well as the same return type as expected by Portaudio. The callback is not invoked directly by our code, but automatically from the Portaudio inner mechanism. This function receives a pointer to the block of incoming samples and a pointer to the block of outgoing samples from the Portaudio mechanism. It is your task to read and, eventually, process the samples of the input block, as well as to calculate the samples of the audio output block at each function call. Notice that this function has a long list of arguments, and returns an int. This is the function head:

```
int audio_callback (void *inputBuffer,void *outputBuffer,
                    unsigned long framesPerBuffer,
                    const PaStreamCallbackTimeInfo* timeInfo,
                    PaStreamCallbackFlags statusFlags,
                    void *userData)
```

However, in our case, we only have to care about the first three arguments and the return value (i.e. inputBuffer, outputBuffer, and framesPerBuffer), since the others are not used in this program. Nevertheless, the Pa_OpenStream() API[26] function requires the address of a function having such a prototype as an argument (so we must declare it as above). That function will register our callback with Portaudio.

Concentrating now on audio_callback(), let us review its code:

```
int audio_callback( const void *inputBuffer, void *outputBuffer,
                    unsigned long framesPerBuffer,
                    const PaStreamCallbackTimeInfo* timeInfo,
```

```
                    PaStreamCallbackFlags statusFlags,
                    void *userData
                    )
{
    float *in = (float*) inputBuffer, *out = (float*)outputBuffer;
    static double phase = 0;
    unsigned long i;
    for( i=0; i < framesPerBuffer; i++ ) {
        float sine = sin(phase);
        *out++ = *in++ * sine; /* left channel */
        *out++ = *in++ * sine; /* right channel */
        phase += si;
    }
    return paContinue;
}
```

The arguments `inputBuffer` and `outputBuffer` are pointers that contain the addresses of the input and output blocks[27] of sample frames. Such variables are void pointers. In order to use them, they must be cast to a pointer of a concrete type. Since, in this case, we plan to deal with samples of 32-bit floating-point format,[28] we have to cast them to `float` pointers (in and out). Since the audio stream was opened as a stereo stream, each buffer frame is made up of two interleaved[29] float samples. The in and out buffers can be considered as arrays of stereo frames, each having `framesPerBuffer` length. The current phase of the modulator is stored in a static double variable, initialized to zero at the start of the program.[30]

The `for` loop is our audio engine, which is iterated `framesPerBuffer` times. Here, the modulator is obtained by calculating the sinus of current phase value, and the output is stored in the temporary `sine` variable. Then the left input channel is ring-modulated (i.e. multiplied) by the sine output and the output is stored to current buffer (i.e. frame block) location. Notice the indirection (asterisk) and post-increment operators of the `out` and `in` pointers:

`*out++ = *in++ . . .`

These asterisks are indirection operators (a unary prefix operator whose purpose is to access, for writing or reading, the location currently pointed to by the corresponding pointer). Don't confuse them with the asterisk of the multiplication operator (a binary infix operator that is placed in between the in pointer and the sine variable):

`*in++ * sine`

This operator simply multiplies the two items. In the statement

`*out++ = *in++ * sine; /* left channel */`

the value of the input buffer location, having the `in` pointer as an address, is extracted and multiplied by the current `sine` value. The result is copied to the output buffer location having the out pointer as an address. After this assignment, the in and out pointers are both incremented (be aware that the increment operation is done on the addresses contained in the pointers, not on the values of the pointed locations), and consequently point to the next locations of corresponding buffers. This statement is applied to the left channel. Given that the buffer is made up of interleaved frames, an identical statement is provided for the right channel. Because of its perceived efficiency, this use of buffer pointer increment is very common in audio applications.[31]

At the last line of the loop, current phase value is incremented by the sampling increment. After the loop has processed all the frames of the input and output blocks in this way, the audio_callback() function returns the paContinue API enumerator constant.[32]

Our main() function is minimal:

```
int main()
{
    init_stuff();
    while(getchar() != ' ') Pa_Sleep(100); /* wait for space-bar
                                               and enter */

    terminate_stuff();
    return 0;
}
```

It calls the init_stuff() function, which gets the modulator frequency and the audio ports from the user, initializes everything, opens the audio stream, and starts the Portaudio callback process. Then it starts a while loop that calls the Pa_Sleep() API function. This function blocks the main thread of execution for 100 milliseconds (this value represents its argument) and yields, for this time interval, all the CPU time to the other threads and processes (among which there is the Portaudio callback mechanism). This loop has, as a testing condition, getchar() != ' '. This function checks the terminal for keyboard input: if the user has pressed space bar followed by enter, the condition becomes false (i.e. getchar() returns the space character) and the loop is exited. In this case, the terminate_stuff() function is called to stop the callback process and destroy the PaStream object.

Now let's look into the details of the init_stuff() function. It contains the code to create the PaStream object and to start the callback process. We get the frequency of the modulator from the user and calculate the sampling increment (si), used in audio_callback() to increment the phase of the modulator.

The Portaudio library is initialized by calling the Pa_Initialize() API function, which must be called before any other API function belonging to Portaudio. The loop

```
for (i=0;i < Pa_GetDeviceCount(); i++) {
    info = Pa_GetDeviceInfo(i); /* get information from current
                                    device */
    hostapi = Pa_GetHostApiInfo(info->hostApi); /*get info from current
                                                    host API */
```

```
    if (info->maxOutputChannels > 0)/* if curr device supports
                                       output */
        printf("%d: [%s] %s (output)\n",i, hostapi->name, info->name );
    }
```

is used to display all the available audio output devices. These devices include all available host APIs supported by Portaudio (for example, MME, DirectX, and ASI in Windows, and OSS and ALSA in Linux). The loop is iterated the number of times equal to the value returned by the `Pa_GetDeviceCount()` API function, which provides the number of available devices belonging to all host APIs.

At each loop iteration, the `info` pointer is filled with the (read-only, or const) address of a variable belonging of the type `PaDeviceInfo`, by calling `Pa_GetDeviceInfo()`. This contains details about a corresponding audio device. Here are all the members of a `PaDeviceInfo` structure[33]:

```
typedef struct PaDeviceInfo {
    int structVersion;
    const char *name;
    PaHostApiIndex hostApi;
    int maxInputChannels;
    int maxOutputChannels;
    PaTime defaultLowInputLatency;
    PaTime defaultLowOutputLatency;
    PaTime defaultHighInputLatency;
    PaTime defaultHighOutputLatency;
    double defaultSampleRate;
} PaDeviceInfo;
```

The relevant members in our case are `name`, `hostApi`, and `maxOutputChannels`. The `name` member is a pointer to a string containing the name of current device; the `hostApi` member contains an *int* value that expresses the host API index of the current audio device. With this, we can get information about a host API by calling `Pa_GetHostApiInfo()`. This function returns a (read-only, or const) pointer to `PaHostApiInfo`, which contains some host API information. Here are all the members of the `PaHostApiInfo` structure[34] (of which we need only name):

```
typedef struct PaHostApiInfo {
    int structVersion;
    PaHostApiTypeId type;
    const char *name;
    int deviceCount;
    PaDeviceIndex defaultInputDevice;
    PaDeviceIndex defaultOutputDevice;
} PaHostApiInfo;
```

The code inside the loop also tests the `maxOutputChannels` member of `PaDeviceInfo`:

```
if (info->maxOutputChannels > 0)
    /* if curr device supports output */
        printf("%d: [%s] %s (output)\n",i, hostapi->name, info->name );
```

This is done to know if the current audio device supports *output* channels. If this test is true, i.e. if there is a number of output channels greater than zero, a line of text is printed to the console displaying the audio device number, its host API, its name, and whether it is an output device. On my computer, the output of the loop displaying the output devices is as follows:

```
7  [MME] Microsoft Sound Mapper - Output (output)
8  [MME] MOTU Analog 1-2 (output)
9  [MME] MOTU Analog 3-4 (output)
10 [MME] MOTU Analog 5-6 (output)
11 [MME] MOTU Analog 7-8 (output)
12 [MME] MOTU TOSLink 1-2 (output)
13 [MME] Avance AC97 Audio (output)
21 [Windows DirectSound] Driver audio principale (output)
22 [Windows DirectSound] MOTU Analog 1-2 (output)
23 [Windows DirectSound] MOTU Analog 3-4 (output)
24 [Windows DirectSound] MOTU Analog 5-6 (output)
25 [Windows DirectSound] MOTU Analog 7-8 (output)
26 [Windows DirectSound] MOTU TOSLink 1-2 (output)
27 [Windows DirectSound] Avance AC97 Audio (output)
28 [ASIO] ASIO DirectX Full Duplex Driver (output)
29 [ASIO] ASIO Multimedia Driver (output)
30 [ASIO] MOTU FireWire Audio (output)
```

Notice how the number of the device begins with 7 (not with zero) and skips several numbers: these devices are skipped because they contain zero output channels (i.e. they don't support audio output). After the list is shown, the user is asked to type the number of the output device he or she intends to choose, and the `id` variable is filled with that number. Information on the chosen device is then printed to the terminal.

Once we have an output device, then we can set it up. We do this by filling the data members of the `outputParameter` variable, which has the type `PaStreamParameters`[35]:

```
typedef struct PaStreamParameters {
    PaDeviceIndex device;
    int channelCount;
    PaSampleFormat sampleFormat;
    PaTime suggestedLatency;
    void *hostApiSpecificStreamInfo;
} PaStreamParameters;
```

This structure contains the following information:

`device`: an *int* number (chosen by the program user) that expresses the index of a supported audio device. Its range is from 0 to (`Pa_GetDeviceCount() - 1`).

`channelCount`: the number of audio channels to be delivered to the stream callback. It can range from 1 to the value of `maxInputChannels` in the `PaDeviceInfo` structure for the device specified by the device parameter.

`sampleFormat`: the sample format of the buffer provided to the stream callback. It may be any of the formats supported by Portaudio.[36]

`suggestedLatency`: The desired latency in seconds. Be aware that an audio device could not support the value of latency set by the user, and so provide a latency quite different than this setting. The actual latency values for an already-opened stream can be retrieved using the *inputLatency* and *outputLatency* members of the `PaStreamInfo` structure returned by the `Pa_GetStreamInfo()` API function.

`hostApiSpecificStreamInfo`: This is an optional pointer to a host API specific data structure containing additional information for device setup and/or stream processing. Often not used, as in *helloRing.c*, in which case it must be set to `NULL`.

The address of `outputParameter` structure will be provided as an argument of the `Pa_OpenStream()` API function, which creates the audio stream object. In addition to output, we must select and set-up audio input. We will proceed similarly by filling the `inputParameters` variable. We can then pass the addresses of both variables to the `Pa_OpenStream()` API function[37]:

```
Pa_OpenStream( /* open the PaStream object and get its address */
    &audioStream, /* get the address of the portaudio stream object */
    &inputParameters, /* provide output parameters */
    &outputParameters, /* provide input parameters */
    SAMPLING_RATE, /* set sampling rate */
    FRAME_BLOCK_LEN, /* set frames per buffer */
    paClipOff, /* set no clip */
    audio_callback, /* provide the callback function address */
    NULL ); /* provide no data for the callback */

    Pa_StartStream(audioStream); /* start the callback mechanism */
}
```

This function has the task of creating (opening) an audio stream object, capable of starting the callback process. Notice that the address of the `audioStream` pointer is passed as an argument. After a call to this function, it will point to the audio stream object, which is now open.

The `paClipOff` item is a bitwise flag that can be used together with other flags[38] to describe the behavior of the callback process. Normally, Portaudio clips[39] out-of-range samples. Since we are dealing with floating-point samples, `paClipOff` disables default clipping of the samples. To set more than one flag, it is possible to use a bitwise OR operator | between flag identifiers. For example, to set the `paClipOff` and the `paDitherOff` flags at the same time, one would provide the following expression as an argument:

`paClipOff | paDitherOff`

We will also provide the `audio_callback` function address[40] as an argument so that the `Pa_OpenStream()` function can register it with Portaudio. The last argument is a pointer to an optional user-defined data pointer that is passed at each call to the audio callback function. In *helloRing.c* we don't make use of this feature, so the pointer is set to NULL.

At the end of the `init_stuff()` function, the callback mechanism is started by a call to the `Pa_StartStream()` API function. It will automatically call the `audio_callback()` function every time the input and output buffers need to be filled, in a completely transparent way.[41] The callback mechanism stops when the `terminate_stuff()` function is called (in response to a user keypress, as discussed above):

```
void terminate_stuff()
{
    Pa_StopStream( audioStream );   /* stop the callback mechanism */
    Pa_CloseStream( audioStream );  /* destroy the audio stream
                                        object */

    Pa_Terminate();                 /* terminate portaudio */
}
```

Both `Pa_StopStream()` and `Pa_CloseStream()` get the pointer to the audio stream object as an argument. The first stops audio streaming, and the second close the stream object (invalidating corresponding pointer). The `Pa_Terminate()` function cleans up Portaudio.

3.5   Conclusion

In this chapter we have explored the concept of audio streams, a concept that is central to audio processing and programming. We have looked at several examples first producing streams as text, then as binary data, generating output to soundfiles and finally real-time audio. This text should have provided the basis for further exploration of the manipulation of audio signals, as discussed in other chapters of this book and on the DVD.

3.6   Exercises

Exercise 3.6.1
The waveform-drawing functions `fill_square()`, `fill_saw()` and `fill_triangle()` in *HelloTable.c* are quite basic and have a major flaw: they are not band limited. This means that the sound synthesized with these always contain aliased components, which contribute to the low quality of the sound. How would you go about generating band-limited versions of

these flawed functions? Please implement these and then substitute them in the example program, comparing the results.

Exercise 3.6.2

The audio callback used in *HelloRing.c* includes the line

```
static double phase = 0;
```

which declares a static variable. The use of static variables is highly discouraged in modern programming, as it can cause problems in large systems. In keeping with a better style of programming, do the following:

(a) Remove the static definition.
(b) Replace the static definition with some externally provided memory. (Hint: The userData argument to the callback is never used. Perhaps you could try giving it something to do.) Rebuild and test your program.

Exercise 3.6.3

Implement a stereo ring modulator with two oscillators, one for each channel, at different frequencies. Remember that each oscillator will have to keep its phase and its increment separate. In complement to what you have done in exercise 2, remove another simplistic feature of *HelloRing*: the use of a global variable to hold the sampling increment. Substitute for it two local variables (to `main`), which will keep the separate increments and use some means of passing their value to the callback. (Hint: You can group the two increments and two phases in a data structure.)

Notes

1. 'Signal' is referred to here with its technical meaning, such as a function describing variations of voltage in an analog device, or the flow of related numbers describing the course of some physical quantity, such as fluctuating air pressure, plotted and displayed as an exponential curve on a computer screen. (See chapter 5 for more background.)

2. In my chapters, the term 'sound' will not always be used with its appropriate meaning, but rather, it will often serve as a synonym for "audio signal."

3. The '.c' file extension of "*helloworld.c*" and "*hellosine.c*" indicates that they are C language source files. Other extensions we will deal with in this book are '.h' (include files of both C and C++ languages), '.cpp' (C++ language source files), and '.hpp' (C++ header files).

4. The "Hello world!" program is famous because it appeared as the first example in *The C Programming Language*, a book by B. W. Kernighan and D. M. Ritchie, the creators of the C programming language. Their book is the "official" C programming tutorial and the most renowned book about the C programming language.

5. A sample is the numerical representation of the instantaneous value of a signal, in this case of the air pressure, given that our signal is a sound signal. It is a single numeric value, and a sequence of samples makes up a digital audio signal.

6. We will see what "standard output" is later in this chapter.

7. In the C language, a *table* is normally implemented as an *array*. Later in this book you will learn what arrays are and their purpose in detail; for now, it is sufficient to know that an *array* is nothing more than a sequence of computer memory locations containing items of the same kind. In the case of audio *tables*, these items are numbers that represent the samples of a sampled sound or of a synthesized wave.

8. Some non-standard libraries are needed: the first, the *portsf.lib* (also known as *Dobson Audio Lib*) provides several useful routines that deal with reading/writing audio files from/to disk; the second, the *Tiny Audio Lib* has already been used for *hellotable.c*, and serves to provide an easy-to-use API for DAC/ soundcard real-time audio in/out.

9. *stdio.h* for the `printf()` function, *portsf.h* for special audio file functions such as *psf_init()*, *psf_sndOpen()*, *psf_sndReadFloatFrames()*, *psf_sndClose()*, *psf_finish()*, and *tinyAudioLib.h* for *outBlockInterleaved()* and *outBlockMono()*.

10. You can find the sources of *crack.c* on the DVD.

11. -, In the previous programs *player.c, player2.c, playerGUIsimple.cpp*, and *playerGUI.cpp*, used the function

```
long psf_sndReadFloatFrames(int sfd, float *buf, DWORD nFrames);
```

from the *portsf* library, instead of our hypothetical `get_new_data()` function. The function `psf_sndReadFloatFrames( )` reads a block of samples from a wave file and copies them into a previously allocated memory block. In this case, the user must provide the address of the block in the *buf* pointer before the function call.

12. This is not to be confused with the term as it is used when referring to analog recording tape, in which a drop-out is a sudden loss of amplitude. In digital audio, 'drop-out' means a total absence of signal due to the temporary lack of available samples to convert. This is much more noticeable and disturbing than in the analog case, because loud clicks can be heard.

13. A block of items of the same type (for example a block of samples) is often called a *buffer*. So, in our case, the term *buffers of samples* refers to the sample block. Consequently, using a multiple buffering technique, means we can deal with something like "buffering of buffers." For example, assuming that we deal with blocks of 512 samples, in the case of double buffering, we have a buffer made up of two data items, each one made up of a block (or buffer) of 512 samples. In the case of triple buffering we deal with a buffer of three elements (i.e. three blocks of samples) and so on.

14. There is another buffer type, these are called *LIFO* (Last-In First-Out) *buffers* or **stacks**. They are used in other cases, but not in streaming data items to an output.

15. In most cases, the processing speed of a computer routine is not constant: in certain moments it can be extremely fast, whereas in others it can remain blocked for a limited time or flow extremely slowly. There are several reasons for this, for example: in an operating system there are normally many concur-

rent processes completely independent from each others, sometimes a process needs more CPU cycles than the other ones and vice versa in other moments; the cache memory of the processor can sometimes help to increase the speed of a loop, and other times might not be available, because it is busy with other processing routines, and so on. For these reasons some kind of buffering scheme is a necessary prerequisite for real-time streaming.

16. The unit of measure for buffer size is the number of data items that can be contained by the buffer itself. For example, a buffer of 512 elements is obviously bigger than a buffer of 256 elements.

17. Such latency calculation is theoretical because, in practice, there is another time lag you have to add to obtain the real latency delay, this lag is determined by the hardware device driver internal mechanism, that is completely hidden from the programmer. Also, sound has a limited propagation velocity in the air medium, so, depending on speaker distance from the listener, the real latency can be proportionally higher. Therefore, real latency delay is always bigger than the theoretical one, obtained by counting the FIFO buffer's data items.

18. Remember that the Tiny Audio Library wraps the blocking part of the Portaudio library, in order to make its use simpler for beginners. A more efficient and versatile (but even more difficult) way can be obtained by using the Portaudio library directly, as will be the case in the following applications. Portaudio not only supports a blocking mechanism, but also a much more efficient callback mechanism, as we will see later.

19. Copyright 1999 and 2000 by Ross Bencina and Phil Burk.

20. The *blocking* API is not as efficient as the *callback-based* API. But it is mainly provided to simplify the programming and development of simple audio utility programs. It consist of a single thread of execution, whose flow is blocked each time an in/out function is called, i.e. such function doesn't return until the corresponding buffers has been flushed. The *Tiny Audio Library* we have used so far is based on the blocking API of Portaudio. For real-world tasks, the callback-based API is highly recommended. In this chapter we deal with the callback-based API of Portaudio only.

21. The ring modulation technique is perhaps the simplest way to modify and process an input signal. Actually, this technique consists of a single multiplication of two signals: the *carrier* and the *modulator*. In a multiplication, the order of the operands is not significant, this means that modulator and carrier are symmetric, i.e. they are swappable without affecting the resulting output. The resulting spectrum of the output signal is made up of the sums and the differences of all the partial frequencies of the two starting signals. Ring modulation is very similar to the *amplitude modulation* technique, the only difference is that, in the latter, a DC offset is added to the modulator, in order to make it positive only. The spectrum of the amplitude modulation contains not only the sums and differences of the frequencies of all carrier and modulator partials (as in the case of ring modulation), but also the original frequencies.

22. In cases like this, the term 'buffer' is often used interchangeably with 'block'.

23. Latency doesn't depend solely on the block size, but also on how many blocks are used. The exact number of blocks used at runtime is transparent to the user of the Portaudio API, so that you do not have to worry about it. In any case, the user of this API does have some control over this number, by setting an approximate suggestion of the latency time by means of specific parameters (we will see such parameters later in this chapter).

24. A `PaStream` object has nothing to do with C++ classes and objects. It is actually a C structure containing pointers, pointers to functions and data that apply in all inner mechanisms of Portaudio. Its type is initially a null pointer.

25. Here is the type definition of an audio stream callback function in Portaudio v19:

```
typedef int PaStreamCallback(void* input, void* output,
    unsigned long frameCount,
    const PaStreamCallbackTimeInfo* timeInfo,
    PaStreamCallbackFlags statusFlags, void* userData );
```

26. The API functions are, in this case, the library functions belonging to the Portaudio library. The `audio_callback()` function is not an API function, because it is written by the Portaudio user, and doesn't belong to the Portaudio library.

27. In this case, 'blocks' and 'buffers' are synonymous.

28. Current Portaudio implementation (v.19) supports blocks of frames having any number of channels, and the following sample formats, expressed by symbolic macro constants:

`paFloat32`	32-bit floating-point samples (floats)
`paInt32`	32-bit signed integers (longs)
`paInt24`	packed 24-bit format
`paInt16`	16-bit signed integers (shorts)
`paInt8`	8-bit signed integers (chars)
`UInt8`	8-bit unsigned integers (unsigned chars)

Even if in *helloRing.c,* we chose a 32-bit floating-point sample format, such a format may not be natively supported by you audio interface (and almost surely it isn't, because most audio interfaces are based on 16-bit or 24-bit integer sample format). However, this fact won't prevent *helloRing.c* from working with your interface because there is a Portaudio internal setting that automatically converts the sample format into a format compatible with your interface, so you needn't worry about explicitly using a sample format natively supported by your interface.

29. Normally Portaudio uses interleaved blocks, made up of frames, in which each frame contains a sample of all channels. However, since v19, Portaudio now optionally supports non-interleaved blocks. By using the `paNonInterleaved` macro constant, one sets a bitwise flag which informs the engine that the user doesn't want a single default frame block for all channels, but rather, multiple separated non-interleaved sample blocks, one for each channel. When non-interleaved blocks are chose, the callback arguments `void *inputBuffer` and `void *outputBuffer` don't point to a single sample-frame block, but rather, to an array of sample blocks. And consequently, the void pointers must be cast in the following way inside the audio callback:

```
float *left = ((float **) inputBuffer)[0];
float *right = ((float **) inputBuffer)[1];
```

30. Remember that local static variables are created at the start of the program and keep their content unchanged between function calls. This is the reason we used a static variable in this context. So, the variable phase will keep the last value assumed in each subsequent function call, and you have to be

aware that it is set to zero only at the program start, not each time the `audio_callback` function is called (different from non-static local variables).

31. Current compilers can generate machine code with the same efficiency, even when using the array style instead of incrementing the pointers. In this case the loop would assume the following style:

```
for( i=0; i < framesPerBuffer; i+=2 ) {
    float sine = sin(phase);
    out[i] = in[i] * sine; /* left */
    out[i+1] = in[i+1] * sine; /* right */
    phase += si;
 }
```

Another reason of convenience in using the pointer-increment style is how easy it is to modify the code for multi-channel audio. For example, if we had to support quadraphonic output, the loop would simply be as follows:

```
for( i=0; i < framesPerBuffer; i++ ) {
    float sine = sin(phase);
    *out++ = *in++ * sine; /* front left */
    *out++ = *in++ * sine; /* front right */
    *out++ = *in++ * sine; /* rear left */
    *out++ = *in++ * sine; /* rear right */
    phase += si;
}
```

32. The `paContinue` API enumerator constant (belonging to the `PaStreamCallbackResult` enumeration type) is equal to zero in Portaudio v19. This value informs the Portaudio mechanism that the callback process has to be continued. There are two other possible return values of the callback function: `paComplete` (equal to one), which informs that the process has completed, so there is no necessity for further calls to the callback functions; and `paAbort` (equal to two), which informs that the callback process must be stopped.

33. See the *portaudio.h* header file, provided with the Portaudio distribution, for more information and documentation about this structure.

34. As in note 33.

35. As in note 33.

36. See note 31.

37. This is the prototype of the `Pa_OpenStream()` API function:

```
PaError Pa_OpenStream( PaStream** stream,
const PaStreamParameters *inputParameters,
const PaStreamParameters *outputParameters,
double sampleRate, unsigned long framesPerBuffer,
PaStreamFlags streamFlags, PaStreamCallback *streamCallback,
void *userData );
```

Notice that this function returns an error value, not used in *helloRing.c*.

38. The possible flags are the following:

`paNoFlag`   no flag is set

`paClipOff`   disable clipping

`paDitherOff`   disable dithering

`paNeverDropInput`   will not discard overflowed input samples without calling the stream callback

`paPrimeOutputBuffersUsingStreamCallback`   call the stream callback to fill initial output buffers, rather than the default behavior of priming the buffers with zeros (silence)

`paPlatformSpecificFlags`   platform-specific flags.

By default, Portaudio clips and dithers the samples.

39. Clipping means making all samples above and below certain thresholds equal to the corresponding threshold values. For example if the allowed range is −1 to +1, and a sample has a value of .8, it passes unmodified by the clipping stage, but if a sample has a value of 1.2 it will be clipped to 1, and if a sample has a value of −2 it will be clipped to −1. By default, the Portaudio mechanism clips samples. Upper and lower clipping limits can vary, depending on the sample formats:

`paFloat32`   −1 to 1

`paInt32`   the limits of a long variable (−2,147,483,648 to 2,147,483,647)

`paInt24`   depends on the implementation, normally the limits are the same of `paInt32`, but the real values are approximate, because the lower eight bits are truncated

`paInt16`   the limits of a short variable (−32,768 to 32,767)

`paInt8`   the limits of a char variable (−128 to 127)

`paUInt8`   the limits of an unsigned char variable (0 to 255).

40. To get the address of a function, it is sufficient to set the function name without round braces, and so, to get the address of the `audio_callback()` function, we can simply provide the `audio_callback` identifier. This identifier returns the address of the target function in both C and C++.

41. Once the `Pa_StartStream()` function has been successfully called, the callback function is repeatedly called without us needing to worry about doing this explicitly. In the case of *helloRing.c*, there is no need to control anything more, because the modulator frequency is constant. If we had to control it in real time, for example via MIDI, some control mechanism would have to be activated and performed during the callback process. Part of this control mechanism can reside in the audio callback function, while other part could reside elsewhere (for example, in an eventual MIDI callback function). But often all control gears reside in the audio callback too.

4   Introduction to Program Design

John ffitch

In the earlier chapters of this book you will have had the opportunity to learn the language aspects of C—how to construct a well-formed statement, a syntactically correct function, and so forth. In this chapter we are considering the totality of the program. To write a useful program, we need not only to know how to express our intent, but to know what it is we are trying to do, and how to achieve our intent. Some people seem to have no troubles with this; it can be most dispiriting to see these people apparently doing this arcane activity as if it were instinctive. Fortunately, for the majority of humanity there are methods to assist us.

In the circles of computer science this is usually called *Software Engineering*, and it has been a major area of both practical and theoretical research. In light of this, it is clear that in an introductory book it is simply not possible to give a comprehensive knowledge of the field, let alone provide sufficient work-experience to gain employment. The aim in this chapter is to show one of the most direct and applicable techniques of software engineering without the weight of formalism with which this subject is so often burdened.

The approach taken here is to work from a simple example; to create a complete program to accomplish a simple audio task. The task chosen is to create a wave-table playback synthesizer. The software engineering methodology is a simplified variant of *object-oriented design*.

You may find it helpful to contemplate an analogy with the composition process. It is given that the work is to be, say, a string quartet. That means that we are to write for strings, and we need to be competent in the way this done, in the same way that we need to be familiar with the C language to write a C program. However that is not the heart of the composition. We need to design the whole work, consider the structure of the entity, what its emotional content is to be, or whatever suits your musical aesthetic. Technique is used in the detailed evolution of the notes, or the temporally local processes. Like all analogies this can be stretched too far, but the major point is that programs need overall design and organization.

4.1   Where to Begin

In many ways the hardest part of programming is starting. Faced with a blank sheet of paper or a blank computer screen it is all too easy for the mind to panic. In order to overcome this natural reaction, object-oriented design suggests a technique to identify the major components of the program. The technique starts by asking for a natural language description of the problem. If one cannot write such a description then it is almost certain that you do not really know what you are trying to do, and while the resulting programming experience can be fun, it is unlikely to be successful.

Thus, our task is to write a wavetable playback system. That is, we need to have a waveform, which is defined either by reading from an external file or mathematically constructed, from which we copy to the output, sometimes speeding it up and sometimes slowing it down. We can take this as our initial description. Later we may find that we need to be more detailed, or add new explanations of what we would like the program to achieve. The next step in the technique is to identify the nouns (words denoting things), and to identify the verbs (words that denote actions) in our initial description.

4.1.1   Data Representation

We need to have a *waveform*, which is defined either by reading from an external *file* or mathematically constructed, from which we copy to the *output*, sometimes speeding it up and sometimes slowing it down.

Let's start with the nouns. In our simple example, the three nouns we have identified are the existence of a waveform, an external file, and an output. The reason we identify these parts is that we are going to have to provide some mechanism to represent the nouns in our description. In the jargon of object-oriented design, these nouns would become *objects*. In fact, if our target were a program in C++ or some other object-oriented language, these nouns would become the *instances* and *classes*. But for the purposes of this chapter, since we are aiming at C, we don't need to concern ourselves directly with this, yet.

We have already made a significant start. Whatever else happens in our program, or in our attempt to create it, we now know that without some way of storing the waveform we are never going to achieve our stated aims. It is tempting to immediately jump to considering exactly how to *represent* the waveform,[1] but this temptation must be resisted, at least of a little longer. The reason for the delay is that in order to get a good solution, rather than just a working one, some ways of representing the object may be preferable to others, and a premature decision may preclude some ways of working. A very good maxim for software design, as in many other forms of design, is to maximize flexibility, and avoid cutting off possible futures until late in the process. As part of the rest of the design the representation may become obvious, or may still remain part of the art of programming.[2]

We have determined that there must be some representation of the waveform, but we defer the specific consideration of how until later. However, before moving on, it is useful to ensure that there is at least one representation we could use. Observing that WAV files exist, we can be sure that there is at least one solution, and so we can move on to the next problem.

The second noun was 'file'. In this case the representation is largely imposed by the computer system, but we will have to consider what kind of file we will use—WAV, AIFF, MP3, or some other format. Again we can, and should, defer this to a later stage.

The third noun we identified was 'output'. This is a potential problem, with much work required to complete even an abstract representation. However we can use another trick from the software engineer's bag—software reuse. We may notice that a particular object in our program has been featured in other programs—either written by ourselves or others. In the specific case of the output representation of audio, there are many libraries that do just that. For this example we will make use of just such an object, a component in an existing software library, the *portsf* library. This completes the first pass: to identify the objects, indicated by nouns, in the original English description.

4.1.2 Actions and Process

Now let's deal with the verbs. In grammar, a verb is sometimes called a "doing" word. For our purposes this is a good concept. Verbs are indications of actions that our program must do to solve the problem. These actions will take nouns, that is data, as their subject and object.

We need a waveform, which is defined either by reading from an external file or mathematically *constructed*, from which we *copy* to the output, sometimes speeding it up and sometimes slowing it down.

In considering the verb 'reading', we can see that it refers to both an external file and the waveform. This indicates that there will need to be a *function*, which will take as arguments or give as a result, the representations of these two entities. As it reads from a file to produce a waveform, one possible formulation is a function with a protocol something like

```
WAVEFORM readform(FILE_HANDLE);
```

However, if one thinks of the waveform as an empty structure that is filled from the file, then it might be more natural to think of a function with no result, or just an error indication, such as

```
int readform(WAVEFORM,FILE_HANDLE);
```

The function that is chosen is part of the intangibles of design, based on personal taste, perhaps personal skill, and a view of what is 'natural'. For a number of reasons that I find hard to explain,[3] I prefer the first form, and so it is that one I will use in this design development.

We also expect that the waveform could be provided by a mathematical formula. This reading of our description turns up yet another noun, 'formula', which will also need a representation. What we are seeing here is that as we investigate each of our nouns and verbs, we can see that our original statement (called a *specification* in software engineering jargon[4]) is not complete, and that we will need to refine it, or to provide a more detailed description. Usually the initial specification of a program is deficient in some respects and the designer has to provide additional specifications or to limit the specification is some way.

In our example there are a large number of ways that a mathematical formula could be specified, let alone represented.[5] However, we will simplify this by considering the kinds of use to which the program might be put. The commonest waveform, from which others can be built, is the sine or cosine function. Thus, we will provide for the creation of just these two, while making it possible to extend the program at some later stage to other pre-defined function.

We now need a representation of a *formula* that only has two possible values, *sine* and *cosine*. With this simplification we deduce that the function we require is

```
WAVEFORM createformula(FORMULA);
```

We now turn to the third verb, which may be seen as the heart of the program. We need to copy the waveform to the output. That suggests a functional form of

```
int copywaveform(WAVEFORM, OUTPUT);
```

—but that would be to miss another aspect of the original specification, where we stated that the copy could *sometimes speeding it up and sometimes slowing it down*. This is part of the copying action, and there is an implied noun that we had not previously noted: the speed of the copy. We will need some representation of *speed*; but in line with our previous policy of not getting to detailed representations yet, we will just note that it is needed and proceed to modify our function prototype to

```
int copywaveform(WAVEFORM, SPEED, OUTPUT);
```

I have returned a value from this function to provide a possible error reporting mechanism. It may happen that the output cannot take the waveform, or the disk is full, or the speed is not acceptable, or other possible conditions that we have not yet identified. It is generally a good practice to make a provision for what could go wrong throughout the design and coding processes.

That completes a first pass through the specification. Just as with the nouns, where we identified the objects that needed representation but did not fully consider the representation; with the verbs, we have identified the actions that will be the *functions* in our solution, but we have not yet considered the actual way, the specific process, in which the functions will work. Processes are achieved through algorithms.

There is a long mathematical tradition of studying algorithms, but the main features that mathematicians have identified for a process to be considered an *algorithm* is that it must have a finite description (that is, our code cannot go on forever[6]), it must be unambiguous (imposed largely by the programming language that cannot accept ambiguous statements), and it must be effective in achieving the result is a finite time.[7]

4.1.3   How to Proceed

With the first pass completed, we can list the tasks that remain. We need representations for the following:

a waveform: `WAVEFORM`
an external file: `FILE_HANDLE`
the output: `OUTPUT`
formulae: `FORMULA`
speed: `SPEED`

The actions mean that we need algorithms for the following:

`readform: FILE_HANDLE -> WAVEFORM`

`createformula: FORMULA -> WAVEFORM`

`copywaveform: WAVEFORM x SPEED x OUTPUT -> INTEGER`

I have described the actions via a name and a signature. This is a formal way of talking about the *arguments* and *results* that does not tie us too closely to any specific programming language. (They could also be presented as C *function prototypes*.)

To proceed, we continue in the same way, taking each of the actions and attempting to give them more detail. In doing this we may uncover more nouns that need representation, and more processes which require functions; but these will be seen as subordinate to the functions we have already identified. In this analysis, we sometimes discover that the same action is required in more than one part of the program, and we can choose to merge two instances, and simplify the resulting solution.

The obvious question about this process is when to stop. Obviously, we could do this successive refinement indefinitely. Again, this is where the "art" comes in. At some stage we should decide that the action is obvious, or similar to what we have done in other programs, and so should not cause us any problem. Another indicator that it is time to stop is when any further refinement depends closely on the representation. Clearly this stage differs between individuals, based on their experience and talents. In our example, we will continue a little further as I am not yet clear how we are to achieve these actions.

The final process is to create concrete representations for the nouns. By leaving this to the end we will know exactly what we want to do to the representation, and this can guide us toward choosing good or appropriate representations. We will consider the concrete representations much later.

4.1.4   Reading a File as a Waveform

In considering the function `readform` that I have determined will have the signature

`FILE_HANDLE -> WAVEFORM`

or equivalently in C

```
WAVEFORM readform(FILE_HANDLE);
```

we can proceed in the same way as the main problem. We start by trying to describe what we expect this function to do, in simple textual form. We then examine this for nouns and verbs, and check that we have captured the required intent.

The function is supposed to *get* a WAVEFORM and *copy* the data contained in the associated file into the representation.

There are no new nouns in that specification, but there are two verbs, which have been underlined. The *get* operation needs to create an empty waveform, and the *copy* operation populates it. To make this clearer, we need to narrow the definition somewhat, and consider, still in an abstract fashion, how a waveform is to be represented.

We could still widen this description, or have a number of possible representations, but I am going to impose the condition that all waveforms will be represented in digital sampled format. This form has a number of variants and at this point I do not wish to decide on exactly which. But it does give some structure to the abstract data object WAVEFORM. It needs to maintain some representation of a number of *samples*, and in addition, we will need to know the number of samples it uses, the size. We may need more components as we continue the analysis, but this is enough to determine that we have some kind of composite object that can be divided into sub-components. We can continue to use our noun/verb methodology to see that there are (at least) two of these subcomponents, identified by the two nouns samples and number.

```
WAVEFORM:
    SIZE
    SAMPLES
```

We are still not saying how the samples are to be represented inside the running program, or how the size of the collection of samples is to be represented. We may be tempted to think that the size will be an integer, but that is a premature thought. However, we can continue the design to the two verbs. The creation of an empty waveform might be expected to require the number of samples that are to be represented,[8] and this implies a function:

```
WAVEFORM getnewform(SIZE);
```

The other function is to read the data from the external file. Again without deciding on the exact format of the file, we can deduce a functional prototype:

```
int readfile(WAVEFORM, FILE_HANDLE);
```

We have, however, introduced a new problem: the need to determine the size of the sample collection. We could for example take this as a fixed constant, or we could assume that the file contains this information. I will take the second as it is a little more general and it fits our general approach. Thus, we will need to ensure that there is a function to get the size from the file. That function is

```
SIZE lengthoffile(FILE_HANDLE);
```

and the complete function `readform` will be approximately as follows:

```
WAVEFORM readform(FILE_HANDLE file)
{
    WAVEFORM xx;
    int err;
    xx = getnewform(lengthoffile(file));
    if ((err=readfile(xx, file)) !=0) return xx;
    error("Failed to read wave form for reason %d", err);
    return NULL;
}
```

The purists say that one should continue moving from an abstract program toward a concrete one in stripes, but in practice we sometimes can complete one component independently. Indeed the whole purpose of this approach to program design is to clarify what is independent and separate.

We can move this part of the program forward by considering how the samples are to represented in the external file. Note that this does not place any constraints on how the internal representation is to be maintained, as the `readfile` function could make any alterations if wished. As the designer of the program, I am going to impose an external format of text-based numbers, one to a line. The first number will be the length of the file in samples, followed by values of the samples at equally spaced time intervals, and the wave repeating after the length.[9] That decision allows us to make a step forward with the design of `readfile`. Clearly we have to read the count, and then, in a loop, read and set the internal structure. Indeed the process we are seeing is one where, as we simplify and define the program structures, we can see more clearly how the data structures should be, and the data structures inform what the program should be. It seems as if the `FILE_HANDLE` of our abstract version can be thought of as the name of the file, and we can use `FILE*` from the standard C library associated with this name as a C string. We will tentatively propose a definition of `readfile`:

```
typedef char *FILE_HANDLE;
. . .
int readfile(WAVEFORM xx, FILE_HANDLE file)
{
    int count, i;
    double val;
    FILE *ff = fopen(file, "r");

    if (ff==NULL)
        return ERR_NO_FILE;
    if (fscanf(ff, "%d", &count)!=1)
        return ERR_NO_COUNT;
```

```
for (i=0; i<count; i++) {
    if (fscanf(ff, "%f", &val)!=1)
        return ERR_NO_DATA;
    put_val(xx, i, val);
}
fclose(ff);
return 0;
}
```

We now have a potential solution to the internal structure of a waveform. (I say this tentatively, as we really need to ensure that there are no fence-post problems with the count, and I have skipped a number of stages of error reporting and design; but we will return to them later.)

A feature of software design that so far I have only hinted at is the need to review and revise decisions taken when later it seems that the solution is not complete or could be made easier. In general, software is a complex entity, and some have even defined the whole subject of computing as managing complexity; that is why so often programmers and software engineers refer to simplicity. We know that a simple program is easier to understand and hence develop or maintain. To paraphrase Einstein, programs should be as simple as possible, but no simpler.

4.1.5 Filling a Waveform from a Formula

In the previous subsection we decided on an initial internal structure for storing a waveform. We can now test that structure by seeing if it can deal with the other way we have suggested for obtaining a waveform: from a mathematical formula. Previously we had a prototype of

```
WAVEFORM createformula(FORMULA);
```

and we had decided that we would limit ourselves to only sine and cosine functions in the first instance. We now have to face up to the problems of specifying the formula. Just to say we want a sine wave is insufficient. We need to have a range of values to store, that is the range of the x axis for which we will store $\sin(x)$ or $\cos(x)$. But what range of x? Starting at 0 seems a good idea. As we know that the circular functions repeat over a range of 2π, we could say that we will store one complete cycle. This is still not a complete description, as we need to decide on the number of points. (See figure 4.1.)

Knowing that we are making a simplifying decision, and marking this as a point we may wish to reconsider later, let us decide to store one cycle in 4,096 points—computer scientists tend to like powers of 2. We will see later how this could give a simpler solution than allowing any value for the size. Even so, we will use a C macro so that this can be changed to a different constant with ease. If we later decide that this value should not be constant, then more drastic changes will be needed.

i	i/trig_size	2πi/trig_size	sin(2πi/trig_size)
0	0.000	0	0.000
512	0.125	π/4	0.707
1024	0.250	π/2	1.000
1536	0.375	3π/4	0.707
2048	0.500	π	0.000
2560	.0625	5π/4	−0.707
3072	0.750	3π/2	−1.000
3584	0.875	7π/4	−0.707
4096	1.000	2π	0.000

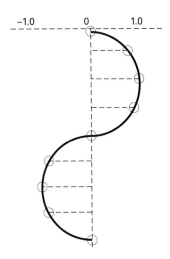

output of sin() function for nine selected values of i

Figure 4.1
A sine waveform function table.

We can then represent FORMULA as a simple label, and the function can be like

```
#define TRIG_SIZE (4096)
#define TWOPIBYSIZE (6.28318530718/(double)TRIG_SIZE)
WAVEFORM createformula(FORMULA trig)
{
 WAVEFORM xx = getnewform(TRIG_SIZE);
 int i;
 double val;

    for (i=0; i<TRIG_SIZE; i++) {
        if (trig==SINE)
            val = sin((double)i*TWOPIBYSIZE);
        else if (trig==COSINE)
            val = cos((double)i*TWOPIBYSIZE);
        else return ERR_NO_FORMULA;
         put_val(xx, i, val);
    }
    return xx;
}
```

We now have most of the program designed and programmed. Only one major component remains: the copying of the waveform to the output. What we have not completed is the actual representation of all the components. Rather than continuing in the strict top-down order of development we will now consider concrete representations.

4.2 Choosing Concrete Representations

The last stage of the development is to choose how to represent the low-level entities we have defined. In order to make this decision we need to know the range of opportunities. Part of this is just knowledge of the C language, but it also includes other aspects, such as the target computer.

4.2.1 The Palette of Options

The C language provides a small number of built-in data types, and two ways in which they can be used to create more complex items. The basic integer types are `char`, `short`, `int`, and `long` ; there are two floating-point types: `float` and `double`. The types `short`, `int`, and `long` can also be given as `unsigned` if strictly negative numbers are not required. Also, `chars` can be used directly, or can be `signed` or `unsigned`. This is very confusing; below I will attempt to explain it.

There is a great deal of confusion about the exact meanings of `char`, `short`, `int`, and `long`. The language standard guarantees that these are in non-decreasing order of size. They can in fact all be the same (and yes there are computers like that), but on most computers today they correspond to 8-bit, 16-bit, and 32-bit numbers, with `long`s the same as `int`s. On the early PCs, the sizes were 8, 16, 16, and 32, and on the coming generation of 64-bit machines the sizes may be 8, 16, 32, and 64 or 8, 16, 64, and 64. One should not make assumptions, and one should rely on a reasonable range.

Why would one use a `short` rather than an `int`? It may save space if only small values are needed, and that is the main reason. Unfortunately, `shorts` are sometimes slower than `ints`, because hardware manufacturers optimize their chips for `int` use.

A similar situation arises with `floats` and `doubles`. Though traditionally these correspond to 32-bit and 64-bit floating-point numbers, this is not guaranteed. Many older compilers were not good at handling `floats`, and `floats` are still often handled more slowly than `doubles`, even though they are smaller.

The problem with `chars` is that some hardware treats 8-bit integers as `signed` and some treat them as `unsigned`. In creating the C standard it was necessary to reconcile these two differing stances, and so the standard does not say which is meant. For most use of `chars` this is not important, but if you wish to compare characters with < or > then they are different. If it really matters to you, you should use the `signed` or `unsigned` versions explicitly, and accept that on some machines this may give slower code. More complex representations can be constructed from `arrays` or from `structs`.

Two other features in C are useful in considering representations. An enum allows a list of names to be treated as basic tokens of the language. In fact they usually are mapped to ints. (For example, they could be useful in our program where we need tokens for SINE and COSINE formulae; we could just use 0 and 1, but there is no logic in that choice.) And typedef that allows us to have our own name for any previously defined structure. Usually this is used with structs, but it can be used well with enum or even the basic types to make the program read more like the problem than the solution.

4.2.2 Making the Choice

As in many parts of software creation, there are no hard rules to making the choices. There are however a number of general principles, like being simple, making use of enumeration types, and using typedef to maintain clarity related to the problem.

In our program-design exercise, we clearly should have the formulae as an enumeration type

```
enum FORMULA {SINE, COSINE};
```

This is simple, and still allows us flexibility to add, say, sawtooth or square waves. One crucial object in our analysis is the WAVEFORM. So far we have only considered the operations we need to do to a WAVEFORM, but I have deliberately not considered the concrete representation. A good software engineer may well say that it is still too soon to generate a concrete representation, as we have not yet considered all the operations. Well, I am going to cheat a little; it is my program and I can break the rules.

In considering the WAVEFORM we can use a simple part of information theory. We can count the number of items that are identified and use that as a start to the process of designing the concrete representation. We already have

```
WAVEFORM:
    SIZE
    SAMPLES
```

We will need to represent the size and the actual samples. The size is a count of the number of samples, and so an integer is appropriate. The char type is certainly too small on many machines, and so I will decide to use int. I could have chosen a short, as it is extremely unlikely that I will need a waveform with a large number of samples. However as a matter of personal style, I like shorts only where I know I am memory restricted, as I have used too many computers where shorts are slow. The samples are a collection of floating-point values or possibly integers. I will decide to use double for each sample, again realizing that this takes more memory than floats. We are still left with the question of how to represent the collection.

Collections are usually represented by either arrays or lists. Lists are a little more complex to code but are much more flexible when wanting to add new data in the middle, or wanting to delete data values. In our application we are reading the data and then using it, and we have not seen any part of the description ask for modifications of an existing waveform. So with relief we can use an `array`. What seems to be sought is

```
struct WaveForm {
    int size;
    double samples[size];
};
```

But that is not allowed in C.[10] Arrays must be declared with a constant size. There are two possible approaches. The simplest is to decide that no waveform will be longer than, say, 8,192 samples, and to declare this in the design document, and in the `struct`. We will also have to police this limit in the function `getnewform`. Better would be to use a true dynamic `array`. We declare the `struct` with an `array` of length 1, and use `malloc` to create instances of the `WAVEFORM`. This translates into

```
typedef struct WaveForm {
    int size;
    double samples[1];
} WAVE;
typedef WAVE *WAVEFORM;

WAVEFORM getnewform(int size)
{
    WAVEFORM xx =
        (WAVEFORM)malloc((size-1)*sizeof(double)+sizeof(WAVE));
    if (WAVEFORM==NULL){
        error("Failed to allocate memory\n");
        exit(1);
    }
    xx->size = size;
    return xx;
}

void put_val(WAVEFORM xx, int i, double val)
{
    xx.samples[i] = val;
}
```

4.2.3 Can One Be Certain Which Choice Is Best?

Whenever there is a choice, one might be concerned that the solution is the "correct" one. This is a rather pointless concern; in software as in composition there is no right solution. Certainly some choices are better than others, and this is largely a matter of experience. Good representations are those that avoid awkward code, and for which the algorithms are easy. Knowing this takes time. But some suggestions can be made. Throughout computing there are trade-offs, and the largest one is between space and time. Often a small representation requires complicated code to use. Fast access often introduces memory under-use.

One of the advantages of this object-oriented design is that the representations are largely decoupled from the program structure, so if it turns out that we made a bad decision, it should be easy to return to the design structure and replace the offending decision with a better one.

4.2.4   Copy Waveform

We now return to the main design. We have design and code to create waveforms in the computer, and we have considered many aspects of program design. We now must face up to the other major task: reading the waveform out at different speeds. We have already decided that

```
int copywaveform(WAVEFORM, SPEED, OUTPUT);
```

and the interpretation of WAVEFORM is largely determined. So let us consider what we mean by SPEED. Our initial description of the problem stated "we copy (the waveform) to the output, sometimes speeding it up and sometimes slowing it down." We have stored the wavetable as one cycle, so we have a choice of two approaches. The first is to know the intended speed of the stored waveform, and so speed would be a multiplicative factor on that base speed; the other is to treat speed as an absolute rate in hertz, giving how many passes a second are needed to give the desired output. I am going to follow the second of these.[11]

The speed will be represented in hertz, that is, cycles per second. While it is tempting to consider only integer values for this, it would be more flexible for this to be any number, and it surely cannot introduce too much complexity.[12]

We now have to ask how we are going to achieve the copying of the waveform to the output at the desired speed. Again we can gain insight into what is required by attempting to describe the process. The first thing to recognize is that the output is going to require that the sound is represented by a series of equally spaced samples, and the spacing is related to the sample rate. We have another choice here, to use a fixed sample rate or to make it variable, or selectable by the user. I expect that the commonest sample rate will be 44,100 Hz, but for some real-time uses people are willing to use a lesser quality with the aim of speed. I suggest that we write the program assuming a sample rate that is a "name," and I will use sr for this value. This allows us to delay the question of constancy or variability of the sample rate until a later stage. If we find a part where there is a difference in algorithm we will be forced to make a decision; if we get to the end of the design without having to make such a choice, then we know that the sample rate can be varied. This is another general principle of software design. Use "names" for entities even if they are constant.[13] This will lead to a more flexible design in most cases. Even if it turns out that it really is a constant, the use of a name makes for more readable code.

If we are to copy the waveform at SPEED hertz, at the sample rate of sr, then we need to take (sr/SPEED) samples from each traverse of the cycle. This formula can be checked by using the *Factor-Label Method* of Units Analysis: sr is in samples/second and SPEED is in copies/second, hence sr/SPEED is in samples/cycle. We can also verify this formula by noting that for high frequencies this number is smaller than for low frequencies, so there are fewer samples in a cycle. (See figure 4.2.)

The problem we have to solve is how to generate (sr/SPEED) samples when the number of sample points we have stored is a fixed number, either from the external file (the size in the file) or a constant in the case of the mathematical formulae. Ideally we would like for have a loop that has a running position in the waveform that is incremented by the size/(sr/SPEED). The problem is that this result is not necessarily an integer, and so it cannot identify or index a single sample. Still, we could take the simplest version (to truncate the result and take the integer below), and use that stored value. With this idea we can code T seconds of output as

```
void copywaveform(WAVEFORM w, SPEED s, OUTPUT out)
{
    double index = 0.0;
    int total_samps = (int)(T*sr);
    int size = waveform_size(w);
    int i;
    for (i=0; i<total_samps; i++) {
        double value = waveform_val(w, (int)index);
        index += size*s/sr;
        if (index >= size) index -= size;
        output_sample(out, value);
    }
}
```

where we have postulated two functions, waveform_size and waveform_val, that extract information from a waveform. This kind of function is often called a "selector," as it only reads a value from the representation.[14] With the decisions above, these functions can be easily coded as

```
int waveform_size(WAVEFORM w)
{
    return w->size;
}

double waveform_val(WAVEFORM w, int which)
{
    return w->samples[which];
}
```

an example

SR = 44100
copy the wave form to the output using
44100 samples per second

SPEED = 11025 Hz
use the above 44100 samples to represent
11025 copies of the wave form in one second.

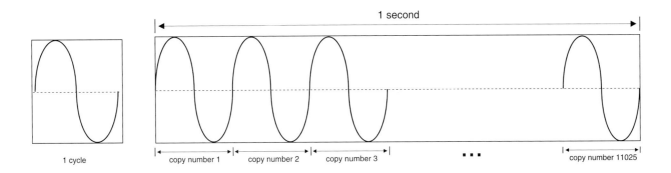

SR/SPEED

$$44100 \frac{\text{samples}}{\text{second}} \Big/ 11025 \frac{\text{copies}}{\text{second}} = 4 \frac{\text{samples}}{\text{second}} \frac{\text{second}}{\text{copies}} = 4 \frac{\text{samples}}{\text{copy}}$$

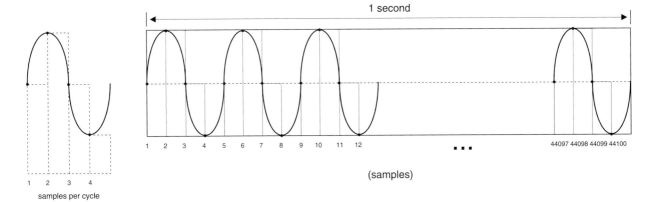

Figure 4.2
Copying a waveform.

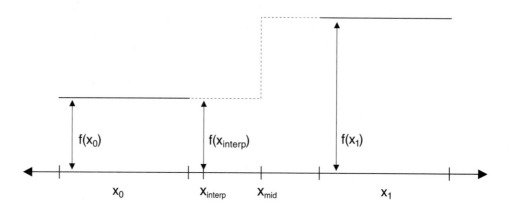

$$f(x_{interp}) = \left\{ \begin{array}{l} f(x_0), \; x_{interp} < x_{mid} \\ f(x_1), \; x_{interp} > x_{mid} \end{array} \right\} \; x_{mid} = \frac{(x_1 - x_0)}{2}$$

Figure 4.3
Interpolation, taking the closest value.

Although this solution will generate some kind of output, it will introduce a significant amount of noise. A different solution would be to use the closest sample, which would only require the change of one line to

```
double value = waveform_val(w, (int)(index+0.5));
```

But while this is better for only a small computational cost, it is hardly ideal. The next idea would be to use some kind of interpolation. Interpolation is the subject of estimating the value of a function at a point that is not stored. What we have considered so far is taking the closest value that we do have and using this, as shown in figure 4.3.

The next suggestion is to determine the two stored values on either side of the value we want, and to assume that the function is a straight line between them (figure 4.4). This is, not surprisingly, called *linear interpolation*. Mathematically, if we want $f(x)$ and we have values at x_0 and x_1 which are either side of x, then the straight line between $f(x_0)$ and $f(x_1)$ is

$$y = f(x_0) + \frac{f(x_1) - f(x_0)}{x_1 - x_0} (x - x_0). \tag{1}$$

We can check that this formula is correct by considering that when x is x_0 then y is $f(x_0)$; if x is x_1 we get $f(x_1)$. This is what we want. If your mathematical skills are not strong, you may not know that if the x only occurs to the power 1 then the formula is a straight line.[15]

Thus, to code a linear interpolating version of our value reader we need code like the following:

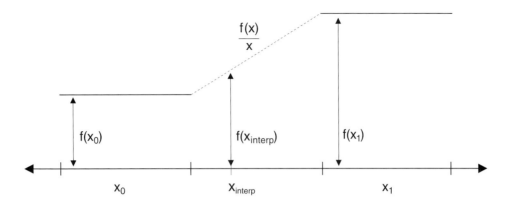

$$\frac{f(x)}{x} = \frac{f(x_1) - f(x_0)}{(x_1 - x_0)}$$

$$f(x_{interp}) = f(x_0) + \frac{f(x_1) - f(x_0)}{(x_1 - x_0)}\,(x_{interp} - x_0)$$

Figure 4.4
Linear interpolation.

```
double waveform_ival(WAVEFORM w, double which)
{
    int x0 = (int)which;
    int x1 = (int)(which+1.0);
    double f0, f1;
    if (x1>=waveform_size(w)) x1 = 0;
    f0 = waveform_val(w,x0);
    f1 = waveform_val(w,x1);
    return f0 + (f1 - f0)*(which-x0);
}
```

The only problem is what happens when x is greater that the last value stored. As we are treating the waveform as endlessly repeating, x_1 beyond the end is the same as if it were the first value stored (the table wraps around).

Notice that I have made a small simplification. When we are storing the waveform at points $0, 1, 2, \ldots$, the value of $x_1 - x_0$ is unity, so I can save the division. It is possible to make other simplifications to the formula, but that will do for the present.

You may feel that just drawing a straight line is a little crude, as indeed it is. If we have enough points stored in the waveform, then the errors introduced may be acceptable; alternatively, we could seek better interpolation methods.

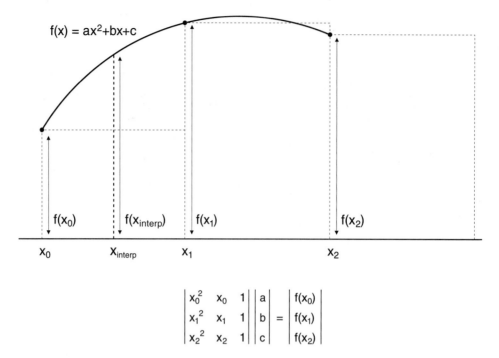

Figure 4.5
Quadratic interpolation.

The obvious idea is to use a curve rather than a line; in order to decide what kind of curve we would need to use additional points.

The next simplest interpolation is *quadratic interpolation* (figure 4.5), where we fit a second-degree polynomial through three points.[16] This is a valid interpolation method, and it is not much harder to code than linear interpolation. However, it suffers from a small oddity: should we take two points before the required x and one after, or one before and two after? This asymmetry is the reason that quadratic interpolation is rarely used for this style of application. (See figure 4.5.)

More common is *cubic interpolation*, with two points before the truncated table position and two points after. This is certainly more complex. Apart from adding a requirement that there are actually four points stored,[17] the code is much harder. The mathematics is left as an exercise to the enthusiastic, but the code would be as follows:

```
double waveform_ival(WAVEFORM w, double which)
{
    int x0 = (int)which;
    int x1 = (int)(which+1.0);
    int x2 = (int)(which+2.0);
```

```
    int xm1 = (int)(which-1.0);
    int x = which-x0
    double f0, f1, f2, fm1;
    if (x1>=waveform_size(w)) x1 -= waveform_size(w);
    if (x2>=waveform_size(w)) x2 -= waveform_size(w);
    (xm1<0) xm1 += waveform_size(w);
    f0 = waveform_val(w,x0);
    f1 = waveform_val(w,x1);
    f2 = waveform_val(w,x0);
    fm1 = waveform_val(w,x1);
    return f0 + (((f2 - fm1 - 3*f1 + 3*f0)*x + 3*(f1 + fm1 - 2*f0))*x -
                (f2 + 2*fm1 - 6*f1 + 3*f0))*x/FL(6.0);
}
```

For our sample program we will use linear interpolation as that gives reasonable results without too much complexity. In line with the general approach I am describing, we may have to reopen this area if it appears later that it is not good enough. To complete this, the nearest point interpolation can be written as

```
double waveform_ival(WAVEFORM w, double which)
{
    int x0 = (int)(which+0.5);
    double f0;
    f0 = waveform_val(w,x0);
    return f0;
}
```

and our main function becomes

```
void copywaveform(WAVEFORM w, SPEED s, OUTPUT out)
{
    double index = 0.0;
    int total_samps = (int)(T*sr);
    int size = waveform_size(w);
    for (i=0; i<total_samps; i++) {
        double value = waveform_ival(w, index);
        index += size*s/sr;
        if (index >= size) index -= size;
        output_sample(out, value);
    }
}
```

It does not take much imagination to realize that there must be a fifth-degree (six-point) interpolation method, and that there must be higher-degree methods. The code tends to be rather complex and costly. Cubic is a good compromise. There are other, non-polynomial interpolation methods, but discussing these is beyond the real topic of this chapter. Interested readers are referred elsewhere.[18]

4.2.5 Output

So far we have largely ignored what we are going to do with the processed samples. In the initial description, I have said that the samples would be sent to the output and that is all. There are two major types of output that could have been meant; it could be expected to become a sound from speakers somewhere, or it may be expected to be stored in the computer as a file for later use. In either case the output has only to be initialized (or created), accept the samples, and possibly be closed down when the program has finished. If we were to use a library, then we would expect that the library would provide these three facilities, and possibly others we do not need. If we were to write our own output system we could, and should, act as if we were writing a library. The critical point, which appears repeatedly in the whole software design process, is "separation." We do not want the details of the output to, say, affect the calculation of the speed. The representation of the output could be a pointer to a `struct`, or an `int`, or almost anything. We would expect the functions

```
OUTPUT initialize_sound(. . .);
int output_sample(OUTPUT, double);
int close_sound(OUTPUT);
```

where the arguments to the initialization function could vary depending on the library. It may include things like the sample rate, sample size and format, the number of channels as well as choosing WAV or AIFF, or the sound card. The results of the other two functions are for error checking. A false value (that is zero) will mean that it failed.[19]

For this example application we are going to use and adapt Richard Dobson's ***Portsf***. The relevant functions in the library interface are `psf_sndCreate`, `psf_sndWriteFloatFrames`, and `psf_sndClose`. The output is represented by an `int`. In addition the library must be initialized with a call to `psf_init`.

We are now in a position to start some code. The file format has been fixed as standard monophonic WAV. The sample rate must come from the variable we have been using, `sr`. I have decided to use 16-bit samples, as they have in use for a long time. This does introduce a small difficulty, as the "natural" range for floating-point samples is from -1 and $+1$ while the equivalent range for 16-bit samples is from $-32,768$ to $+32,767$. We will deal with this with a little scaling inside the output function. If at some later stage it is decided to support other sample sizes, this code will have to be revisited. To implement these ideas, we can provide some functions:

```
typedef OUTPUT int; /* For Portsf library */

OUTPUT initialize_sound(char *name, int sr)
```

```
{
    PSF_PROPS inprops;

    inprops.srate = (long)sr;
    inprops.chans = 1L;
    inprops.samptype = PSF_SAMP_16;
    inprops.format = PSF_STDWAVE;
    inprops.chformat = MC_MONO;
    return psf_sndOpen(name, &inprops,0);
}

int output_sample(OUTPUT out, double sample)
{
    short buffer[1];
    buffer[0] = (short)(sample*32767.0);
    if (psf_sndWriteShortFrames(out, buffer, 1) != 1L)
        return 0;
    return 1;
}

int close_sound(OUTPUT out)
{
    psf_sndClose(out);
    return 1;
}
```

and we need to call `psf_init` in the main program. It is also a good idea to call the `close_sound` function at the end of the main program to ensure that the sounds are written to the disk (or to the output device if we were using a more advanced library).

4.3   User Interface

An aspect of the whole program that we have so far ignored is how the user of this program is going to specify which waveform to use, at what speed to play it back, and for how long. When this information is specified, we know what to do with it, with the program fragments previously developed. This aspect is often called the *user interface*. In some ways this is very important; it is the aspect of the program that is most obvious to the user community. Its style is what is remembered. In another way, it is the least important aspect. It does nothing, does not solve the problem, and computationally is usually simple.

We can compare the user interface to the ending of a musical piece. It may be what some of the audience remember, and so skill and artifice must be used, but that is not (usually) what the musical creation is about, or what is important. The interface is similar to a musical "hook." We need one.

There are two fundamentally different approaches to the user interface: the command-line approach and the graphical approach. Traditionally, the former has been favored by computer professionals[20] and the latter by consumers and users. From our standpoint, in designing this simple program, the graphical user interface (GUI) is much more complex to use, and if we have any intention of being cross-platform or platform-neutral, this introduces a large number of problems which we would rather not face at this time. We will develop a command-line system, and then consider briefly how this can be adapted to a GUI with simple tools.[21]

4.3.1   The Command-Line Interface

In designing the user interface the same design technique can be used. We need to identify what information the user needs to specify, and what we should do if this information is omitted. We have already made a start on this when we said that the user of this program is going to specify which waveform to use, at what speed to play it back, and for how long. Identifying the nouns provides three entities that must be defined: the waveform, the speed, and the length. For each of these we can consider the kinds of value we might expect integers, floating-point numbers, characters, or character strings. When we have thought of the range we are willing to accept, we can consider the programming aspects. The fourth entity that I did not mention in the original design is the "name of the output" file to receive the results.

Let us consider the three items in turn. The first is the waveform. Looking back at our analysis, the waveform comes either from a file or from a mathematical formula. The file would be naturally specified by its name, which is a character string, but with the formula it is not obvious what to do. We could use a name like 'sine' to stand for that formula, surreptitiously limiting the names we can use for files. An alternative would to make the formulae a fifth item to be specified, as long as we checked that both were not given, or more weakly we documented which one took precedence in that case. Which one we choose is largely a matter of personal style. No doubt there are experts[22] who can produce learned reasons in favor of either. I am going to choose the second version, mainly because I do not like the restriction of names. You may of course disagree, in which case you will have to reconstruct this section to suit your own concepts.

We conclude that the waveform can have an external (to the program) representation of a file name as a character string. The mathematical formula could be represented either by an integer (1 for sine, 2 for cosine) or a name. To my mind there is no obvious way of relating the formulae to numbers,[23] so I will use a character string. This is also easily extensible if we decide to introduce sawtooth waves or square waves later. (See exercises.) As these are different specifications to the file names there is no potential for the interface language changing, as might happen if we had used a single name, and suddenly more file names had a different meaning.

The speed of playback has a natural representation in hertz in our program, and as this is a terminology that we may hope our target user community may be familiar with, I am going to specify the speed as a floating-point number in hertz. You should not however think that this is the only possible choice. If we were expecting the program to be used within a mainstream western musical context, we might think note names more appropriate (A for 440 Hz, and so on for A#, B, C, C#, ...). If the use is expected to be within MIDI systems, the MIDI note number might be a candidate.

The length of time to play the sound is naturally thought of in seconds, and so a floating-point representation suggests itself. Again there are alternatives. We could restrict ourselves to integer numbers of seconds, or we could specify the integer number of times we should scan the waveform. While these may seem less useful, it does depend on the use we are expecting. You may also note that the program itself is not really affected. The interface could easily translate the external specification into something very different for internal use. The last item, the output file name, is similar to the waveform name.

The next stage in designing the command-line interface is to determine how we are going to know which item is which. There are two basic forms: *positional* and *tagged*. In a positional system, we decree that the items must appear in a fixed order, which we must document. In a tagged system, the items appear after some kind of symbol to identify how it is to be interpreted. (And of course there are hybrid systems, where some arguments are tagged and some are positional.) A simple rule of thumb is that if an argument is always required, then making it positional is probably acceptable. A few options can be positional, but are usually better tagged. (If you look at the command of UNIX or the DOS component of Windows, you will see these options used, and not always in a consistent fashion.) As the waveform and formula are alternatives it seems logical that they should be tagged. The speed and length could be positional, but I would prefer to make them both *optional*, with default values of 440 Hz and 3 seconds. I seem to have come to an all-tagged solution; and that decision was based on both my experience and my belief of how my program will be used. For now I suggest that you accept it and we see how it goes. What we do need to decide is how to tag the information. There are a number of tagging systems in general use. In traditional UNIX, the normal method is to introduce a *tag* with a "minus sign," and the tag is a single character. In DOS a similar system is used, except that a solidus (/) introduces the tag. In GNU/ Linux there is an increasing use of a double minus followed by a word to introduce a tag (e.g. `--waveform`). For this program I am going to use the single minus tradition, and so I will use `-w`, `-f`, `-s`, `-t`, and `-o` to introduce the `waveform`, `formula`, `speed`, `duration`, and the `output`, respectively.

Remember that in a standard C implementation the command-line arguments are available in an array of strings, usually called `argv`, and that there is a count in an `int` variable called `argc`. The count includes the name of the program as the first value (stored in `argv[0]`). To decode the command line, we have to loop through the arguments, see what they are, and act accordingly. We look at the next item, see that it begins with a `-`, and then

see which argument it describes. The code is familiar to most programmers from the UNIX
tradition:

```c
double duration = 3.0;
double speed = 440.0;
char *output = NULL;
char *wavename = NULL;
int formula = -1;
enum ARG_RES {WAVEFORM_GIVEN, FORMULA_GIVEN};
typedef enum ARG_RESE ARG_RES;

ARG_RES decode_arguments(int argc, char **argv)
{
    int i = 0;
    char *a = argv[0];
    while (--argc) {
        a = argv[i];
        if (a[0]=='-') { /* tag found */
            switch (a[1]) {
                case 'w': /* Waveform */
                    if (argc == 0) {
                        printf("No waveform argument\n"); exit(1);
                    }
                    wavename = argv[i+1];
                    argc--; i += 2;
                    break;
                case 'f':
                    if (argc == 0) {
                        printf("No waveform argument\n"); exit(1);
                    }
                    if (strcmp(argv[i+1], "sine")==0)
                        formula = SINE;
                    else if (strcmp(argv[i+1], "cosine")==0)
                        formula = COSINE;
                    else {
                        printf("No valid formula name\n"); exit(1);
                    }
                    argc--; i += 2;
                    break;
                case 's':
                    if (argc == 0) {
                        printf("No speed given\n"); exit(1);
                    }
                    speed = atof(argv[i+1]);
```

```
                    argc--; i += 2;
                    break;
                case 't':
                    if (argc == 0) {
                        printf("No duration given\n"); exit(1);
                    }
                    duration = atof(argv[i+1]);
                    argc--; i += 2;
                    break;
                case 'o':
                    if (argc == 0) {
                        printf("No output argument\n"); exit(1);
                    }
                    output = argv[i+1];
                    argc--; i += 2;
                    break;
            }
        }
        else {
            printf("No tag found\n"); exit(1);
        }
    }
    /* Now the checks */
    if (output == NULL) {
        printf("No output file given\n"); exit(1);
    }
    if (waveform == NULL && formula == -1) {
        printf("Neither waveform nor formula specified\n"); exit(1);
    }
    if (waveform != NULL && formula != -1) {
        printf("Both waveform and formula specified\n"); exit(1);
    }
    if (waveform == NULL) return FORMULA_GIVEN;
    else return WAVEFORM_GIVEN;
}
```

There are a variety of different forms to this function. One common interface is to allow either -t 10 or -t10. Modifying this program to allow that format is not very hard, and you might like to think about how to do it.

4.3.2 Graphical User Interface

The major issue with graphical user interfaces is that every platform has a different way of dealing with and supporting graphics. One way to overcome this is to use a different programming system, one that is designed entirely to deal with user interfaces. There are a small number of these; the simplest in many ways is Tcl/Tk.[24] The language is slow to run, and to some eyes it produces a rather simplistic and dull interface. Still, it is easy to create a prototype interface, and if we already have the complete command-line interface then we can use Tcl/Tk to call the existing program.[25]

The following fragment provides a form into which a user can type waveform names or output names, select a formula, and/or give duration and speed. This form is used to call the program we have been developing with a suitable command line. We have assumed that our C program is called *waveform*.

```
message .title -width 10c -justify center \
    -text "Waveform Interface"
pack .title
set formula 0
radiobutton .f0 -text "none" -variable formula -value 0
radiobutton .f1 -text "sine" -variable formula -value 1
radiobutton .f2 -text "cosine" -variable formula -value 2
pack .f0 .f1 .f2
set waveform ""
message .tw -width 10c -justify center -text "waveform"
entry .w -width 25 -relief sunken -borderwidth 2 \
    -textvariable waveform
pack .tw .w
set output ""
message .to -width 10c -justify center -text "output"
entry .o -width 25 -relief sunken -borderwidth 2 \
    -textvariable output
pack .to .o
set speed -1
message .ts -width 10c -justify center -text "speed"
entry .s -width 25 -relief sunken -borderwidth 2 \
    -textvariable speed
pack .ts .s
set duration -1
message .tt -width 10c -justify center -text "duration"
entry .t -width 25 -relief sunken -borderwidth 2 \
    -textvariable duration
pack .tt .t
button .ok -text "OK" -command do_it
button .bad -text "Exit" -command exit
pack .ok -side left
pack .bad -side right
```

```
proc do_it {} {
    global formula; global waveform
    global output;
    global speed; global duration
    set cc(0) "./waveform"
        set cnt 1
        if { $formula == 1} {
            set cc(1) "-f"
            set cc(2) "sine"
            set cnt 3
            } else {
                if { $formula == 2} {
                    set cc(1) "-f"
                    set cc(2) "cosine"
                    set cnt 3
                }
            }
            if { $waveform != ""} {
                set cc($cnt) "-w"
                incr cnt 1
                set cc($cnt) "$waveform"
                incr cnt 1
            }
            if { $output != ""} {
                set cc($cnt) "-o"
                incr cnt 1
                set cc($cnt) "$output"
                incr cnt 1
            }
            if { $speed != -1} {
                set cc($cnt) "-s"
                incr cnt 1
                set cc($cnt) "$speed"
                incr cnt 1
            }
            if { $duration != -1} {
                set cc($cnt) "-t"
                incr cnt 1
                set cc($cnt) "$duration"
                incr cnt 1
            }
            if { $cnt == 1 } {
                exec $cc(0)
```

```
        } else {
            if { $cnt == 3 } {
                exec $cc(0) $cc(1) $cc(2)
            } else {
            if { $cnt == 5 } {
                exec $cc(0) $cc(1) $cc(2) $cc(3) $cc(4)
            } else {
                if { $cnt == 7 } {
                    exec $cc(0) $cc(1) $cc(2) $cc(3) \
                        $cc(4) $cc(5) $cc(6)
                } else {
                    if { $cnt == 9 } {
                        exec $cc(0) $cc(1) $cc(2) $cc(3) \
                            $cc(4) $cc(5) $cc(6) $cc(7) \
                            $cc(8)
                    } else {
                        if { $cnt == 11 } {
                            exec $cc(0) $cc(1) $cc(2) $cc(3) \
                                $cc(4) $cc(5) $cc(6) $cc(7) \
                                $cc(8) $cc(9) $cc(10)
                        }
                    }
                }
            }
        }
    }
    tk_messageBox -message "Success! Output file: $output" -icon info
}
```

As a C programmer you may understand some of this. The first section defines a number of buttons and text boxes that are packed into a display box. The "OK" button has the function do_it associated with it. This long but simple function constructs a call to exec with the command-line arguments. The exec function is very similar to the C function for calling an external programs execl(). This program is run using the Tcl/Tk interpreter wish.[26]

4.4   The Whole Program

We now have all the components of the program we started to write. The next stage is the assembly of the whole program. There are still some organizational decisions to make. The main one is between how many files to distribute the code. One could decide on a single file, but except for very simple programs, or "throw-away" programs, it is usually better to divide the program into logically connected units. The analysis process can be used for this as well. The first level of decomposition would be a suitable breakdown, and so we will have three files: one for the creation of waveforms, one for the playing of waveforms, and one for interface and control. There will also be the library code, with which we will link our code.

4.4.1 Creation

Collecting the code from above, we get the following, after adding a few forward declarations and including a header for the definitions of the types and functions:

```
#include "waveform.h"
#include <math.h>
WAVEFORM getnewform(int);
int readfile(WAVEFORM, FILE_HANDLE);
void put_val(WAVEFORM, int, double);
WAVEFORM getnewform(int);

enum ERRORS { ERR_NO_FILE=100,
              ERR_NO_COUNT,
              ERR_NO_DATA,
              ERR_NO_FORMULA,
              ERR_NO_MEMORY
};
void errormsg(char *format, enum ERRORS err)
{
    fprintf(stderr, format, (int)err);
    switch (err) {
    case ERR_NO_FILE:
        fprintf("\nfile not found\n");
        return;
    case ERR_NO_COUNT:
        fprintf("\nno count in file\n");
        return;
    case ERR_NO_DATA:
        fprintf("\ndata malformed\n");
        return;
    case ERR_NO_FORMULA:
        fprintf("\nnot a valis formula\n");
        return;
    case ERR_NO_MEMORY:
        return;
    }
}
```

```c
int lengthoffile(FILE_HANDLE file)
{
    FILE *ff = fopen(file, "r");
    int count;
    if (ff==NULL) return 0;
    if (fscanf(ff, "%d", &count)!=1) {
        fclose(ff);
        return 0;
    }
    fclose(ff);
    return count;
}

WAVEFORM readform(FILE_HANDLE file)
{
    WAVEFORM xx;
    int err;
    xx = getnewform(lengthoffile(file));
    if ((err=readfile(xx, file)) ==0) return xx;
    error("Failed to read wave form for reason %d", err);
    return NULL;
}

int readfile(WAVEFORM xx, FILE_HANDLE file)
{
    int count, i;
    double val;
    FILE *ff = fopen(file, "r");

    if (ff==NULL)
        return ERR_NO_FILE;
    if (fscanf(ff, "%d", &count)!=1)
        return ERR_NO_COUNT;
    for (i=0; i<count; i++) {
        if (fscanf(ff, "%f", &val)!=1)
            return ERR_NO_DATA;
        put_val(xx, i, val);
    }
    fclose(ff);
    return 0;
}

#define TRIG_SIZE (4096)
#define TWOPIBYSIZE (6.28318530718/(double)TRIG_SIZE)
WAVEFORM createformula(FORMULA trig)
```

```
{
    WAVEFORM xx = getnewform(TRIG_SIZE);
    int i;
    double val;

    for (i=0; i<TRIG_SIZE; i++) {
        if (trig==SINE)
            val = sin((double)i*TWOPIBYSIZE);
        else if (trig==COSINE)
            val = cos((double)i*TWOPIBYSIZE);
        else return NULL;
        put_val(xx, i, val);
    }
    xx->size = size;
    return xx;
}

WAVEFORM getnewform(int size)
{
    WAVEFORM xx =
        (WAVEFORM)malloc((size-1)*sizeof(double)+sizeof(WAVE));
    if (xx==NULL) {
        error("Failed to allocate memory\n");
        exit(1);
    }
    return xx;
}

void put_val(WAVEFORM xx, int i, double val)
{
    xx->samples[i] = val;
}
```

This is still not satisfactory as production level code, as it is totally without comments. As we have developed the code, the comments we did not provide can be found in the text of this chapter. So we can now revisit the final program and transfer the salient points of this discussion into the code. As one gets more experience, this happens as one writes; but it should not be neglected. In large projects sometimes the comments may be references to some formal design document.

The header file, which includes the types and main declarations, is as follows:

```
#include <stdio.h>

enum FORMULAE { SINE, COSINE};
typedef enum FORMULAE FORMULA;
```

```
typedef struct WaveForm {
    int size;
    double samples[1];
} WAVE;
typedef WAVE *WAVEFORM;

typedef char *FILE_HANDLE;

typedef double SPEED;

typedef int OUTPUT; /* For Portsf library */

#define sr (44100)

WAVEFORM readform(FILE_HANDLE);

WAVEFORM createformula(FORMULA);

void copywaveform(WAVEFORM, SPEED, OUTPUT, double);
```

4.4.2 Output Waveforms

The second major section of the program deals with the output from the waveforms stored by the previous section. In addition to the header for this project we need to include the header for the *Portsf* library that we will use. Apart from that, the program code is just a collection of the fragments we have developed above.

```
#include "waveform.h"

#include "portsf.h"

double waveform_val(WAVEFORM, int);
int output_sample(OUTPUT, double);

void copywaveform(WAVEFORM w, SPEED s, OUTPUT out, double T)
{
    double index = 0.0;
    int total_samps = (int)(T*sr);
    int size = waveform_size(w);
    int i;
    for (i=0; i<total_samps; i++) {
        double value = waveform_ival(w, index);
        index += size*sr/s;
        if (index >= size) index -= size;
        output_sample(out, value);
    }
}
```

```
int waveform_size(WAVEFORM w)
{
    return w->size;
}

double waveform_val(WAVEFORM w, int which)
{
    return w->samples[which];
}

double waveform_ival(WAVEFORM w, double which)
{
    int x0 = (int)which;
    int x1 = (int)(which+1.0);
    double f0, f1;
    if (x1>=waveform_size(w)) x1 = 0;
    f0 = waveform_val(w,x0);
    f1 = waveform_val(w,x1);
    return f0 + (f1 - f0)*(which-x0);
}

OUTPUT initialize_sound(char *name, int srate)
{
    PSF_PROPS inprops;

    inprops.srate = (long)srate;
    inprops.chans = 1L;
    inprops.samptype = PSF_SAMP_16;
    inprops.format = PSF_STDWAVE;
    inprops.chformat = MC_MONO;
    return psf_sndOpen(name, &inprops,0);
}

int output_sample(OUTPUT out, double sample)
{
    short buffer[1];
    buffer[0] = (short)(sample*32767.0);
    if (psf_sndWriteShortFrames(out, buffer, 1) != 1L)
        return 0;
    return 1;
}

int close_sound(OUTPUT out)
{
    psf_sndClose(out);
    return 1;
}
```

4.4.3   The Main Program

The final section of the program is the top level, the main function, which includes decoding of the arguments. I am only considering the C component, so the code is simple:

```c
#include "waveform.h"

#include "portsf.h"
#include <string.h> /* for strcmp */
#include <stdlib.h> /* for atof */

double duration = 3.0;
double speed = 440.0;
char *output = NULL;
char *wavename = NULL;
int formula = -1;
enum ARG_RESE {WAVEFORM_GIVEN, FORMULA_GIVEN};
typedef enum ARG_RESE ARG_RES;

/* Decode the command line and indicate which style of input is
   given */
ARG_RES decode_arguments(int argc, char **argv)
{
    int i = 0;
    char *a = argv[0];
    while (--argc) {
        a = argv[i];
        if (a[0]=='-') { /* tag found */
            switch (a[1]) {
            case 'w': /* Waveform */
                if (argc == 0) {
                    printf("No waveform argument\n"); exit(1);
                }
                wavename = argv[i+1];
                argc--; i += 2;
                break;
            case 'f': /* formula name */
                if (argc == 0) {
                    printf("No waveform argument\n"); exit(1);
                }
                if (strcmp(argv[i+1], "sine")==0)
                    formula = SINE;
                else if (strcmp(argv[i+1], "cosine")==0)
                    formula = COSINE;
                else { /* we do not have this function yet */
```

```
                        printf("No valid formula name\n"); exit(1);
                }
                argc--; i += 2;
                break;
            case 's':
                if (argc == 0) {
                    printf("No speed given\n"); exit(1);
                }
                speed = atof(argv[i+1]);
                argc--; i += 2;
                break;
            case 't':
                if (argc == 0) {
                    printf("No duration given\n"); exit(1);
                }
                duration = atof(argv[i+1]);
                argc--; i += 2;
                break;
            case 'o':
                if (argc == 0) {
                    printf("No output argument\n"); exit(1);
                }
                output = argv[i+1];
                argc--; i += 2;
                break;
            }
        }
        else {
            printf("No tag found\n"); exit(1);
        }
    }
    /* Now the checks */
    if (output == NULL) {
        printf("No output file given\n"); exit(1);
    }
    if (wavename == NULL && formula == -1) {
        printf("Neither waveform nor formula specified\n");
        exit(1);
    }
    if (wavename != NULL && formula != -1) {
        printf("Both waveform and formula specified\n");
        exit(1);
    }
```

```
        if (wavename == NULL) return FORMULA_GIVEN;
        else return WAVEFORM_GIVEN;
}

int main(int argc, char **argv)
{
        int format = decode_arguments(argc, argv);
        OUTPUT ff;
        WAVEFORM xx;
        psf_init();
        if (format==WAVEFORM_GIVEN)
            xx = readform(wavename);
        else
            xx = createformula(formula);
        ff = initialize_sound(output, sr);

        copywaveform(xx, speed, ff, duration);
        close_sound(ff);
        return 0;
}
```

4.4.4 Compiling and Linking with the Library

The last stage in the creation of the program is to arrange that it all gets compiled and linked with the library. The details of how to achieve this goal depend somewhat on the operating system and the compiler suite you are using. If you are using Visual Studio Express on Windows or Xcode on the Macintosh, you expect to use the provided IDE. I, on the other hand, have been writing this program on a GNU/Linux machine, and so I expect to write my own Makefile.

The creation of Makefiles is sometimes considered a black art, but if the application is not too complex it is not really that complex or difficult. The Makefile consists of rules with three parts: what we want to create, what needs to exist previously, and how to perform the task. The main pitfall is that the tab character is considered to be different from a sequence of single-character spaces.[27]

I have called the three files *rd.c*, *out.c*, and *main.c*. So, at least for GNU/Linux, the rules are as follows:

```
rd.o: rd.c waveform.h
   cc -c -g rd.c

out.o: out.c waveform.h portsf.h
   cc -c -g out.c

main.o: main.c waveform.h portsf.h
   cc -c -g main.c
```

where the lines with initial spaces (e.g. 'cc -c -g rd.c' actually start with tabs. You will see that the object files depend on the sources and the headers. The make program is ensures that if a file is changed (as shown by a date change) then things that depend on it will be rebuilt. The target is before the colon, the dependencies are on the same line, and the commands are on a number of lines that start with a tab. The default target is the first rule, so we may add an initial rule:

```
waveform: rd.o out.o main.o portsf.a
    cc -o waveform rd.o out.o main.o portsf.a -lm
```

This assumes that the library exists, but just for completeness I have added lines to create the library; these could be improved but are sufficient for now. The whole makefile becomes

```
waveform: rd.o out.o main.o portsf.a
    cc -o waveform rd.o out.o main.o portsf.a -lm

rd.o: rd.c waveform.h
    cc -c -g rd.c

out.o: out.c waveform.h portsf.h
    cc -c -g out.c

main.o: main.c waveform.h portsf.h
    cc -c -g main.c

portsf.a: portsf.c ieee80.c portsf.h ieee80.h
    cc -c portsf.c
    cc -c ieee80.c
    ar rv portsf.a portsf.o ieee80.o
    rm portsf.o ieee80.o
```

4.5 Principles of Testing

It is tempting to think that we have finished, but that would be too easy. We have not checked in any way that the program works. Privately I have run the make command[28] and had no errors in the build. I also have run it with no arguments and got the message No output file given (which was true). But that is hardly enough to give one any sense of confidence or belief in the program. We have to test it.

In the field of software engineering, testing is a process that has its own methodologies and language. This is not the time to go into great detail, but there are a few basic lessons to learn.

The main purpose of testing it to see that the program does what the initial specification of the program asked for. Obviously, if we had been asked to design and build a waveform player it would not be acceptable to deliver a Web browser, even if it was a good Web browser. The purpose of systematic testing it to ensure that we have written the correct program; which is to say that it does what it was asked, and that it satisfies other, often un-written requirements: not crashing, possibly running at a sufficient speed, or using limited machine resources. In our case we need to ensure that it can read a waveform, or create one from all of our formulae, and that it can create the output specified. This is where we hit the first problem. Except in trivial cases, we cannot test all possible inputs, so we must select examples that we think will typify all. It also shows that when we run a test, we should have determined in advance what output we expect. Formal testing methods want: a list of tests, reasons for the tests, and the expected outcome of the tests; but we can be a little less formal for this simple program.

In this process, we realize the fact that since not "all" inputs can be tested, testing can show the existence of bugs but not the absence of bugs. Thus, if we test it carefully and thoroughly, we may have confidence in the program, but we cannot be certain that there are no bad cases. The only way to achieve that is via the processes of *program proving*, and that is both hard and currently unreliable. There is a technique called *bebugging* where a known number of errors are deliberately inserted into a program before the testers start (who must be a different team of programmers). If the testers find all the inserted bugs then we may believe that they have been thorough, and they are unlikely to be unknown bugs remaining. If the testers only find half the inserted bugs, then they probably only found about half of the unknown ones.

There are two main styles of testing: *white-box* and *black-box*. In black-box testing, the testers are not allowed to look at the code, but test the whole program, as if it were an opaque black box, to see if it conforms with the specification. In white-box testing, the testers are allowed to look at the code, and so devise tests aimed at specific components. Typically these are loops which might be "off by one," running either one time too many or one time too few. This type of error is also known as a *fencepost problem*.[29]

So to test our program we need to devise a small set of examples, the results of which we know. I suggest that there are two basic cases we need to address—the formula and the "read-in" wave. To test the formulae, we need to specify both sine and cosine, and to output it at a small number of frequencies. As long as we can plot the output with a sound editor we should be able to see that the output is the correct function, and we should be able to test that the frequency is the requested value. For the file-based input we could use a sine wave, and compare it with the formula system, and use square-waves and impulse waves which should allow the results to be easily examined.

4.5.1 Initial Tests

The first test is to create a sine wave by formula:

```
waveform -f sine -o xxx.wav
```

If we try this, we get the error message No tag found. That is not what we want, so there is an error that we must fix before we can perform any more testing. Looking at the code, we see that that this error message comes from the function decode_arguments, so we will look there first.

There are about three main techniques for finding the source of bugs. The best is to think. The second, and perhaps most common, is to add print statements at various places in the program; this can generate rather a lot of information, and then one needs to resort to thinking again. The third method is to do a paper calculation of what the computer should do—a simple variant of this is to use *single stepping* of the program, either at the source or at the binary level.

Using this method, just by reading the code I saw one error; the first argument to be decoded was argv[0], which is the program name, rather that argv[1]. We started the variable i from 0 rather than 1. We can correct this, recompile, and try again. As is common, our first error was a fencepost error.

Our second attempt is more encouraging; the program runs to completion, but on looking for the output there is none. This suggests that the program has generated the answers, but either we did not output them or we have not created the output file correctly. A little more thought suggests the later, as there is no file generated at all. Either it was not opened correctly, or was not closed correctly. We will start by looking at the functions initialize_sound that opens the output file, and close_sound that terminates it. Finding the error may be quick for you, but for me it took quite a time. My program has misused the **Portsf** library; I have called the function to read a soundfile rather than the function to create a new soundfile. Before correcting this error, it is worth reflecting on how it was made. Was it bad documentation in the library, or carelessness on my part? Figuring out this mistake now, we may be able to ensure that we do not make the same mistake again, or at the very least recognize it quicker next time. Actually in this case, it is a personal problem of mild dyslexia; I frequently have problems distinguishing in and out, and read and write, and I tend to flip them.

Fixing the code is now a bit more complex. The function we wanted was psf_sndCreate. It takes two more arguments: a minimum header and an access code. My revised function is now

```
OUTPUT initialize_sound(char *name, int srate)
{
    PSF_PROPS inprops;

    inprops.srate = (long)srate;
    inprops.chans = 1L;
    inprops.samptype = PSF_SAMP_16;
    inprops.format = PSF_STDWAVE;
    inprops.chformat = MC_MONO;
    return psf_sndCreate(name, &inprops, 0, 0, PSF_CREATE_RDWR);
}
```

Now I can rebuild (remake) and retest. This time I get output. Looking at it with a sound editor such as Audacity, I see that it is a sine wave, it is 3 seconds long, and the default frequency sounds correct. To confirm that the frequency output "is" correct, my next test is

```
waveform -o xxx.wav -f sine -s 10
```

This should produce a 3-second sine wave at 10 Hz. Counting up to 10 cycles in a second is easy, and it worked as expected.

Further experiments I made with the -t also seem to work, as do tests with `cosine`:

```
./waveform -o xxx.wav -f cosine -s 2 -t 1
```

Testing the file input is the next stage. First we need to create a suitable input file. There are many ways of doing this but my way would be to write a small program. I suppose it could be argument that we ought to do a formal design exercise for this, but I am not going to. We can create a 1,024-point sine wave using the code from `createformula`:

```
#define SIZE (1024)
#define TWOPIBYSIZE (6.28318530718/(double)SIZE)
int main(void)
{
 int i;
 printf("%d\n", SIZE);
 for (i=0; i<SIZE; i++)
 printf("%f\n", sin((double)i*TWOPIBYSIZE));
}
```

Testing with this wavetable worked. We can build and run this as shown below:

```
cc -o sine1024 create_test.c
```

```
./sine1024
```

```
./sine1024 > sine1024.txt
```

```
./waveform -o xxx.wav -w sine1024.txt -s 4 -t 2
```

```
./waveform -o xxx.wav -w sine1024.txt -s 440 -t 2
```

There are still a number of tests that should be considered, but for now this will do.

4.5.2 Maintenance and Development

After initial testing, a program is rarely finished. In use, a program can be seen to have deficiencies in design, or new requirements may emerge. Even in our simple program one might wish to add more formulae, or improve the user interface with respect to checking. This is the area of maintenance.

Whenever a report is received about a deficiency in the program, one must distinguish a *bug report* from a *new feature request*. After the release of a program, reported bugs are an indication of a testing failure or a testing weakness. Getting a small, simple bug example is a useful exercise. It is much easier to find a bug in a small program rather than one that exercises more of the code. The other advantage is that the example can be kept for future testing. This is called *reversion testing*, where a new version is run against all previously reported errors; it is quite amazing how errors that one thinks they have fixed can reappear. Over time this can strengthen the test suite. Finding bugs is much the same as in the testing process: thinking, printing, and stepping.

Developing new facilities can be a little different. It can be useful to revisit the design documentation to see how the facility fits within the overall design. If, for example, there is a request for a formula for a square wave (if we do not concern ourselves with issues of band-limiting), then it will be clear that we need to change decode_arguments so we can recognize the word 'square':

```
case 'f':
    if (argc == 0) {
        printf("No waveform argument\n"); exit(1);
    }
    if (strcmp(argv[i+1], "sine")==0)
        formula = SINE;
    else if (strcmp(argv[i+1], "cosine")==0)
        formula = COSINE;
    else if (strcmp(argv[i+1], "square")==0)   /* New code */
        formula = SQUARE;
    else {
        printf("No valid formula name\n"); exit(1);
    }
    argc--; i += 2;
    break;
case 's':
 if (argc == 0) {
 printf("No speed given\n"); exit(1);
 }
. . .
```

We would have to extend the enumeration type in *waveform.h*:

```
enum FORMULAE { SINE, COSINE, SQUARE};
```

And we would have to make a small change in createformula:

```
for (i=0; i<TRIG_SIZE; i++) {
    if (trig==SINE)
```

```
        val = sin((double)i*TWOPIBYSIZE);
    else if (trig==COSINE)
        val = cos((double)i*TWOPIBYSIZE);
    else if (trig==SQUARE)   /* New code */
        val = (i<TRIG_SIZE/2 ? 1.0 : -1.0);
    else return NULL;
    put_val(xx, i, val);
}
```

We can see from the design that this is all that would be required if we wanted to add square waves to the test system.[30]

If the requested development is more extensive, such as changing the output to optionally generate sound directly, then the design documents show what components need to be changed and which will still be functional. Consider some developments to the system, such as other formulae. Also consider how difficult is would be to add a band-limited version of the square wave. In software development there is always a possibility that a requested change would be so great that it does not fit the overall design. In this case it will be a judgment call based on experience whether to expand the current design (a redesign), to refuse to implement the feature, or to design a whole new program.

Another aspect of maintenance that is problematic is to review the whole program and consider if there are any oddities of inefficiencies. In the program above, I noticed that the design of the reading of waveforms from a file has an inelegance and inefficiency. We open the file to read the length of the form in the function `lengthoffile`, and then close the file, only to reopen it in `readfile`. There are two attitudes to this kind of thing; the first is summarized in the phrase "If it ain't broke, don't fix it." The second is to view such things as design failures, and as a maintenance activity this is an area of the code to redesign and rebuild. Doing this is left as an exercise.

4.6   Conclusion

In this chapter we have followed the processes by which we can go from an idea for a program, through design by object refinement, to a working program that is tested and so we have reasonable confidence in its accuracy. The traditional model of software development acknowledges that half of the effort goes into continuing maintenance and development, which is often not apparent when caught up in the difficulties of learning to write a program at all. We have seen how the design document can be a continuing help, in understanding errors and in guiding the long-term maintenance of the system. Programs are rarely finished, and frequently live for many years.[31] A good design is a firm foundation on which to build, or even survive.

4.7   Exercises

Exercise 4.7.1

The waveform program does not have any control of amplitude (or gain, or volume). Design a new user interface option and implement a way of changing the amplitude of the output.

Exercise 4.7.2

A useful addition to the program is a "help—usage" message, printing options (tags) and their use. This can be printed when a wrong option is used, or when the program is given no arguments. Design and implement a solution to add this functionality to the program.

Exercise 4.7.3

Currently, our program produces sounds a wave table that is defined in a file or by a formula. The latter is limited to 'sine' or 'cosine,' as well as non-band-limited 'square'. Extend these options to incorporate band-limited sawtooth (harmonics with a $1/N$ weight, where N is harmonic number), square ($1/N$ but only odd harmonics), and triangle (odd harmonics, $1/N^2$) using a Fourier series method. Note that some design decisions will have to be made: How many harmonics? How would they be defined? How to set up the user interface?

Exercise 4.7.4

Design a third modification to the program that will apply a trapezoidal amplitude envelope to the sound output. This envelope is characterized by a rise time, when the amplitude goes from 0 to the maximum; and a decay time, calculated backward from the end of the total duration, when the amplitude goes from maximum to 0. (Hint: the amplitude control added in exercise 1 will now need to be a time-varying function.)

Notes

1. *Representation*: We say that a waveform must be "represented" in the computer rather than simply put into the computer. At the most basic level, a digital computer can only store binary bit-patterns. Thus, if we are storing numbers, characters or more complex entities, like fragments of audio, we need to decide how to represent these complex entities in this trivial binary format. Languages like C provide direct representation for numbers and characters; but representing anything more complex must be constructed from numbers and characters using the *arrays* and *structs* of C. We distinguish the *abstract* from the *concrete* representation of an object. An *abstract* representation concerns the way an object is built from simpler components; whereas a *concrete* representation directly concerns the mapping of the abstract representation to numbers, characters, and bit patterns.

2. In saying this, I am consciously using the title of Donald Knuth's seminal work, *The Art of Computer Programming*. It remains one of the professional programmer's main references. The title itself reflects the fact that while there may be technology or even science in the subject, at the heart of a computer program is inspiration and intelligent design. Like a painter when choosing and creating the perfect blend

of colors; or the composer's brilliant orchestration of a beautiful melody, a good programmer makes good choices. And these "good choices" are informed by both knowledge and experience. If you really want to go deeply into programming, Knuth's multi-volume work is required reading; but beware that Knuth is a mathematician, and the book can be daunting to the algebraically and numerically challenged.

3. I can try! The first form might make it easier to have multiple waveforms in existence, and if we ever wish to extend the program to include mixing of different waveforms, then I suspect that this formulation will make it easier. The second form still begs the question of how one creates an empty representation, and so will lead to another function being required. Also, I have had a mathematical education that has emphasized the function as creating things rather than modifying things. I can well understand that you may have the other view, and you are entitled to it. However you will have to do the exercise of reproducing this chapter with the other decision.

4. *Specification*: A clear description of what the program is to do, either in text or possibly using some formal system.

5. There is a whole area of computing, algebraic computation, which is concerned with the representation and manipulation of algebraic forms. Its scope is beyond this book, but the interested reader may find interest in a rather old paper (David Barton and John Fitch, "The Application of Symbolic Algebra Systems to Physics," *Reports on Progress in Physics* 35, 1972: 235–314) or in a more detailed book (James Davenport, Yvon Siret, and Evelyne Tournier, *Computer Algebra, Systems and Algorithms for Algebraic Computation*, Academic Press, 1993).

6. Of course we could write a program to generate the program, but then this new program must be finite; we could have a tower of such programs creating programs, but the tower must be finite to qualify as an algorithm.

7. Strictly we do not require finite time, but if we are generating an infinite sequence, like the primes, the nth answer must appear in finite time.

8. This is not a deduction, but is actually a design decision. It would be possible to create a design that started with an empty waveform and, as it was defined from the file, its internal representation changed and expanded to the given size. I chose not to do things that way, as my experience tells me that that is likely to be more complex that the version in the text, and I like to write the simple solutions first, and reconsider the issue later if necessary. The methodology does however identify and isolate these decisions, so if I do decide to revisit this decision, then I have an idea of how much of the program will be affected.

9. I take this format for simplicity, but if one wanted to have a sample rate as part of the file then that is an easy extension and you may like to consider how much it changes the overall program. I just decided to maintain simplicity at this initial stage. I like the evolutionary development of software, whereby we add features in an incremental way, using the initial analysis as the guide. For now we will stick to monophonic samples.

10. This is certainly true in C89; more recent C standards have made changes in this area, but it is still better to avoid variable-sized arrays for cross-platform compilation.

11. I suppose strictly, as we posed the problem, only the first is a direct solution; but as when we started we were rather unclear as to what we meant, I feel that we can even at this late stage revise what we had in mind. Of course, if you object to this, you are at liberty to take the other route. You will need to modify the WAVEFORM representation to remember the initial speed, and similar changes will be needed in the sine and cosine functions. The other differences should become obvious as we progress.

12. You might like to think about this when the program is complete, and see if this decision added complexity, or was neutral.

13. I am reminded of a cartoon I saw in an Indian newspaper, where a teacher is saying: "The problems for the exam will be similar to those discussed in class. Of course the numbers will be different; but not all of them—Pi will still be 3.14159...."

14. You may ask why these are coded as functions rather than directly reading from the structures. The answer lies in the whole approach to software design we are using. The actions are logically separated from the representation, and we use these selector functions to provide the final link. This would allow a total change of the representation without changing the main code, and avoids the problems of searching for all relevant occurrences.

15. But this is the case. If the x is squared, then the function is a quadratic; if the x is cubed, then it is a cubic, and so forth. We will use these ideas in a short while.

16. In take two points to define a straight line, three points for a quadratic, four for a cubic and so forth. You might like to think about why this is so.

17. If you are excessively clever, you will realize that cubic interpolation can be done with only one point, but the code is even harder, and if you are willing to admit such poor waveforms then it is hardly worth bothering with interpolation.

18. For technical overviews, see the following: T. Laakso, V. Valimaki, M. Karjalainen, and U. Laine, "Splitting the Unit Delay," *IEEE Signal Processing Magazine* 13 (1996), no. 1: 30–60; R. Schafer and L. Rabiner, "A Digital Signal Processing Approach to Interpolation," *Proceedings of the IEEE* 61(1973, no. 6:. 692–702.

19. I am never certain whether to use true to mean success and false to mean failure or to use 0 to mean OK and a non-zero value to be an error code. This latter version is more general and extensible, but the simplicity of Boolean values is also attractive.

20. Geeks.

21. Yes they are "simple," but they will involve learning some new computer language.

22. I was told many years ago that 'expert' came from 'ex' (meaning used-to-be or has-been) and 'spurt' (meaning drip under pressure).

23. Why not 0 for sine and 1 for cosine?

24. Perl/Tk is perhaps more flexible, but with a much steeper initial learning curve, and systems like Qt can generate more aesthetically beautiful interfaces, but are also more complex. Tcl/Tk is well described in John K. Ousterhout's book *Tcl and the Tk Toolkit* (Addison-Wesley, 1994).

25. Superficially the Tcl language is like C, but in fact there are major differences.

26. If you have the Tcl script in a file called *interface.tcl*, and the waveform program is in the same directory, you can run this using the wish command: `$ wish interface.tcl`.

27. Stu Feldman, who invented the "Make" idea, admits that this was a mistake, but by the time he realized it, he had a user community of about 10 whom he did not want to upset. This is considered by some people to be one of the largest mistakes in the history of software development, as now thousands of programmers are confused by this decision.

28. To run make, provided you are in the same directory as your Makefile, just type: `$ make`. Once this is built, you can run your program by typing its name preceded by './' (to indicate you mean the program that is in the same directory you are in): `$ ./waveform`.

29. One possible source for this name is the problem of how many fence posts you need for a 100-yard-long fence with posts every yard.

30. Note that the square wave as defined here is non-band-limited as it contains "straight corners" at the transitions between −1 and 1. A better implementation would be to add band-limited square waves using the Fourier series (see exercises).

31. In the late 1960s I wrote an algebra system for use in my research into cosmology; the program survived and was used by a small community and myself for more than 20 years. My design was not good in many ways, and in fixing errors I frequently complained about the original author who did not know how to design, and left no documentation. Unfortunately, I was that original programmer. I am attempting to protect you from the pain I suffered from that program.

Audio Programming Essentials

5   Introduction to Digital Audio Signals

Victor Lazzarini

5.1   Signals

Signals can be defined as information carriers and, more compactly, as functions that can describe that information. In the case of music, signals are generally defined as one-dimensional functions of time, or sometimes space, but can also assume other forms. These functions will describe a pattern of variation of some parameter; in the case of musical signals, this parameter can be the pressure measured at a point in space, the velocity of air particles, voltage changes in a circuit, etc. The value of such functions at a certain time t is known as the signal amplitude. A function of time describing an arbitrary musical signal (which can be anything from a sinusoid to Stockhausen's *Kontakte*) is normally notated as $f(t)$ and read as function f of t. This means that we are interested in the pattern variations that are associated with the independent variable t, in this case, conventionally, the "passing time." Such functions can assume either continuous or discrete forms. The former occurs when the function is defined for all possible (infinitesimal) values of t, so it depends on continuous variables and describes a *continuous-time signal*. The latter is related to functions that are only defined for discrete values of t, representing sequences of values that make up a *discrete-time signal*. If certain conditions are met, these two types of signals can be considered equivalent.

Continuous-time functions whose output, the signal amplitude, is also a continuous value describe what is called an *analog* signal. Examples of such functions can be found in the air pressure measured at the tympanic membrane, the output voltage of a microphone, the magnetic imprints on an audio cassette tape. This type of signal cannot be handled by computers, which are limited by their available memory and internal data representations. In order to process audio in a computer, we will have to use a signal that is both discrete-time and discrete-amplitude, in other words, using a function whose output will assume only a certain number of discrete values. This type of signal is called a *digital signal*.

The class of discrete-time signals, to which digital signals belong, will be defined by functions in which the independent variable is not continuous, so that it can be treated as an index to a sequence of values. To avoid confusion, we can notate such functions as $f(n)$,

Table 5.1
A function table.

n	0	1	2	3	4	5	6	...
$f(n)$	0	-1	2	0	-2	0	4	...

where n, which represents time, is effectively a time index. Such discrete-time signals are sequences of values, as in

$$f(n) = \{0, -1, 2, 0, -2, 0, 4, \ldots\},$$

in which a value in the sequence can be accessed by its index n:

$$f(0) = 0, f(4) = -2.$$

A function table can also be built out of such functions—see table 5.1. Such structures can be useful to hold pre-calculated functions, so that the program has to do the math only once, after which it need only look up the function values in the table.

5.2   Digital Signals

As defined above, digital signals are discrete-time signals whose output will only assume a finite number of values, or states. They can be obtained from an analog signal by a process of sampling followed by quantization. The former operation measures and obtains values from the analog signal at discrete points in time. Each value is known as a *sample*. The output of this operation, which is a continuous-amplitude signal, is then passed through a quantizer. This assigns discrete states to each value of its input, producing a digital signal. The exact components and operation of an analog-to-digital converter (ADC) are not of interest here. However, it is important to investigate the two steps of sampling and quantization in order to gain an insight into the generated signal.

5.2.1   Sampling

For the type of discrete-time signals we will be discussing here, the sampling process is one of obtaining values off an input signal at evenly spaced time points. This means that the process is *periodic*, i.e. that it happens at a fixed time interval. The period of time that elapses between each sampling operation is called the *sampling period*. Its reciprocal, or the number of sampling operations in a given space of time, is the *sampling frequency* or *rate*. This is the fundamental attribute of the process, which will determine the amount of data that is obtained from the analog signal for a given signal duration.

Another consequence of this operation, directly related to the sampling rate, is that it limits the type of signals that can be successfully converted. This means that the output signals are effectively equivalent to their analog inputs, and that they can be recovered, or

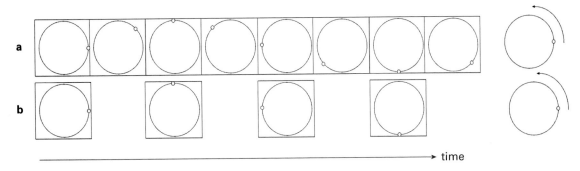

Figure 5.1
Snapshots from a rotating wheel: (a) 8 frames per cycle, (b) 4 frames per cycle.

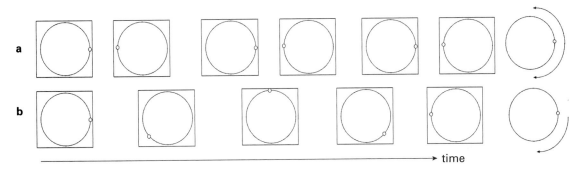

Figure 5.2
Snapshots from a rotating wheel: (a) 2 frames per cycle, (b) 1.75 frame per cycle.

re-converted, back into continuous-time counterparts. In order to understand this, let us use a visual metaphor for the sampling process.

Consider a steadily rotating wheel from which we take regular snapshots at a certain time interval (figure 5.1). This is equivalent to sampling, and the time interval between snapshots is the sampling period. If we take eight pictures each revolution, we will be picking up the movement of the wheel perfectly; if we animate the pictures at the right rate, we will see the wheel rotating at its original speed. Now let us reduce the number of pictures by half and pick up one snapshot out of every two. In this case, although we have increased the sampling interval (and reduced the sampling rate), we can still plot the rotating wheel's movement correctly.

If we double the sampling interval again, the speed of the wheel's rotation will still be plotted correctly (figure 5.2a). However, we seem to be at the limit, as now we are only picking up two different positions in its movement. In fact, there can be an ambiguity in relation to the direction of the wheel movement (clockwise or counterclockwise). Things start to go wrong here.

Consider now increasing the sampling interval by a small amount, by say 25 percent of the previous value (figure 5.2b). Now we will be picking up the wheel moving a little beyond halfway in relation to the start position in one sampling interval. The result is that it would appear as if the wheel is rotating in the opposite direction to which it was originally. On top of that, if we animate it at the right rate, the speed of the wheel will appear to be slower than what it was originally. In other words, our discrete-time representation of the rotating wheel is defective; it does not match the original continuous-time rotating wheel. This was rotating at a speed that was beyond what our sampling process could represent. This movement produced a signal that was impossible to represent in discrete-time using that particular sampling frequency, resulting in a misrepresentation, which is often referred to as aliasing. (On the DVD, you will find a simple animation program that demonstrates this principle.)

We have discovered the fundamental theorem of sampling that tells us that in order to pick up something that changes at a certain frequency, we need to use at least twice that frequency for sampling. The wheel moved at X rpm, we needed a sampling frequency of at least $2X$ shots per minute. Transferring this analogy to audio signals, we will see that the highest frequency that can be represented will be half the sampling frequency. The audio CD standard sets the sampling rate at 44,100 hertz (Hz), so it means that we will be able to encode signals up to 22,050 Hz. Since, for all practical purposes, our hearing will have a frequency range of 20–20,000 Hz, this should be enough to convert analog musical signals to discrete-time signals.

5.2.2   Quantization

So far we have been discussing discrete-time signals, which are not always digital. To make them digital, we will have to apply the operation of quantization to the output of the sampling process. This involves finding a numerical value that will represent the input signal, mapping it to that value. Digital conversion is an example of audio coding, because it involves an encoding (and decoding) process. It is important to bear that in mind, even though for practical reasons we tend to think that digital signals are the same as the analog ones our ears capture.

The numerical value that is the result of the encoding process will apply to a range of inputs. The process generally involves checking if an input falls within a particular region and then output the numerical code that corresponds to that region. There will be a finite number of regions or *quantizing levels* between the maximum and minimum values of an input signal. The number of them and their ranges will be determined by the form and precision of encoding. The most common types of digital signals, including the ones that are discussed in most parts this book, are generated using Pulse Code Modulation (PCM) encoding.

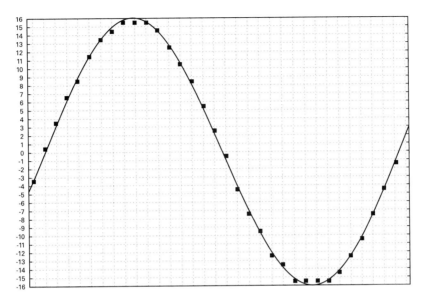

Figure 5.3
Linear PCM quantization using 5 bits (32 states) of a sinusoid. The squares indicate the samples output by the quantizer.

5.2.3 Pulse Code Modulation

Digital signals generated by PCM conversion have two basic characteristics:

1. The quantization process is linear. (The full name for PCM is Linear PCM.)
2. The numerical codes generated represent discrete signal amplitude steps, making it easy to understand and manipulate.

Linear quantization splits up the available amplitude range into a number of regions of equal width (figure 5.3). This can be seen as an equivalent to the sampling process, but now applied to the amplitudes, not the time. The number of regions used will depend on the available range of numbers for encoding, or, effectively, the number of bits allocated to each output value.

   Computer hardware uses a binary format to represent data, manipulating information on a basis of two states: on (1) and off (0). The aforementioned bit is the basic unit of information in the binary system; in fact it is short for 'binary digit'. In order to be able to represent more than two states, a computer uses a group of bits. For instance, a bit can only have two states (0 and 1), but two bits can have four states (00, 01, 10, and 11). In general, n bits can have 2^n unique states. Thus, with eight bits we can count from 0 to 255 (256 states), and with 16 bits we can have 65,536 states. For a bipolar signal, such as a waveform, conventionally the amplitude range in this case will be from $-32,768$ to $+32,767$. In the case of these signals, the maximum absolute amplitude is said to be 2^{n-1}. Encoding then can use any number of bits, which will determine the number of quantization levels. This process effectively means that there will be some loss of information along the way. The amount of loss will depend largely on the precision of the encoding, so that with more regions covering the signal amplitude range, the smaller the loss will be and the closer the output will be to the input.

The loss of information known as *quantization error* is the difference between the value output by the quantizer and the continuous-amplitude input. In PCM, we can assume that the quantized output will be equivalent to a continuous-value input at the center of the region. So the maximum error will happen when the detected value is at the boundary between two regions, or half the region width. The error will be then subject to the region width, which in turn is determined by the number of bits used in coding.

Quantization error is generally described as system noise and thus can determine the signal-to-noise ratio (SNR) of a digital signal. The SNR can be described, in simple terms,[1] as the ratio of the maximum absolute signal amplitude (2^{n-1}, with region width 1 and a bipolar signal) to the maximum quantization error (0.5):

$$\text{SNR} = \frac{2^{n-1}}{0.5} = 2^n.$$

It is often more common to express the SNR in terms of signal pressure (amplitude) levels (SPL), in the dB scale, which is equivalent to the root-mean-square (RMS) level of a signal. This is defined as 20 times the base-10 logarithm of the SNR, as in the following equation:

$$\text{SNR}_{\text{dB}} = 20 \log_{10} 2^n = n \times 20 \log_{10} 2 = 6.02 \times n.$$

Thus, for 24-bit PCM we would have roughly 144 dB of dynamic range. However, this indicates the maximum SNR, and applies only to a full-scale signal (using all the possible range); the actual value will decrease with the signal level. This is because the average amount of quantization error, and thus the noise amplitude, is generally said to be constant and independent of the signal amplitude. Lower signal amplitudes would be more severely affected by noise. This is one of the most problematic aspects of linear PCM.

On the upside, PCM gives us signals that are easy to understand and comparable to their analog counterparts. In an analog signal, such as a continuous waveform, we have a quantity (amplitude) that varies continuously in time. In PCM, we have equivalently the same signal, except that amplitudes are defined discretely and the signal is a sequence of such amplitudes. We can assume that, if the conditions for equivalence are met, we are dealing with similar types of signals. This effectively means that many concepts that were evolved to deal with analog signals can be easily adapted to deal with PCM signals. Unless, otherwise stated, we will assume PCM encoding for all digital signals discussed in this book.

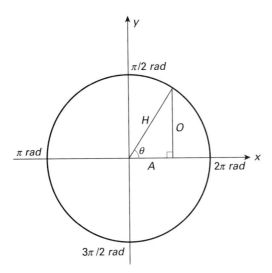

Figure 5.4
The trigonometric circle.

5.3   Simple Signals: Sinusoids

A very basic type of musical signal is the sinusoid waveform. In fact, it is so basic that we can describe more complicated signals as collections or sums of sinusoids. So it is a signal that is worth investigating. The sinusoid is a general name given to waves that have a particular shape, of which the sine and cosine waves are special cases. These types of waves are conventionally described as functions of time (but could as well be defined as functions of space, etc.). Such functions will output the value of the sine (or cosine) of an angle as it varies in time:

$$s(t) = \sin(\omega t). \tag{1}$$

You can see why the above expression defines a function of time (t): the sine angle changes as t increases. So for a given ω, the angle will change by that amount every time t increases by 1.

From trigonometry, we remember that the sine of an angle is the ratio of the length of the side of the right triangle opposite to it (0 in figure 5.4) to the hypotenuse H. Conventionally, we make $H = 1$, so that the sine becomes 0. The cosine is then the adjacent side A to the angle. As shown in the figure, the values of the sines and cosines are effectively the amplitudes of y and x (on the vertical and horizontal axes), corresponding to the plot of the different points in the circle (called a trigonometric circle), as the angle that the line from the origin to the circle makes with the horizontal axis varies from 0 to 2π radians.[2] In other words, sines and cosines can be seen as plots of rotating wheels. The rate of rotation ω is how fast the angle varies with time, determining the frequency of the sine wave (the number of revolutions per unit time). If our time is being measured in seconds, the frequency f will be measured in cycles per second, or hertz. In this case we define ω as $2\pi f$ so that we will make the angle vary from 0 to $2\pi f$ times every second. The sinusoid described by equation 1 will have a peak amplitude of 1 (varying from -1 to $+1$), so it can be scaled to whatever amplitude, as in

$$s(t) = a \sin(\omega t). \tag{2}$$

In terms of waveform shape, there will be no distinction between sines and cosines. The only difference between them is in relation to their starting angle, or phase offset. The sine wave is delayed by one-fourth of the circle ($\pi/2$) in relation to the cosine wave:

$$a \sin(\omega t) = a \cos(\omega t - \pi/2). \tag{3}$$

In fact, any sinusoid, of whatever amplitude and phase offset, can be described as a sum of cosine and sine functions:

$$s(t) = a \cos(\omega t + \phi) = m \cos(\omega t) + n \sin(\omega t). \tag{4}$$

We can obtain the amplitude and phase of such sinusoid by looking at the relative amounts (amplitudes, weights) of cosine and sine components, m and n, in the signal. The amplitude a of the sinusoid is the square root of the sum of the squares of m and n:

$$a = \sqrt{m^2 + n^2}. \tag{5}$$

The phase offset ϕ can be obtained from m and n as the arctangent of the ratio of n and m:

$$\phi = \arctan(n/m). \tag{6}$$

In other words, arbitrary sinusoid waves can be seen as a combination of sines and cosines; these are special cases of sinusoids where either the cosine or the sine amounts (m and n) are zero. Sinusoids of different frequencies, amplitudes, and phase offsets can be used as building blocks for other signals.

5.3.1 Digital Sinusoids

So far, we have examined the continuous case of sinusoids. The digital forms of these signals are very close to what we have already seen. If we consider that a discrete-time signal (such as a digital signal) has an independent variable n that is discrete and we can obtain such variable from its continuous cousin by sampling the signal at a periodic interval T, then we can introduce it as

$$s(n) = a \cos(\omega nT + \phi), \tag{7}$$

with the relationship between the sample index n and the continuous time t defined as

$$n = \text{int}[t/T],\tag{8}$$

where int[x] means the integer part of x.

Using the sampling rate sr for $1/T$, and redefining ω as $2\pi f$/sr, we can write our sinusoid in a more compact form:

$$s(n) = a \cos(\omega n + \phi).\tag{9}$$

Effectively, this makes the difference between the digital sinusoid in equation 9 and the analog one in equation 4 a matter of using the sample index n instead of the continuous time t. However, the digital signal $s(n)$ is defined only for integral values of n. Digital-to-analog conversion can, of course, generate a signal $s(t)$, which is continuous, from it.

Here is a simple C code fragment that will generate a simple, steady-frequency, full-amplitude sinusoidal signal (of length N, or N/sr seconds) with 16-bit precision:

```
int n;                          /* sample index */
short sig[N];                   /* 16-bit (2-byte) signal */
float amp = 32767.f, freq = 440.f, sr = 44100.f; /* signal params */
float phase = 0.75;             /* phase, in fractions of a cycle */
double twopi = 8*atan(-1.);     /* 2*PI, a constant */
phase *= twopi;                 /* phase in radians */
for(n=0; n < N; n++)            /* the signal generation loop */
    sig[n]=(short)(amp*cos(twopi*n*freq/sr + phase));
```

(On the DVD you will find a synthesis program that generates sinusoid tones.)

5.3.2 Aliasing

An important point to be made about this type of signal is that not all analog sinusoids can be successfully represented by a digital version. Returning to the question of sampling, we remember that, in order to represent a signal in discrete time, we need to sample it at least twice its frequency. This means that the maximum frequency that our sinusoid can reach is sr/2. We saw that once this frequency has been exceeded by the analog signal, strange things start to happen with its discrete representation. In the visual metaphor of figures 5.1 and 5.2, we saw that the rotating wheel is misrepresented, making it slower (and rotating backward).

With sinusoids, 'slower' means with a lower frequency. This means that a sinusoidal signal whose frequency is higher than sr/2 will be misrepresented by a sinusoid at a frequency below sr/2 (figure 5.5). The exact relationship between the frequency of a digital sinusoid and its analog original is

$$f_{\text{digital}} = f_{\text{analog}} - \text{int}\left[\frac{2f_{\text{analog}}}{\text{sr}}\right] \times \text{sr}.\tag{10}$$

The "rotating backward" effect seen in the wheel metaphor is also shown by equation 10, as the resulting misrepresented frequency will have an inverted sign. For instance, if the

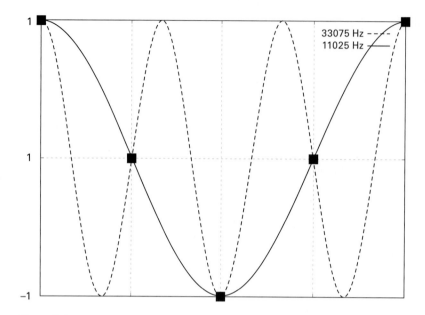

Figure 5.5
Cosine waves at 11,025 (blue) and 33,075 Hz (red), sampled at 44.1 KHz. The first is properly sampled; the second produces an alias that is not distinguishable from the first signal.

sampling rate is 44,100 Hz, a sinusoid at 33,075 Hz will appear in the digital signal as a −11,025-Hz sinusoid. Such signals, with negative frequencies, will sound to us just as if they had positive frequencies, except that they will, in some cases, have a different phase offset (unless they are pure cosines, as in figure 5.5). They are produced by sinusoidal functions whose angles decrease instead of increase ("rotate backward").

Misrepresented sinusoidal signals are known as *aliases*, because they are indistinguishable from non-aliased signals. In the example above, it is impossible to distinguish an aliased −11,025-Hz signal produced by sampling a 33,075-Hz sinusoid from the one produced by sampling a −11,025-Hz sinusoid. Aliasing will occur every time a signal whose frequency is above sr/2 is sampled. It is therefore crucial that the analog-to-digital conversion eliminate any analog signals above that frequency. Although we might not be able to hear it, high-frequency components might be present in a signal. These would cause aliased components to be added to the signal, which are generally undesirable.

The solution is to use a low-pass filter, which would eliminate all frequencies above sr/2. For a 44,100-Hz conversion, we would expect to set the filter cutoff frequency at around 20,000 Hz, so that its curve rolls off to eliminate anything above 22,050 Hz. In practice, since good analog filters are expensive to make, oversampling is used (effectively sampling at higher frequencies), so that we can use a simpler analog filter combined with some digital filtering (which is cheap).

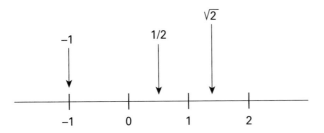

Figure 5.6
The real numbers -1, 0.5, and $2^{0.5}$.

It is also important to note that the low-pass filtering that is done at the ADC stage is mirrored by a similar operation at the DAC stage. This has the effect of smoothing the transitions between the samples in the signal output by the converter (which generate a staircase-like signal). This produces a continuous signal without frequencies above sr/2, which were present in the signal as it was converted from the digital form.

5.3.3   Real and Complex Signals

Audio signals, such as the sinusoids we have been looking at, are said to be real-valued. This means that the signal function will generate a real number, a one-dimensional quantity. Such numbers can be visualized as always lying on a line (figure 5.6). In the trigonometric circle shown in figure 5.4, the values of a sine function will lie in on the vertical axis, whereas the values of the cosine function lie in on the horizontal axis. These two functions are real-valued, and each one of them, on its own, will generate a signal that has only one dimension.

It is possible, however, to have numbers and signals that are two-dimensional, i.e., that occupy a plane (figure 5.7). Although time-domain audio signals will not normally be of this kind, it is worth exploring the concepts of two-dimensional functions, as they will be useful in certain types of signal processing, such as spectral analysis and filter theory. These types of functions are said to be complex-valued, as their output will generate a complex number. It is possible to combine two real functions to make up a complex one. For instance, consider the circle that is described by the intersection of the values of a sine and a cosine function as the angle varies from 0 to 2π (figure 5.8). This is a typical example of a two-dimensional, complex-valued signal generated by a combination of two real functions. A special point about the way these two functions are combined is that they are evaluated on axes that are at right angles to each other, making it possible to combine them to generate a signal that lies on the plane. So in order to make the right-angle combination explicit, we include a symbol, j,[3] which labels the function that is to be evaluated on the vertical axis. Such a complex (digital) signal then can be defined as

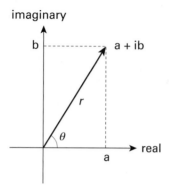

Figure 5.7
The complex (bi-dimensional) number $a + jb$.

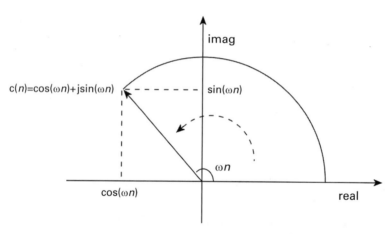

Figure 5.8
A complex signal $c(n)$, which plots a rotating circle on a plane.

$$c(n) = a[\cos(\omega n) + j \sin(\omega n)] \tag{11}$$

and its output is the figure of a circle with radius a in the complex plane. The symbol j can have more than one interpretation. In algebra, it is defined as the square root of -1, which is not possible to define in real-number terms. Here, it is more useful to think of it as a 90° rotating operator. When we multiply a quantity by it, we rotate it by 90°. Take for instance the real number 1, which can be said to lie on the horizontal axis. Multiplying it by j puts it on the vertical axis (making it complex). Multiplying it twice by j puts it back on the horizontal axis, but on the negative side, as $j^2 = -1$, and so on.

The signal $c(n)$ defined above is a complex sinusoid, which is going to be a very useful signal for many types of signal-processing operations. It can be represented in different ways. The form introduced above uses a rectangular combination of cosine and sines, defining its x and y coordinates, or its real and imaginary parts. We could alternatively define it using the length of the line from the rim of the circle to the origin (the radius) and the angle that the line makes with the horizontal axis. This second form is known as a *polar representation* of the signal, wherein the length of the line is also known as the *magnitude* or *modulus*:

$$c(n) = a \angle \omega n, \tag{12}$$

where $\angle$ means "at an angle." The magnitude is obtained by taking the square root of the sum of the squares of the real and imaginary part. The angle is obtained by the arctangent of the ratio of the imaginary and real parts:

$$a = \sqrt{\text{real}[c(n)]^2 + \text{imag}[c(n)]^2}. \tag{13}$$

$$\omega n = \arctan \frac{\text{imag}[c(n)]}{(\text{real}[c(n)])}.$$

A third representation links the two previous ones together in a very compact form. This is based on the Euler's famous formula

$$c(n) = a[\cos(\omega n) + j \sin(\omega n)] = a \times e^{j\omega n}. \tag{14}$$

So a complex sinusoid is also a complex exponential. A rotating circle is effectively described by the number e raised to increasing powers. It does not really matter to us what e is exactly, but we can think of it simply as a constant value (also known as the natural base of logarithms).

It was mentioned previously that audio signals are real-valued, so at first it might appear that this study of complex signals is not relevant to the present discussion. In fact, it is true to say that this area will only really come to play a significant role in audio signal processing in more advanced topics. However, there is one basic and crucial aspect of audio signals that should be highlighted here: connecting real-valued and complex sinusoids.

Two complex sinusoids of the same amplitude and same positive and negative frequencies can be combined to make up a real-valued sinusoid. This is because sine waves with negative frequencies (or phases) are equivalent to negative sines with positive frequencies, $\sin(-\omega t) = -\sin(\omega t)$, making the sine an odd function. Equally, cosine waves of the same positive and negative frequencies are the same signal, $\cos(\omega t) = \cos(-\omega t)$, making the cosine an even function. Thus, if we call these two sinusoids the signals $c(n)$ and $d(n)$, their sum is

$$c(n) + d(n) = a[\cos(\omega n) + j \sin(\omega n)] + a[\cos(-\omega n) + j \sin(-\omega n)]$$

$$= a[\cos(\omega n) + j \sin(\omega n) + \cos(\omega n) - j \sin(\omega n)] = 2a \cos(\omega n). \tag{15}$$

Summing these two complex sinusoids, we end up with a (real-valued) cosine wave. The reason why we obtained a cosine and not a sine is that the complex sinusoid had a phase offset of 0. (See equation 4.) It is also important to bear in mind the following relationship, inferred from equation 14:

$$a \cos(\omega n) = \tfrac{1}{2}a(e^{j\omega n} + e^{-j\omega n}). \tag{16}$$

Conversely, it is possible to say that a real sinusoid is actually composed of a pair of positive and negative complex sinusoids. The relationship between these two complex sinusoids is called complex conjugation. A complex number is said to be the complex conjugate of another when they only differ in the sign of the imaginary part. Because of this relationship, it can be said that real signals will actually be made up of positive and negative frequencies. This will have very important implications for many areas of signal processing, two of which, ring modulation and delays, will be discussed in the next section.

We can generate a complex digital sinusoid if we are careful to keep the real and imaginary parts separate. This can actually be used in some signal-processing operations, such as single-sideband modulation. This is a complex version of the real-valued sinusoid code fragment shown above. Here, the signal is now a complex number represented by the C structure[4] _cmplx_ and we will generate a signal in the ±1.0 range:

```
int n;                                     /* sample index */
struct _cmplx_ {
    float re;
    float im;
} sig[N];                                  /* complex signal */
float amp = 1.f, freq = 440.f, sr = 44100.f;  /* signal params */
float phase = 0.75;                        /* phase, in fractions of
                                              a cycle */
double twopi = 8*atan(-1.);                /* 2*PI, a constant */
phase *= twopi;                            /* phase in radians */
for(n=0; n < N; n++){                      /* the signal generation
                                              loop */
    sig[n].re =(float)(amp*cos(twopi*n*freq/sr + phase));
    sig[n].im =(float)(amp*sin(twopi*n*freq/sr + phase));
}
```

(The DVD examples for this chapter include a demonstration of how complex sinusoids can be used in sound synthesis and processing.)

5.4 Basic Operations on Digital Signals

Now that we have some idea of what simple digital signals are, it would be interesting to examine the basic operations that can be applied to them. These will lay the foundation for all the more advanced signal processing that will be discussed in this book. Four of the six processes that we will explore here will be directly concerned with two arithmetic operations only, addition and multiplication. The fifth one will involve both, and the sixth, although not apparently using it, can also be represented by a multiplication (by a complex number).

As you will see, it is quite an accomplishment that we can get such signal-processing mileage from two such simple mathematical operations.

5.4.1   Mixing Signals

The first basic operation we will introduce is one of the most used of all signal processing: mixing signals. It is very simple in essence: the addition of two or more signals, as in

$$mix(n) = s1(n) + s2(n). \tag{17}$$

What this operation does is sum, sample by sample, the signals involved. It is important to stress this so that we can understand why sometimes we can get unexpected results. Consider for instance the mixing of these two signals:

$$mix(n) = \sin(\omega n) + \sin(\omega n + \pi). \tag{18}$$

The output of this mix will be a muted signal; all samples will be zero. At first it might puzzle us as to why this has happened, but a look at the two signals will tell us why. Both of them are sinusoids, the first in the sine phase and the second with a shift of π, or half a cycle. This means that whenever the first signal is positive, the second is negative, and the mixed signal is the result of a destructive interference between the signals. If the signals were in the same phase, we would experience a doubling in amplitude (constructive interference). This phenomenon can be used musically with a lot of effect. Consider, for instance, summing two arbitrary waveform signals with a very small frequency difference. Because of the minimal difference, the result will be that the waveforms will start to drift apart and the interference will vary from a constructive to a destructive one (when the two signals are in opposite phase). If the two signals are sinusoids, we will hear a very slow amplitude fluctuation; if they are any other type of periodic wave, we will hear a *phasing* effect, similar to the one used by Risset in *Inharmonique*. The second case is explained by the fact that the harmonics will drift in and out of phase, each at a different time.

Mixing can be effected in C code by a loop that sums every sample of one signal to its corresponding sample of the other signal:

```
for(n=0; n < N; n++)            /* mixing loop */
   mix[n]= sig1[n] + sig2[n];
```

(A simple mixing program in the DVD examples folder for this chapter demonstrates the principle.)

5.4.2   Scaling Signals

Scaling is another basic operation that involves a signal and a constant (or a slowly varying control signal, such as an envelope). It is performed by multiplying the signal by a constant; and the effect is to change its peak amplitude:

$$\text{scaled}(n) = s(n) \times g. \tag{19}$$

In fact, the scaling factor has already been introduced in this chapter; the amplitude a of a sinusoidal signal (equation 4) is basically the scaling factor. Another name given to it is *the gain constant*, and scaling is also known as *gain adjustment*.

Scaling is used in all sorts of operations. In fact a basic mixer is made up of a scaling operation followed by mixing as defined above. Another important use of scaling is to ensure that our signals are in the right range for PCM quantization at the right precision. Generally, signal-processing operations, such as the synthesis of sound, are performed using numbers with decimal points, which in computers are called *floating-point numbers*. These numbers can have a wider range than certain integer formats, such as 8-bit and 16-bit precision numbers. So it is possible to generate a signal that exceeds the range of a certain quantizer's precision. Scaling is then necessary to reduce the amplitude by multiplying the signal by a scaling factor between 0 and 1.

Furthermore, certain synthesis and processing systems, such as Pure Data, conventionally work with floating-point signals in the range of ± 1.0, which are then scaled to the right quantizer range before conversion. When programming applications in these systems, it is sometimes necessary to scale signals down to that range, if they are originally, say, in the 16-bit range. They also might need scaling up if they are supposed to be in a different range (to be written to a soundfile, for instance). A signal in the range of ± 1.0 is said to be *normalized*.

Scaling can be done using a constant or a control signal. By the latter, we mean a slowly varying signal, such as envelope or a low-frequency (sub-audio) modulation. If, however, the scaling signal is at audio frequencies (generally above 20 Hz), then the multiplication operation is not going to be performing signal scaling; but rather, ring modulation, which will be discussed below.

Some C code for scaling would loop through a signal multiplying every sample by a gain variable:

```
for(n=0; n < N; n++)          /* scaling loop */
   scaled[n] = sig[n]*gain;
```

(The DVD examples for this chapter include a programming example implementing gain adjustment for soundfiles that demonstrates this concept.)

5.4.3 Offset

The arithmetic operation of sum, when applied to a signal and a constant, will not perform mixing, but will result in signal offsetting (more specifically, DC offsetting). The term DC, which comes from "direct curren," is related to what is described as a 0-Hz signal, one that does not vary with time. By adding a constant value to a signal, we will raise or lower its mean value. For instance, consider a sinusoid $\sin(n)$ that has a peak amplitude of 1.0 and is a bipolar signal with a mean value of 0. If we offset it by a, as in

$$\text{offset}(n) = s(n) + a, \tag{20}$$

its mean value will now be a (also known as the DC component of the signal), and the signal will vary from $a - 1$ to $a + 1$.

Typically, offsetting is used when we need to make a bipolar signal positive-only, in order, for instance, to modulate a parameter such as frequency or amplitude. In this case we generally combine an offset value with a scaling factor, so that the range of values is correct. For example, if we need to place the output of a sinusoid in the range of 0–1, we will need to offset it by 1 and scale it by 0.5.

The so-called *Hanning window*, used to envelope sounds prior to spectral analysis, is generated by offsetting and scaling one cycle of a cosine wave:

$$\text{hanning}(n) = 0.5 - 0.5 \cos\left(\frac{2\pi n}{N}\right), \qquad 0 \leq n < N. \tag{21}$$

The following C code fragment creates a Hanning window in a float array:

```
for(n=0; n < N; n++)              /* hanning window generation */
    hanning[n]= 0.5-0.5*cos(n*twopi/N);
```

5.4.4 Ring Modulation

As was hinted above, the multiplication of two audio-frequency signals does not result in scaling, but in what is called *ring modulation*. The net effect of this process is that a signal will be generated containing components with frequencies equivalent to the sum and difference of the frequencies of all components of the two inputs. It is easier to see what is happening if we consider simple signals such as sinusoids, which contain only one component. If we multiply two sinusoids, as in

$$ring(n) = \cos(\omega_1 n) \times \cos(\omega_2 n) = 0.5[\cos([\omega_1 - \omega_2]n) + \cos([\omega_1 + \omega_2]n)], \tag{22}$$

we get the two components mixed and scaled at half of the original component amplitudes. This is based on a well-known trigonometric identity. This principle then can be expanded to an arbitrary waveform with any number of components.

The general-purpose ring modulator is then implemented as a multiplication of two signals, such as shown in the C code fragment below:

```
for(n=0; n < N; n++)              /* ring modulation */
    mix[n]= sig1[n]*sig2[n];
```

(You will find an example program on DVD that implements a general-purpose ring modulation effect applied to two input soundfiles.)

Another way of understanding what happens here is through the concepts developed for complex sinusoids. Since a complex sinusoid is also a complex exponential, a multiplication of signals can also be seen as an addition of their frequencies:

$$cring(n) = (\cos(\omega_1 n) + j \sin(\omega_1 n)) \times (\cos(\omega_2 n) + j \sin(\omega_2 n)) \tag{23}$$

$$= e^{j\omega_1 n} e^{j\omega_2 n}$$

$$= e^{j(\omega_1 + \omega_2)n}.$$

Since a real sinusoid can be seen as two complex sinusoids with opposite signs for their frequencies, we can infer that when we multiply two such signals, we will have a result which will have components at the sum (frequencies having the same sign) and difference (frequencies having opposite sign) of the two sinusoid frequencies. In addition, we can expect that the resulting real-valued signal with two components will also be a mixture of four complex sinusoids, two with positive frequencies and two with negative frequencies. In fact, equation 22 shows two of these, with positive frequencies; for a real signal, there would also be two negative ones (the sinusoids will differ only by the imaginary sign). Apart from providing some musically interesting transformations, used in many works of contemporary music, ring modulation is also the basis for a very useful operation on signals, called heterodyning. This operation is used in some important spectral analysis processes, such as the phase vocoder.

5.4.5   The Fourier Series

The next operation we will explore is fundamental to many synthesis techniques. It will use the two arithmetic operations of addition and multiplication to generate an arbitrary waveform signal from elementary ones, the sinusoids. From the work of Fourier, and later Helmholtz, we learn that periodic waveforms can be deconstructed as a series of weighted sinusoids. Periodic waveforms are a very useful musical signal, because of one of its basic characteristics: at the right frequency range, they produce a sensation of pitch. It is therefore possible to recompose such waveforms by adding up (mixing) weighted (scaled) sinusoids of different frequencies. We only need to know what frequencies to chose, which is a simple matter, as we are told that they will be integer multiples of the fundamental frequency (which is generally the one that conveys the pitch height).

How many of these sinusoids will we need? That will depend on the type of waveform we are creating, but since we are generating a digital signal, the absolute maximum must have a frequency that is less than or equal to sr/2. The Fourier series can be defined, then, as this operation of mixing weighted sinusoids, as in

$$s(n) = \sum_{k=1}^{N} a_k \cos(k\omega n + \phi_k), \tag{24}$$

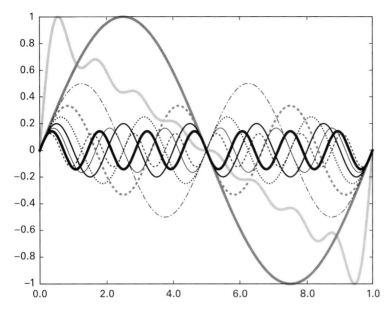

Figure 5.9

Fourier-series operation: the plot of a sawtooth wave (in light gray) against its eight component sinusoids, also known as harmonics.

where a_k and ϕ_k are the weight and the phase offset of each sinusoid.

The fundamental frequency is defined by ω (or f, in Hz, as we are using the convention of $\omega = 2\pi f/\text{sr}$), and the highest-frequency component, N, cannot have a frequency higher than $\text{sr}/2$ if we want to avoid aliasing. The sum operator mixes all the sinusoids together to provide the output (figure 5.9). We usually call each of these integer-related sinusoidal components a *harmonic*.

From very basic recipes, a number of standard waveforms can be generated with this operation:

• A sawtooth wave is generated by setting $a_k = 1/k$ (and, for its characteristic shape, we should use a phase offset $\phi_k = -\pi/2$ for each component, i.e. sines instead of cosines)
• A square wave recipe is (also with $\phi_k = -\pi/2$)

$$a_k = \begin{cases} 1/k & \text{for } k \text{ odd} \\ 0 & \text{for } k \text{ even} \end{cases}$$

• A pulse waveform (buzz) has $a_k = 1$.
• A triangle wave can be obtained with

$$a_k = \begin{cases} 1/k^2 & \text{for } k \text{ odd} \\ 0 & \text{for } k \text{ even} \end{cases}$$

The following two C functions implement the generation of arbitrary wavetables using the Fourier series:

```
#define TWOPI 6.283185307
/* this takes the number of harmonics, an array of harmonic weights,
the table length and a phase offset in fractions of a cycle */
float* fourier_table(int harms, float *amps,
  int length, float phase){
    int i,n;   /* harmonic index, sample index */
    float a;   /* amplitude */
    double w;   /* freq in rads of each harmonic */
    float *table = (float *) malloc(length*sizeof(float));
    phase *= (float)PI*2;
    memset(table,0,(length)*sizeof(float));
    for(i=0; i < harms; i++)
        for(n=0; n < length; n++){
        a = amps ? amps[i] : 1.f;    /* use 1, if amps not supplied */
        w = (i+1)*(n*TWOPI/length); /* freq of each harmonic */
        table[n] += (float) (a*cos(w+phase)); /* scale and mix */
    }
    normalize_table(table, length); /* normalize the table */
    return table;
}

/* this takes a table and normalizes it */
void normalize_table(float *table, int length,
                    float scale){
    int n;
    float max = 0.f;
    for(n=0; n < length; n++) /* find the peak value */
        max = table[n] > max ? table[n] : max;
    if(max) for(n=0; n < length; n++) table[n] /= max;
}
```

(An example of the application of such function tables can be found in a simple synthesis program on the DVD.)

The Fourier series is a basic operation for simple additive synthesis.[5] A little modification of the formula will transform it into a general description for an additive synthesizer:

$$additive(n) = \sum_{k=1}^{N} a(n)_k \cos(\omega(n)_k + \phi_k),$$

(25)

where now it is not necessary to restrict the sinusoid frequencies to multiples of a fundamental frequency. In addition, the amplitude and phase of each component, $a(n)_k$ and

$\omega(n)_k$, are themselves functions of time, so we can synthesize signals whose timbres change dynamically change (as all interesting and musical sounds do).

5.4.6 Delays

Last, but not least, I would like to introduce the operation of signal delay. This, at first, seems to be disconnected from what we have previously seen, but in fact, it can be explained as a particular type of scaling. As the name implies, a signal delay means modifying the time coordinate of a signal, 'holding' it for a certain time. In a general sense, a delay operation can be described as

$$\text{delayed}(n) = s(n - d), \tag{26}$$

where d is the delay in samples.

Delays are used everywhere in signal processing, from filters to echo and reverberation. For instance, we can use this operation to generate a slap-back echo effect on a signal, using this simple C code fragment:

```
d = delaytime*sr;          /* delaytime is the delay in secs */
for(n=0; n < N, n++)       /* we'll make the echo 1/2 amp */
   echo[n] = sig[n] + (n >= d ? 0.5*sig[n-d] : 0.f);
```

An important insight into what is actually happening when we delay a signal can be given using a complex number description (actually using a complex sinusoid as an input). With it, it is simpler to demonstrate the point, which can be then be extrapolated for all signals. Starting with a complex signal, such as a sinusoid $\cos(\omega n) + j \sin(\omega n)$, we can generate a delayed (by one sample) version as follows:

$$s(n - 1) = \cos(\omega(n - 1)) + j \sin(\omega(n - 1)). \tag{27}$$

We can rewrite this as a complex exponential:

$$\cos(\omega(n - 1)) + j \sin(\omega(n - 1)) = e^{j\omega[n-1]}. \tag{28}$$

Changing from a sum of exponents to a multiplication of exponentials, we have

$$e^{j\omega n - j\omega} = e^{j\omega n} e^{-j\omega} = e^{-j\omega} s(n). \tag{29}$$

Effectively, what we have is

$$s(n - 1) = e^{-j\omega} s(n), \tag{30}$$

which means that here the one-sample delay is equivalent to a multiplication by the complex exponential $e^{-j\omega}$. Similarly, a delay of d samples will be equivalent to the multiplication by $e^{-jd\omega}$. This complex number is so common in signal processing that it is given the shorthand

$$e^{-j\omega} = z^{-1}. \tag{31}$$

The multiplication by z is a special one, normally occurring in what is called the *z-domain*, where time-domain signals such as $s(n)$ are represented by their z-transforms.[6] An alternative view is to see z as an operator that acts on the signal as a whole. We can generalize the ideas above for all signals employing this concept. For instance, if we want to represent the mix of two signals in the slap-back echo example above, we can notate it, using this operator, as

$$Y = S + 0.5z^{-d}S, \tag{32}$$

where Y represents the output and S the input (in fact, these are the z-transforms of the time-domain signals $y(n)$ and $s(n)$).[7] So, we can see now that all the basic operations with signals are in one way or another based on addition and multiplication.

5.5   Some Applications of Signal Processing

Complementing the study of basic signal operations are two examples of applications that use the ideas discussed above. The first demonstrates a method of signal transformation; the second is a classic technique of sound synthesis.

5.5.1   Transforming Signals with Filters

Filtering is a signal-processing operation that is designed to transform sounds in different ways. The most common application of filters is to boost, attenuate, or block out certain components of an input sound, i.e. to change the amplitude of its different sinusoidal components. Other filter applications involve modifying the phase offsets of different components. These two types of processes correspond to the two aspects of the action of a filter: its amplitude and phase responses, respectively. In most music signal-processing applications, we tend to be more interested in the filter amplitude response, as this is generally the most directly perceived effect. However, in certain cases, the phase response might play an important part in the signal transformation.

Filters are built by combining an input signal with scaled and delayed signals, which can be of two forms:

- input delays: delayed copies of the input signals
- output delays, i.e. delayed copies of the filter input signal, which can be seen as a form of feedback (plugging the output back into the input of the filter).

These two forms of delays give rise to two distinct classes of filters: finite impulse response (FIR), when using only input delays, and infinite impulse response (IIR), when using output delays (with or without input delays). These two filter classes are also known as feedforward or non-recursive filters and feedback or recursive filters, respectively.

In order to understand these concepts, we will examine a simple FIR filter and study its characteristics. One of the simplest such filters is obtained by combining a signal with its one-sample delay copy and scaling both signals by 0.5, as in

$$y(n) = 0.5x(n) + 0.5x(n-1), \tag{33}$$

where we conventionally notate the filter output as $y(n)$ and its input as $x(n)$. Equation 33 is what is called a *filter equation*.

The scaling values of 0.5 are known as the filter coefficients, which in this case are the same for the input and one-sample delay terms of the filter. This particular filter is also known as an *averaging first-order filter*, because it takes the average of the current input and its previous value and because it uses only a delay of one sample; a filter with a delay of N samples is an Nth-order filter. This filter can be implemented in C with the following code fragment:

```
for(n=0; n < N; n++){
    out[n] = (in[n] + delayed)*0.5; /* filter equation */
    delayed = in[n];                /* keep previous input */
}
```

To examine the effects of this filter,[8] we need to find what its amplitude and its phase response are. We can do this first by rewriting the filter using a complex exponential as its input. (See equation 31.) This will give us (with $x(n) = e^{j\omega n}$ and $z = e^{j\omega}$)

$$y(n) = 0.5[x(n) + z^{-1}x(n)]. \tag{34}$$

We moved the scaling by 0.5, and we can, for simplicity, ignore it for the moment (it is only equivalent to turning the output volume down by half). What this expression gives us is the possibility of evaluating what the filter will do to different sinusoids of different frequencies by re-interpreting z^{-1} as a complex exponential:

$$y(n) = x(n) + z^{-1}x(n) = x(n) + e^{-j\omega}x(n) = x(n)[1 + e^{-j\omega}]. \tag{35}$$

This complex expression shows filtering as yet another use of scaling in signal processing, as we are effectively multiplying the signal $x(n)$ ($= e^{j\omega n}$) by the complex function $F(\omega) = 1 + e^{-j\omega}$. The result of this multiplication is that the output will be the input signal with a modified amplitude and phase.

What is the amplitude of the output going to be? As we vary the frequency of the input sinusoid, the amplitude of the output will vary. This demonstrates the action of the filter; in this case, attenuation of the different frequency components of the input signal. How this attenuation varies with frequency can be found by plotting the amplitude of the signal in equation 34 for different values of the frequency ω.

As the filter expression is a complex one, we have to find its magnitude (see equation 13, which is indicated by $|1 + e^{-j\omega}|$ and is equivalent to the amplitude response of the filter[9]:

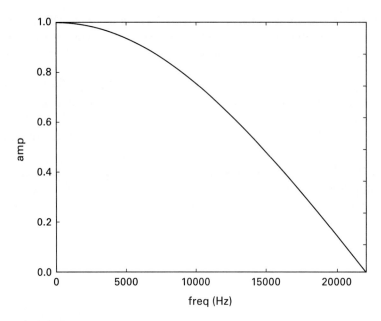

Figure 5.10

Amplitude response of an averaging first-order filter, with sr = 44.1 KHz.

$$A(\omega) = |1 + e^{-j\omega}|$$

$$= |1 + \cos(\omega) - j\,\sin(\omega)|$$

$$= \sqrt{[1 + \cos(\omega)]^2 - [j\,\sin(\omega)]^2}$$

$$= \sqrt{1 + 2\,\cos(\omega) + \cos^2(\omega) - [-\sin^2(\omega)]}$$

$$= \sqrt{1 + 2\,\cos(\omega) + \cos^2(\omega) + \sin^2(\omega)}$$

$$= \sqrt{2 + 2\,\cos(\omega)} = \sqrt{4\,\cos^2(\omega/2)} = 2\,\cos(\omega/2). \tag{36}$$

Now, remembering that we had omitted scaling the signal by 0.5, we can plot the amplitude response of the filter (figure 5.10). This is done by re-casting ω as $2\pi f/\mathrm{sr}$ (with f now the frequency in Hz), which gives us the expression $\cos(\pi f/\mathrm{sr})$ for the filter amplitude response, the first one-fourth of a cosine wave, from 0 Hz to sr/2. The shape of the filter makes it a low-pass filter, i.e. one that attenuates high-frequencies, letting low-frequencies pass more or less unaltered.

The second aspect of the filter complex scaling action on the signal is the fact that it will alter the phase offsets of the different sinusoidal components of an input signal. This means that a certain time delay will be imposed on the signal, which is expected, since we are using a delay operation. Similarly to the amplitude response, the phase response will vary with fre-

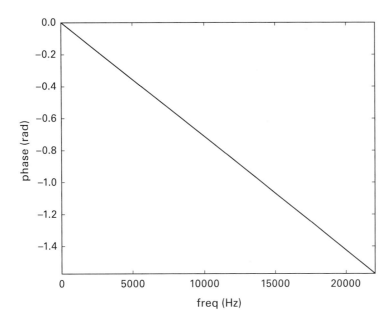

Figure 5.11
Phase response of first-order averaging filter, with sr $= 44.1$ KHz.

quency, so we can also evaluate it using the same principles above, except that we will now have to extract the angle of the complex scaling function $F(\omega) = 1 + e^{-j\omega}$. This is done, as shown in equation 13, by taking the arctangent of the ratio of its imaginary and real parts:

$$PH(\omega) = \angle\,(1 + e^{-j\omega})$$
$$= \angle\,(1 + \cos(\omega) - j\sin(\omega))$$
$$= \arctan\left(\frac{-\sin(\omega)}{1 + \cos(\omega)}\right)$$
$$= -\omega/2. \tag{37}$$

In other words, the phase offset varies linearly with frequency, as figure 5.11 demonstrates. A delay of $\omega/2$ or $\pi f/\text{sr}$ represents a delay of half a sample, since a sinusoidal signal with such delay, $\cos(\omega n - \omega/2)$, would be equivalent to $\cos(\omega[n - 0.5])$.

In fact, we could predict the phase response of this filter, because FIR filters, with coefficients that are symmetrical about a central point have exhibit a linear phase response, with a delay of $N/2$ samples, where N is the order of the filter. In this case, the coefficients are 0.5 and 0.5, meeting the pre-requisite for linear phase response and its delay is predictably half a sample. Not all filters will be linear-phase, some in fact can have very complicated phase responses, but an FIR can be made so by carefully choosing its coefficients.

The complex function $F(\omega) = 1 + e^{-j\omega}$, which we have been using to obtain the amplitude and phase responses, is also called the *frequency response* of the filter. It is actually a special case of a more general expression called the *transfer function*.[10] The action of a filter is a multiplication[11] of a signal by its transfer function. The combination of the amplitude and phase responses of a filter is called its *frequency response*. The general form for a transfer function of a first-order FIR filter $y(n) = a_0x(n) + a_1x(n-1)$ is $H(\omega) = a_0 + a_1e^{-j\omega}$, and its amplitude response $A(\omega)$ is

$$A(\omega) = \sqrt{a_0^2 + 2a_0a_1 \cos(\omega) + a_1^2}. \tag{38}$$

Different values for coefficients will yield different amplitude responses for the same filter design. For instance high-pass response can be obtained from the above filter by setting the coefficient a_1 to a negative value.

The type of filter discussed above is, as mentioned, very simple, and it provides only a gentle transformation of the input signal. However, the concepts introduced here can be applied to more complicated types of filters. For musical uses, we often choose to use feedback filters, as they provide a more dramatic effect. Although they exhibit a more involved amplitude and phase response description, they can be studied with the same principles explored above. The main difference is that we will use delayed copies of the filter output, as shown by the equation below, describing a first-order feedback filter, with coefficients a and b:

$$y(n) = ax(n) - by(n-1). \tag{39}$$

Using the same tools and definitions as before, we can derive the complex frequency response for this filter, using some extra manipulations of the equation:

$$y(n) = ax(n) - bz^{-1}y(n)$$

$$= y(n) + bz^{-1}y(n) = ax(n)$$

$$= y(n)[1 + bz^{-1}] = ax(n)$$

$$= y(n) = x(n)\frac{a}{1 + bz^{-1}}. \tag{40}$$

Its frequency response is

$$F(\omega) = \frac{a}{1 + be^{-j\omega}}. \tag{41}$$

The main difference in the transfer functions of a feedback and feedforward filter is that in the latter case the variable z^{-1} ends up in the denominator.

For the amplitude response, which is what interests us the most, this expression indicates that for frequencies that make the modulus of the $1 + be^{-j\omega}$ expression zero, the scaling factor will be infinite. In the case of feedback filters, we have the inverse situation: for those frequencies, the scaling would be zero. The name given to a frequency that makes a transfer function infinite is a *pole*, whereas the name for a frequency that makes it zero is, of course, a *zero*.

Generally, we do not want filters to have an infinite value anywhere in their amplitude response, because that would make it unstable. So with feedback filters, we will have to be careful in designing our coefficients so that we avoid such situations. Ideally, we will try to choose coefficients that make the denominator close to, but never, zero. In the case of the simple feedback filter shown above, this will be reduced to making sure that b is close to, but not equal to or bigger than, 1 (also not equal to or smaller than -1). The amplitude response $A(\omega)$ of the above filter, derived similarly to equation 35, will be

$$A(\omega) = |F(\omega)| = \frac{a}{\sqrt{1 + b^2 + 2b \cos(\omega)}}. \tag{42}$$

First-order filters, such as the ones discussed above, will only be able to implement either low-pass or high-pass responses, because they only have one zero and/or one pole. For other shapes, we will have to use more delays, in order to be able to create more poles or zeros. For instance, a second-order filter can implement band-pass filters, and higher-order filters can implement more complicated shapes.

5.5.2 Synthesizing Sound with FM and PM

The additive synthesis algorithm outlined by equation 25 is very powerful and general. However, it uses a little too much brute force to achieve its goals. In doing so, it is very demanding in terms of computation. Alternative techniques have been sought to provide similar possibilities with less computation effort. One such technique is frequency modulation (FM), developed in the late 1960s by John Chowning. The main advantage of FM is its compactness, allowing for interesting time-evolving sounds with the use of only a few operations. In order to understand FM, we will describe first a variant form of it, called phase modulation (PM), which produces similar results. This technique is in fact used in many hardware-based FM implementations, such as Yamaha's DX series of synthesizers. In certain situations, it is actually better to use the PM form rather than FM. The term 'phase' used here in relation to this technique is a little more general than the one we were using before, relating to phase offset. So in the sinusoid below, the term $\theta(n)$ is what we call the phase of the sinusoid, i.e. its angle:

$$s(n) = a \cos(\theta(n)). \tag{43}$$

We have the phase of a cosine function of (discrete) time n, in order to make explicit the fact that it will be changing in time. Modulating it means to apply a periodic signal that will time-vary it. We can use another sinusoid to do that. The sinusoid angle will then be defined as

$$\theta(n) = \omega_c n + I \sin(\omega_m n) \tag{44}$$

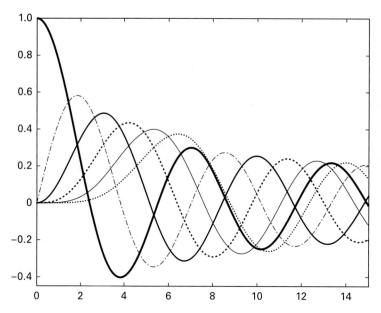

Figure 5.12
Bessel functions of orders 0–5 plotted against index of modulation I.

and so the PM signal is generated by

$$pm(n) = a \cos(\omega_c n + I \sin(\omega_m n)). \tag{45}$$

The expression above implements the PM technique. The peak amplitude I of the modulating signal is called the index of modulation. It controls how much modulation is inserted in the signal, so that if it is set to zero, the output is the original sinusoid. The resulting signal $s(n)$ will have components at the sum and differences of k integer multiples of ω_m, the modulator signal frequency, and ω_c, the carrier signal frequency. The signal resulting from PM synthesis is equivalent to the (additive synthesis) expression

$$\cos(\omega_c n + I \sin(\omega_m n)) = \sum_{k=-\infty}^{\infty} J_k(I) \cos([\omega_c + k\omega_m]n). \tag{46}$$

The scaling functions used for each pair of components (called a sideband), $J_k(I)$, are a well-known family of functions called *Bessel functions of the first kind*. The best way of understanding how they work is by looking at their plots in figure 5.12. The negative-order Bessel functions can be obtained from the positive ones using the identity

$$J_{-k}(I) = (-1)^k J_k(I). \tag{47}$$

As can be seen in figure 5.12, as the index of modulation rises, the amplitude of the signal gets more spread between the different components. With $I = 0$, all Bessel functions have the value 0, except for the order-zero one. This means that the output signal has only one component, at the carrier frequency. As I rises, the other Bessel functions kick in and the amplitude of the different components fluctuates between positive and negative values (which result in inverted-phase signals). So it is possible to generate time-varying timbres by varying the value of I. This is one of the most important aspects of the technique.

Another important point of PM (and FM) is that the frequencies of signal components will depend on the ratio of the carrier and modulator frequencies, $\omega_c : \omega_m$. Because of this, it is possible to generate a variety of sounds, with or without pitch, from drums and bells to woodwind and brass emulations. Many of these sounds would have a very complicated description in terms of additive synthesis parameters, as shown by equation 46, but can be created very easily with two sound-generating sinusoidal functions, by equation 45 instead.

PM has some similarities with ring modulation. However, here, instead of a simple multiplication of two signals, we use a complex exponentiation of one of the signals. To show this, we can define it in terms of a complex signal expression (by taking only its real part):

$$pm(n) = \cos(\omega_c n + I \sin(\omega_m n))$$

$$= \mathrm{real}[e^{j(\omega_c n + I \sin(\omega_m))}]$$

$$= \mathrm{real}[e^{j\omega_c n} e^{jI \sin(\omega_m n)}]. \tag{48}$$

Now we can see where the Bessel functions come from. They arise from the expansion of the exponential expression

$$e^{jI \sin(\omega_m n)} = \sum_{k=-\infty}^{\infty} j^k J_k(I) \left(\cos k \left[\omega_m n + \frac{\pi}{2} \right] \right)$$

$$= J_0(I) + 2 \sum_{k=1}^{\infty} J_{2k}(I) \cos(2k\omega_m n) + j J_{2k-1}(I) \sin([2k-1]\omega_m n). \tag{49}$$

So in fact the result of PM of two sinusoids is the ring modulation of a sinusoid by a signal with several components. We can compare the equations above to equation 23 to spot the differences and similarities. From equation 49 we can see how it is possible to arrive at equation 46, the additive expression for the signal.

Frequency modulation is very similar to PM,[12] but generally easier to implement in software systems, such as Csound. The main difference is that the signal being modulated is not the phase angle, but the instantaneous frequency, its time derivative. As we are now modulating a different parameter, a few adjustments have to be made to the PM formula. The basic difference is that, for FM, the scaling gain of the modulation signal is not the index of modulation anymore, but a frequency deviation, an amount of absolute change in the carrier signal frequency. This parameter, d, is defined as

$$d = I \times f_m, \tag{50}$$

where f_m is the modulating frequency and I is the index of modulation. With this change, we can adapt the PM formula as defined above for FM synthesis. Using If_m for the modulation signal amplitude, and remembering that $\omega_c = 2\pi n f_c / \text{sr}$ and $\omega_m = 2\pi n f_m / \text{sr}$, we will modulate the carrier frequency f_c, instead of the phase. In this case the varying (modulated) frequency $f(n)$ of the carrier oscillator becomes

$$f(n) = f_c + If_m \cos\left(\frac{2\pi n f_m}{sr}\right). \tag{51}$$

(The DVD examples include some comparative implementations of PM and FM in Csound.)

In order to implement FM, one last important consideration has to be made. If we are implementing the sinusoidal signal generation as in equation 43, we have to be careful to generate the varying phase angle $\theta(n)$ using the update expression

$$\theta(n + 1) = \theta(n) + \Delta\theta, \tag{52}$$

where $\Delta\theta$, the difference between two consecutive phase values, is the instantaneous radian frequency $2\pi f / \text{sr}$. This is because of the fact that the instantaneous frequency is the derivative of the phase, as mentioned above. If the frequency f is constant, the expression is simpler: $\theta(n) = 2\pi n f / \text{sr}$. With FM, however, the instantaneous carrier frequency will not be constant, so we have to use the expression above for updating the phase of the carrier signal. With that in mind, we can apply the FM formula more or less directly to the following C code fragment:

```
for(n=0; n < N; n++) {
    s[n] = amp*cos(pha);
    /* tpisr is 2pi/sr, ndx is I and the rest is self-explanatory */
    pha = pha + tpisr*(fc+ndx*fm*cos(tpisr*n*fm));
}
```

It is important to note that in signal-processing systems, such as Csound, FM is implemented using table-lookup oscillators. This is a more efficient way to implement synthesis than using a direct evaluation of a cosine (or sine) function as in the code examples shown in this text. In addition, FM synthesis is generally described and implemented using sine functions instead of cosines. Although there will be a number of important differences in the generated signal, all the principles explored in this text also apply to sine-wave PM/FM.

Conclusion

We have seen in this chapter a number of basic concepts relating to signals, in general, and digital audio signals, in particular. These form the foundation of the discipline of digital signal processing, which is itself the basis for audio programming. A number of more advanced topics, such as spectral analysis and advanced synthesis and filter theory, were not discussed here, but will be introduced in other chapters. However, it is important to note that the ideas explored here will be very useful in understanding even the more complex aspects of audio signal processing to come.

Notes

1. Some will argue that we hear quantization noise as a continuous noise, so that our perception of it will be defined by its average power, which is less than its peak value. The average power of the max quantization error 0.5 is $12^{-0.5}$. In that case, the SNR will be $2^{n-1}/12^{-0.5}$, or $3^{0.5}2^n$, giving us a $\text{SNR}_{dB} = 4.77 + 6.02n$.

2. In signal processing, angles are more likely to be defined in radians. The reason for this is that the radian 'scale' is defined in relation to the radius of a circle. So for a circle of radius 1, it actually givens the length of the circle's circumference (the outer line that makes up the circle boundary). For that reason, angles need no conversion to linear measurements. The ratio of a circle's circumference (c) and its diameter (d) (which is twice the radius), is described by $\pi = c/d$. This relationship is then used to define an angle in radians: the whole circumference is πd, or $2\pi r$ (r standing for radius), giving that angle (360°) the value of 2π radians. Other angles then are measured as fractions of this amount: $\pi/2$ (90°), π (180°), $3\pi/2$ (270°), etc.

3. This is also commonly written as i instead of j, depending on the name of other variables in the expression (so not to be confused with them).

4. C structures are very useful programming devices for creating new data types that do not exist in the language. As there are no types for complex numbers (as there are for integers and real numbers), we need to create one. So, by defining a structure with two separate slots for real and imaginary parts we can do just that. This facility allows us to manipulate this type in a more controlled fashion. In fact, C structures are so useful that in the C++ language, they are expanded to hold functions (known in that context as methods) as well as data types, to support a way of programming known as object-oriented.)

5. Additive synthesis is one of the most powerful techniques of synthesis. It can be implemented by using a bank of oscillators, each one with different amplitude and frequency envelopes. The data for such envelopes can get quite large if we want to create more realistic sounds. To help with this, analysis-synthesis techniques are used, where real sounds are analyzed and data for amplitude and frequency envelopes are extracted, which is then used to drive oscillator banks. One popular technique for analysis-synthesis is the phase vocoder, which will be discussed in detail in later chapters.

6. The z-transform is used to obtain a frequency domain representation of a discrete-time signal. This means that what we have then is a function of frequency (which in this particular case is a complex variable, so the z-domain is a complex frequency domain), rather than time. There are other ways of obtaining other frequency-domain representations of signals, such the Fourier Transform and the Discrete Fourier Transform, which are closely related to the z-transform. The details of this are beyond the scope of the this text, but one of the applications of the z-transform is to obtain the transfer function of a system.

7. You can think of the z-transform of the signal as representing all of it, instead of individual samples. So when we use an operator such as z^{-d} we are acting on the whole signal.

8. Filters present perhaps the best illustration of the usefulness of complex numbers. So far with the simple processing of waveforms we have been studying, we really had no need for the extra complication of complex arithmetic. However, when we look at filters, we see that they have two effects on an input signal. They change the signal's amplitude as well as delay the signal (change its phase). These two effects are independent of each other, but the same filter causes them. So, to measure them it is handy to use a number that has two components: a complex number. This measurement is called the filter frequency response and it contains two independent values. One of the numbers will tell us how the filter changes the amplitude of the signal at a certain frequency, the magnitude of the filter frequency response. The other number gives the amount of delay, or phase change, that the filter effects, the phase of the filter frequency response. The complex frequency response in this case is in polar form, but it can also be written in Cartesian form, which is the more usual way we see complex numbers (with "real" and "imaginary" parts).

9. The following derivation uses the fact that $j^2 = -1$ and two trigonometric identities: $\cos^2 x + \sin^2 x = 1$ and $0.5 + 0.5\cos(2x) = \cos^2(x)$.

10. The transfer function is generally notated $H(z) = 1 + z^{-n}$, to indicate that it is a function of z, a complex-valued variable; the frequency response is obtained when we set z to $e^{j\omega}$, as in the example above. For that filter, the transfer function would be $H(z) = 1 + z^{-1}$. The z-transform of the impulse response of a system (i.e. the time-domain signal obtained by feeding it with a single impulse) is equivalent to its transfer function.

11. Here we mean the whole signal, as in its z-transform, so actually this is the "special type of multiplication" seen in equation 32.

12. FM and PM yield effectively very similar results, although for the same parameters of modulation frequency, carrier frequency and index of modulation, they can result in different spectra. The initial phases of the modulator and carrier signals will also be influential, as say using sines instead of cosines will yield slightly different results. In general, FM is simpler to implement in software systems such as Csound, because it only requires oscillators. To implement PM, we need to break an oscillator apart into its constituent components, so it is slightly more involved. However, in hardware synthesizers, such as Yamaha's DX7, PM is the technique actually implemented. The reason is that PM is more resilient to rounding errors, allowing for the implementation of stacked modulation (modulators connected in series) and feedback (the carrier signal being fed back into itself as a modulator). These effects cannot be implemented using FM synthesis.

6 Time-Domain Audio Programming

Victor Lazzarini

This chapter will provide an overview of audio programming for time-domain signal process-ing (i.e. sound waveforms[1]). We will look at the essential and basic recipes for synthesis and effects, from wavetable synthesis to delay lines. All concepts will be discussed in terms of C++ examples, with fully working programs as a demonstration of each component studied. We will assume the reader is generally fluent in C and C++ (although examples are compli-ant with the latter language, most of them are written in a style that is very close the former).

6.1 Synthesis: Table-Lookup Oscillators

6.1.1 Before We Start: A Soundfile Interface

Before we study components for synthesis, such as the table-lookup oscillator, we would per-haps want to define a simple soundfile interface for sound output (and later we will add sound input). We could use the *libsndfile* library[2] as it is, but perhaps we can simplify it even further. We'll add a function interface to open a file for output, to write to it and to close it. This can be done taking the advantage of default parameters, and using *libsndfile* for its implementation:

```
SNDFILE *soundout_open(char* name, int chans=def_chans,
                       float sr=def_sr);

/** close output soundfile.
*/
void soundout_close(SNDFILE *psf_out);

/** soundfile output.

   psf_out: soundfile handle
   buffer: signal buffer, interleaved if multichannel
   vecsize: signal vector size in frames
   returns: number of frames output to file
*/
int soundout(SNDFILE *psf_out, float *buffer, int vecsize=def_vsize);
```

With this interface in place, we do not need to worry about the output anymore, we can just treat it as a "black box." An implementation of these functions is easily done using *libsndfile* or another similar library.

6.1.2 Oscillators: Some Important Issues

Frequency and Phase Increment

The first component we will look at is the oscillator. These are used primarily to generate periodic signals, such as a sine wave. If we start with this type of signal, we can discuss some important issues about oscillator implementation. Sine waves can be synthesized with a simple call to the `sin()` function:

```
a[n] = sin(n*2*pi*f/sr).
```

This will generate a sine wave signal with the frequency f at the sampling rate sr. This is a simple implementation that will work for limited cases, but not for all applications. The basic issue with this code is that, whereas it allows fixed values of frequency, it will fail when the frequency vary, as in a glissando. The reason for this is that the `sin()` function expects an angle, i.e. a *phase* angle, as its input. So when we supply with an expression that depends on a *frequency* value, we will have to transform that frequency value into a phase angle. That is in fact what is being done in the first example above. The phase angle changes with time (*n*, in samples) and is calculated by the expression `n*2*pi*f/sr`. However, if we change the frequency, the phase angle will not be calculated properly. We will have to update the phase using the fact that the frequency is equivalent to the phase difference between two calls of the `sin()` function. In other words, we will generate a new phase angle each time we call `sin()`, based on an increment according to the expression `2*pi*f/sr`:

```
a[n] = sin(pha);
pha += 2*pi*f/sr;
```

For the fixed frequency case, the two examples are equivalent. However, this example will work even it the frequency varies, whereas the first example will not.

Generality and Efficiency

The example above would work perfectly well to generate sine waves. However, in most applications, we would like to generate more than sine waves, and we would like to do it efficiently. One way of generating waveforms other than sines is to perform additive synthesis, based on the Fourier principles. This would mean calling `sin()` several times, once for each harmonic that we try to generate. This would be in many cases very slow and inefficient. Even for sine waves, a better method exists for signal generation.

Instead of calling `sin()` or any other periodic function for each sound sample, we could pre-calculate the function used, store it in memory and look it up whenever we want to get the value off the function. This is the table-lookup method of function evaluation and the basis for the table-lookup oscillator.

6.1.3   Table-Lookup Oscillator Basics

Wavetables

Wavetables will contain one cycle of a waveshape that is going to be used in synthesis. They will have a certain length and will usually be normalized (with values ranging from −1 to 1). In C++ terms, wavetables are arrays of floats of any size. The size of the wavetable will determine the precision of the function evaluation. A sine wave table can be created as follows:

```
for(int i=0; i < length; i++) table[i] = sin(i*2*pi/length);
```

Table Lookup

The output of the oscillator is based primarily on the table-lookup procedure, which is, in its simplest form, based on obtaining a value from the table array and scaling it with an amplitude value:

```
out[n] = a*table[(int)index];
```

The casting operation is needed because we will have to use a floating-point index (for precision) and array indices can only be integral.

Frequency Control

The fundamental frequency of the oscillator will depend on the increment of the phase index, as discussed above. This increment, called *sampling increment*, will depend on the user-defined frequency, the size of the table, and the sampling rate:

```
incr = f*length/sr;
index += incr;
```

For instance, if the table length is the same as the sampling rate, then for a frequency of 1 Hz the increment is 1. In this case we will reach the end of the table only after 1 second.

Modulus Operation

In order to make the lookup operation loop around the wavetable, we will have to check the index and apply a *generalized modulus* operation if it is beyond the required range. We are using the generalized modulus because we want to allow for negative frequencies, i.e. decrementing the phase index (looping backward). This is how we implement it:

```
while(index >= length) index -= length;
while(index < 0) index += length;
```

(See figure 6.1.)

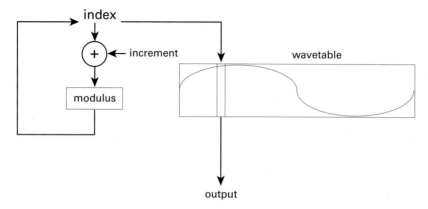

Figure 6.1
The elements of a table-lookup oscillator.

6.1.4   A Truncating Table-Lookup Oscillator

The basic elements discussed above can be put together to make a C++ function implementation of an oscillator. The simplest form will be the truncating oscillator, which truncates the floating-point index to obtain a value from the wavetable. One important point here is that we will need to provide some 'permanent' external memory for the phase index, as we will be calculating the next index position based on the previous one (and it is important to create a separate variable to hold this for each oscillator, if we want to have more than one, otherwise we will get in tangle).[3] Here is a basic prototype for such function:

```
float oscil(float amp, float freq, float* table, float* index,
    int len=1024, float sr=44100);
```

This function has as parameters the amplitude, the frequency, the wavetable, the index (an external variable), the table length, and the sampling rate. For simplicity, we will be using a single-precision float for the index, but in more robust implementations double precision is preferred. Here is the implementation:

```
float oscil(float amp, float freq, float* table, float* index,
            int len, float sr){
    float out;
    out = amp*table[(int) *index];
    *index += freq*len/sr;
    while (index >= len) index -= len;
    while (index < 0 ) index += len;
    return out;
}
```

Such a function could be used to generate a signal, when called in a processing loop:

```
for(int i=0; i < durs; i++) out[i] = oscil(0.5f, 440.f, wtab, &ndx);
```

Here we are using a normalized amplitude (in the range from -1.0 to $+1.0$) to facilitate things. The external variable ndx has been declared and initialized to 0 (notice how we have to pass it indirectly, by its address). The wavetable wtab[ ] has been allocated and filled with an arbitrary waveshape.

6.2   Oscillators: Implementation Issues

6.2.1   Processing Audio Vectors

The version of oscillator we have presented so far is simple conceptually, but still requires one more addition. At the moment, we are outputting one sample at a time, so for each sample we have to do a function call. For simple applications, this is not a problem. However, for larger systems using several such oscillators, the overhead involved in the function call might be problematic. Instead what can be done is to process audio in blocks, or vectors, of samples. In this case, our function will implement a loop that will process one vector of samples at a time. The function will only be called once for a number of output samples, which will increase efficiency. As a consequence, we will be splitting the processing into two rates: an audio sampling rate and a control rate. The latter is the rate at which we are calling the oscillator function, whereas the former is the inverse of the number of samples we will be expected to produce in one second.

   The new-look oscillator will have the following interface:

```
/** truncating table-lookup oscillator.

    output: output signal vector \n
    amp: amplitude \n
    freq: frequency \n
    table: function table \n
    index: lookup index \n
    length: function table length \n
    vecsize: signal vector size\n
    sr: sampling rate\n
                    \n
    returns: first output sample
*/
float osc(float *output, float amp, float freq,
          float *table, float *index,
          int length=def_len, int vecsize=def_vsize,
          long sr=def_sr);
```

The constants `def_len`, `def_vecsize`, and `def_sr` are previously defined (e.g. as 1,024,256 and 44,100). The implementation of the oscillator will then include a signal-generating loop:

```
float osc(float *output, float amp, float freq,
          float *table, float *index,
          int length, int vecsize, long sr)
{
    // increment
    float incr = freq*length/sr;

    // processing loop
    for(int i=0; i < vecsize; i++){
        // truncated lookup
        output[i] = amp*table[(int)(*index)];
        *index += incr;
        while(*index >= length) *index -= length;
        while(*index < 0) *index += length;
    }
    return *output;
}
```

Instead of just returning the output sample, we are filling an input buffer with the output signal. In fact, we are also returning the first output sample, for convenient use of this function with vectors of 1. The osc function will be called in a control loop, as in (here, dur is the total duration in *control samples*):

```
for(int i=0; i < dur; i++){
    osc(buffer,amp,freq,wave,&ndx);
    soundout(psf,buffer);
}
```

6.2.2 Control Rate

The preceding subsection introduced the concept of control rate, as well as, indirectly, control period (its inverse), control samples (the components of a control signal), and vector size (the number of audio samples in a control period). For efficiency reasons, we can have some synthesis components running at the control rate (cr) and others at the sampling rate (sr). For example, if we want to modulate the frequency or amplitude of an oscillator at sub-audio rates, we can generate a control signal from an oscillator and insert it at the right place, as in the following:

```
for(int i=0; i < dur; i++){
    osc(buffer,amp,
        freq+osc(&cs,10.f,5.f,wave,&ndx2,def_len,1,def_cr),
        wave,&ndx);
    soundout(psf,buffer);
}
```

Here we are using two oscillators: one that is running at the audio rate and another that is running at the control rate (notice also that we have to use two separate phase index variables). You can see that the latter has an output vector of one sample and it has the sampling rate of def_cr (def_sr/def_vecsize). Sub-audio modulation is one of the examples of the use of control-rate oscillators. However, if we are modulating a signal at audio ranges, then we will need control-rate oscillators (i.e. both oscillators at the same rate and with the same vector size).

6.2.3 Wavetable Generation

The best method for generating waveshapes to be used with oscillators for sound generation is by Fourier addition. Here we will generate and add the partials, which are integral multiples of a fundamental, scaled according to a certain principle, to the wavetable:

```
float* Fourier table(int harms, float *amps,
                int length, float phase){
    float a;
    float *table = new float[length+2];
    double w;
    phase *= (float)pi*2;

    memes(table,0,(length+2)*size of(float));

    for(int i=0; i < harms; i++)
        for(int n=0; n < length+2; n++){
            a = amps ? amps[i] : 1.f;
            w = (i+1)*(n*2*pi/length);
            table[n] += (float) (a*cos(w+phase));
        }

    normalize_table(table, length);
    return table;
}
```

The function allocates the table, resets it to 0, and then, if an array exists with the amplitudes, it uses the array values as the weights of each harmonic, otherwise it assumes all harmonics have the same amplitude. All harmonics are summed into the table and then the table is normalized. This function can be called to construct a series of standard shapes, such as sawtooth, square, and triangle (note that the first two use sums of sines, whereas the third uses cosines):

```
float* saw_table(int harms, int length){
    float *amps = new float[harms];
    for(int i=0; i < harms; i++) amps[i] = 1.f/(i+1);
    float *table = fourier_table(harms,amps,length, -0.25);
    delete[] amps;
    return table;
}

float* sqr_table(int harms, int length){
    float *amps = new float[harms];
    memset(amps, 0, sizeof(float)*harms);
    for(int i=0; i < harms; i+=2) amps[i] = 1.f/(i+1);
    float *table = fourier_table(harms,amps,length, -0.25);
    delete[] amps;
    return table;
}

float* triang_table(int harms, int length){
    float *amps = new float[harms];
    memset(amps, 0, sizeof(float)*harms);
    for(int i=0; i < harms; i+=2) amps[i] = 1.f/((i+1)*(i+1));
    float *table = fourier_table(harms,amps,length);
    delete[] amps;
    return table;
}
```

6.2.4   A Simple Example

Here is an example program using a sine-wave oscillator with vibrato:

```
#include <stdio.h>
#include <stdlib.h>
#include <snd_defs.h>

/** Simple synthesis program.

    Generates a sine-wave sound. This program shows the use of
    truncating oscillators.\n
    \n
    oscillator sndfile.wav amp freq(Hz) dur(secs)
*/
int main(int argc, char** argv) {
```

```
        SNDFILE *psf;
        float *buffer;
        int dur;

        float amp, freq, *wave, cs, ndx=0, ndx2=0;

        if(argc == 5){
            amp = (float) atof(argv[2]);
            freq = (float) atof(argv[3]);
            dur = (int) (atof(argv[4])*def_cr);

            // allocate buffer & table memory
            buffer = new float[def_vsize];
            wave = sinus_table();

            // now we open the file
        if(!(psf = soundout_open(argv[1]))){
            printf("error opening output file\n");
            exit(-1);
        }

            for(int i=0; i < dur; i++){
                osc(buffer,amp,
                    freq+osc(&cs,10.f,5.f,wave,&ndx2,
                    def_len,1, def_cr),
                    wave,&ndx);
                soundout(psf,buffer);
            }

            // close file & free memory
            soundout_close(psf);
            delete[] buffer;
            delete[] wave;

            return 0;
        }
        else {
            printf("usage: oscillator sndfile.wav "
                    "amp freq(hz) dur(s)\n");
            return 1;
        }
    }
```

6.3   Interpolation

Interpolation is an operation that is used in many applications in digital audio. Its basic use is to "fill in the gaps" when needed. For instance, if we decide to obtain a sample from a wavetable, fractionally between two table positions, we can interpolate between the two values to obtain the result. This is the basis for the interpolating oscillator.[4] Also, if we want to generate a curve between two points, we will be using interpolation to obtain the values for the curve.

6.3.1   Interpolating Oscillators

The simplest type of interpolation, which will be enough for most of the typical oscillator applications, is linear interpolation. If an index pos p falls between points x_1 and x_2, whose table values are y_1 and y_2, then, by linear interpolation we have

$$y = y_1 + (y_2 - y_1) \times (p - x_1). \tag{1}$$

Here x_1 and x_2 are consecutive integral indexes and p is the floating-point index. Linear interpolation is nothing more than a first-order function, a very simple mathematical device, with the general definition:

$$y = cx + d, \tag{2}$$

where $d = y_1$ and $c = y_1 - y_2$ (x being the fractional index position $p - x_1$).

A more complex but also more accurate interpolation for table-lookup oscillators is provided by cubic interpolation, where instead of taking just two points around the target position we will use four points by including the two outside values, y_0 and y_3. Cubic interpolation uses a third-order polynomial function of the form

$$y = ax^3 + bx^2 + cx + d. \tag{3}$$

Here we have a heavier computational load than the simple linear interpolation. Cubic (sometimes also called four-point) interpolation can use the following coefficients:

$$a = 0.5[y_1 - y_2] + [y_3 - y_0],$$
$$b = [y_0 + y_2]0.5 - y_1,$$
$$c = y_2 - 0.333y_0 - 0.5y_1 - 0.166y_3, \tag{4}$$
$$d = y_1.$$

Another important fact relating to interpolating oscillators is that we will need extra points at the end of the table for the mechanism to work. For linear interpolation, we will need one extra point at the end. For cubic interpolation, we will need two points at the end, plus we will have to take care when the index is below 1, so that the point equivalent to x_0 is read from the end of the table.

The following code implements linear interpolation. It expects the wavetable to have one extra point (at least) at its end:

```
float osci(float *output, float amp, float freq,
           float *table, float *index, float phase,
           int length, int vecsize, float sr)
{
    // increment
    float incr = freq*length/sr, frac, pos,a ,b;
    phase = phase < 0 ? 1+phase : phase;
    int offset = (int)(phase*length)%length;

    // processing loop
    for(int i=0; i < vecsize; i++){
        pos = *index + offset;

        // linear interpolation
        frac = pos - (int)pos;
        a = table[(int)pos];
        b = table[(int)pos+1];
        output[i] = amp*(a + frac*(b - a));

        *index += incr;
        while(*index >= length) *index -= length;
        while(*index < 0) *index += length;
    }

    return *output;

}
```

The next function implements cubic interpolation, as discussed above, and expects two extra points at the end of the table:

```
float oscc(float *output, float amp, float freq,
           float *table, float *index, float phase,
           int length, int vecsize, float sr)
{
    // increment
    float incr = freq*length/sr, frac, fracsq, fracb;
    float pos,y0,y1,y2,y3, tmp;
    phase = phase < 0 ? 1+phase : phase;
    int offset = (int)(phase*length)%length;

    // processing loop
    for(int i=0; i < vecsize; i++){

        pos = *index + offset;
```

```
    // cubic interpolation
    frac = pos - (int)pos;
    y0 = (int) pos > 0 ? table[(int)pos-1] : table[length-1];
    y1 = table[(int)pos];
    y2 = table[(int)pos+1];
    y3 = table[(int)pos+2];

    tmp = y3 + 3.f*y1;
    fracsq = frac*frac;
    fracb = frac*fracsq;

    output[i] = amp*(fracb*(- y0 - 3.f*y2 + tmp)/6.f +
                    fracsq*((y0+y2)/2.f—y1) +
                    frac*(y2 + (-2.f*y0 - tmp)/6.f) + y1);

    *index += incr;

    while(*index >= length) *index -= (length);
    while(*index < 0) *index += length;

  }

  return *output;

}
```

6.4 Envelopes

Envelopes can be generated in several ways. The basic principle is to have a certain curve, which will shape the amplitude (or any other parameter) of the sound. Curves can be created during processing by an interpolating function, or can be drawn into tables to be accessed by oscillators.

6.4.1 Envelope Tables

Interpolating linearly between two points generates the simplest envelope table, using basically the same principles outlined in subsection 6.3.1. For instance, to generate an N-point table, with linear interpolation, between 0 and 1, we can use the following code:

```
for(int i =0; i < N; i++)
    table[i] = (float)i/N;
```

More generally, we have

```
table[i] = start + i*(end—start)/N;
```

which can also be implemented as

```
tmp = start;
incr = (end—start)/N;
for(int i =0; i < N; i++) {
    table[i] = tmp;
    tmp += incr;
}
```

This will generate a single line segment. Multi-section envelopes can be built by splitting the table into similar sections. Linear envelopes can be enhanced by adding the concept of a curve coefficient. A curve coefficient can be used to bend the linear shape in two ways: (a) making it change quickly to start with and the straighten out; (b) the reverse, starting with small changes and increasing the rate of change as it reaches the end of the line segment

$$y(x) = y_1 + (y_2 - y_1)x^\alpha, \tag{5}$$

where x is the position in the range 0–1. The curve coefficient α determines the shape of the curve: if $\alpha < 1$, we have (a) ; if $\alpha > 1$, we have (b); if $\alpha = 1$, we have a linear segment.

Equation 5 will yield the following modification to the code:

```
table[i] = start + (end—start)*(pow((double)i/N, alpha);
```

6.4.2 Exponential Interpolation

Linear envelopes work well with simple controls, but for perceptually accurate envelopes it sometimes is necessary to use exponential interpolation. For instance, a constant-interval glissando requires this type of interpolation, because intervals are frequency ratios. The expression for exponential interpolation is

$$y(x) = y_1 \times (y_2/y_1)^x. \tag{6}$$

This type of interpolation requires that the values of y_1 and y_2 be non-zero and positive. Exponential interpolation can be used instead of linear interpolation for cases where the rate of a parameter change does not match what is expected, as in the case of continuous glissando.

The implementation of the exponential interpolation is quite simple:

```
for(int i =0; i< N; i++)
    table[i] = start*pow(end/start, (double) i/N);
```

Alternatively, it can be implemented as

```
tmp = start;
mult = pow(end/start, 1./N);
for(int i=0; i < N; i++){
    table[i] = tmp;
    tmp *= mult;
}
```

6.4.3   Examples of Envelope-Table Generators

Here are two examples of functions that can generate tables containing envelopes made up of segments of linear and exponential curves. A linear envelope-table generator can look like this:

```
float* line_table(int brkpts, float* pts, int length){
    float start,end,incr,*table = new float[length+2];

    for(int n=2; n < brkpts*2; n+=2){
        start = pts[n-1];
        end = pts[n+1];
        incr = (end - start)*1.f/(pts[n]-pts[n-2]);
        for(int i=(int)pts[n-2]; i < pts[n] && i < length+2; i++)
        {
            table[i] = start;
            start += incr;
        }
    }
    normalize_table(table, length);
    return table;
}
```

The following generator builds a table with exponential segments:

```
float* exp_table(int brkpts, float* pts, int length){
    float mult,*table = new float[length+2];
    double start, end;

    for(int n=2; n < brkpts*2; n+=2){
        start = pts[n-1] + 0.00000001;
        end = pts[n+1] + 0.00000001;
        mult = (float) pow(end/start,1./(pts[n]-pts[n-2]));
        for(int i=(int)pts[n-2]; i < pts[n] && i < length+2; i++)
        {
            table[i] = (float) start;
            start *= mult;
        }
    }
    normalize_table(table, length);
    return table;
}
```

These tables can be used with oscillators for envelope generation. Here is an example:

```
float pts[6] = {0,0,100.f, 1.f, 400.f, 0.f};
env = line_table(3, pts, 400);
```

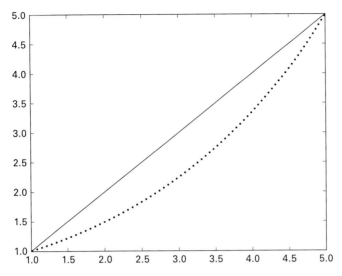

Figure 6.2
Linear (solid line) and exponential (dotted line) envelope segments.

This builds a table with three segments, from 0 to 1 (at pos 100) and back to 0 at the end of the table (400). Now we can use it in an oscillator by reading it with another oscillator:

```
oscc(buffer,
    osc(&out,amp,1/dur,env,&ndx2,400,1,def_cr),
    freq,wave,&ndx);
```

The oscillator is made to read once through the table (notice that its frequency is defined as 1/dur, where dur is the duration of the sound in seconds). Also note, and this is very important, that we have used separate variables to hold the indexes for each oscillator (don't mix them up).[5] See figure 6.2.

6.5   Envelope Generators

One of the disadvantages of using tables and oscillators as envelopes is that the size of each envelope segment will be stretched or compressed as the total duration of the sound changes. A solution for this is to employ fixed-length envelope generators. These generators can be used to provide controls for any parameter. Since they are producing control signals, we can implement them to run at the control rate. This means that they will always output a single sample, instead of a vector, and that they will take the control rate as their sampling rate. They will also have to keep track of the time, so an external time index (a sample count) will have to be supplied to them in the form of an integer variable address.

6.5.1 Linear

A linear generator is the simplest of these types of control-signal generators. It will draw a line between two points for a certain duration. What happens after that is not defined, but we can limit the output to the maximum value:

```
float line(float pos1, float dur, float pos2, int *cnt
          float cr){
   int durs = (int) (dur*cr);
   if((*cnt)++ < durs)
       return pos1 + *cnt*(pos2-pos1)/durs;
   else return pos2;
}
```

6.5.2 Exponential

An exponential generator can be built on the same principle, using the following code:

```
float expon(float pos1, float dur, float pos2, int *cnt,
           float cr){
   int durs = (int) (dur*cr);
   if((*cnt)++ < durs)
       return (float)(pos1*pow((double)pos2/pos1,(double)*cnt/durs));
   else return pos2;
}
```

6.5.3 Using Curve Coefficients

A linear envelope with a curve coefficient control can be a very flexible generator:

```
float interp(float pos1, float dur, float pos2, double alpha,
            int *cnt, float cr){
   int durs = (int) (dur*cr);
   if((*cnt)++ < durs)
   return (float) (pos1 + (pos2-pos1)*pow((double) *cnt/durs, alpha));
   else return pos2;
}
```

6.5.4 An ADSR Envelope

The typical envelope generator used to control the amplitude of synthesized sounds is the ADSR envelope. This is a four-stage envelope, comprising an attack (A) or rise period, a decay period (D), a sustain(S) portion, and a release (R) segment. Typically, in synthesizers, the ADSR t kicks into action in response to an external "trigger." The release stage is entered after

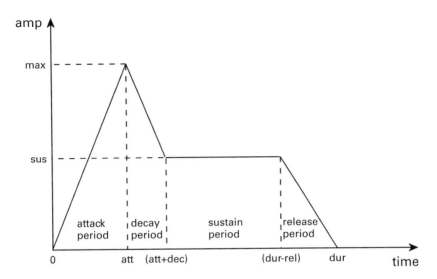

Figure 6.3
The ADSR envelope and its parameters.

a "note release" trigger (often a MIDI NOTE OFF command), so the overall length of the envelope is indeterminate.

Here, since we are not using controls of the aforementioned kind, we will run the ADSR from the start with a set total duration. We will then fit the different stages as portions of this total duration. The sustain period does not have a duration of its own, but it lasts for the amount of time that is left between the first two stages and the release period. This one is calculated backward from the end. The basic design problem that has to be solved is how to organize these four segments and provide the (linear) interpolation to generate the lines between the points. (See figure 6.3.)

The following is the ADSR prototype:

```
/** adsr envelope.

    maxamp: maximum amplitude\n
    dur: total duration (s)\n
    at: attack time (s)\n
    dt: decay time (s)\n
    sus: sustain amplitude\n
    rt: release time (s)\n
    cnt: time index\n
    cr: control rate\n
\n
    returns: output control sample
```

```
*/
float adsr(float maxamp, float dur, float at, float dt,
           float sus, float rt, int* cnt, float cr=def_cr);
```

Durations are in seconds, so we will have to convert them all to be in (control) samples. The attack period comes first:

```
// attack period
if(*cnt <= at) a = *cnt * (maxamp/at);
```

It goes from 0 to maxamp in at samples. Then the code moves into the rest of the envelope, starting with the decay period:

```
// decay period
else if(*cnt <= (at+dt))
    a = ((sus - maxamp)/dt)*(*cnt - at) + maxamp;
```

The counter cnt is incremented every sample, so now we check to see if there is any time left for the sustain period:

```
// sustain period
else if(*cnt <= (dur - rt))
    a = sus;
```

Otherwise we just move into the release period, which brings the amplitude back to zero:

```
// release period
else if(*cnt > (dur - rt))
    a = -(sus/rt)*(*cnt - (dur - rt)) + sus;
```

The complete ADSR envelope function is as follows:

```
float adsr(float maxamp, float dur, float at, float dt,
           float sus, float rt, int *cnt, float cr)
{
      float a;
      // convert to time in samples
    at = at*cr;
    dt = dt*cr;
    rt = rt*cr;
    dur = dur*cr;

    if(*cnt < dur) { // if time < total duration
        // attack period
        if(*cnt <= at) a = *cnt * (maxamp/at);
        // decay period
        else if(*cnt <= (at+dt))
            a = ((sus - maxamp)/dt)*(*cnt - at) + maxamp;
            // sustain period
```

```
        else if(*cnt <= (dur - rt))
            a = sus;
        // release period
        else if(*cnt > (dur - rt))
            a = -(sus/rt)*(*cnt - (dur - rt)) + sus;
    }
    else a = 0.f;

    // update time counter
    (*cnt)++;
    return a;
        }
```

6.5.5   An Example Program

The following example shows the use of envelopes to control amplitude and frequency of an oscillator:

```
#include <stdio.h>
#include <stdlib.h>
#include <snd_defs.h>

/** simple synthesis program with envelopes.

        Generates a sawtooth sound with frequency and amplitude
        envelopes. This program also shows the use of
        interpolating oscillators.\n
        \n
        envelope sndfile.wav amp freq(Hz) dur(secs)

*/
int main(int argc, char** argv) {

 SNDFILE *psf;
 float *buffer;
 int smps, cnt1=0, cnt2=0;

 float dur, amp, freq, *wave, ndx=0;

 if(argc == 5){
   amp = (float) atof(argv[2]);
   freq = (float) atof(argv[3]);
   dur = (float)atof(argv[4]);
   smps = (int) (dur*def_cr);

   // allocate buffer & table memory
   buffer = new float[def_vsize];
   wave = sinus_table();
```

```
    // now we open the file
    if(!(psf = soundout_open(argv[1]))){
    printf("error opening output file\n");
    exit(-1);
    }

    for(int i=0; i < smps; i++){
        oscc(buffer,
            amp*adsr(1.f,dur,0.05f, 0.1f, 0.7f, 0.2f, &cnt1),
            expon(freq,dur/2,freq*2, &cnt2),
            wave,&ndx);
        soundout(psf,buffer);
    }
// close file & free memory
    soundout_close(psf);
    delete[] buffer;
    delete[] wave;

return 0;
}
else {
    printf("usage: envelope sndfile.wav amp freq(hz) dur(s)\n");
    return 1;
}
}
```

6.6   Filters

6.6.1   Filter Basics

Filters are implemented by combining signals with their delayed copies, in different ways. There are two basic families of filters: filters that use delayed copies of their input, called feedforward or finite impulse response (FIR), and filters that use delayed outputs, called feedback or infinite impulse response (IIR). Filters of the second kind can also include feedforward elements.

In some digital filters, delays will be as small as one sample. The order of the filter is determined by the order of the delays used. If a filter uses a max of two-sample delays, it is classed as second-order. Filters are defined by their equations. These will show the delays used in the filter and the coefficients (gain multipliers) associated with each delay.

Here is an example of a second-order filter equation:

$$y(n) = a_0x(n) + a_2x(n-2) - b_1y(n-1) - b_2y(n-2), \tag{6}$$

where n is the current sample of a signal, $y(n)$ is the output, $x(n)$ is the input, with its coefficient a_0, a_2 is the coefficient associated with a two-sample delay of the input, and b_1 and b_2 are the coefficients associated with one-sample and two-sample delays of the filter output.

The frequency response is how a filter alters an input signal's amplitude and phase at different frequencies. The amplitude response is the part of the frequency response that has to do with boosting or attenuating the different input frequencies. The phase response determines the timing delays imposed on different frequencies. It can be linear (the same phase change at all frequencies) or non-linear. From the filter equation (and coefficients) we can determine the frequency response, and vice versa.

IIR filters are generally simple to implement but complex to design. One way around this is that they are generally offered in "pre-packed" formats—resonators, Butterworth filters, ellipticals, and so on. Their cutoff frequencies and bandwidths can be made time-varying, which is an important characteristic for musical applications.

FIR filters are simpler to design and can offer linear-phase characteristics, so they are often preferred by engineers. Implementing them is also easy; however, they can be computationally intensive, and time-varying can be difficult.

6.6.2 Resonators and Other IIR Filters

Resonators are basic general-purpose filters. They are well understood and provide good results for most applications. Resonators are feedback filters; that is, they use a combination of previous output samples with the current input sample. The basic resonator equation is

$$y(n) = x(n) - b_1 y(n-1) - b_2 y(n-2). \tag{7}$$

This equation defines a second-order filter, with coefficients b_1, and b_2. The frequency response of the filter will be determined by its coefficients. Conversely, we can determine the coefficients according to the filter characteristics we require.

The resonator will be defined by two main characteristics: center frequency and bandwidth. The coefficients b_1 and b_2 will be determined according to these parameters (f is the filter center frequency, BW is the filter's bandwidth, and sr is the sampling rate, all in hertz):

$$R = 1 - \pi(\text{BW/sr}), \tag{8}$$

$$b_1 = -[4R^2/(1 + R^2)]^* \cos(2\pi f/\text{sr}), \tag{9}$$

$$b_2 = R^2. \tag{10}$$

The output of the resonator will tend to vary with the center frequency and bandwidth, depending also on the input signal. With sharp resonances, it is possible that the filter will cause clipping distortion in most systems. To avoid that, we set a scaling factor to be applied to the input signal. To scale a signal at the center frequency to 1, we can use

$$scaling = (1 - R^2) \sin(2\pi f/\text{sr}). \tag{11}$$

Table 6.1
The second-order Butterworth coefficients.

	λ	ϕ	a_0	a_1	a_2	b_1	b_2
LP	$1/\tan(\pi f/\mathrm{sr})$	—	$1/(1 + 2\lambda + \lambda^2)$	$2a_0$	a_0	$2a_0(1 - \lambda^2)$	$a_0(1 - 2\lambda + \lambda^2)$
HP	$\tan(\pi f/\mathrm{sr})$	—	$1/(1 + 2\lambda + \lambda^2)$	$2a_0$	a_0	$2a_0(\lambda^2 - 1)$	$a_0(1 - 2\lambda + \lambda^2)$
BP	$1/\tan(\pi \mathrm{BW}/\mathrm{sr})$	$2\cos(2\pi f/\mathrm{sr})$	$1/(1 + \lambda)$	0	$-a_0$	$-\lambda\phi a_0$	$a_0(\lambda - 1)$
BR	$\tan(\pi \mathrm{BW}/\mathrm{sr})$	$2\cos(2\pi f/\mathrm{sr})$	$1/(1 + \lambda)$	$-\phi a_0$	a_0	$-\phi a_0$	$a_0(\lambda - 1)$

One of the problems with resonators is that there is a deformation on its amplitude response curve, when the frequency is close to 0 Hz or the Nyquist limit. The attenuation below (or above) is not as good in these situations. A proposed solution is to add a two-sample feedforward delay to the filter. This has the effect of creating a "zero" (attenuation) at 0 Hz and the Nyquist frequencies.[6] The tradeoff is that the filter rolloff at the other side of the band becomes less steep:

$$y(n) = x(n) - a_2 x(n - 2) - b_1 y(n - 1) - b_2 y(n - 2), \tag{12}$$

where a_2 can either be set to 1 or to the value of R.

There are a number of other "ready-made" digital filter designs, based on analog filters of particular characteristics.[7] A typical example of these is found in the Butterworth design. Butterworth filters offer a maximally flat *passband* and a good *stopband* attenuation and come in BP, LP, HP, and Band-Reject (BR) flavors. They employ both feedback and feedforward delays and are realized in second-order sections, as in:

$$y(n) = a_0 x(n) + a_1 x(n - 1) + a_2 x(n - 2) - b_1 y(n - 1) - b_2 y(n - 2). \tag{13}$$

It is possible to have a basic filter "engine" for a second-order Butterworth section, which can be made into any amplitude response shape by just modifying how its coefficients are calculated. The "recipes" for LP, HP, BP, and BR are shown in table 6.1 (f is the filter centre or cutoff frequency, BW its bandwidth, and sr the sampling rate, all in hertz).

6.7   Filters: Implementation

6.7.1   Direct Forms

A filter equation can be implemented in two basic ways:

(a) direct form I: using separate delays for feedback and feedforward sections (see figure 6.4):

$$y(n) = a_0 x(n) + a_1 x(n - 1) + a_2 x(n - 2) - b_1 y(n - 1) - b_2 y(n - 2) \tag{14}$$

(b) direct form II: the filter equation is re-arranged in two separate equations and the same delays can be used for feedforward and feedback signal paths (see figure 6.5):

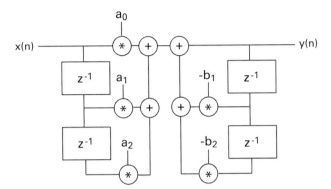

Figure 6.4
Direct Form I filter flow chart.

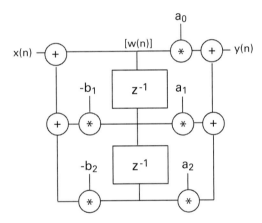

Figure 6.5
Direct Form II filter flow chart.

$$w(n) = x(n) - b_1 w(n-1) - b_2 w(n-2) \qquad \text{[feedback]}, \tag{15}$$

$$y(n) = a_0 w(n) + a_1 w(n-1) + a_2 w(n-2) \qquad \text{[feedforward]}. \tag{16}$$

6.7.2 Low-Pass and High-Pass Filters: First Order

Simple tone-control-type filters, which provide a gentle low-pass or high-pass amplitude response, can be implemented with a basic first-order recursive (or feedback) filter based on the equation

$$y(n) = ax(n) - by(n-1). \tag{17}$$

Table 6.2
First-order IIR coefficients.

	a	b
LP	$1 + b$	$\sqrt{[2 - \cos(2\pi f/\mathrm{sr})]^2 - 1} - 2 + \cos(2\pi f/\mathrm{sr})$
HP	$1 - b$	$2 - \cos(2\pi f/\mathrm{sr}) - \sqrt{[2 - \cos(2\pi f/\mathrm{sr})]^2 - 1}$

The coefficients a and b can be calculated as shown in table 6.2 (f is the filter cutoff frequency and sr the sampling rate, both in hertz).

As can be seen from the above, changing the low-pass response to a high-pass one is just a matter of multiplying the b coefficient by -1 while keeping a unchanged.

Here is the C++ code for these two filters. We will use an externally allocated memory variable to hold the one-sample feedback delay.

```
float lowpass(float* sig, float freq, float *del,
              int vecsize, float sr){

   double costh, coef;
   costh = 2. - cos(2*pi*freq/sr);
   coef = sqrt(costh*costh - 1.) - costh;

   for(int i =0; i < vecsize; i++){
       sig[i] = (float) (sig[i]*(1 + coef) - *del*coef);
       *del = sig[i];
   }

   return *sig;
}

float highpass(float* sig, float freq, float *del,
               int vecsize, float sr){

   double costh, coef;
   costh = 2. - cos(2*pi*freq/sr);
   coef = costh - sqrt(costh*costh - 1.);

   for(int i =0; i < vecsize; i++){
       sig[i] = (float) (sig[i]*(1 - coef) - *del*coef);
       *del = sig[i];
   }

   return *sig;
}
```

6.7.3 Resonators

The resonator filter uses one-sample and two-sample feedback delays. The resonator filter expression and coefficients have already been discussed. Here is a C++ function that implements this filter:

```
float resonator(float* sig, float freq, float bw, float *del,
                int vecsize,float sr){

    double r, rsq, rr, costh, scal;
    rr = 2*(r = 1. - pi*(bw/sr));
    rsq = r*r;
    costh = (rr/(1.+rsq))*cos(2*pi*freq/sr);
    scal = (1 - rsq)*sin(acos(costh));

    for(int i=0; i < vecsize; i++){
        sig[i] = (float)(sig[i]*scal + rr*costh*del[0] - rsq*del[1]);
        del[1] = del[0];
        del[0] = sig[i];
    }
    return *sig;
}
```

The improved version of the resonator filter, using a two-sample feedforward delay, can be implemented using the basic resonator coefficients, but modifying the scaling factor and adding the a_2 term as follows:

$$scaling = 1 - R, \tag{18}$$

$$a_2 = R, \tag{19}$$

where R is the filter radius, calculated from the bandwidth. Since we are using feedback and feedforward delays, we will use direct form II as discussed above, separating the filter into two equations:

```
float bandpass(float* sig, float freq, float bw, float *del,
                int vecsize,float sr){

    double r, rsq, rr, costh, scal, w;
    rr = 2*(r = 1. - pi*(bw/sr));
    rsq = r*r;
    costh = (rr/(1.+rsq))*cos(2*pi*freq/sr);
    scal = (1 - r);

    for(int i=0; i < vecsize; i++){
        w = scal*sig[i] + rr*costh*del[0] - rsq*del[1];
        sig[i] = (float)(w - r*del[1]);
```

```
        del[1] = del[0];
        del[0] = (float) w;
    }
    return *sig;
}
```

Note that in this design we will scale the signal as it enters the filter, as the scaling factor here is not the a_0 coefficient. For general-purpose second-order sections (such as those used in Butterworth filters), we would apply the a_0 coefficient to the feedforward section of the equation.

6.7.4   RMS Estimation and Signal Balancing

When using filters, sometimes it is necessary to provide a signal-rescaling facility, as the overall amplitude of the output might be very different from the input. This is often the case when a cascading connection of filters is used. If we estimate the root-mean-square (RMS) of the filter output and the RMS of a comparator signal, we can rescale the output to match the amplitude of the comparator. This is the basis of the balance or envelope follower processor.

The RMS is estimated by rectifying the signal (taking its absolute values) and low-pass filtering it (also, instead of rectification, we could have taken its square root). The scaling gain to be applied will be the ratio of the comparator RMS to the input RMS. Here is the code for the balance processor:

```
float balance(float *sig, float *cmp, float* del, float freq,
              int vecsize, float sr){

    double costh, coef;
    costh = 2. - cos(2*pi*freq/sr);
    coef = sqrt(costh*costh - 1.) - costh;

    for(int i=0; i < vecsize; i++){
        del[0] = (float)((sig[i] < 0 ? -sig[i] : sig[i])*(1+coef)
                 - del[0]*coef);
        del[1] = (float)((cmp[i] < 0 ? -cmp[i] : cmp[i])*(1+coef)
                 - del[1]*coef);
        sig[i] *= (float)(del[0] ? del[1]/del[0] : del[1]);
    }
    return *sig;
}
```

Notice that the LP design used is the basic first-order feedback low-pass filter discussed above. The rectification is combined with the filter equation in one single expression. Two delays are used, one for each filter and the input is scaled by the RMS ratio of the two signals.

6.7.5   A Programming Example

Here is a simple program employing an oscillator, a filter, and a balance processor:

```
#include <stdio.h>
#include <stdlib.h>
#include <snd_defs.h>

/** subtractive synthesis program with envelopes.

    Generates a filtered sawtooth sound with amplitude
    and filter cf envelopes. This program also shows the use
    of interpolating oscillators.\n
    \n
    envelope sndfile.wav amp freq(Hz) dur(secs)

*/
int main(int argc, char** argv) {
    SNDFILE *psf;
    float *buffer;
    int smps, bytes = sizeof(float)*def_vsize, cnt1=0, cnt2=0;

    float dur, amp, freq, *wave, *comp, ndx=0;

    if(argc == 5){
        amp = (float) atof(argv[2]);
        freq = (float) atof(argv[3]);
        dur = (float)atof(argv[4]);
        smps = (int) (dur*def_cr);

        // allocate buffer, delay & table memory
        buffer = new float[def_vsize];
        comp = new float[def_vsize];
        float del[2]={0.f, 0.f}, del1[2]={0.f,0.f};
        wave = saw_table(30);

        // now we open the file
        if(!(psf = soundout_open(argv[1]))){
            printf("error opening output file\n");
            exit(-1);
        }

        for(int i=0; i < smps; i++){
            oscc(buffer,
                adsr(amp,dur,0.05f, 0.1f, amp*0.7f, 0.2f, &cnt1),
                freq,
                wave,&ndx);
```

```
        memcpy(comp, buffer, bytes);
        resonator(buffer, expon(freq*8,dur,freq*4, &cnt2), 50, del);
        balance(buffer, comp, del1);
        soundout(psf,buffer);
    }
    // close file & free memory
    soundout_close(psf);
    [] buffer;
    delete[] comp;
    delete[] wave;

    return 0;
}
else {
    printf("usage: filter sndfile.wav amp freq(hz) dur(s)\n");
    return 1;
}
}
```

6.8   Delay-Based Sound Processing

The majority of the classic techniques of time-domain signal processing involve the use of signal delays. These uses range from the use small delays already discussed examples of IIR filters to longer delays in reverberation and variable delays in flanging, pitch effects, etc.

6.8.1   Soundfile Input

Before examining the use of delays in processing techniques and their implementation, we will have to introduce some means of signal input. Here we will define a simple soundfile interface for sound input, similarly to what we have already done with output. We will add a function interface to open a file for input, to read from it and to close it. This can be done using libsndfile for its implementation (or a similar library; in any case, we can treat this as a "black box"):

```
SNDFILE *soundin_open(char* name, int *chans, float *sr);

/** close output soundfile.
*/
void soundin_close(SNDFILE *psf_in);

/** soundfile output.

    psf_out: soundfile handle
    buffer: signal buffer, interleaved if multichannel
```

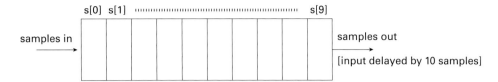

Figure 6.6
Conceptual view of a delay line.

```
    vecsize: signal vector size in frames
    returns: number of frames output to file
*/
int soundin(SNDFILE *psf_out, float *buffer, int vecsize=def_vsize);
```

The basic difference from the `soundout()` interface is that, since we are reading from a file, the basic parameters relating to number of channels and sampling rate can be obtained from the file (or at least checked for consistency). These parameters are copied into the `*chans` and `*sr` variables by the `soundin_open()` function.

6.8.2   Delay Lines

Delay lines are the basic component of all the processing techniques discussed here. Their basic function is to delay a signal by a certain amount of time, which can be set in seconds, milliseconds, or samples (taking the sampling rate in consideration).

The amount of actual time delay in figure 6.6 will be determined by the sampling rate as well as the size of the delay line in samples. For a ten-sample delay at 44,100 hertz, this will be 10/44,100 seconds, or 0.227 millisecond.

6.8.3   Circular Buffers

Small delays, in the case of the ones used in second-order filters, are implemented by a first-in first-out (FIFO) structure, where samples are copied from one memory location to the next, as in the conceptual example above. However, for larger delays, this will mean an unnecessary number of sample shifts, because the same thing can be implemented more efficiently without moving any samples in the delay line. In this case, we will use a programming construct called a *circular buffer*.

A circular buffer works by keeping the samples in place and moving the reading and writing positions along the buffer, wrapping around when at the end of the buffer. (See figure 6.7.) In this case, all we need do is keep track of the writing pointers. Moreover, in the simplest cases, we need to keep track of only one pointer, as the writing operation can be preceded by the reading operation on the same memory position. In order to effect a certain

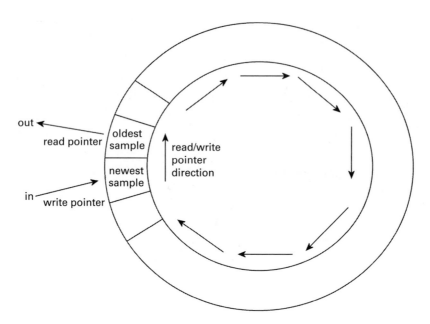

Figure 6.7
The circular buffer.

time delay, we will allocate the necessary number of samples and then, using an index, read and write to memory, incrementing the pointer after the writing operation. Nothing could be simpler.

6.8.4 Fixed Delays

Here is an example of a fixed-delay implementation, based on a circular buffer. The function will require the delay buffer to be allocated externally and the index (pointer) also to exist as an externally allocated variable. Three basic actions will have to be implemented, in the following order:

1. Read the delay buffer at the current position to generate the output.
2. Write the input signal that position.
3. Increment the position index (r/w pointer), checking if we have not reached the end of the buffer.

This can be done as follows:

```
float delay(float *sig, float dtime, float *del,
            int *p, int vecsize, float sr){
    int dt;
```

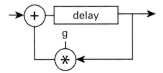

Figure 6.8
Comb-filter flow chart.

```
float out;
dt = (int) (dtime*sr);

    for(int i=0; i < vecsize; i++){
    out = del[*p];
    del[*p] = sig[i];
    sig[i] = out;
    *p = (*p != dt-1 ? *p+1 : 0);
}
    return *sig;
}
```

This function, if combined with the input signal, will create a single slap-back echo. The amount of delay will be dependent on the delay time parameter (in seconds, generally set to the size of the delay buffer, possibly less but never exceeding it).

Reverberation and echo are examples of effects that employ fixed delays. Reverberators can be constructed quite efficiently by connecting together small units such as comb filters and allpass filters.[8] These can be also used on their own for a variety of effects.

6.8.5   Comb Filters

Comb filters are based on a fixed delay line with a feedback circuit inserted into it. The amount of feedback is controlled by the parameter

$$g = 0.001^{\tau/\text{RVT}}, \tag{19}$$

where τ is the delay time and RVT is the total reverb time of the comb filter. (See figure 6.8.) The reverb time is defined as the time it takes for the output of the comb filter to fall to 1/1,000 of its original amplitude (-60 dB) once its input has stopped. A simple modification of the above code for fixed delays will implement a comb filter:

```
float comb(float *sig, float dtime, float gain,
           float *delay, int *p, int vecsize, float sr){
    int dt;
    float out;
```

```
    dt = (int) (dtime*sr);
    for(int i=0; i < vecsize; i++){
        out = delay[*p];
        delay[*p] = sig[i] + out*gain;
        sig[i] = out;
        *p = (*p != dt-1 ? *p+1 : 0);
    }
    return *sig;
}
```

Comb filters can be used in a variety of applications. On their own they can be employed for echo effects and as resonating chambers (with very short delays and high feedback gain values). In reverberators, they are usually connected in parallel, their output feeding one or more allpass filters in series.

6.8.6   Allpass Filters

These component reverberators are very similar to comb filters, but they also include a feed-forward section in addition to the feedback. Here is the code:

```
float allpass(float *sig, float dtime, float gain,
                float *delay, int *p, int vecsize, float sr){
    int dt;
    float dlout;
    dt = (int) (dtime*sr);
    for(int i=0; i < vecsize; i++){
        dlout = delay[*p];
        delay[*p] = sig[i] + dlout*gain;
        sig[i] = dlout - gain*sig[i];
        *p = (*p != dt-1 ? *p+1 : 0);
    }
    return *sig;
}
```

(See figure 6.9.)

This type of allpass filter is often employed in series connections to create thick reverberation effects.

6.9   Variable and Multitap Delays

So far we have only discussed the aspects relating to delays that are fixed, or at least, that change only occasionally. The possibility of modulating the delay time will open the doors for a variety of effects, including flanging, chorusing, vibrato, doppler, and pitch shifting.

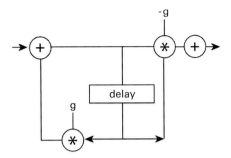

Figure 6.9
Allpass-filter flow chart.

6.9.1   Implementing a Variable Delay Line

In order to implement variable delays using circular buffers, we should consider these four points:

1. Since the writing to the delay line will always proceed sample by sample, we will have to calculate our delay in relation to the writer pointer position, in order to obtain a reading position index.
2. The reading position, when calculated as an offset from the writing position, might fall beyond the delay buffer memory; in this case we will have to provide a modulus operation to bring it to the right range.
3. The reading position index might fall between buffer positions, if we are to calculate precise delays. To get a good result, we will have to interpolate to generate the output.
4. When interpolating linearly, we need the next sample to our truncated read-position. A special case arises when this position is the last sample in the delay buffer; in this case we will read the first position of the array as the next point.

Once these points are considered, all we need is a little editing of the fixed-delay code.

6.9.2   Flanger

As an example of the use of variable delay lines, we can implement a simple flanger effect. First, we introduce a variable delay implementation, which is based on a variation of the code in subsection 6.8.4:

```
float vdelay(float *sig, float vdtime, float maxdel,
             float *delay, int *p, int vecsize, float sr){
    int mdt,rpi;
    float out, rp, vdt, frac, next;
    vdt = vdtime*sr;
```

```
    mdt = (int) (maxdel*sr);
    if(vdt > mdt) vdt = (float) mdt;
    for(int i=0; i < vecsize; i++){
        rp = *p - vdt;
        rp = (rp >= 0 ? (rp < mdt ? rp : rp - mdt) : rp + mdt);
        rpi = (int) rp;
        frac = rp - rpi;
        next = (rpi != mdt-1 ? delay[rpi+1] : delay[0]);
        out = delay[rpi] + frac*(next - delay[rpi]);
        delay[*p] = sig[i];
        sig[i] = out;
        *p = (*p != mdt-1 ? *p+1 : 0);
    }
    return *sig;
}
```

The delay time can be modulated by a periodic source or an envelope. In the programming example below, we are using a simple envelope to change the delay time. The actual `flanger()` function used in the programming example is a variation on the `vdelay()` function that includes a feedback path (as in the comb filter), with the following prototype:

```
float flanger(float *sig, float vdtime, float fdb,
              float maxdel,float *delay, int *p,
              int vecsize=def_vsize, float sr=def_sr);
```

The feedback path is created by modifying one line from the `vdelay()` code, writing the delay as follows:

```
delay[*p] = sig[i] + out*fdb;
```

Here is the full program code for our flanger effect:

```
/** flanging program with envelopes.
    Flanges an input sound with a delay time envelope.
    \n
    delay infile.* outfile.wav maxdelay(s) env_dur(s)
*/
int main(int argc, char** argv) {
    SNDFILE *psfo, *psfi;
    float *buffer;
    int chans, bytes = sizeof(float)*def_vsize, cnt=0, pt=0, ts=0;

    float sr, dur, dtime, *comp, *del, del1[2]={0.f, 0.f};

    if(argc == 5){
        dtime = (float) atof(argv[3]);
        dur = (float) atof(argv[4]);
```

```
        // allocate buffer and delay memory
        buffer = new float[def_vsize];
        comp = new float[def_vsize];
        del = new float[(int)(dtime*def_sr)];
        memset(del, 0, sizeof(float)*(int)(dtime*def_sr));

        // now we open the files
        if(!(psfi = soundin_open(argv[1], &chans, &sr))){
            printf("error opening input file\n");
            exit(-1);
        }

        if(chans > 1 || sr != def_sr) {
            printf("unsupported channels or sr\n");
            exit(-1);
        }

        if(!(psfo = soundout_open(argv[2]))){
            printf("error opening output file\n");
            exit(-1);
        }
        do {
            cnt = soundin(psfi, buffer);
            memcpy(comp, buffer, bytes);
            flanger(buffer, line(.0001f, dur, dtime, &ts), 0.8f,
                    dtime, del, &pt);
            balance(buffer, comp, del1);
            soundout(psfo,buffer, cnt);
        } while(cnt);

        // close file & free memory
        soundin_close(psfi);
        soundout_close(psfo);
        delete[] buffer;
        delete[] comp;
        delete[] del;

        return 0;
    }
  else {
     printf("usage: flanger infile.* outf.wav maxdelay(s)
            env_dur(s)\n");
     return 1;
     }
  }
```

6.9.3   Other Effects

The `vdelay()` function shown above can be used to implement most of the other variable delay effects. Chorusing can be performed by adding a few delayed signals (without feedback), modulated by an LFO a low-frequency oscillator (LFO). Vibrato can be created by using an LFO to modulate the delay time (again without feedback). Doppler shift can be created by calculating a variable delay based on the distance from a moving source.

6.9.4   Multitap Delays and Convolution

In addition to fixed and variable delays, another interesting possibility is that of adding other "taps" to the delay line. Here, instead of only extracting the output at a single point in the circular buffer (at the end or at variable points), we will get it at more than one position; thus it is a *multitap delay*. The typical application of such a unit is to reproduce early reflections for reverberation, where, for instance, each tap models the echo from a surface in a room. In fact the extreme case of multitap delays is found where we place a tap at each position in a delay line. This can be used to implement the operation of convolution,[9] which is one of the means used to recreate realistic early reverberation effects.

In this case, we will also apply a gain multiplier to each tap. Each output sample will be a sum of N taps, where N is the size of the delay line. The sequence of gain values is also N-size and is often called the *impulse response* (IR). This is can be seen as a digital signal with N samples, which could be obtained, for instance, by recording the result of a very short burst of noise played into a room (the noise is the *impulse* and the recording is of the room's response to it). Another way of looking at this is to think of the IR as the amplitude of each individual reflection of the room's surfaces. Furthermore, the operation can be generalized as a method of imparting the characteristics of a system into an input sound. It is also a means of implementing FIR filters, as the IR is effectively a sequence of feedforward filter coefficients.

The time-domain implementation of convolution is shown schematically in figure 6.10. We need two basic components: a circular buffer (seen in the center of the figure), tapped at each point, and a table containing the impulse response in positions ranging from 0 to $N-1$ (the 'imp' array in the figure).

The mechanism is effectively the same seen in fixed delays, the write pointer being incremented for each input sample, except that now we will have to sum up all the scaled outputs of each tap (so we have N read pointers). This is implemented as an inner loop that cycles through all positions in the buffer, extracting their samples and scaling them. Here is a function that performs the convolution of an input signal and an impulse response:

```
float fir(float *sig, float *imp, float *del,
          int length, int *p, int vecsize, float sr){

    float out=0.f; int rp;
```

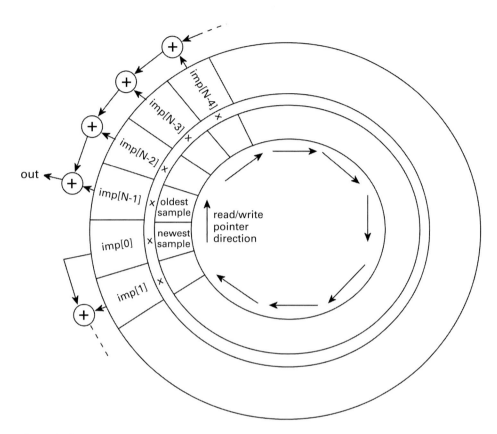

Figure 6.10
Time-domain convolution with a circular buffer.

```
for(int i=0; i < vecsize; i++){
    del[*p] = sig[i];
    *p = (*p != length-1 ? *p+1 : 0);
    for(int j=0; j < length; j++){
        rp = *p+j;
        rp = (rp < length ? rp : rp - length);
        out += (del[rp]*imp[length-1-j]);
    }
    sig[i] = out;
    out = 0.f;
}
return *sig;
}
```

This function can then be used in a program that implements time-domain convolution of two soundfiles (one the input signal and the other the IR). We allocate the delay buffer and the impulse table depending on the size of the latter and then apply the process to the stream of input samples. This process is quite processor intensive and becomes slow with large IRs (because it does N additions and multiplications per sample), so we might want to display its progress to inform the impatient user that the program is still running. Also, depending on the files used, clipping can occur, so it is good to have a gain control for attenuation or boost of the output signal. Here is an example program:

```
#include <stdio.h>
#include <stdlib.h>
#include <snd_defs.h>

/** convolution program.

    Convolution of an input file and an impulse

    \n
    conv infile.* impulse.* outfile.wav gain

*/
int main(int argc, char** argv) {
    SNDFILE *psfo, *psfi[2];
    float *buffer, gain;
    int chans,i,j=0,cnt=0,pt=0,size;
    float sr, *imp, *del;

    if(argc == 5){

        // allocate buffer, delay & table memory
        buffer = new float[def_vsize];
        gain = atof(argv[4]);

        // now we open the files
        if(!(psfi[0] = soundin_open(argv[1], &chans, &sr))){
            printf("error opening input file\n");
            exit(-1);
        }

        if(chans > 1 || sr != def_sr) {
            printf("unsupported channels or sr\n");
            exit(-1);
        }

        if(!(psfi[1] = soundin_open(argv[2], &chans, &sr))){
            printf("error opening impulse file\n");
            exit(-1);
```

```
    }
    if(chans > 1 || sr != def_sr) {
        printf("unsupported channels or sr\n");
        exit(-1);
    }

    if(!(psfo = soundout_open(argv[3]))){
        printf("error opening output file\n");
        exit(-1);
    }

    size = dataframes(psfi[1]);
    del = new float[size];
    imp = new float[size];
    memset(del, 0, sizeof(float)*size);

    // copy impulse into table
    do {
        cnt = soundin(psfi[1],buffer);
        for(i=0; i < cnt; i++,j++) imp[j] = buffer[i];
    } while(cnt);

    printf("Processing (this might take a while). . . \n");
    // process
    j=0;
    do {
        cnt = soundin(psfi[0], buffer);
        fir(buffer,imp,del,size,&pt);
        for(i=0; i < def_vsize; i++) buffer[i] *= gain;
        soundout(psfo,buffer);
        memset(buffer,0,sizeof(float)*def_vsize);
        if(j%(def_vsize*50)==0) printf("%.3f secs..\n", j/def_sr);
        j+=def_vsize;
    } while(cnt);

    // tail (last N-1 samples)
    cnt = size - 1;
    do {
        fir(buffer,imp,del,size,&pt);
        (i=0;i < def_vsize; i++) buffer[i] *= gain;
        soundout(psfo,buffer);
        memset(buffer,0,sizeof(float)*def_vsize);
        cnt -= def_vsize;
    }   while(cnt >= 0);
```

```
        // close file & free memory
        soundin_close(psfi[0]);
        soundin_close(psfi[1]);
        soundout_close(psfo);
        delete[] buffer;
        delete[] imp;
        delete[] del;

        return 0;
    }
    else {
        printf("usage: conv infile.* impulse.* outfile.wav gain \n");
        return 1;
    }
}
```

6.10   An Essential Application: An Audio Effect Plug-in

Audio plug-ins are now so ubiquitous in computer systems that we could consider them the "essential" application for our "essential" components. They have some advantages over full programs and other types of development, as the work is focused on audio programming tasks rather than other aspects of making the software work. This section describes the steps in putting together a plug-in, for which we will choose a popular (albeit proprietary) application programming interface[10] called VST.[11] Other types of plug-ins, including Audio Units and Csound opcodes, are discussed elsewhere in the book.

What is a plug-in? First of all, it is different from the full programs developed in our previous examples in an important aspect: it is designed to be a component of an existing system (i.e. the plug-in *host*), rather than a stand-alone application. Because of this, it will not need to implement any of the infrastructures of a program, such as connections to the soundcards, file IO, user interfaces,[12] and application control.

From the OS point of view, plug-ins are dynamic-loadable modules, a type of software library that a running program, the host, can load up and use. On Windows these are known as DLLs and have a *.dll file extension; on Linux they generally have *.so extension (with some exceptions); on OSX these types of libraries are known as *bundles*. In addition, on OSX, the bundle file is often hidden under a small directory structure, which might contain some associated resource files.

A plug-in API, such as VST, allows developers to create the code elements (classes, functions, and so on) that the host application expects to see when it loads and runs it. Generally speaking, a plug-in is a class[13] that is instantiated[14] (i.e. created in memory, initialized, etc.) by the host, creating one or more objects of this plug-in type that can be run to process audio. Some APIs are based on the C language. Others are written in C++, and this is the case with VST.

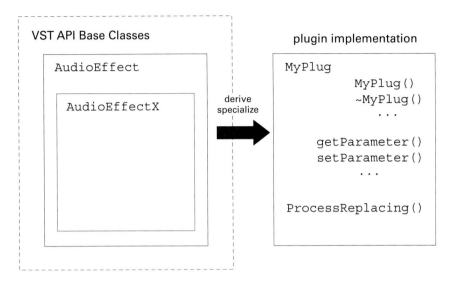

Figure 6.11
VST plug-in base and derived classes.

This API offers two base classes, which the developer will specialize[15] (i.e. write new classes derived from them). VST hosts then are able to call methods (functions) of the base class to run the specialized code we have written. A plugin host developer does not need to know about the internal details of the process implemented in a plug-in. This is possible because the host and the plug-in share the same interface provided by the API.

6.10.1   Deriving a Plug-in Class from the VST Base Classes

A VST plug-in is derived from the `AudioEffectX` class, which in turn is derived from `AudioEffect`. Both of these classes provide the interface that our plug-in is expected to implement (figure 6.11). They also offer some functionality that we might find useful, such as getting the sampling rate of the host, retrieving parameters, and receiving MIDI. Not all of this functionality is needed at all times, and we can use and implement only the relevant parts of the interface.

In our present application, we will be doing the following:

1. initializing: allocating any memory needed, setting initial values for variables and parameters, etc.; also termination (freeing up memory)
2. retrieving parameters from the host, so we can have real-time control of our processes; this will also include keeping track of programs (which are stored sets of parameter values)
3. processing audio.

We will then implement some of the base class methods that the host will use to perform them. Let's go straight to our class definition, which looks like this (with some bits missing):

```
class MyPlug : public AudioEffectX
{
    protected:

    /* our internal variables, we'll leave this for later */

    public:
    /* initialization and termination */
        MyPlug (audioMasterCallback audioMaster);
        ~MyPlug ();
        virtual void resume ();
        virtual bool getEffectName (char* name);
        virtual bool getVendorString (char* text);
        virtual bool getProductString (char* text);
        virtual VstInt32 getVendorVersion () { return 1024; }
        virtual VstPlugCategory getPlugCategory ()
            { return kPlugCategEffect; }

    /* processing */
    virtual void processReplacing (float** inputs, float** outputs,
                                    VstInt32 sampleFrames);

    /* parameters and programs */
    virtual void setParameter (VstInt32 index, float value);
    virtual float getParameter (VstInt32 index);
    virtual void getParameterLabel (VstInt32 index, char* label);
    virtual void getParameterDisplay (VstInt32 index, char* text);
    virtual void getParameterName (VstInt32 index, char* text);
    virtual void setProgram (VstInt32 program);
    virtual void setProgramName (char* name);
    virtual void getProgramName (char* name);
    virtual bool getProgramNameIndexed (VstInt32 category,
                                    VstInt32 index, char* text);

    /* plus any extra methods we might create specially for our
        class */

};
```

As the comments indicate, we have the three tasks clearly laid out in the class definition. We will be specializing base-class methods (named "virtual") to implement the functionality we need. Their names are good indicatives of what they are supposed to do, as we will see later. Later we will also add any variables we require for our processing and some of our own methods (to set variables etc.), which we omitted here. Now it is a good time to introduce our effect.

6.10.2   A Pitch Shifter

A notable side effect of the variable delays introduced above can be used to create pitch effects. When delays increase, we have an upward change in pitch; when they decrease, a downward change is noticed. Constantly increasing delays will cause a fixed pitch transposition effect, whereas slowing-down and speeding-up delay changes can create modulation effects like vibrato.

Let us concentrate on the pitch shifter effect, which is created by increasing or decreasing the delay by a fixed amount. If we look at this from a different angle, we can think of the circular delay line as a wavetable that is constantly re-written. The delay reading point then proceeds through the table at the desired pitch transposition rate. If its position increment is 1, there is no pitch change (and no delay change—the writing point always has an increment of 1); above 1, we have an upward pitch shift, as we are playing the "wavetable" at a rate faster than the rate at which it was written; conversely, if the increment is between 0 and 1, the pitch is shifted downward. This appears to be straightforward, but there is one complication: the delay line is finite and circular, so at some point either the reading point will overtake the writing point or vice versa. This will create a nasty click in the signal, as we go from, say, maximum delay to minimum delay. The best way to avoid the click is to add an envelope (sometimes called a *window*) that goes to zero at that discontinuity. This can be a simple triangle shape, going from 0 at its ends to 1 in the middle.

This is not the end of the story, as we are left with a transposed but amplitude-modulated signal. In order to reduce this tremolo effect, which is generally undesirable, we can use a second reading point, or tap, that is offset by half a delay length, and enveloped in the same way. So when one tap is at the discontinuity point (and thus its amplitude is zero), the other tap is at its maximum amplitude. This results in a smoother output, with no clicks and a less intrusive amplitude fluctuation.

That is our pitch shifter effect, illustrated schematically in figure 6.12. One further addition to it is a feedback path, which can be used to create arpeggiation effects as we feed the transposed output back to be further shifted. We have all the tools we need to implement this already in place from previous sections: circular buffer, variable delay readout, multiple taps, envelopes.

Our effect will have four parameters: pitch transposition ratio, gain, feedback, and delay time. These parameters and our delay, envelope, writing pointer and reading pointer will determine what internal variables we will need. We will also include an array of programs to store our parameters. These make up our class member variables:

```
protected:
    MyPlugProgram* programs; // program storage
    float *delay, *env; // circular buffer and envelope arrays
    float gain, pitch, rp, fdb, sr; // parameters etc
    int taps, dsize, wp; // no of taps, delay size, write-point
```

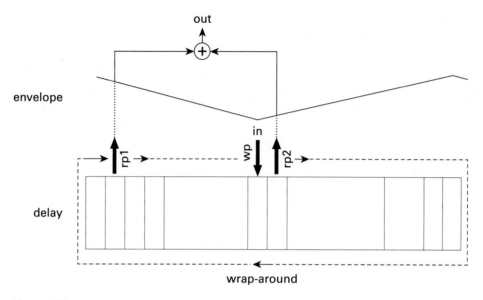

Figure 6.12
The pitch-shifter effect.

Program storage is handled by a data structure, which holds the four parameters together. Each program can also be given a name. Note that delay size is stored in seconds:

```
struct MyPlugProgram
{
    MyPlugProgram (){
        gain = 0.5; pitch = 0.5; fdb = 0.0, dsize = 0.045;
        strcpy (name, "Init");
    }
    float gain;
    float pitch;
    float fdb;
    float dsize;
    char name[64];
};
```

6.10.3   Initialization

Now let us focus on the initializing element of our class. Here is the constructor:

```
MyPlug::MyPlug (audioMasterCallback audioMaster)
    : AudioEffectX (audioMaster, PROGS, PARAMS)
{
```

```
    int i;
    // allocate program memory
    programs = new MyPlugProgram[numPrograms];
    // parameters, initial values
    gain = 0.5;
    pitch = 1.0;
    fdb = 0.0;
    taps = 2;
    // getSampleRate() returns the host SR
    sr = getSampleRate();
    dsize = (int) (0.045*sr);
    // allocate a 1-sec delay line and envelope
    delay = new float[(int)sr];
    env = new float[(int)sr];
    // write a triangular envelope (ramp up, ramp down)
    for(i=0; i < dsize/2; i++) env[i] = i*2./dsize;
    for(i=dsize/2; i >= 0; i--) env[dsize-i-1] = i*2./dsize;
    // set init program as number 0
    if(programs)setProgram(0);
    setNumInputs(1);      // 1 channel
    setNumOutputs(1);     // input & output
    setUniqueID('MpLg'); // this should be unique
    resume();             // zero delay etc
}
```

Most of the lines here are self-explanatory. PROGS and PARAMS are constants holding the numbers of programs (64) and parameters (4) that have been defined previously. The major bit of initialization is writing the envelope (made up of up and down ramps, each half the delay size). The delay and envelopes are created with the maximum allowed delay size (1 sec), but we can set the delay to be smaller than that (initially it is 45 msec). The final call is to resume():

```
void MyPlug::resume ()
{
    wp = 0;
    rp = 0.;
    memset (delay, 0, sr * sizeof (float));
    AudioEffectX::resume ();
}
```

This clears the delay line and zeroes the writer and reader point positions. It calls the base class method for any other initialization implemented in there (which we don't need to know about). When the plug-in is closed, a termination method (destructor) is called automatically, where the memory we previously allocated is released:

```
MyPlug::~MyPlug ()
{
    if(delay) delete[] delay;
    if(env) delete[] env;
    if(programs) delete[] programs;
}
```

The other initialization-related methods deal with registration and name setting:

```
bool MyPlug::getEffectName (char* name)
{
    strcpy (name, "PitchShift");
    return true;
}

bool MyPlug::getProductString (char* text)
{
    strcpy (text, "PitchShift");
    return true;
}

bool MyPlug::getVendorString (char* text)
{
    strcpy (text, "Acme Audio Ltd");
    return true;
}
```

6.10.4   Parameters

VST treats parameters in a very straightforward manner. A parameter is linked to numerical index, which is used by the host to set and get it from the plug-in. Two methods implement this. setParameter() is called when a parameter changes in the host (notice how we set the parameter variables and their corresponding program values):

```
void MyPlug::setParameter(VstInt32 index, float value)
{
    MyPlugProgram &ap = programs[curProgram];
    switch (index)
        {
        case PITCH:
            setPitch(ap.pitch = value);
            break;
        case GAIN:
            setGain(ap.gain = value);
            break;
```

```
        case DSIZE:
            setDsize(ap.dsize = value);
            break;
        case FDB:
            setFdb(ap.fdb = value);
        }
    }
```

`getParameter()` returns the parameter asked for:

```
float MyPlug::getParameter(VstInt32 index)
{
    float param = 0;

    switch (index)
        {
        case GAIN:
            param = gain;
            break;
        case PITCH:
            param = pitch;
            break;
        case FDB:
            param = fdb;
            break;
        case DSIZE:
            param = dsize/sr;
        }
    return param;
}
```

The constants PITCH, GAIN, FDB, and DSIZE are the parameter numerical indexes. To make matters simple, we define these in an enumeration (together with the other constants used before):

```
enum { PROGS = 64, GAIN = 0, PITCH, FDB, DSIZE, PARAMS };
```

To set the parameter variables we have previously defined some class functions, which we employed above. These are

```
void setGain(float g) { gain = g;}
```

```
void setPitch(float p) { pitch = p;}
```

```
void setFdb(float f) { fdb = f;}
```

and the delay setting, which also resets the envelope (because its length is tied to the delay size):

```
void MyPlug::setDsize(float d){
    dsize = (int)(sr*d);
    int i;
    for(i=0; i < dsize/2; i++) env[i] = i*2./dsize;
    for(i=dsize/2; i >= 0; i--) env[dsize-i-1] = i*2./dsize;
}
```

In addition, we implement functions to give parameters their names, labels, and display values:

```
void MyPlug::getParameterName (VstInt32 index, char *label)
{
    switch (index)
        {
        case GAIN:
            strcpy (label, "Gain");
            break;
        case PITCH:
            strcpy (label, "Pitch");
            break;
        case DSIZE:
            strcpy (label, "Delay");
            break;
        case FDB:
            strcpy (label, "Feedback");
        }
}

void MyPlug::getParameterLabel (VstInt32 index, char *label)
{
    switch (index)
        {
        case PITCH:
            strcpy (label, "ratio");
            break;
        case GAIN:
            strcpy (label, "dB");
            break;
        case DSIZE:
            strcpy (label, "secs");
            break;
        case FDB:
            strcpy (label, "gain");
        }
}
```

```
void MyPlug::getParameterDisplay (VstInt32 index, char *text)
{
    switch (index)
        {
    case PITCH:
            float2string ((pitch*1.5+0.5), text, kVstMaxParamStrLen);
            break;
    case GAIN:
            dB2string (gain, text, kVstMaxParamStrLen);
            break;
    case DSIZE:
            float2string (dsize/sr, text, kVstMaxParamStrLen);
            break;
    case FDB:
            float2string (fdb, text, kVstMaxParamStrLen);
    }
}
```

Notice in this last method that the pitch parameter is stored normalized (0.0–1.0) but displayed in the range it is used (0.5–2.0) using the conversion `pitch*1.5+0.5`, which is also used in the processing method to set the read pointer increment. This way, the parameter value displayed will correspond correctly to its use. VST parameter ranges are normalized, so we use this as a work-around.

Finally, we also implement some functions to deal with programs, setting their values and getting or setting their names:

```
void MyPlug::setProgram (VstInt32 program)
{
    MyPlugProgram* ap = &programs[program];
    curProgram = program;
    setParameter (GAIN,ap->gain);
    setParameter (PITCH,ap->pitch);
    setParameter (FDB,ap->fdb);

}

void MyPlug::setProgramName (char *name)
{
    strcpy (programs[curProgram].name, name);
}

void MyPlug::getProgramName (char *name)
{
    if(!strcmp (programs[curProgram].name, "Init"))
        sprintf(name, "%s %d", programs[curProgram].name,
                curProgram + 1);
```

```
    else
        strcpy(name, programs[curProgram].name);
}

bool MyPlug::getProgramNameIndexed (VstInt32 category,
                                    VstInt32 index, char* text)
{
 if (index < PROGS)
    {
        strcpy(text, programs[index].name);
        return true;
    }
 return false;
}
```

6.10.5 Processing

The core of the plug-in is implemented by the `processReplacing()` method. This takes as parameters two arrays of input and output sample vectors (one per channel each way, but since we only have one channel, these are arrays of one item) and their sizes as arguments. We can implement this more or less as in the processing functions of previous sections, except that we have separate input and output arrays and that our "permanent" variables (read and write pointers, delay, envelope) are class members, so we can access them directly (and don't have to use "external" memory to hold them).

The code is very similar to the variable-delay circular buffer examples, but we will output from multiple (well, at least two) taps, offsetting the reader pointer positions. We will also apply the envelope to these taps. The envelope index position is offset against the current writer pointer position, as this marks where the jump from minimum to maximum delay (or vice versa) happens:

```
void MyPlug::processReplacing(float** inputs,
                              float** outputs, VstInt32 vecframes)
{
    float* in = inputs[0];
    float* out = outputs[0];
    int rpi, ep;
    float s=0.f,rpf, frac, next, p = (pitch*1.5) + 0.5;
    // processing loop
    for(int i=0; i < vecframes; i++){
        // taps loop (taps = 2)
        for(int j=0; j < taps; j++){
            // tap position, offset
            rpf = rp + j*dsize/taps;
```

```
                rpf = rpf < dsize ? rpf : rpf - dsize;
                rpi = (int) rpf;
                frac = rpf - rpi;
                next = (rpi != dsize-1 ? delay[rpi+1] : delay[0]);
                // envelope index
                ep = rpi - wp;
                if(ep < 0) ep += dsize;
                s += (delay[rpi] + frac*(next - delay[rpi]))*env[ep];
            }
            // increment reader pointer and check bounds
            rp += p;
            rp = rp < dsize ? rp : rp - dsize;
            // feed the delay line
            delay[wp] = in[i] + s*fdb;
            // output the signal
            out[i] = (s/taps)*gain;
            s = 0.f;
            // increment write pointer
            wp = (wp < dsize ? wp+1 : 0);
        }
    }
```

This method will be called by the host repeatedly to process audio. You can see what I had to do to transform the function/procedural code of previous sections to the method/object-oriented way of doing things. First, as the key data items are held in the class (delay size, write and read positions, delay, and envelope buffers: dsize, wp, rp, delay, and env), we don't have to pass them as parameters anymore. If the host needs to create another running pitch shifter effect, all it needs to do is to create a new MyPlug object. Each of these objects will have its own separate delay buffer, envelope, and so on. There will be no chance of these being mixed up and shared by different instances of the effect (which is a real possibility in the function way of doing things). This is a safer and more satisfactory way of doing things. In fact, object orientation is really an important concept for audio systems programming, whether it is implemented in C or in C++.

6.10.6 Building a Plug-in

The final step is to build the plug-in. We will need some of the source code and header files from the VST SDK, which define and implement the base classes and the plug-in entry point.[16] The host starts a new plug-in effect by invoking this function:

```
AudioEffect* createEffectInstance(audioMasterCallback audioMaster)
{
    return new MyPlug(audioMaster);
}
```

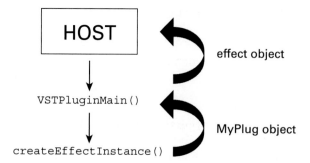

Figure 6.13
VST host plug-in instantiation.

and passing it an audioMasterCallback object (which we do not need to know much about). We implement this function somewhere in our source code (e.g. in the same file as the MyPlug class), and all it needs to do is to create a new MyPlug object and return it. Note that the return type is AudioEffect*, which is a VST base class object, as expected by the host. This small function completes all the code we need to write.

Figure 6.13 illustrates this process schematically. The host calls the entry point function, which in its turn calls createEffectInstance(). This returns a newly created plug-in object. VSTPluginMain() in its turn returns an audio effect instance. This is an internal representation of the plug-in, used by the host, that has access to the newly created MyPlug object.

Now we are in a position to build our plug-in. If we drop the vstsdk2.4 package[17] directory inside our working directory, we can do this with these commands on the various platforms:

Linux

```
g++ -shared -o myplug.so myplug.cpp
    vstsdk2.4/public.sdk/source/vst2.x/audioeffect.cpp
    vstsdk2.4/public.sdk/source/vst2.x/audioeffectx.cpp
    vstsdk2.4/public.sdk/source/vst2.x/vstplugmain.cpp
    —D__cdecl=""
    -I vstsdk2.4/public.sdk/source/vst2.x/ -I vstsdk2.4
```

Windows

```
g++ -shared -o myplug.dll myplug.cpp
    vstsdk2.4/public.sdk/source/vst2.x/audioeffect.cpp
    vstsdk2.4/public.sdk/source/vst2.x/audioeffectx.cpp
    vstsdk2.4/public.sdk/source/vst2.x/vstplugmain.cpp
    -I vstsdk2.4/public.sdk/source/vst2.x/ -I vstsdk2.4
```

OSX

```
g++ -bundle -o myplug myplug.cpp
    vstsdk2.4/public.sdk/source/vst2.x/audioeffect.cpp
    vstsdk2.4/public.sdk/source/vst2.x/audioeffectx.cpp
    vstsdk2.4/public.sdk/source/vst2.x/vstplugmain.cpp
    I vstsdk2.4/public.sdk/source/vst2.x/ -I vstsdk2.4
```

On OSX we have to drop the dynamic module (bundle) inside a certain directory structure (also called a bundle), together with a couple of files. The first one of them is called *info.plist* and is an XML file that looks like this:

```
<?xml version="1.0" encoding="UTF-8"?>
<!DOCTYPE plist PUBLIC "-//Apple Computer//DTD PLIST 1.0//EN"
"http://www.apple.com/DTDs/PropertyList-1.0.dtd">
<plist version="1.0">
<dict>
    <key>CFBundleDevelopmentRegion</key>
    <string>English</string>
    <key>CFBundleExecutable</key>
    <string>myplug</string>
    <key>CFBundleIdentifier</key>
    <string>com.apple.carbonbundletemplate</string>
    <key>CFBundleInfoDictionaryVersion</key>
    <string>6.0</string>
    <key>CFBundleName</key>
    <string>myplug</string>
    <key>CFBundlePackageType</key>
    <string>BNDL</string>
    <key>CFBundleShortVersionString</key>
    <string>1.0</string>
    <key>CFBundleSignature</key>
    <string>????</string>
    <key>CFBundleVersion</key>
    <string>1.0</string>
    <key>CSResourcesFileMapped</key>
    <true/>
</dict>
</plist>
```

Notice that most of this XML code is self-explanatory. The only important thing here is to give the correct name of the plug-in bundle (library) file we compiled (shown above in bold-face). The bundle structure is created with the following commands:

```
mkdir myplug.vst
```

```
mkdir myplug.vst/Contents
```

```
mkdir myplug.vst/Contents/MacOS

cp myplug myplug.vst/Contents/MacOS

cp info.plist myplug.vst/Contents/
```

The second file we need is just a text file with eight characters BNDL????, which can be created as follows:

```
echo "BNDL????" > myplug.vst/Contents/PkgInfo
```

The complete bundle directory structure looks like this:

```
myplug.vst
        /Contents
                        /info.plist
                        /PkgInfo
                        /MacOS/myplug
```

It is also possible to add an optional Resources subdirectory (of Contents) to hold any extra resources (not needed here). Finally, we want to hide the directory structure inside the bundle, so the Finder sees it as a single file. We can use the command

```
/Developer/Tools/SetFile -a B myplug.vst
```

6.11   Conclusion

This chapter has provided a survey of various time-domain signal processing techniques and some recipes for their implementation in the C++ language. The elements covered in the text are perhaps the most basic and essential ones for audio programming of synthesis and effects. I hope that this text has given the reader the background and tools for the discovery of other, more advanced techniques.

6.12   Exercises

Exercise 6.12.1

Create a command-line subtractive synthesizer program using the components discussed in this chapter. This can be structured with one oscillator, one filter, and two envelopes (one controlling amplitude and the other filter center frequency). Here are some possibilities (you can implement each one at a time):

(a) Users might have a choice of waveform and filter type.
(b) The parameters to the synthesizer can be read from a text file.
(c) You could also read a separate text file with frequencies and durations of a sequence of notes. This will enable the program to become a small full-featured mono-synth sequencer.

Exercise 6.12.2

Using the comb and allpass filters, implement a Schroeder reverb, made up of four parallel comb filters feeding two allpass filters in series. You will find details of this design in some of the suggested readings cited in the notes.

Exercise 6.12.3

Implement a vibrato effect by modifying the variable delay code discussed in the last section of this chapter. Note that you will need an LFO to control the delay time, which can be implemented with one of the oscillators presented in the text. Remember that the vibrato effect does not use feedback.

Exercise 6.12.4

Adapt one of the filter functions presented in this text to create a VST plug-in. You can use the plug-in class presented in section 6.10 as a starting point.

Notes

1. Here *time domain* refers to signals that are functions of time, such as an acoustic wave from an instrument or the vibration of a loudspeaker cone. This term is also used to distinguish these from *frequency-domain* or *spectral* signals, which are functions of frequency (and which are discussed in later chapters).

2. *Libsndfile* is a specialized programming library written by Erik de Castro Lopo for input and output to soundfiles. It is available at http://www.mega-nerd.com/libsndfile.

3. Keeping indexes and such "permanent" variables separate will happen naturally when we shift to an object-oriented way of doing things in the last section of this chapter. However, a procedural approach as used here is more "to the point" in explaining the essential algorithms.

4. One of the reasons for interpolating is precision, which also means a better signal-to-noise ratio. This topic is covered in some detail in the following article: F. R. Moore, "Table Lookup Noise for Sinusoidal Digital Oscillators," *Computer Music Journal* 1 (1977), no. 2: 26–29.

5. This is another good reason for using object orientation.

6. These ideas can be found in the following articles: J. Smith and J. Angell, "A Constant-Gain Digital Resonator Tuned by a Single Coefficient," *Computer Music Journal* 6 (1982), no. 4: 36–40; K. Steiglitz, "A Note on Constant-Gain Digital Resonators," *Computer Music Journal* 18 (1994), no. 4: 8–10.

7. With the development of DSP theory, techniques were developed to translate analog filters into digital forms. Two pioneering texts on these ideas are K. Steiglitz, *The General Theory of Digital Filters with Applications to Spectral Analysis* (Sc.D. dissertation, New York University, 1963) and J. F. Kaiser, "Design Methods for Sampled Data Filters," in *Proceedings of the First Allerton Conference on Circuit and System Theory* (University of Illinois, 1963).

8. For some ideas on how to create reverberators out of comb and allpass filters, see 2000, *The Csound Book*, ed. R. Boulanger (MIT Press, 2000) and C. Dodge and T. Jerse 1985, *Computer Music* (Schirmer Books, 1985).

9. For further technical details on convolution, see chapter 7.

10. An application programming interface (API) is a collection of code elements (functions, classes, etc.) that provide an "interface" to a particular software system, in this case the plug-in architecture.

11. VST stands for Virtual Studio Technology. We will be using its 2.4 version, which is at the time of writing the most commonly supported one. The concepts discussed here can also serve as the basis for plug-in writing in later versions (as well as for other APIs).

12. Although we don't need to implement a UI (hosts will generally provide one), many plug-ins offer a GUI of their own. Since this text is not about computer graphics, we will ignore this aspect.

13. You will recall, from other chapters that discuss programming, that classes are *models* of things we want to implement, in this case an audio plug-in. Classes can then be created into computing *objects* that will do the actions they model, in this case process audio.

14. This is an important concept of object orientation: classes are the model, "the kinds" of things we want; objects are their concrete realization, their individual "instances," of which there can be many, each one separate and individual from the others. For instance, we have a plug-in class for an effect, and the host can have many individual and separate effects running in parallel. The plug-in is the model (the kind of effect) and the running effects are the objects. The object-oriented way of doing things guarantees that the objects will not get entangled with other objects.

15. This works well because the base class will declare methods to do various tasks, and since the host knows about these, it can call them whenever it needs. If they are implemented in the derived class, then that code is the one called, rather than the original in the base class (which in most cases does nothing). The host does not need to know anything about a particular plug-in, because all it expects is that certain actions are implemented by it. So all we need to do is to specialize, i.e. to provide an implementation for the methods we require.

16. Just as stand-alone programs do, plug-ins have an equivalent "main" function (in the case of VST, this is called `VSTPluginMain()`), where its execution starts, which is called an "entry point." The difference is that, while for a program the entry point is called by the operating system to run the program, in plug-ins it is called by the host. This function is implemented by the VST SDK, and you do not, in general, need to touch it (just add the relevant file when building the plug-in).

17. The vstsdk2.4 is available from http://www.steinberg.net.

Spectral Audio Programming

7 Spectral Audio Programming Basics: The DFT, the FFT, and Convolution

Victor Lazzarini

In this chapter we will start looking at techniques that work with frequency-domain or spectral representations of signals. In order to transform the time-domain data into spectral data and modify it in different ways, we will be using methods of processing based on the Fourier transform. The discussion of these spectral techniques will be mostly non-mathematical, focusing on the practical aspects of each technique. However, wherever necessary we will examine the underlying mathematical concepts and formulations.

7.1 Frequency Analysis: The Discrete Fourier Transform

The discrete Fourier transform (DFT) is an analysis tool that is used to convert a time-domain digital signal into its frequency-domain representation. It is a variation on the original continuous-time/continuous-frequency Fourier transform, which is adapted for discrete signals, thus perfectly suited for digital audio applications. The underlying principles of the DFT are derived from the Fourier transform, which is effectively a theoretical tool. We will concentrate on the DFT and try to explore its potential for audio processing.

The DFT transforms a signal into its frequency representation and a complementary tool, the IDFT, does the inverse operation. In the process of transforming the spectrum, we start with a real-valued signal composed of the waveform samples, and we obtain a complex-valued signal composed of the spectrum samples. Each pair of values (that make up a complex number) generated by the transform represents a particular frequency point in the spectrum. Similarly, each single (real) number that composes the input signal represents a particular time point. The DFT is said to represent a signal at a particular time, as if it was a "snapshot" of its frequency components.

One way of understanding the "magic" of the DFT is by looking at its formula and trying to understand what it does:

$$DFT(x(n), k) = \frac{1}{N}\sum_{n=0}^{N-1} x(n) \times e^{-j2\pi kn/N}, \qquad k = 0, 1, 2, \ldots, N-1. \tag{1}$$

The whole process is one of multiplying an input signal by complex exponentials and adding up the results to obtain a series of complex numbers that make up the spectral signal. The complex exponentials are nothing more than a series of complex sinusoids made up of cosine and sine parts:

$$e^{-j2\pi kn/N} = \cos(2\pi kn/N) - j\sin(2\pi kn/N). \tag{2}$$

The exponent $j2\pi kn/N$ determines the phase angle of the sinusoids, which in turn is related to its frequency. When $k = 1$, we have a sinusoid with its phase angle varying as $2\pi n/N$. This will of course complete a whole cycle in N samples, so we can say its frequency is $1/N$. (To obtain a value in hertz, we need only multiply it by the sampling rate.) All other sinusoids are going to be whole-number multiples of that frequency, for $1 < k < N - 1$. N is the number of points in the analysis, or the number of spectral samples (each one a complex number), also known as the *transform size*. For each particular frequency point k, we multiply the input signal by a sinusoid and then we sum all the values obtained (and scale the result by $1/N$). The DFT formula is very simple to program and can give us an insight into how the calculation is performed[1]:

```
const double twopi = 2*acos(-1.);

// dft takes an input signal *in of size N
// outputs spectrum *out with N pairs of
// complex values [real, imag]
void dft(float *in, float *out, int N){
    for(int i = 0,k = 0; k<N; i+ = 2, k++){
        out[i] = out[i+1] = 0.f;
        for(int n = 0; n < N; n++){
            out[i] += in[n]*cos(k*n*twopi/N);
            out[i+1] -= in[n]*sin(k*n*twopi/N);
        }
        out[i] / = N;
        out[i+1] / = N;
    }
}
```

(A short program that generates one cycle of a waveform and then analyzes it is provided in the DVD ROM examples for this chapter. It uses the above code for the spectral analysis and it demonstrates how the process works.)

Consider the simple case where the signal $x(n)$ is a sine wave with a frequency $1/N$, defined by the expression $\sin(2\pi n/N)$. The result of the DFT operation for the frequency point 1 is

$$DFT(x(n), 1) = \frac{1}{N}\sum_{n=0}^{N-1} \sin(2\pi n/N) \times \cos(2\pi n/N) - j\sin^2(2\pi n/N)$$

$$= -0.5\,j. \tag{3}$$

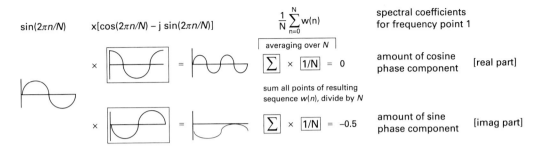

Figure 7.1

The DFT operation on frequency point 1, showing how a complex sinusoid is used to detect the sine and cosine phase components of a signal.

Here, what happened was that the complex sinusoid has detected a signal at that frequency and the DFT has output a complex value [0, −0.5] for that spectral sample (the meaning of −0.5 will be explored later). This complex value is also called the *spectral coefficient* for frequency $1/N$. The real part of this number corresponds to the detected cosine phase component and its imaginary part relates to the sine phase component. The DFT operation for frequency $1/N$ is presented graphically in figure 7.1. If we slide the sinusoid to the next frequency point ($k = 2$) we will obtain the spectral sample [0, 0], which means that the DFT has not detected a sinusoid signal at the frequency ($2n/N$). This shows that the DFT uses the "sliding" complex sinusoid as a detector of spectral components. When a frequency component in the signal matches the frequency of the sinusoid, we obtain a non-zero output. This is, in a nutshell, how the DFT works (and, by extension, how the Fourier transform works). Of course, this example shows the analysis of a very simple signal. We will have to develop our understanding a bit further to get a more general idea of how it can work for *any* signal (not just sinusoids at frequency multiples of $1/N$). In any case, the frequency $1/N$ is a special one, known as the *fundamental frequency of analysis*. As was mentioned above, the DFT will analyze a signal as composed of sinusoids at multiples of this frequency.

Consider now a signal that does not contain components at any of these multiple frequencies. How would the DFT cope with this kind of input? It would simply analyze it in terms of the components it has at hand, namely the multiples of the fundamental frequency of analysis. For instance, take the case of a sine wave at $1.3/N$, $\sin(2\pi 1.3n/N)$ (figure 7.2). The result of the DFT is shown in table 7.1. The transform was performed using the C++ code above with $N = 16$. Although this result is confusing at first, it is what we would expect, since we have tried to analyze a sine wave with a length of 1.3 cycle. We can, however, observe that one of the two largest pairs of absolute values is found on point 1. From what we saw in the first example, we might guess that the spectral peak is close to the frequency $1/N$, as in fact it is $1.3/N$. Nevertheless, the result shows a large amount of spectral spread, contaminating all

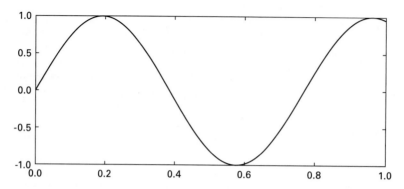

Figure 7.2
Plot of $\sin(2\pi 3n/N)$.

Table 7.1
Spectral coefficients for a 16-point DFT of $\sin(2\pi 1.3n/N)$.

Point (k)	Real part (re[$X(k)$])	Imaginary part (im[$X(k)$])
0	0.127	0.000
1	0.359	0.221
2	−0.151	0.127
3	−0.071	0.056
4	−0.053	0.034
5	−0.046	0.022
6	−0.042	0.013
7	−0.041	0.006
8	−0.040	0.000
9	−0.041	−0.006
10	−0.042	−0.013
11	−0.046	−0.022
12	−0.053	−0.034
13	−0.071	−0.056
14	−0.151	−0.127
15	0.359	0.221

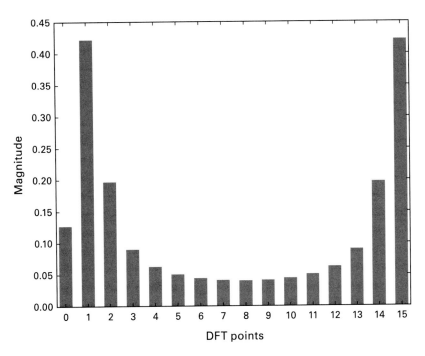

Figure 7.3
Magnitude spectrum from a 16-point DFT of $\sin(2\pi 3n/N)$. The plot shows the positive half of the spectrum from 0 Hz to the Nyquist frequency (points 0–8), followed by the negative side (8–15).

frequency points (see also figure 7.3). This has to do with the discontinuity between the last and first points of the waveform, which is clearly visible in figure 7.2.

7.1.1 Reconstructing the Time-Domain Signal

Table 7.1 can be used to reconstruct the original waveform by applying the inverse operation to the DFT, the inverse discrete Fourier transform, defined as

$$IDFT(X(k), n) = \sum_{k=0}^{N-1} X(k) \times e^{j2\pi kn/N}, \qquad n = 0, 1, 2, \ldots, N-1. \tag{4}$$

In other words, the values of $X(k)$ are [complex] coefficients, which are used to multiply a set of complex sinusoids. These will be added together, point by point, to reconstruct the signal. This is, basically, a form of additive synthesis that uses complex signals. The coefficients are the amplitudes of the sinusoids (cosine and sine), and their frequencies are just multiples of the fundamental frequency of analysis. If we use the coefficients in the table above as input, we will obtain the original 1.3-cycle sine wave. The IDFT formula yields this very simple code:

```
// idft takes an input spectrum *in as N complex pairs
// outputs real signal *out, consisting of N samples
void idft(float *in, float *out, int N){
    for(int n = 0; n<N; n++){
        out[n] = 0.f;
        for(int k = 0, i = 0; k < N; k++, i+ = 2){
            out[n] += in[i]*cos(k*n*twopi/N) - in[i+1]*sin(k*n*twopi/N);
        }
    }
}
```

We start with a complex spectrum and somehow end up with a real waveform. This is, of course, because we are concerned only with audio signals that are real-valued. If we started with such a signal, it will return to its original form when we recompose it. How is that possible? First, I am assuming that the output of the IDFT is real-valued, so its imaginary part is zero. So I need to program only the real part of the operation. Now, if we check the imaginary part of the IDFT output, we will see that it is, as expected, zero-valued. In addition, by looking at the coefficients in table 7.1, we see that all absolute values of points 1–7 are mirrored by points 9–15. This is one of the properties of real signals: half of the spectrum will be a mirror of the other half. This will be understood a bit better when we look at what frequencies the spectral points refer to. We saw above that point 1 refers to the frequency $1/N$, and point 2 to $2/N$, and so on. As has been mentioned, the fundamental frequency of analysis in hertz will depend on how many samples are representing our signal in a second, namely, the sampling rate (SR). Thus our frequency points will be referring to kSR/N Hz, with $k = 0, 1, 2, \ldots, N-1$. Because of this, we will be able to quickly determine the frequencies for points 0 to $N/2$, ranging from 0 Hz to SR/2 (the Nyquist frequency—the highest possible frequency for a digital signal).

What about the other half of the coefficients, to which frequencies do they belong? The answer is inferred by looking at the frequency points in table 7.1, realizing that points 9–15 basically have the same complex values as points 1–7 (in reverse order and except for the sign of the imaginary part). It is reasonable to assume that they refer to the same frequencies, which is part of the answer. The sign of the imaginary parts give the rest of the answer away: since they refer to amplitudes of sine waves, they might refer to negative frequencies. This is because a negative frequency sine wave is the same as positive one with negative amplitude (or out-of-phase): $\sin(-x) = -\sin(x)$. In addition, $\cos(-x) = \cos(x)$, so the real parts are the same for negative and positive frequencies.

The conclusion is simple: the second half of the points refer to negative frequencies, from $-SR/2$ to $-SR/N$. It is important to point out that the point $N/2$ refers to both SR/2 and $-SR/2$ (these two frequencies are indistinguishable). Also, it is important to note that the coefficients for 0 Hz and the Nyquist frequency are always purely real (no imaginary part). If our SR is 32 KHz, then, for $N = 16$, the points will be at 0, 2, 4, 6, 8, 10, 12, 14, ± 16, -14, -12, -10, -8, -6, -4, and -2 KHz. We can see that the output of the DFT splits the spectrum of a digital waveform into equally spaced frequency points, or bands. Looking at this conclusion and the coefficients above, we note that the negative side of the spectrum can always be inferred from the positive side, so it is, in a way, redundant.

7.1.2   Rectangular and Polar Formats

In order to understand further the information provided by the DFT, we can convert the representation of the complex coefficients, from real/imaginary pairs to one that is more useful to us. One of the most interesting aspects of the DFT analysis is that, by breaking a waveform into components, we can determine how much energy (or, more precisely, amplitude) each of these components have. This is given by the magnitude of each complex spectral coefficient. The magnitude (or modulus) of a complex number z is

$$|z| = \sqrt{re[z]^2 + im[z]^2}. \tag{5}$$

This is Pythagoras' famous formula, which yields a real-valued number. The magnitude will tell what the amplitudes of each component in the spectrum are. However, because a real signal is always split into positive and negative frequencies, the amplitude of a point will be half the "true" value. Recall the first example above. Point 1 yields magnitude 0.5, but the original signal had amplitude 1.0 for the frequency SR/N. If we look at point $N - 1$, we will see that its coefficient will also have magnitude 0.5. The same can be said for the second example here, where the magnitudes at the second half of the table mirror the ones in the first half (figure 7.3). The values obtained by the magnitude conversion are known as the *amplitude spectrum* of a signal. The amplitude spectrum of a real signal is always mirrored at 0 Hz. It is a real-valued function of the frequency.

The other conversion that complements the magnitude provides the phase angle of the coefficient, in relation to a cosine wave. This yields the phase offset of a particular component, and it is expressed by the following relationship:

$$\theta(z) = \arctan\left(\frac{im[z]}{re[z]}\right). \tag{6}$$

This conversion of the DFT output, called the *phase spectrum*, is also a real-valued function of frequency. The phase spectrum of real signals is always anti-symmetrical around 0 Hz.

The process of obtaining the magnitude and phase spectrum of the DFT is called *Cartesian-to-polar* conversion, because the original spectral coefficients are the Cartesian coordinates of complex numbers. The amplitude and phase representation is called the polar form of a complex number. The amplitude corresponds to the modulus, the length of the line from the center of a Cartesian plane to the point defined by the coordinates. The phase is the angle that this line makes with the horizontal axis.

If we take the first example and look at the two non-zero coefficients, at points 1 and 15, we have [0, −0.5] and [0, 0.5]. These two complex pairs tell us that at frequencies SR/N and −SR/N the amplitude is 0.5 and that the phase offset of frequency SR/N is arctan(−0.5/0) = −π/2 – 90°), which means, in relation to a cosine wave, that the wave is in the sine phase (cos(x − π/2) = sin x). In complement, the phase of frequency −SR/N is arctan(0.5/0) = π/2 (90°), denoting an inverted sine wave. If we add these two components together, we obtain a sine wave at SR/N with amplitude of 1 (or a sine wave at −SR/N with amplitude of −1):

$$x(n) = 0.5 \sin(2\pi n/N) + 0.5[-\sin(-2\pi n/N)]$$

$$= \sin(2\pi n/N)$$

$$= -\sin(-2\pi n/N).$$

This is, of course, the signal we started with.

Similarly, if we take all the magnitude and phase of all components that were found in the second example and used these parameters to do an additive synthesis operation as above, we would obtain the original signal. The additive synthesizer could be defined by the formula

$$x(n) = \sum_{k=0}^{N-1} |X(k)| \cos\left(\frac{2\pi kn}{N} + \theta[X(k)]\right),\tag{7}$$

with $X(k) = \text{DFT}(x(n), k)$, the spectral coefficients of $x(n)$.

We can see from figure 7.3 that the results are not always clear. In fact, unless the signal has all its components at multiples of the fundamental frequency of analysis, there will be a spectral spread over all frequency points. However, if we plot the amplitude spectrum values of a finer analysis (using more points) and smooth the curve between the points, we will obtain a better representation of the spectral content. Although this will not reveal the exact component frequencies of a sound, it will provide an idea of the distribution of energy at the different frequency bands.

In addition to the problems identified above, the DFT, in its present form as a one-shot, single-frame transform, will not be able to track spectral changes. This is because it takes a single "picture" of the spectrum of a waveform at a certain time. We might conclude that in the present form, the DFT is almost useless as an analysis tool for real-life applications. We will, nevertheless, be able to improve considerably on this bare-bones method. However, before we look into tweaking it, it is important to point out that the single-frame DFT is not completely useless for audio processing. In fact, there are some interesting sound transformation applications that employ this technique more or less in the format described in this section.

The above discussion of the DFT tried to focus on the practical aspects of the DFT.[2] For this reason, the scope of the mathematical discussion of the concepts involved in the DFT was somewhat limited.[3]

7.2   Applications of the DFT: Convolution

The single-frame DFT analysis as explored above has one important application, the convolution of time-domain signals through spectral multiplication. Before we proceed to explore this technique, it is important to note that the DFT is very seldom implemented in the direct form shown above. More usually, we will find optimized algorithms that will calculate the DFT much more efficiently. These are called the *fast Fourier transform* (FFT). Their result is in all aspects equivalent to the DFT as described above. The only difference is in the way the calculation is performed. Also, because the FFT is based on specialized algorithms, they will only work with a certain number of points (N, the transform size). For instance, the standard FFT algorithm uses only power-of-2 (2, 4, ..., 512, 1,024, ...) sizes. The technique of fast convolution uses the DFT implemented with FFT algorithms, as the direct form calculation does not provide any advantage to ordinary time-domain convolution. From now on, when we refer to the DFT, we will imply the use of a fast algorithm for its computation.

Convolution is defined as

$$w(n) = y(n) \star x(n) = \sum_{m=0}^{n} y(m)x(n - m). \tag{8}$$

The simplest way to look into this operation is to examine some simple examples.

1. Consider the convolution of two signals $x(n)$ and $u(n)$, where $u(0) = 1$ and $u(n) = 0$ for all other values of n. This is sometimes called the *unit sample function* or the *unit impulse*. The result is the original signal $x(n)$, unchanged:

$$u(n) \star x(n) = \{1, 0, 0\} \star \{0, 1, 3, 2, 1, 0, -1\} = \{0, 1, 3, 2, 1, 0, -1, 0, 0\}.$$

2. If we create a third signal, $s(n) = u(n - d)$, a delayed version of $u(n)$, and we convolve it with $x(n)$, we will obtain $x(n - d)$, a delayed version of $x(n)$:

$$s(n) \star x(n) = \{0, 0, 1, 0\} \star \{0, 1, 3, 2, 1, 0, -1\} = \{0, 0, 0, 1, 3, 2, 1, 0, -1\}.$$

3. If we create a scaled version of $u(n)$, $g(n) = au(n)$, and we convolve it with $x(n)$, we will obtain a scaled version of it, $ax(n)$:

$$g(n) \star x(n) = \{2, 0, 0\} \star \{0, 1, 3, 2, 1, 0, -1\} = \{0, 2, 6, 4, 2, 0, -2, 0, 0\}.$$

4. Combining examples 2 and 3, $f(n) = au(n - d)$, and convoluting with $x(n)$, we have a delayed, scaled version of $x(n)$, $ax(n - d)$:

$$s(n) \star x(n) = \{0, 0, 0, 3\} \star \{0, 1, 3, 2, 1, 0, -1\} = \{0, 0, 0, 0, 3, 9, 6, 3, 0, -3\}.$$

5. If we apply these ideas more explicitly, we can consider any arbitrary signal as a sequence of scaled and delayed unit sample functions added together. We can therefore apply this method to the convolution of any two signals. Take the example of two signals $f(n) = \{1, 2, 3\}$ and $g(n) = \{5, 9, 6, 2, 3\}$. The first signal can be considered the sum of three functions: (1) unit

sample function $u(n) = \{1, 0, 0\}$, scaled by $f(0) = 1$, $\{1, 0, 0\}$; (2) $u(n)$ delayed by one sample and scaled by $f(1) = 2$ $\{0, 2, 0\}$; and (3) $u(n)$ delayed by two samples and scaled by $f(2) = 3$. We can convolve the second signal by scaling it by these three signals separately (generating three copies) and adding these together (mixing them) to get the result:

5	9	6	2	3			[slide by 0 positions, scale by $f(0) = 1$]
	10	18	12	4	6		[slide by 1 position, scale by $f(1) = 2$]
		15	27	18	6	9	[slide by 2 positions, scale by $f(2) = 3$]

5	19	39	41	25	12	9

As we can see, in terms of signal processing, convolution can be seen as a tapped delay line, with a gain multiplier applied to each tap. In fact, direct convolution is achieved by that method. It is also fair to conclude that one of the applications of convolution is in the modeling of reverberation.

One important aspect of time-domain convolution is that it is equivalent to the multiplication of spectra (and vice versa). In other words, if $y(n)$ and $h(n)$ are two waveforms whose Fourier transforms are $Y(k)$ and $H(k)$, then

$$DFT[y(n) * h(n)] = Y(k)H(k)$$

and   (9)

$$DFT[y(n)h(n)] = Y(k) * H(k).$$

This means that if the DFT is used to transform two signals into their spectral domain and the two spectra can be multiplied together, the result can be transformed back to the time domain as the convolution of the two inputs. In this type of operation, we generally have an arbitrary sound that is convoluted with a shorter signal, called the *impulse response*. The latter can be thought of as a mix of scaled and delayed unit sample functions and also as the list of the gain values in a tapped delay line. The convolution operation will impose the spectral characteristics of this impulse signal into the other input signal. There are four basic applications for this technique:

1. Early reverberation: the impulse response is a train of pulses, which can be obtained by recording room reflections in reaction to a short sound
2. Filtering: the impulse response is a series of FIR filter coefficients, and its amplitude spectrum determines the shape of the filter
3. Cross-synthesis: the impulse response is an arbitrary sound, whose spectrum will be multiplied with the other sound; their common features will be emphasized, and the overall effect will be one of cross-synthesis
4. Sound localization: if we have impulse responses measured at our ears for sounds at different positions, by applying these to sounds using convolution, the illusion of sound localization at different positions can be created for binaural (i.e. headphone) listening.

Depending on the application, we might use a time-domain impulse response, whose transform is then used in the process. In other situations, we might start with a particular spectrum, which is directly used in the process. The advantage of this is that we can define the frequency-domain characteristics that we want to impose on the other sound.

7.2.1 A DFT-based Convolution Application

We can now look at the details of the application of the DFT in convolution, called *fast convolution*, with some programming examples. The first thing to consider is that, since we are using real signals, there is no reason to use a DFT that outputs both the positive and negative sides of the spectrum. We know that the negative side can be extracted from the positive, so we can use FFT algorithms that are optimized for the real signals. The discussion of specific aspects of these algorithms is beyond the scope of this text, but whenever we refer to the DFT, we will imply the use of a real input transform. There are several programming libraries that provide FFT routines, such as the FFTW library. They will also provide a variety of FFT algorithms, for different transform sizes. As stated above, the most common of these is the one for the power-of-2 size. In our discussion, we will assume the use of existing routines for forward and inverse FFT, which work on the basis of that algorithm with real signals. We will assume that the spectral output of the forward DFT will be in the form of a sequence of $N/2$ pairs of numbers (N values). The first pair will contain the real parts of the 0 Hz and Nyquist frequency points, respectively. The following pairs will be complex numbers (real, imaginary) for all other frequency points, from 1 to $N/2 - 1$.

The inverse DFT will assume its input to be in the same format. Let's say, then, that our routines are defined as follows[4]:

```
void fft(float *sig, float *spec, int N);
void ifft(float *spec, float *sig, int N);
```

The time-domain signal is held in the `sig` vector, the spectrum is placed in the `spec` vector, the number of points in the transform is N (always a power of 2). Any real-signal FFT/IFFT library routines can replace these with a little adaptation.

The central point of the implementation of convolution with the DFT is the use of the *overlap-add* method after the inverse transform. Since our impulse response will be of a certain length, this will determine the transform size (we will capture the whole signal in one DFT). The other input signal can be of arbitrary length, all we will have to do is keep taking time slices of it that are the size of the impulse response. We know that the resulting length of the convolution of two signals is the sum of their lengths minus 1. This will determine the minimum size of the transform, because the IDFT output signal, as a result of the convolution, will have to be of that length.

The need for an *overlap-add* operation arises as a consequence of the length of the convolution being larger than the original time slice. For this reason, we will have to make sure the input signal blocks

| impulse response | length S |

| sound input | | | | S-length time slices |

DFT signal blocks

| inputs | zero-padding |

length: next power-of-two to 2S - 1
S-length inputs zero-padded to the DFT length

| output [non-zero samples] | null samples |

the first 2S - 1 samples contain the convolution signal

overlap-add output

| block 1 | block 2 |

block 1 length S, block 2 length S-1

| block 1 | block 2 |

align end of previous block 1
to start of next block 1

| block 1 | block 2 |

| block 1 | block 2 |

| sound output, length: input length + S - 1 |

Figure 7.4
Convolution input and output block sizes and the overlap-add operation.

tail part of it is mixed with the next output block. This will align the start of each output block with the original start of each time slice in the input signal.

If the impulse response size is S, we will slice the input signal in blocks of S samples. The convolution output size will be $2S - 1$, and the size of the transform will be the first power of 2 not less than that value.

The inputs to the transform will be padded to the required size. After the multiplication and the IDFT operation, we will have a block of $2S - 1$ samples containing the signal output (the zero padding will be discarded). All we need to do is to time-align it with the original signal by overlapping the first $S - 1$ samples of this block with the last $S - 1$ samples of the previous output. The overlapping samples then are mixed together to form the final output. Figure 7.4 shows the input signal block sizes and the overlap-add operation.

Now it is just a matter of putting these ideas into code. The following example takes two signals, an impulse response and an arbitrary input, of any sizes (but we expect the impulse response to be the smaller of the two). It outputs the convolution of these two signals. The length of the output, as discussed above, will be the sum of the two input sizes minus 1, so we expect an output vector that is at least of that size.

The code is quite simple and commented throughout. Its main structure is as follows: The signal vectors are allocated and we take the DFT of the impulse response (which only needs to be calculated once). In the processing loop, we first fill a vector that will hold one time slice of the input. When the vector is ready, we copy the overlapping samples from the output block and we zero-pad the vector holding the input time slice. This is followed by the DFT of that signal; the complex multiplication of the two spectra; and the IDFT of that product. As soon as the first convolution operation is performed, we start to overlap-add the signal blocks to obtain the output. The processing loop will run until the last sample of the convolution is output.

Here is the code:

```
void convol(float* impulse, float* input, float* output,
            int impulse_size, int input_size){

    float *impspec, *inspec, *outspec; // spectral vectors
    float *insig, *outsig, *overlap; // time-domain vectors
    int fftsize = 1, convsize; // transform and convolution sizes
    int overlap_size; // overlap size
    int count, i, j; // counter and loop variables

    overlap_size = impulse_size - 1;
    convsize = impulse_size + overlap_size;

    while(fftsize < convsize) fftsize * = 2;

    impspec = new float[fftsize]; // allocate memory for
    inspec = new float[fftsize]; // spectral vectors
    outspec = new float[fftsize];

    insig = new float[fftsize];
    outsig = new float[fftsize];
    overlap = new float[overlap_size];

    // get the impulse into the FFT input vector
    // pad with zeros
    for(i = 0; i < fftsize; i++){
        if(i < impulse_size) insig[i] = impulse[i];
        else insig[i] = 0.f;
    }

    // Take the DFT of impulse
    fft(insig, impspec, fftsize);

    // processing loop
    for(i = count = 0; i < input_size+convsize; i++, count++){

        // if an input block is ready
        if(count == impulse_size && i <(input_size+impulse_size)){

            // copy overlapping block
            for(j = 0; j < overlap_size ; j++)
                overlap[j] = outsig[j+impulse_size];
```

```
            // pad input signal with zeros
            for(j = impulse_size; j < fftsize; j++)
                insig[j] = 0.f;

            // Take the DFT of input signal block
            fft(insig, inspec, fftsize);

            // complex multiplication
            // first pair is re[0Hz] and re[Nyquist]
            outspec[0] = inspec[0]*impspec[0];
            outspec[1] = inspec[1]*impspec[1];

            // (a+ib)*(c+id) = (ac - bd) + (ad + bc)i
            for(j = 2; j < fftsize; j+ = 2){
                outspec[j] = inspec[j]*impspec[j]
                                  - inspec[j+1]*impspec[j+1];
                outspec[j+1] = inspec[j]*impspec[j+1]
                                  + inspec[j+1]*impspec[j];
            }

            // IDFT of the spectral product
            ifft(outspec, outsig, fftsize);

            // zero the sample counter
            count = 0;
        }

        // get the input signal
        // stop when the input is finished
        if(i < input_size)
            insig[count] = input[i];

        // overlap-add output starts only
        // after the first convolution operation
        if(i > = impulse_size)
            output[i-impulse_size] = outsig[count] +
                (count < overlap_size ? overlap[count] : 0);
    }
    // de-allocate memory
    delete[] overlap;
    delete[] outsig;
    delete[] insig;
    delete[] outspec;
    delete[] inspec;
    delete[] impspec;
}
```

The code expects the impulse, input, and output signal vectors to be allocated externally. (The DVD examples for this chapter show a complete program that implements the convolution of two soundfiles, an impulse response and an input sound, using this function.)

This function, in the present format, will not serve for real-time purposes. However, it can be modified for this kind of application, by processing one FFT block at a time and leaving the overlap-add to be performed by the invoking code. The only caveat is that there is an implicit delay in this process, which is determined by the length of the impulse response. So with longer responses, the real-time use is somewhat compromised. A further development of fast convolution, designed to overcome this, is called *partitioned convolution*. This process breaks the impulse signal into smaller partitions and applies the FFT-based convolution using each one of these separately. Then the results of each convolution are re-combined to provide the output signal.

7.3 Conclusion

The discrete Fourier transform is a cornerstone of modern audio signal processing. Understanding it is very important for any type of spectral processing. Although in its straight form it is not used in many applications, it provides the basis for many other methods of analysis and processing, including short-time Fourier transform and the phase vocoder. Its main application, fast convolution, is an important technique that has many applications, among them reverberation, filtering, and sound localization.

7.4 Exercises

Exercise 7.4.1
Using the DFT and IDFT functions as defined in section 7.1, create a convolution program based on the convolution function of section 7.2. Because we are not using the FFT, zero-padding is not necessary. Adjust your code to reflect this fact. Compare the computation time required for this program with the FFT-based example in the DVD-ROM.

Exercise 7.4.2
Modify your program and the convolution example to allow for the timing of the process. Look for a C function in your system that can obtain the system time. (Tip: In OSX and Linux, use the 'man' command for searching system subroutines.) Compare the timings of your convolution code with the FFT-based example for different impulse response sizes.

Exercise 7.4.3
Write a program to implement direct convolution by applying equation 8 directly. (Tip: Use a circular buffer tapped at every sample.) Add the timing functions as in exercise 2 and compare the resulting processing times with the two previous versions.

Notes

1. The best way to look at a summation formula, such as that in the DFT equation, is as a loop. That is exactly what it means (an example of how programming is effectively mathematics), with the "looping variable" going from the value stated under the Σ to the value on the top. In this case, the variable is n and it goes from 0 to $N - 1$ (increasing by one each time), and N is the DFT size (and also the size of the input array). This, in the code example, is the inner loop, which uses the variable n as its counter:

```
for(int n =0; n < N; n++){
    out[i] += in[n]*cos(k*n*twopi/N);
    out[i+1] -= in[n]*sin(k*n*twopi/N);
}
```

The other loop in the code, incidentally, is basically a way of applying the DFT function to create all the output samples and to increment the frequency index (k).

2. The DFT and the FFT are effectively the same thing, as far as their inputs and outputs are concerned (the same goes for the IDFT and the IFFT). The only difference is that the FFT is implemented differently than the straight DFT shown above. For large transform sizes, the FFT is much faster than the DFT. The FFT is a fast algorithm for calculating the DFT, and in fact there are several different FFT algorithms, optimized for different transform sizes. As the DFT is very seldom used directly in applications, we normally use the term FFT for it, but it is important to make the distinction between the two: DFT is the operation, FFT is the algorithm.

3. For a further overview of the mathematics of the DFT, a two-part article by David Jaffe is of particular interest for musical applications: "Spectrum Analysis Tutorial, Part 1: The Discrete Fourier Transform," *Computer Music Journal* 11 (1987), no. 2: 9–24; "Spectrum Analysis Tutorial, Part 2: Properties and Applications of the Discrete Fourier Transform," *Computer Music Journal* 11 (1987), no. 3: 17–35.

4. The following code adapts the `fft()` and `iff()` interface functions to use the FFTW 2.1.3 library for FFT processing. The only caveat here is that the interface allows for only one set of parameters for forward and one set of parameters for inverse transform per program, because only two FFTW plans are used as global static variables. For most applications this should not be problematic. The interface can also be wrapped in a C++ class, if multiple variable FFT parameters are required. The basic job of this code is to rearrange the FFTW FFT array into the format used in this text, which contains the pair (0 Hz, Nyquist) followed by (real, imag) of all other bins in ascending order. The FFTW formats the real-fft frame differently: all real coefficients from 0 to the Nyquist frequency, inclusive, followed by all imaginary coefficients, in descending order from bin $N/2 - 1$ to 1. Here is the code:

```
#include "rfftw.h"
/* these check if the FFTW plan was created */
bool ft=true,ift=true;
static rfftw_plan forward, inverse; /* these are the FFTW plans */

void fft(float *in, float *out, int N){
    int i, k;
    if(ft){
```

```
        /* create the plan only once, first time it is called*/
        forward=
        rfftw_create_plan(N, FFTW_REAL_TO_COMPLEX, FFTW_ESTIMATE);
        ft=false;
    }
    /* copy input to the output */
    for(i =0; i < N; i++) out[i] = in[i];
    /* transform array out[] into in[] */
    rfftw_one(forward, out, in);
    /* move Nyquist to pos 1 */
    out[0] = in[0]/N;
    out[1] = in[N/2]/N;
    /* re-arrange array into [re, im] pairs */
    for(i = 2, k=1; i < N; k++, i+=2){
        out[i] = in[k]/N;
        out[i+1] = in[N-k]/N;
    }
}
void ifft(float *in, float *out, int N){
    int i, k;
    if(ift){
        /* create the plan only once, first time it is called*/
        inverse=
        rfftw_create_plan(N, FFTW_COMPLEX_TO_REAL, FFTW_ESTIMATE);
        ift=false;
    }
    /* re-arrange array into the FFTW format */
    for(i = 2, k=1; i < N; k++, i+=2){
        out[k] = in[i];
        out[N-k] = in[i+1];
    }
    /* move Nyquist to pos N/2 */
    out[0] = in[0];
    out[N/2] = in[1];
    /* transform array in[] into out[] */
    rfftw_one(inverse, out, in);
    for(i =0; i < N; i++) out[i] = in[i];
}
```

8 The STFT and Spectral Processing

Victor Lazzarini

In this chapter we will build on the concepts of the DFT and the FFT to develop a time-varying method of spectral analysis. This will be useful for the processing of any arbitrary input sound, as we can apply effects that vary in time and change the signal dynamically. We will start by seeing how the methods introduced in the earlier chapter can be adapted to provide the time-varying possibilities we are looking for.

8.1 Analyzing Time-Varying Spectra: The Short-Time Fourier Transform

So far we have been using what we described as a single-frame DFT, one "snapshot" of the spectrum at a specific time point. In order to track spectral changes, we will have to find a method of taking a sequence of transforms, at different points in time. In a way, this is similar to the process we used in the convolution application: we will be looking at extracting blocks of samples from a time-domain signal and transforming them with the DFT. This is known as the *short-time Fourier transform*. The process of extracting the samples from a portion of the waveform is called *windowing*. In other words, we are applying a time window to the signal, outside which all samples are ignored.

8.1.1 Windowing

Time windows can have various shapes. The one we used in the convolution example is equivalent to a rectangular window, where all the window contents are multiplied by one. This shape is not very useful in STFT analysis, because it can create discontinuities at the edges of the window (figure 8.1). This is the case when the analyzed signal contains components that are not integer multiples of the fundamental frequency of analysis. These discontinuities are responsible for analysis artifacts, such as the ones observed in the previous chapter on the DFT, which limit its usefulness.

Other shapes that tend toward 0 at the edges will be preferred. As the ends of the analyzed segment meet, they eliminate any discontinuity (figure 8.2). In fact, except for the rectangular

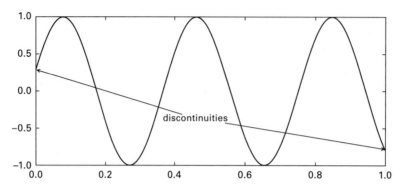

Figure 8.1
Rectangular window and discontinuities in the signal.

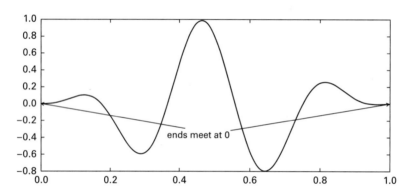

Figure 8.2
A windowed signal where the ends tend toward 0.

case, the windowing process will always involve the application of an envelope to the extracted samples.

The effect of a window's shape can be explained by remembering that (as in equation 9 in the previous chapter), when we multiply two time-domain functions, the resulting spectrum will be the convolution of the two spectra. This is of course, the converse case of the convolution of two time-domain functions as seen in the previous chapter.[1] The effect of convolution in the amplitude spectrum can be better understood graphically. As we saw before, it is the shifting and scaling of the samples of one function by every sample of the other. This operation can be as seen in figure 8.3, where the spectrum of the ring modulation of two sinusoids is shown. When we use a window function in the DFT, we are multiplying the series of complex sinusoids that compose it by that function. Since this process results in spectral convolution, the resulting amplitude spectrum of the DFT after windowing will

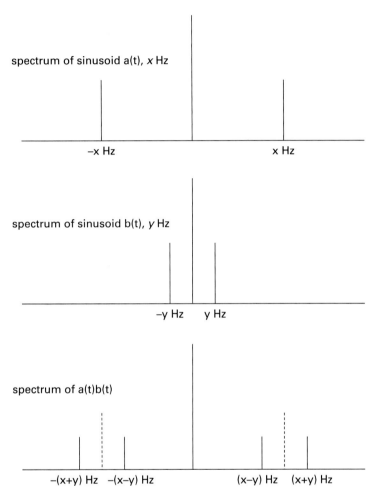

Figure 8.3
A graphic convolution of two amplitude spectra. Thicker lines represent components of spectra.

be imposition of the spectral shape of a window function on every frequency point of the DFT of the original signal (figure 8.4). A similar effect will also be introduced in the phase spectrum.

As I have already said, windowing always happens when we apply the DFT to an arbitrary segment of a signal. In all our previous cases, since we had only extracted samples from the signal, a rectangular window was used. The spectral shape of that window is not very suitable for attenuating analysis artifacts, such as the leakage observed when analyzing non-integral wave periods. (See the spectral plot of the rectangular window in figure 8.6.) However, when we choose a window with an amplitude spectrum that has a peak at 0 Hz and fades away

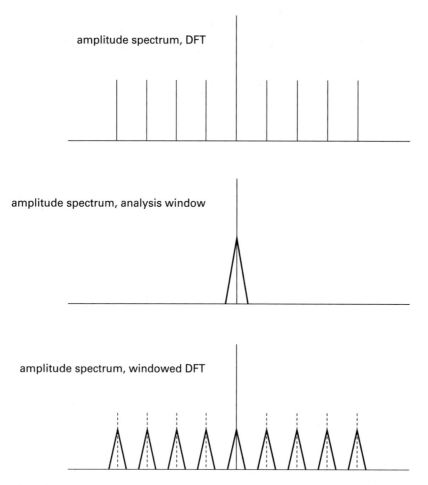

Figure 8.4
A simplified view of the amplitude spectrum of a windowed DFT as a convolution of the DFT sinusoids and the window function. Dotted lines mark positions of DFT frequency points.

quickly to zero as the frequency rises, we will have a more reasonable result. This is case of the ideal shape in figure 8.4, where each analysis point will capture components around it and ignore spurious ones further away from it.[2]

In practice, several windows with such low-pass characteristics exist. The simplest and more widely used are the ones based on raised inverted cosine shapes, the Hamming and Hanning ("Von Hann") windows (figures 8.5 and 8.6), defined as

$$w(n) = \alpha - (1 - \alpha) \cos\left(2\pi \frac{n}{N-1}\right), \qquad 0 \leq n < N \tag{1}$$

where $\alpha = 0.5$ for the Hanning window and 0.54 for the Hamming window.

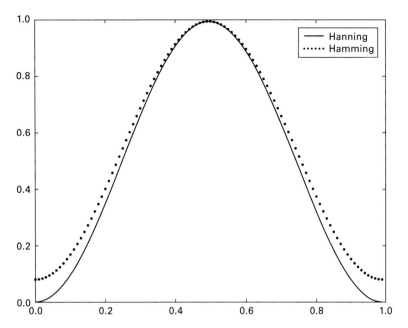

Figure 8.5
Time-domain plots of Hanning and Hamming windows.

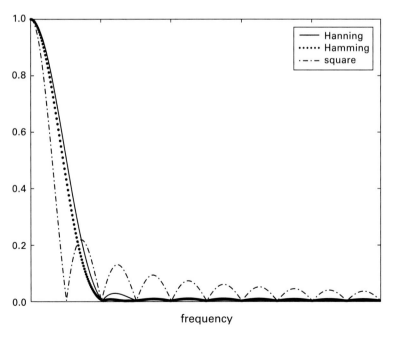

Figure 8.6
Spectral plots for rectangular, Hamming, and Hanning windows (positive frequencies only).

8.1.2   Performing the STFT

In order to perform the STFT, we will apply a time-dependent window to the signal and take the DFT of the result. This will mean also that we are making the whole operation a function of time, as well as frequency. Here is a definition for the discrete STFT of an arbitrary-length waveform $x(n)$ at a time point t:

$$STFT(x(n), k, t) = \frac{1}{N} \sum_{n=-\infty}^{\infty} w(n - t)x(n)e^{-j2\pi kn/N}, \qquad k = 1, 2, \ldots, N - 1. \tag{2}$$

This of course implies the use of a window function $w(n)$, which is defined in the range $0 \leq n < N$ and is zero elsewhere. When implementing the STFT as given above, we will be initially simple-minded, by just using the real-signal DFT (as implemented by the FFT algorithm) on N-size slices of the input signal. This will not be, in reality, the exact implementation of (2). However, it will suffice for the moment.

The STFT provides a full spectral frame for each time point, in the form of overlapped measurements, so we can view each one of the these as the result of an ordinary DFT applied to the windowed signal. For each time point, we will generate N values ($N/2$ complex pairs), so the amount of data generated by this operation is very large. However, we do not have to compute the DFT for each sample of a waveform; we can hop the window along a certain number of samples before extracting the next sample frame. The space between each frame is referred to as the *hopsize* and this will determine the time resolution of the analysis. Often it is possible to take as little as four overlapped transforms (hopsize = $N/4$) to have a good resolution. Effectively, when using the STFT output for signal processing, the smallest hopsize will be determined by the type of window used ($N/4$ is the actual value for Hamming and Hanning windows). This will guarantee that we are able to reconstruct the original signal in resynthesis.

The overlapped spectral frames can be transformed back into the time domain by performing an inverse DFT on each signal frame. In order to smooth any possible discontinuities introduced when processing the signal in the spectral domain, we will also apply a window to each transformed signal block. The waveform is reconstituted by applying an overlap-add method that is very similar to the one employed in the convolution example. Here we will overlap each sample block by *hopsize* samples, adding them together to get the output signal. Each sample will be the sum of N/*hopsize* samples, one from each overlapping block.

With these ideas in mind, we can program the forward and inverse STFT:

```
int stft(float *input, float *window, float *output,
         int input_size, int fftsize, int hopsize){

  int posin, posout, i;
  float *sigframe, *specframe;
  sigframe = new float[fftsize];
  specframe = new float[fftsize];
```

```
        for(posin=posout=0; posin < input_size; posin+=hopsize){
            // window a signal frame
            for(i=0; i < fftsize; i++)
                if(posin+i < input_size)
                    sigframe[i] = input[posin+i]*window[i];
                else sigframe[i] = 0;
            // transform it
            fft(sigframe, specframe, fftsize);
            // output it
            for(i=0; i < fftsize; i++, posout++)
                output[posout] = specframe[i];

        }
        delete[] sigframe;
        delete[] specframe;
        return posout;
}

int istft(float* input, float* window, float* output,
          int input_size, int fftsize, int hopsize){

    int posin, posout, i, output_size;
    float *sigframe, *specframe;
    sigframe = new float[fftsize];
    specframe = new float[fftsize];
    output_size = input_size*hopsize/fftsize;

    for(posout=posin=0; posout < output_size; posout+=hopsize){
        // load in a spectral frame from input
        for(i=0; i < fftsize; i++, posin++)
            specframe[i] = input[posin];
        // inverse-transform it
        ifft(specframe, sigframe, fftsize);
        // window it and overlap-add it
        for(i=0; i < fftsize; i++)
            if(posout+i < output_size)
                output[posout+i] += sigframe[i]*window[i];
    }
    delete[] sigframe;
    delete[] specframe;
    return output_size;
}
```

These two example functions show the process again in a non-real-time form, but are easily adaptable to any application. They use the fft() and ifft() functions used in chapter 7 of this volume.

The forward short-time transform takes the whole signal and outputs overlapped spectral frames. The input, output and the window signal vectors are expected to be allocated externally. Every `fftsize` block of floats in the output signal composes a spectral frame relative to consecutive time points. The size of the output is determined by the number of overlaps (`fftsize/hopsize`) times the input size, but it can exceed that by a little if the input size is not an integral multiple the hop period. The function returns the length of the output. The inverse transform takes a sequence of overlapped frames, transforms them, and overlap-adds them. In the following sections, we will see these functions in action in small example programs.

8.2   Spectral Transformations: Manipulating STFT Data

Each spectral frame can be considered as a collection of complex pairs relative to the information found on equally spaced frequency bands at a particular time. These bands are sometimes called *DFT (or frequency) bins*. They will contain information on the amplitude and frequency contents detected at that band. The rectangular, or Cartesian, format that is the output of the transform packs these two aspects of the spectrum in the real and imaginary parts of each complex coefficient. To separate them, all we need do is convert the output into a polar representation. The magnitudes will give us the amplitude of each bin, and the phases will be indicative of the detected frequencies. A single STFT frame can give us the amplitudes for each band, but we will not be able to obtain proper frequency values for them. This would imply extracting the *instantaneous frequency*, which is not really possible with one STFT measurement. Instead, the phases will contain the frequency information in a different form. Nevertheless, we will be able to transform the amplitude and frequency aspect of a sound, by manipulating the magnitudes and phase values of each bin.

8.2.1   Cross-Synthesis of Frequencies and Amplitudes

The first basic transformation that can be achieved in this way is *cross-synthesis*. There are different ways of crossing aspects of two spectra. The spectral multiplication made in the convolution example is one. By splitting amplitude and frequency aspects of spectra, we can also make that type of operation separately on each aspect. Another typical cross-synthesis technique is to combine the amplitudes of one sound with the frequencies of another. This is a spectral version of the time-domain *channel vocoder*. Once we have the STFT spectra of two sounds, there could not be an easier process to implement.

1. Convert the rectangular spectral samples into magnitudes and phases.
2. Take the magnitudes of one input and the phases of the other and make a new spectral frame, on a frame-by-frame basis.
3. Convert the magnitudes and phases to rectangular format.[3] This is done with the following relationships:

$re[z] = Mag_z \times \cos(Pha_z),$

$im[z] = Mag_z \times \sin(Pha_z).$

$$(3)$$

The resulting spectral frames in rectangular format can then be transformed back to the time domain using the ISTFT and the overlap-add method. This three-step procedure yields the following code, which processes one STFT frame at a time:

```
void crosspec(float *maginput, float *phasinput, float *output,
            int fftsize){

    int i;
    float mag, phi;

    // take care of real-valued points at 0Hz and Nyquist
    output[0] = maginput[0];
    output[1] = maginput[1];

    for(i=2; i< fftsize; i+=2){

        // get the magnitudes of one input
        mag = (float) sqrt(maginput[i]*maginput[i]
                +maginput[i+1]*maginput[i+1]);
        // get the phases of the other
        phi = (float)
            atan2(phasinput[i+1], phasinput[i]);
        // combine them and convert to rectangular form
        output[i] = (float) (mag*cos(phi));
        output[i+1]= (float) (mag*sin(phi));
    }
}
```

The code above (and the code that follows) expects the inputs and outputs to exist externally as *N*-size arrays of floats. In fact, the output signal could be the same as one of the inputs (i.e. an "in-place" process). Here is a short program demonstrating this function:

```
/** cross-synthesis main program

    \b usage: cross infile1 infile2 outfile dur(s) \n
    \n
        infile1: input1 (magnitudes) filename \n
        infile2: input2 (phases) filename \n
        outfile: output filename \n
        dur: duration of input in seconds \n
    \n
    all files are supposed to be mono \n

*/
```

```
int
main(int argc, char **argv){
    SNDFILE *fin, *fin2, *fout;
    SF_INFO input_info, input_info2;
    float *win, *in, *in2, *out, *spec, *spec2;
    int outsize, specsize, fftsize=1024,hopsize=256;
    int dataratio=fftsize/hopsize;
    int frames, extraframes;
    int read=0, written = 0, i,j, dur;
    float *buff;

    if(argc < 3) {
        printf("%s: unsufficient number of
                arguments(got %d, needed 2)", argv[0], argc-1);
        usage();
        exit(-1);
    }
    if(!(fin = sf_open(argv[1], SFM_READ, &input_info))){
        printf("could not open %s \n", argv[1]);
        exit(-1);
    }

    if(!(fin2 = sf_open(argv[2], SFM_READ, &input_info2))){
    printf("could not open %s \n", argv[2]);
    exit(-1);
    }

    if(!formats_equal(input_info, input_info2)){
        sf_close(fin2);
        sf_close(fin);
        printf("%s and %s formats are not equal
                or files not mono\n",
                argv[1], argv[2]);
        exit(-1);
    }
    dur = input_info.frames > input_info2.frames ?
    input_info2.frames : input_info.frames;
    buff = new float[100];
    win = new float[fftsize];
    in = new float[dur];
    in2 = new float[dur];
    /* number of full dataframes */
    frames = ((dur*dataratio)/fftsize);
    /* extra frames [not completely filled] */
    extraframes = 1 +
```

```
        (frames*fftsize - dur*dataratio)/fftsize;
   /* size of spectral data */
   specsize = (frames + extraframes)*fftsize;
   spec = new float[specsize];
   spec2 = new float[specsize];
   outsize = specsize/dataratio;
   out = new float[outsize];

   if(!(fout = sf_open(argv[3], SFM_WRITE, &input_info))){
      printf("could not open %s \n", argv[3]);
      exit(-1);
   }

   for(i=0; i< fftsize; i++) win[i] = 0.5f -
             (float)(0.5*cos(i*twopi/fftsize));

   for(j=0; j < dur; j+=read){
      read = sf_read_float(fin, buff, 100);
      for(i=0; i < read; i++) in[i+j] = buff[i];
   }

   for(j=0; j < dur; j+=read){
      read = sf_read_float(fin2, buff, 100);
      for(i=0; i < read; i++) in2[i+j] = buff[i];
   }

   outsize = stft(in, win, spec, dur, fftsize, hopsize);

   stft(in2, win, spec2, dur, fftsize, hopsize);

   for(i=0; i < outsize; i += fftsize)
      crosspec(&spec[i], &spec2[i], &spec[i], fftsize);

   dur = istft(spec, win, out, outsize, fftsize, hopsize);

   for(j=0; j < dur;j+=written){
      for(i=0; i < 100 && j < dur; i++){
         if(i+j < dur) buff[i] = out[i+j];
         else buff[i] = 0.f;
      }
      written = sf_write_float(fout, buff, i);
   }
   delete[] out;
   delete[] in;
   delete[] in2;
   delete[] spec;
```

```
        delete[] spec2;
        delete[] win;
        delete[] buff;

        sf_close(fout);
        sf_close(fin);
        sf_close(fin2);
        return 0;
}


void
usage(){

 puts("\n\n usage: cross input1 input2 output \n");

}
```

8.2.2   Spectral-Domain Filtering

If we manipulate the magnitudes separately, we will be able to create some filtering effects by applying a certain contour to the spectrum. For instance, to generate a simple low-pass filter we can use one-fourth of the shape of the cosine wave and apply it to all points from 0 to N/2. The function used for shaping the magnitude will look like

$$mag[k] = \cos\left(\frac{\pi k}{N}\right), \qquad 0 \le k \le N/2. \tag{4}$$

Here is the code for this simple filter, which, again, processes one frame at a time:

```
void simplp(float *input, float *output, int fftsize){

    int i,k;
    float mag, magin, phi;
    // The low-pass contour is 1 at 0Hz
    // and 0 at the Nyquist
    output[0] = 1.f;
    output[1] = 0.f;

    for(i=2, k=1; i < fftsize; i+=2, k++){

        // get the magnitudes of input
        magin = (float)
            sqrt(input[i]*input[i]+input[i+1]*input[i+1]);
        // apply the spectral contour
        mag = (float) cos(pi*k/fftsize)*magin;
        // get the phases
        phi = (float) atan2(input[i+1], input[i]);
```

```
        // convert to rectangular form
        output[i] = (float) (mag*cos(phi));
        output[i+1]= (float) (mag*sin(phi));
    }
}
```

This function can be used with the `stft()` and `istft()` functions to create a filtering program. (See the DVD examples for the full code, in *simpfl_main.c*.) A high-pass filter could be designed by using a sine function instead of cosine in the example above. In fact, we can define any filter in spectral terms and use it by multiplying its spectrum with the STFT of any input sound. This leads us back into the convolution territory. Consider a typical two-pole resonator filter. Its transfer function is

$$H(z) = \frac{A_0}{1 - 2R \cos \theta z^{-1} + R^2 z^{-2}}. \tag{5}$$

Here θ is the pole angle and R is its radius (or magnitude), parameters that are related to the filter center frequency and bandwidth, respectively. The scaling constant A_0 is used to scale the filter output so that it does not run wildly out of range. Now, if we evaluate this function for evenly spaced frequency points $z = e^{j2\pi k/N}$, we will reveal the discrete spectrum of that filter. All we need do is perform a complex multiplication of the result with the STFT of an input sound.[4]

The mathematical steps used to obtain the spectrum of the filter are based on Euler's relationship, which splits the complex sinusoidal $e^{j\omega}$ into its real and imaginary parts, $\cos(\omega)$ and $j \sin(\omega)$.[5] Once we have the spectral points in the rectangular form $A_0(a + ib)^{-1}$, all we need do is multiply them with the STFT points of the original signal. This will in reality turn out to be a complex division:

$$Y[k] = (real\{X[k]\} + j \times imag\{X[k]\} + j \times imag\{F[k]\})^{-1}$$

$$= A_0 \left(\frac{real\{X[k]\} + j \times imag\{X[k]\}}{real\{F[k]\} + j \times imag\{F[k]\}} \right), \tag{6}$$

where $X[k]$, $A_0 F[k]^{-1}$, and $Y[k]$ are, respectively, the spectra of the input signal, the filter, and the output.

Here is some code that takes the pole angle and radius characterizing a resonator and apply filtering to an input signal. The scaling constant A_0 is also taken as an argument. These three parameters can be calculated from the filter's center frequency and bandwidth. This C++ function operates on frame-by-frame basis; thus the filter parameters can be varied dynamically every hop period.

```
void specreson(float *input, float *output, float scale,
               double angle, double radius, int fftsize) {
```

```
int i, k;
double sinw, cosw, cos2w, w, costheta, radsq, rad2;
float re, im, div, rout, imout;

costheta = cos(angle);
radsq = radius*radius;
rad2 = 2*radius;

// 0 Hz and Nyquist taken care of
output[0] = (float)((scale*input[0])/(1. - rad2*costheta + radsq));
output[1] = (float)((scale*input[1])/(1. + rad2*costheta + radsq));

for(i=2, k=1; i <fftsize; i+=2, k++){

    w = (twopi*k)/fftsize;
    sinw = sin(w);
    cosw = cos(w);
    cos2w = cos(2*w);

    // real and imag parts of filter spectrum
    re = (float) (1. - rad2*costheta*cosw + radsq*cos2w);
    im = (float) (sinw*(rad2*costheta - 2*radsq*cosw));

    // complex division
    div = re*re + im*im;
    rout = (input[i]*re + input[i+1]*im)/div;
    imout = (input[i+1]*re - input[i]*im)/div;

    output[i] = scale*rout;
    output[i+1] = scale*imout;
}
}
```

(This function is used in the DVD example program specreson.. The source code for it is found in *specreson_main.c*.)

Similarly, we can implement a spectral comb filter by multiplying the filter transfer function, evaluated as above, by the input signal. The comb filter transfer function depends on the delay D (in samples) and the pole radius R:

$$H(e^{j2\pi k/N}) = \frac{e^{-jD2\pi k/N}}{1 - Re^{-jD2\pi k/N}}, \qquad k = 0, 1, 2, \ldots, N - 1. \tag{7}$$

The following code implements the comb filter, which can be used in flanging and filtering applications. As in the delay-line version, the amplitude spectrum will resemble an upside-down comb, with the reciprocal of the delay parameter determining the spacing of the spectral peaks. The maxima and minima of the curve will depend on the pole radius. In this code, delay is expected to be in seconds.

```
void specomb(float *input, float *output, float scale, float delay,
             double radius, int fftsize, float sr) {

    int i, k;
    double sinw, cosw, w, radsq, rad2;
    float re, im, div;
    radsq = radius*radius;
    rad2 = 2*radius;
    delay *= sr;

    // 0 Hz and Nyquist taken care of
    output[0] = (float)(input[0]*(1.-radius)/(1. - rad2 +
                        radsq))*scale;
    output[1] = (float)(input[1]*-(1+radius)/(1. + rad2 +
                        radsq))*scale;

    for(i=2, k=1; i <fftsize; i+=2, k++){
        w = (delay*twopi*k)/fftsize;
        sinw = sin(w);
        cosw = cos(w);

        // real and imag parts of filter spectrum
        div = (float) (1. - rad2*cosw + radsq);
        re = (float) (cosw - radius)/div;
        im = (float) (sinw - rad2*cosw*sinw)/div;

        // complex multiplication
        output[i] = (input[i]*re - input[i+1]*im)*scale;
        output[i+1]= (input[i+1]*re + input[i]*im)*scale;
    }
}
```

The use of a delay parameter here is somewhat misleading, as the output does not contain the full length of all of the delayed signals. Since the STFT process effectively cuts off the decay tail of the sound, this implementation cannot be used for reverb applications. For these, we would have to use a method similar to the DFT-based convolution discussed previously. In that case, we would use a suitably long transform size to accommodate the expected impulse response. (This code is the basis of the DVD example program `speccomb`; the source code for it is found in *speccomb_main.c*.)

8.3   Conclusion

There are many more processes that can be devised for transforming the output of the STFT. Two spectra can be interpolated, for instance, to generate a sound with characteristics that are midway between the two. Convolution can be performed as the two input sounds evolve in time. Noise suppression can be implemented by a variety of methods, e.g. by using a simple amplitude threshold mechanism. The examples given here are only the start. They represent what we can call the "classic" approach. But several other more radical techniques could certainly be explored. The STFT is a rich source of very interesting sound effects and a key to the development of useful spectral processing programs.

8.4   Exercises

Exercise 8.4.1
Design a cross-synthesis function based on the multiplication of two input spectra, using the structure of the processing functions explained in this chapter. Write a new program (or modify one of the programming examples) to use this function.

Exercise 8.4.2
Create a version of the cross-synthesis function of exercise 8.4.1 that only multiplies together the magnitudes of the STFT outputs, and uses the phases of the inputs unchanged. Write a program to use the function.

Exercise 8.4.3
Write a filtering program that filters out specific frequency bands, by changing the magnitude of the bins in these bands. Design it so that the user has control over the range of the band and the amount of filtering (attenuation or boost).

Notes

1. Time-domain (i.e. waveform) multiplication results in frequency-domain (spectral) convolution. Spectral multiplication is the same as waveform convolution. So if we want to filter a sound, we can do it in two ways: we can take the filter spectrum and multiply it by the input sound spectrum or we can take the filter impulse response and combine it with the input sound waveform using convolution. The filter's spectrum is closely linked to its frequency response. So in polar form the magnitude is how the filter changes the input amplitudes at different frequencies and the phase is how the input delays different frequencies. In many cases, we are only interested in the magnitude effect. In the case of windowing, what we are doing is multiplying the input by the window, so if we will be performing spectral convolution: the shape of the window magnitude spectrum will be shifted and scaled by every component of the input sound spectrum. (See the discussion of convolution in chapter 7.)

2. Windows are effectively envelopes. Different window shapes will have an effect on the analysis because their magnitude spectra will have different shapes. Some windows also do not go all the way to 0 at their ends, so their use can lead to artifacts if the spectral data is modified in certain ways. There are a variety of different windows for spectral analysis in addition to the ones shown here. Bartlett, Kaiser, and Blackman-Harris are the names of other commonly found windows.

3. Spectral data can be represented either in Cartesian (real-imaginary) or in polar (magnitude-phase) forms. For musical applications, the polar format is probably more meaningful: the magnitudes tell us how much energy is present at certain bands and the phases are correlated to the frequencies detected at each bin. If we have the data in that format, we will be able to manipulate these two parameters separately, which is an advantage. If we, for instance, change the magnitudes but do not modify the phases, we will still get quite a lot of the original sound characteristics, but with some timbral changes. This is a powerful form of filtering. In fact, the STFT allows for some very interesting ways of changing the timbre of sounds.

4. Another way of implementing a filter, not as rigorous as the spectral resonator example, would be to modify only the spectral magnitudes. We could first define a magnitude shape (or envelope), either by finding the magnitude response function of an existing filter, or by creating an arbitrary curve. Then we could apply this curve to a signal by multiplying the signal's magnitudes with our filter magnitudes and keeping the phases unchanged. In fact, we could derive this curve from an arbitrary input signal, by obtaining its magnitudes for the same purpose. In this case, we would be creating a version of the cross-synthesis program presented earlier in the chapter. (See exercise 8.4.2.)

5. By setting $z = e^{j\omega}$, with $\omega = 2\pi k/N$, we obtain the DFT of the filter impulse response:

$$H(e^{j\omega}) = \frac{A_0}{1 - 2R \cos \theta e^{-j\omega} + R^2 e^{-j2\omega}}.$$

Using Euler's relationship $e^{j\omega} = \cos \omega + j \sin \omega$, we obtain the spectrum of the filter in rectangular format:

$$H(e^{j\omega}) = \frac{A_0}{1 - 2R \cos \theta \cos \omega + R^2 \cos \omega + j \sin \omega (2R \cos \theta - 2R^2 \cos \omega)}.$$

9 Programming the Phase Vocoder

Victor Lazzarini

The phase vocoder[1] (PV) is one of the most frequently used tools in spectral processing. It produces an output that is simple to understand, to manipulate, and to resynthesize. In this chapter, I will discuss the details of implementing this technique, starting from the principles explored in chapter 8. I will show how the short-time Fourier transform (STFT) can be modified and enhanced to perform PV analyses.

9.1 Tracking the Frequency

Although we can manipulate the frequency content of spectra through their phases, the STFT does not have enough resolution to tell us what frequencies are present in a sound. We will have to find a way of tracking the instantaneous frequencies in each spectral band. A well-known technique known as the PV can be employed to do just that. The PV analysis process is sometimes described in the time domain as the use of a bank of filters tuned to equally spaced frequencies, from 0 hertz to the Nyquist frequency. The filter-bank outputs are made up of values for amplitudes and frequencies at each band. Here we will take a frequency-domain approach, starting with the STFT and adapting it to fit the PV output characteristics.[2]

The STFT followed by a polar conversion can also be seen as a bank of parallel filters. Its output is composed of the values for the magnitudes and phases at every time point or hop period for each bin. The first step in transforming the STFT into a phase vocoder is to generate values that are proportional to the frequencies present in a sound. Ideally, this is done by the taking the time derivative of the phase; but we can approximate it by computing the difference between the phase value of consecutive frames for each spectral band. This simple operation, although not yielding the *right* value for the frequency at a spectral band, will output one that is related to it.

With these small changes we will be able to process sound in a way that was not possible before. By keeping track of the phase differences, we can time-stretch or compress a sound without altering its frequency content (or, put simply, its pitch). We can perform this by repeating or skipping spectral blocks, to stretch or compress the data. Because we are keeping the phase differences between the frames, when we accumulate them before resynthesis, we will be able to reconstruct the signal back using the correct relative phase values.

The code below takes a rectangular STFT input and converts it to magnitudes and phase differences (conversion in place):

```
const double pi = twopi/2.;

void deltaphi(float *spec, float *lastphs, int fftsize){
    int i, k;
    float mag, phi;

    for(k=0, i=2; i < fftsize; i+=2, k++){

        mag = (float) sqrt(spec[i]*spec[i]+spec[i+1]*spec[i+1]);
        phi = (float) atan2(spec[i+1], spec[i]);
        spec[i] = mag;
        spec[i+1] = phi - lastphs[k];
        lastphs[k] = phi;

        // bring the diffs to the -pi and pi range
        while(spec[i+1]> pi) spec[i+1] -= (float) twopi;
        while(spec[i+1]< -pi) spec[i+1] += (float) twopi;
    }
}
```

The inverse tangent function outputs the phase in the range of $-\pi$ to π. When the phase differences are calculated, they might exceed this range. In this case, we have to bring them down to the expected interval (known as *principal values*). This process is sometimes called *phase unwrapping*.

The next function does the inverse operation, as it integrates the values to calculate the current phase value for each frequency point. This operation is complemented by a polar to rectangular conversion:

```
void sigmaphi(float *spec, float *lastphs, int fftsize) {

    int i, k;
    float mag, phi;

    for(k=0, i=2; i < fftsize; i+=2, k++){
        mag = spec[i];
        phi = spec[i+1] + lastphs[k];
        lastphs[k] = phi;
        spec[i] = (float)(mag*cos(phi));
        spec[i+1] = (float)(mag*sin(phi));
    }
}
```

This is an improvement on the basic STFT, but it does not provide much flexibility even for time-scale modifications, as we have to keep the same hopsize for analysis and resynthesis. Therefore, depending on the length of the hop period, fine changes in time scale will not be possible. Nevertheless, much more can be achieved. We can, for instance, scale the phase difference to match the change in the hopsize from analysis to resynthesis. For instance, if we start with a hopsize of D samples and resynthesize the sound using a hopsize of I samples, the ratio $I:D$ will give us the appropriate scaling figure. This idea will be incorporated in the implementation of the phase vocoder.

9.1.1 Frequency Estimation

So far we have been working with values that are proportional to the frequencies at every analysis band. In order to obtain the proper values in hertz, we will have to first modify the input to the STFT slightly. We will rotate the windowed samples inside the analysis frame, relative to the time point n (in samples, and take modulus N) of the input window. If our window has 1,024 samples and we are hopping it every 256 samples, the moduli of the successive time points n will be 0, 256, 512, 768, 0, 256, ... The rotation will imply that for time point 256 we will move samples from positions 0–767 into positions 256–1,023. The last 256 samples will be moved to the first locations of the block. A similar process is applied to the other time points (figure 9.1). The mathematical reasons for this input rotation are

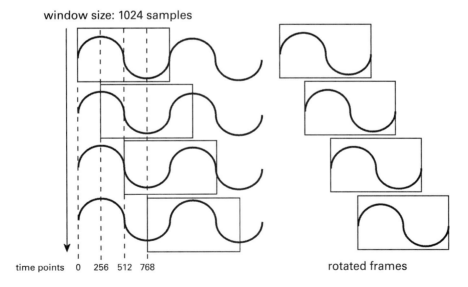

window size: 1024 samples

time points 0   256 512 768

rotated frames

Figure 9.1
Signal frame rotation, according to input time point.

somewhat complex, but the graphic representation in figure 9.1 goes some way on helping us understand the process intuitively. As we can see, the rotation process has the effect of aligning the phase of the signal in successive frames. This will help us obtain the right frequency values, but we will understand it better after seeing the rest of the process. In fact, the input rotation renders the STFT formulation mathematically correct. Previously, in chapter 8, we had been using a non-rigorous and simpler approach (which so far had worked for us).[3]

After the rotation, we can take the DFT of the frame as usual and convert the result into polar form. The phase differences for each band are then calculated. This now tells us how much each detected frequency deviates from the center frequency of its analysis band. The center frequencies are effectively the DFT analysis frequencies $2\pi k/N$, in radians. To obtain the proper detected frequency value, we need only add the phase differences to the center frequency for each analysis band, scaled by the hopsize. The values in hertz can be obtained by multiplying the result, which is given in radians per hopsize samples by $sr/(2\pi \times \text{hopsize})$, where sr is the sampling rate in samples per second.

Now we can go back to the rotation and understand the process. Figure 9.1 shows a very simple case, a sine wave with the same period as the analysis window. After we rotate the signal and obtain the phase-aligned result, there is no phase difference between the successive frames. Accordingly, when we take STFT of this signal, we will detect the most energy on the first frequency band, and the phase difference for that band will be null. This is what we expect, since this particular wave has the same frequency as the first frequency point. Now if we proceed by converting this phase difference in hertz, we will of course obtain $sr/1{,}024$ Hz, the expected result (43.07 Hz at 44.1 KHz). If the input were not rotated, we would detect a phase difference of $\pi/2$, which would result in an 86.14 Hz, twice the right value. This intuitive understanding can be extrapolated to more complex signals.

Here is a summary of the steps involved in phase vocoder analysis:

1. Extract N samples from a signal and apply an analysis window.
2. Rotate the samples in the signal frame according to input time $n \bmod N$.
3. Take the DFT of the signal.
4. Convert rectangular coefficients to polar format.
5. Compute the phase difference and bring the value to the range from $-\pi$ to $+\pi$.
6. Add the difference values to $2\pi kD/N$, and multiply the result by $sr/2\pi D$, where D is the hopsize in samples.
7. For each spectral band, the result from step 6 yields its frequency in hertz, and the magnitude value, its peak amplitude.

The following C++ code implements the algorithm outlined above. A lot of it was already in place in the `stft()` code.

```
int pva(float *input, float *window, float *output,
        int input_size, int fftsize, int hopsize, float sr){

    int posin, posout, i, k, mod;
    float *sigframe, *specframe, *lastph;
    float fac, scal, phi, mag, delta, pi = (float)twopi/2;

    sigframe = new float[fftsize];
    specframe = new float[fftsize];
    lastph = new float[fftsize/2];
    memset(lastph, 0, sizeof(float)*fftsize/2);

    fac = (float) (sr/(hopsize*twopi));
    scal = (float) (twopi*hopsize/fftsize);

    for(posin=posout=0; posin < input_size; posin+=hopsize){
        mod = posin%fftsize;
        // window & rotate a signal frame
        for(i=0; i < fftsize; i++)
            if(posin+i < input_size)
                sigframe[(i+mod)%fftsize]
                    = input[posin+i]*window[i];
            else sigframe[(i+mod)%fftsize] = 0;
        // transform it
        fft(sigframe, specframe, fftsize);

        // convert to PV output
        for(i=2,k=1; i < fftsize; i+=2, k++){

            // rectangular to polar
            mag = (float) sqrt(specframe[i]*specframe[i]
                            + specframe[i+1]*specframe[i+1]);
            phi = (float) atan2(specframe[i+1], specframe[i]);
            // phase diffs
            delta = phi - lastph[k];
            lastph[k] = phi;

            // unwrap the difference, so it lies between -pi and pi
            while(delta > pi) delta -= (float) twopi;
            while(delta < -pi) delta += (float) twopi;

            // construct the amplitude-frequency pairs
            specframe[i] = mag;
            specframe[i+1] = (delta + k*scal)*fac;

        }

        // output it
```

```
        for(i=0; i < fftsize; i++, posout++)
            output[posout] = specframe[i];

    }
    delete[] sigframe;
    delete[] specframe;
    delete[] lastph;

    return posout;
}
```

9.1.2 Phase Vocoder Resynthesis

Phase vocoder data can be resynthesized using a variety of methods. Since we have blocks of amplitude and frequency data, we can use some sort of additive synthesis to playback the spectral frames. However, a more efficient way of converting to time-domain data for arbitrary sounds with many components is to use an overlap-add method similar to the one in the ISTFT. All we need do is retrace the steps taken in the forward transformation:

1. Convert the frequencies back to phase differences in radians per I samples by subtracting them from the center frequencies of each channel, in hertz, ksr/N, and multiplying the result by $2\pi I/sr$, where I is the synthesis hopsize.
2. Accumulate them to compute the current phase values.
3. Perform a polar to rectangular conversion.
4. Take the IDFT of the signal frame.
5. Unrotate the samples and apply a window to the resulting sample block.
6. Overlap-add consecutive frames.

The code is as follows:

```
int pvs(float* input, float* window, float* output,
        int input_size, int fftsize, int hopsize, float sr){

    int posin, posout, k, i, output_size, mod;
    float *sigframe, *specframe, *lastph;
    float fac, scal, phi, mag, delta;

    sigframe = new float[fftsize];
    specframe = new float[fftsize];
    lastph = new float[fftsize/2];
    memset(lastph, 0, sizeof(float)*fftsize/2);

    output_size = input_size*hopsize/fftsize;

    fac = (float) (hopsize*twopi/sr);
    scal = sr/fftsize;
```

```
for(posout=posin=0; posout < output_size; posout+=hopsize){

    // load in a spectral frame from input
    for(i=0; i < fftsize; i++, posin++)
            specframe[i] = input[posin];

    // convert from PV input to DFT coordinates
    for(i=2,k=1; i < fftsize; i+=2, k++){
        delta = (specframe[i+1] - k*scal)*fac;
        phi = lastph[k]+delta;
        lastph[k] = phi;
        mag = specframe[i];

        specframe[i] = (float) (mag*cos(phi));
        specframe[i+1] = (float) (mag*sin(phi));

    }
    // inverse-transform it
    ifft(specframe, sigframe, fftsize);

    // unrotate and window it and overlap-add it
    mod = posout%fftsize;
    for(i=0; i < fftsize; i++)
        if(posout+i < output_size)
            output[posout+i] +=
                sigframe[(i+mod)%fftsize]*window[i];
}
delete[] sigframe;
delete[] specframe;
delete[] lastph;

return output_size;
}
```

PV analysis has several advantages over the straightforward STFT. The first advantage is independence of time scale and frequency scale, already discussed above. Another is the flexibility of the representation, which can be used in many applications. Dealing with amplitude and frequency is more musically meaningful, when compared to the manipulation of raw spectral coordinates. In addition, all of the already discussed STFT data processing techniques are also available to the PV format, with a little adaptation. This makes the phase vocoder a more versatile tool for spectral processing than the STFT. However, conversion to PV format involves a little more computation than straight STFT processing. Thus, for certain applications, if the STFT is sufficient, there is no need to look beyond it.

All DFT-based algorithms will have some limits in terms of frequency resolution. The analysis will be able to resolve a maximum of one sinusoidal component per frequency band. If two or more partials fall within one band, the phase vocoder will fail to output the right values for the amplitudes and frequencies of each of them. Instead, we will have an amplitude-modulated composite output, in many ways similar to beat frequencies. In addition, because the DFT splits the spectrum in equal-size bands, this problem will mostly affect lower frequencies, where bands are perceptually larger. This also implies that the phase vocoder is more suitable to the analysis of harmonic spectra. Nevertheless, there are many different types of manipulations of phase vocoder data to which these problems are not relevant. In general, the phase vocoder is a powerful tool for transformation of arbitrary signals.

9.1.3   Spectral Morphing

A typical transformation of PV data is spectral interpolation, or morphing. It is a more general version of the spectral cross-synthesis example discussed previously. Here, we interpolate[4] between the frequencies and amplitudes of two spectra frame by frame. The code below implements this operation by interpolating linearly between the frequencies and exponentially between the frequencies. The arguments morpha and morphfr define the amount of interpolation and should be in the range 0–1.

```
void pvmorph(float* input1, float *input2, float *output,
             float morpha, float morphfr, int fftsize, float sr){

    int i;
    float amp1, amp2, fr1, fr2;
    double div;

    for(i=0; i< fftsize; i+=2){
        amp1 = input1[i];
        amp2 = input2[i];
        output[i] = amp1 + (amp2-amp1)*morpha;

        if(i){
            // interpolate frs
            fr1 = input1[i+1];
            fr2 = input2[i+1];
            div = fr1 ? fr2/fr1 : HUGE_VAL;
            div = div > 0 ? div : -div;
            output[i+1] = (float)(fr1*pow(div, morphfr));
        }
        else {
            // this is the nyquist frequency band
            amp1 = input1[i+1];
            amp2 = input2[i+1];
            output[i+1] = amp1 + (amp2-amp1)*morpha;
        }
    }
}
```

Here is the full code of an example program using the above function for a spectral morphing application:

```c
#include <stdio.h>
#include "spec.h"
#include "fourier.h"

/** pv morphing main program

    \b usage: pvmorph infile1 infile2 outfile dur(s) \n
    \n
        infile1: input1 (start sound) filename \n
        infile2: input2 (final sounds) filename \n
        outfile: output filename \n
        dur: duration of input in seconds \n
    \n
        all files are supposed to be mono \n

*/

int
main(int argc, char **argv){
    SNDFILE *fin, *fin2, *fout;
    SF_INFO input_info, input_info2;
    float *win, *in, *in2, *out, *spec, *spec2;
    int outsize, specsize, fftsize=1024,hopsize=256;
    int dataratio=fftsize/hopsize;
    int frames, extraframes;
    int read=0, written = 0, i,j, dur;
    float *buff,sr;

    if(argc < 3) {
        printf("%s: unsufficient number of
                arguments(got %d, needed 3)", argv[0], argc-1);
        usage();
        exit(-1);
    }
    if(!(fin = sf_open(argv[1], SFM_READ, &input_info))){
        printf("could not open %s \n", argv[1]);
        exit(-1);
    }

    if(!(fin2 = sf_open(argv[2], SFM_READ, &input_info2))){
        printf("could not open %s \n", argv[2]);
        exit(-1);
    }
```

```
    if(!formats_equal(input_info, input_info2)){
        sf_close(fin2);
        sf_close(fin);
        printf("%s and %s formats are not equal
                or files not mono\n",
                argv[1], argv[2]);
        exit(-1);
    }
    dur = input_info.frames > input_info2.frames ?
    input_info2.frames : input_info.frames;
    sr = input_info.samplerate;
    buff = new float[100];
    win = new float[fftsize];
    in = new float[dur];
    in2 = new float[dur];
    /* number of full dataframes */
    frames = ((dur*dataratio)/fftsize);
    /* extra frames [not completely filled] */
    extraframes = 1 +
    (frames*fftsize - dur*dataratio)/fftsize;
    /* size of spectral data */
    specsize = (frames + extraframes)*fftsize;
    spec = new float[specsize];
    spec2 = new float[specsize];
    outsize = specsize/dataratio;
    out = new float[outsize];

    if(!(fout = sf_open(argv[3], SFM_WRITE, &input_info))){
        printf("could not open %s \n", argv[3]);
        exit(-1);
    }

    for(i=0; i< fftsize; i++) win[i] = 0.5f -
                        (float)(0.5*cos(i*twopi/fftsize));

    for(j=0; j < dur; j+=read){
        read = sf_read_float(fin, buff, 100);
        for(i=0; i < read; i++) in[i+j] = buff[i];
    }

    for(j=0; j < dur; j+=read){
        read = sf_read_float(fin2, buff, 100);
        for(i=0; i < read; i++) in2[i+j] = buff[i];
    }

    outsize = pva(in, win, spec, dur, fftsize, hopsize, sr);
```

```
    pva(in2, win, spec2, dur, fftsize, hopsize, sr);

    for(i=0; i < specsize; i+=fftsize) {
        pvmorph(&spec[i], &spec2[i], &spec[i],
        (float)i/outsize, (float)i/outsize, 1024, (float) sr);
    }

    dur = pvs(spec, win, out, specsize, fftsize, hopsize, sr);

    for(j=0; j < dur;j+=written){
        for(i=0; i < 100 && j < dur; i++){
            if(i+j < dur) buff[i] = out[i+j];
            else buff[i] = 0.f;
        }
        written = sf_write_float(fout, buff, i);
    }

    delete[] out;
    delete[] in;
    delete[] in2;
    delete[] spec;
    delete[] spec2;
    delete[] win;
    delete[] buff;

    sf_close(fout);
    sf_close(fin);
    sf_close(fin2);
    return 0;
}

void
usage(){

 puts("\n\n usage: morph input1 input2 output \n");

}
```

Spectral morphing can produce interesting results. However, its effectiveness depends very much on the spectral qualities of the two input sounds. When the spectral data does not overlap much, interpolating will sound similar to cross-fading, which can be achieved in the time domain with much less trouble.

There are many more transformations that can be devised for modifying PV data. In fact, any number of manipulation procedures that generate a spectral frame in the right format can be seen as valid spectral processes. Whether they will produce a musically useful output is another question. In general, we should not have any problems with any amplitude data transformation, but care should be taken with changes in frequency data. If the PV data is to be resynthesized using the inverse overlap-add operation, we will have to keep the frequencies within the bandwidth of a bin. If the frequency of a bin is modified so that it is actually in another bin's range, then that component (its amplitude and frequency) should be moved to the right bin. This is the basis of general-purpose frequency scaling of PV data.[5] But if additive synthesis is used, no such restriction applies. Understanding how the spectral data is generated in analysis is the first step in designing transformations that work.

We have explored the phase vocoder from the DFT perspective, as a modification of more basic spectral analysis algorithms. However, it is important to remember that the original theory also involves a time-domain interpretation of the process, as the use of a bank of overlapping band-pass filters. Each of these filters, in that interpretation, is constructed using a heterodyne algorithm, which consists in the multiplication of the signal by cosine and sine waves (in parallel), followed by low-pass filtering. This, of course, turns out to be the same as the STFT operation (windowing works as low-pass filtering). The frequency-domain interpretation of the technique seen here is, nevertheless, very important, as it has more practical implementations (because of the availability of FFT algorithms).[6]

9.2 The Instantaneous Frequency Distribution

The instantaneous frequency distribution (IFD) algorithm, proposed by Toshihiko Abe, gives an alternative method of frequency estimation.[7] It uses some of the principles already seen in the phase vocoder, but its mathematical formulation is more complex. The basic idea, also present in the PV algorithm, is that the frequency (more precisely, the instantaneous frequency detected at a certain band) is the time derivative of the phase. We saw in chapter 7 how to obtain the phase output from rectangular coordinates. Using Euler's relationship, we can also define the output of the STFT in polar form. This is shown below, using $\omega = 2\pi k/N$:

$$STFT(x(n), k, t) = R(\omega, t) \times e^{j\theta(\omega, t)}. \tag{1}$$

The phase detected by band k at time point t is $\theta(2\pi kn/N, t)$, and the magnitude is $R(2\pi kn/N, t)$. The instantaneous frequency distribution of $x(n)$ at time t is then the time derivative of the STFT phase output:

$$IFD(x(n), k, t) = \frac{\partial}{\partial t}\theta(\omega, t). \tag{2}$$

This can be intuitively understood as the measurement of the rate of rotation of the phase of a sinusoidal signal. In the phase vocoder, we estimated it by crudely taking the difference between phase values in successive frames. The IFD actually calculates the time derivative of the phase directly, from data corresponding to a single time point. The downside is that it will require the calculation of two DFTs per frame. Also, there is the need for some mathematical muscle in the outlining of the process. We will start by using the STFT, taken as a series of DFTs of a rotated and windowed input signal:

$$STFT(x(n), k, t) = e^{-j2\pi kt/N}\frac{1}{N}\sum_{m=0}^{N-1}w(m)x(m+t)e^{-j2\pi km/N}$$

$$= e^{-j2\pi kt/N}DFT(x_t(m), k). \tag{3}$$

Each *DFT* is taken from $x_t(m) = w(m)x(m+t)$, the windowed input signal at time point t. The multiplication by the complex exponential can be done in the time domain as a rotation of the input (as demonstrated in figure 9.1). Now we proceed by isolating the phase from the magnitude spectrum. This can be done by first taking the logarithm of the DFT output in polar form:

$$\ln[DFT(x_t(m), k)] = \ln[R(\omega, t) \times e^{j\theta(\omega, t)}]$$

$$= \ln[R(\omega, t)] + j\theta(\omega, t), \qquad \omega = 2\pi k/N. \tag{4}$$

It is clear from the above that the phase is the imaginary part of the natural logarithm of the DFT, $imag\{\ln(DFT)\}$. This is in fact an alternative way of obtaining the phase output of a transform, to the one seen in previous chapters. Now we can put the derivative of the phase in terms of the DFT of the signal:

$$\frac{\partial}{\partial t}\theta(\omega, t) = \frac{\partial}{\partial t}imag\{\ln[DFT(x_t(m), k)]\}$$

$$= imag\left\{\frac{\partial}{\partial t}\ln[DFT(x_t(m), k)] \times \frac{\partial}{\partial t}DFT(x_t(m), k)\right\}$$

$$= imag\left\{\frac{1}{DFT(x_t(m), k)} \times \frac{\partial}{\partial t}DFT(x_t(m), k)\right\}. \tag{5}$$

Now all we have to do is find the derivative of the DFT. This can be done by changing the summation variable of the transform using $r = m + t$, so that the only function of the time variable t left inside the summation is the window:

$$DFT(x_t(m), k) = \frac{1}{N}\sum_{m=0}^{N-1}x(m+t)w(m)e^{-j\omega m}$$

$$= \frac{1}{N}\sum_{r=0}^{N-1}x(r)w(r-t)e^{-j\omega(r-t)}$$

$$= e^{j\omega t}\frac{1}{N}\sum_{r=0}^{N-1}x(r)w(r-t)e^{-j\omega r}. \tag{6}$$

Now we are left with the simple matter of taking the derivative (with respect to time) of the above product. This is easier, because the derivative of the complex exponential is trivial and we are left only with the derivative of the window function:

$$\frac{\partial}{\partial t}DFT(x_t(m),\,k) = \frac{\partial}{\partial t}\left\{e^{j\omega t}\frac{1}{N}\sum_{r=0}^{N-1}x(r)w(r-t)e^{-j\omega r}\right\}$$

$$= \frac{\partial}{\partial t}e^{j\omega t}\times\frac{1}{N}\sum_{r=0}^{N-1}x(r)w(r-t)e^{-j\omega r} + \frac{\partial}{\partial t}\left\{\frac{1}{N}\sum_{r=0}^{N-1}x(r)w(r-t)e^{-j\omega r}\right\}\times e^{j\omega t}$$

$$= j\omega e^{j\omega t}\frac{1}{N}\sum_{r=0}^{N-1}x(r)w(r-t)e^{-j\omega r} + e^{j\omega t}\frac{1}{N}\sum_{r=0}^{N-1}x(r)\left\{\frac{\partial}{\partial t}w(r-t)\right\}e^{-j\omega r}.$$

Reverting to the previous formulation of the DFT (using the converse of equation 6, with $m = r - t$), we have

$$\frac{\partial}{\partial t}DFT(x_t(m),\,k) = \frac{j\omega}{N}\sum_{r=0}^{N-1}x(m+t)w(m)e^{-j\omega m} + \frac{1}{N}\sum_{r=0}^{N-1}x(m+t)\left\{\frac{\partial}{\partial(r-m)}w(m)\right\}e^{-j\omega m}$$

$$= j\omega DFT(x_t(m),\,k) + DFT(x'_t(m),\,k),\tag{8}$$

where

$$x'_t(m) = -\frac{\partial}{\partial m}w(m)x(m+t).$$

Substituting this expression for the derivative of the DFT in equation 5, we obtain

$$\frac{\partial}{\partial t}\theta(\omega,\,t) = imag\left\{\frac{1}{DFT(x_t(m),\,k)}\times\left[j\omega DFT(x_t(m),\,k) + DFT(x'_t(m),\,k)\right]\right\}.\tag{9}$$

Using the definition of the IFD given in equation 2, we arrive at its final formulation, as a quotient of two DFTs. The top one is taken from the signal windowed by the negative derivative of the window and the bottom one from the ordinarily windowed signal:

$$IFD(x(n),\,k,\,t) = \omega + imag\left\{\frac{DFT(x'_t(m),\,k)}{DFT(x_t(m),\,k)}\right\}.\tag{10}$$

The mathematical steps involved in the derivation of the IFD are quite involved. Since they show a newer alternative to the well-known phase vocoder algorithm, it was important to spell them out in detail. However, if we want to implement the IFD, all we need is to employ its definition in terms of DFTs, as given above. We can use the straight DFT of a windowed frame to obtain the amplitudes and use the IFD to estimate the frequencies. Because we are using the straight transform of a windowed signal, there is no need to rotate the input, as in the phase vocoder. If we look back at the DFT as defined in chapter 7, we see that it, in fact, does not include the multiplication by a complex exponential (as does the STFT). Finally, computing the differences between its consecutive samples can generate the derivative of the analysis window.

9.2.1 An IFD Analysis Application

The following steps can be used to implement IFD + magnitude (amplitude or spectrogram) analysis from overlapped time-domain signal blocks:

1. On each hop period, take N samples from a signal, multiply them by a window and its negative derivative. Generate the derivative by taking the differences between its samples.
2. Take the DFT of the two windowed signals.
3. Calculate the magnitude of the rectangular output of the DFT of the windowed signal. This, as we have seen, is the square root of the sum of the squared real and imaginary parts. This will give us the output amplitudes.
4. Calculate the frequencies by first taking the imaginary part of the quotient of the two DFTs. This gives the amount of detected frequency deviation (in *radians per sample*) from the channel center frequency. Convert this value into hertz by multiplying it by $sr/2\pi$. Now we just add it to the channel center frequency in hertz (ωsr or $2\pi ksr/N$).

Here is the code implementing the IFD in similar fashion to previous analysis algorithms, with the window, input, and output allocated and defined externally:

```
int ifd(float *input, float *window, float *output,
        int input_size, int fftsize, int hopsize, float sr){
   int posin, posout, i, k;
   float *sigframe, *specframe1, *specframe2, *diffwin;
   double a,b,c,d,powerspec;
   float fac = (float)(sr/twopi), fund = sr/fftsize;
   sigframe = new float[fftsize];
   specframe1 = new float[fftsize];
   specframe2 = new float[fftsize];
   diffwin = new float[fftsize];

   for(i=0; i < fftsize; i++){
      diffwin[i] = (i ? window[i-1] : 0.f) - window[i];
   }

   for(posin=posout=0; posin < input_size; posin+=hopsize){
   // multiply an extracted signal frame
   // by the derivative of the window
   for(i=0; i < fftsize; i++)
      if(posin+i < input_size)
         sigframe[i] = input[posin+i]*diffwin[i];
      else sigframe[i] = 0;
      // transform it
         fft(sigframe, specframe1, fftsize);
      // multiply the same signal frame
      // by the window
```

```
        for(i=0; i < fftsize; i++)
            if(posin+i < input_size)
                sigframe[i] = input[posin+i]*window[i];
            else sigframe[i] = 0;
        // transform it
        fft(sigframe, specframe2, fftsize);
        // take care of 0Hz and Nyquist freqs
        output[posout++] = specframe2[i];
        output[posout++] = specframe2[i+1];
        for(i=2, k=1; i < fftsize; i+=2, k++, ut+=2){
            a = specframe1[i];
            b = specframe1[i+1];
            c = specframe2[i];
            d = specframe2[i+1];
            powerspec = c*c+d*d;
        // compute the amplitudes
            output[posout] = (float) sqrt(powerspec);
        // compute the IFD
        if(powerspec)
            output[posout+1] =
            (float) ((b*c - a*d)/powerspec)*fac + k*fund;
        else output[posout+1] = k*fund;
        }
    }
    delete[] diffwin;
    delete[] sigframe;
    delete[] specframe2;
    delete[] specframe1;
    return posout;
}
```

The output of the IFD is very similar to the phase vocoder. However, a direct inverse transformation is not defined for the IFD. In order to resynthesize the frequency-domain data, we would ideally use some sort of additive synthesis method, with a bank of oscillators. Alternatively, an ISTFT-based algorithm can be formulated, by integrating the successive frequency values for each time point and converting them to get the current phases in radians, as outlined above for the phase vocoder.

9.2.2   Additive Resynthesis

The additive synthesis method of signal reconstruction is not always as computationally efficient as the inverse DFT-based algorithms. However, it is a little bit more flexible when it comes to certain processes, such as pitch-shifting and other frequency modifications.

Because we are using oscillators[8] to produce the sound, we can introduce any changes we like to bin frequencies before resynthesis. It is very easy to create a program that changes the pitch of a sound without changing its length. One way of making the resynthesis more efficient is to employ oscillators to resynthesize only the components that have a significant presence in the spectrum, using a thresholding method.

The following code implements a generalized additive synthesis method, which can be used with data in real-FFT-based amp-freq format (0 hertz and Nyquist followed by amplitude and frequency pairs in hertz). As with the previous examples, we will expect the spectral signal to be present in the `input` array and we will synthesize it into the `output` array, which should be allocated externally. The code will use a truncating table oscillator, reading from a 10,000-point sine-wave table.

The principle of additive synthesis is very straightforward: we will use the amplitudes and frequencies as control signals to drive a bank of oscillators. In order to provide a smooth output, we will linearly interpolate these control signals from one time point to the next. The frequencies will then be used to increment the phase of each oscillator and the amplitudes will scale their output. The signal will be accumulated in the `outsum` buffer, before it is sent to the output.

```
const int tablen = 10000;

int
addsyn(float* input, float *window, float* output, int inputsize,
      float thresh, float pitch, float scale,
      int fftsize,int hopsize, float sr) {

    int n, i, k, posin, posout, output_size, bins, s=1;
    float *amp, *freq, *tab, *outsum, ratio;
    float ampnext, freqnext, *phase,incra,incrf;

    //allocate memory
    bins = fftsize/2;
    outsum = new float[hopsize];
    amp = new float[bins];
    phase = new float[bins];
    freq = new float[bins];
    tab = new float[tablen];

    // initialize parameters
    output_size = inputsize*hopsize/fftsize;
    ratio = (float)tablen/sr;
    for(i=0; i <bins; i++){
        amp[i] = phase[i] = 0.f;
        freq[i] = i*(float)fftsize/sr
    }

    for(n=0; n<tablen; n++) tab[n] = (float)sin(n*twopi/tablen);
```

```
for(posin=0, posout=0; posout < output_size;
    posout+=hopsize, posin+=fftsize){
// zero outsum vector
for(n=0; n<hopsize; n++) outsum[n] = 0.f;
// for each bin
for(i=1,k=2; i < bins; i++, k+=2){
    // get the amps & freqs from input
    ampnext = scale*input[k+posin];
    freqnext = pitch*input[k+posin+1];
    // calculate the interpolation increment
    incra = (ampnext - amp[i])/hopsize;
    incrf = (freqnext - freq[i])/hopsize;
    // if the amplitude is above a threshold
    if(ampnext > thresh){
    // synthesize and mix in the partial
        for(n=0; n < hopsize; n++){
            phase[i] += freq[i]*ratio;
            while(phase[i] < 0) phase[i] += tablen;
            while(phase[i] >= tablen) phase[i] -= tablen;
            [n] += amp[i]*tab[(int)phase[i]];
            amp[i] += incra;
            freq[i] += incrf;
        }
    }
    // otherwise zero the amplitude
    else amp[i] = 0.f;
            }
    // send the signal to the output
    for(n=0; n<hopsize; n++) output[posout+n] = outsum[n];
}
// de-allocate memory
delete[] outsum;
delete[] tab;
[] phase;
delete[] freq;
delete[] amp;
return posout;
}
```

9.3   Conclusion

As we have seen, there are many applications for spectral processing of audio signals. The use of the PV techniques for frequency analysis is quite widespread in audio programming. The availability of fast computation algorithms makes these techniques a very practical proposition for the development of sound processing and synthesis software. In fact, most of the modern music processing languages, including Csound and Pure Data, provide facilities for PV-based frequency analysis and resynthesis.

9.4   Exercises

Exercise 9.4.1

Design a "spectral freeze' function" that holds on to fixed amplitude and/or frequency bin values for a certain amount of time. Write a program (or modify one of the examples) that uses the function, creating a freeze-frame application.

Exercise 9.4.2

In two straight analysis-synthesis programs (i.e. no processing of spectral data), one using PV resynthesis and another using Additive synthesis, implement a way of checking the processing time (using system time functions) and check the difference in efficiency of each method.

Exercise 9.4.3

Modify the additive synthesis function to allow for pitch-shifting. Implement a program that shifts the pitch of a sound without changing its length.

Notes

1. The original phase vocoder was introduced in J. Flanagan and R. Golden, "Phase Vocoder," *Bell System Technical Journal* 45 (1966): 1493–1509.

2. There are two equally valid ways of interpreting the PV operation. One is to think of it as several filters working in parallel (i.e. the same input is sent to all filters), each covering a fixed band and all of them with the same bandwidth. These filters cover the entire spectrum, from 0 Hz to the Nyquist frequency, and because they are all of the same bandwidth they will be spaced equally. Each filter outputs a pair of time-varying signals, one containing the detected amplitude and the other the detected frequency. The other way of seeing PV analysis is to think of it as a series of spectral analysis frames out of a STFT operation, containing frequency bins with amplitude and frequency pairs of values. The second interpretation is more closely related to the way we are implementing it here.

3. The STFT was defined in chapter 8 as

$$\text{STFT}(x(n), k, t) = \frac{1}{N} \sum_{n=-\infty}^{\infty} w(n - t)x(n)e^{-j2\pi kn/N}, \qquad k = 0, 1, 2, \ldots, N - 1.$$

Since the windowed signal is non-zero in the range from 0 to $N - 1$, we can rewrite the STFT expression as

$$\text{STFT}(x(n), k, t) = \frac{1}{N} \sum_{n=t}^{t+N-1} w(n-t)x(n)e^{-j2\pi kn/N}.$$

Now we will change the summation index n, using $n = m + t$, so that we can bring the formula into the 0 to $N - 1$ range in the right format for DFT evaluation:

$$\text{STFT}(x(n), k, t) = \frac{1}{N} \sum_{m=0}^{N-1} w(m)x(m+t)e^{-j2\pi k(m+t)/N}$$

$$= e^{-j2\pi kt/N} \frac{1}{N} \sum_{m=0}^{N-1} w(m)x(m+t)e^{-j2\pi km/N}.$$

Multiplying by a complex exponential is the same as shifting the input samples circularly according to the input time $t \bmod N$. This is due to the so-called shift theorem of the DFT. Thus, by rotating the input signal we avoid the complex multiplication in the spectral domain.

4. Interpolation is a way of generating intermediary values between two points. The simplest type, and generally the one that is more often used, is called linear interpolation. It is possible to see it as making a straight line between the points and reading the interpolated values off this line. This implies that you are taking the *difference* between the values and then scaling it to cover smaller intervals. Say the difference between the first and second points is 2 and the interval between these points is 1. Then if we want to find the interpolated values in between, say at 0.1 intervals, we multiply the difference by the ratio of the target interpolation interval (0.1) and the interval (1), $2*0.1 = 0.2$. That will give us the differences at the interpolation intervals, which we just cumulatively add to our initial value to create to interpolate $(x, x + 0.2, x + 0.2 + 0.2, \ldots, x + 2)$. To find a specific value between the two points, multiply the difference by the interpolated position (between 0 and 1) we want to find and add to the value of position 1: $y = x_1 + (x_2 - x_1) \times pos$. If, on the other hand, we would like to interpolate based on *ratios* of values instead of differences, we use exponential interpolation. In this case, all we need do is to exchange the sums for multiplications, differences for divisions and multiplication for exponentiation: $y = x^1 \times (x^2/x^1)^{pos}$.

Exponential interpolation is useful in music because of the way we perceive frequency, pitches, and musical intervals, which is based on ratios rather than differences. For instance, we perceive the change from 1,10 Hz to 2,20 Hz (an octave) as being the same as the change from 220 Hz to 440 Hz. These changes (of octave) are in the ratio 2:1.

5. The secret of general-purpose frequency scaling of PV data (for pitch-shifting applications, for instance) is not only to scale the frequencies, but also to scale the bins. So when we want to pitch shift a sound an octave higher (frequency scaling by 2), we need to scale the bin frequency by 2 and move the bin frequency and amplitude data to a bin 2 times this bin's number. Example: say that in bin 3 we have freq $= 110$ and amp $= 1000$. Then we multiply the frequency by 2, and move the data to bin $2*3$. Bin 6 will then contain freq $= 220$ and amp $= 1,000$. This operation has to be performed on all bins for pitch shifting to occur. Scaling by other factors or other intervals works on the same basis. Note that these frequency modifications are not artifact-free and can be problematic with certain input sounds and large amounts of scaling.

6. For a more detailed look at this alternative view of the phase vocoder, see James Flanagan's original article on the technique. For other descriptions of the technique, both in terms of its time-domain and

spectral perspectives, see M. Dolson, "The Phase Vocoder Tutorial," *Computer Music Journal* 10(1986), no. 4): 14–27; F. Moore, *Elements of Computer Music* (Prentice-Hall, 1990).

7. T. Abe, "The IF spectrogram: a new spectral representation," in *Proceedings of ASVA 97*: 423–430. The technique had also been proposed independently by D. Friedman ("Instantaneous-frequency distribution vs. time: An interpretation of the phase structure of speech," in *Proceedings of the ICASSP*, 1985). The IFD is related to what elsewhere is called *frequency reassignment* (because the bin frequencies get "reassigned" other values that might be different from the original bin center frequencies).

8. Oscillators are usually implemented as wrap-around table readers. They have three basic elements: phase (or index) increment, table lookup, and amplitude scaling. The phase increment makes sure we read the right table location each time we need to produce a sample of audio. This is based on the fundamental frequency we want to generate, the sampling rate and the size of the table. The amount of increment we need each time is

$$incr = freq \times \frac{table\_size}{sr}.$$

We will also have to make sure we wrap around at the ends of the table, so a generalized modulus is applied there too. Table lookup is just a matter of looking up values in an array and scaling is multiplying those values, which are generally normalized by the correct amplitude. The additive synthesis code has also an extra bit of code to interpolate between amplitude and frequency values at adjacent frames, so that the synthesized signal is generated smoothly.

Programming Csound Opcodes

10 Understanding an Opcode in Csound

John ffitch

A computing skill which is often mentioned but rarely taught is the ability to read a program and understand what it does, and how. In cases where there is a design document this can be a little easier, but in the real world of fifty years of software evolution in many cases such documentation does not exist, and you must develop reading skills.

It has been said that the teaching of computing concentrates too much on writing programs and too little on reading, unlike the learning of literacy, where reading is usually afforded the higher place.[1] To better understand what we are reading, we begin with a glossary of some Csound terms (table 10.1).

In the spirit of program reading, we are going to consider a few opcode implementations in Csound, with the intention of understanding how they work, and how they relate to the main Csound engine. We will take first a very simple filter, where the body of code to be understood is small, and then a number of increasingly complex opcodes, each of which introduces new mechanisms.

10.1 The tone Opcode

The filter opcode we will consider is the **tone** opcode, an implementation of a first-order recursive low-pass filter. There are three places where there is code related to this opcode, in the entry table (`Engine/entry1.c`), and a header in `H/ugens5.h` for the type RESON, and the source code in `OOps/ugens5.c`.

In `entry1.c` there is the line

```
{ "tone", S(TONE), 5, "a", "ako", tonset, NULL, tone },
```

The header type declaration in `H/ugens5.h` is

```
typedef struct {
    OPDS h;
    MYFLT *ar, *asig, *khp, *istor;
    double c1, c2, yt1, prvhp;
} TONE;
```

Table 10.1

A glossary of some Csound terms.

FL	a C macro to deal with single and double precision floating-point numbers
MYFLT	a C type that is either float or double
OENTRY	a *structure* maintained as an *array*, where each entry defines an *opcode*
a rate	audio rate, referring to operations that generate output at the sample-rate
engine	the fundamental Csound control system that starts, maintains, and stops *instruments* playing
instrument	a collection (network) of *opcodes* that together defines a particular sound or operation; a "patch," a "preset," a "voice," an effect, or a combination of a voice(s) with effect(s); a sound generating or processing algorithm
k rate	the control rate, a rate slower that the sample rate at which changes occur
ksmps	the number of samples generated on each control cycle; the sample rate divided by the control rate
opcodes	the atomic operation from which instruments are built

and the base code in OOps/ugens5.c is

```c
int tonset(CSOUND *csound, TONE *p)
{
    double b;
    p->prvhp = (double)*p->khp;
    b = 2.0 - cos((double)(p->prvhp * csound->tpidsr));
    p->c2 = b - sqrt(b * b - 1.0);
    p->c1 = 1.0 - p->c2;

    if (!(*p->istor))
        p->yt1 = 0.0;
    return OK;
}

int tone(CSOUND *csound, TONE *p)
{
    MYFLT *ar, *asig;
    int n, nsmps = csound->ksmps;
    double c1 = p->c1, c2 = p->c2;
    double yt1 = p->yt1;

    if (*p->khp != (MYFLT)p->prvhp) {
        double b;
        p->prvhp = (double)*p->khp;
        b = 2.0 - cos((double)(p->prvhp * csound->tpidsr));
        p->c2 = c2 = b - sqrt(b * b - 1.0);
        p->c1 = c1 = 1.0 - c2;
    }
```

```
    ar = p->ar;
    asig = p->asig;
    for (n=0; n<nsmps; n++) {
        yt1 = c1 * (double)(asig[n]) + c2 * yt1;
        ar[n] = (MYFLT)yt1;
    }
    p->yt1 = yt1;
    return OK;
}
```

At first sight this may appear frightening, but with basic knowledge of C syntax it ought to be possible to understand the main local structure. In order to get further in understanding will require some information on the overall structure on Csound, which in not a small topic.

10.1.1   A Quick Guide to Csound as a Program

At the most basic level, Csound[2] is a specialized object-oriented system that arranges to initiate instruments at the time requested by the score, and to continue to play them until the end of the note. Each instrument consists of a number of opcodes generally obeyed in sequence, and there is a fairly complex system to pass the arguments to the opcodes (figure 10.1). Technically the arguments are passed *by reference* and so each opcode gets the arguments as pointers. This does have some implication for the programming of opcodes, especially if the answer is the same variable as one of the inputs.[3]

The main purpose of the Csound engine, as the major control system is often called, is to perform the initiation of the new notes (using a function called `insert` to be found in the file `Engine/insert.c`), and remove them when their duration has expired. Between these events each active instrument is called, that is the sequence of opcodes are obeyed and are expected to generate `ksmps` of audio results for a-rate opcodes or one k-rate answer for k rate. In effect for speed Csound generates short vectors of audio before changing any parameters. The **out** family of opcodes mix these short vectors into the output, whether to file or directly to the audio output. The implication of this is that for each k-rate cycle a function is

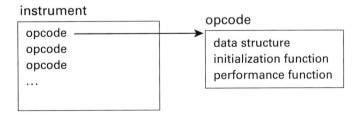

Figure 10.1
Instruments and opcodes in Csound.

called for each opcode. There is another function associated with the opcode that is called once to initialize the operation (figure 10.1). In fact there is provision for a third function to be called at termination time, but this is not widely used. Above is a very simple sketch of the Csound engine, and as one gets more expert one discovers many other details, but this description is sufficient to understand the **tone** opcode that is our initial task.

In summary, each opcode has two functions, one to initialize the operation and one to generate a small `ksmps` vector of audio. Both functions are provided with a pointer to a structure that holds the pointers to the arguments and to any local state that the opcode may require.

The association of the opcode name with the structures and functions is done in an `entry`, that is, a line in an `OENTRY` array. Each line has nine fields: name, size of `struct`, a bit pattern to say which combination of init-time, k-rate and a-rate occasions the opcode needs attention, a string specifying the answer(s) type(s), a string specifying the arguments, and the possible four functions: one for init-time, one for k-rate, one for a-rate, and one for deactivation time. For the **tone** opcode we will see the following line:

```
{ "tone", S(TONE), 5, "a", "ako", tonset, NULL, tone },
```

The macro `S` is just shorthand for `sizeof`. The third component, 5, should be read as $1 + 4$, or in binary 101. The 001 indicates a function to be called at init time, and the 100 indicates a function at a rate. If this had been a k-rate function then there would have been a 010 bit. The answer is specified by "a" which indicates a single a-rate answer. The engine has to arrange space for the necessary short vector. The arguments of "ako" indicate an a-rate argument, a k-rate argument, and an optional i-rate argument that defaults to 0 if not specified. The coding here is rather arcane, and is extended from time to time, but currently the possibilities are those listed in table 10.2. The parser and orchestra translation and loading components of Csound read these `OENTRY` tables to determine the syntax of each opcode, as well as adding the optional arguments and checking types. The rest of the entry gives the names of the functions that need to be called. Advocates of object-oriented programming may notice that in effect what we have is an object with up to four methods and a set of private variables. There are also some inherited members.

10.1.2 The TONE Structure

The `TONE` structure, which is the representation of the state of the opcode, is declared in the file `ugens5.h`, where

```
typedef struct {
    OPDS h;
    MYFLT *ar, *asig, *khp, *istor;
    MYFLT c1, c2, yt1, prvhp;
} TONE;
```

Table 10.2
Entry codes for opcode specification in OENTRY.

i	initialization
k	k rate
a	a rate
f	frequency variable
w	spectral variable
x	k-rate scalar or a-rate vector
S	string
T	string or i rate
U	string or i/k rate
B	Boolean
l	label
m	begins an indefinite list of iargs (any count)
M	begins an indefinite list of args (any count or rate)
n	begins an indefinite list of iargs (nargs odd)
N	begins an indefinite list of args (any count/rate i, k, a, S)
y	begins an indefinite list of aargs (any count)
z	begins an indefinite list of kargs (any count)
Z	begins an alternating kakaka ... list (any count)
h	optional, defaulting to 127
j	optional, defaulting to −1
o	optional, defaulting to 0
p	optional, defaulting to 1
q	optional, defaulting to 10
v	optional, defaulting to 0.5
O	optional k rate, defaulting to 0
P	optional k rate, defaulting to 1
V	optional k rate, defaulting to 0.5

This defines a structure and also makes it into a type for C.[4] The first member of the structure is a variable of type OPDS. This is the inherited component; all opcode structures must begin with this. It is used by the engine to maintain information about progress; to decide on what to do after; and other housekeeping information. It is not necessary to understand this part of Csound to understand the opcodes, or to understand how to read them and eventually how to write them. Just remember that it must be present.

The second line of the struct declares four members, all of type MYFLT: *ar, asig, khp, and istor. This type is a pointer to a floating-point number. Because Csound exists in both single and double precision forms, we use this type, which is actually float or double, but we do not need to know or care which it is in any compilation. The only time we need to be careful about this is when printing, which is a minor problem. Examples of this problem can be found in Engine/rdscor.c, where the code reads

```
if (sizeof(MYFLT)==4)
    fscanf(scfp, "%f", pfld);
else
    fscanf(scfp, "%lf", pfld);
```

These four variables are the answer and three arguments to the opcode. If you check the Csound manual, you will see that the opcode is defined as

ar **tone** asig, khp [, iskip]

so the structure members `ar`, `asig`, `khp`, and `istor` correspond directly to the user's parameter. The two a-rate entities will be pointers to a `ksmps` vector; the others will be pointers to single floating-point[5] values. The rest of the structure is entirely decided by the programmer, and is used for values that we wish to be preserved between the initialization and the execution, or from one execution cycle to another. This will become clearer as we read the code.

Now we can read the implementation of this filter opcode with a good chance of understanding what it is doing.

10.1.3 Initialization of tone

The initialization function, as most functions in Csound, takes as its first argument a pointer to an instance of the CSOUND structure. This structure carries all the constants for the particular run of Csound, as well as pointers to useful functions generally used. The use in the tone opcode is very slight, but it is always needed.

The initialization function for this particular opcode is quite short. It has three distinct parts.

The first part reads

```
p->prvhp = (double)*p->khp;
```

This simply copies the input k-rate value to a variable, ensuring that it is double precision, which is preserved between execution cycles. This could be seen as a minor speed optimization, saving one indirection, but in fact it is more that that as we will see when we consider the execution cycle.

The second part reads

```
b = 2.0 - cos((double)(p->prvhp * csound->tpidsr));
p->c2 = b - sqrt(b * b - 1.0);
p->c1 = 1.0 - p->c2;
```

It is important to know that `csound->tpidsr` is a global value in Csound, calculated when the system starts, and denoting "two π divided by sample rate" (`tpidsr`), a simple example of the kinds of values stored in this structure. The code here calculates two "constants" for the filter: `c1` and `c2`. They are defined by

$$b = 2 - \cos(2\pi \, hp/sr), \tag{1}$$

$$c_2 = b - \sqrt{b^2 - 1}. \tag{2}$$

and

$$c_1 = 1 - c_2. \tag{3}$$

If you are an expert in digital signal processing, you may recognize these equations as the coefficients for a simple infinite impulse response (IIR) low-pass filter, where hp is the response amplitude's half-power point (that is, the frequency displacement in hertz at which the output falls to half the peak).[6] The values of the computed constants are stored in the TONE structure so they can be used by the execution cycles. This explains the structure members—c1, c2, and prvhp. They are declared as double to improve the accuracy of the filter.

The last part of the initialization reads

```
if (!(*p->istor))
    p->yt1 = 0.0;
```

Here we are setting another state variable to zero, but only if the last argument to the opcode, that is the optional one, is zero. Reading the manual for this opcode you will see that the optional argument, called *iskip* in the text, is used to control the use of the filter in legato cases, when we wish to skip the initialization. The default usage leads to the member yt1 being initialized to zero. Again with any knowledge of digital filters the name of the variable should be suggestive, as the value of the last output, which will be needed in a recursive filter. If you do not have such detailed knowledge of digital filters, just wait a short while until we consider the execution cycle.

In summary, we can see that the initialization is mainly concerned with initializing the structure state variables. Other more complex initializations may do some checking of argument ranges, or perform some quite complex calculations; commonly they arrange local vectors for the opcode. We will consider that later, as it is another level of complication, unnecessary until we have understood the simplest opcode, in order to see the structure.

10.1.4 Execution of tone

The a-rate execution function also has four components. They are to some extent interleaved, so the code is given here with the four parts identified:

```
int tone(CSOUND *csound, TONE *p)
{
    MYFLT       *ar, *asig;           /***organize */
    int n, nsmps = csound->ksmps; /***organize*/
    double c1 = p->c1, c2 = p->c2;/***organize*/
    double yt1 = p->yt1;           /***organize*/
```

```
    if (*p->khp != (MYFLT)p->prvhp){        /***control*/
        double b;                            /***control*/
        p->prvhp = (double)*p->khp;          /***control*/
        b = 2.0 - cos((double)(p->prvhp *
            csound->tpidsr));                /***control*/
        p->c2 = c2 = b - sqrt(b * b - 1.0);/***control*/
        p->c1 = c1 = 1.0 - c2;               /***control*/
    }                                        /***control*/
    ar = p->ar;/***organize*/
    asig = p->asig;/***organize*/
    for (n=0; n<nsmps; n++){/***generate*/
        yt1 = c1 * (double)(asig[n]) + c2 * yt1;/***generate*/
        ar[n] = (MYFLT)yt1;/***generate*/
    }/***generate*/
    p->yt1 = yt1; /***tidyup*/
    return OK; /***result*/
}
```

I have labeled a number of lines as `organize`; these include variable declarations, but one of the main components is to create local variables copied from the argument structure. This is largely for performance rather than necessary. If we look at the parts labeled `generate` this will become clearer.

When we remember that the value `p->asig` is a pointer to the input signal, usually denoted by x_t in filter descriptions, and `p->ar` is a pointer to the output, the generation code is just a loop which is repeated `ksmps` times, that is the length of the audio vector, which calculates $y_t = c_1 x_t + c_2 y_{t-1}$ and then remembers y_t as the variable `yt1` for the next cycle. This is a classic recursive filter loop. The k rate is stored in `csound->ksmps`, but this is read into a local variable `nsmps` for efficiency. The only additional features are the type coercions from `MYFLT` to `double` and back.

The component labeled `control` may be seen to be substantially the same as the calculations of `p->c1` and `p->c2` in the initialization. Indeed this is what it is doing; if the value of *khp* changes, which it can only do at the k rate, then the constants are recalculated, and in addition to being used in local variables, they are written to the structure state. Again this is part of an optimization. We could just calculate the constants on every execution cycle, but as these tend not to change very often, it would take significant additional time.

If we expected the half-power point to change on every cycle, we could instead have a conceptually simpler implementation:

```
int slowtonset(CSOUND *csound, SLOWTONE *p)
{
    if (!(*p->istor))
        p->yt1 = FL(0.0);
    return OK;
}
```

```
int slowtone(CSOUND *csound, SLOWTONE *p)
{
    MYFLT *ar, *asig;
    int n, nsmps = csound->ksmps;
    double c1, c2;
    double yt1 = p->yt1;
    double b;

    b = 2.0 - cos((double)(*p->khp * tpidsr));
    c2 = b - sqrt(b * b - 1.0);
    c1 = 1.0 - c2;
    for (n=0; n<nsmps; n++) {
        p->yt1 = c1 * (double)p->asig[n] + c2 * p->yt1;
        p->ar[n] = (MYFLT)p->yt1;
    };
    return OK;
}
```

We still need to remember the previous output, and to remember that between execution cycles it must be stored in the structure, but this version obviates the need to the other variables. The structure would be simplified to

```
typedef struct {
    OPDS h;
    MYFLT *ar, *asig, *khp, *istor;
    MYFLT yt1;
} SLOWTONE;
```

10.1.5 Conclusions from tone

We have read through the sources that define the actions of the **tone** filter, and used it to get a first understanding of the execution structure of Csound, and hence how the code must be structured to use this system. This opcode is fairly simple, but it does show the way in which an opcode is initialized and can pre-calculate values which are saved in a structure for the execution time. This opcode also has the possibility of varying one parameter between successive cycles.

But the one part of this opcode that can be found in nearly all a-rate opcodes is a loop structure of the general form

```
MYFLT      *ar = p->ar;
int    n, nsmps = csound->ksmps;
. . . .
for (n=0; n<nsmps; n++) {
    . . . . . .
```

```
    ar[n] = . . . .
  }
```

that writes `ksmps` to the output variable-vector. A read through almost any file of opcode implementations will find this. Some opcodes use a `do. . .while` loop and pointer arithmetic, but the purpose is the same.[7] We have also seen how the line in one of the entry tables controls the opcode, both for parsing and for execution.

10.2   A k-rate Opcode: rms

In order to understand the way in which a k-rate opcode works let us read the implementation of the **rms** opcode. I have chosen to look at this opcode as this opcode as it is fairly simple, but does show how to return a k-rate value.

The algorithm for the **rms** operation is to use an IIR low-pass filter on the square of the signal. One might expect a root-mean-square to average over a short time window, but the filtering method gives a more useful answer and is incremental.

The specification of the opcode (in `Engine/entry1.c`) is

```
{ "rms", S(RMS), 3, "k", "aqo", rmsset, rms }
```

Notice that the third field is 3, which in binary is $1 + 2$ and so indicates that there is an initialization function and a k-rate function. Specified later in the line there is one result, of type control, and the input arguments are an audio signal and two optional arguments. The engine handles optional arguments. From the point of view of the implementation there is no difference between optional and required arguments; they are all present at run time.

Looking at the manual, we can see that the last two arguments are the half-power point (in hertz) of the internal low-pass filter, and the initial disposition of internal data space:

```
typedef struct {
    OPDS h;
    MYFLT *kr, *asig, *ihp, *istor;
    double c1, c2, prvq;
} RMS;
```

Like the tone example above, this structure, from `H/ugens5.h,` has local fields for the filter coefficients and the previous output.

The initialization code (from `OOps/ugens5.c`)

```
int rmsset(CSOUND *csound, RMS *p)
{
    double b;

    b = 2.0 - cos((double)(*p->ihp * csound->tpidsr));
    p->c2 = b - sqrt(b*b - 1.0);
    p->c1 = 1.0 - p->c2;
```

```
    if (!*p->istor)
        p->prvq = 0.0;
    return OK;
}
```

is very similar to the initialization of tone and should not cause any further problems in understanding.

The performance function is

```
int rms(CSOUND *csound, RMS *p)
{
    int n, nsmps = csound->ksmps;
    MYFLT *asig;
    double q;
    double c1 = p->c1, c2 = p->c2;

    q = p->prvq;
    asig = p->asig;
    for (n=0; n<nsmps; n++) {
        double as = (double)asig[n];
        q = c1 * as * as + c2 * q;
    }
    p->prvq = q;
    *p->kr = (MYFLT) sqrt(q); /***result*/
    return OK;
}
```

The structure of rms is very similar to that of the previous opcode, using local variables as copies of the structure values for speed given that the bandwidth of this filter is fixed at initialization time, and so the filter coefficients cannot change. In effect, the only change is the line marked result, as this is where it updates the k-rate answer, which is naturally a single value.

One can also have initialization-time only opcodes, for example **seed**, which initializes the pseudo random number generator, or the **filelen** opcode, which returns the length of a soundfile.

10.3   Memory Allocation in Opcodes: vdelay

The two opcodes considered above require a small amount of data, but a definite quantity only, and these can easily be accommodated within a structure that maintains the state of each instance. But some opcodes need a variable amount of data, and this needs an additional mechanism. Naturally such an opcode will be more complex that the previous opcodes we have seen. Memory may be needed in either k-rate or a-rate opcodes. The opcode we will consider is **vdelay**, which provides a variable length delay line. Naturally such an opcode needs space to hold the values in the delay. The **vdelay** opcode also introduces another variant; it can be used in either a rate or k rate. The definition is `entry` is

```
{ "vdelay", S(VDEL), 5, "a", "axio", vdelset, NULL, vdelay },
```

so we can tell immediately the name used in the syntax, and that it returns an a-rate (audio vector) answer. There are initialization (`vdelset`) and a-rate performance (`vdelay`) functions. What is different is the specification of the arguments, which includes an `x` (which can be either an a-rate or a k-rate argument). In some ways there is not much difference, as all arguments are passed by reference, which is passed as a pointer to them, but the code needs to be written differently for the cases of the argument is a single value or a vector.

The Csound manual states

ar **vdelay** asig, xdel, imaxdel [, iskip]

This is an interpolating variable time delay. It is not very different from the alternative implementation (**deltapi**), but it is easier to use. See also the precision versions of these opcodes. This opcode's Csound manual page continues as follows:

INITIALIZATION

imaxdel Maximum value of delay in milliseconds. If *xdel* gains a value greater than *imaxdel* it is folded around *imaxdel*. This should not happen.

iskip Skip initialization if present and non zero (compare *iskip* argument of other filter opcodes).

PERFORMANCE

With this unit generator it is possible to do Doppler effects or chorusing and flanging.

asig Input signal.

xdel Current value of delay in milliseconds. Note that linear functions have no pitch change effects and that fast changing values of *xdel* will cause discontinuities in the waveform resulting in noise.

Reading this, one might begin to think about what one expects to find in the structure. The answer and arguments are clear, and of course there will be the standard header. The code is in `H/vdelay.h`:

```
typedef struct {
    OPDS    h;
    MYFLT   *sr, *ain, *adel, *imaxd, *istod;
    AUXCH   aux;
    long    left;
} VDEL;
```

The new material here is the type `AUXCH`, and one other member field related to the implementation, `left`. This is used between performance runs to remember where the start point is in the circular buffer. This will become clearer when we consider the performance implementation. But first let us look at the initialization function:

```
#define ESR (esr/FL(1000.0))

int vdelset(CSOUND *csound, VDEL *p) /* vdelay set-up */
{
    unsigned long n = (long)(*p->imaxd * ESR)+1;

    if (!*p->istod){ /* allocate space for delay buffer */
        if (p->aux.auxp == NULL ||
            (int)(n*sizeof(MYFLT))>p->aux.size)
                csound->AuxAlloc(csound,
                        n * sizeof(MYFLT), &p->aux);
        else{ /* make sure buffer is empty */
            memset(p->aux.auxp, 0, n*sizeof(MYFLT));
        }
        p->left = 0;
    }
    return OK;
}
```

Notice that the majority of the code is conditional on `*p->istod` being zero. This corresponds to the skipping of initialization described in the manual above, so that should not be a surprise. If there is to be initialization, then the main decision is based on whether `p->aux.auxp` is NULL or is already a pointer. The type `AUXCH` is defined in `H/csoundCore.h` as

```
typedef struct auxch {
    struct auxch *nxtchp;
    long size;
    void *auxp, *endp;
} AUXCH;
```

This is used to maintain a chain of allocated memory, chained through the first field. Each chunk of memory has a length (in bytes) recorded in `size` and starts at `auxp` and ends at `endp`. The allocation is done by the function `csound->AuxAlloc` which takes the ubiquitous `CSOUND` pointer, a size and a pointer to an `AUXCH` structure. This code, which you can find in the file `Engine/auxfd.c`, deals with returning previous space, and maintaining the necessary housekeeping to control the space. Read the code if you wish, or just accept the definition.

The maximum size of the delay line we need is in the variable `*p->imaxd`, but this is measured in milliseconds. The delay line length has to be in samples, so we need to convert to seconds and multiply by the sampling rate that is in samples per second. There is a rather pathological case if the requested maximum delay line is under 1 sample long, and to avoid the problems this causes the length has 1 added, which deals with the rounding as well. The length, calculated in the variable n, and then we can check if there already is a buffer, and it is sufficiently large, when we can just reuse it, taking care to zero it. If either of these are not the case we allocate a new buffer (which would return any old small one to the system). This is an optimization, and the code would do the same, but at the cost of always reallocating a buffer which would be slower than the additional tests.

```
if (!*p->istod) { /* allocate space for delay buffer */
    csound->AuxAlloc(csound, n * sizeof(MYFLT), &p->aux);
    p->left = 0;
}
```

Let us now turn to the main performance function, vdelay. The first noticeable feature is that there are two variants based on the value of XINARG2, which is actually a complex macro. The value is a Boolean taken from a bit-pattern stored in the OPDS structure of each opcode instance that indicates which arguments are k-rate and which are a-rate. The bit used is the nth bit being 1 if the nth argument is a-rate. To help with this Csound has introduced macros XINARG1, XINARG2, XINARG3, XINARG4, and XINARG5 to hide the exact coding.

```
int vdelay(CSOUND *csound, VDEL *p) /* vdelay routine */
{
    long nn, nsmps = csound->ksmps, maxd, indx;
    MYFLT *out = p->sr;       /* assign object data to */
    MYFLT *in = p->ain;       /* local variables */
    MYFLT *del = p->adel;
    MYFLT *buf = (MYFLT *)p->aux.auxp;

    if (buf==NULL) {                /* RWD fix */
        return
            csound->PerfError(csound,Str("vdelay: not initialized"));
    }
    maxd = (unsigned long) (1+*p->imaxd * ESR);
    indx = p->left;

    if (XINARG2) { /* if delay is a-rate */
        for (nn=0; nn<nsmps; nn++) {
            MYFLT fv1, fv2;
            long v1, v2;

            buf[indx] = *in[nn;
            fv1 = indx - (del[nn]) * ESR;
            /* Make sure Inside the buffer */
            /*
             * The following has been fixed by adding a cast
             * and making a ">=" instead of a ">" comparison.
             * The order of the comparisons has been swapped
             * as well (a bit of a nit, but comparing a possibly
             * negative number to an unsigned isn't a good
```

```
            * idea--and broke on Alpha).
            * heh 981101
            */
           while (fv1 < FL(0.0))
               fv1 += (MYFLT)maxd;
           while (fv1 >= (MYFLT)maxd)
               fv1 -= (MYFLT)maxd;
               /* Find next sample for interpolation */
           if (fv1 < maxd - 1)
               fv2 = fv1 + FL(1.0);
           else
               fv2 = FL(0.0);

           v1 = (long)fv1;
           v2 = (long)fv2;
           *out++ = buf[v1] + (fv1 - v1)*(buf[v2] - buf[v1]);
           /* Advance current pointer */
           if (++indx == maxd) indx = 0;
       }
   }
   else {                          /* and, if delay is k-rate */
       MYFLT fdel=*del;
       for (nn=0; nn<nsmps; nn++) {
           MYFLT fv1, fv2;
           long v1, v2;

           buf[indx] = in[nn];
           fv1 = indx - fdel * ESR;
           /* Make sure inside the buffer */
           /*
            * See comment above--same fix applied here.
            */
           while (fv1 < FL(0.0))
               fv1 += (MYFLT)maxd;
           while (fv1 >= (MYFLT)maxd)
               fv1 -= (MYFLT)maxd;
           /* Find next sample for interpolation */
           if (fv1 < maxd - 1)
               fv2 = fv1 + FL(1.0);
           else
               fv2 = FL(0.0);

           v1 = (long)fv1;
           v2 = (long)fv2;
```

```
                *out++ = buf[v1] + (fv1 - fv1)*( buf[v2] - buf[v1]);
                /* Advance current pointer */
                if (++indx == maxd) indx = 0;
            }
        }
        p->left = indx; /* and keep track of where you are */
        return OK;
    }
```

The code is fairly straightforward. The output is subjected to linear interpolation.[8] The new incoming audio is placed in the delay line and the output value retrieved, with care being taken to remain inside the buffer. By now the code should be taking on a familiar style.

A few cautionary words should be said about the AUXCH system. In some opcodes there is a need for more than one flexible buffer. This can be achieved with two or more fields of type AUXCH in the structure, or by using one of these and considering it as a collection for the operation. What you must not do is have an AUXCH object pointed at by a word in another one. This may seem tempting, and indeed some would-be Csound programmers have done this, but the effect is to confuse the automatic return mechanism for these flexible arrays, and usually Csound crashes when this is attempted.

10.4   Polymorphic Opcodes: taninv2 and divz

A particular case of opcodes that is moderately common in Csound is the case where the same opcode is used in different contexts. We will consider a couple of examples of this, the **taninv2** opcode and the **divz** opcode.

The **taninv2** opcode calculates the inverse tangent (arctangent or $\tan^{-1}$), and has two arguments. The problem is that there really are three different but closely related operations: the inverse tangent of initialization values, k-rate values, and a-rate values. The OENTRY lines for these operations are as follows:

```
{ "taninv2", 0xffff },
{ "taninv2.i",S(AOP), 1, "i", "ii", atan2i },
{ "taninv2.k",S(AOP), 2, "k", "kk", NULL, atan2i },
{ "taninv2.a",S(AOP), 4, "a", "aa", NULL, NULL, atan2aa },
```

The tags .i, .k, and .a refer to the three rates. If for a moment we ignore the tags, it is clear that the lines correspond to the earlier examples in this chapter. We have an answer type, argument types, and functions run at initialization time, k-rate or a-rate. The first line is the oddity. What this is doing is declaring that the user can use the opcode **taninv2** and the parser will decide from the type of the answer provided which case is needed, and add the tag internally. This is a class of polymorphism in which **taninv2** has three forms. If you look at the various OENTRY lines, you will see a number of similar opcodes with this declaration, each with a structure size of 65535 (0xFFFF).[9] This does place an extremely minor restriction on what structures can be used, but in reality this is no problem. The code for adding the tags can be found in the files `Engine/csound_orc_semantics.c` in the function `handle_polymorphic_opcode` for the new parser, and in `Engine/rdorch.c` in the function `getoptxt` for the older parser.

There are in fact four different cases of polymorphism provided in Csound. The others provide different forms depending on different criteria. The flag `0xFFFE` is used for opcodes like `oscil` that have multiple forms depending on the types of the first two arguments, which `0xFFFD` is used for opcodes whose form depends on the first argument type.

The last case is exemplified by the opcode `divz`. It uses the flag `0xFFFC`, which is a division operation with a specified value used when the division is by zero, rather than giving a numerical error at run time.

```
{ "divz", 0xfffc },
{ "divz_ii", S(DIVZ), 1, "i", "iii", divzkk, NULL, NULL },
{ "divz_kk", S(DIVZ), 2, "k", "kkk", NULL, divzkk, NULL },
{ "divz_ak", S(DIVZ), 4, "a", "akk", NULL, NULL, divzak },
{ "divz_ka", S(DIVZ), 4, "a", "kak", NULL, NULL, divzka },
{ "divz_aa", S(DIVZ), 4, "a", "aak", NULL, NULL, divzaa },
```

The type depends on the first two arguments.

10.5   Opcodes That Use f-tables: dconv

A common desire in Csound opcodes is to use an f-table declared in the score and passed to the opcode by a parameter, and so there is a common code section to access a table. As an example we will consider the **dconv** opcode, in the plug-in file `Opcodes/ugmoss.c`. The manual describes the actions as

ar   **dconv**   asig, isize, irfn.

The output is the result of two signals directly convolved together, rather than the spectral based method of the convolve opcode. Let us look at the Csound manual to see how it works:

INITIALIZATION

isize   the size of the convolution buffer to use. If the buffer size is smaller than the size of *irfn*, then only the first *isize* values will be used from the table.
irfn   table number of a stored function containing the *Impulse Response* for convolution.

PERFORMANCE

Rather than the analysis/resynthesis method of the **convolve** opcode, **dconv** uses direct convolution to create the result. For small tables it can do this quite efficiently, however larger table require much longer time to run. The **dconv** opcode does (`isize`, `ksmps`) multiplies on every k-cycle. Therefore, reverb and delay effects are best done with other opcodes (unless the times are short).

The **dconv** opcode was designed to be used with time varying tables (using the *table write* opcodes) to facilitate new real-time filtering capabilities. In contrast to convolve there is no need for a pre-analyzed file, there is no initial delay in output, and the impulse can change over time.

The following diagram demonstrates the operation:

```
[A]    [B]    [C]    convolution coefficients
 *      *      *
[z]    [y]    [x]]   input signal
```

The incoming signal is multiplied and delayed on every a-time interval. The sum is then taken to produce the output.

```
[A]    [B]    [C]    convolution coefficients
 *      *      *
[x]    [0]    [0]    input signal
 |      \      \
A*x + B*0 + C*0      output signal
```

On the next sample:

```
[A]    [B]    [C]    convolution coefficients
 *      *      *
[y]    [x]    [0]    input signal
 |      \      \
A*y + B*x + C*0      output signal
```

and so on (see figure 10.2).

If you put the filter coefficients in the table, then this opcode will act as a filter. If you put in a 1 followed by zeros in the table, then it will spit out whatever comes into it. From this it

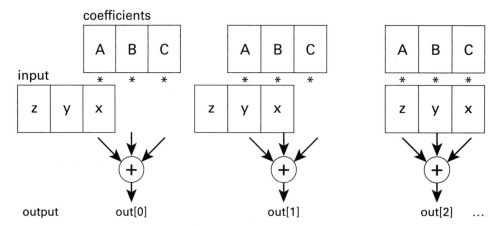

Figure 10.2
Schematics of the operation of convolution.

can be seen that the input signal is convolved with a signal stored in a table, and it is that aspect of the opcode we will consider in particular.

The OENTRY line is

```
{ "dconv", S(DCONV), 5, "a", "aii", dconvset, NULL, dconv }
```

Thus, we can see exactly what we expect; that the table is given at initialization time, and so we need to look at the dconvset function. The controlling structure is in Opcodes/ ugmoss.h:

```
typedef struct {
    OPDS            h;
    MYFLT           *ar, *ain, *isize, *ifn;
    MYFLT           *curp;
    FUNC            *ftp;
    AUXCH           sigbuf;
    unsigned int    len;
} DCONV;
```

It contains familiar components, as well as an AUXCH structure for internal space. The new element is the pointer to a FUNC type, which is actually a structure. The initialization function does three things; obtains the length of the convolution, locates the table, and allocates space.

```
static int dconvset(CSOUND *csound, DCONV *p)
{
    FUNC *ftp;

    p->len = (int)*p->isize;
    if ((ftp = csound->FTFind(csound, p->ifn)) != NULL) {
        /* find table */
        p->ftp = ftp;
        if ((unsigned)ftp->flen < p->len)
            p->len = ftp->flen; /* correct len if flen shorter */
    }
    else {
        return csound->InitError(csound, Str("No table for dconv"));
    }
    if (p->sigbuf.auxp == NULL ||
        p->sigbuf.size < (int)(p->len*sizeof(MYFLT)))
                    auxalloc(p->len*sizeof(MYFLT), &p->sigbuf);
    p->curp = (MYFLT *)p->sigbuf.auxp;
    return OK;
}
```

The first of these activities is in the line `p->len = (int)*p->isize;` remember that the arguments to an opcode are passed as pointers to `MYFLT`, so this line not only removes one level of indirection, but also makes an integer, which is what is needed for the convolution.

The new code style is the second action, finding the table. Again the table number is passed via a pointed to a `MYFLT`. The function `csound->FTFind`, defined in the file `Engine/fgens.c` as `ftfind`, has a signature of `FUNC *(*)(CSOUND*, MYFLT *);` it takes the pointer to the table number, and returns a pointer to a `FUNC`, which is a small structure that encodes various aspects of a table, but also checks to see that the table exists. Amongst the data that is extracted is the actual length of the table (the `flen` member), and the table data (in the member `ftable`).[10] If the table does not exist then a null pointer is returned. So we can see that the initialization function finds the table, remembers the structure in its local state, and also corrects the convolution length if the table is too short. We can also see the use of initialization errors and the `Str` macro for error messages.

The third component, declaring local memory, follows the pattern described above, and should not cause you any problems to read and understand.

The performance function depends critically on the algorithm, and while it may be educational to read it, that is not the purpose of this section. There is one line in the `dconv` function where the table is referenced. As part of the initialization a pointer `ftp` is made to point to the data in the table. This is in `FUNC` structure, and is found with `ftp = p->ftp->ftable`.

```
static int dconv(CSOUND *csound, DCONV *p)
{
    long i = 0;
    int n, nsmps = csound->ksmps;
    long len = p->len;
    MYFLT *ar, *ain, *ftp, *startp, *endp, *curp;
    MYFLT sum;

    ain = p->ain;              /* read saved values */
    ar = p->ar;
    ftp = p->ftp->ftable;
    startp = (MYFLT *) p->sigbuf.auxp;
    endp = startp + len;
    curp = p->curp;

    for (n=0; n<nsmps; n++) {
        *curp = ain[n];        /* get next input sample */
        i = 1, sum = *curp++ * *ftp;
        while (curp<endp) /* start the convolution */
            sum += (*curp++ * *(ftp + i++));
        curp = startp; /* correct the ptr */
        while (i<len) /* finish the convolution */
```

```
                 sum += (*curp++ * *(ftp + i++));
          if (--curp < startp)
              curp += len; /* correct for last curp++ */
          *ar++ = sum;
          ar[n] = sum;
      }
      p->curp = curp; /* save state */
      return OK;
}
```

10.6 General Information about the Csound Process

Inside an opcode there may be a need for knowledge of a general nature about the Csound process. We have already seen that there is a global value, `csound->ksmps`, that says how long the vector of audio is for either input or output. This is actually part of a single global structure that maintains the state for each instance of Csound. This structure, usually pointed to by `csound` of type `CSOUND*` holds a wide variety of values. It is declared in the main header file `H/csoundCore.h`.

Values that are often used include `esr`, the sample rate, `nchnls` for the number of output channels, but it also gives access to things like the names of the input files `orchname` and `scorename`. Sometimes useful is the value `kcounter`, which counts the number of k-rate cycles that have been performed. It can be used to tell which performance cycle is being called.

There is a substantial amount of information available inside an opcode, accessed via the compulsory header component of the instance structure. The `OPDS` structure, defined in `H/csoundCore.h`, is rather complex. There may not be many fields, but this hides a great deal.

```
typedef struct opds {
    /** Next opcode in init-time chain */
    struct opds * nxti;
    /** Next opcode in perf-time chain */
    struct opds * nxtp;
    /** Initialization (i-time) function pointer */
    SUBR iopadr;
    /** Perf-time (k- or a-rate) function pointer */
    SUBR opadr;
    /** Orch file template part for this opcode */
    OPTXT *optext;
    /** Owner instrument instance data structure */
    INSDS *insdshead;
} OPDS;
```

From this structure we can move through the opcodes that will be done, either at init time or performance tine; we can see the functions that implement the methods for the opcode also. These are not particularly useful for writing opcodes, but the last two fields are useful. They allow access to the information about the opcode, its arguments type, result type, the strings passed to the opcode, the rates of the arguments, and with some navigation to the line number and source of the instrument where it was called; the instrument number in which this instance of the opcode is use is there, and, more importantly for MIDI operation, the releasing flag, how long the instrument has to run, and many other things. For a deep understanding of Csound, following the `OPTXT` and `INSDS` structures tells most of the profundity. You can see use of some of this information in the various physical modeling opcodes in particular, but elsewhere as well.

10.7 Writing Your Own Opcode: *negate*

If you have understood the descriptions above for how existing opcodes are constructed it is time to consider writing ones own. We know from above that an opcode has the following:

- an entry in the `OENTRY` table
- a structure that carries the arguments and locals
- an initialization function
- a performance function
- a function called at note end (rarely found)
- user documentation.

The opcode that one writes must conform to this pattern.

Here we will rehearse the stages that are needed to add an opcode to the base system. This is not the preferred method, which will be described in the next section, but it does serve to identify the main stages.

As a first example let us construct a particularly simple (and quite useless) opcode that negates a signal. It is clear that there must be a single a-rate output and a single a-rate input, and so we know that the entry in the `OENTRY` table but be something like

```
{ "negate", S(???), ?, "a", "a", ???, NULL, ??? }
```

where the question marks is a placeholder for elements we have not yet determined. There are some informal rules about the name you choose for your opcode. Opcode names are made from words starting with a letter and followed by letters and/or digits. Names should not start with the lower-case letters a, k or i, and preferable not f or w. This is because these letters introduce Csound types of variables, and so if they are used for opcode names it might break existing orchestras if this word were to become an opcode. Except in polymorphic opcodes, a period should not be used in the name, as it could confuse the polymorphic system. Apart from these restrictions, the choice is free. I have used the word **negate** here, and that did not break any of these rules.

Next we need to decide on a name for the structure. A common choice is to use the opcode name, only in all upper case. Until we have completed the implementation we do not know if any state variables are needed, but we can write

```
typedef struct {
    OPDS h;
    MYFLT *ar, *asig;
} NEGATE;
```

and add any other variables later.

It is often easier to write the performance function first, as it indicates any need for initialization.

The general layout of the performance function is

```
int negate(CSOUND *csopund, NEGATE *p)
{
    int n, nsmps = csound->ksmps;
    . . . .
    for (n=0; n<nsmps; n++) {
        . . . .
        p->ar[n] = ???;
    }
    return OK;
}
```

Based on what we now know from above, the implementation is

```
int negate(CSOUND *csound, NEGATE *p)
{
    int n, nsmps = csound->ksmps;
    MYFLT *ar = p->ar;
    MYFLT *as = p->asig;
    for (n=0; n<nsmps; n++) {
        ar[n] = - as[n]
    }
    return OK;
}
```

and there is no need for any initialization.

We now have the performance and (empty) initialization functions, so we can see that the field in the OENTRY table for when to call the functions will be 4, meaning a-rate performance only. The line can be completed as follows:

```
{ "negate", S(NEGATE), 4, "a", "a", NULL, NULL, negate }
```

We now have to add this code into the system. For this purpose, we have to change two or three files (depending on your platform). We need to add the OENTRY line above to the file `Engine/entry1.c`, and to give a prototype for the function `negate`, in the form below to `H/entry1.h`:

```
int negate(CSOUND*, void*);
```

For a number of reasons, this should be declared with a void * argument instead of a `NEGATE*` one. I leave the reasons to you as an exercise; but they are not very easy. If you cannot work it out, just accept it for the moment, but do it this way.

We also need to ensure that the structure `NEGATE` is declared. It is best to do this by including (with `#include`) the header file that defines the `typedef` above. Again the name can be anything, but a trivial choice would be `H/negate.h`, and so we would add `#include "negate.h"` in the other file inclusions.

We can similarly place our function in a file `OOps/negate.c`, which would read as follows:

```
#include "csoundCore.h"
#include "negate.h"

/* Performance a-rate function for negating a signal */
int negate(CSOUND *csound,NEGATE *p)
{
    int n, nsmps = csound->ksmps;
    MYFLT *ar = p->ar;
    MYFLT *as = p->asig;
    for (n=0; n<nsmps; n++) {
        ar[n] = - as[n]
    }
    return OK;
}
```

where we have added the `includes` for the basic Csound definitions and the header particular to this code.

We now have to arrange to compile this code. Csound uses a build system called **SCons**, which is controlled by a file called `SConstruct`. For a section of code in the base system the name of the code file must be added to the list called `libCsoundSources` about a third of the way down the file.[11]

We still need to create documentation for the opcode in the standard format (which is controlled by XML); that is a line of syntax, and a very short description. This is followed by descriptions of initialization and performance (as above). The documentation is finished with an example of use:

```
<refentry id="negate">
<indexterm id="IndexNegate"><primary>negate</primary></indexterm>
   <refentryinfo><title>Mathematical Operations</title></refentryinfo>
```

```
<refmeta>
    <refentrytitle>negate</refentrytitle>
</refmeta>

<refnamediv>
    <refname>negate</refname>

    <refpurpose>
        Negate a signal
    </refpurpose>
</refnamediv>

<refsect1>
    <title>Description</title>
    <para>
        Returns the negative of the input signal.
    </para>
</refsect1>

<refsect1>
    <title>Syntax</title>
    <synopsis>ares <command>negate</command> asig</synopsis>
    <para>
        Returns the negative of the signal
<emphasis>asig</emphasis>.
    </para>
    </refsect1>

<refsect1>
    <title>Performance</title>
    <para>
        <emphasis>asig</emphasis> -- audio signal input.
    </para>
</refsect1>

<refsect1>
    <title>Examples</title>
    <para>
        Here is an example of the negate opcode.
    a1 oscil 32000, 440, 1
    a2 negate a1
        out a1, a2

    </para>
</refsect1>

<refsect1>
```

```
      <title>Credits</title>
      <para>
         <simplelist>
             <member>Author: YOUR NAME</member>
             <member>THE DATE WRITTEN</member>
         </simplelist>
      </para>
   </refsect1>
</refentry>
```

10.8   A k-rate Plug-in Opcode: trigger

The **trigger** opcode is not your typical opcode; but rather it is a **plug-in** opcode that is loaded optionally. Much of the implementation should be familiar if you have followed this chapter, but it does introduce the way in which a plug-in opcode is defined. The manual describes the **trigger** opcode as follows:

kout   **trigger**   ksig, kthreshold, kmode

DESCRIPTION

Informs when a k-rate signal crosses a threshold.

PERFORMANCE

ksig   input signal
kthreshold   trigger threshold
kmode   can be 0, 1 or 2

Normally **trigger** outputs zeroes: only each time *ksig* crosses *kthreshold* **trigger** outputs a 1. There are three modes of using *ktrig*:

- *kmode* = 0 (down-up) *ktrig* outputs a 1 when current value of *ksig* is higher than *kthreshold*, while old value of *ksig* was equal to or lower than *kthreshold*.
- *kmode* = 1 (up-down) *ktrig* outputs a 1 when current value of *ksig* is lower than *kthreshold* while old value of *ksig* was equal or higher than *threshold*.
- *kmode* = 2 (both) *ktrig* outputs a 1 in both the two previous cases.

With this description we should be able to predict in many ways what code we will see. We have a single k-rate answer and three k-rate arguments. It is likely that there will be an initialization function and a performance function. There will be a structure that carries the pointers to the arguments and answer space, and possibly additional information. So when we read in the OENTRY table at the end of the file Opcodes/uggab.c we see

```
{ "trigger", S(TRIG), 3, "k", "kkk", trig_set, trig, NULL },
```

which is not going to be a surprise. We may not have predicted the actual names of the functions, but even they are fairly obvious.

The next component is the `TRIG` structure, which can be found in the file `Opcodes/uggab.h`; but before looking at it we can predict what we will find, and even guess that the variable names will follow the documentation. Thus we expect to see

```
typedef struct {
    OPDS h;
    MYFLT *kout, *ksig, *kthreshold, *kmode;
    . . . .
} TRIG;
```

Note in particular that kout, *ksig, *kthreshold, and *kmode are all pointers to `MYFLT`. It is important that all arguments and answers are of this type. Until we consider the actual implementation we do not know if there are any more members, but if there are they will be in the place of the ellipses. In fact if you now look at the real code you will find that there is one floating-point value, called `old_sig`, which is an indication of its use, to retain the signal from the previous cycle. This should come as no surprise, as the documentation for this opcode is all about a signal changing between successive calls. The actual structure is

```
typedef struct {
    OPDS h;
    MYFLT *kout, *ksig, *kthreshold, *kmode;
    MYFLT old_sig;
} TRIG;
```

We can now look at the implementation found in the file `Opcodes/uggab.c`. It is a little easier to read the k-rate function before the initialization.

```
#include <csdl.h>                                    /**** 0 */

. . . . . .

static int trig(CSOUND *csound, TRIG *p)
{
    switch ((int) (*p->kmode + FL(0.5))) {           /**** 1*/
    case 0:        /* down-up */
        if (p->old_sig <= *p->kthreshold &&
                *p->ksig > *p->kthreshold)
            *p->kout = FL(1.0);
        else
            *p->kout = FL(0.0);
        break;
    case 1:        /* up-down */
        if (p->old_sig >= *p->kthreshold &&          /**** 2*/
                *p->ksig < *p->kthreshold)           /**** 2*/
            *p->kout = FL(1.0);
        else
```

```
            *p->kout = FL(0.0);
        break;
    case 2:          /* both */
        if ((p->old_sig <= *p->kthreshold &&
                *p->ksig > *p->kthreshold) ||
            (p->old_sig >= *p->kthreshold &&
                *p->ksig < *p->kthreshold) )
                    *p->kout = FL(1.0);
        else
            *p->kout = FL(0.0);
        break;
    default:
        return
            csound->PerfError(csound,
                    Str(" bad imode value"));     /**** 4*/
        return;                                   /**** 4*/
    }
    p->old_sig = *p->ksig;                        /**** 3*/
    return OK;
}
```

The basic structure here is a switch statement that deals with the differences between the various kinds of triggering, as controlled by the kmode parameter. This parameter controls whether we are looking for an event of down-up, up-down or either. Each case is similar, so we will look at the second case in detail, and the others will be left as an exercise. But there is some advantage in looking at the line annotated with a 1. The value on which the switch is made is (int) (*p->kmode + FL(0.5)). Remember that the argument is provided as a pointer embedded in the TRIG structure, and we are given a pointer to this structure as the argument to the performance function.

To get the pointer to the argument, we need p->kmode; and we need *p->kmode to get the value. All arguments and results in Csound are of MYFLT type, and hence the need for a cast to an integer. The addition of FL(0.5) is to make this a rounded operation rather than a truncation toward zero. In theory the user would always have provided an integer value, which has an exact representation in floating point, but in practice it is usually better to be safe in cases like this.

In the case of looking for an up-down transition of the ksig, that is case 1, we are interested in the case when the current value is strictly negative[12] and the previous one was positive. We have to ensure that one of these is a strict interpretation. The test we find in the code, annotated with a 2 above. Again we need to use the *p->kthreshold form. The previous value is remembered in the TRIG structure in the member old_sig. We can (and should) remember the value here rather than a pointer to the value, which may well have changed—indeed that is the purpose of the opcode. We set the answer to 0 or 1 (as floating point) as required based on this test. The last operation that must be done is to remember the previous value of the signal, which we can find in the line labeled with a 3.

Before leaving this function there are a couple of issues left to be explored. You will see that the function checks that the mode is 0, 1, or 2. The default case is an error. It is good practice to include checks such as this. The question that immediately arises is what to do in the case of an error. There are two major actions, to ignore the error, with or without a message, or to cause the opcode to abort, and hence the instance of the instrument to cease. To give a warning message the function csound->Warning is provided, with the signature

```
void (*)(CSOUND*, char *);
```

This prints the argument to the output if the overriding parameters to Csound want messages to appear.[13] You should use this function rather than invent one of your own if you ever wish to write an opcode. To cause the instrument instance to stop the function csound->PerfError

```
int (*)(CSOUND*, char *s);
```

that not only writes the message but causes the current instrument-instance to be removed from the chain of active notes, and signals an error to the engine. It should be used as the value of a return statement.

Another issue is the macro Str. Csound was originally written in American English, and this can be a problem in some parts of the world where the language can be a barrier.[14] The macro Str allows a system for translation of all messages into the language of the user. There is a possibility for an external database of translated strings being used. If you want to translate the messages from Csound into an alternative language, then the first stage is to translate the messages in the last of these into your target language, and add them to the top-level language database.

That completes the consideration of the performance function. It is simple to see that all that is needed in initialization is to give a value to the last signal:

```
static int trig_set(CSOUND *csound, TRIG *p)
{
    p->old_sig = FL(0.0);
    return OK;
}
```

As this opcode is in a plug-in module, it is acceptable (and usual) to use static functions as they will not be seen elsewhere. We also need to communicate the OENTRY line to the main Csound program. This is achieved in the code at the end of the file Opcodes/uggab.c where there is a local array localops of opcodes defined in the file, and formulaic init function. If you write a new plug-in opcode then you need to copy this code, or the slightly simpler example at the end of Opcodes/date.c.

We have now considered a simple opcode that operates at the audio rate and a slightly more complex one that works at control rate. If you have understood this material you should be able to read and get at least a basic understanding of many of Csound's opcodes.

There are a number of additional complications that need to be comprehended before one could pretend to be an expert. These include the allocation of memory in opcodes, and the creation of opcodes that can work at different rates. We will consider these in the next section with a more complex opcode.

10.8.1   More about Plug-in Opcodes

The alternative to adding our **negate** opcode to the base system is to provide it as a plug-in which can be loaded when required. Most of the previous sections still apply, but there are a few differences, especially since we don't want to modify the system files like `Engine/entry1.c`. The Csound plugin mechanism is arranged to obviate that need. The idea is to build a shared library[15] that includes not only the initialization and performance code but also additional code to add the opcode to the syntax tables, and to give the shared library access to the state and functions of base Csound. This additional communication requires one of two methods; both require a table and the inclusion of a different header from the basic `csoundCore.h`, but differ in the degree of control they provide. As an example of how this is done we will re-implement the negate opcode but as a loadable library.

```
#include "csdl.h"

typedef struct {
    OPDS h;
    MYFLT *ar, *asig;
} NEGATE;

static int negate(CSOUND *csound, NEGATE *p)
{
    int n, nsmps = csound->ksmps;
    MYFLT *ar = p->ar;
    MYFLT *as = p->asig;
    for (n=0; n<nsmps; n++) {
        ar[n] = - as[nn]
    }
    return OK;
}

static OENTRY localops[] = {
{ "negate", sizeof(NEGATE), 4, "a", "a", NULL, NULL, negate }
};

LINKAGE
```

The macro LINKAGE is a new concept. It provides a couple of functions that the engine can use to initialize the entry table into the system. The details of how this works is beyond the current need.

At the start of the file the header file csdl.h replaces the base csoundCore.h header in plug-ins. This adjusts for the way in which certain internal functions and values are accessed. It is worth emphasizing that a plug-in code segment cannot call other parts of Csound except through the CSOUND structure, which contains pointers to all relevant functions.

You will also note that in this example the structure is not in a separate header file. This is acceptable as there is no inclusion of the header for one of the entry files. Of course if the opcode being implemented is of sufficient complexity it could be in a header file used by a number of files. Similarly there is no need for the initialization and performance functions to be globally visible, so in this example they are declared static. This is an issue of programming style; in general functions should be static unless there is a need for them to be global. I know that the C language rather encourages the opposite, but that is no reason to give in to laziness.

Finally we need to build the library. If one is using the **Scons** system, one needs to add a line like

```
makePlugin(pluginEnvironment, 'negate, ['Opcodes/negate.c'])
```

to the similar lines.[16]

It is possible to compile a plug-in without the rest of the sources, but then the construction of a suitable Makefile is left to the user.

10.9 Plug-in Table Generators: *fgens*

Csound provides a number of table generator (*fgens*) to initialize tables to sines, Gaussians, envelopes, and similar operations. It is possible to write plug-in code to add new table generators. As an example of this, consider the code in Opcodes/ftest.c:

```
#include "csdl.h"
#include <math.h>

static int tanhtable(FGDATA *ff, FUNC *ftp)
{
    /* CSOUND *csound = ff->csound; */
    MYFLT *fp = ftp->ftable;
    MYFLT range = ff->e.p[5];
    double step = (double) range / (double) ftp->flen;
    int i;
    double x;

    for (i = 0, x = 0.0; i <= (int) ftp->flen; i++, x += step)
        fp[i] = (MYFLT) tanh(x);
```

```
        return OK;
}

static NGFENS localfgens[] = {
    { "tanh", tanhtable },
    { NULL, NULL }
};
```

FLINKAGE

The function `tanhtable` is the implementation of a table generator to fill a table with the hyperbolic tangent function, where the range is zero until the fifth argument to the `f` score opcode. When it is called, the second argument is the table structure so all it needs to do is write the values into the table of `MYFLT`s.

The static table `localfgens` is a list of the new generators, with a name and the function; the table is terminated by a `NULL` name. The macro `FLINKAGE` includes the necessary initialization code. It includes creating score macros for the given names so the generators can be used; the numbers are generator internally and cannot be relied on from one run to the next.

10.10   Localization and Internationalization

Csound is a widely used program, and not all users speak the same language. While it has become accepted that English is the language of computing this can be a barrier to composers and sound designers who could benefit. In recent years there has been a move in computing to provide internationalization and localization service within the existing frameworks. Csound also is moving in this way, ever since the 1999 announcement.[17] In fact there have been three different methods used. The first attempt was to wrap every message string in the sources in a function call with two arguments—an index number and the string. It was possible to create a file of translations with the index number providing the linkage. This scheme may be found in some older Csound systems, from version 3.54 until 4.23f02. There are obvious drawbacks to this indexing method when plug-ins are introduced and the system allows for local, private or commercial plug-in opcodes that would not necessarily have access to the allocation of index numbers.

Starting with Csound5, a new scheme was adopted. The numerical index was removed and the string itself was used as the index, implemented with hashing. The wrapping of the strings continued but now the form was that any string that might need a translation at any time is passed via a macro `Str`, and it is this format that is used earlier in this chapter. If you are adding new code it is a very good idea to follow this method, even if you are not expecting to translate the messages yourself.

The implementation of the translation tables is fairly complex, and can be seen in the file `Top/getstings.c`, together with tools to assist in the creation of translation files; here we will not consider the details as a third scheme is in the process of incorporation.

The GNU project has been faced with this localization problem in many software packages, and they have produced a very general system that is very like the second Csound method. They wrap the strings with a functions call, gettext, very like Str, but there are also mechanisms for dealing with plurals and duals, and changing the order of arguments in printf formats, as word order is not the same in all languages. In addition the **GNU gettext** project[18] provides a number of tools to assist in the creation and maintenance of translations. In versions of Csound after 5.07 it is this scheme that will be developed.

From the point of view of the programmer the simple rule is to wrap all strings in the Str macro. The more complex rule is to look at the recommendations in the GNU **gettext** documentation[19] about making messages clear and translatable. As in the case in many long-standing software packages, the error messages in Csound are often terse and written in jargon. Part of the move to internationalization is to revise all these strings to make the messages clear; and to this end, all advice is welcome.

10.11   Conclusion

This chapter should assist you in understanding the way in which Csound works, and in particular how to add new opcodes and other operations. Some of the information may seem rather detailed and almost pernickety, but this is central to programming. One must not only get the structure correct, but also the details must be correct. Computers are very unforgiving of sloppy details, at both the syntactic and the semantic level.

10.12   Exercises

Exercise 10.12.1
Modify the *negate* opcode to add more functionality to it.

(a) First try to add an extra parameter, which would be a k-rate variable to control the "negation": when it is zero, the "effect" is bypassed (no negation), when it is non-zero, the opcode behave as the original version. Make this a plug-in opcode.
(b) Add another parameter, now an i-time one, which controls the gain of the signal (i.e. a multiplier), so that we can attenuate or boost the signal.
(c) Try to design a third variation on the original opcode by adding another parameter (i time, k, or a rate).

Exercise 10.12.2
Make a version of the **tone** opcode (called **newtone**), where the cutoff frequency parameter (khp) is now an audio rate parameter. First figure out what the differences are in terms of the expected input, then consider how often the filter coefficients have to be update (and so where the update code should go). Make this an internal opcode.

Exercise 10.12.3

Create a new plug-in f-table which would tabulate the function $f(x) = x^3$ within a range defined by the p-fields 5 and 6 (start and end points).

Notes

1. See Donald E. Knuth, *The Art of Computer Programming* (Addison-Wesley, 1973).

2. Csound can be built from its sources with just a few commands. However, since it is a large system with several components, it has a number of dependencies (i.e. software on which it depends for its operation). These will need to be present if you want to build a particular element of Csound. For this chapter, we might only need one extra component, *PortAudio* IO module, in addition to the basic system. In this case, we will require as dependencies the *libsndfile* (for the basic system) and PortAudio libraries. The former can be downloaded from http://www.mega-nerd.com/libsndfile and the latter from http://portmedia.sourceforge.net. These sites contain full instructions for the installation of these libraries.

   Csound is built using a build system called scons, which can be downloaded from http://www.scons.org, where again full instructions can be found for its installation. The sources for Csound can be downloaded from http://csound.sourceforge.net. Once you have these, building Csound is just a matter of running the following command in the top-level directory of the source code: $ scons. This will build the software in the top-level sources directory. You can then run Csound from there without the need for anything else: $ ./csound. If instead you would like to work from other directories, you can always place that directory in your $PATH environment variable. In this case, you will also want to set the $OPCODEDIR variable to contain this directory as well, so that Csound can find its plug-ins. If you are doing this, to avoid confusion, you should not have more than one build of Csound in your system (e.g. this one you have built yourself and another from an installer distribution). Alternatively, by running your own build of Csound only from the top-level sources directory, you should avoid any mix-up of versions and builds (this is what we will recommend for the work covered in this chapter). More details on building Csound with other components and other options can be found in the Csound manual (also found in http://csound.sourceforge.net)

3. If you look at the sources of some filter opcodes you will see that care is taken to read the inputs before any output is written, in case there is this kind of variable sharing. A simple example can be found in **areson** where the output signal is remembered in a local variable until after the last use of the input signal. More extreme cases can be found elsewhere.

4. In C++ this is not necessary, as a struct is automatically a type in that language.

5. This is of MYFLT type.

6. For more on filters, see *The Csound Book*, ed. R. Boulanger (MIT Press, 2000); K. Steiglitz, *A Digital Signal Processing Primer* (Addison-Wesley, 1996).

7. The pointer arithmetic form was universal in earlier versions of Csound, but the for loop is better optimized by modern compilers and is thus preferred.

8. This is described in chapter 4 of the present volume.

9. Remember that the second field in an OENTRY is an unsigned short that is typically a 16-bit quantity.

10. Much of the rest is related to looping, and to the use of tables in oscillators.

11. As was mentioned in note 2 above, Csound uses the scons build system. This software uses a script file called SConstruct, which contains all details of how to compile and link the various components of the software. SConstruct has lists of all the required source files inside it. In the specific case of internal opcodes, these files are in a list called 'libCsoundSources', which starts at around line 1106 in the file:

```
else:
    libCsoundSources = Split('''
    Engine/auxfd.c
    . . .
    Top/utility.c
    ''')
```

Placing the name (and directory location) of your source code file anywhere inside this list (for instance after the last line but before the triple quotes) will compile it as an internal component of Csound.

12. Strictly negative means less that zero; a non-strict negative would include zero as negative.

13. There is a -m option that controls the kind of messages that actually are printed.

14. Some of the "American English" messages it produced are, in fact, not compatible with the English that I speak and write.

15. That is a DLL in Windows, a .so in UNIX and GNU/Linux or a.dylib in OS X.

16. Again in SConstruct we find a section that starts with the following big comment:

```
##########################################################
#
# Plugin opcodes.
##########################################################
```

Just after these lines you can add your own call to makePlugin as discussed in the text:

```
makePlugin(pluginEnvironment, 'negate, ['Opcodes/negate.c'])
```

17. R. Boulanger and J. ffitch, "Teaching software synthesis: From hardware to software synthesis," in *Global Village—Global Brain—Global Music*: *KlangArt-Kongreß 1999*, ed. B. Enders and J. Strange-Elbe (Electronic Publishing, 2003).

18. Information for the GNU gettext project is available at http://www.gnu.org/software/gettext/. The code is available at http://ftp.gnu.org/pub/gnu/gettext/. The gettext FAQ is available at http://www.gnu.org/software/gettext/FAQ.html.

19. The online manual for gettext is available at http://www.gnu.org/software/gettext/manual/gettext.html.

11 Spectral Opcodes

Victor Lazzarini

Developing opcodes that process spectral data is as simple as writing ordinary unit generators. Csound has a special data type, fsig, that was designed to hold self-describing spectral data. The fsig was created alongside a series of unit generators known as the "streaming phase vocoder"[1] opcodes. These include, among other things, the analysis opcode **pvsanal** and the synthesis opcode **pvsynth**, which can be used to transform signals from waveforms (in the time domain) into spectra (in the frequency domain) and vice versa. With spectral data, it is possible to design interesting and unique effects. This chapter will introduce the main elements of fsigs and how opcodes to process them can be created.

11.1 Processing Spectral Signals

As was discussed in chapter 10, Csound provides data types for control and audio, which are all time-domain signals. For spectral domain processing, there are actually two separate signal types, wsig and fsig. The former is a signal type introduced by Barry Vercoe to hold a special, non-standard, type of logarithmic frequency analysis data and is used with a few opcodes originally provided for manipulating this data type. The latter is a self-describing data type designed by Richard Dobson to provide a framework for spectral processing, in what is called "streaming phase vocoder processing." Opcodes for converting between time-domain audio signals and fsigs, as well as a few processing opcodes, were provided as part of the original framework by Dobson. In addition, support for a self-describing, portable, spectral file format PVOCEX has been added to Csound, into the analysis utility program pvanal and with a file reader opcode.

Fsig is a self-describing Csound data type that will hold frames of spectral analysis data based on the discrete Fourier transform (DFT). Each frame will contain the positive side of the spectrum, from 0 hertz to the Nyquist frequency (inclusive). The framework can support different spectral formats: real-imaginary, phase-amplitude, frequency-amplitude, and sinusoidal tracks. We will be discussing here the most common of these formats: amplitude-frequency, which will hold pairs of floating-point numbers with the amplitude and frequency (in hertz) data for each DFT analysis bin. This is probably the most musically meaningful of the DFT-based output formats and can be generated by the phase vocoder (PV) analysis (implemented by the already mentioned opcode pvsanal and the utility analysis program pvanal).

The fsig data type is defined by the following C structure:

```
typedef struct pvsdat {
    long N; /* framesize-2, DFT length */
    long overlap; /* number of frame overlaps */
    long winsize; /* window size */
    int wintype; /* window type: hamming/hanning */
    long format; /* format: we will be using AMP:FREQ */
    unsigned long framecount; /* frame counter */
    AUXCH frame; /* spectral sample is a 32-bit float */
} PVSDAT;
```

The structure holds all the data needed to describe the signal type: the DFT size (N), which will determine the number of analysis bins ($N/2 + 1$) and the framesize; the number of overlaps, or decimation, which will determine analysis hopsize (N/overlaps); the size of the analysis window, generally the same as N; the window type: currently supporting PVS_WIN_HAMMING, PVS_WIN_HANN, PVS_WIN_KAISER and PVS_WIN_CUSTOM; the data format: we will be using PVS_AMP_FREQ only, (PVS_TRACKS is also used in Csound); a frame counter, for keeping track of processed frames; and finally the AUXCH structure, which will hold the actual array of floats with the spectral data.

11.1.1   Spectral Opcode Specifics

A number of implementation differences exist between spectral and time-domain processing opcodes. The main one is that new output is produced only if a new input frame is ready to be processed. Because of this implementation detail, the processing function of a streaming PV opcode is actually registered as a k-rate routine. In addition, opcodes allocate space for their fsig frame outputs, unlike ordinary opcodes, which simply take floating-point buffers as input and output. The fsig dataspace is allocated externally, in similar fashion to audio-rate vectors and control-rate scalars; however the DFT frame allocation is done by the opcode that generates the signal. With that in mind, and observing that type of data we are processing is frequency-domain, we can implement a spectral unit generator as an ordinary (k-rate) opcode.

The code example we will develop here takes advantage of one of the main aspects of the PV data format: the separation between amplitudes and frequencies.[2] We will implement a spectral highlighter, or spectral arpeggiator. We are borrowing the idea from Trevor Wishart's *specarp* program from the original Composers Desktop Project suite of PV data transformation software. The concept (and implementation) is very simple, yet effective: we will emphasize one central bin, while attenuating all others. This will happen for every output frame, depending on three k-rate controls: bin index, depth of attenuation and highlight gain. In order to provide a frame-size-independent bin index, we will take it as a normalized value, between 0 and 1, scaling it to the fftsize. The depth will control how much all bins, except the highlighted one, will be attenuated, from 0 (no attenuation) to 1 (full attenuation). The highlight gain is simply the positive gain applied to the selected bin. This transformation only concerns the amplitudes of each spectral bin, so we will pass all frequencies unchanged.

The opcode dataspace is as follows:

```
#include <csdl.h>
#include <pstream.h>

typedef struct _pvsarp {
    OPDS h;
    PVSDAT *fout;
    PVSDAT *fin;
    MYFLT *cf,*kdepth, *gain;
    unsigned long lastframe;
} pvsarp;
```

The opcode dataspace contains pointers to the output and input fsig, as well as the k-rate input parameters and a frame counter. The init function has to allocate space for the output fsig DFT frame, as well as setting the various PVSDAT parameters:

```
int pvsarp_init(CSOUND *csound, pvsarp *p)
{
    long N = p->fin->N; /* fftsize */

    /* allocate output fsig frame if needed */
    if (p->fout->frame.auxp==NULL ||
        p->fout->frame.size < sizeof(float) * (N+2))
        csound->AuxAlloc(csound,(N+2)*sizeof(float),&p->fout >frame);
    /* initialize the PVSDAT structure */
    p->fout->N = N;
    p->fout->overlap = p->fin->overlap;
    p->fout->winsize = p->fin->winsize;
    p->fout->wintype = p->fin->wintype;
    p->fout->format = p->fin->format;
    p->fout->framecount = 1;
    p->lastframe = 0;

    if (!(p->fout->format==PVS_AMP_FREQ) ||
        (p->fout->format==PVS_AMP_PHASE))
            return csound->InitError(csound,
    "pvsarp: signal format must be amp-phase or amp-freq.\n");
    return OK;
}
```

The processing function keeps track of the frame count and only processes the input, generating a new output frame, if a new input is available. The framecount is generated by the analysis opcode and is passed from one processing opcode to the next in the chain. As mentioned before, the processing function is called every control period, but it is independent of it, performing only when needed. The only caveat is that the fsig framework requires that the control period, in samples (ksmps), be smaller than or equal to the analysis hopsize. As mentioned above, this process only alters the amplitudes of each bin, indexed by i, passing the frequencies (i+1).[3]

```c
int pvsarp_process(CSOUND *csound, pvsarp *p)
{
    long i,j,N = p->fout->N, bins = N/2 + 1;
    float g = (float) *p->gain;
    MYFLT kdepth = (MYFLT) *(p->kdepth), cf = (MYFLT) *(p->cf);
    float *fin = (float *) p->fin->frame.auxp;
    float *fout = (float *) p->fout->frame.auxp;

    if(fout==NULL)
        return csound->PerfError(csound, "pvsarp: not initialized\n");

    /* if a new frame is ready for processing */
    if(p->lastframe < p->fin->framecount) {
        /* limit cf and kdepth to 0-1 range */
        /* scale cf to the number of spectral bins */
        cf = cf >= 0 ? (cf < 1 ? cf*bins : bins-1) : 0;
            kdepth = kdepth >= 0 ? (kdepth <= 1 ? kdepth :
            (MYFLT)1.0): (MYFLT)0.0;
            /* j counts bins, whereas i counts frame positions */
            for(i=j=0;i < N+2;i+=2, j++) {
            /* if the bin is to be highlighted */
            if(j == (int) cf) fout[i] = fin[i]*g;
            /* else attenuate it */
            else fout[i] = (float)(fin[i]*(1-kdepth));
            /* pass the frequencies unchanged */
            fout[i+1] = fin[i+1];
        }
        /* update the internal frame count */
        p->fout->framecount = p->lastframe = p->fin->framecount;
    }
    return OK;
}
```

Finally, the localops OENTRY structure for this opcode will look like this (not forgetting the LINKAGE macro):

```
static OENTRY localops[] = {
    {"pvsarp", sizeof(pvsarp), 3, "f", "fkkk", (SUBR)pvsarp_init,
    (SUBR)pvsarp_process}
};
LINKAGE
```

11.2 Modifying the Frequencies

The next example shows how frequencies can be manipulated in a pitch-shifting opcode, **pvtranspose**. In contrast with amplitudes, some care has to be taken when changing the values of frequencies in bins. If they exceed the bin bandwidth, i.e. they are actually moving into another bin's frequency range, then they need to be moved to a different bin. So the principle of modifying frequencies involves changing them and moving the bin's contents (amplitude and frequency) to a new bin.

The opcode data space defines one fsig output, one fsig input, and two extra k-rate parameters, the pitch transposition ratio and an amplitude scaling factor:

```
typedef struct _pvstransp {
    OPDS h;
    PVSDAT *fout;
    PVSDAT *fin;
    MYFLT *kscal;
    MYFLT *gain;
    unsigned long lastframe;
} pvstransp;
```

The initialization function is pretty much the same as in the previous example:

```
static int pvstransp_init(CSOUND *csound, pvstransp *p)
{
    long N = p->fin->N;

    if (p->fout->frame.auxp == NULL ||
        p->fout->frame.size < sizeof(float) * (N + 2))
        csound->AuxAlloc(csound,
                          (N + 2) * sizeof(float), &p->fout->frame);
    p->fout->N = N;
    p->fout->overlap = p->fin->overlap;
    p->fout->winsize = p->fin->winsize;
    p->fout->wintype = p->fin->wintype;
    p->fout->format = p->fin->format;
    p->fout->framecount = 1;
    p->lastframe = 0;

    return OK;
}
```

The main part of the opcode is found in the processing function. Here in the inside code section, after the "ready for processing" test, where the last frame is compared to the current input's frame count, we have the following steps:

1. Copy the 0 Hz and Nyquist amplitudes unchanged (these might actually change in later steps).

2. Zero the output amplitudes and set frequencies to −1.0. This is used later to check that empty bins are not amplitude-scaled.

3. In a loop from bin 1 upward, find the target bin then copy the input amplitude to that bin. Scale the input frequency and copy it to the target bin.

4. Make sure we are not overstepping the array when doing the previous operation. This will actually get rid of any possible aliasing when transposing upward.

5. Scale the bins that have moved data onto them (the ones not marked −1.0, since negative frequencies will never occur).

The code is as follows:

```
static int pvstransp_process(CSOUND *csound, pvstransp *p)
{
    long i, bin, j, N = p->fout->N;
    float max = 0.0f;
    MYFLT pscal = (MYFLT) fabs(*p->kscal);
    float g = (float) *p->gain;
    float *fin = (float *) p->fin->frame.auxp;
    float *fout = (float *) p->fout->frame.auxp;

    if (fout == NULL)
        return csound->PerfError(csound,
                                  Str("pvscale: not initialized"));

    if (p->lastframe < p->fin->framecount) {
        /* do not change the 0hz and Nyquist bins */
        fout[0] = fin[0];
        fout[N] = fin[N];
        /* zero the output amplitudes */
        for (i = 2; i < N; i += 2) {
            fout[i] = 0.f;
            fout[i+1] = -1.0f;
        }

        for (i=2,bin=1; i < N; bin++, i += 2) {
            /* find the target new bin */
            j = (int) (bin * pscal)*2;
            /* scale frequency and move bins */
```

```
            if (newbin < N && newbin > 0) {
                fout[j] = fin[i];
                fout[j+1] = (float) (fin[i+1] * pscal);
            }
        }
        for (i = 2; i < N; i += 2) {
            if (fout[i+1] != -1.0f)
                fout[i] *= g; /* scale amplitude */
        }
        p->fout->framecount = p->lastframe = p->fin->framecount;
    }
     return OK;
    }

    static OENTRY localops[] = {
            {"pvstransp", sizeof(pvstransp), 3, "f", "fkk",
            (SUBR)pvstransp_init, (SUBR)pvstransp_process}
    };
```

LINKAGE

Processing frequencies requires a little more care than processing amplitudes. However, once the above limitations are understood, processes can be devised that manipulate them successfully.

11.3 Documentation—The Final Frontier

It is generally assumed that software development stops here (when the finished code is tested and works), but a final and important stage is still to be completed. This is of course the writing of suitable documentation for our work. Without it, any software is of limited use, perhaps only for its developers, but even in this case, its usability is not guaranteed. Therefore, it is important that a manual page and some examples are supplied with every new opcode.

A Csound manual page template for opcode reference is very well established. The manual currently exists in many formats: plain text, help file, html, xml, etc. The latter is particularly flexible as it can itself generate documentation in different forms. For those interested in that format, a quick look at some opcode entries will be enough for learning the xml tags used in the manual.

In general, the manual page should have the following format:

title (generally the opcode's name)
short description: one line on what it does
description: under that heading, a longer discussion of what the opcode does and how to use it

syntax: the opcode's csound syntax
initialization parameters and their description
performance parameters and their description, including their expected ranges
a csound instrument example of opcode usage.

As an example, here is the plain-text manual entry for the **pvsarp** opcode discussed in the preceding section:

```
PVSARP
```

```
Spectral filtering and arpeggiation of PV streams.
```

```
DESCRIPTION
Pvsarp takes an input fsig and arpeggiates it according to bin index,
effect depth and boost amplitude controls. On each fsig input frame,
it will apply a gain to the target bin, as well as attenuating all the
other frequency bins according to the depth control.
```

```
fsig pvsarp fin, kcf, kdepth, kgain
```

```
[INITIALIZATION: this is omitted as the opcode does not have i-type
parameters]
```

```
PERFORMANCE
fin—input fsig
kbin— bin index (normalized, 0-1, equivalent to the 0 Hz—Nyquist
range), determining the target bin for arpeggiation.
kdepth—depth of attenuation of surrounding bins (0 <= kdepth <= 1)
kgain—gain (multiplier), applied to the target bin.
```

```
EXAMPLE
This example arpeggiates the spectrum of an input signal, using an LFO
(with a triangle wave) to control the bin index. The modulation width
is 0.05*SR/2 (1102.5 at 44.1 KHz) and the lowest frequency is
0.005*SR/2 (110.25).
```

```
instr 1
```

```
ifftsize = 1024
iwtype = 1
ifr = 0.2
idepth = 1
```

```
asig in
kbin oscil 0.05, ifr, 1
kbin = kbin + 0.005
```

```
fsig pvsanal asig, ifftsize, ifftsize/4, ifftsize, iwtype
ftps pvsarp fsig, kbin, 0.95, 15
atps pvsynth ftps
```

```
    out atps
endin

f1 0 1024 7 0 512 1 512 0
i1 0 20
```

11.4   Conclusion

Spectral processing and opcode development have become more accessible with the introduction of the plug-in framework and the fsig data type. Now, users with a basic understanding of C can design frequency-domain processing unit generators. This is a feature that makes Csound one of the most flexible synthesis and processing systems to extend and customize.

11.5   Exercises

Exercise 11.5.1
Design and implement an opcode that filters out a certain user-defined band of frequencies. Allow for control-rate changes in the bandwidth and amount of filtering.

Exercise 11.5.2
Write a manual page for the **pvstransp** opcode, providing a usage example and explaining its parameters.

Exercise 11.5.3
Design and implement an opcode that (a) takes two fsigs, (b) splits their spectra in half, (c) combines the lower half of one with the upper half of the other, (d) outputs the composite fsig.

Notes

1. The phase vocoder is a popular algorithm for spectral analysis and re-synthesis. It is based on a DFT analysis followed by amplitude and frequency estimation of each analysis point (bin). It results in a series of frames of amp-freq data pairs, one for each analyzed frequency bin from 0 Hz to the Nyquist frequency, inclusive. The analysis is performed at a certain time interval and the number of points in the analysis determines the frequency precision of the result. A typical size is 1,024, giving $512 + 1$ analysis bins (the extra bin is at the Nyquist frequency). Often the interval between the analysis is $\frac{1}{4}$ of the analysis size, here 256 samples. So in this case, we will be producing one frame of 513 bins (with amp + freq) every 256 samples. For more details on how the PV algorithm works, see chapter 9.

2. One of the great things about fsigs is that we do not even need to know how the PV works in detail. All we need to know is how the data is presented to us. We know that the first pair of values in the

spectral frame correspond to the 0-Hz bin and the following pairs are in incremental frequency steps all the way to the Nyquist. Each bin has equal bandwidth, so for 1,024 points we will have 512 equal-sized bins from 0 to the $\frac{1}{2}$ sampling rate: at 44.1 KHz we have bins of $22,050/512 = 43.3$ Hz. So the lowest bin after 0 Hz will be centered at 43.3 Hz, the next one at 86.6 Hz, and so on. If we want to isolate a particular frequency band, we need only identify the correct bin.

3. Filters can be quite successfully implemented as streaming PV opcodes. For this type of application, the idea is that we will not touch the frequencies, but only change the amplitudes. The spectral envelope (the shape of the amplitude spectrum) will determine what frequencies get emphasized and what frequencies get cut off. Generally, the best method to impose a filter shape onto an input sound is by multiplying the two together. The only thing to watch out for is that the resulting amplitudes do not get out of hand. One handy way of making sure they are OK is to keep your filter amplitudes between 0 and 1 (or not too much above 1).

Algorithmic Synthesis and Music Programming

12 A Modular Synthesizer Simulation Program

Eric Lyon

In this chapter I will develop a tool for algorithmic sound design based on a digital simulation of an analog synthesizer. This is not a new idea but rather one of the oldest in computer music. Researchers at Bell Labs during the 1950s, including Max Mathews, had the fundamental insight that analog electronic circuits could be understood to be performing mathematical operations that could be modeled digitally, and then programmed and simulated on the computer. The digital signal in such programs represented analog signal flowing through analog electronic components, thus allowing engineers to model electronic circuits without physically building them. Bell Labs researchers Kelly, Lochbaum, and Vyssotsky wrote the program BLODI (block diagram) to simulate electronic circuits.[1] Mathews wrote a series of programs (Music I–V)[2] to simulate the circuitry for analog musical synthesizers, and to facilitate their use in musical composition. Thus was born the first *acoustic compiler*, with many descendents still in use today, such as Csound, cmusic, and Cmix.

12.1 Basic System Design

The basic method of analog synthesis is to patch together self-contained modules that generate or modify electronic signals into configurations with particular sound qualities. This paradigm is adopted in Csound where sound modules are replaced with unit generators, and patch cords are replaced with signal variables. This project has two parts. First we will write a very simple language that translates patch specifications into Csound orchestras. Second, we will write a program that algorithmically generates patch specifications, automating the sound design process.

There are a few reasons why we take the intermediary step of designing a patch specification language rather than directly generating Csound code. A patch language designed to represent specific Csound code configurations will be easier to use than writing the Csound code directly. This will make patch specification more convenient, thus encouraging the creation of more complex patches. Given the large number of unit generators in Csound, narrowing to the use of a small subset of available unit generators will focus the project, leading to uses of Csound that might not otherwise be attempted.

The first decision is which analog modules we wish to model and manipulate in Csound. We will start with four very basic modules: an oscillator, a filter, a sample and hold unit, and noise. We will also bear in mind that we will probably wish to add more modules as the project develops. Therefore the design of the overall program should make the addition of more modules a relatively simple matter. Let's start with the oscillator.

12.1.1   Patch Specification for an Oscillator

Primarily we can control the oscillator's waveform and its frequency. But to make things more interesting, we can add the capability to frequency modulate and amplitude modulate the oscillator. Since we may wish to use the oscillator as an LFO (low-frequency oscillator) controller for another oscillator (or some other module), we would like to be able to specify the range of its output signal (for example have it slowly vary between 500 and 550 Hz and use it as a frequency control signal). Since the oscillator will be implemented with Csound, we also need to give the name of an audio variable to hold its output.

The possible parameters to our oscillator are frequency, FM signal, AM signal, output variable, output minimum, and output maximum.

12.1.2   Designing the Interface

Consider a simple case in which the oscillator is a sine wave with a frequency of 880.0 and the output is assigned to variable a1. The Csound code will look like this:

```
a1 oscil 1.0, 880.0, isine
```

where `isine` will be defined to point to a stored sine-wave table. If we wish to frequency modulate a1 with the signal in a2, the code is not much more complex:

```
a1 oscil 1.0, 880.0 * (1.0 + a2) , isine
```

This appears to restrict us to an FM index of 1 (since presumably a2 will vary between −1 to 1), but as we will later see, this is not the case. AM with signal a2 can be implemented with

```
a1 oscil a2, 880.0, isine
```

Finally, scaling output from an oscillator to between 100 and 600 for use as an LFO at speed 7 Hz gives us this code:

```
a1 oscil 1.0, 7.0, isine
a1 = 100 + (500 * ((a1+1.) * 0.5))
```

The first part of our project will be to transform simple specifications into actual Csound code. The first decision is how to specify our oscillator. Let's assume that we will read in data a line at a time, and the first word in the line will indicate that we are calling an oscillator. (Remember we plan to implement other modules.)

The simplest approach is to decide on all the parameters we need for the oscillator, and list them in series. Let's list the data we need: output variable, frequency, waveform, AM signal, FM signal, output minimum, output maximum. So we could write

```
OSC a1 440 SINE NONE NONE −1 1
```

That is the format we will use here, since it is the simplest and we don't want to spend too much time on parsing. If our intent was to make a lot of these patches by hand rather than through automation, we might consider other formats that would allow us to only specify the required information, such as

```
OSC OUT=a1 FREQ=440
```

The ideal parser will anticipate everything that could be thrown at it, and will have an elegant and informative response to surprises. Ours, however, will be just good enough to parse data in the form we require. It will fail catastrophically if given any data that does not conform to our rigid specifications. Since we plan to ultimately generate this data from a program rather than enter it manually, this is not as irresponsible as it may seem at first glance.

12.2   Building the Code

We need to make specification conventions for each module we wish to support. We therefore need C code to read in the patch specifications, turn them into Csound code, embed this code inside a working instrument, and finally write a Csound orchestra that can synthesize the patch. We will work from the inside out, first writing code to read in lines of patch specification and convert them to Csound code. First we make a structure to contain the data we need for oscillators. We will put it in a header file called synmod.h. We also define constants for the maximum number of characters for each variable, and the maximum number of units that may be contained in a single patch:

```
#define SYNMOD_CHARS (128)
#define MAXMODS (256)

typedef struct {
    char frequency[SYNMOD_CHARS];
    char sig_out[SYNMOD_CHARS];
    char sig_am[SYNMOD_CHARS];
    char sig_fm[SYNMOD_CHARS];
    char waveform[SYNMOD_CHARS];
    char omin[SYNMOD_CHARS];
    char omax[SYNMOD_CHARS];
} OSCMOD;
```

It may seem odd that we are defining all these variables as strings, rather than floats. But this gives us greater flexibility since we can specify the frequency to be a Csound audio variable as well as a simple frequency value in hertz. We will later convert the string to a float with the sscanf() function when necessary.

Now we will write code into a file called synmod.c. First we write code to read in a patch file, line by line. If the module is an OSC, we read the rest of the data. We use the C function strcmp() to check if the two strings match. This function returns a **false** value (zero) when its two arguments match. For now all the modules will be OSCs. We also print the data to assure that we read it correctly.

```c
#include <stdio.h>
#include <stdlib.h>
#include "synmod.h"

main(int argc, char **argv)
{
    OSCMOD *oscs;
    int osc_count = 0;
    char modname[64];

    oscs = (OSCMOD *) malloc(MAXMODS * sizeof(OSCMOD));

    while(scanf("%s", modname) != EOF){
        if(! strcmp(modname, "OSC")){
            /* READ IN THE DATA */
            scanf("%s", oscs[osc_count].sig_out);
            scanf("%s", oscs[osc_count].frequency);
            scanf("%s", oscs[osc_count].waveform);
            scanf("%s", oscs[osc_count].sig_am);
            scanf("%s", oscs[osc_count].sig_fm);
            scanf("%s", oscs[osc_count].omin);
            scanf("%s", oscs[osc_count].omax);

            /* PRINT IT TO MAKE SURE IT'S OK */

            printf("%s %s %s %s %s %s %s\n",
                oscs[osc_count].sig_out,oscs[osc_count].frequency,
                oscs[osc_count].waveform, oscs[osc_count].sig_am,
                oscs[osc_count].sig_fm,oscs[osc_count].omin,
                oscs[osc_count].omax);
            ++osc_count;
        }
    }
}
```

12.2.1   Introducing the Command-Line Interface

We will be using *synmod* within a command-line interface (CLI), a rawer interface than the GUI that is found on Max/MSP and most other modern music programs. The interface to the CLI is text; you type commands at a prompt. Although the CLI is relatively primitive, in some cases it is possible to accomplish tasks faster by typing into a CLI than by manipulating a mouse over a GUI. In Mac OS X, the CLI is accessed with the program Terminal, which is found in the Utilities sub-folder of Applications. Most of work of this chapter will be consist of typing commands into a terminal window.

Compile *synmod* by running the gcc compiler in a terminal window as shown below. You must be in the same directory where you created the `synmod.c` file. This will create an executable program file called synmod[3]:

```
$ gcc —o synmod synmod.c
```

Write the following data into a file called mpatch1, using your favorite text editor[4]:

```
OSC a1 440 SINE NONE NONE -1 1
OSC a2 770 SINE NONE NONE -1 1
```

Now test the program[5]:

```
$ synmod < mpatch1
a1 440 SINE NONE NONE —1 1
a2 770 SINE NONE NONE —1 1
```

Here < is the UNIX redirect symbol, which in this case means take the data in the file *mpatch* and use it as input to the *synmod* program.[6]

12.3   Tightening the Structure and Making It Safer

If there are more than 256 OSCS in the patch file, this program will fail. This could be prevented by checking if we are at the limit, and if so, allocating more memory with `realloc()`. We will take the middle path and simply shut down the program if more that 256 OSCS are requested. In the current form of the program, reading in the data will clutter up the main program loop. This will be worse if we decide to do some checking on the data. Therefore, we will rewrite the program to localize data reading into a function call[7]:

```
void read_osc(OSCMOD *oscs, int count)
{
    scanf("%s %s %s %s %s %s %s",oscs[count].sig_out,
        oscs[count].frequency, oscs[count].waveform,
        oscs[count].sig_am, oscs[count].sig_fm,
        oscs[count].omin, oscs[count].omax);
```

```
    if(count >= MAXMODS){
        fprintf(stderr,
                "Number of oscillators has exceeded maximum: %d\n",
                MAXMODS);
        exit(1);
    }
}
```

We must put the function prototype into `synmod.h`:

```
void read_osc(OSCMOD *oscs, int count);
```

We also need a function to write the Csound code for each stored oscillator. We'll call it `print_osc()`. We will support some basic waveforms, all of which can easily be generated with the Csound GEN10 function:

```
void print_osc(OSCMOD osc)
{
    float omin, omax;
    float mo2;
    printf("%s oscil ", osc.sig_out);
    if(!strcmp(osc.sig_am, "NONE")){
        printf("1.0, ");
    } else {
        printf("%s, ", osc.sig_am);
    }
    if(!strcmp(osc.sig_fm, "NONE")){
        printf("%s, ", osc.frequency);
    } else {
        printf("%s * (1.0 + %s), ",osc.frequency, osc.sig_fm);
    }
    if(!strcmp(osc.waveform, "SINE")){
        printf("isine\n");
    }
    else if(!strcmp(osc.waveform, "TRIANGLE")) {
        printf("itriangle\n");
    }
    else if(!strcmp(osc.waveform, "SAWTOOTH")){
        printf("isawtooth\n");
    }
    else if(!strcmp(osc.waveform, "SQUARE")){
        printf("isquare\n");
    }
```

```
    else if(!strcmp(osc.waveform, "PULSE")){
        printf("ipulse\n");
    }
    else {
        fprintf(stderr,"print_osc: %s is unknown"
                        "- using sine instead\n",osc.waveform);
        printf("isine\n");
    }
    sscanf(osc.omin,"%f",&omin); // convert strings to floats
    sscanf(osc.omax,"%f",&omax);
    if(omin != -1.0 || omax != 1.0){ // rescale output if necessary
        mo2 = (omax - omin) / 2.0;
        printf("%s = %s + (%f*%s + %f)\n",
                osc.sig_out, osc.omin, mo2, osc.sig_out, mo2);
    }
}
```

You should add the function prototype of print_osc to synmod.h as we did for the prototype to read_osc().

We finally rewrite the main program as shown below. Notice how we avoid clutter in the main program by moving the nitty-gritty action elsewhere. In anticipation of different kinds of unit generators, we have added a test for an opcode at the beginning of the line. At present we only test for OSC, but that will soon change.

```
main(int argc, char **argv)
{
    OSCMOD *oscs;
    int osc_count = 0;
    char modname[64];
    int i;

    oscs = (OSCMOD *) malloc(MAXMODS * sizeof(OSCMOD));

    while(scanf("%s", modname) != EOF){
        if(!strcmp(modname, "OSC")){
            read_osc(oscs, osc_count++);
        } else {
            fprintf(stderr,"%s is an unknown module\n", modname);
        }
    }
    for(i = 0; i < osc_count; i++){
        print_osc(oscs[i]);
    }
}
```

Having changed our line parsing scheme, we now need to change our `mpatch2` file to read as follows:

```
OSC a1 440 SINE NONE NONE -1 1
OSC a2 770 SINE NONE NONE -1 1
```

At this point we can test the program to see if it is spitting out valid Csound code. The output

```
$ synmod < mpatch1
a1 oscil 1.0, 440, isine
a2 oscil 1.0, 770, isine
```

is exactly what we hoped to see. Now let's test the FM and AM. Put the following data into a file called `mpatch2`.

```
OSC a1 440 SINE NONE NONE -1 1
OSC a2 770 SINE a1 NONE -1 1
OSC a3 330 TRIANGLE NONE a2 -1 1
```

```
$ synmod < mpatch2
a1 oscil 1.0, 440, isine
a2 oscil a1, 770, isine
a3 oscil 1.0, 330 * (1.0 + a2), itriangle
```

and test the remapping capability with the following data in `mpatch3`:

```
OSC a1 3.0 SINE NONE NONE 440 660
OSC a2 a1 SINE NONE NONE -1 1
```

```
$ synmod < mpatch3
a1 oscil 1.0, 3.0, isine
a1 = 440 + (110.000000*a1 + 110.000000)
a2 oscil 1.0, a1, isine
```

All that is needed to turn this into a working Csound instrument is an output statement.[8] We need to specify that in our patchfile, so we will make another module called MIXOUT with this simple format:

```
MIXOUT variable amplitude
```

We add a MIXOUT struct to the header file `synmod.h`:

```
typedef struct {
    char outvar[SYNMOD_CHARS];
    char amplitude[SYNMOD_CHARS];
} MIXOUT;
```

We now create functions to read and write the `MIXOUT` module. To avoid annoying clicks, we will apply a simple envelope as part of the mix print function:

```
void read_mix(MIXOUT *mix, int count )
{
    scanf("%s %s", mix[count].outvar, mix[count].amplitude );
}

void print_mix( MIXOUT mix )
{
    float amp;
    sscanf(mix.amplitude, "%f", &amp);
    printf ("kenv linseg 0,.05,%f,p3-0.1,%f,.05,0\n",amp, amp);
    printf("out (%s)*kenv\n", mix.outvar);
}
```

Note the parentheses around the output variable. This enables us to use expressions like a1+a2 as output, in order to mix out more than one variable at a time.

Add the prototypes to synmod.h:

```
void read_mix(MIXOUT *mix, int count);
void print_mix(MIXOUT mix);
```

Finally, update the main function to allocate space for the MIXOUT modules, and scan for a MIXOUT opcode in addition to scanning for OSC:

```
main(int argc, char **argv)
{

    OSCMOD *oscs;
    MIXOUT *mixes;

    int osc_count = 0;
    int mix_count = 0;
    char modname[64];
    int i;

    oscs = (OSCMOD *) malloc(MAXMODS * sizeof(OSCMOD));
    mixes = (MIXOUT *) malloc(MAXMODS * sizeof(MIXOUT));

    while(scanf("%s", modname) != EOF){
        if(! strcmp(modname, "OSC")){
            read_osc(oscs, osc_count++);
        }
        else if(! strcmp(modname, "MIXOUT")){
            read_mix(mixes, mix_count++);
        } else {
            fprintf(stderr,"%s is an unknown module\n", modname);
        }
    }
```

```
    for(i = 0; i < osc_count; i++){
        print_osc(oscs[i]);
    }
    for(i = 0; i < mix_count; i++){
        print_mix(mixes[i]);
    }
}
```

Add a mixout line to `mpatch3`:

```
OSC a1 3.0 SINE NONE NONE 440 660
OSC a2 a1 SINE NONE NONE -1 1
MIXOUT a2 5000
```

Compile and test:

```
$ synmod < mpatch3
a1 oscil 1.0, 3.0, isine
a1 = 440 + (110.000000*a1 + 110.000000)
a2 oscil 1.0, a1, isine
kenv linseg 0,.05,5000.000000,p3-0.1,5000.000000,.05,0
out (a2)*kenv
```

Everything seems to work as intended. The next step is to wrap all of these ideas up in a working Csound orchestra.

12.4 Writing the Csound Wrapper Code

Originally Csound code was divided between an "orchestra" file containing synthesis instrument definitions and a "score" file containing calls to those instruments. We will find it more convenient to use the Unified File Format, designed by Michael Gogins, that combines orchestra and score information into a single file.[9]

We will create two new functions, `print_header()` and `print_score()`, that when combined with the main program will write a functioning `.csd` file to `stdout`:

```
void print_header(void)
{
    printf("<CsoundSynthesizer>\n\n");
    printf("sr = 44100\n");
    printf("kr = 4410\n");
    printf("ksmps = 10\n");
    printf("nchnls = 1\n\n");
    printf("<CsInstruments>\n\n");
    printf("\tinstr 1\n");
    printf("isine = 1\n");
```

```
    printf("itriangle = 2\n");
    printf("isawtooth = 3\n");
    printf("isquare = 4\n");
    printf("ipulse = 5\n");
}
```

The score will have a duration parameter to specify the length of the note:

```
void print_score(float duration)
{
    printf("\tendin\n\n");
    printf("</CsInstruments>\n");
    printf("<CsScore>\n\n");
    printf("f1 0 8192 10 1 ; sine\n");
    printf("f2 0 8192 10 1 0 .111 0 .04 0 .02 0 ; triangle\n");
    printf("f3 0 8192 10 1 .5 .333 .25 .2 .166 .142 .125 ;
            sawtooth\n");
    printf("f4 0 8192 10 1 0 .333 0 .2 0 .142 0 .111; square\n");
    printf("f5 0 8192 10 1 1 1 1 1 1 1 1 1 1 1 1 1; pulse\n\n");
    printf("i1 0 %f\n\n", duration);
    printf("</CsScore>\n");
    printf("</CsoundSynthesizer>\n");
}
```

As before, you will have to add function prototypes to the header file synmod.h. I will assume that you now know how to do this by yourself.

We now sandwich our main code generation with calls to the header and score functions:

```
/* WRITE .csd FILE FOR CSOUND */
print_header();

for(i = 0; i < osc_count; i++){
    print_osc(oscs[i]);
}
for(i = 0; i < mix_count; i++){
    print_mix(mixes[i]);
}

print_score(10.0); /* TEN SECOND NOTE */
```

The entire main function now looks as follows:

```
main(int argc, char **argv)
{
    OSCMOD *oscs;
    MIXOUT *mixes;
```

```
    int osc_count = 0;
    int mix_count = 0;
    char modname[64];
    int i;

    oscs = (OSCMOD *) malloc(MAXMODS * sizeof(OSCMOD));
    mixes = (MIXOUT *) malloc(MAXMODS * sizeof(MIXOUT));

    /* WRITE .csd FILE FOR CSOUND */
    print_header();

    while(scanf("%s", modname) != EOF){
        if(! strcmp(modname, "OSC")){
            read_osc(oscs, osc_count++);
        }
        else if(! strcmp(modname, "MIXOUT")){
            read_mix(mixes, mix_count++);
        } else {
            fprintf(stderr,"%s is an unknown module\n", modname);
        }
    }

    for(i = 0; i < osc_count; i++){
        print_osc(oscs[i]);
    }
    for(i = 0; i < mix_count; i++){
        print_mix(mixes[i]);
    }
    print_score(10.0); /* TEN SECOND NOTE */
}
```

Compile synmod yet again. At this point, the code will generate a working Csound .csd file. Type the following into a file called mpatch4:

```
OSC a1 100 PULSE NONE NONE -1 1
OSC a2 100.1 PULSE NONE NONE -1 1
OSC a3 100.2 PULSE NONE NONE -1 1
OSC a4 100.3 PULSE NONE NONE -1 1
OSC a5 100.4 PULSE NONE NONE -1 1
OSC a6 100.5 PULSE NONE NONE -1 1
MIXOUT a1+a2+a3+a4+a5+a6 2000
```

Look at the output:

```
$ synmod < mpatch4
synmod < mpatch4
<CsoundSynthesizer>
```

```
sr = 44100
kr = 4410
ksmps = 10
nchnls = 1

<CsInstruments>

    instr 1
isine = 1
itriangle = 2
isawtooth = 3
isquare = 4
ipulse = 5
a1 oscil 1.0, 100, ipulse
a2 oscil 1.0, 100.1, ipulse
a3 oscil 1.0, 100.2, ipulse
a4 oscil 1.0, 100.3, ipulse
a5 oscil 1.0, 100.4, ipulse
a6 oscil 1.0, 100.5, ipulse
kenv linseg 0,.05,2000.000000,p3-0.1,2000.000000,.05,0
out (a1+a2+a3+a4+a5+a6)*kenv
    endin

</CsInstruments>
<CsScore>

f1 0 8192 10 1 ; sine
f2 0 8192 10 1 0 .111 0 .04 0 .02 0 ; triangle
f3 0 8192 10 1 .5 .333 .25 .2 .166 .142 .125 ; sawtooth
f4 0 8192 10 1 0 .333 0 .2 0 .142 0 .111; square
f5 0 8192 10 1 1 1 1 1 1 1 1 1 1 1 1 1; pulse

i1 0 10.000000

</CsScore>
</CsoundSynthesizer>
```

Route the output to a .csd file. The UNIX redirect symbol ">" here means "send the output from *synmod* into a new file called mpatch4.csd which will be created, or written over if it already exists"[10]:

```
$ synmod < mpatch4 > mpatch4.csd
```

Run Csound[11] on this file. We will use the CLI version of Csound here. For convenience we will write the output to the DACs of your computer with the —odac flag, effectively generating the sound in real time.

```
$ csound -odac mpatch4.csd
```

You should hear a flanging effect as the detuned harmonics gradually reinforce or cancel each other. Now would be a good time to take a break and play around with some patches. Here are a few ideas to get you started.

FM:

```
OSC a1 0.25 SINE NONE NONE 0.1 1
OSC a2 102 SINE a1 NONE -8 8
OSC a3 100 SINE NONE a2 -1 1
MIXOUT a3 10000
```

Tonal:

```
OSC a1 4.76 SINE NONE NONE 0.6 1
OSC a2 5.33 SINE NONE NONE 0.6 1
OSC a3 3.15 SINE NONE NONE 0.6 1
OSC a4 7.54 SINE NONE NONE 0.6 1
OSC a5 4.78 SINE NONE NONE 0.6 1
OSC av1 7.56 SINE NONE NONE -.01 .01
OSC av2 7.08 SINE NONE NONE -.01 .01
OSC av3 5.26 SINE NONE NONE -.01 .01
OSC av4 3.82 SINE NONE NONE -.01 .01
OSC av5 6.85 SINE NONE NONE -.01 .01
OSC a6 261.6256 TRIANGLE a1 av1 -1 1
OSC a7 329.6276 SAWTOOTH a2 av2 -1 1
OSC a8 391.9954 SQUARE a3 av3 -1 1
OSC a9 493.8833 SAWTOOTH a4 av4 -1 1
OSC a10 587.3295 TRIANGLE a5 av5 -1 1
MIXOUT a6+a7+a8+a9+a10 2000
```

More complex:

```
OSC atr1 .15 SINE NONE NONE 0.6 1.0
OSC a1 131 SINE atr1 NONE -25 25
OSC a2 93.3 SAWTOOTH NONE atr1 0.6 1
OSC a3 200.5 TRIANGLE a2 a1 -1 1
OSC a4 17.1 SQUARE a2 a1 -1 1
MIXOUT a3+a4 5000
```

12.5   Enabling Oscillator Feedback

One attractive feature of analog oscillators that we lack at present is the ability to route the output of an oscillator back into itself or into another oscillator that controls it. Routing a signal output to its input is called feedback. Csound is capable of implementing oscillator feedback, with a few small modifications to the current orchestra. First we must change the local a variables to global variables. In order to use global variables with feedback, they must first be initialized. This requires a small bit of additional code. We will write a function to generate this initialization code, called `initialize_globals()`. We will later modify this function to initialize other global variables as well.

```
void initialize_globals(OSCMOD *oscs, int osc_count)
{
    int i;
    for(i = 0; i < osc_count; i++){
        printf("%s init 0.0\n", oscs[i].sig_out);
    }
}
```

Add this function to the code file, and its prototype to the header file.[12] This function will get called in `main()` just before we call `print_oscs()`. Here is the new `main()` function:

```
main(int argc, char **argv)
{
    OSCMOD *oscs;
    MIXOUT *mixes;

    int osc_count = 0;
    int mix_count = 0;
    char modname[64];
    int i;

    oscs = (OSCMOD *) malloc(MAXMODS * sizeof(OSCMOD));
    mixes = (MIXOUT *) malloc(MAXMODS * sizeof(MIXOUT));

    print_header();
    initialize_globals(oscs, osc_count);

    while(scanf("%s", modname) != EOF){
        if(! strcmp(modname, "OSC")){
            read_osc(oscs, osc_count++);
        }
        else if(! strcmp(modname, "MIXOUT")){
            read_mix(mixes, mix_count++);
        } else {
            fprintf(stderr,"%s is an unknown module\n", modname);
        }
    }

    for(i = 0; i < osc_count; i++){
        print_osc(oscs[i]);
    }
}
```

```
    for(i = 0; i < mix_count; i++){
        print_mix(mixes[i]);
    }
    print_score(10.0);
}
```

Here is a simple patch that utilizes feedback. We are now using global audio variables in the patch. Try this with the new version of synmod.

```
OSC ga1 100 SINE NONE ga2 -1 1
OSC ga2 113 SINE NONE ga1 -1 1
MIXOUT ga2 20000
```

More complex configurations yield more complex behavior.

```
OSC ga1 450 SINE NONE ga4 -1 1
OSC ga2 1.41 SINE NONE ga1 -1 1
OSC ga3 6.5 SINE NONE ga2 -1 1
OSC ga4 1001.15 SINE NONE ga3 -1 1
MIXOUT ga1 20000
```

A longer duration would be preferable for this patch. Rather than hard coding the duration, we will add an opcode called DURATION, so that duration may be set from inside the patch.[13] Here is our updated main() function. Since we are not adding any new functions, we do not have to update the header file this time.

```
main(int argc, char **argv)
{
    OSCMOD *oscs;
    MIXOUT *mixes;

    int osc_count = 0;
    int mix_count = 0;
    char modname[64];
    int i;
    float duration = 10.0; /* Our default duration is 10 seconds */

    oscs = (OSCMOD *) malloc(MAXMODS * sizeof(OSCMOD));
    mixes = (MIXOUT *) malloc(MAXMODS * sizeof(MIXOUT));

    print_header();

    while(scanf("%s", modname) != EOF){
        if(! strcmp(modname, "OSC")){
            read_osc(oscs, osc_count++);
        }
        else if(! strcmp(modname, "MIXOUT")){
            read_mix(mixes, mix_count++);
```

```
        }
        /* Now we scan for duration too */
        else if(! strcmp(modname, "DURATION")){
            scanf("%f", &duration);
        }
        else {
            fprintf(stderr,"%s is an unknown module\n", modname);
        }
    }

    initialize_globals(oscs, osc_count);

    for(i = 0; i < osc_count; i++){
        print_osc(oscs[i]);
    }
    for(i = 0; i < mix_count; i++){
        print_mix(mixes[i]);
    }
    /* now we use our duration variable, but we do not have to
    change print_score() since we planned ahead! */
    print_score(duration);
}
```

We can now revisit that last patch:

```
DURATION 30
OSC ga1 450 SINE NONE ga4 -1 1
OSC ga2 1.41 SINE NONE ga1 -1 1
OSC ga3 6.5 SINE NONE ga2 -1 1
OSC ga4 1001.15 SINE NONE ga3 -1 1
MIXOUT ga1 20000
```

12.6   Adding Noise

Most of the hard work on this part of the project is done. We need only add a few more module types, following the existing model of the oscillator module. Each new addition will increase the variety of possible sounds that can be teased from our algorithmic sound design strategy.

Next we will add a module for interpolated noise.[14] This will be useful both as an audio signal and as a control source. We must specify the Csound variable name, the speed of change, the random seed, and output minimum and maximum values. For example:

```
NOISE ga1 4.5 .111 -1 1
```

Here is the structure, which will go into the header file:

```
typedef struct {
    char speed[SYNMOD_CHARS];
    char sig_out[SYNMOD_CHARS];
    char seed[SYNMOD_CHARS];
    char omin[SYNMOD_CHARS];
    char omax[SYNMOD_CHARS];
} NOISEMOD;
```

Definition and allocation:

```
NOISEMOD *noises;
int noise_count = 0;
. . .
noises = (NOISEMOD *) malloc( MAXMODS * sizeof(NOISEMOD));
```

Functions:

```
void read_noise(NOISEMOD *unit, int count)
{
    scanf("%s %s %s %s %s", unit[count].sig_out unit[count].speed,
            unit[count].seed, unit[count].omin, unit[count].omax);
}

void print_noise(NOISEMOD noise)
{
    float omin, omax, mo2;

    printf("%s randi 1.0, %s, %s\n", noise.sig_out, noise.speed,
                noise.seed);
    sscanf(noise.omin,"%f",&omin); // convert strings to floats
    sscanf(noise.omax,"%f",&omax);

    if(omin != -1.0 || omax != 1.0){
        mo2 = (omax - omin) / 2.0;
        printf("%s = %s + (%f*%s + %f)\n", noise.sig_out,
                noise.omin, mo2, noise.sig_out, mo2);
    }
}
```

The slightly difficult part is that we will now need to modify the initialize_globals() function and function call as follows:

```
initialize_globals(oscs, osc_count, noises, noise_count);

void initialize_globals(OSCMOD *oscs, int osc_count, NOISEMOD
                        *noises, int noise_count)
{
    int i;
```

```
    for(i = 0; i < osc_count; i++){
        printf("%s init 0.0\n", oscs[i].sig_out);
    }
    for(i = 0; i < noise_count; i++){
        printf("%s init 0.0\n", noises[i].sig_out);
    }
}
```

Now that we have changed the `initialize_globals()` function, we must also change its prototype in the header file. At this point, you should be able to rewrite the `main()` function on your own. Try doing so before reading further.

The updated `main()` function is as follows:

```
main(int argc, char **argv)
{

    OSCMOD *oscs;
    MIXOUT *mixes;
    NOISEMOD *noises; /* We now define a pointer for the noise
                         modules here. */

    int osc_count = 0;
    int mix_count = 0;
    int noise_count = 0; /* We now keep count of noise modules. */
    char modname[64];
    int i;
    float duration = 10.0;

    oscs = (OSCMOD *) malloc(MAXMODS * sizeof(OSCMOD));
    mixes = (MIXOUT *) malloc(MAXMODS * sizeof(MIXOUT));
    /* Here is our new allocation call */
    noises = (NOISEMOD *) malloc( MAXMODS * sizeof(NOISEMOD));

    print_header();

    while(scanf("%s", modname) != EOF){
        if(! strcmp(modname, "OSC")){
            read_osc(oscs, osc_count++);
        }
        /* Notice that we put noise before the MIXOUT. Otherwise
        the noise would not be mixed out. */
        else if(! strcmp(modname, "NOISE")){
            read_noise(noises, noise_count++);
        }
        else if(! strcmp(modname, "MIXOUT")){
            read_mix(mixes, mix_count++);
```

```
        }
        else if(! strcmp(modname, "DURATION")){
            scanf("%f", &duration);
        }
        else {
            fprintf(stderr,"%s is an unknown module\n", modname);
        }
    }
    /* Our call to initialize_globals now initializes noise too. */
    initialize_globals(oscs, osc_count, noises, noise_count);

    for(i = 0; i < osc_count; i++){
        print_osc(oscs[i]);
    }
    /* We print the noise here: */
    for(i = 0; i < noise_count; i++){
        print_noise(noises[i]);
    }
    for(i = 0; i < mix_count; i++){
        print_mix(mixes[i]);
    }
 print_score(duration);
}
```

Here are a few patch files you can use to test the NOISE opcode.

Simple random control of oscillator frequency:

```
DURATION 15
NOISE ga1 2.5 .222 57 670
OSC ga2 ga1 SAWTOOTH NONE NONE -1 1
MIXOUT ga2 10000
```

Interpolated noise modulation of a sine wave creates a formant region centered on the sine frequency:

```
NOISE ga1 100 .222 -1 1
OSC ga2 380 SINE ga1 NONE -1 1
MIXOUT ga2 10000
```

Here is a patch where similar noise units gradually go out of phase:

```
DURATION 30
NOISE ga1a 6.0 .522 80 1200
NOISE ga1b 6.15 .522 80 1200
NOISE ga1c 6.3 .522 80 1200
OSC ga2 ga1a TRIANGLE NONE NONE -1 1
```

```
OSC ga3 ga1b TRIANGLE NONE NONE -1 1
OSC ga4 ga1c TRIANGLE NONE NONE -1 1
MIXOUT ga2+ga3+ga4 7000
```

12.7   Sample and Hold

Now let us quickly build a sample and hold unit.[15] It is essentially the same as the NOISE unit, except without interpolation between random values. In fact the only difference is that we use Csound opcode *randh* rather than *randi* so we'll be able to reuse most of the NOISE code. We'll use the label SAH for these sample-and-hold units.

We just require a print_sah() function. We can use the NOISE structure.

```
void print_sah(NOISEMOD noise)
{
    float omin, omax, mo2;

    printf("%s randh 1.0, %s, %s\n", noise.sig_out, noise.speed,
            noise.seed);
    sscanf(noise.omin,"%f",&omin); // convert strings to floats
    sscanf(noise.omax,"%f",&omax);

    if(omin != -1.0 || omax != 1.0){
        mo2 = (omax - omin) / 2.0;
        printf("%s = %s + (%f*%s + %f)\n",
                noise.sig_out, noise.omin, mo2, noise.sig_out, mo2);
    }
}
```

We add this code in the appropriate places. We will use the function read_noise() to get data for the SAH, since the input formats for SAH and NOISE are identical.

```
else if(! strcmp(modname, "SAH")){
        read_noise(sahs, sah_count++);
}
. . .
for(i = 0; i < sah_count; i++){
    print_sah(sahs[i]);
}
```

We must, of course, create new variables and allocate memory as well.

```
NOISEMOD *sahs;
int sah_count = 0;
sahs = (NOISEMOD *) malloc(MAXMODS *sizeof(NOISEMOD));
```

Finally, we have to update the initialize_globals() function, and its prototype in the header file.

```
void initialize_globals(OSCMOD *oscs, int osc_count, NOISEMOD *noises,
                        int noise_count, NOISEMOD *sahs, int sah_count)
{
    int i;

    for(i = 0; i < osc_count; i++){
        printf("%s init 0.0\n", oscs[i].sig_out);
    }
    for(i = 0; i < noise_count; i++){
        printf("%s init 0.0\n", noises[i].sig_out);
    }
    for(i = 0; i < sah_count; i++){
        printf("%s init 0.0\n", sahs[i].sig_out);
    }
}
```

This time I will not show you the updated main() function, but if you get stuck you can find it on the DVD.

We can test with the last patch, replacing the NOISEs with SAHs.

```
DURATION 30
SAH ga1a 6.0 .522 80 1200
SAH ga1b 6.15 .522 80 1200
SAH ga1c 6.3 .522 80 1200
OSC ga2 ga1a TRIANGLE NONE NONE -1 1
OSC ga3 ga1b TRIANGLE NONE NONE -1 1
OSC ga4 ga1c TRIANGLE NONE NONE -1 1
MIXOUT ga2+ga3+ga4 7000
```

It's also fun to add SAH units together to create terraced melodies:

```
DURATION 30
SAH ga1 6.0 .522 20 150
SAH ga2 7.15 .499 20 200
SAH ga3 1.33 .131 20 500
OSC ga4 ga1+ga2+ga3 SQUARE NONE NONE -1 1
MIXOUT ga4 10000
```

or sum and difference melodies:

```
DURATION 30
SAH ga1 1.45 .332 20 150
SAH ga2 2.73 .619 20 200
OSC ga3 ga1+ga2 SQUARE NONE NONE -1 1
OSC ga4 ga1-ga2 SQUARE NONE NONE -1 1
MIXOUT ga3+ga4 10000
```

12.8   Adding the Filter

A modular synthesizer would be somewhat lacking without a filter. Csound has many attractive filters to choose from. We will use the *moogvcf* filter for sentimental reasons, as it is based on an analog filter from the Moog synthesizer. The two main parameters are cutoff frequency and resonance. The format will be

```
VCF OUTPUT INPUT CUTOFF RESONANCE
```

At this point, you should be able to fully implement the new opcode on your own.[16] As a simple test we can use an SAH to filter noise with a fairly high resonance. For *moogvcf*, 1.0 is the maximum resonance. Here is an example:

```
DURATION 20
SAH ga1 7.45 .1384 200 1400
NOISE ga2 8000 .1 -1 1
VCF ga3 ga2 ga1 0.98
MIXOUT ga3 10000
```

Below is a fixed chord with three randomly sweeping filters:

```
DURATION 30
OSC ga1 100 SAWTOOTH NONE NONE -1 1
OSC ga2 125.1 SAWTOOTH NONE NONE -1 1
OSC ga3 150.25 SAWTOOTH NONE NONE -1 1
OSC ga4 187.6 SAWTOOTH NONE NONE -1 1
OSC ga5 225.8 SAWTOOTH NONE NONE -1 1
NOISE ga6 1.5 .845 100 1500
VCF ga7 (ga1+ga2+ga3+ga4+ga5)*0.2 ga6 0.9
NOISE ga8 0.3 .225 100 1500
VCF ga9 (ga1+ga2+ga3+ga4+ga5)*0.2 ga8 0.9
NOISE ga10 0.3 .125 400 2500
VCF ga11 (ga1+ga2+ga3+ga4+ga5)*0.2 ga10 0.9
MIXOUT ga7+ga9+ga11 10000
```

To summarize, here are the input formats for all the modules we wrote.

OSC OUTPUT FREQUENCY WAVEFORM AM FM OUTMIN OUTMAX
NOISE OUTPUT SPEED SEED OUTMIN OUTMAX
SAH OUTPUT SPEED SEED OUTMIN OUTMAX
VCF OUTPUT INPUT CUTOFF RESONANCE
MIXOUT OUTPUT AMPLITUDE
DURATION DURATION

The available waveforms are SINE, TRIANGLE, SAWTOOTH, SQUARE, and PULSE.

Conclusion

This concludes the first part of the project, but there is more on the DVD. For now, consider what other Csound units might be useful to add to this program. What are some of the limitations of this model? How could you improve on it? Finally, experiment with creating patches by hand. That will give you a good feel for what is possible with *synmod*.

After you finish exploring the musical use of your own additions to the basic *synmod* system in this chapter, you can learn to add more features and functionality to the *synmod* system from the DVD chapters Algorithmic Patch Design for Synmod and Algorithmic Sound Design.

Notes

1. J. Kelly, C. Lochbaum, and V. Vyssotsky, "A Block Diagram Compiler," *Bell System Technical Journal* 40 (1961): 669–676.

2. M. Mathews, "An Acoustic Compiler for Music and Psychological Stimuli," *Bell System Technical Journal* 40 (1961): 677–694.

3. The dollar sign ($) is a typical UNIX "prompt." You may see a different prompt, depending on how your system is configured. The prompt appears at the leftmost point in the input line of your terminal window. It means "type text here."

4. We can do this a bit faster in UNIX by redirecting text into a new file with the `cat` command, rather than firing up a text editor. First type $ `cat > mpatch1`. Then type

```
OSC a1 440 SINE NONE NONE -1 1
OSC a2 770 SINE NONE NONE -1 1
```

Finally, type control-D to close and save the file. (Control-D means hold down the control key and then press d.)

5. The working code and patches can be found on the DVD.

6. There is a small chance that when you try to execute `synmod` above you may receive the following warning: `synmod: Command not found`. What this means is that the shell that your terminal is running could not find *synmod* even though it is in the current directory. The shell is the command interpreter run by the Terminal application. You may not have control over what shell is initially launched as that decision might have been made by your sysadmin. There are two solutions if you run into this problem. The first is to type $ `tcsh`. That will bring up the `tcsh` that is smart enough to find executables in the current directory. Alternatively, each time you execute `synmod`, you can type $ `./synmod`. Here `./` refers to the current directory and removes any potential ambiguity about the location of the desired file.

7. This next modification and refinement of our code and patches can be found on the DVD.

8. This `MIXER` modification and refinement of our code and patches can be found on the DVD.

9. A description of this format is available at http://www.csounds.com/manual/html/CommandUnifile .html.

10. This ADDITIVE and FM modification and refinement of our code and patches can be found on the DVD.

11. If you are reading this book, you almost certainly have Csound installed on your computer. But just in case you don't, the current version of Csound can be downloaded from http://www.csounds.com/, where you can find the version of Csound most appropriate to your computer and OS.

12. This OSCILLATOR FEEDBACK modification and refinement of our code and patches can be found on the DVD.

13. This DURATION modification and refinement of our code and patches can be found on the DVD.

14. This INTERPOLATED NOISE modification and refinement of our code and patches can be found on the DVD.

15. This SAMPLE AND HOLD modification and refinement of our code and patches can be found on the DVD.

16. If you run into any snags, you can find this final FILTER modification and refinement of our code on the DVD.

13 Using C to Generate Scores

John ffitch

This chapter is a case study in algorithmic composition, following the development of a piece from initial concept to first completion—one hesitates to say that the work is complete. The computation will be done in C, generating a Csound score that can be rendered out of real time. Before continuing it is worth noting that there are more complex systems available. Csound, in fact, has had a library of manipulation functions collectively called Cscore since its beginning. Rather than using one of these systems we are going to develop our own low-level C code as the composition and compositional ideas develop.

13.1 The Musical Concept

In order to be definite rather than general, we are going to consider a piece from my *Drums and Different Canons* (table 13.1). These pieces are explorations of the cyclical nature of certain classes of differential equations—cycles that do not repeat exactly. From that it should be clear that there are two significant components of the process; the first is to generate the raw stream of values from the differential equation and the second is to map these onto musical events, as exemplified by a Csound score. We are not directly concerned with sound design in this project, and so we will borrow Csound instruments from others. It would be possible to use the raw data stream to generate audio directly, but this is not done here.

The piece we are going to develop is number 4 in the sequence, *Unbounded Space*. We will not necessarily follow the exact path of the composer, but it will be sufficiently close for the relationship between the programming, the concept and the music to be audible. For this piece, the Csound instruments are taken from Richard Boulanger's *Trapped in Convert*, a fine set of sounds that Boulanger has continued to explore in works like *At Last, Free. . . .* The main data source was decided *a priori* to be the *Henon* difference equation, which was used for the first in the series. These decisions leave a great deal to be determined as the work develops. We have decided to explore the near-cyclical behavior using Boulanger's sound design. Questions not yet raised include: pitch system, duration, selection of individual events and many more details.

Table 13.1
Catalog of *Drums and Different Canon* works.

Year	Number	Title	Length
1996	1	*Henon, Gruneberg, Distance*	7:00
2000	2	*Stalactite*	7:37
2001	3	*For Connie (Piano)*	4:00
2002	4	*Unbounded Space*	6:50
2002–03	5	*Charles á Nuit*	5:00

We will start by considering the raw data stream, and then explore various mappings of this to events.

13.2   The Raw Process

The basis of a whole family of algorithmic compositions is some mathematical (or other) process that generates an infinite stream of numbers. There are a large number of such processes, but for interesting music one needs the process not to just cycle through the same values. This is at the heart of the interest in chaotic processes for artistic use. These chaotic processes divide into two main groups: differential equations and difference equations. They are in fact very closely related as we can see.

Consider the (non-chaotic) equation

$$x'' = -x, \tag{1}$$

which can be recast as a pair of coupled equations by defining $y = x'$, we have

$$x' = y \tag{2}$$

and

$$y' = -x. \tag{3}$$

We need to develop a small C function that, every time it is called, delivers (x, y) pairs of values. (This is not the correct place to start to teach the intricacies of numerical analysis. There are a great number of unexpected problems in numerical calculations, and a full treatment requires some sophistication in linear algebra and other areas of mathematics.[1]) In this case we will use a simple technique. Recall that the meaning of a derivative dx/dt is the gradient (slope, tangent) of the function x at some time t. If we take a small time $\delta\tau$ and draw a chord to the function from its value at times τ and $\tau + \delta\tau$ then we have an approximation to the tangent. (See figure 13.1.)

As $\delta\tau$ gets smaller, the chord gets closer to the tangent. The slope of the chord is

$$x' \approx \frac{x(\tau + \delta\tau) - x(\tau)}{(\tau + \delta\tau) - \tau}. \tag{4}$$

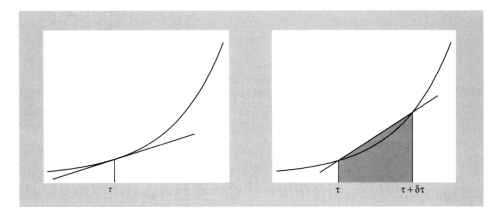

Figure 13.1
Tangents and chords.

Rearranging this equation, we see that

$$x(\tau + \delta\tau) = x'\delta\tau + x(\tau). \qquad (5)$$

Thus, if we choose some small value for $\delta\tau$ we can calculate the value of x at the next value of $n\delta\tau$ from a starting value and the derivative. Equations 4 and 5 above define the derivative in terms of x, and so we have a complete method:

$$x(t + \delta t) = \delta t \times y(t) + x(t), \qquad (6)$$

$$y(t + \delta t) = -\delta t \times x(t) + y(t). \qquad (7)$$

We can convert this to a sequence, using the notation of a suffix to count the number of iterations:

$$x_{n+1} = x_n + hy_n, \qquad (8)$$

$$y_{n+1} = y_n - hx_n. \qquad (9)$$

For the piece of music we are considering, the decision is to use the Henon map, or more strictly a member of the Henon map indexed by two constants, A and B:

$$x_{n+1} = 1 + y_n - Ax_n^2, \qquad (10)$$

$$y_{n+1} = Bx_n. \qquad (11)$$

We can choose different values of A and B to get different streams.

When coding this process in C, the first problem is that we require two answers from each call. We could arrange that the function returned a structure, but that is usually a wrong-minded idea in C, in part due to the implementation issues, but in part because there is a much simpler way. If we call the function with the address where the current values of x and y are stored, the function replaces them[2]:

```
extern double A, B;

void henon(double *x, double *y)
{
    double new_x;
    double new_y;
    double xx = *x;
    double yy = *y;

    new_x = 1.0 + yy - A * (xx*xx);
    new_y = B * xx;
    *x = new_x;
    *y = new_y;
}
```

In this function, we have to take a little care that we do not overwrite the old values before we finish needing them. The code above is overcautious: the value `yy` is used only once. The squaring is done by repeated multiplication rather than by calling the `pow` function (which would be considerably slower).[3]

13.3   Applying the Henon Map

We now have the ability to generate a stream of numbers, but this is not yet music. We have to consider how to map the numbers onto musical events. Having chosen to "borrow" the sound design from Boulanger, we have 13 primary instruments and two effects instruments. An initial idea might be to take the data stream, and take the integer values of the stream $x_0, x_1, \ldots$ to select the instrument, and the values of the y stream to say how long each sound will last. A slight problem with that plan is that since we do not know the range of values that can be in x we may never use more than one instrument. We can easily run the henon function for a length of time and record the maximum and minimum values.

```
#include <stdio.h>

double A = 1.3, B = 0.21;

int main(int argc, char **argv)
{
    double maxx = 1.0, maxy = 1.0;
    double minx = 1.0, miny = 1.0;
    int iterations = 1000000;
    double x = 1.0, y = 1.0; /* Initial values */
    int i;
```

```
    for (i=0; i<iterations; i++) {
        henon(&x, &y);
        if (x>maxx) maxx = x;
        if (x<minx) minx = x;
        if (y>maxy) maxy = y;
        if (y<miny) miny = y;
    }
    printf("x has range (%f,%f)\ny has range (%f,%f)\n",
            minx,maxx,miny,maxy);
}
```

Running this program with the henon function from above gives $(-0.860850, 1.193449)$ as the range of x and $(-0.180779, 1.000000)$ as the range of y. If one increases the number of iterations to 2 million, the values do not change. Thus, we can be reasonably confident in this range; besides, we are not likely to need that many raw values unless we are expecting the piece to last a very long time.

What this does show is that taking the integer part of x is not sufficient. We could of course scale x so that it was in the range $[1,13]$. If we add 0.860850 to x, the range becomes $[0,2.054299]$, so if we want a range of 0 to 12 we need to multiply by a number that makes 2.054299 into 12, or $12/2.054299 = 5.841409$, and so we get the formula for a range of $[1,13]$ as $X = 1+(x+0.860850)*5.841409$. It is a good idea to check this formula. If $x = 0$ this gives a value of 1, while if $x = 1.193449$ it yields $1+(1.193449+0.860850)*5.841409$, which is 13, which checks. Coding this formula as C, and for the moment ignoring the pitch, amplitude, and other parameters:

```
#include <stdio.h>

double A = 1.3, B = 0.21;

int main(int argc, char **argv)
{
    int iterations = 1000;
    double x = 1.0, y = 1.0; /* Initial values */
    int i;

    for (i=0; i<iterations; i++) {
        henon(&x, &y);
        printf("i%d %d\n", (int)(1.0+(x+0.860850)*5.841409), i);
    }
}
```

We can run this program for 1,000 note events, but in order to get any evaluation of the utility of this approach it might be useful to count how many of each value is generated. Here is a program to gather some statistics:

```c
#include <stdio.h>

double A = 1.3, B = 0.21;

int main(int argc, char **argv)
{
    int iterations = 1000;
    int count[13];
    double x = 1.0, y = 1.0; /* Initial values */
    int i;

    for (i=0; i<13; i++) count[i] = 0;

    for (i=0; i<iterations; i++) {
        int instr;
        henon(&x, &y);
        instr = (int)(1.0+(x+0.860850)*5.841409);
        count[instr-1]++;
        printf("i%d %d\n", instr, i);
    }
    printf("\nSTATICS:\n");
    for (i=0; i<13; i++) printf("%d ",count[i]);
    printf("\n");
}
```

The statistics for 1,000 iterations are

133 6 3 3 126 9 129 144 26 143 132 145 0.

The first thing we notice here is that we do not generate an instrument 13 at all. The reason why is fairly clear; our formula took us to a range of [1,13] but only just reaches 13. With a little rounding error it is quite possible for the 13 to never actually occur. We can adjust this by mapping x to the range [1,13.9] and then the integer part will be a better range. It is easy to see that this can be achieve by changing the 12 in the above calculation to 12.9, and I get a revised multiplier of 6.279514, and for 1,000 iterations the statistics

133 5 4 3 6 128 5 253 23 148 17 130 144

This may be a usable allocation of instruments, and so we can move to consider the other parameters of the note events; pitch, onset time and duration—we will continue to delay consideration of the other parameters of the timbre until later. But we do need to know how many parameters each instrument needs, and also typical range of values.

13.3.1 Outputting Note Events

The plan is to create a function for each instrument that outputs a single score event with appropriate parameters. We will call these functions instr_1 through instr_13, and we

Table 13.2
Parameter ranges for Boulanger's *Trapped in Convert* instruments.

Instr	Para	Min	Max	Para	Min	Max	Para	Min	Max	Para	Min	Max
1	p3	5	24	p6	200	700	p7	0.0	5.2	p8	3	18
	p9	0	0.99									
2	p3	4	9	p6	500	6000	p7	0	1	p8	17	60
	p9	3	21	p10	0	0.38						
3	p3	5	8	p6	600	900	p7	0.5	0.8	p8	45	70
4	p3	0.7	3.1	p6	850	5001	p7	5699	10000	p8	18	7000
	p9	5	50	p10	0.2	0.9						
5	p3	0.9	2.4	p6	2000	4500	p7	0.1	0.4	p8	0.1	1
	p9	2	11	p10	3	11	p11	12	20	p12	27	37
6	p3	4.3	8.5	p4	0.81	17	p5	3000	6000	p6	17	9000
	p7	10	100	p8	0.4	0.6	p9	0.9	1.6			
7	p3	1.9	6.4	p4	8000	9999	p6	0.01	0.2	p7	0.7	1
	p8	0.3	1	p9	2	3	p10	2	3	p11	0.1	0.23
8	p3	3.1	26.9	p4	0.79	4	p5	20	10000	p6	100	11000
	p7	10	1000	p8	2	33	p9	1.3	22	p10	0.1	1
9	p3	2.85	9.1	p4	0.1	0.9	p6	600	3100	p7	0.1	0.9
	p8	3.8	39									
10	p3	1.6	34	p6	300	6000	p7	0.1	0.8	p8	1.4	68
	p9	27	300									
11	p3	4	8	p4	0.2	0.5	p6	1200	3300	p7	0.1	0.5
12	p3	0.6	3	p4	0.3	11	p6	1000	3000	p7	200	7000
	p8	4	30	p9	0.1	0.3						
13	p3	4	4.5	p4	0.4	0.4	p6	1500	2000	p7	30	40
	p8	5	7									

will call them with the time, duration, and pitch of the note (where that is appropriate), and use fixed timbral parameters until we have the basic design under control. In order to determine "typical" values for the other p fields, it is necessary to inspect the score of *Trapped in Convert* to see what values are used there. This is a little tedious. I did the calculations by first sorting the score as text, and then deleting the comment and blank lines.[4] The relevant values are given in table 13.2, where the pitch values have been omitted. From this table we can construct the first version of our output functions (assuming that the start time, the duration, and the pitch are provided as parameters), by using typical values for the other parameters. Later we will consider more sophisticated modification of these. Here is the code:

```
int instr_1(double tt, double dur, double pitch)
{
/* i1: p6=amp,p7=vibrat,p8=glisdeltime (default < 1),
     p9=frqdrop */
```

```
        double amp, vibrat, glis, frqdrop;
        amp= 500.0;
        vibrat= 0.001;
        glis = 10.0;
        frqdrop = 0.99;
        printf("i1 %f %f 0 %f %f %.3f %f %.2f\n",
               tt, dur, pitch, amp, vibrat, glis, frqdrop);
}

int instr_2(double tt, double dur, double pitch)
{
/* i2: p6=amp,p7=rvbsnd,p8=lfofrq,p9=num of harmonics,
       p10=sweeprate */
        double amp, rvbsnd, lfofrq, numh, sweeprate;
        amp= 2000;
        rvbsnd = 0.5;
        lfofrq = 11;
        numh = 10;
        sweeprate =0.5;
        printf("i2 %f %f 0 %f %f %f %f %f %f\n",
               tt, dur, pitch, amp, rvbsnd, lfofrq,
               numh, sweeprate);
}

int instr_3(double tt, double dur, double pitch)
{
/* i3: p6=amp,p7=rvbsnd,p8=rndfrq */
        double amp, rvbsnd, rndfrq;
        amp= 700.0;
        rvbsnd = 0.8;
        rndfrq = 57.0;
        printf("i3 %f %f 0 %f %f %f %f\n",
               tt, 10*dur, pitch, amp, rvbsnd, rndfrq);
}

int instr_4(double tt, double dur, double pitch)
{
/* i4: p6=amp,p7=fltrswp:strtval,p8=fltrswp:endval,
       p9=bdwth,p10=rvbsnd */
        double amp, strtval, endval, bdwth, rvbsnd;
        amp = 3000.0;
        strtval = 7000;
        endval = 40;
        rvbsnd = 0.5;
```

```
    printf("i4 %f %f 0 %f %f %f %f %f %f\n",
            tt, dur, pitch, amp, strtval, endval,
            bdwth, rvbsnd);
}
int instr_5(double tt, double dur, double pitch)
{
/* i5: p6=amp,p7=rvbatn,p8=pan:1.0,p9=carfrq,p10=modfrq,
        p11=modndx,p12=rndfrq */
    double amp, rvbatn, pan, carfrq, modfrq, modndx, rndfrq;
    amp =
    rvbatn = -0.3;
    pan =
    carfrq = 5;
    modfrq = 7;
    modndx = 17;
    rndfrq = 25;
    printf("i5 %f %f 0 %f %f %f %f %f %f %f\n",
            tt, dur, pitch, amp, rvbatn, pan, carfrq,
            modfrq, modndx, rndfrq);
}

int instr_6(double tt, double dur, double pitch)
{
/* i6: p5=swpfrq:strt,p6=swpfrq:end,p7=bndwth,p8=rvbsnd,p9=amp */
    double strt, end, bndwth, rvbsnd, amp2;
    strt = 3000;
    end = 17;
    bndwth = 10;
    rvbsnd = 0.6;
    amp2 = 1.6;
    printf("i6 %f %f 17 %f %f %f %f %f\n",
            tt, dur, strt, end, bndwth, rvbsnd, amp2);
}

int instr_7(double tt, double dur, double pitch)
{
/* i7: p4=amp,p5=frq,p6=strtphse,p7=endphse,p8=ctrlamp(.1-1),
        p9=ctrlfnc, p10=mainfnc, p11=revb */
    double amp, frq, trtphse, endphse, ctrlamp, ctrlfnc,
        mainfnc, revb;
    amp = 9000.0;
    trtphse = 0.2;
    endphse = 0.7;
```

```
    ctrlamp = 0.5;
    ctrlfnc = 2;
    mainfnc = 3; /* Should choose 2, 3 or 14 */
    revb = 0.12;
    printf("i7 %f %f %f %f %f %f %f %f %f %f\n",
            tt, dur, amp, pitch, trtphse, endphse, ctrlamp,
            ctrlfnc, mainfnc, revb);
}

int instr_8(double tt, double dur, double pitch)
{
/* i8: p4=amp,p5=swpstrt,p6=swpend,p7=bndwt,p8=rnd1:cps,
        p9=rnd2:cps,p10=rvbsnd */
    double amp, swpstrt, swpend, bndwt, cps1, cps2, rvbsnd;
    amp = 1.95;
    swpstrt = 2000;
    swpend = 5000;
    bndwt = 300;
    cps1 = 8;
    cps2 = 5.6;
    rvbsnd = 0.4;
    printf("i8 %f %f %f %f %f %f %f %f %f\n",
            tt, dur, amp, swpstrt, swpend, bndwt,
            cps1, cps2, rvbsnd);
}

int instr_9(double tt, double dur, double pitch)
{
/* i9: p4=delsnd,p5=frq,p6=amp,p7=rvbsnd,p8=rndamp,p9=rndfrq */
    double delsnd, amp, rvbsnd, rndamp, rndfrq;
    delsnd = 0.4;
    amp = 1200;
    rvbsnd = 0.2;
    rndamp = 25;
    rndfrq = 100;
    printf("i9 %f %f %f %f %f %f %f %f\n",
            tt, dur, delsnd, pitch, amp, rvbsnd,
            rndamp, rndfrq);
}

int instr_10(double tt, double dur, double pitch)
{
/* i10: p4=0,p5=frq,p6=amp,p7=rvbsnd,p8=rndamp,p9=rndfrq */
    double amp, rvbsnd, rndamp, rndfrq;
```

```
    amp = 2000;
    rvbsnd = 0.3;
    rndamp = 6.9;
    rndfrq = 160;
    printf("i10 %f %f 0 %f %f %f %f %f\n",
            tt, dur, pitch, amp, rvbsnd, rndamp, rndfrq);
}

int instr_11(double tt, double dur, double pitch)
{
/* i11: p4=delsnd,p5=frq,p6=amp,p7=rvbsnd */
    double delsnd, amp, vbsnd;
    delsnd = 0.3;
    amp = 2330;
    vbsnd = 0.2;
    printf("i11 %f %f %f %f %f %f\n",
            tt, dur, delsnd, pitch, amp, vbsnd);
}

int instr_12(double tt, double dur, double pitch)
{
/* i12: p6=amp,p7=swpstrt,p8=swppeak,p9=bndwth,p10=rvbsnd */
    double amp, swpstrt, swppeak, bndwth, rvbsnd;
    amp = 2000.0;
    swpstrt = 1500;
    swppeak = 6000;
    bndwth = 4.0;
    rvbsnd = 0.2;
    printf("i12 %f %f 0 %f %f %f %f %f %f\n",
            tt, dur, pitch, amp, swpstrt, swppeak, bndwth,
            rvbsnd);
}

int instr_13(double tt, double dur, double pitch)
{
/* i13: p6=amp,p7=vibrat,p8=dropfrq */
    double amp, vibrat, dropfrq;
    amp = 2000;
    vibrat = 40;
    dropfrq = 7;
    printf("i13 %f %f 0 %f %f %f %f\n",
            tt, dur, pitch, amp, vibrat, dropfrq);
}
```

As a first attempt we can construct a main program that uses these functions to write a score. There are still a number of arbitrary decisions, like each note lasting 1 second, and the mapping of y into a pitch using the following formula:

```
1000.0 (y + 0.180779) + 150.
```

The code for the main program is

```c
int main(int argc, char **argv)
{
    int iterations = 1000;
    double x = 1.0, y = 1.0; /* Initial values */
    double tt = 0.0, pitch;
    int i;

    printf("; amp envelopes\n");
    printf("f1 0 8192 10 1\n");
    printf("f2 0 8192 10 10 8 0 6 0 4 0 1\n");
    printf("f3 0 8192 10 10 0 5 5 0 4 3 0 1\n");
    printf("f4 0 2048 10 10 0 9 0 0 8 0 7 0 4 0 2 0 1\n");
    printf("f5 0 2048 10 5 3 2 1 0\n");
    printf("f6 0 2048 10 8 10 7 4 3 1\n");
    printf("f7 0 2048 10 7 9 11 4 2 0 1 1\n");
    printf("f8 0 2048 10 0 0 0 0 7 0 0 0 2 0 0 0 1 1\n");
    printf("f9 0 2048 10 10 9 8 7 6 5 4 3 2 1\n");
    printf("f10 0 2048 10 10 0 9 0 8 0 7 0 6 0 5\n");
    printf("f11 0 2048 10 10 10 9 0 0 0 3 2 0 0 1\n");
    printf("f12 0 2048 10 10 0 0 0 5 0 0 0 0 0 3\n");
    printf("f13 0 2048 10 10 0 0 0 0 3 1\n");
    printf("f14 0 8192 9 1 3 0 3 1 0 9 .333 180\n");
    printf("f15 0 8192 9 1 1 90 \n");
    printf("f16 0 2048 9 1 3 0 3 1 0 6 1 0\n");
    printf("f17 0 9 5 .1 8 1\n");
    printf("f18 0 17 5 .1 10 1 6 .4\n");
    printf("f19 0 16 2 1 7 10 7 6 5 4 2 1 1 1 1 1 1 1\n");
    printf("f20 0 16 -2 0 30 40 45 50 40 30 20 10 5 4 3 2 "
            "1 0 0 0\n");
    printf("f21 0 16 -2 0 20 15 10 9 8 7 6 5 4 3 2 1 0 0\n");
    printf("f22 0 9 -2 .001 .004 .007 .003 .002 .005 .009"
            ".006\n");

    for (i=0; i<iterations; i++) {
        int instr;
        henon(&x, &y);
        instr = (int)(1.0+(x+0.860850)*6.279514);
```

```
    pitch = (y+0.180779)*1000.0 + 150;
    switch (instr) {
    case 1:
        instr_1(tt, 1.0, pitch); tt += 1.0; break;
    case 2:
        instr_2(tt, 1.0, pitch); tt += 1.0; break;
    case 3:
        instr_3(tt, 1.0, pitch); tt += 1.0; break;
    case 4:
        instr_4(tt, 1.0, pitch); tt += 1.0; break;
    case 5:
        instr_5(tt, 1.0, pitch); tt += 1.0; break;
    case 6:
        instr_6(tt, 1.0, pitch); tt += 1.0; break;
    case 7:
        instr_7(tt, 1.0, pitch); tt += 1.0; break;
    case 8:
        instr_8(tt, 1.0, pitch); tt += 1.0; break;
    case 9:
        instr_9(tt, 1.0, pitch); tt += 1.0; break;
    case 10:
        instr_10(tt, 1.0, pitch); tt += 1.0; break;
    case 11:
        instr_11(tt, 1.0, pitch); tt += 1.0; break;
    case 12:
        instr_12(tt, 1.0, pitch); tt += 1.0; break;
    case 13:
        instr_13(tt, 1.0, pitch); tt += 1.0; break;
    }
  }
  printf("\ne\n");
}
```

If you run this program and synthesize the score with the Boulanger orchestra (*henonTrapped* *.orc*), you get an algorithmic composition that has some merit, but it gets somewhat stuck into a seven-beat cycle with insufficient variations. Of course one could attack this problem by shortening the number of interactions, and modifying the mapping of the pitch. It is also possible to consider the other parameters, possibly using other parts of the two input variables x and y. In particular, the current program does not use most of the value of x, and the lower digits of y have very little effect. You might want to experiment with these mappings. However, to my ears, while the equation gives some structure, the overall effect is not as interesting as I would like. What seems to be missing is the intrinsic structure of the original piece, and it would be better if we could draw some inspiration from that creative incitement.

13.3.2   Alternative Mapping of Henon Map

In the Boulanger piece *Trapped in Convert* the individual instruments play in a certain order. If we study it, we will see that, ignoring the two effects instruments, there are not many note events and the sequence is as follows:

```
int squence[] = { 1, 1, 1, 1, 1, 2, 2, 1, 1, 1, 1, 4, 2, 2, 2,
                  4, 3, 1, 1, 1, 1, 5, 5, 6, 9, 9, 9, 9, 9, 9,
                  3, 6, 7, 7, 7, 3, 7, 8, 8, 8, 7, 7, 9, 9, 9,
                  9, 9, 9, 9, 9, 2, 2, 2, 2, 2, 2, 2, 4, 4, 9,
                  9, 9, 9, 11, 13, 9, 9, 2, 11, 2, 8, 11, 9,
                  9, 9, 9, 11, 11, 13, 13, 9, 9, 9, 2, 8, 2,
                  11, 8, 2, 2, 11, 11, 11, 11, 4, 4, 4, 5, 5,
                  5, 5, 4, 4, 4, 4, 5, 5, 4, 4, 4, 4, 12, 12,
                  12, 4, 4, 4, 12, 10, 10, 12, 10, 4, 4, 4, 4,
                  4, 4, 4, 4, 12, 10, 10, 10, 10, 10, 10, 10,
                  10, 10, 10, 10, 10, 10, 10, 8, 8, 8, 8, 8,
                  8, 8, 4, 10, 10, 10, 10, 2, 2, 4, 4, 10, 10,
                  10, 10, 10, 10, 10 };
```

We could use this order in our piece too, but it would be too much of a constraint to have exactly this number of note events, as this result in little more than an arrangement of the Boulanger. Rather, what we shall do is to decide on a total length (I decided on 323 seconds for no clear reason) and just stretch the sequence out. There are 167 note events. To choose the instrument at time `tt` we can use a short sequence such as the following:

```
int selectinstr(double tt)
{
    int which;
    double ch = 168.0*tt/323.0;
    which = (int)(ch+0.5);
    if (which>167) return 1; /* Force last event */
    if (which== 0) return 0; /* and start event */
    return squence[which];
}
```

We still need to decide on the start time and duration of each event, and the pitch, the amplitude, and other parameters. At present the Henon map is not enough to control so many parameters, so we need another sequence of numbers. Based on my experience from the first piece in the set, I decided to use the Standard Map on a torus in addition to Henon to get a sequence of four numbers.

13.4   Standard Map on a Torus

Following Bidlack's description,[5] we can derive the standard map from a model of a pendulum that is perturbed with a periodic function. There are two variables; however, they are both angles measured in radians, in the range $[0, 2\pi]$, and 2π is the same as 0. This wrapping round is topologically equivalent to a torus:

$$I_{n+1} = I_n + K \sin \Theta_n, \tag{12}$$

$$\Theta_{n+1} = \Theta_n + I_{n+1}, \tag{13}$$

where K is a constant. For our purposes we will take K as 1.2. These equations have chaotic behavior for K larger than 1 and tend to regular behavior for K smaller, and we would like a mildly chaotic sequence so some coherence remains, at least locally.

In the same way as we coded the Henon map, we need code for this map:

```
#include <math.h>

double K = 1.2;

void torus(double *Iota, double *Theta)
{
    double new_iota;
    double new_theta;
    double theta = *Theta;

    new_iota = *Iota + K*sin(theta);
    new_theta = theta + new_iota;
                                /* Normalize */
    while (new_iota < 0.0) new_iota += TWO_PI;
    while (new_iota >= TWO_PI) new_iota -= TWO_PI;
    while (new_theta < 0.0) new_theta += TWO_PI;
    while (new_theta >= TWO_PI) new_theta -= TWO_PI;
    *Iota = new_iota;
    *Theta = new_theta;
}
```

The comments made earlier on the Henon map apply here as well. The new feature is to arrange that the wrap around the torus is effected. Of course we need a value for TWO_PI to complete this. One might use a #define to give it the value 6.2831853071795864769, or one might initialize a variable to be 8 $\tan^{-1}$(1); the latter has the slight merit of giving the answer to machine accuracy—remember that tan $\pi/4 = 1$.[6]

Unlike before, in order to use this map we do not need to check the range as that is implicit in the toroidal topology, so we can return to the main compositional effort. We do require a set of starting values for I and Θ, however. An idea of the values from this map can be given by figure 13.2.

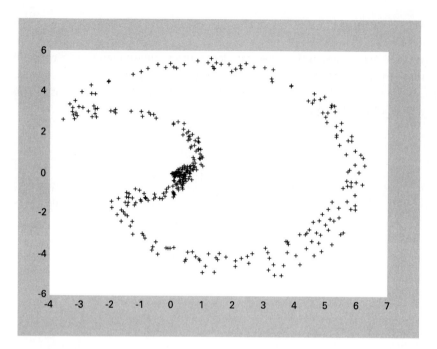

Figure 13.2
The standard torus map.

13.4.1   Generating Notes from Henon and Torus

With the two maps for every cycle, we have four values to use for algorithmic purposes: x and y from the Henon map and I and Θ from the torus. We will write a function that takes these values and generates a score event. To make this function shorter we use an array of functions, each one to output an event for each instrument:

```
double tt = 0.0;              /* Total time */
int pitch;                    /* Last main pitch */
typedef void (*INSTR)(double,double,double,double,double);
INSTR instruments[] = {instr_0, instr_1, instr_2, instr_3,
                       instr_4, instr_5, instr_6, instr_7,
                       instr_8, instr_9, instr_10, instr_11,
                       instr_12, instr_13};
void event_output(double iota, double theta, double x, double y)
{
    double dur;
    int ins;
    double iotaa;
```

```
    iotaa = fabs(iota);
    pitch = 1+(int)(iotaa*400.0/TWO_PI);
    tt += fabs(3.0*theta);
    /* Make duration dependent on pitch */
    dur = fabs(theta) *60.0/(double)pitch;
    if (dur>1) dur = 3.0*sqrt(dur);
    ins = selectinstr(tt, dur);
    (instruments[ins])(tt, dur, pitch, x, y);
}
```

This function contains some results from experiment; scaling Θ by 3 so the events are spaced, and the durations are also scaled so lower pitch sounds last longer. This seems to improve the effects and allows lower notes to develop their character. This was identified by experiment, but there are good psycho-acoustic reasons for it as well. You might care to experiment with different values to see if the effect can be improved. Or even more advanced, there is no *a priori* reason to believe that there should be a linear (simple multiplicative) relationship, so you might consider other expressions.

We can now use these ideas to get a new version of our piece. If you try this there are moments of music but the overall effect is weak. This can be improved greatly by looking at each individual instrument, using the two additional arguments to control parameters, and also adjusting the duration and pitch parameters for each instrument to get a better individual sound. For example:

```
void instr_1(double tt, double dur, double pitch,
            double xx, double yy)
{
/* p6=amp,p7=vibrat,p8=glisdeltime(default < 1),p9=frqdrop */
    double amp, vibrat, glis, frqdrop;
    amp = fabs(xx*1000);
    vibrat = 0.001;
    glis = fabs(0.9*yy)/6.0;
    frqdrop = 0.99;
    /* Should be a table */
    pitch = 440.0*pow(2.0,((int)pitch-40.0)/12.0);
    printf("i1 %f %f 0 %f %f %.3f %f %.2f\n",
            tt, 3.0*dur, pitch, amp, vibrat, glis, frqdrop);
}

void instr_2(double tt, double dur, double pitch,
    double xx, double yy)
{
/* p6=amp,p7=rvbsnd,p8=lfofrq,p9=#harmonics,p10=sweeprate */
    double amp, rvbsnd, lfofrq, numh, sweeprate;
    amp = fabs(xx*1800);
```

```
rvbsnd = 0.5;
lfofrq = 20*fabs(yy);
while (lfofrq>50)
    lfofrq -= 15;
numh = 10;
sweeprate = 0.5;
while (dur>20.0)
    dur -= 10.0;
pitch = 440.0*pow(2.0,((int)pitch-34.0)/12.0);
printf("i2 %f %f 0 %f %f %f %f %f %f\n",
       tt, 81.0*dur, pitch, amp, rvbsnd, lfofrq,
       numh, sweeprate);
}
```

We are now a long way toward a piece, and we are now in the process of experimental modifications of the detailed mapping from the two chaotic processes to note events, and in particular the parameters to each instrument.

13.4.2   Developing the Piece

The main computational stages of the composition are now complete. It is necessary to add some effects, using the original instruments 98 and 99 throughout. To give the whole work context, that the sounds are all from *Trapped in Convert*, I decided to make a couple of quotations from the original. After a few experiments it seemed right to start the same way as *Trapped*, making my first four notes the last four notes of the first section, which seem to have a "lead in" effect. To include them is just a collection of `printf` statements near the beginning of the main program, after the f-tables.

```
printf(";; Quotation from \"Trapped in Convert\" by"
                        "Richard Boulanger\n\n");
printf("i98 2.9 15.1\n");
printf("i99 2.9 15.1 3\n");
printf("i9 2.9 2.9 0.4 31.407 600 0.2 6.2 320\n");
printf("i9 2.93 2.85 0.43 31.770 640 0.23 6.1 300\n");
printf("i9 7.1 7.9 0.2 33.467 700 0.4 4.5 289\n");
printf("i9 7.14 7.78 0.17 34.050 700 0.43 4.4 280\n");
printf("s\n");
```

The second quotation I wanted was the bit that starts 43 seconds into the second section, but after trying it directly after the first quotation, it seemed better to insert it after 196 seconds into the algorithmic component. At first thought this seems difficult, but it is possible to use the "b" score operation in Csound to reset the clock, so the second quotation can be coded:

```
printf(";; Second quotation from Trapped\n");
printf("b 196\n");
printf("i9 0 5 0.4 1108.668 1200 0.2 28 39\n");
printf("i9 0 5 0.3 1040.410 1200 0.4 29 37\n");
printf("i3 0.5 6.5 0 6163.728 600 0.6 47\n");
printf("i99 4.5 2 7\n");
printf("i6 4.5 4.3 17 6000 9000 100 0.4 0.9\n");
printf("i99 6.5 9.9 0.7\n");
printf("i7 6.5 3.2 9999 37.349 0.2 0.7 0.6 2 3 0.12\n");
printf("i7 8 1.9 9800 40.965 0.01 0.9 1 3 2 0.23\n");
printf("i7 9 3.8 9900 1052.541 0.99 0.1 0.3 3 2 0.12\n");
printf("i3 9.1 5.5 0 1154.427 900 0.5 67\n");
printf("i7 9.2 2.5 9890 44.158 0.1 1.0 0.7 2 3 0.23\n");
printf("i8 11 4.6 4 20 8000 590 2 9.9 0.6\n");
printf("i8 15.5 3.1 3 50 4000 129 8 2.6 0.3\n");
printf("i8 16.2 4.3 2 10000 9000 200 12 17.9 1\n");
printf("i99 16.4 10.3 0.3\n");
printf("i7 16.4 3.5 8000 36.496 0.2 0.7 0.5 2 3 0.1\n");
printf("i7 19.3 6.4 8000 41.439 0.01 0.9 1 3 2 0.1\n");
printf("i9 20.2 4 0.4 590.702 1000 0.2 4 100\n");
printf("i9 21 4.2 0.4 926.926 1100 0.4 4 167\n");
printf("i9 21.1 8 0.4 670.752 1000 0.6 4 210\n");
printf("i9 21.25 5 0.4 748.553 1200 0.9 5 200\n");
printf("i99 26.7 5.3 11\n");
printf("i9 26.7 1.9 0.5 31.588 3100 0.1 5.9 300\n");
printf("i9 29.1 2.1 0.1 35.252 2900 0.2 4.2 390\n");
printf("i99 32 6.2 0.28\n");
printf("i9 32 9.1 0.34 43.904 2300 0.5 3.8 420\n");
printf("i9 32.1 9.0 0.4 44.083 2500 0.4 4 430\n");
printf("b 0\n");
```

It was necessary to make a few small modifications to the original orchestra, mainly to ensure that the effects did not generate glitches, and to separate the two effects systems (mine and the original). This was achieved by adding 100 to the modified instrument numbers, and by making a few inconsequential changes. The final version of the program features a few small hand tweaks and includes some statistics-gathering code (which enabled me to check that the various instruments and pitches were being used as I intended).

Conclusion

In this chapter I have shown programs of the kind that I write to support my algorithmic composition methodology. It is not my intent to suggest that this is the "correct" or best way to write algorithmic music, and naturally your own compositional style may require very different processes. But I do want to suggest that small programs are not difficult, and that despite all the teaching of Software Engineering there are times when a small program can be very easily created. For example, checking the range of the values from the raw process generators takes only a few lines of C, and there is no need to fear this. In the algorithmic style I am developing, I frequently write these small programs, and usually throw them away afterward as I know I can re-create them with ease if I have to. The lesson I want you to take from this chapter is that programming is not a hard mysterious activity, but can be made part of our musical activity. Of course the hard part will always remain deciding what to compute, not how.

Notes

1. For further study, I recommend these texts: S. Forman, *Numerical Algorithms That (Usually) Work* (Mathematical Association of America, 1990); W. Cody and W. Waite, *Software Manual for the Elementary Functions* (Prentice-Hall, 1980).

2. For a longer explanation of chaotic processes, see R. Bidlack, "Chaotic Systems as Simple (but Complex) Compositional Algorithms," *Computer Music Journal* 16 (1992), no. 3: 33–47.

3. The function pow is capable of calculating not only integer powers but also fractional powers. It is likely that it uses a more complicated variant of the formula $x^y = \exp(y \log x)$. If the second argument is a positive integer it is clear that a simple loop will be more efficient:

```
double intpow(double x, int n)
{
    int i;
    double ans = 1.0;
    for (i=0; i<n; i++)
    ans = x * ans;
    return ans;
}
```

There is an even faster way, based on the binary decomposition of the positive integer n. The idea is to use the identities $x^{2m} = (xx)^m$ and $x^{2m+1} = x(x)^{2m}$. This suggests that we can test the bottom bit of the binary representation of n (to see if it is even or odd), and if it is 1 we multiply the answer by x. In any case we then square x and shift n down one bit (which is equivalent to a division by two ignoring any fractional part). This gives the simple function

```
double intpow(double x, int n) /* Binary power function */
{
    double ans = 1.0;
    while (n!=0) {
        if (n&1) ans = ans * x;
        n >>= 1;
        x = x*x;
    }
}
```

```
    return ans;
}
```

If you can follow that, you must have a good grasp of the concept of binary numbers.

4. I did this with *emacs*, but it could have been done with standard UNIX tools, including `sort`, `uniq`, `sed`, and similar command-line tools. A possibility that I did not consider seriously was to write a C program, using the function `qsort`, and calculating the ranges using this program. I decided on the ranges by eye, but some would describe me as lazy for this.

5. See note 2.

6. As a mathematician I am used to thinking of angles in radians. If you are more familiar with degrees, then $360°$ is 2π radians and $45°$ is $\pi/4$ radians.

14   Modeling Orchestral Composition

Steven Yi

14.1   Introduction

The musical sounds and effects of orchestral composition are a result of both the ensemble's physical characteristics and the way music is written for it. By studying orchestral composition, computer music composers and programmers can expand the models of musical representation underlying their music-making software to incorporate the many techniques and ways of thinking about music that are inherent to orchestral composition. This article will make observations about the orchestra as a performance ensemble and discuss some of the techniques composers have used in writing for it. It will then derive a model for music making from these observations. Finally, the article will present a C++ class library implementing this model, along with a program demonstrating how the library can be used.[1]

14.2   Observations on Orchestral Composition

Orchestral composition involves the concrete qualities of the orchestra as a performance ensemble, as well as the abstract musical ideas and techniques that a composer may work with—ideas and techniques that are ultimately performed by the ensemble to achieve the end musical result.

14.2.1   The Orchestra as Performance Ensemble

Generally, when one speaks about the *orchestra*, one is referring to a particular ensemble of performers and the instruments they play (woodwinds, brass, strings, percussion, etc.). Aspects that may vary from one orchestra to another can include the locations of the performers onstage (such as basses on the left or on the right), the number of instruments per section (such as eight violins versus ten violins in the Violin I section), the technical capability of each performer, as well as the types and quality of their instruments. Some aspects of the orchestra might be determined by the conductor, while others are decided by the composer, and still other parameters are influenced by non-musical limitations (such as budgetary constraints, physical size of a stage, etc.).

Ultimately, these variable aspects are *properties* of an orchestra that are *configured* by one person or another. If the person configuring the ensemble is the composer, then little can be done by the conductor or individual performers unless they want to compromise the composer's requirements for the piece. If the composer does not exactly specify some properties of the ensemble that is to perform the work, the conductor or performer may make decisions that ultimately affect the orchestral configuration (such as the number of performers to use in a section or the location of the groups of performers on stage).

Orchestral properties that are typically configured include the following:

- Instruments
  Type of instrument required
  Number of each instrument to use
  Quality of each instrument used
- Performers
  Technical proficiency of performer
   Accuracy of timing
   Accuracy of pitch
  Spatial location of performer
- Performer Groups
  Number of performers per group
  Types of performers per group

In general, the properties that most directly affect the end musical result are the individual performers' capabilities and the quality of their instruments. In a professional orchestra, the difference in technical skill between the first and last chair within an instrument section may be very little, while the differences in an amateur group might be considerably more pronounced. It is worth noting that the same music, played on the same instrument, but played by different performers may sound noticeably different due to individual fluctuations in pitch and timing. Instruments may also vary widely in their properties: if a performer plays the same music on different instruments, the end result will change depending on each instrument's unique timbral qualities. The combination of the number and quality of performers that make up an orchestral ensemble, as well as the quality of instruments they use, all together contribute to the end musical result.

14.2.2   Composing for the Orchestra

The properties of the orchestra as an ensemble provide the composer with possibilities for sound production, a palette of sound which the composer can draw on in creating a piece of music. Using that palette of sound, a composer notates a score that instructs performers on what to perform and when to do so, thereby creating a musical product that results both from the composer's instructions and the performers' realization of them. The notation of scores can range from precise descriptions of the sounds to be generated to an abstract idea or image that the performer can interpret freely; the identity of a musical part may stand alone as a distinct entity or it may exist as part of a much larger musical gesture or idea. The relationship between the compositional idea, the performance instructions used to attain this idea, and the mapping of performance instructions to performers are all factors that will be considered in modeling the orchestral composition programming library.

14.2.3   Performance Instructions

Traditionally, composers have used musical notation, including staffs, clefs, notes, and other symbols, as a tool to record instructions for creating the musical piece they have in mind. *Common practice musical notation* is written relative to a single tempo; pitch, duration, and other musical qualities are fixed. The meanings of these symbols have been established over time and constitute a lexicon of commonly used symbols.

Many composers in the twentieth century sought to describe musical ideas and performance techniques that could not be expressed using common practice notation. To convey their ideas to performers, these composers developed new kinds of notational symbols and directions. Some of these dictated the performer's physical actions, leading to extended performance techniques when musicians were instructed to play their instruments in nonstandard ways. Others allowed musicians to fluidly interpret musical parameters that had conventionally been fixed in common practice notation, such as duration, pitch, and amplitude. To ensure understanding of their ideas, composers have typically defined the meanings of unfamiliar symbols at the beginning of the score in which these symbols appear. Some pieces forgo symbols altogether and provide only a written text as instructions for the performer. The use of symbols and instructions not commonly defined and requiring definition in the piece before use will be called here *uncommon practice musical notation*.

Whether common practice or uncommon practice notation is used, in order for a piece to be performed, the meaning of the instructions must be defined so that the notation of musical ideas can be understood by the performer. The instructions may precisely specify the parameters of the sounds the performer is to create, or it may simply give the performer a generalized set of boundaries in which to generate sound.

14.2.4   Mapping Performance Instructions to Performers

In an orchestra, the end musical result is a product of each member's contributions. The musical idea as notated by the composer and realized by the performer may differ; these differences are a result of performance instruction mapping. The mapping of performance instructions to performers may occur in four different ways (table 14.1).

On a practical level, the many-to-many relationship will not often need to be considered separately as it will naturally grow out of working with the other three relationships and merging together instances of them.

Table 14.1
Four ways of "mapping" instructions to performers.

Relationship	Description
One-to-one	One musical instruction is given to one performer to perform. The musical idea notated is exactly what is intended for the one performer to perform.
One-to-many	One musical idea is given to many performers to perform. A common case of this is notating music for an instrument section like "Violin I" to perform. While the composer may notate performance instructions once and designate it for the group to perform, from the performer's perspective, they each receive a copy of the musical instruction to perform and thus there are multiple copies of the musical instruction. This is a case where the composer intent to direct a group of performers with a single set of instructions maps out to be performed by many performers with multiple copies of the original instructions.
Many-to-one	Multiple musical instructions are given to one performer to perform. This kind of mapping may be commonly seen in music written for the piano where multiple musical lines may be given to a single performer to perform.
Many-to-many	Multiple musical instructions are given to multiple performers. This is a general description of the overall notated musical score given to groups of performers to perform.

14.2.5 Mapping Compositional Ideas to Performance Instructions

Just as performance instructions can be mapped to single or multiple performers, a single compositional idea may also be mapped to single or multiple sets of performance instructions. A one-to-one relationship between compositional ideas and performance instructions is commonly found in most Western music, popular or otherwise, and each set of performance instructions is a reflection of a single musical idea. A one-to-many relationship is more often found in orchestral composition from the mid-twentieth century onward. An example of a one-to-many compositional idea can be found in Iannis Xenakis's *Metastasis* where a singular mass of glissandi sounds is made up of a large number of unique parts.

Taken on its own, each set of musical instructions that makes up a one-to-many musical idea may not be enough to understand the overall group sound effect. Only when the parts are performed together does the singular large-scale musical idea come into focus. Also, while the composer may be working with a singular musical idea in the conception of the piece, the composer may need to notate many different performance instructions to achieve that goal. The dissonance between what can be notated and what is desired as the singular group outcome necessarily arises within the context of common practice notation. We will see, however, that this dissonance can be resolved when working with computers, where the composer is free to work with the overall compositional idea, rather than constantly shifting his attention between the desired group effect and the notation of individual parts to create that outcome.

14.3   Designing the Orchestral Composition Library

In the previous section we observed that orchestral composition is a combination of many things:

- the instruments that are being played and generating sound
- the performers playing those instruments
- the physical layout of the performers and their organization into performer groups
- the performance instructions given to performers and performer groups
- the composer's musical ideas, notated as performance instructions.

All these factors are important for the composer of an orchestral work. As a result, each requires representation within the orchestral composition library in order for the library to adequately create an experience similar to that of composing for an orchestra. Each of the above factors is represented in the composition library using the following object-oriented programming constructs: classes with their properties, configuration of those classes, and methods called on those classes. By using these aspects of object-oriented programming, we can create a model that reflects our observations about orchestral composition. The following subsections will address each of the aforementioned aspects of orchestral composition.

14.3.1   Using Csound for Instruments and Notes

We need either software or hardware musical instruments to create sound. We also need a way to perform those instruments, passing in different parameters to affect musical qualities such as the instrument's pitch and volume. At this point we have a number of options on how to proceed. While it is possible for us to develop a software library for musical instruments and create a music software engine to drive those instruments with control information, this would take a great deal of time to develop. Since the focus of this library is on higher levels of compositional abstraction, the choice was made to target an existing music software synthesis system. By reusing an existing music software system, we can leverage the solutions already available and focus more closely on our compositional interests.

Although MIDI-based instruments and software are ubiquitous and popular, this option was passed over for a number of reasons. First, since MIDI is a binary protocol, this makes software development for it more complicated than text-based protocols. Working with MIDI requires either knowing the specification rather well in order to compose for it directly or using a MIDI programming library that adds higher level abstractions on top of the protocol to ease development. While neither is complicated to do, there are simpler alternatives.

Beyond the fact that the protocol is binary, the MIDI specification has limitations in its capability for musical expression that would not be able to meet the needs of the orchestral composition library. Most values in MIDI are defined as a seven-bit range of 0–127 integers, too coarse to express subtle gradations in the differences in pitch and amplitude between instruments and performers that our compositional model needs. While the MIDI specification may very well represent a large range of musical needs and the availability of high quality instruments that can communicate via MIDI is attractive, the expressive needs of the orchestral composition library are beyond what MIDI is capable of performing.

Passing over MIDI as a target system for our model of instruments, several established software solutions are available. Of these, the computer music software Csound was chosen for its cross-platform availability, the flexibility and power of its synthesis system, and its ease of targeting as a programmer. As a synthesizer and music engine, Csound has a large number of audio processing opcodes included that are capable of creating sound-generating instruments more than satisfactorily. The Csound score system also uses either 32-bit float or 64-bit double values with values constrained only by what those formats are limited to expressing, both of which are more than capable of expressing the subtle gradations of values we will need for the library. Finally, being that the score system is a text format, it is extremely easy to program as text generation and manipulation is a core capability found in most programming languages and is also a fundamental skill that most programmers learn. This reduces the complexity required to develop the library and adds no new library dependencies for the project, thus making it simpler to get started and to maintain.

To be able to work with Csound, we need to know some basics about how it works. Traditionally, Csound projects are split into two text files: an orchestra file[2] (ORC) containing definitions of instruments and a score file (SCO) containing a list of notes to play for the instruments used. ORC files can be used with multiple SCO files and vice versa, so one can experiment with the same orchestra and different musical scores, or one may experiment with the same score but different orchestras. Csound instruments are defined in the ORC file with a numerical or string ID that is later used when writing the SCO file. For the SCO file, notes are defined as starting with i, followed by a space delimited list of values (p-fields). Here is an example of a note in Csound SCO format:

```
i1   0   2   440.0   80
```

The letter i denotes that this line is a note. (Lines starting with other characters have different meanings to Csound.) After the i are three mandatory p-fields that all notes must have: p-field 1 (p1) is the instrument for which this note is for, p2 is the start time for this note, and p3 is the duration of this note. In the example note above, the first three p-fields say that this note is for instrument 1, starting at time 0 and lasting for 2 beats. After p3 come optional p-fields whose meanings are defined by the user and are a part of the programming of the instrument. In the example above, p4's value of 440.0 may well represent a frequency value and p5's value of 80 may represent amplitude in decibels.

By having a user-definable amount of p-fields, we have degree of flexibility on a note-to-note basis to set values to describe the qualities of that note. Compared to a MIDI note-on message, whose properties are only the MIDI note number (0–127) and the MIDI key velocity (0–127), we find that Csound offers the user the ability to describe much more about the musical nature of the note.

The flexibility of arbitrarily defining each instrument's allowable p-fields comes at a price for interoperability. If different instruments do not use the same number and meanings for p-fields, then the SCO written for one instrument cannot be reused with a different instrument, and, consequently, the programming library written for one instrument could not be used with a different instrument. The solution to this problem, then, is to define a standard p-field signature, one that can handle the musical needs of the orchestral composition library and can also be implemented by all Csound instruments. By having a standard format that we agree to use, we can create both instruments that accept information in that format and a programming library that can generate that format. As a result, different instruments can be swapped in and out of the project and different score generating programs can be swapped in and out as well.

For the orchestral composition library we will be using instruments that accept an 8 p-field note format with the following values:

p1—instrument identifier

p2—start time

p3—duration

p4—pitch 1 (in either frequency or Csound PCH notation)

p5—pitch 2 (in either frequency or Csound PCH notation)

p6—amplitude in dB

p7—spatial location (from -1.0 to 1.0 corresponding with left and right panning)

p8—articulation (the type of amplitude and filter envelope to use, may be either 0 for ADSR envelope, 1 for triangular envelope, or 2 for ramp envelope)

This eight p-field note format will be flexible enough to handle the compositional needs of the examples provided below. The p4 and p5 fields are used by the example instruments to indicate a starting pitch and ending pitch, although alternative interpretations of those values may be implemented with the instruments used (for example, pitch 1 may be interpreted as a base pitch, while pitch 2 could be interpreted as a pitch to trill to as part of a trill). The p6 field will be used to enter in the amplitude of the note to be played.

The p7 field is interesting in that in a non-computer music setting, the spatial location is not typically a factor of the note to be played, but is rather a quality of the performer. In a music system where we might be handling the audio signals generated by instruments directly instead of delegating the task to another software like Csound, we might have a programming model where a Performer object's perform method consists of calling an Instrument's generateAudio method and then the performer processes the generated signal with its spatial location properties and returns that processed sound to the sound engine. However, since the task of audio processing has been delegated, we will pass the value for the spatial location in as a parameter of the note and the instrument will apply the spatial location processing of the signal. We will later find that although each note within this system will carry that information, the user of the library will not have to notate that information but will instead configure that property on the Performer object and the Performer object will then fill in that information when notes are generated.

The p8 field is the articulation field, which has been set up in the example Csound instruments to accept values of 0, 1, and 2, denoting amplitude and filter envelopes for a standard attack-decay-sustain-release (ADSR) envelope, a pyramid envelope, and ramp envelope, respectively. The articulation field is flexible in that should the user of the orchestral composition library want to extend the instruments to include more articulations, the user may do so in the programming of the instruments without having to make changes in the programming library.

By delegating audio processing tasks to Csound, we can focus on higher-level musical abstractions in our orchestral composition library. Interfacing with Csound from our composition library requires only that we be able to generate a text file in the SCO format that Csound understands. By using an eight p-field note format as the standard for our library's output and our instrument designs' input, we create a system that allows for the experimentation of different musical ideas with different instruments.

14.4   Designing the Programming Library

Having decided to use Csound as the instrument part of our orchestral composition model and having established the means by which we will communicate with Csound (using SCO-formatted text output), we will now model the rest of the factors of orchestral composition we have observed by defining a few classes and establishing conventions for using these classes in ways that parallel the conventions of orchestral composition.

Although the class library here is designed for use with Csound, the general overall design and architecture is valid to be used with different musical data representations such as MIDI or OSC or whatever custom music model the user may decide to build.

14.4.1   Note

The Note class is used to represent the Note information given to performers. It is designed so that when notating musical ideas using this class, the user need only define the essential musical parameters inherent to the musical fragment, leaving out parameters which are normally associated with Performers: what instrument to perform this Note on as well as what the spatial location of the generated sound will be. In acoustic music, notated scores are given to performers to perform. The performers in turn will play that music on the instrument assigned to them; the spatial location is dependent on where they are sitting. Given that a comparable instrument on which the notated music can be performed is given to the same performer, that performer can perform the same music using the different instrument to get different results. Similarly, given the same music and same instrument but moving to another location, the performer will yield different end results. It is for these reasons that the spatial location and assigned instrument are properties that are part of our Performer class and not our Note class.

However, because of the decision to use Csound and to use the text note format that does define an instrument number and spatial location (p1 and p7), we will need to have the Note class ultimately converted to that eight p-field text format for use by Csound. We facilitate this when generating string text from our Note classes by having the Performer class which is performing the Note data pass in the spatial location and instrument number to use in the generated output.

The following is the header definition for the Note class:

```
class Note {
    public:
        float startTime;
        float duration;
        float pitch;
        float pitch2;
        float amp;
        int envType;
        bool isRest;

        Note(float startTime, float duration, float pitch,
            float pitch2, float amp, int envType);

        // This constructor is used to denote a Rest
        // and sets isRest to true
        Note(float startTime, float duration);

        string getNote(int instrumentNum, float space);
};
```

The Note class has seven member variables, six of which map to the Csound note format discussed in the previous sections, and one which is used to determine if the note is a played note or a rest:

float **startTime**—start time (p2)
float **duration**—duration (p3)
float **pitch**—starting pitch (p4)
float **pitch2**—ending pitch (p5)
float **amp**—amplitude in db (p6)
int **envType**—which amplitude envelope to use (p8)
bool **isRest**—determines if this note is to be treated as a rest (a rest generates no note text)

The two forms of the Note constructor methods are each used depending on if a normal performed note is being notated by the user or if it is a rest. When a Note is constructed as a normal performed note, Performer and PerformerGroup objects will take that Note data and create Csound SCO format text. When a Note is constructed as a rest, it will not generate any Csound SCO text but rather will be used to increment time to function as a silence.

The getNote method is used to ultimately generate the string representation of the Note and will be what is used as output to be captured into the SCO file to be used with Csound. Users of the library will not normally need to call the getNote method themselves but rather it will be used by the Performer class to facilitate a *performance* of that note.

14.4.2   Performer

The `Performer` class represents performers within our orchestral composition music model. The following is the header definition for the Performer class:

```
class Performer
{
    public:
    string name;
    int instrumentNum;
    float space;
    float baseAmp;

    Performer(int instrumentNum, float baseAmp, float space,
             string name);

    string toString();

    string perform(vector<Note> noteList, float startTime);

    string performAleatorically(vector<Note> noteList,
        float timeVariance, float ampVariance,
        float pitchVariance, float durationOfSection,
        float startTime);
};
```

The performer class has four member variables, configured as parameters to the Performer object's constructor method:

- string **name**—used for reference and debugging
- int **instrument**—maps to a Csound instrument ID (only numeric instrument ID's will be supported by this library)
- float **space**—denotes the location within the stereo field the performer will be (-1.0 = left, 0.0 = center, 1.0 = right)
- float **ampBase**—a float multiplier(0.0–1.0) value that a Performer will apply to amplitudes of notes that a Performer is given to perform; a simplified way to represent space in terms of depth (i.e. given that they perform at the same volume relative to each other, a performer

further upstage playing the same music and same instrument as someone further downstage will generally be not as loud as the one further downstage)

The Performer object also has three methods:

- string **toString()**—a utility method to display the performer's properties, useful for debugging compositional projects
- string **perform(vector<Note> noteList, float startTime)**—the primary performance method of the Performer class, used to give a Performer object a section of music to perform, resulting in generating Csound performance information (SCO)
- string **performAleatorically(...)**—a performance method used to perform a section of music in an aleatoric manner given a time to start and duration of time to perform, applying randomization to parameters given the modifier arguments.

The performance methods of the Performer class represent the performance techniques that performers understand how to perform. The user of the library will create and configure Performers, define musical ideas using a vector of Notes, and then have the Performers perform those musical ideas at a given start time. By defining musical material and separating the time at which the whole block of material is to be performed, we gain the ability to reuse the same material and have it performed at different times. This closely parallels the way music is generally conceived, i.e. "that this motive is played at this time and played again that time."

14.4.3   PerformerGroup

The `PerformerGroup` class represents sections of performers within our orchestral composition music model. The following is the header definition for the `PerformerGroup` class:

```
class PerformerGroup {
    public:
        string name;
        vector<Performer *> performers;

        PerformerGroup(string name);

        string toString();

        string perform(vector<Note> noteList, float startTime);

        string performAleatorically(vector<Note> noteList,
                    float timeVariance, float ampVariance,
                    float pitchVariance,float durationOfSection,
                    float startRange);

        string performSurface(float amp, int envType,
                    float time1a, float pch1a,
```

```
                                float time1b, float pch1b,
                                float time2a, float pch2a,
                                float time2b, float pch2b);
};
```

The performer group has two member variables:

- string **name**—used for reference and debugging
- vector<Performer *> **performers**—holds references to Performers to put in this group; uses pointers so that different groups may share references to the same Performers.

The performer object also has four methods:

- string **toString**()—a utility method to display the performer group's properties, useful for debugging compositional projects
- string **perform**(vector<Note> noteList, float startTime)—calls all performers in the group to perform the given noteList at the given startTime
- string **performAleatorically**(…)—calls all performers in the group to perform the given noteList aleatorically passing along randomization parameters, starting at a given time and randomizing when each performer should start within the startRange parameter
- string **performSurface**(…)—given the boundary parameters of the surface, calculate the individually unique glissandi notes each performer member of the group will perform to create the group glissandi musical surface

The performance methods of the performer group build upon the available performance methods of the individual performers: the group as an object does not do any performing itself. These group performance methods use one-to-many relationships in that the composer notates an idea for the group, which the group object then interprets as instructions for each individual performer. The result is that the user of the library can focus on notating a musical idea that will be performed by a group without having to individually notate and direct what each performer is to perform. This allows the user to continue to work with the abstract musical ideas, delegating to the library to convert the group instruction into individual directions for each performer in the group.

14.5   Using the Library for Composition

The general steps to using the orchestral composition library are very similar to composing for a live orchestra (table 14.2).

In general, the composer using the orchestral composition library will be working with musical ideas in much the same way that he might work with notating a score for a live orchestra. One advantage to using the orchestral composition library is that in notating for a live orchestra, all musical ideas require notating lines for each performer, even if the musical idea is a singular group sound and conceived as a single idea. With the orchestral

Table 14.2

Comparing the steps of composing for live orchestra and composing with the *orchestra library*.

Composing for live orchestra	Composing with orchestra library
Decide on what instruments to use for the piece (woodwinds, brass, strings, percussion, electronic).	Decide on what Csound instruments to use for the piece and place them in a Csound orchestra (ORC) file.
At the beginning of a score, define number and layout of performers of chosen instruments (some aspects may not be explicitly defined and left to the conductor to choose at performance time).	Create a C++ program to use the orchestra library and define the number and layout of performers of chosen instrument, achieved by creating instances of the Performer class and configuring the instances, optionally grouping into PerformerGroup objects.
Notate a score full of performance instructions to be performed by the performers on their instruments, giving times at which to play and what techniques to use; instructions for performing extended performance techniques are defined at the start of score.	In C++ program, call performance methods on Performer and PerformerGroup objects with Note data or other arguments; calling different methods is equivalent to composing for different performance techniques and the program being written is equivalent to the notated score for live orchestra; composer can define new performance techniques by adding methods to Performer or PerformGroup classes.
Perform the score with an orchestra, using a conductor as a source of time to drive the performance; at this time performers interpret the instruction into physical actions to generate the end musical result with their instruments.	Run the program to generate the Csound score (SCO) file that will be the performance instructions for the instruments in the ORC file. Run Csound with the ORC and SCO to create the end musical result.

composition library, the singular group sound idea can be notated and worked with as a single entity by the composer and the library can handle translating the instruction from the composer into sets of instructions for multiple performers. With this kind of mapping the composer can stay closer to working with the overall musical idea rather than constantly having to notate for one performer after another—switching mental contexts between the group idea and the singular parts making up that idea.

The following example program demonstrates the use of the orchestral composition library. Comments are added inline into the program to demarcate different musical examples. Other notes and explanations of the different parts of the program and musical examples follow.

```
#include <iostream>
#include <ctime>

#include "Note.hpp"
#include "Performer.hpp"
#include "PerformerGroup.hpp"
```

```cpp
using namespace std;

int main()
{
    // INITIALIZING RANDOM SEED
    srand( (unsigned)time( NULL ) );

    /*****************************/
    /* SETTING UP PERFORMER GROUPS */

    // PERFORMER GROUP A
    Performer a1(1, 0.997, -.3, "Performer A1");
    Performer a2(1, 1.0, 0.0, "Performer A2");
    Performer a3(1, .997, .3, "Performer A3");

    PerformerGroup groupA("Group A");
    groupA.performers.push_back(&a1);
    groupA.performers.push_back(&a2);
    groupA.performers.push_back(&a3);

    // PERFORMER GROUP B
    Performer b1(1, 1.0, -.2, "Performer B1");
    Performer b2(1, 0.95, -.15, "Performer B2");
    Performer b3(1, 0.9, -.1, "Performer B3");

    PerformerGroup groupB("Group B");
    groupB.performers.push_back(&b1);
    groupB.performers.push_back(&b2);
    groupB.performers.push_back(&b3);

    // PERFORMER GROUP C
    Performer c1(1, 1.0, .2, "Performer C1");
    Performer c2(1, 0.95, .15, "Performer C2");
    Performer c3(1, 0.9, .1, "Performer C3");

    PerformerGroup groupC("Group C");
    groupC.performers.push_back(&c1);
    groupC.performers.push_back(&c2);
    groupC.performers.push_back(&c3);

    // PERFORMER GROUP D
    Performer d1(1, 0.95, -.1, "Performer D1");
    Performer d2(1, 1.0, 0.0, "Performer D2");
    Performer d3(1, 0.95, .1, "Performer D3");

    PerformerGroup groupD("Group D");
    groupD.performers.push_back(&d1);
```

```
groupD.performers.push_back(&d2);
groupD.performers.push_back(&d3);

/********************/
/* MUSICAL EXAMPLES */
/********************/

/* EXAMPLE 1 - USING NOTE DIRECTLY */

Note direct(0, 1, 8.00, 8.00, 80, 0);
Note directCopy = direct;
directCopy.startTime = 1.00;
directCopy.pitch = 9.00;
directCopy.pitch2 = 9.00;

cout << direct.getNote(1, 0.0) << endl;
cout << directCopy.getNote(1, 0.0) << endl;

/* EXAMPLE 2 - USING PERFORMER AND PERFORMER GROUP
 * PERFORM METHODS */

// DEFINE NOTE DATA
Note a (0, 1, 8.00, 8.00, 80, 0);

vector<Note> noteList;

noteList.push_back(a);
noteList.push_back(Note(1, 1, 8.04, 8.04, 80, 0));
noteList.push_back(Note(2, 1, 8.07, 8.07, 80, 0));
noteList.push_back(Note(3, 1, 9.00, 9.00, 80, 0));
noteList.push_back(Note(0, 3));

// PERFORM NOTE DATA

cout << ";Begin Orchestra Output" << endl << endl;

cout << ";Testing Note" << endl;
cout << a.getNote(1, 0.0) << endl;

cout << endl << ";Testing Performers" << endl;

cout << a1.toString() << endl;
cout << a1.perform(noteList, 5.00) << endl;

cout << a2.toString() << endl;
cout << a2.perform(noteList, 10.0);

cout << a3.toString() << endl;
cout << a3.perform(noteList, 15.0);
```

```
cout << endl << ";Testing Performer Group" << endl << endl;
cout << groupA.toString() << endl;
cout << groupA.perform(noteList, 20.0) << endl;

/* EXAMPLE 3 - FOUR PART HARMONY WITH INDIVIDUAL
 * PERFORMERS AND PERFORMER GROUPS */

// DEFINE MUSICAL PARTS

vector<Note> harmonyPart1;
vector<Note> harmonyPart2;
vector<Note> harmonyPart3;
vector<Note> harmonyPart4;

harmonyPart1.push_back(Note(0, 1, 9.00, 9.00, 80, 0));
harmonyPart1.push_back(Note(1, 1, 9.00, 9.00, 80, 0));
harmonyPart1.push_back(Note(2, 1, 9.02, 9.02, 80, 0));
harmonyPart1.push_back(Note(3, 3, 9.00, 9.00, 80, 0));

harmonyPart2.push_back(Note(0, 1, 8.04, 8.04, 80, 0));
harmonyPart2.push_back(Note(1, 1, 8.05, 8.05, 80, 0));
harmonyPart2.push_back(Note(2, 1, 8.05, 8.05, 80, 0));
harmonyPart2.push_back(Note(3, 3, 8.04, 8.04, 80, 0));

harmonyPart3.push_back(Note(0, 1, 7.07, 7.07, 80, 0));
harmonyPart3.push_back(Note(1, 1, 7.09, 7.09, 80, 0));
harmonyPart3.push_back(Note(2, 1, 7.11, 7.11, 80, 0));
harmonyPart3.push_back(Note(3, 3, 7.07, 7.07, 80, 0));

harmonyPart4.push_back(Note(0, 1, 7.00, 7.00, 80, 0));
harmonyPart4.push_back(Note(1, 1, 6.05, 6.05, 80, 0));
harmonyPart4.push_back(Note(2, 1, 6.07, 6.07, 80, 0));
harmonyPart4.push_back(Note(3, 3, 7.00, 7.00, 80, 0));

// PERFORM MUSICAL PARTS

cout << endl << ";Four-Part Harmony - One per part" << endl;
cout << groupA.performers[0]->perform(harmonyPart1, 25) << endl;
cout << groupB.performers[0]->perform(harmonyPart2, 25) << endl;
cout << groupC.performers[0]->perform(harmonyPart3, 25) << endl;
cout << groupD.performers[0]->perform(harmonyPart4, 25) << endl;

cout << endl << ";Four-Part Harmony - Group per part" << endl;
cout << groupA.perform(harmonyPart1, 32) << endl;
cout << groupB.perform(harmonyPart2, 32) << endl;
cout << groupC.perform(harmonyPart3, 32) << endl;
cout << groupD.perform(harmonyPart4, 32) << endl;
```

```
/* EXAMPLE 4 - GROUP ALEATORY */

// SCORE FOR ALEATORY

vector<Note> alea1;
vector<Note> alea2;
vector<Note> alea3;
vector<Note> alea4;

alea1.push_back(Note(0, 3, 10.08, 10.07, 70, 1));
alea1.push_back(Note(4, 4.3, 10.09, 10.06, 70, 1));
alea1.push_back(Note(8, 4, 10.085, 10.065, 70, 1));
alea1.push_back(Note(0, 3));

alea2.push_back(Note(0, 2, 8.04, 8.04, 76, 1));
alea2.push_back(Note(2, 2, 8.05, 8.05, 76, 1));
alea2.push_back(Note(4, 2, 8.06, 8.06, 76, 1));
alea2.push_back(Note(6, 2, 8.05, 8.05, 76, 1));
alea2.push_back(Note(0, 3));

alea3.push_back(Note(0, 4, 7.10, 7.11, 75, 2));
alea3.push_back(Note(5, 4.3, 7.095, 7.115, 75, 2));
alea3.push_back(Note(10, 4, 7.105, 7.11, 75, 2));
alea3.push_back(Note(0, 3));

alea4.push_back(Note(0, 3, 7.02, 7.01, 77, 2));
alea4.push_back(Note(4, 3.3, 7.03, 7.015, 77, 2));
alea4.push_back(Note(8, 3.6, 7.025, 7.005, 77, 2));
alea4.push_back(Note(0, 3));

// PERFORMANCE OF ALEATORY

cout << endl << ";Testing PerformAleatorically Method" << endl;

cout << groupA.performAleatorically(alea1, 0.3, 0.1, .2, 35, 55, 5)
        << endl;

cout << groupB.performAleatorically(alea2, 0.2, 0.02, .02, 50,
        50, 7) << endl;

cout << groupC.performAleatorically(alea3, 0.01, 0.02, .02, 55,
        45, 6) << endl;

cout << groupD.performAleatorically(alea4, 0.1, .05, .05, 60,
        40, 8) << endl;


/* EXAMPLE 5 - SURFACES (GLISSANDI SOUND MASSES) */

cout << endl << ";Testing PerformSurface Method" << endl;
```

```
// CONTRACTING SURFACE
cout << groupA.performSurface(80, 1, 150.0, 9.10, 150.5, 10.04,
        162.0, 10.01, 162.5, 10.01) << endl;

// TWISTED SURFACE
cout << groupB.performSurface(80, 1, 135.0, 8.00, 135.5, 8.05,
        150.0, 9.00, 149.5, 7.07) << endl;

// EXPANDING SURFACE
cout << groupC.performSurface(80, 1, 145.0, 8.03, 145.5, 8.03,
        160.0, 7.11, 159.5, 8.08) << endl;

// EXPANDING SURFACE PROJECTING UPWARDS
cout << groupD.performSurface(80, 1, 135.0, 6.00, 135.5, 6.02,
        160.0, 7.00, 159.5, 7.04) << endl;

cout << endl << ";End Orchestra Output" << endl;

    return 0;
}
```

14.5.1   Initial Setup

This program starts off with a call to seed the random number generator with the current time, a common call to make before generating random numbers. Afterward is the initial setup section of the Performer and PerformerGroup objects that we will be using to perform the music we create. The Performers are all created with a parameter for their panning location and amplitude adjustment to simulate their spatial location as well as what Csound instrument they are to "play" or generate output for. For these musical examples we have chosen to use a single instrument type for all performers and groups, modeled somewhat on the string sections of a live orchestra. Four PerformerGroups are created, each with three Performers within them. They are laid out so that groupA is spread evenly and wide across panning spectrum, groupB is laid out slightly to the left of center, groupC is laid out slightly to the right of center, and groupD is laid out evenly like groupA but not as wide. Each group will perform music in similar registers to the Violin, Viola, Cello, and Bass sections of an orchestra.

14.5.2   Example 1: Using The Note Class Directly (0:00)

The first example does not use any Performers or Performer groups but instead uses the Note class directly to create Csound SCO output. This would normally not be used when using this library but can be useful when working with a sound idea directly that does not involve any abstractions like Performers or PerformerGroups. It is available to the composer to use for situations where direct control over the output of a note is desired.

14.5.3   Example 2: Using the Performer and PerformerGroup Perform Methods (0:05)

The second musical example is an arpeggio of the first, third, fifth, and octave scale degrees of a major scale. It is notated as a vector of Note objects. The musical example first demonstrates using the musical example with each of the individual performers from groupA, then using that same musical example calls groupA to perform it all together. Notice that in the same way that one may notate a musical line or motive and give it to a single performer to play or a group of performers to play, one can have the same representation and manner of operation in the orchestral composition library and achieve a similar solo and group audible result as one would expect from a live orchestra.

14.5.4   Example 3: Four-Part Harmony (0:25)

The third musical example is short four-part harmony (I-IV-V^7-I). It is notated as four lines of music using four vectors of Note objects. The four parts are first played by an individual member of each of the four PeformerGroups, and then performed a second time with each of the groups playing each of the parts. This example demonstrates more clearly the audible differences between using individual performers to perform musical lines and groups of performers. The example also shows the simplicity in switching between directing individual members of a group to perform a musical line and directing a group of performers to perform that musical line.

14.5.5   Example 4: Group Aleatory (0:40)

The fourth musical example is a demonstration of aleatoric music performed by groups. Four different musical fragments are notated and each of the four groups are directed to perform those fragments, starting at different times and with different parameters for degrees of variation in amplitude, pitch, duration, and a range of start times staggered for each member within each group. The fragment is given to the group and the group then staggers the start times and calls each member of the group to perform that fragment aleatorically, each applying their own spatial characteristics to their results. Because the algorithm for the aleatoric performance makes use of random number generators, each run of the program will result in uniquely generated output, much like how aleatoric music would be performed by a live orchestra. By having the ability to have unique performances, the composer can experiment with aleatoric musical ideas and rapidly test to see if the results match what he or she imagines they will be.

14.5.6   Example 5: Surfaces (Glissandi Sound Mass) (2:15)

The fifth and final example demonstrates composing with glissandi sound masses to create a surface of sound, modeled after musical structures used by Iannis Xenakis in his orchestral work *Metastasis*. Unlike the other examples, this one does not use a list of notes but instead calls the performSurface method on the PerformerGroup with a set of parameters to denote the two outer boundary lines of the surface, using time-pitch pairs for the starting and ending point of each boundary line. By denoting the start and end points of the boundary lines, the start and end points of each note for each member of the group can be calculated.

Four types of surfaces are used in the example: a contracting surface where the members start out at different pitches and converge to a single pitch, a twisted surface where members start out at different pitches from high to low and end up in opposite order from low to high, an expanding surface where all members of the group start at a single pitch and end up on different pitches above and below the starting pitch, and an expanding surface projecting upward where the overall mass starts at one set of pitches with a small range and ends up at another set of pitches all pitched higher than the first set and also with a larger range.

Conclusion

Orchestral music is a result of both the physical characteristics of the orchestra as well as the conventions of notating music for that ensemble. By developing a small C++ library used in conjunction with Csound, a model for orchestral composition was created that offers composers a similar experience to writing music for a live orchestra. Examples of composing for single performers as well as groups of performers demonstrated the flexibility of the library design to handle different compositional needs. The reader is encouraged to explore further usage of the library, to extend the library to accommodate new performance techniques, and to experiment with developing other interfaces for entering in and configuring data, such as building a graphical user interface.

Notes

1. This library was originally created using the Python programming language. The library and example are written here in C++ to better match the other content of this book. The most recent Python version of this library is included with the author's music composition software *blue*.

2. The Csound orchestra is not a model of orchestral composition but simply the collection of instrument definitions for a Csound project.

Appendix A: Command-Line Tools Reference

Jonathan Bailey

The command line was once the only means for interaction with a computer and, in some cases, still provides certain advantages over a graphical user interface for computation. This appendix functions as both a reference and overview for commonly available and widely utilized commands, tools and techniques within a UNIX-compatible command-line environment. Though not a tutorial, beginners should consider opening a terminal and following along with the commands outlined in this text to gain greater familiarity with the abilities of the command-line interface.

The first section of this appendix covers basic navigation and usage of the command-line interface. Next, we delve deeper into how to compile and build programs using **gcc** and **make**, and conclude with some tips on how to create and edit files from the command line using the **emacs** editor.

A.1 Bash Shell Fundamentals

In this first section, we cover the basics of using Bash, the most commonly encountered command-line shell.[1] Some of these examples make use of special characters—sometimes called "meta-characters"—that are available from the command line and provide shorthand notation for performing certain tasks or referencing standard file system locations. Refer to table A.1. for a list of these characters. Many of the commands and techniques covered in this section will work with other shells, though meta-character specifics, command syntax and outputted results may vary slightly.

A.1.1 Basic Navigation

There are a number of basic navigation commands built into Bash.

pwd—print working directory
This displays the current location on the file system. The following example shows that the author is currently situated in a directory called `jonb`, located within a directory called `Users`, located within the root directory of the computer:

Table A.1
Bash shell meta-characters and key shortcuts.

Character or command	Description
*	Wild card; matches all characters
.	Current directory
..	Parent directory
~/	Home directory
~foo	Home directory belonging to user "foo"
&	Execute process in the background
Key: ctrl-c	Cancel execution of a progress
Key: ctrl-z	Suspend process
Key: ctrl-d	Send EOF (end-of-file) character from standard input, or delete next character from the command shell
Key: Up-Arrow	Previous command history item
Key: Down-Arrow	Next command history item
Key: Left-Arrow	Move left one character
Key: Right-Arrow	Move right one character

```
jonb@oberheim:~$ pwd
/Users/jonb
```

cd—change directory

This moves the current user to a new location on the file system. When no argument is passed, cd changes to the location of the user's home directory (defined in the $HOME environment variable). Example:

```
jonb@oberheim:~$ cd /usr/local/bin
jonb@oberheim:/usr/local/bin$ cd
jonb@oberheim:~$
```

ls—list files

This reveals the contents of a directory. When no argument is passed, it lists the contents of the current working directory. A large variety of flags reveal additional information, including file permissions, creation data, modification date, size, and other file attributes. Example:

```
jonb@oberheim:~/book$ ls
appendix.doc      example_script.sh notes.txt
jonb@oberheim:~/book$ ls -al
total 32
drwxr-xr-x 6 jonb staff 204 Jun 19 14:02 .
drwx------ 70 jonb staff 2448 Jun 19 12:13 ..
-rw-r--r-- 1 jonb staff 4 Jun 19 14:02 .hidden
-rw-r--r-- 1 jonb staff 4 Jun 19 12:14 appendix.doc
```

```
-rwxr-xr-x 1 jonb staff 5 Jun 19 12:14 example_script.sh
-rw-r--r-- 1 jonb staff 8 Jun 19 12:14 notes.txt
jonb@oberheim:~/book$ ls -S
notes.txt     example_script.sh appendix.doc
```

mkdir—make directory

This creates a local directory on the filesystem. It requires a valid path and sufficient permissions to create the directory in the specified location.

rm—remove file

This deletes a file or directory from the disk. It requires a valid path and sufficient permissions to delete. Flags are provided to force file removal (–f) and recursively delete nested files and directories (–r). Example:

```
jonb@oberheim:~/book$ ls
appendix      example_script.sh notes.txt
appendix.doc      my_trash
jonb@oberheim:~/book$ ls my_trash/
foo
jonb@oberheim:~/book$ rm -rf my_trash/
jonb@oberheim:~/book$ ls
appendix      example_script.sh
appendix.doc      notes.txt
```

cp—copy file

This copies a file or directory from one location on disk to another. Use with –r flag to copy directory contents. It requires valid read permissions for the source files/directories and write permissions for the destination directory. Example:

```
onb@oberheim:~/book$ cp -r ~/Downloads/csound5/ .
```

mv—move file

This moves a file or directory from one location on disk to another. It requires valid read permissions for the source files/directories and write permissions for the destination directory.

ln—link file

This creates a hard or symbolic link between files, similar (but with slight implementation differences) to an "alias" in Mac OS or a symbolic link in recent versions of Windows. A symbolic or "soft" link is simply a reference to another file, and any modifications to the link itself will not affect the target file. In contrast, modifications to a hard link also apply to the target file, and hard links often may only be applied to files, not directories. Example:

```
jonb@oberheim:~$ ln -s /Applications/ apps
```

Table A.2
Examples of permissions settings.

`-rwxrwxrwx`	Read, write, and execute for owner, group, and others
`-rwx------`	Read, write, and execute for owner only
`-rw-r-r--`	Read and write for owner; read-only for group and others
`-rwx-x---`	Read, write, and execute for owner; execute-only for group

open—open a Finder window

This opens a Finder window from the specified location in the file system (MacOS X only).

A.1.2 Permissions and Accounts

Each file in a UNIX-like file system possesses three sets of read, write, and execute permissions (viewed in shorthand as `rwx`)—one set each for the user that owns the file, the group that owns the file, and the rest of the world ("others," sometimes called "global permissions"). These permissions can be viewed using the `ls` command, as shown in the above example, and are organized in the following order: owner permissions, group permissions, and other permissions. Continue below for commands that demonstrate modification of permissions. Refer to table A.2 for examples of different permissions schemes.

chmod—modify file permissions

This changes the permissions of a file or directory. Example:

```
jonb@oberheim:~/book$ ls -al example_script.sh
-rw-r--r-- 1 jonb staff 4 Jun 19 15:31 example_script.sh
jonb@oberheim:~/book$ chmod u=rwx,go=x example_script.sh
jonb@oberheim:~/book$ ls -al example_script.sh
-rwx--x--x 1 jonb staff 4 Jun 19 15:31 example_script.sh
```

chown—modify file owner

This changes the user or group that possesses ownership permissions over a given file. This naturally requires sufficient permissions—otherwise, one could steal files.

whoami—display current user

This reveals which system account the current user session is operating under.

su—substitute user

This allows a user to become another user given as the argument, after quoting a password or having sufficient permission by other methods. As a special case if no user name is given it logs in to the administrative account—known as "super user" or "root"—on a system. On UNIX systems this is user number 1. Example:

```
jonb@oberheim:~$ su
Password:
sh-3.2# whoami
root
```

sudo—execute a command as super user

This executes a command as the super user, or any other user. There is a complex mechanism to control this; users will normally have to quote the root password, or their own password, or for some commands no password. This is all controlled by the sudoer system, controlled by the super-user. Often this control is achieved by membership of a special group, often called "sudoers" or "wheel." Example:

```
jonb@oberheim:~$ whoami
jonb
jonb@oberheim:~$ sudo whoami
root
```

A.1.3   Locating and Viewing Files and Data

echo—view input

This prints out supplied input to the standard output. This is more useful that one might suppose, as it expands all special characters and shell variables before echoing, so it is a way to determine the values.

cat—view a file

This prints out a file to the terminal, all at once. The name is an abbreviation of concatenate as it will concatenate a number of files before printing. Example:

```
jonb@oberheim:~$ echo "foo" > bar
jonb@oberheim:~$ cat bar
foo
jonb@oberheim:~$ cat bar bar
foo
foo
```

more—view a file

This prints out a file to the terminal, scrolling forward one page at a time. It also incorporates simple searching.

less—view a file

This prints out a file to the terminal, allows navigating forward, backward, and line by line, as well as various search options. On some systems the commands more and less are actually identical.

head—view file head

This prints out only the beginning of a file. It defaults to 10 lines but can be controlled with a flag.

tail—view file tail

This prints out only the end of a file, again defaulting to 10 lines.

strings—print all strings in a file

This prints out string data from a file, especially useful for obtaining ASCII string data from binary files.

sort—sort file

This prints out the lines within a file, sorted alphabetically, numerically, or using various other sort criteria.

grep—find specified text within a file

This searches contents of readable files to determine if they contain a given term. grep uses a simple regular expression for the search; indeed the name stands for general regular expression. The variant **fgrep** (for fast grep) searches for the exact text and the **egrep** variant can be used to match search terms using extended regular expressions.[2] The following example searches files in all subdirectories (-r for recursive) of the directory "Opcodes" within the "Csound5.09.0" directory for the case-insensitive (-i) term "waveset," and returns resulting line and line number (-n). Example:

```
jonb@oberheim:~/Csound5.09.0$ grep -rin "waveset" Opcodes/
Opcodes/pitch.c:1953:int wavesetset(CSOUND *csound, BARRI *p)
Opcodes/pitch.c:1971:int waveset(CSOUND *csound, BARRI *p)
```

find—find a file on disk

This locates files that match a certain criteria, using related to their file name or type. The following example locates all files that end in the case-insensitive extension .c within the *Csound5.09.0* directory. Example:

```
jonb@oberheim:~$ find Csound5.09.0 -iname \*.c
Csound5.09.0/Engine/auxfd.c
Csound5.09.0/Engine/cfgvar.c
Csound5.09.0/Engine/csound_orc_compile.c
(etc)
```

The following example makes use of the ability to execute a nested command while searching for files using find. In this case, we incorporate the use of grep to locate all files within the current directory hierarchy that end in the case-insensitive extension `.c` and contain the case-insensitive phrase "moog":

```
jonb@oberheim:~$ find . -iname \*.c -exec grep -i "moog" {} \;
static int moogvcfset(CSOUND *csound, MOOGVCF *p)
static int moogvcf(CSOUND *csound, MOOGVCF *p)
(etc)
```

The reader should note that even though a semicolon terminates the command, it needs to be "escaped" with a backslash so that it will not be seen as the termination of the `find` command. As `*` is expanded to match all files, it too must be escaped. Clearly `find` is a very powerful command, but one with difficult syntax.

A.1.4 Compressed Formats

`zip` or `unzip`
This compresses or uncompresses one or more files using the PKZIP format. Example:

```
jonb@oberheim:~/book$ ls -F
dir1/  file1
jonb@oberheim:~/book$ zip -r stuff.zip dir1/ file1
    adding: dir1/ (stored 0%)
    adding: dir1/file2 (stored 0%)
    adding: file1 (stored 0%)
jonb@oberheim:~/book$ mv stuff.zip ..
jonb@oberheim:~/book$ cd
jonb@oberheim:~$ unzip stuff.zip
Archive: stuff.zip
    creating: dir1/
    extracting: dir1/file2
    extracting: file1
```

`gzip`—compression utility
This compresses files with the Lempel-Ziv compression algorithm, often in conjunction with the `tar` command for archiving. Use the `gunzip` command to uncompress files. Usually produces smaller files than `zip`.

`bzip2`—compression utility
This is yet another compression standard that is commonly encountered, employing the Burrows-Wheeler algorithm. It is also often used in conjunction with the `tar` command for archiving. Use the `bunzip2` command to uncompress files. It usually produces smaller files than `gzip`.

tar—archiving utility

This is used to archive files, commonly in conjunction with some kind of file compression. The name comes from **tape ar**chive although these days it is rarely used with tape. There is also an **ar** command, rarely used. The following example illustrates the use of tar with GZIP compression to archive and compress a directory, moves the file to a new location, and decompresses and extracts the file contents:

```
jonb@oberheim:~/book$ ls -F
dir1/   file1
jonb@oberheim:~/book$ tar zcvf stuff.tar.gz *
dir1/
dir1/file2
file1
jonb@oberheim:~/book$ mv stuff.tar.gz ..
jonb@oberheim:~/book$ cd
jonb@oberheim:~$ tar zxvf stuff.tar.gz
dir1/
dir1/file2
file1
```

A.1.5   Settings and Preferences

alias—create an alias for a command

This substitutes one command string for another. Remove the substitution using the **unalias** command. Example:

```
jonb@oberheim:~/book$ alias lf='ls -F'
jonb@oberheim:~/book$ lf
dir1/   file1
```

set—set a shell or environment variable

Set a local variable within the current instance of this shell, and do not export that variable to child processes or other shells spawned from the current shell. Remove the variable with **unset** command.[3]

export—set a shell or environment variable

Set a shell or environment variable and export it to all spawned processes and shells. The following example modifies the PATH environment variable, which determines the search path for executed commands:

```
jonb@oberheim:~/book$ which testcommand
jonb@oberheim:~/book$ export PATH=$PATH:~/book/bin
jonb@oberheim:~/book$ which testcommand
/Users/jonb/book/bin/testcommand
```

printenv—print all environment variables

This prints out all environment variables for the current user. Printing and setting of environment variables can also be accomplished using the env command.

In addition to manually specifying these shell and environment preferences at the command line, the user can utilize a special bash file in their home directory, *.profile*, as a means for storing these preferences across sessions. The following contents could be from an example *.profile*:

```
export PATH=$PATH:~/bin
export MANPAGER='less -R'
export VISUAL=/usr/bin/emacs
# aliases
alias l="ls -l"
alias ll="ls -al"
alias enw="emacs -nw"
alias buchla="ssh jonb@buchla"
```

source—read in shell variables, settings, and commands

This reads a file of shell commands as if they had been typed at the terminal. It is particularly useful to reload the shell settings from a specified file. For example, after modifying your *.profile* file, reload the new version with the following command:

```
jonb@oberheim:~/book$ source ~/.profile
```

A.1.6   Pipes, Redirection, and Streams

In addition to providing access to a rich set of command-line tools and programs, the shell allows users to route input and output between commands, files, and shell input/output streams. Three such i/o streams exist in the Bash environment—standard output, standard error, and standard input—and each stream can be accessed by a unique numeric *descriptor*. The ability to access i/o streams by descriptor and to route input and output between different commands greatly increases the power of the shell environment. See table A.3 for a list of meta-characters related to pipes and redirection within the command shell.

Here are some examples of how redirections and piping can be useful. The first is to request the web root from csounds.com and search the text for references to Barry Vercoe, suppressing error messages:

```
jonb@oberheim:~$ curl www.csounds.com 2>/dev/null | grep -i vercoe
```

The second example is to create a file called *moog_findings* that catalogs all instances of the case-insensitive string "moog" in Csound C source-code files and strip out any C-style comment lines:

```
jonb@oberheim:~$ find Csound5.09.0/ -iname \*.c -exec grep -i
    moog {} \; -print face| grep -v "/\*" >> moog_findings
```

Table A.3
Pipe and redirection meta-characters.

|	Direct output from one program to input of another program
>	Direct output from a program to a file
<	Direct contents of a file to standard input
>>	Direct output from a program and concatenate to a file
0	Standard input descriptor
1	Standard output descriptor
2	Standard error descriptor
&	File handle for i/o descriptors
2>&1	Redirect standard error to standard output
2>/dev/null	Redirect standard error to system "null" device (i.e., suppress error output)

A.1.7   System and Process Status

top—print system and process status information

This prints detailed information about current system status, including process owner, CPU utilization, memory utilization, and execution time.

ps—user process status

This prints status information for running processes. Flags can be supplied to constrain or expand search results. Here is an example of processes owned by current user:

```
jonb@oberheim:~/book$ ps
```

And here is an example of processes owned by a super user:

```
jonb@oberheim:~/book$ ps aux | grep root
```

As referenced in table A.1, bash provides the ability to launch processes in the background, thereby providing continued access to the shell and the ability to execute additional commands while the first command operates—and to suspend processes currently running in the foreground. Processes (sometimes called "jobs") running in the background can be listed using the jobs command, repositioned to the foreground using the **fg** command, or terminated using the **kill** command.

jobs—display shell jobs

This prints a numbered list of jobs running in the background.

fg—foreground

This moves a job running in the background to the foreground. Example:

```
jonb@oberheim:~/book$ jobs
[1]+ Stopped emacs
jonb@oberheim:~/book$ fg %1
```

kill—kill a process

This terminates or restarts a process via process identifier (pid). Use killall command to terminate all processes by command name. Use kill-9 to force quit. Here is an example of this command:

```
jonb@oberheim:~/book$ ps
   PID TTY TIME CMD
   879 ttys000 0:00.03 -bash
   520 ttys001 0:00.29 -bash
   1118 ttys001 0:00.09 emacs
jonb@oberheim:~/book$ kill -9 1118
jonb@oberheim:~/book$ ps
   PID TTY TIME CMD
   879 ttys000 0:00.03 -bash
   520 ttys001 0:00.30 -bash
[1]+ Killed emacs
jonb@oberheim:~/book$
```

nice—specify run time process priority

This allows the user to designate a priority level for an executed command. For example, this is useful to constrain the execution of a process—such as a full-disk find—that can otherwise consume system resources excessively. The super-user can also increase the priority by using negative priority. Example:

```
nice -n -10 find / -iname moog.c
```

time—time process execution

This measures and displays the execution time of a process. Example:

```
jonb@oberheim:~/book$ time sort file1
real    0m0.088s
user    0m0.001s
sys 0m0.004s
```

who—list system users

This displays who is on the system and which terminal they are accessing.

date—list system time

This displays the current system date and time.

A.1.8 Scripting

One of the most powerful features within Bash is the ability to create scripts and small programs, and execute those scripts directly within the command line or from a saved file. Though the subject of Bash scripting goes well beyond the scope of this chapter, we include a few examples of common script below to illustrates how scripts can help to automate and facilitate certain repetitive or complex command-line tasks.

The basic syntax of shell scripts is in many ways similar to other programming languages, such as C, but many small but noteworthy differences do exist. Most importantly, the treatment of variables is slightly different in Bash shell scripts. Whereas in C, you may assign to and read from a defined variable using exactly the same syntax, Bash uses a separate descriptor for reading from a defined shell variable. To set a shell variable "foo" to the value of "bar," use the familiar syntax

```
jonb@oberheim:~$ foo=bar
```

but there must not be any white space around the = sign. However, to read the value of foo that we have set you must use the $ character as a prefix to the variable name:

```
jonb@oberheim:~$ echo $foo
bar
```

In addition, bash supports the use of backticks (`` ` ``) to execute nested commands within a script. For example, in the following example, backticks are used to echo the string ls to the command shell, which has the equivalent effect of executing the ls command directly:

```
jonb@oberheim:~/book$ ls
bin dir1    file1    test
jonb@oberheim:~/book$ `echo ls`
bin dir1    file1    test
```

Loop syntax also differs in Bash scripts, in that the keywords do and done must be incorporated into the loop structure to define the start and end points of the scripted loop. To learn more about other specific idiosyncrasies of Bash scripting, consult one of the books listed in the reference for this appendix. Example: Print all of the valid MIDI note numbers to a file.

```
for i in `seq 0 127`; do echo $i >> midi_notes; done
```

Example: Convert all WAVE files in a directory to AIF format using sed and the **SoX** audio utility:

```
jonb@oberheim:~/book$ ls *.wav
file1.wav file2.wav file3.wav
jonb@oberheim:~/book$ for wav in `ls *.wav`; do aif=`echo $wav | sed
-e s/\.wav/\.aif/`; sox $wav $aif; done
```

```
jonb@oberheim:~/book$ ls *.aif
file1.aif  file2.aif  file3.aif
```

Example: Here is a script to convert MIDI notes to approximate pitch frequencies—i.e., a command-line version of the **mtof** program. This script reads in note values from standard input and makes use of the bash calculator, bc, to perform the mathematical computation:

```
jonb@oberheim:~/dev/audio$ while read note; do echo 'scale=6;
((220 * (1.0594631 ^ 3.0)) * (.5 ^ 5.0)) * ((1.0594631)^'$note')'
| bc 2>/dev/null; done
```

A.1.9 Command Help

man—manual pages for commands
This prints help files for all shell commands. Manual information for some built-in shell commands may require reading the manual for Bash itself, i.e., man bash, and searching for the desired command.

A.2 Compiling Code

UNIX-like systems offer a vast array of command-line source code compilers and interpreters for every conceivable programming language. The most utilized and popular command-line tool is the GNU C/C++ Compiler, **gcc**—a powerful open-source and cross-platform compiler, assembler and linker for C, C++, and Objective-C. This free tool functions as the compiler of choice for this book, and the following section will highlight some common options and techniques for compiling and building software projects using **gcc**. This section will also show some basic techniques for usage of the **make** command to compile and build larger software projects.

A.2.1 Compilation

Compilation is the process by which code written in a high-level programming language, such as C or C++, is translated into machine code for a target computing platform. Though often referred to using the singular term "compilation," the actual process involves several steps—"preprocessing" C or C++ source code to strip comments, include definitions from header files and replace macro and constant definitions; "compilation" of C or C++ code into assembly code; "assembling" of assembly code into machine binary code; and "linking" of binary objects into an executable program or shared library. Table A.4 lists several flags and options often used when processing, compiling, and assembling code with **gcc**. Note that although **gcc** can be used to compile both C and C++ by itself, we recommend the use of the **g++** program (part of the **gcc** tools package) for building C++ applications to ensure

Table A.4

The gcc/g++ compilation and assembly options.

gcc/g++ Flag	Description
`-c`	Compile and assemble into an object file, but do not link.
`-o <file>`	Place compiled output into specified file.
`-g`	Compile with debugging symbols.
`-Wall`	Enable all warnings for the GCC assembler.
`-W<warning>`	Enable a specific warning. For example, to warn that a variable is used before being initialized, use `-Wuninitialized`. See the GCC manual (man gcc) for all supported warnings.
`-std=<standard>`	Compile using designated C Standard. For example, to compile using the C99 standard instead of ANSI C, use the `-std=c99` flag.
`-E`	Pre-process code and print to standard output without compiling or assembling. The resulting effect is that of replacing all included headers, constant definitions, macros, and other pre-processor directives with their code equivalents and stripping out all comments.
`-S`	Translate C (or C++ or Objective-C) code into assembly code and output an assembly source file, but do not assemble into machine code or link. Useful for viewing and editing C or C++ code as assembly code.
`-I<dir>`	Include `<directory>` in the search path for included header files.
`-isystem <dir>`	Specify vendor-supplied system include location.
`-F <dir>`	Include header files from the specified framework (MacOS X only).
`-iwithsysroot <dir>`	Specify base SDK to build against (MacOS X only).
`-O(1-3)`	Specify the code optimization level—shorthand mechanism for turning on many of the specific optimizations that are available as individual flags.
`-D<name>`	Define a macro or constant from the command line. For example `-Dpi=3.14159` would define an approximation for pi. When value is omitted, assigned a value of 1.
`-arch`	Specify processor architecture: i386, ppc, or ppc64.
`--version`	Print detailed version information.
`--help`	Print help text.

that the correct standard C++ libraries and search paths are used when you compile your programs. (See table A.4.)

Example: Compile, assemble, and link the file test1.c into the executable program, *a.out*:

```
jonb@oberheim:~/book$ gcc test1.c
```

Example: Compile, assemble, and link the file *test1.c* into the executable program *test* with debug symbols:

```
jonb@oberheim:~/book$ gcc -o test -g test1.c
```

Example: Compile and assemble the file *test1.c* into the binary output file, *test.o*, for subsequent linking. Use the C99 standard and print out all warnings. Here is the command line:

```
jonb@oberheim:~/book$ gcc -c -o test.o -std=C99 -Wall test1.c
```

A.2.2   Linking

In linking (the final stage of the overall compilation process), compiled binary resources are combined into a single executable program or library. Linking can be performed either "dynamically" or "statically." Static linking embeds all the dependent code that is needed for a program or library into a single executable or library file. For example, if you write a program that makes use of Richard Dobson's **portsf** library for opening or saving audio files, and you statically link **portsf**, then the binary code for all of the functions implemented in **portsf** will be copied into your program's resulting binary executable file, along with the binary code created from your source code. Dynamically linking, by contrast, establishes references to shared resources, such as third-party libraries, without requiring a copy of that code within the resulting binary program or library. When the program is executed, the run time environment will resolve references to any dependent libraries and load those resources as needed before execution. There are advantages and disadvantages to both approaches, but developers normally recommend dynamic linking because of the space saved by sharing a single common library resource between multiple programs and the freedom from having to recompile a program whenever a dependent library implementation changes.

Note that linking with **gcc/g++** really passes along the linking instructions to the tools **ld** and **libtool**. This **ld** tool is the standard linking tool and can handle all required linking tasks within the GNU development environment, and **libtool** is a specialized front-end to **ld** that facilitates the creation of libraries. Most of the features of both **ld** and **libtool** are accessible from the front-end provided by **gcc/g++**, as can be seen in the following example. (Also see table A.5.)

Example: Link binary output files *test1.o* and *test2.o* and the **portaudio** library into the program **test**:

```
jonb@oberheim:~/book$ gcc test1.o test2.o -lportaudio -o test
```

Table A.5

The gcc/g++ linking options.

gcc/g++ flag	Description
-print-search-dirs	Prints out search directories for included headers and libraries
-l<library>	Links to binary code from <library>. For example, to build against the portaudio library, use the option -lportaudio. This has the equivalent effect of passing a direct path to liblibrary.a on the command line to gcc/g++.
-L<directory>	Includes <directory> in the search path for included library files
-framework <name>	Includes named OS X framework (MacOS X only)
-o <file>	Places compiled output into specified file
-bundle	Outputs linked results in mach-o bundle file format (MacOS X only)
-dynamiclib	Creates a dynamic library (dylib) instead of an executable file (MacOS X)
-shared	Creates a shared library (.so, .dll) instead of an executable file (other platforms)

A.2.3   The make Utility

A real-world project of any appreciable complexity will undergo compilation many times as it evolves through the software lifecycle of design, development, testing and release. As you can imagine, having to manually recompile large projects as they evolve, or as they are ported and distributed to new platforms, would present an unnecessary headache for programmers. The **make** command addresses this issue by allowing custom compilation and linking steps to be stored in a file, called a *Makefile*, that is saved to disk for repeated use. The utility also provides a mechanism for only re-compiling and re-linking resources whenever they are modified or updated.

The compilation settings stored in a working Makefile are actually quite simple—they comprise a set of variables, or "macros" in **make** nomenclature, and compilation rules. Required syntax for a Makefile macro is very similar to the syntax for shell variables. To define a macro, you must use the form name = value. To read a macro, you must use the form $(name).

Makefile rules contain two parts: the "dependency," which informs **make** when to perform a compilation, and the "shell lines," which inform **make** how to perform the compilation. The dependency always occurs on a dedicated line and follows the form target: dependency1 dependency2 . . . . Each dependency must possess a corresponding shell line, which is prefixed by a tab and occurs immediately after the dependency line[4]: compiler/linker (flags) file1 file2. For example, the contents of a simple Makefile to compile and link the program **test** from the source file *test.c* could look like this:

```
CC = gcc
test: test.o
    $(CC) -o test test.o
test.o: test1.c
    $(CC) -c -o test.o test1.c
```

When run using the command make test, the contents of this Makefile instruct **make** to build the target program test whenever test.o needs to be updated—i.e., it is missing or has changed. During the first compilation, **make** determines that test.o does not yet exist, and thus it will recursively resolve that dependency and ensure that the target test.o is built before continuing. The dependency for test.o is similarly dependent on test1.c, and will be rebuilt whenever the file *test1.c* changes. To build the target test.o, the command line following that dependency is executed on the shell, using the compiler defined in the macro, CC.

A specialized and useful type of Makefile rule called an "inference rule" makes reduces the need for redundant rules for similar types of resources in a Makefile. Consider the following Makefile:

```
CC = gcc
LINKER = gcc
CFLAGS = -c -ggdb
test: test1.o test2.o
    $(LINKER) -o test test1.o test2.o
test1.o: test1.c
    $(CC) $(CFLAGS) -o test.o test1.c
test2.o: test2.c
    $(CC) $(CFLAGS) -o test.o test2.c
```

As you can see, each of the two source files requires a separate Makefile rule that differs only by filename. A version of the same Makefile that makes use of an inference rule to eliminate the redundancy might work as follows:

```
CC = gcc
LINKER = gcc
CFLAGS = -c -ggdb
OBJECTS = test1.o test2.o
default: test
test: $(OBJECTS)
        $(LINKER) $(OBJECTS) -o test
.o: $*.c
        $(CC) $(CFLAGS) $*.c
clean:
        /bin/rm -rf *.o test
```

The rules for building each object file have been replaced by a generic object file extension that uses a wildcard character to match the source code filename with the object. All dependent object files are now defined in the macro, OBJECTS. Note also the presence of rules for the targets `clean` and `default`. The `clean` rule simply executes a shell command to delete all object and program files, and is very commonly used within Makefiles. The `default` rule allows the program to be built by simply running the command, `make`, from the command line.

A.3   Editing Files

Command-line text editors are much like digital audio workstation programs—engineers love to talk themselves in circles about which one works the best, and in the end they all have similar enough capabilities that the most logical approach is simply to pick one and learn it inside and out. The two main protagonists in the so-called editor war are the two most common command-line text editors, **emacs** and **vi**. Both are fully featured and stable applications that are capable of performing tasks far beyond anything you actually have to do in order to get some work done, and the author does not recommend one over the other. That said, since at a certain point in time, the author learned **emacs**, and never had a good enough reason to learn anything else, that's what we'll cover in this editor reference.

To launch **emacs**, assuming the program is installed in your shell, simply type

```
jonb@oberheim:~/book$ emacs
```

You can also pass a filename as an argument to open that file by default:

```
jonb@oberheim:~/book$ emacs test1.c
```

If you pass multiple files as arguments, they will all be opened into separate "buffers" in **emacs**. Think of these buffers as being separate "documents," each in a separate floating window or frame within a traditional GUI text editor.

A.3.1   Basic Commands

In any text editor, it is important to know how to get around. See table A.6 for a set of basic navigation commands for **emacs**, some of which will seem intuitive and some of which will require some getting used-to. Some of these commands refer to a "Meta" key—this is usually the "esc" key as a prefix, but is often remapped to "alt" or "option" in most shell environments for ease. In addition, some commands reference the "kill ring"—this is a special buffer in **emacs** for text that has been deleted, but it can be reclaimed after deletion by certain other commands. This becomes a very useful tool for actions such as cutting and pasting.[5]

Table A.6
Basic emacs navigation and editing commands.

`ctrl-x` `ctrl-s`	Save file.
`ctrl-x` `ctrl-f`	Open a file.
`ctrl-x` `ctrl-w`	Write current buffer to a new file.
`ctrl-x` `ctrl-q`	Quit emacs.
`ctrl-x k`	Kill buffer.
Key: `Up-Arrow or Control-p`	Move up one line.
Key: `Down-Arrow or ctrl-n`	Move down one line.
Key: `Left-Arrow or ctrl-b`	Move left one character.
Key: `Right-Arrow or Control-f`	Move right one character.
`Meta-f`	Move forward one word or token.
`Meta-b`	Move back one word or token.
`ctrl-a`	Move to beginning of the current line.
`ctrl-e`	Move to the end of the current line.
`ctrl-v`	Page forward.
`Meta-v`	Page back.
`Meta-<`	Go to beginning of buffer.
`Meta->`	Go to the end of the buffer.
`Meta-x goto-line`	Go to line number.
`ctrl-d`	Delete the following character.
`Alt-d`	Delete the following word/token (place into "kill ring").
`ctrl-k`	Delete the following line, up to the newline character (place into "kill ring").
`ctrl-y`	"Yank" or return text from the "kill ring."
`ctrl-s`	Forward search.
`ctrl-r`	Reverse search.
`Meta-%`	Replace text.
`ctrl-spacebar`	Define the start of a copy/cut region.
`Meta-w`	Define the end of a copy region and copy.
`ctrl-w`	Define the end of a cut region and cut.
`ctrl-x` `ctrl-b`	View list of available buffers.
`ctrl-x b`	Move to another buffer.
`ctrl-x 2`	Split screen horizontally between two buffers.
`ctrl-x 3`	Split spleen vertically between two buffers.
`ctrl-x 1`	Return to a single screen.
`ctrl-l`	Re-center page view around cursor line location.
`ctrl-x u`	Undo.
`ctrl-g`	Cancel in-progress command.
`Meta-x help`	Help subsystem for emacs.

Table A.7
Additional emacs commands for developers.

`Meta-x compile`	Compile code with the specified compile command.
`Meta-x shell`	Open a shell within the editor.
`ctrl-c ctrl-c`	Scroll to next error in the compile buffer.
`Meta-x comment-region`	Turn the region into comments.
`Meta-x gdb`	Run the GNU debugger within emacs.

A.3.2   Useful Commands for Development

The **emacs** editor, long used for development, was originally developed by the same author of the GNU development tools **gcc** and **gdb**. Thus, there are a variety of features in **emacs** that are useful for developers, some of which are listed in table A.7.

A.3.3   Running Macros

For automating repeated tasks, **emacs** also supports the creation of simple keyboard macros. The process works as follows:

- Enter the command "Meta-x(" to signal the start the macro.
- Perform some combination of keyboard commands.
- Enter the command "Meta-x)" to signal the end of the macro.
- Enter the command "ctrl-x e" to execute the macro.
- Enter the command "e" to continue executing the macro.

A.3.4   Stored User Preferences in the *.emacs* File

Upon launch, **emacs** reads the `.emacs` file in the user's home directory to obtain any preferences and settings, including custom key bindings and definitions for custom functions. For example, here is a line that can be placed in a `.emacs` file to remap the command Meta-x goto-line to the key combination Meta-g:

```
(define-key global-map "\M-g" 'goto-line)
```

Function definitions for **emacs** must be implemented in the lisp programming language, whose details and syntax are beyond the scope of the book. However, the author recommends self-study of this topic for readers with particular interest in **emacs** and, as inspiration, has included a custom function definition below to insert a custom code header into a source file. Copy the entire passage below into your `.emacs` file and execute using Meta-/ to see the results.

```
(defun jb-insert-code-header ()
   (interactive)
   (insert "//\n")
   (insert "// " (buffer-name) "\n")
   (insert "// (Project Name)\n")
   (insert "//\n")
   (insert "// Author: Jonathan Bailey, drumwell@gmail.com\n")
   (insert "// Created on: ")
   (insert (shell-command-to-string "date +%m/%d/%Y"))
   (insert "// Copyright Drumwell Group " (shell-command-to-string
      "date +%Y"))
   (insert "//\n"))

(global-set-key "\M-/" 'jb-insert-code-header)
```

One of the major features of emacs is indeed its extensibility. With custom lisp code one can change emacs to ones personal taste, add commands, and change the keystrokes for others.

A.4 Learning More

The UNIX-compatible command line is far too complex and powerful to cover in full detail in a short appendix. But many books have been written about both the shell environment as a whole, and even about distinct commands, including **emacs** and **sed**. Further, **bash**, **gcc**, and **emacs** are only singular examples of the many shells, compilers, and text editors that are available for use in the command line. Refer to the references section for more links and books to learn more about this powerful computing environment and tool set.

Notes

1. There is an alternative family of shell interfaces based strongly on the C language, called the C shell; the common variant at present is the **tcsh** program. In many ways it is very similar to **bash**, as it uses arguments, environment, variables as so forth, but with different syntax. It is a matter of personal choice which shell one uses.

2. A regular expression is a character sequence used for matching patterns in text strings.

3. This behavior is significantly different in the C shell.

4. One can have a dependency with no shell line, as long as it is somewhere. Also, one can have multiple lines each starting with a tab. As there is no tab, we know the dependency line has ended.

5. Note that **emacs** also has a built-in tutorial, accessed with the ctrl-h t key combination; and an extensive help and documentation system. One can query any key combination by prefacing it with ctrl-h k, and one can query the documentation for a function with ctrl-h f.

Appendix B: Debugging Software with the GNU Debugger

Jonathan Bailey

Software bugs—logical, algorithmic, and/or syntactical flaws that cause undesired behavior or output within a program—are an unfortunate fact of life in the world of programming. Every software developer writes buggy code, and a mastery of the techniques required to locate and remediate bugs is essential for success in any programming endeavor. In this chapter we outline a set of core techniques for debugging software using code examples from the preceding sections of the book. This overview makes use of the cross-platform and freely available GNU Debugger, **gdb**, to illustrate this set of common debugging practices; however, the underlying concepts apply equally well to any other debugger or integrated development environment.

B.1 Basic Debugging Techniques

Before we delve into a debugging session using **gdb**, we must first understand something about what a debugger is and how it works, and how we can make use of such a tool to better understand the inner workings of our code. Fundamentally, a debugger is simply a piece of software that runs another program in a manner that better illuminates the run time state of that program in a controlled setting. A debugger can provide a clearer view of a program's internal functionality by allowing the developer to run the compiled code step by step and to view the program's data structures and variables as their values change.

In most cases, before a program can be run within a debugger it must undergo a small amount of additional preparation to allow the debugger to correlate the compiled version of the program with the original source code. Most integrated development environments support this by specifying different build modes for a project, such as a "development" and "deployment," but in the **gcc/gdb** environment we prepare a program for debugging by specifying the '-ggdb'[1] flag during compilation. Using Richard Dobson's frequency-to-MIDI conversion utility, **ftom** (located on the DVD), as our first example, we can compile *ftom.c* as required using the following command[2]:

```
$ gcc -ggdb -o ftom ftom.c
```

The debugging information must be stored somewhere, and there are two main mechanisms used in different platforms. One scheme, used on Linux for example, is to write a larger binary file with debugging tables at the end of the executable part. The other way is to create a new file for this information, as used on OS X. On that platform, listing the contents of the directory containing the source file and the newly compiled program, we can see that an additional file has been created that contains the desired "debug symbols" for debugging the program using **gdb**.[3] We can now load this program into the debugger as follows.

```
$ gdb ftom
```

At this point, you should see some version, copyright, and license information for **gdb**, and a command prompt that provides the main user interface for the command-line version of **gdb**. Entering the `help` command at the prompt will reveal a list of commands, organized into various topics, that can be executed from this prompt:

```
(gdb) help
List of classes of commands:

aliases -- Aliases of other commands
breakpoints -- Making program stop at certain points
data -- Examining data
files -- Specifying and examining files
internals -- Maintenance commands
obscure -- Obscure features
running -- Running the program
stack -- Examining the stack
status -- Status inquiries
support -- Support facilities
tracepoints -- Tracing of program execution without stopping the
program
user-defined -- User-defined commands

Type "help" followed by a class name for a list of commands in that
class.
Type "help" followed by command name for full documentation.
Command name abbreviations are allowed if unambiguous.
```

As the instructions indicate, to learn more about a "class" of commands, you can enter `help` followed by the class name. For example, you can learn more about the set of commands that relay status information about the current debugging sessions as follows:

```
(gdb) help status
Status inquiries.

List of commands:

info -- Generic command for showing things about the program being
debugged
```

```
macro -- Prefix for commands dealing with C preprocessor macros
show -- Generic command for showing things about the debugger

Type "help" followed by command name for full documentation.
Command name abbreviations are allowed if unambiguous.
```

Again, per the displayed the instructions, to learn more about any individual command, type help and the command name.

```
(gdb) help macro
Prefix for commands dealing with C preprocessor macros.

List of macro subcommands:

macro define -- Define a new C/C++ preprocessor macro
macro expand -- Fully expand any C/C++ preprocessor macro invocations
in EXPRESSION
macro expand-once -- Expand C/C++ preprocessor macro invocations
appearing directly in EXPRESSION
macro list -- List all the macros defined using the 'macro define'
command
macro undef -- Remove the definition of the C/C++ preprocessor macro
with the given name

Type "help macro" followed by macro subcommand name for full
documentation.
Command name abbreviations are allowed if unambiguous.
```

The scope of this overview will cover only a small selection of the available commands within **gdb**, but we encourage you to learn more about all of the features of this debugger by exploring the help command further.

B.1.1 Running the Program and Viewing Memory

The first step in actually debugging a program is usually to identify sections of the code that we would like to review as the program executes, which we can accomplish by setting a "breakpoint" on those particular lines of code in the program. The purpose of a breakpoint is to inform the debugger to pause the execution of a program whenever the line of code that contains the breakpoint is encountered during the debugging session. By pausing a running program temporarily, we can step through the code at a slower pace, reviewing the state of variables and confirming that the path of execution actually occurs as expected.

To set a breakpoint in our example program, **ftom**, we start by first reviewing the source code from within **gdb** by using the list command to display the first 37 lines from the *ftom.c*. This will reveal the entire program source, numbered line by line, within **gdb**'s output.

```
(gdb) list 1,37
1    /* listing 1.2. Calculate frequency of a MIDI Note number */
2    #include <stdio.h>
3    #include <math.h>
4
5    int main()
6    {
7        double semitone_ratio;
8        double fracmidi;
9        double c0;
10       double c5;
11       double frequency; /* which we want to find, */
12       int midinote; /* given this note. */
13
14       /* calculate required numbers */
15       /* find nearest MIDI note to a given frequency in Hz */
16       /* uses the log rule:
17        log_a(N) = log_b(N) / log_b(a)
18        to find the log of a value to base 'semitone_ratio'.
19        */
20
21       semitone_ratio = pow(2, 1/12.0); /* approx. 1.0594631 */
22
23       /* find Middle C, three semitones above low A = 220 */
24       c5 = 220.0 * pow(semitone_ratio, 3);
25
26       /* MIDI Note 0 is C, 5 octaves below Middle C */
27       c0 = c5 * pow(0.5, 5);
28       frequency = 400.0;
29       fracmidi = log(frequency / c0) / log(semitone_ratio);
30
31       /* round fracmidi to the nearest whole number */
32       midinote = (int) (fracmidi + 0.5); //casting
33       printf("The nearest MIDI note to the
34       frequency %f is %d\n", frequency, midinote);
35       return 0;
36   }
37
```

As we can see from the output above, the first 20 or so lines of code simply define variables and contain comments. The first real expression is contained at line 21, so we can set a breakpoint here to view the results of the semitone ratio calculation.

```
(gdb) break 21
Breakpoint 1 at 0x1e93: file ftom.c, line 21.
```

Let's set another breakpoint at the last line in the program, which, as we saw from the output of the `list` command, occurs where the `printf` function is called on line 33.

```
(gdb) break 33
Breakpoint 2 at 0x1f69: file ftom.c, line 33.
```

We can now execute the program within **gdb** using the `run` command. This will cause **gdb** to execute the program as though run from the command line, however **gdb** will pause execution whenever a breakpoint is encountered. This will occur almost immediately in our example because we have placed our first breakpoint on the first logic expression in the program.

```
(gdb) run
Starting program: /path/to/ftom
Reading symbols for shared libraries ++. done

Breakpoint 1, main () at ftom.c:21
```

As we expect, as soon as **gdb** reaches line 21, the first breakpoint is encountered and the execution of **ftom** pauses. We can now view the current contents of the program's variables in memory, whose values we cannot at this stage predict because they have not yet been initialized with any valid data. One of several options of viewing these variables is the `print` command, which literally prints the data stored in each variable to the debugger's console.

```
(gdb) print semitone_ratio
$1 = 0
(gdb) print c5
$2 = 8.6928873489885679e-311
(gdb) print frequency
$3 = 0
(gdb) print midinote
$4 = -1881141193
```

We continue running the program up until the next breakpoint using the `continue` command. The debugger will execute all of the intermediary program code between the current and subsequent breakpoints and pause again. When we `print` the same values from memory as above, we will see the expected modifications performed by the program code from line 21 up to, but not including, 33. This is an important point to keep in mind—a breakpoint on a given line of code pauses the run time execution of a program *before* that line of code is executed.

```
(gdb) continue
Continuing.
```

```
Breakpoint 2, main () at ftom.c:33
33      printf("The nearest MIDI note to the frequency %f is %d\n",
frequency, midinote);
(gdb) print semitone_ratio
$5 = 1.0594630943592953
(gdb) print c5
$6 = 261.62556530059868
(gdb) print frequency
$7 = 400
(gdb) print midinote
$8 = 67
```

At this point, we can continue to the end of the program to view the results of the call to printf.

```
(gdb) continue
Continuing.
The nearest MIDI note to the frequency 400.000000 is 67

Program exited normally.
(gdb)
```

B.1.2   Exerting Greater Control over the Debugging Sessions

Setting breakpoints within a program and running between those breakpoints is a useful debugging technique, but sometimes we'd like to slow down the execution of the program even further and step through each line of a program at our own pace. Additionally, the task of manually printing each variable value we wish to monitor could quickly become cumbersome. Below we will run the program, **ftom**, again to execute the code and view data with greater control using the commands step and display.

```
(gdb) run
Starting program:
/Users/jonb/dev/audio/class/apb/redux/debug/ftom

Breakpoint 1, main () at ftom.c:21
21      semitone_ratio = pow(2, 1/12.0); /* approx. 1.0594631 */
(gdb) display midinote
1: midinote = -1881141193
(gdb) display fracmidi
2: fracmidi = 0
(gdb) step
24      c5 = 220.0 * pow(semitone_ratio, 3);
2: fracmidi = 0
1: midinote = -1881141193
```

```
(gdb) s
27      c0 = c5 * pow(0.5, 5);
2: fracmidi = 0
1: midinote = -1881141193
(gdb) s
28      frequency = 400.0;
2: fracmidi = 0
1: midinote = -1881141193
(gdb) s
29      fracmidi = log(frequency / c0) / log(semitone_ratio);
2: fracmidi = 0
1: midinote = -1881141193
(gdb) s
32      midinote = (int) (fracmidi + 0.5); //casting
2: fracmidi = 67.349957715000727
1: midinote = -1881141193
(gdb) s

Breakpoint 2, main () at ftom.c:33
33      printf("The nearest MIDI note to the frequency %f is %d\n",
frequency, midinote);
2: fracmidi = 67.349957715000727
1: midinote = 67
```

As can be seen, we selected two variables for continuous monitoring using the `display` command, which accepts a variable name as argument. Using the `step` command (and subsequently `s` for shorthand), we are able to step through each line of code manually and review the current value for the variables `midinote` and `fracmidi` after each line. This not only saves us the time of printing out the values of the variables manually but also allows us to view how and when their values changed as the program executes.

B.2 Debugging a More Complex Program

The previous example illustrated several techniques for debugging a fairly simplistic program that contained a small amount of code and only one function. Most real-world applications are much larger in size and scope, often containing thousands of lines of code across hundreds of functions defined in many different files. In the next example, we look at some additional debugging techniques for evaluating a larger application whose logic and code spans several files and different functions, **simple_oscil**. This program is a simple monophonic synthesizer, based on an oscillator, that runs from the command-line and makes use of the **portaudio** library for playback of generated audio, and can be found on the DVD.

Once we have succeeded in building **simple_oscil**, we can load the program into **gdb**, as before, and begin setting breakpoints wherever we want to pause the execution of the program. In this case, because we have multiple files that comprise the logic for this project, we must specify a filename wherever we want to view source from a particular file within **gdb**. Below, we view the code surrounding the function definitions for main in *simple_oscil.c* and create_wave_square function in *simple_waveforms.c*, using the ability of the list command to accept a function name in addition to the range of line numbers used previously.

```
(gdb) list simple_oscil.c:main
184         }
185     }
186
187
188     int main(int argc, char *argv[])
189     {
190         simpleOscil data; // data structure that will contain the
defined waveshapes and be passed to portaudio
191
192         if(argc < 4) {
193             usage();
(gdb)  list simple_waveforms.c:create_wave_square
34             triangle[i] = 1 - (i-halfway)*2.0/(float)(halfway);
35         }
36     }
37
38     // square wave - 1 until the middle of the period, and then
back down to -1
39     void create_wave_square(float *square, int wave_length) {
40         float halfway = ((float)wave_length)/2.;
41         int i;
42         for(i = 0; i < wave_length; i++)
43             square[i] = (i < halfway) ? 1 : -1;
```

As we did when viewing code form multiple files within **gdb**, we must also specify file names when setting breakpoints for multi-file projects. In the following section, we'll show how to set a breakpoint on a function, using the examples create_wave_sine and create_wave_square in the file *simple_waveforms.c*.

B.2.1 Conditional Debugging

Setting a breakpoint on a function name is a useful technique and saves the developer the trouble of determining lines numbers for code that requires inspection during debugging.

In actual fact, when we set a breakpoint on a function, we are really setting a breakpoint on the first line of code contained in that function. For this debugging session, we will also make use of an additional feature of **gdb** that allows developers to have greater control over the debugging session by assigning conditions to breakpoints.

```
(gdb) b simple_waveforms.c:create_wave_sine
Breakpoint 1 at 0xf2c5: file simple_waveforms.c, line 12.
(gdb) b simple_waveforms.c:create_wave_saw
Breakpoint 2 at 0xf334: file simple_waveforms.c, line 20.
(gdb) info b
Num Type       Disp Enb Address  What
1 breakpoint   keep y 0x0000f2c5 in create_wave_sine
                                 at simple_waveforms.c:12
2 breakpoint   keep y 0x0000f334 in create_wave_saw
                                 at simple_waveforms.c:20
(gdb) condition 1 wave_length < 1024
(gdb) condition 2 wave_length > 1024
```

The output above shows that **gdb** associates a number with each breakpoint we set, which we can view at any time using the `info breakpoints` (or `info b`, for shorthand) command. A breakpoint's number can be used to associate a conditional expression with a given breakpoint. The expression must be valid within the scope of the location of the breakpoint in the program—for example, an expression that is dependent on a variable must reference a variable that resides within the scope of the breakpoint location.

Conditional breakpoints can be very useful in debugging—they will only cause the execution of the program to pause whenever **gdb** reaches the associated line within the running program *and* the condition assigned to that breakpoint evaluates to true. In this case, the condition that we have set will cause the first breakpoint, on the first line of the function `create_wave_sine`, to pause the program execution only when the program reaches that function and supplies an argument within `wave_length` that contains a value of less than 1,024. Correspondingly, the second breakpoint, on the first line of the function `create_wave_saw`, will only cause a break when the `wave_length` argument is greater than 1,024. Assuming that the main body of the program creates wave tables of a constant size (which it does), these two conditions should prove to be mutually exclusive, and only one of the breakpoints should trigger during run time.

As we saw in the first example, **gdb** informs the user whenever a breakpoint is encountered, thus we can empirically confirm which breakpoint triggers by simply running the program and reviewing the output. As a quick aside, this program differs from the first example in that we need to supply a set of command-line arguments to the program; if we enter the `run` command without any arguments, the program will execute the `usage` function (which displays required call-time syntax to the user), and exit, as follows.

```
(gdb) run
Starting program: path/to/simple_oscil
Reading symbols for shared libraries +++++++. . .. . .. . .. . .. . ..
. .. . .. . .. . .. . .. done
usage: simple_oscil <waveform> <frequency> <duration>
(waveforms)    1 - sine
               2 - sawtooth
               3 - triangle
               4 - square

Program exited with code 04.
(gdb) run 1 200 3
Starting program: path/to/simple_oscil 1 200 3

Breakpoint 2, create_wave_saw (saw=0x2d000, wave_length=8192) at
simple_waveforms.c:20
20   for(i = 0; i < wave_length; i++) {
```

As expected, the initial attempt to run failed because we did not supply the expected arguments to **simple_oscil**. After specifying a set of valid arguments, the program executed until breakpoint 2, located on the first line of create_wave_saw, was reached. We also see from the output the values of the two parameters that were passed to the create_wave_saw function—the value of pointer to an address in memory for the waveform array, saw, and the desired waveform length, wave_length. That we did not pause the program execution until we reached the second breakpoint makes sense—elsewhere in the code we define the table length for each waveform to be 8,192 and pass that value to both the create_wave_sine and create_wave_saw functions. Clearly 8,192 is never less than 1,024, and so the condition we set for the first breakpoint will always evaluate to false, which correctly explains why we did not stop on the breakpoint located on the first line of create_wave_sine.

Previously we looked at two options of monitoring memory within **gdb**: manual output of a variable using print and continuous output of a variable using display. A third option for viewing memory during debugging is to make use of conditional structure similar to a conditional breakpoint, known as a "watchpoint." Whereas a breakpoint is always associated with a line of code within the program, a watchpoint is always associated with the state of a program variable and does not need to be tied to a specific line of code. Whenever the variable that a watchpoint is associated with changes, the watchpoint will inform **gdb** to output the variable's current value to the console.

Continuing with our current example, we will set a watchpoint on the value of the current sample value of the sawtooth wave, saw[i], so we can review each point in the waveform as it is generated.

```
(gdb) list create_wave_saw
13              sine[i] = sin(2.0*M_PI*i/(float)wave_length);
14          }
15      }
16
17      // sawtooth wave - ramp from 1 to -1 across the period
18      void create_wave_saw(float *saw, int wave_length) {
19          int i;
20          for(i = 0; i < wave_length; i++) {
21              saw[i] = 1-i*2.0/(float)(wave_length);
22          }
(gdb) watch saw[i]
Hardware watchpoint 3: saw[i]
(gdb) s
21   saw[i] = 1-i*2.0/(float)(wave_length);
(gdb) s
Hardware watchpoint 3: saw[i]

Old value = 0
New value = 1
create_wave_saw (saw=0x2d000, wave_length=8192) at
simple_waveforms.c:20
20   for(i = 0; i < wave_length; i++) {
(gdb) s
Hardware watchpoint 3: saw[i]

Old value = 1
New value = 0
0x0000f381 in create_wave_saw (saw=0x2d000, wave_length=8192) at
simple_waveforms.c:20
20 for(i = 0; i < wave_length; i++) {
(gdb) s
21   saw[i] = 1-i*2.0/(float)(wave_length);
(gdb) s
Hardware watchpoint 3: saw[i]

Old value = 0
New value = 0.999755859
create_wave_saw (saw=0x2d000, wave_length=8192) at
simple_waveforms.c:20
20 for(i = 0; i < wave_length; i++) {
(gdb) s
Hardware watchpoint 3: saw[i]
```

```
Old value = 0.999755859
New value = 0
0x0000f381 in create_wave_saw (saw=0x2d000, wave_length=8192) at
simple_waveforms.c:12
20 for(i = 0; i < wave_length; i++) {
(gdb) s
21   saw[i] = 1-i*2.0/(float)(wave_length);
(gdb) s
Hardware watchpoint 3: saw[i]

Old value = 0
New value = 0.999511719
create_wave_saw (saw=0x2d000, wave_length=8192) at
simple_waveforms.c:20
20 for(i = 0; i < wave_length; i++) {
(gdb) s
Hardware watchpoint 3: saw[i]

Old value = 0.999511719
New value = 0
0x0000f381 in create_wave_saw (saw=0x2d000, wave_length=8192) at
simple_waveforms.c:20
20 for(i = 0; i < wave_length; i++) {
(gdb) s
21   saw[i] = 1-i*2.0/(float)(wave_length);
(gdb) s
Hardware watchpoint 3: saw[i]

Old value = 0
New value = 0.999267578
create_wave_saw (saw=0x2d000, wave_length=8192) at
simple_waveforms.c:20
20 for(i = 0; i < wave_length; i++) {
(gdb)
```

As we can see, **gdb** outputs the value of saw[i] for each step because each time the loop index, i, increments, a new value of saw[i] is obtained and then assigned a valid point from the waveform. If we wish to limit the amount of information **gdb** generates, we can always associate a condition with the watchpoint, as we did with breakpoints previously.

```
(gdb) info b
Num Type      Disp Enb Address  What
1 breakpoint  keep y 0x0000f2c5 in create_wave_sine at
simple_waveforms.c:12
    stop only if wave_length < 1024
```

```
2 breakpoint  keep y 0x0000f334 in create_wave_saw at
simple_waveforms.c:20
    stop only if wave_length > 1024
    breakpoint already hit 1 time
3 hw watchpoint keep y saw[i]
    breakpoint already hit 7 times
(gdb) condition 3 saw[i] > .5
(gdb) info b
Num Type        Disp Enb Address  What
1 breakpoint  keep y 0x0000f2c5 in create_wave_sine at
simple_waveforms.c:12
 stop only if wave_length < 1024
2 breakpoint  keep y 0x0000f334 in create_wave_saw at
simple_waveforms.c:20
    stop only if wave_length > 1024
    breakpoint already hit 1 time
3 hw watchpoint keep y saw[i]
    stop only if saw[i] > 0.5
    breakpoint already hit 7 times
```

Finally, though we have not shown it explicitly in this overview, any breakpoint that is set in **gdb** may be deleted, disabled and re-enabled, using the commands `delete`, `disable` and `enable`, respectively, along with the breakpoint number.

B.2.2 A Closer Examination of the Program and Memory

Thus far we have only viewed memory during our debug session, and only in whatever format **gdb** has designated for us. However, **gdb** does provide use with the ability to view a piece of memory in other formats that we designate. We can also modify memory, as the following session will illustrate, to alter the program in real time:

```
(gdb) break simple_oscil.c:extract_data
Breakpoint 1 at 0xf0f3: file simple_oscil.c, line 160.
(gdb) run 1 100 20
Starting program: /path/to/simple_oscil 1 100 20
Reading symbols for shared libraries +++++++. . .. .. .. .. . ..
. .. .. .. .. . .. . .. done

Breakpoint 1, extract_data (data=0xbffff45c, argv=0xbffff4a0) at
simple_oscil.c:160
160     int itemp = atoi(argv[1]);
(gdb) backtrace
#0 extract_data (data=0xbffff45c, argv=0xbffff4a0) at
simple_oscil.c:160
```

```
#1 0x0000f296 in main (argc=4, argv=0xbffff4a0) at
simple_oscil.c:198
(gdb) x/s argv[1]
0xbffff5d1:    "1"
(gdb) x/a argv[1]
0xbffff5d1:    0x30310031
(gdb) s
161     if(itemp < MIN_TABLE || itemp > MAX_TABLE) {
(gdb) print itemp
$1 = 1
(gdb) set itemp = 2
(gdb) print itemp
$2 = 2
```

In this session, we began by restarting **gdb** and reloading **simple_oscil** to clear out all of our breakpoints and watchpoints, and then immediately set a breakpoint on the extract_ data function in the file *simple_oscil.c*. We then ran the program with the arguments '1 100 20,' which instructed the program to play a pure sine waveform at a frequency of 100 Hz for a duration of 20 seconds. As expected, our first breakpoint triggered as soon as we reached the first line of the extract_data function. This function parses and validates the command-line data passed by the user to **simple_oscil** and assigns those values to our program data structure. To confirm the execution of the program according to our expectations, we made use of the backtrace to command to reveal the state of the call stack. The function call stack shows that the program is currently executing the extract_data function, which was called by the main function.

```
#0 extract_data (data=0xbffff45c, argv=0xbffff4a0) at
simple_oscil.c:160
#1 0x0000f296 in main (argc=4, argv=0xbffff4a0) at simple_oscil.c:198
```

At this point, we reviewed the value of the second item in the argv command-line parameter array by using the examine command, x, and specifying a data encoding format.

```
(gdb) x/s argv[1]
0xbffff5d1:    "1"
(gdb) x/a argv[1]
0xbffff5d1:    0x30310031
```

This first call to x instructs gdb to display the contents of the second argv array index formatted as a character string (/s), and we can clearly view the value we entered represented in character form as "1." We then also display this same value as an address in memory because, as we know, strings values in C are stored as pointers to arrays of characters. We step one instruction to copy this integer equivalent of this value into the temporary parameter itemp, and then confirm success by printing out the value of itemp. We finish by making use of the set command to assign a new value to `itemp`, which we confirm is 2 by printing out the value again.

```
(gdb) s
158  if(itemp < MIN_TABLE || itemp > MAX_TABLE) {
(gdb) print itemp
$1 = 1
(gdb) set itemp = 2
(gdb) print itemp
$2 = 2
```

On your computer there may be small differences in the **gdb** output, but these are slight and unimportant.

B.3 Other Commands

There are a large number of other command understood by **gdb**, and every user get to be familiar with a subset that allows working in a personally satisfactory way. In this section we will outline some of those that the writer has found particularly useful.

We have already seen the use of the step command **s** to step through a program; a similar command is **next**, usually abbreviated to **n**. While **s** steps to the next line in the whole program, **n** goes to the next written line, that is normally when the line number in the current function changes. Often these two are the same, but not always. In particular, **step** will step into a function call, while **next** will step over the function call. This is especially useful when the programs call library routines that were not written by you and may not be compiled with the **-g** flag.

```
$ gdb simple_oscil
(gdb) break simple_oscil.c:extract_data
Breakpoint 1 at 0xf0f3: file simple_oscil.c, line 160.
(gdb) run 1 100 20
Starting program: /home/jpff/BOOK/C_baileyGDB(9p)/examples/simple
1 100 20
[Thread debugging using libthread_db enabled]

Breakpoint 1, extract_data (data=0xbffff45c, argv=0xbffff4a0)
 at simple_oscil.c:160
160 int itemp = atoi(argv[1]);
(gdb)) s
161 if(itemp < MIN_TABLE || itemp > MAX_TABLE) {
(gdb) list
156 // simple user interaction function that queries input from the
user until they provide an acceptable value,
157 // defined by the ranges set above.
```

```
158
159 void extract_data(simpleOscil *data, char **argv) {
160 int itemp = atoi(argv[1]);
161 if(itemp < MIN_TABLE || itemp > MAX_TABLE) {
162 printf("Error: enter a valid wave shape (1=sin, 2=sawtooth,
3=triangle)\n");
163 exit(1);
164 } else {
165 data->table_num = itemp-1;
(gdb) s
165 data->table_num = itemp-1;
(gdb) s
168 float ftemp = atof(argv[2]);
(gdb) s
169 if(ftemp < MIN_FREQ || ftemp > MAX_FREQ) {
(gdb) s
175 data->table_inc = ftemp * TABLE_LENGTH/SAMPLE_RATE;
(gdb) s
178 ftemp = atof(argv[3]);
(gdb) s
179 if(ftemp < MIN_DUR || ftemp > MAX_DUR) {
(gdb) s
183 data->duration = ftemp;
(gdb) s
185 }
(gdb) s
main (argc=4, argv=0x7fffffffe168) at simple_oscil.c:202
202 create_waveshapes(&data);
```

At this point, if we use s the tracing will step into the function create_waveshapes:

```
(gdb) s
create_waveshapes (data=0x7fffffffe070) at simple_oscil.c:85
85          data->tables = (float**)malloc(sizeof(float*)*MAX_TABLE);
(gdb) s
88          for(i = 0; i < MAX_TABLE; i++) {
(gdb) s
89              data->tables[i] =
                    (float*)malloc(sizeof(float)*TABLE_LENGTH);
(gdb) s
88 for(i = 0; i < MAX_TABLE; i++) {
(gdb) list
83          // allocate space for the pointers to each array
84          // data->tables => float **;
```

```
85 data->tables = (float**)malloc(sizeof(float*)*MAX_TABLE);
86
87        // allocate space for the arrays themselves
88        for(i = 0; i < MAX_TABLE; i++) {
89            data->tables[i] =
                    (float*)malloc(sizeof(float)*TABLE_LENGTH);
90        }
91
92        // now generate the waveforms within the data structure//
(gdb) list
93        create_wave_sine(data->tables[0], TABLE_LENGTH);
94        create_wave_saw(data->tables[1], TABLE_LENGTH);
95        create_wave_triangle(data->tables[2], TABLE_LENGTH);
96        create_wave_square(data->tables[3], TABLE_LENGTH);
97    }
98
99    // this function simply initializes portaudio, creates a stream
and registers our
100 // callback function, and starts processing. after a delay
corresponding to our
101 // duration, playback is stopped, the stream is closed and
portaudio is terminated.
102
(gdb) b 93
Breakpoint 2 at 0x400fbc: file simple_oscil.c, line 93.
(gdb) c
Continuing.

Breakpoint 2, create_waveshapes (data=0x7fffffffe070) at
simple_oscil.c:93
93     create_wave_sine(data->tables[0], TABLE_LENGTH);
(gdb)
```

There are two new features here. The first is that the break command can be abbreviated to **b**, and we have used the **continue** command or **c** to continue from the current location until the next breakpoint or until the program terminates.

At this point we decide that we do not need to inspect the operation of the function create_wave_sine so we move to the next line with **next** or **n**.

```
(gdb) n
94     create_wave_saw(data->tables[1], TABLE_LENGTH);
(gdb)
```

If one was stepping through a function and by mistake stepped into an uninstrumented library function, or one that is not of interest, what can one do? There is a gdb command

finish that runs to the finish of the current function and then stops as if there were a breakpoint.

```
(gdb) s
create_wave_saw (saw=0x60b050, wave_length=8192) at
simple_waveforms.c:20
20      for(i = 0; i < wave_length; i++) {
(gdb) s
21          saw[i] = 1-i*2.0/(float)(wave_length);
(gdb) finish
Run till exit from #0 create_wave_saw (saw=0x60b050, wave_length=8192)
 at simple_waveforms.c:21
create_waveshapes (data=0x7fffffffe070) at simple_oscil.c:95
95      create_wave_triangle(data->tables[2], TABLE_LENGTH);
(gdb)
```

There are many other commands, and an effective help system to help explore them.

B.4   Debugging after a Crash

A common problem is when one runs a program and it crashes for an unknown reason with a cryptic error message, such as "segmentation fault." It is possible to use **gdb** is a simple way to find out the problem. Most modern computers run without the creation of "core dumps" on error, but if you are running that way **gdb** can read a core file. This is illustrated in the program broken.c on the DVD.

More often the process is to run the program under **gdb** and with no breakpoints, use the **run** command:

```
$ gdb broken
(gdb) run 6
Starting program: /path/to/examples/broken 6

Program received signal SIGSEGV, Segmentation fault.
0x00000000004006a1 in main (argc=2, argv=0x7fffffffe178) at broken.c:36
36          list = list->next;
(gdb) print list
$1 = (struct data *) 0x0
```

We can see that the program stopped on line 31, and a little investigation shows the null pointer being followed.

In more complex crashes, it is useful to know not only where the program faulted but also how that point was reached. Using the broken program with a different option illustrates this:

```
(gdb) run
Starting program: /home/jpff/BOOK/C_baileyGDB(9p)/examples/broken

Program received signal SIGFPE, Arithmetic exception.
0x00000000004005fc in fact (n=0) at broken.c:18
18              if (n==0) return fact(1/n);
(gdb) where
#0 0x00000000004005fc in fact (n=0) at broken.c:18
#1 0x0000000000400616 in fact (n=1) at broken.c:19
#2 0x0000000000400616 in fact (n=2) at broken.c:19
#3 0x0000000000400616 in fact (n=3) at broken.c:19
#4 0x0000000000400616 in fact (n=4) at broken.c:19
#5 0x0000000000400616 in fact (n=5) at broken.c:19$ gdb broken
#6 0x000000000040064b in main (argc=1, argv=0x7fffffffe188) at
broken.c:27
(gdb)
```

We can see the functions that led to the crash, the names of variables, and the line numbers of the call. We can investigate the local variables of each of these functions by using the command **up** and then the printing and listing commands. The **up** command changes the focus of function in the stack; there is also a **down** command to allow general navigation on the stack.

```
(gdb) up
#1 0x0000000000400616 in fact (n=1) at broken.c:19
19         else return n*fact(n-1);
(gdb) up
#2 0x0000000000400616 in fact (n=2) at broken.c:19
19         else return n*fact(n-1);
(gdb)
```

Conclusion

In this debugging overview, we have looked at a variety of different techniques for debugging a piece of software: how to compile an application for debugging; debugging features such as *breakpoints, conditional breakpoints*, and *watchpoints*; and how to view and manipulate memory in a running program in various different ways. These techniques represent a common set for debugging software projects through they are by no means comprehensive and in reality comprise only a subset of the features of **gdb**. The majority of bugs, are usually just a simple discrepancy between what a developer expects either a value in memory, or an execution flow, to be, and what that value or flow actually is when a program runs. This particular set of techniques addresses exactly those issues. Slowing down the processing of data and closely observing the code as it runs - line by line and value by value—should provide a solid foundation for attacking bugs in your own programs.

Notes

1. On Linux and other systems it is only necessary to use the flag -g in order to get the necessary additional information. The gcc package provides a number of options to control the format of this information. The -g flag uses the operating system native format, while -ggdb uses a gdb-specific form. There are other formats for specific systems. In general, use -g if it works and -ggdb if there are problems.

2. This chapter assumes that both gcc and gdb are located within your path. For more information on UNIX and command paths, refer to appendix A on the UNIX command line.

3. Under OS X, this file is a package called *ftom.dSym*, and may be organized differently on different platforms.

Appendix C: Soundfiles, Soundfile Formats, and *libsndfile*

Victor Lazzarini

In this appendix, we first review the basic methods of accessing files using the standard C input and output library, which are universally used. This is followed by a discussion of soundfiles and their characteristics, looking at "raw" files and self-describing formats. We then examine two popular soundfile formats, RIFF-Wave and AIFF. To complete the text, we introduce a cross-platform library for soundfile manipulation, *libsndfile*.

C.1 File Input and Output

The most general way of handling files for input and output is to use the standard C library. It provides ways for writing text files or, more importantly, binary data files, such as soundfiles.

To open a file, use `fopen()`. Its prototype is shown here:

```
#include <stdio.h>
FILE *fopen(char *fname, char *mode);
```

The `fopen()` function, like all the standard IO functions, is declared in the header file `stdio.h`. The name of the file to open is `fname`. The string `mode` determines how the file may be accessed; see table C.1.

If the open operation is successful, `fopen()` returns a valid file handle. This file handle will be used with all other functions that operate on the file. It is "opaque"; that is, it is not to be touched or changed directly. If `fopen()` fails, it returns a `NULL pointer`. For example:

```
FILE *fp;

if ((fp = fopen("myfile", "r")) ==NULL){
    printf("Error opening file\n");
    exit(1);
}
```

To close a file, use `fclose()`, whose prototype is

```
int fclose(FILE *fp);
```

Table C.1

The modes of the `fopen()` function.

Mode	Meaning
r	Open a text file for reading.
w	Create a text file for writing.
a	Append to a text file.
rb	Open a binary file for reading.
wb	Open a binary file for writing.
ab	Append to a binary file.
r+	Open a text file for read/write.
w+	Create a text file for read/write.
a+	Append or create a text file for read/write.
r+b	Open a binary file for read/write.
w+b	Create a binary file for read/write.
a+b	Append a binary file for read/write.

The `fclose()` function closes the file associated with `fp`, which must be a valid handle previously obtained using `fopen()`, and which disassociates the `stream` from the file. The `fclose()` function returns 0 if successful and `EOF` (end of file) if an error occurs.

C.1.1   Text File Functions

Four functions are provided for text file IO. First we have `fputs()` and `fgets()`, which write or read a string from a file, respectively. Their prototypes are

```
int fputs(char *str,FILE *fp);
```

and

```
char *fgets(char *str, int num, FILE *fp);
```

The `fputs()` function writes the string `str` to the file `fp`. It returns `EOF` if an error occurs and a non-negative value if successful. The *null* that terminates `str` is not written. The `fget()` function reads characters from the file `fp` into a string `str` until *num* − 1 characters have been read, a new-line character is encountered, or the end of the file is reached. The string is *null-terminated* and the newline character is retained. The function returns `str` if successful or `NULL` if an error occurs.

The other two functions are `fprintf()` and `fscanf()`. These functions operate exactly like `printf()` and `scanf()` except that they work with files. Their prototypes are

```
int fprintf(FILE *fp, char *control-string, . . .);
```

and

```
int fscanf(FILE *fp, char *control-string . . .);
```

and they read or write to a file rather than to the standard input/output (console).

C.1.2   Binary File Functions

The standard C library includes two general-purpose file functions: `fread()` and `fwrite()`. These functions can read and write any type of data, using any kind of representation. Their prototypes are

```
size_t fread(void *buffer, size_t size, size_t num,FILE *fp);
```

and

```
size_t fwrite(void *buffer, size_t size, size_t num, FILE *fp);
```

The `fread()` function reads from the file `fp` num number of items, each item `size` bytes long, into a buffer pointed to by `buffer`. It returns the number of items actually read. If this value is 0, no objects have been read. You can use the functions

```
int feof(FILE *fp);
```

and

```
int ferror(FILE *fp);
```

to see if there was an error or if the end of file has been reached.

The `feof()` function returns true (non-0) if the reading or writing pointer for `fp` has reached the end of file; otherwise it returns false (0). The `ferror()` function returns non-0 if the reading of or writing to `fp` has experienced an error; otherwise it returns 0.

The `fwrite()` function is the opposite of `fread()`. It writes to file `fp` num number of items, each item `size` bytes long, from the buffer pointed to by `buffer`. It returns the number of items written. This value will be less than num only if an output error has occurred.

C.1.3   Reading/Writing Pointer Functions

You can position a file reading/writing position to the start of the file using `rewind()`. Its prototype is

```
void rewind(FILE *fp);
```

You can point to a certain position in bytes along a file by using

```
int fseek(FILE *fp, long offset, int whence);
```

This positions the read or write pointer at position `offset` (in bytes), which is also determined by the parameter `whence`. There are three options for this parameter:

1. SEEK_SET, offset is the absolute position from the beginning of file.
2. SEEK_CUR, offset is the position from the current read/write pointer position..
3. SEEK_END, offset is calculated in relation to the end of the file, offset can then be negative or positive (extending the length of the file).

The fseek function returns 0 if successful and the constant EOF if not.

Finally, you can also find the current position by using int ftell(FILE *fp).

C.2   Raw Soundfiles

In this section we will be discussing the basic aspects of sound storage in computer files. Soundfiles are very important for music programming, as they provide a medium for manipulating audio in a computer. They were the first type of support for computer music, and until very recently they were the typical means of input and output of a sound-generating program. Soundfiles provide a way of implementing computer musical signal processing in a platform/device-independent way, without the need to consider more complex issues relating to real-time performance, ADC/DAC, etc.

C.2.1   What's in a Soundfile?

Sound in computers is treated, as everything else, in a digitally encoded way. There are different types of digital encoding, some using compressed data, some uncompressed. The most common of all these, and the one we will be using, is known as *pulse code modulation* (PCM). This type of encoding is the one used in most professional soundfiles and in other types of digital audio applications, such as CDs, DATs, and ADATs. PCM data is basically a stream of binary numbers, which represent samples of a waveform at certain points in time. Each number (which will be a group of binary digits, one or more bytes long) represents a specific amplitude measured at that time point; we call that number a *sample*. It is important not to confuse this definition of a sample as a single number describing a waveform at a time point with the more colloquial use of the word to mean a *sampled signal* (as in a "piano sample").

A soundfile holds a certain number of binary numbers, or samples, describing a digital waveform. This is what we should expect when reading a soundfile and what we should output when writing a soundfile. It is, in fact, very simple, just a sequence of numbers. It is important, however, to point out that these numbers are written in binary, not in ASCII (text) form. That is the only proviso in handling soundfiles.

By writing a program that opens a file for reading/writing in binary, we are able to manipulate audio data. However, in order to do so in a more complete way, we will have to understand the characteristics of the digital signal we are handling. Audio data, the sequence of samples, is nothing more than a series of zeroes and ones. To interpret it, we need to know how many bits (or bytes) make up a single sample (the *precision*), what time interval the samples are supposed to be separated by (the *sampling period*), and how many channels of audio are represented in the sequence of samples (*samples per frame*). Once we know these things, and we are not reading/writing data produced by or meant for a different computer system, we are ready to make computer music.

C.2.2 Sample Precision

The first thing we need to know about our digital data is how many bits (or bytes) were used in the encoding of each sample. With this information, we will know how to group the bits in the sample, so when we read a file, we know that every so many bytes represent a different number. Generally speaking, the typical PCM-format soundfile will represent samples as integers, either as single byte (8-bit) samples (the lowest precision) or as two-, three-, or four-byte samples.

The CD/DAT standard precision is based on 16-bit, or two-byte, samples. In the C language these are called `short int`(egers) or `shorts`. Single-byte samples are `chars`, and three-byte or four-byte samples are going to be stored in `long ints` or just `ints`. (There are no 3-byte, 24-bit data types in C.) Since 8-bit precision is not used in professional computer music systems, we will ignore it. Because 16-bit is a popular norm, and is more than good enough for most applications, we will be concentrating on it. Higher precisions can be handled in similar ways.

Short integer values range between $-32,768$ and $32,767$, so the maximum possible signal-to-noise ratio in CD format audiois 96 dB. It is important not to exceed these maximum and minimum values in order to avoid clipping distortion.

You can open and read a binary file containing PCM audio samples, stored as 16-bit integers, with the following code:

```
#include <stdio.h>
#include <stdlib.h>

int main(){

FILE *fpin;
short *audioblock;
int samples = 0;

fpin = fopen("soundfile," "rb");
audioblock = (short *) malloc(sizeof(short)*256);

while(!feof(fpin))
  samples += fread(audioblock, sizeof(short), 256, fpin);

printf("%d samples read from file," samples);
```

```
free(audioblock);
fclose(fpin);

return 0;

}
```

This code, of course, is just an example, and it does not do anything but report how many samples were read. However, it shows some important aspects of what we have to do to read audio: open a file, allocate some memory to hold the samples we read from the file, and read them in a loop until we reach the end of the file. Note that the program reads a block of samples from the file. We could have read a single sample at a time. However, this would not be as efficient as reading a whole block every time we call the `fread()` function.

The loop conditional control here is the simplest: check if we reached the end of the file; if we have not, keep reading. In this program we are overwriting the memory we reserved to hold samples, but in a real-life situation we would ideally do something with the data before overwriting it. In order to do so, we normally would have to know a little more about it.

C.2.3   Sampling Rate

The next parameter that defines what our sample data represents in terms of audio is the *sampling rate* (sr). This is the number of samples in one period of time, say a second (in which case we are measuring it in hertz). This is the inverse of the time lapse between each sample point. The CD standard is 44,100 Hz. It is generally acceptable. At this sr, one second of a single channel of 16-bit audio will occupy 88,200 bytes of storage (44,100 `shorts`).

The sr has two important side effects on the computer system, one having to do with size of storage and one having to do with real-time capabilities. In general, modern systems are well capable of handling high sampling rates and have enough disk storage to hold long soundfiles. However, the use of high sampling rates (above the usual 44,100 Hz) will require more storage space and may put some limits on simultaneous playback of multiple files. For this course, we will be sticking to 44,100-Hz sampling rate and to 16-bit samples. The sampling rate also limits the frequency range of a system, limiting the highest possible frequency (before aliasing occurs) to half the sr frequency, also known as the Nyquist frequency (that is, to 22,050 Hz in the present case).

C.2.4   Audio Channels

The third characteristic of digital audio data is the number of channels present in a soundfile. Multiple channels are generally stored in an *interleaved* way: adjacent samples will belong to different channels. A group of samples representing a single time point of a multichannel audio data is known as a *sample frame*. The size of the sample frame is thus equivalent to the number of channels present in the data.

A two-channel block of data will contain a sequence of two-sample sample frames; each frame will contain samples for channel 1 (left) and channel 2 (right), in that order. Similarly, a four-channel file will contain a sequence of four-sample sample frames. It is very important to know how many channels we are dealing with, so that the sample streams of different channels get separated accordingly.

As an example, consider the following code, which takes a one-second extract from a two-channel soundfile (sr = 44,100) and splits the channels into two separate files:

```c
#include <stdio.h>
#include <stdlib.h>

int main(){

FILE   *fpin, *fpleft, *fpright;
short  *audioblock, *left, *right;
int    frames, samples, end, i, j;
int    sr = 44100;
int    blockframes = 100, blocksamples;
int    channels = 2;
blocksamples = blockframes*channels;
end = sr;

fpin = fopen("soundfile," "rb");
fpleft = fopen("left_channel," "wb");
fpright = fopen("right_channel," "wb");

audioblock = (short *) malloc(sizeof(short)*blocksamples);
left = (short *) malloc(sizeof(short)*blockframes);
right = (short *) malloc(sizeof(short)*blockframes);

for(i=0; i < end && !feof(fpin); i+=blockframes){

    samples = fread(audioblock, sizeof(short), blocksamples, fpin);
    frames = samples/2;

    for(j=0; j < frames; j++){
        left[j] = audioblock[j*2];
        right[j] = audioblock[j*2+1];
    }

    fwrite(left,sizeof(short), frames, fpleft);
    fwrite(right,sizeof(short), frames,fpright);
}

free(audioblock);
free(left);
free(right)
```

```
fclose(fpleft);
fclose(fpright);
fclose(fpin);

return 0;

}
```

C.3　Self-Describing Soundfile Formats

The fact that sample data is meaningless without any information as to how it is representing a digital signal points to the need for additional elements to be stored with the sound itself. So far, we have been handling "raw" soundfiles, because we know what to expect from the sample data. However, if we want to make our soundfiles more flexible and portable, we will have to use a *self-describing soundfile format*. This will store, along with the audio, information about the sr, the number of channels, the sample width (precision), the number of sample frames in the file, and other useful information. The simplest way to do this is through an agreed soundfile header format. One of the first formats around was the SUN/Next .au audio file format. This carried a fixed-size header containing all pertinent information at the start of the file. In this format, the header is defined in a simple C structure. The structure is used to read or write the header information. To create such a file, all that is necessary is to fill the structure fields with the required values and then write the whole structure to disk. The sound data is written after the header. Accessing .au files involves reading the whole header structure before getting the sound data.

The most common formats, *AIFF* and *RIFF-Wave*, are slightly different from this. They are known as "chunked" formats, where the data resides in chunks, rather than being composed of a fixed header plus sound data. Each "chunk" can be defined by a separate C language structure and can exist anywhere in a file (not necessarily at the beginning). However, we can mimic these types of files using a fixed-header structure that agglutinates the basic required chunks plus the sound data.

A complete discussion of *AIFF* and *Wave* soundfiles is presented later in this appendix. In this section, we will show how a fixed-header file works by generating a simple *RIFF-Wave* file based on a fixed header.

First it is necessary to define a header structure:

```
typedef struct riff_wave_header {
    int magic;            /* 'RIFF' */
    int len0;             /* file size—8 (in bytes) */
    int magic1;           /* 'WAVE' */
    int magic2;           /* 'fmt ' */
    int len;              /* chunk length (16 bytes) */
```

```
   short format;          /* 1 is PCM, rest not important */
   short nchns;           /* channels */
   int rate;              /* sampling frequency */
   int aver;              /* nBlockAlign * rate */
   short nBlockAlign;     /* nchns * size / 8 */
   short bits;            /* size of each sample (8,16,32) */
   int magic3;            /* 'data' */
   int datasize;          /* sound data size in bytes */
} wavehead;
```

This structure combines two required RIFF-Wave chunks: format (fmt) and data. If we write to the beginning of a file, we will mimic a RIFF-Wave with the minimum required chunks in a straightforward order. This will work without any restriction for newly generated files. It is not guaranteed to work for reading all sorts of wave files, as some might have chunks in a different order, or possibly other chunks in between the format and data chunk. Nevertheless, it works for simple cases.

Next it is necessary to define the "magic numbers" that are needed to name the chunks in the header structure:

```
static char RIFF_ID[4] = {'R','I','F','F'};
static char WAVE_ID[4] = {'W','A','V','E'};
static char FMT_ID[4] = {'f','m','t',' '};
static char DATA_ID[4] = {'d','a','t','a'};
```

We define them as "static," so that there is only one copy each of those variables in a program unit. Now we can write a function that will fill the header structure with the appropriate values:

```
void update_header(wavehead* header, int sr, int channels,
                   int precision, int databytes){
   header->magic = (*(long *)RIFF_ID);
   header->len0 = databytes + sizeof(wavehead) - 8;
   header->magic1 = (*(long *)WAVE_ID);
   header->magic2 = (*(long *)FMT_ID);
   header->len = 16;
   header->format = 1;
   header->nchns = (short) channels;
   header->rate = sr;
   header->aver = sr*channels*precision/8;
   header->nBlockAlign = (short) (channels*precision/8);
   header->bits = (short) precision;
   header->magic3 = (*( long *)DATA_ID);
   header->datasize = databytes;
}
```

We can use this to write a synthesis program that will output a wave file that can be read on any Windows soundfile editor:

```c
#include <math.h>
#include <stdio.h>
#include <stdlib.h>
#include "wave.h" /* header file containing the wavehead struc
                     and the declaration of update_header() */

int main(int argc, char** argv){
    FILE *fpout;              /* output file pointer */
    short *audioblock;        /* audio memory pointer */
    int end, i, j;            /* dur in frames, counter vars */
    int sr = 44100;           /* sampling rate */
    int blockframes = 256;    /* audio block size in frames */
    int databytes ;           /* audio data in bytes */
    unsigned int ndx = 0;     /* phase index for synthesis */
    float  dur, freq;         /* duration, frequency */
    double twopi;             /* 2*PI */
    wavehead *header;

    if(argc != 4) {
        printf("usage: %s outfile dur freq \n", argv[0]);
        exit(-1);
    }

    dur = atof(argv[2]);
    freq = atof(argv[3]);
    twopi = 8*atan(1.);
    end = (int)(dur*sr);
    fpout = fopen(argv[1], "wb");
    audioblock = (short *) malloc(sizeof(short)*blockframes);

    /* set the data size */
    databytes = end*sizeof(short);

    /* write the header */
    header = (wavehead *) malloc(sizeof(wavehead));
    update_header(header, sr, 1, 16, databytes);
    fwrite(header, 1, sizeof(wavehead), fpout);

    for(i=0; i < end; i+=blockframes){
        for(j=0; j < blockframes; j++, ndx++){
            audioblock[j] = 16000*sin(ndx*twopi*freq/sr);
        }
```

```
        fwrite(audioblock,sizeof(short), blockframes, fpout);
    }
    free(audioblock);
    free(header);
    fclose(fpout);
    return 0;
}
```

The only caveat about this program is that it is not portable to big-endian machines (see below).

C.3.1   Byte-Ordering Confusion

The final reason for using established self-describing formats is to solve the problem of data portability between machines. This is due to the different byte-ordering conventions used in Intel-based hardware (e.g. PCs and Intel Macs) and Motorola/PowerPC/Sun/etc-based processors (e.g. PPC Macs). The Intel ordering is known as "little-endian"; the Motorola/etc ordering is known as "big-endian." They have to do with the way bytes are ordered in a multi-byte data type.

Little-endian ordering puts the least significant byte (LSB) first and the other bytes in order of increasing significance. The LSB is the byte where a change of, say, 0 to 1 leads to the smallest change in actual decimal values; e.g. (for two byte integers),

```
LSB            MSB
0000  0000  0000  0000  [0]
0000  0001  0000  0000  [1]
0000  0000  0000  0001  [256]
```

Big-endian ordering puts the MSB first and the other bytes in decreasing significance order. File formats are generally either little-endian or big-endian and this generally depends to which platform they are native: AIFF files are big-endian, as they are the preferred Mac format (because traditionally Macs had used big-endian hardware, but now are based on little-endian Intel processors). RIFF-Wave was designed by Microsoft and is native to the PC and Windows. When writing programs that deal with these formats, they have to provide byte-order conversion if the native format is different from the expected ordering. An example of such conversion is provided below.

C.4   RIFF-Wave Soundfiles

In this section, we will describe the structure of a Wave file format. This format is based on the RIFF (Resource Interchange File Format) framework, which has other applications besides audio. As all RIFF files, the Wave file format is a "chunked" file format and is native to the Windows operating system. In this format (which was created for Intel processors), all integer data is stored in little-endian (least significant byte first) order.

Chunks are blocks of data, each one storing a different type of information. Each chunk has its own mini-header, consisting of its ID and the number of bytes of data it contains. Both header components are 32-bit integers, making the chunk header only 8 bytes long. (The chunk size is the file size minus this header size.) All chunks of a Wave file are subchunks contained in a `RIFF` chunk. The sole data that this chunk contains is the resource ID, which is always the ASCII characters `WAVE`. Since the chunk header is always the same for all `RIFF` chunks, it will be excluded from the chunk definitions in the next sections. We will assume it to precede any chunk-specific data.

The usual file format has the following structure:

[RIFF chunk]	chunk ID: `RIFF`
	chunk datasize: total file size minus this header size (8 bytes)
	RIFF Type ID: `'WAVE'`
[format subchunk]	chunk ID: `fmt`
	chunk datasize: the size of the format chunk
	chunk data (data format info)
[data subchunk]	chunk ID: `'data'`
	chunk datasize: the size of audio data
	sample data
[other subchunks]	

This is the basic `RIFF` structure. It groups the files contents (sample format data, samples, etc.) into separate chunks, with their own headers and data bytes. The chunk header specifies the type and size of the chunk data bytes. This organization method allows programs to easily skip over unwanted chunks of data and then continue processing relevant chunks. Certain types of chunks may also contain subchunks. `RIFF` file chunks must be word-aligned (16-bit aligning). This means that their total size must be a multiple of two bytes (2, 4, 6, 8, and so on). If a chunk contains an odd number of data bytes, an extra padding byte with a value of zero must follow the last data byte. This extra padding byte is never counted in the chunk size. A program must always check for a word-aligned size (even) in chunks when calculating the offset of the following chunk.

C.4.1   Wave File Chunks

A wave file must contain at least two chunks: the format chunk and the data chunk (or a wave-list chunk instead). These are the two chunks needed to describe the data format and to hold the samples themselves. According to the original file format documentation, the format chunk must be placed before the data chunk.

C.4.2   Format Chunk

The format chunk specifies the format of the wave data present in the data chunk. Its ID is 'fmt ' (four characters, including a space). Its data fields are made up of two sections: common fields and format-specific fields. The first is defined by the following data structure (WORD is a 16-bit integer, DWORD a 32-bit integer):

```
struct {
    WORD    wFormatTag;
    WORD    wChannels;
    DWORD   dwSamplesPerSec;
    DWORD   dwAvgBytesPerSec;
    WORD    wBlockAlign;
}
```

wFormatTag is the data format code: 1 for PCM; other codes for different encoding/ compressed data formats. wChannels is the number of interleaved audio channels. dwSamplesPerSec is the data sampling rate. dwAvgBytesPerSec is the average number of bytes per second for data transfer and can be used to estimate playback buffer sizes. wBlockAlign is the alignment of data in bytes, which can be used for buffer alignment.

The format-specific data is dependent on the format code. For the specific case of PCM audio, it takes the form

```
WORD wBitsPerSample;
```

wBitsPerSample is the number of bits in a single sample, i.e., the encoding precision. The lowest allowed precision is 8 bits (in the unsigned range 0–256). PCM data are generally expected to be integral in the Wave format (i.e., there is no way of distinguishing integers from floating-point numbers). Other formats will have different (and possibly more) fields— this has to be taken into account when setting the chunk size, which is just 16 bytes for PCM.

For PCM data, the value of wAvgBytesPerSample is

```
wChannels * wSamplesPerSecond * wBitsPerSample / 8
```

and wBlockAlign is

```
wChannels * wBitsPerSample / 8
```

These values may change, depending on the encoding or compression format.

C.4.3   Storage of Audio Data

Audio data in a Wave-format file can be stored using either a single data chunk or, rarely, a wave-list chunk. The data chunk contains the sample data in the format and compression method specified in the Wave Format Chunk. Wave files usually contain only a single data chunk. If a wave-list chunk is used, then several data chunks can be used, together with silent chunks.

The data chunk ID is data, its size is the audio data size in bytes, and its contents are audio samples. Multi-channel data are stored as interleaved samples, in "frames" containing two or more samples for each channel. As was mentioned above, 8-bit precision samples are stored as unsigned values. All other sample bit sizes are specified as signed values. All RIFF chunks (including WAVE "data" chunks) must be word aligned. If the sample data uses an odd number of bytes, a padding byte with a value of zero must be placed at the end of the sample data. Note that the "data" chunk header's size should not include this byte.

The wave-list chunk contains a series of subchunks (data chunks or silent chunks). Its chunk ID is wavl. The silent chunk content (its ID being slnt) is defined as

```
DWORD dwSamples;
```

dwSamples is the number of "silent" samples. These are a series of samples that must be silent, in between the samples of each data chunk. The wave-list chunk has rarely been used; it should be avoided, because many programs do not recognize it.

C.4.4   Fact Chunk

The fact chunk is required only if the file is storing compressed data. Its ID is fact, and currently it contains only one field:

```
DWORD dwFileSize;
```

dwFileSize is the number of samples of waveform data in this file. This chunk was originally designed to be expanded if and when new formats were added to the Wave format specification. New formats would add format-dependent information in new fields added to this chunk.

C.4.5   Cue Chunk

This optional chunk identifies a series of positions (cue points) in the sample data stream. The cue chunk ID is 'cue ' (with a space at the end). The first member of the cue chunk is

```
DWORD dwCuePoints;
```

dwCuePoints is the number of cue points defined in this chunk. This is followed by one or more cue point descriptions, defined by the following data structure:

```
struct {
    DWORD dwName;
    DWORD dwPosition;
```

```
    FOURCC fccChunk;
    DWORD dwChunkStart;
    DWORD dwBlockStart;
    DWORD dwSampleOffset;
}
```

`dwName` is the cue-point identifier; it must be unique. `dwPosition` specifies the position of the cue in a sequential order. `fccChunk` is either `data` or `slnt`; it specifies which of the chunks contains the cue. `dwChunkStart` is used only with wave-list data; it specifies the file position of the data or silent chunk relative to the start of the data section of the wave-list chunk; otherwise, it is zero. `dwBlockStart` is also used only with wave-list data; it specifies the file position of the data section of the `slnt` or `data` chunk relative to the start of the data section of the wave-list chunk; otherwise, it is zero. `dwSampleOffset` is the sample position of the cue point relative to the start of the block.

C.4.6   Playlist Chunk

This specifies a play order for a series of cue points. Its ID is `plst`. It contains a number of playlist segments:

```
DWORD play-segments;
```

Each segment is defined by the following data structure:

```
struct {
    DWORD dwName;
    DWORD dwLength;
    DWORD dwLoops;
}
```

Here `dwName` is the cue point identifier (found in the cue chunk), `dwLength` is the length of the play segment in samples, and `dwLoops` is the number of times the segment should be played. A series of such playlist segments is stored in the chunk.

C.4.7   Associated Data Chunk

This provides a list of attached information, including labels, to the waveform data. Its ID is `adtl`. It can contain four different types of subchunks: labels (`labl`), notes (`note`), text (`ltxt`), and file (`file`). The label and note chunks have the same structure:

```
struct {
    DWORD dwName;
    ZSTR data;
}
```

Here `dwName` is the cue-point identifier to which the label (`labl` chunk) or text (`note`) is associated, and `data` is a NULL-terminated string containing the label or text to be associated.

The text chunk is used to associate a text with a data segment of specific length. It data structure is as follows:

```
struct {
    DWORD dwName;
    DWORD dwSampleLength;
    DWORD dwPurpose;
    WORD wCountry;
    WORD wLanguage;
    WORD wDialect;
    WORD wCodePage;
    BYTE* data;
}
```

The `dwName` element is the cue-point identifier to which the text is associated, `dwSampleLength` specifies the number of samples in the segment, `dwPurpose` specifies a type or code for the text (e.g. `'scrp'` for script), `wCountry` specifies the country code for the text, `wLanguage` and `wDialect` specifies the language and dialect codes for the text, `wCodePage` specifies the code page for the text, and `data` is the associated text characters.

The final subchunk to be examined is the file subchunk, which has the structure

```
struct {
    DWORD dwName;
    DWORD dwMediaType;
    BYTE *fileData;
}
```

and is used to store attached information in other file formats. Here `dwName` is the cue-point identifier to which the file is associated, `dwMediaType` is the file type in the filedata field, it can be either a known type or 0, and `fileData` contains the file associated with the cue point.

C.5   AIFF Soundfiles

Audio Interchange File Format (AIFF) is another common soundfile format. It has been mostly used in the MacOS platform. This file format is also a chunked format. In general it is quite similar to RIFF-Wave. One major difference is that all multi-byte integral data in this format is stored in big-endian format. AIFF files require only two chunks to be present: the common chunk and the sound data chunk. These are actually subchunks of the form AIFF chunk, as shown below:

[FORM chunk:]	chunk ID: `'FORM'`
	form Type ID: `'AIFF'`
[comm subchunk :]	chunk ID: `'COMM'`
	chunk data (common format info)
[sound subchunk:]	chunk ID: `'SSND'`
	sample data
[other subchunks]	

C.5.1 Common Chunk

The common chunk is equivalent to the format chunk of RIFF-Wave files and contains the file format information:

```
struct {
    ID              chunkID;
    long            chunkSize;
    short           numChannels;
    unsigned long   numSampleFrames;
    short           sampleSize;
    extended        sampleRate;
}
```

Here `chunkID` (ID is a four-character data type) is `'COMM'`, `chunkSize` is the number of bytes in the chunk (as with the RIFF-Wave `'fmt '` chunk, it does not include the eight bytes preceding it, so it will be 18 bytes), `numChannels` is the number of audio channels (multiple channels are interleaved), `numSampleFrames` is the number of sample frames (the total number of data samples divided by `numChannels`), `sampleSize` is the number of bits in each sample (sample data are supposed to be integral), and `sampleRate` is the sampling frequency (held in a special data type: the 80-bit IEEE Standard 754 floating-point number, which is 10 bytes long and will need special translation to a standard double-precision type).

C.5.2 Sound Data Chunk

The Sound Data Chunk contains the sample data:

```
struct {
    ID              chunkID;
    long            chunkSize;
    unsigned long   offset;
    unsigned long   blockSize;
    unsigned char   WaveformData[];
}
```

The chunkID is 'SSND', and chunkSize is the number of bytes in the chunk (as with the RIFF-Wave data chunk, it does not include the eight bytes preceding it, so it will be size in bytes of the waveform data). The size of the chunk must be even (word-aligned), so extra padding bytes will have to be added at the end of the waveform data. These bytes are not counted here. offset is where the first sample frame in the WaveformData starts. It is in bytes, and it is generally zero. blockSize is the size in bytes of the blocks to which waveform data is aligned. It can be set to zero, as most applications will not use it. WaveformData is an array containing the audio data in the format and precision defined in the common chunk.

C.5.3   Marker Chunk

This optional chunk is used to define markers that point to positions in the sample data. A marker is defined by the following structure:

```
struct {
    MarkerID          id;
    unsigned long     position;
    pstring           markerName;
}
```

Here id is a unique ID identifying the marker within a FORM AIFF, and MarkerID is a 16-bit integer. position is the marker's position in the waveform data in frames. markerName field is a text string containing the name of the mark. The datatype used here is a Pascal string, which uses the first character of an array as the string length and the remaining characters as the actual string.

The marker chunk itself is defined by the following structure:

```
struct {
    ID                chunkID;
    long              chunkSize;
    unsigned short    numMarkers;
    Marker            Markers[];
}
```

The chunkID is 'MARK', chunkSize is the number of bytes in the chunk, numMarkers is the number of marker structures in the Marker Chunk, and Markers is an array of numMarkers markers.

C.5.4   Instrument Chunk

This optional chunk defines basic parameters for waveform playback in an instrument.

AIFF audio can be looped, allowing a portion of the waveform to be repeated. A loop is defined as follows:

```
struct {
    short       PlayMode;
    MarkerId    beginLoop;
    MarkerId    endLoop;
}
```

playMode specifies which type of looping is to be performed: 0 (no looping), 1 (forward), or 2 (forward-backward). beginLoop is a marker ID that marks the begin position of the loop segment. endLoop is a marker id with the end position of a loop.

The instrument chunk is defined by the following data structure:

```
struct {
    ID      chunkID;
    long    chunkSize;
    char    baseNote;
    char    detune;
    char    lowNote;
    char    highNote;
    char    lowvelocity;
    char    highvelocity;
    short   gain;
    Loop    sustainLoop;
    Loop    releaseLoop;
}
```

Here chunkID is 'INST', chunkSize is 20 bytes, and baseNote is the MIDI note number of the waveform reference (base) frequency. detune defines any fine tuning, in cents, within a range from −50 to +50. lowNote and highNote are the suggested range of sample placement (in MIDI note numbers). lowVelocity and highVelocity are the suggested range of MIDI velocities in which this sample should be placed. gain is any attenuation or boosting of the waveform data on playback, in dB. sustainLoop is a Loop structure describing any sustain-period loop. releaseLoop is a Loop structure describing any release-period loop.

C.5.5 MIDI Data Chunk

This optional chunk is used to store MIDI data, mainly system-exclusive messages:

```
struct {
    ID              chunkID;
    long            chunkSize;
    unsigned char   MIDIdata[];
}
```

The chunkID is 'MIDI', chunkSize is the number of bytes in the chunk, and MIDIData is any MIDI data. There should be as many bytes as chunkSize specifies, plus a pad byte if the total number of bytes is not even.

C.5.6   Audio Recording Chunk

This optional chunk stores information relating to audio recording devices:

```
struct {
    ID              chunkID
    long            chunkSize;
    unsigned char   AESChannelStatusData[24];
}
```

The chunkID is 'AESD', chunkSize is 24 bytes, and AESCChannelStatusData contains 24 bytes as specified in *AES Recommended Practice for Digital Audio Engineering—Serial Transmission Format for Linearly Represented Digital Audio Data.*

C.5.7   Application-Specific Chunk

This is an optional chunk that can be customized by application developers:

```
struct {
    ID      chunkID;
    long    chunkSize;
    char    applicationSignature[4];
    char    data[];
}
```

The chunkID is 'APPL', chunkSize is the number of bytes in the chunk, applicationSignature is used by programs for the Apple platform that contain an application identifier, and data is the application-defined data.

C.5.8   Comments Chunk

This optional chunk is used to store any comments, which can optionally be linked to a marker ID. Each comment is defined by

```
struct {
    unsigned long    timeStamp;
    MarkerID         marker;
    unsigned short   count;
    char             text[];
}
```

Here `timeStamp` is the computer time of creation of the comment, `marker` is a marker ID to link the comment to (otherwise zero), `count` is the number of characters in the comment string (and does not include the extra pad byte that might be required), and `text` contains the comment itself, possibly with an extra pad byte.

The comment chunk is defined as

```
struct {
    ID                chunkID;
    long              chunkSize;
    unsigned short    numComments;
    Comment           comments[];
}
```

The `chunkID` is `'COMT'`, `chunkSize` is the number of bytes in the chunk, `numComments` contains the number of Comment structures in the chunk, and `comments` hold comment data.

C.5.9 Text Chunks: Name, Author, Copyright, and Annotation

These four optional text chunks have the same format:

```
#define NameID 'NAME'    /* chunkID for Name Chunk */
#define NameID 'AUTH'    /* chunkID for Author Chunk */
#define NameID '(c) '    /* chunkID for Copyright Chunk */
#define NameID 'ANNO'    /* chunkID for Annotation Chunk */

struct {
    ID     chunkID;
    long   chunkSize;
    char   text[];
}
```

Here `chunkID` is either `'NAME'`, `'AUTH'`, `'(c) '`, or `'ANNO'`. `chunkSize` is the number of bytes in the chunk. `text` is a character array containing the chunk text.

C.5.10 Converting to Big-Endian Format

Since AIFF files are by definition in the big-endian (BE) byte ordering, it is important to make sure that integers written to disk are always in that format. This will of course be redundant on native BE machines (such as the PPC Macintosh), but will be necessary for little-endian (LE) processors, such as Intel machines. A portable way of converting to BE format is demonstrated here, based on code found in earlier Csound versions. This will not affect natural BE integers, so the byte swap is done only when a LE integer is input.

The 16-bit conversion takes a short in native format and outputs a BE short. This then can be safely written to disk. the output will not be meaningful for LE machines without conversion, so this conversion should be used only before disk writing.

The principle involved is to use a two-item char (single-byte) array to do the swap. We will fill the first position of the array with the most significant byte (MSB) and then fill the second position with the least significant byte (LSB). The MSB and LSB are extracted from the input short integer by shifting the bytes to the right and using a single-byte bit-mask and the bit-wise AND operator (&). Here is the code:

```
short benshort(short sval)
{
    char benchar[2];
    char *p = benchar;

    // extract the MSB
    *p++ = 0xFF & (sval >> 8);
    // extract the LSB
    *p = 0xFF & sval;
    // output in BE format
    return(*(short *)benchar);
}
```

The main part of the conversion requires further explanation. The line

```
*p++ = 0xFF & (sval >> 8);
```

does several important things:

1. It takes the input and shifts it eight positions to the right. This shifts the first native byte to the right, e.g.,

```
0x0F01 >> 8 -> 0xFF0F
```

2. It uses a bit mask 0xFF to pass only the required byte, e.g.,

```
0x00FF & 0xFF0F -> 0x000F
```

3. It stores the byte in the first position of the char array, the MSB byte.
4. It increments the char pointer to make it point to the next array position, the LSB byte.

The next line of the code does a similar job, except that, because it does not shift the bytes, it will actually let the second byte be assigned to the second array position.

Physically, in a LE machine, the following things would happen:

1. An input, say 0x0F01, represented physically as 010F (0000 0001 0000 1111), when shifted right and masked, would yield 0x0F:

```
010F (shift eight positions) -> 0FFF
FF00 & 0FFF -> 0F
```

2. The LSB byte then, as above, would be extracted by using a bitmask:

```
FF00 & 010F -> 01
```

3. Then the MSB and LSB are stored in the right order.

In a BE machine, the byte ordering would remain intact, e.g.,

```
0F01 (shift eight positions) -> FF0F
FF0F & 00FF -> 0F
0F01 & 00FF -> 01
```

Similarly, when reading BE integers from the disk, we will have to convert them into a native format:

```
short natshort(short sval)
{
    unsigned char benchar[2];
    short natshort;
    *(short *)benchar = sval;
    natshort = benchar[0];
    natshort <<= 8;
    natshort |= benchar[1];
    return(natshort);
}
```

This code gets a BE short and splits it into two bytes (benchar[0] and benchar[1]). It then takes the MSB (benchar[0]) and assigns it to the natural short LSB, which is shifted to the left, making it a MSB. Then it combines that byte with the original LSB (using a bit-wise OR operation). For 32-bit integers a similar procedure can be used, except that instead of moving two bytes around we will be moving four bytes:

```
long benlong(long lval) // coerce a natural long into a bigendian long
{
    char benchar[4];
    register char *p = benchar;
    *p++ = (char) (0xFF & (lval >> 24));
    *p++ = (char) (0xFF & (lval >> 16));
    *p++ = (char) (0xFF & (lval >> 8));
    *p = (char) (0xFF & lval);
    return(*(long *)benchar);
}

long natlong(long lval) // coerce a bigendian long into a natural long
{
    unsigned char benchar[4];
    register unsigned char *p = benchar;
    register long natlong;
```

```
    *(long *)benchar = lval;
    natlong = *p++;
    natlong <<= 8;
    natlong |= *p++;
    natlong <<= 8;
    natlong |= *p++;
    natlong <<= 8;
    natlong |= *p;
    return(natlong);
}
```

C.5.11   Converting Extended Floating-Point Data

The special operation needed to convert extended IEEE ten-byte floating-point data to or
from a standard C data type is as follows:

```
unsigned long IEEE2long(unsigned char *ieeefl)
{
    unsigned long mant;
    unsigned long tmp = 0;
    unsigned char exp;

    mant = natlong((unsigned long *)(ieeefl+2));
    exp = 30 - *(ieffl+1);
    while (exp--)
    {
        tmp = mant;
        mant >>= 1;
    }
    if tmp & 0x00000001) mant++;
    return mant;
}

void long2IEEE(unsigned int longval, unsigned char *ieeefl)
{
    unsigned long exp;
    unsigned char i;

    memset(ieefl, 0, 10);
    exp = longval;
    exp >>= 1;
    for (i=0; i<32; i++)
    {
        exp >>= 1;
        if (!exp) break;
```

```
    }
    *(buffer+1) = i;

    for (i=32; i; i--)
    {
        if (value & 0x80000000) break;
        longval <<= 1;
    }
    memcpy((unsigned long *)(ieeef1+2), &benlong(longval), 8)
}
```

C.6   *libsndfile*

An alternative to implementing soundfile IO from basic principles, as discussed previously, is to use a library of functions that provides support for a variety of formats. Currently, *libsndfile* is one of the best such libraries, supporting several soundfile types with a transparent interface. The advantage is that all the nasty things about headers, chunks, endian-ness, and precision are all hidden away and the library provides a single way of accessing all formats. The same code can be used to access a file, whether it is WAVE, AIFF, SND, or something else.

C.6.1   Basics

The library is designed to resemble the C standard IO library mode of operation. We have a file open function, which returns a handle that is our reference to the open file. This function can open a file for reading, writing, or both. As usual, I suggest either reading or writing, rather than trying to do both operations on the same file. The file open function is

```
SNDFILE *sf_open(const char *path, int mode, SF_INFO *sfinfo);
```

That function takes a name (or full path) as a string , a mode of operation (SFM_READ, SFM_WRITE or SFM_RDWR), and the address of a SF_INFO data structure. The function returns a handle (SNDFILE *) to the open file. The SF_INFO structureholds the format data for the soundfile. Its members are self-explanatory:

```
typedef struct SF_INFO
{   sf_count_t frames ;
    int     samplerate ;
    int     channels ;
    int     format ;
    int     sections ;
    int     seekable ;
} SF_INFO;
```

The way to use an `SF_INFO` object is to declare one instance of such structure for each sound-file used, then pass its address to the `sf_open` function. If the file is being read, then the data structure will contain the number of frames, the sampling rate, the channels, and the format taken from the soundfile after the call to `sf_open`. Otherwise, for writing, you will fill these attributes with your own chosen values, then pass the structure to `sf_open` in the same manner. The soundfile data structures on disk will be created accordingly.

You will fill the format attribute using one or more of the *libsndfile* constants. These are separated into two basic groups—a type and a subtype—which you can combine using a bitwise OR (|), as follows:

Types

```
SF_FORMAT_WAV       /* Microsoft WAV (little endian default). */
SF_FORMAT_AIFF      /* Apple/SGI AIFF format (big endian). */
SF_FORMAT_AU        /* Sun/NeXT AU format (big endian). */
SF_FORMAT_RAW       /* RAW PCM data. */
SF_FORMAT_PAF       /* Ensoniq PARIS file format. */
SF_FORMAT_SVX        /* Amiga IFF / SVX8 / SV16 format. */
SF_FORMAT_NIST       /* Sphere NIST format. */
SF_FORMAT_VOC        /* VOC files. */
SF_FORMAT_IRCAM      /* Berkeley/IRCAM/CARL */
SF_FORMAT_W64        /* Sonic Foundry's 64 bit RIFF/WAV */
SF_FORMAT_MAT4       /* Matlab (tm) V4.2 / GNU Octave 2.0 */
SF_FORMAT_MAT5       /* Matlab (tm) V5.0 / GNU Octave 2.1 */
SF_FORMAT_PVF        /* Portable Voice Format */
SF_FORMAT_XI         /* Fasttracker 2 Extended Instrument */
SF_FORMAT_HTK        /* HMM Tool Kit format */
SF_FORMAT_SDS        /* Midi Sample Dump Standard */
SF_FORMAT_AVR        /* Audio Visual Research */
SF_FORMAT_WAVEX      /* MS WAVE with WAVEFORMATEX */
SF_FORMAT_SD2        /* Sound Designer 2 */
SF_FORMAT_FLAC       /* FLAC lossless file format */
SF_FORMAT_CAF        /* Core Audio File format */
```

Subtypes

```
SF_FORMAT_PCM_S8    /* Signed 8 bit data */
SF_FORMAT_PCM_16    /* Signed 16 bit data */
SF_FORMAT_PCM_24    /* Signed 24 bit data */
SF_FORMAT_PCM_32    /* Signed 32 bit data */
SF_FORMAT_PCM_U8    /* Unsigned 8 bit data (WAV and RAW only) */
SF_FORMAT_FLOAT     /* 32 bit float data */
SF_FORMAT_DOUBLE    /* 64 bit float data */
```

```
SF_FORMAT_ULAW              /* U-Law encoded. */
SF_FORMAT_ALAW              /* A-Law encoded. */
SF_FORMAT_IMA_ADPCM         /* IMA ADPCM. */
SF_FORMAT_MS_ADPCM          /* Microsoft ADPCM. */
SF_FORMAT_GSM610          /* GSM 6.10 encoding. */
SF_FORMAT_VOX_ADPCM         /* OKI / Dialogix ADPCM */
SF_FORMAT_G721_32         /* 32kbs G721 ADPCM encoding. */
SF_FORMAT_G723_24         /* 24kbs G723 ADPCM encoding. */
SF_FORMAT_G723_40         /* 40kbs G723 ADPCM encoding. */
SF_FORMAT_DWVW_12         /* 12 bit Delta Width Variable Word */
SF_FORMAT_DWVW_16         /* 16 bit Delta Width Variable Word */
SF_FORMAT_DWVW_24         /* 24 bit Delta Width Variable Word */
SF_FORMAT_DWVW_N          /* N bit Delta Width Variable Word */
SF_FORMAT_DPCM_8          /* 8 bit differential PCM (XI only) */
SF_FORMAT_DPCM_16         /* 16 bit differential PCM (XI only) */
```

For instance, if we want to create a WAVE file with 24-bit encoding, we will use

```
sfinfo.format = SF_FORMAT_WAV | SF_FORMAT_PCM_24;
```

With this interface, we can handle several different types of soundfiles using the same code.

C.6.2   Reading and Writing

For reading and writing to soundfiles we have a number of options. These functions are divided into two basic ways of dealing with audio samples: (1) as individual samples (items) and (2) as sample frames. These are just two ways of counting samples, the first type of function counts sample by sample and expects a block of samples as one of its arguments, the second counts frames and expect a block of sample frames.

Then there are functions for each C data type: `char`, `short`, `int`, `float`, and `double`. Most important, these functions always work with native data formats, doing any conversion that is needed (say little-endian to big-endian, or to the bit length required) behind the scenes. For instance, to write a block of floats as samples, you would use

```
sf_count_t sf_write_float(SNDFILE *sndfile,float *ptr,sf_count_t
items);
```

Here the first argument is the soundfile handle, the second is the array with the audio data as floats, and the third is the number of samples in the array. The function returns the number of samples written. If instead you wanted to read the soundfile data, as a block of frames, into a short (16-bit) array, you would use

```
sf_count_t sf_readf_short(SNDFILE *sndfile,short *ptr,sf_count_t
frames);
```

Now, instead of counting in samples, we will count in sample frames, which will contain one sample for each channel. The function will also return the number of frames actually read.

If you want to be precision-neutral, so that a 16-bit file can be treated in the same way as a 24-bit file, it is probably better to use the floating-point reading/writing functions (float or double), rather than the integer ones. These will work with samples in the range from −1.0 to 1.0 (by default, but this can be changed) and will scale to or from the desired precision. A float will have enough range to deal with up to 24 bits integral precision; above that it is better to use doubles. To use these functions in the usual way, we need only make sure that our data is within the range, which is quite simple.

As with the standard C file IO, we can fast-forward or rewind the file position to any place. But now we can do it specifically within the waveform data. This is done using the `sfseek()`, which will offset the position in the same way as `fseek()`, but now in relation to the start of the audio data block:

```
sf_count_t sf_seek(SNDFILE *sndfile, sf_count_t frames, int whence);
```

Now, also instead of offsetting bytes, we will be counting in frames. The `whence` parameter is also `SEEK_SET`, `SEEK_CUR`, or `SEEK_END`, relating to the start of the waveform data, the current position, and the end of data, respectively.

C.6.3   An Example Program: Soundfile Conversion

This simple example shows how to use *libsndfile* in a simple soundfile conversion program. We will start with a AIFF file and convert it to WAV, with the desired user-supplied precision. This program will demonstrate how to check for formats and how to create a file of a certain type using the ideas introduced above.

First, don't forget the *libsndfile* header:

```
#include <sndfile.h>
```

The first action is to open the file for reading and to check whether the file has been open:

```
if(!(psf_in = sf_open(argv[1],SFM_READ,psfinfo_in))){
    printf("error opening input file\n");
    exit(-1);
 }
```

Next, check whether we have the right soundfile type. Checking the relevant SF_INFO field does this. If the format is right, we proceed:

```
if((psfinfo_in->format & SF_FORMAT_TYPEMASK) == SF_FORMAT_AIFF){
```

The `SF_INFO` structure for the file we want to write is then filled with values from the input file:

```
psfinfo_out->samplerate = psfinfo_in->samplerate;
psfinfo_out->channels = chans = psfinfo_in->channels;
psfinfo_out->format = SF_FORMAT_WAV | (psfinfo_in->format &
                                       SF_FORMAT_SUBMASK);
```

With this function we open (create) a new file for writing, making sure it opens correctly:

```
if(!(psf_out = sf_open(argv[2], SFM_WRITE,psfinfo_out))){
    printf("error opening output file\n");
    exit(-1);
}
```

Now all we need do is to copy the data, frame by frame, from one file to another, until there is no more data to copy:

```
do {
    count = sf_readf_float(psf_in, buffer, BUFITEMS/chans);
    sf_writef_float(psf_out, buffer, count);
}
while(count);
```

Assuming that the libsndfile header (`sndfile.h`) is in /usr/local/include and that the library file is in `/usr/local/lib`, we would build this example using gcc with the command

```
gcc -o aiff2wave aiff2wave.c -I/usr/local/include
        -L/usr/local/lib -lsndfile
```

Here is the full program code:

```
/* aiff2wave.c:
    libsndfile example
    converts an AIFF into a WAVE file
*/
#include <stdio.h>
#include <stdlib.h>
#include <sndfile.h>

#define BUFITEMS 512

void usage();

int main(int argc, char** argv) {
    SNDFILE *psf_in, *psf_out;
    SF_INFO *psfinfo_in, *psfinfo_out;
    float *buffer;
    sf_count_t count;
    int chans;
```

```c
if(argc < 3) {
usage();
exit(-1);
}

/* memory for SF_INFO structures */
psfinfo_in = (SF_INFO *) malloc(sizeof(SF_INFO));
psfinfo_out = (SF_INFO *) malloc(sizeof(SF_INFO));

/* open input */
if(!(psf_in = sf_open(argv[1],SFM_READ,psfinfo_in))){
    printf("error opening input file\n");
    exit(-1);
}
/* check to see if format is AIFF */
if((psfinfo_in->format & SF_FORMAT_TYPEMASK) == SF_FORMAT_AIFF){

    /* allocate buffer memory */
    buffer = (float *) malloc(sizeof(float)*BUFITEMS);

    /* Now we initialize the SF_INFO structure
       with the same sampling rate. . . */
    psfinfo_out->samplerate = psfinfo_in->samplerate;
    /* . . . same number of channels. . . */
    psfinfo_out->channels = chans = psfinfo_in->channels;
    /* and WAV format with the same precision */
    psfinfo_out->format = SF_FORMAT_WAV | (psfinfo_in->format &
                                         SF_FORMAT_SUBMASK);
    /* now we open the file */
    if(!(psf_out = sf_open(argv[2], SFM_WRITE,psfinfo_out))){
        printf("error opening output file\n");
        exit(-1);
    }
        /* and we copy the data, frame by frame */
    do {
    count = sf_readf_float(psf_in, buffer, BUFITEMS/chans);
    sf_writef_float(psf_out, buffer, count);
    }
    while(count);

    sf_close(psf_in);
    sf_close(psf_out);
    free(psfinfo_in);
    free(psfinfo_out);
    free(buffer);
    return 0;
```

```
    }
    else {
        printf("Not an AIFF file\n");
        sf_close(psf_in);
        return 1;
    }
}

void usage(){
    printf("\nusage: aiff2wave input.aif output.wav\n");
}
```

C.7   Finding Out More

Another great thing about *libsndfile* is that it is very well documented. To start with, a lot can be found out just by reading `sndfile.h` and its comments. But also the library has a very good reference manual that can be found online (at www.mega-nerd.com/libsndfile) or together with the library sources. The reference manual is well written and informative. I strongly advise anyone interested in using the library to read the documentation, as there many extra features that are beyond the scope of this text.

Appendix D: An Introduction to Real-Time Audio IO with PortAudio

Victor Lazzarini

Most modern operating systems will provide application programming interfaces[1] (APIs) for accessing audio devices (soundcards) present in the system for input/output (IO). For instance, on Windows we have the MME (Multimedia Extensions) and DirectX, among other APIs, for this purpose; on OS X these services are offered by the CoreAudio framework; on Linux the most common "back-end" API is ALSA (Advanced Linux Sound API). In addition, we also have other higher-level cross-platform APIs for audio IO that often are built on top of the basic sound systems, such as the Jack Connection Kit (Linux and OS X, mostly), PulseAudio (Linux and Windows), and PortAudio (OS X, Windows, Linux).

The major drawback of writing programs using a platform-specific API is that porting a program involves major re-implementation of the audio IO parts. For this reason, using cross-platform APIs is often a good idea, even though sometimes using the back-end API might allow slight better performance. This appendix will introduce some basic aspects of real-time audio processing using the PortAudio API for audio IO. PortAudio is part of a set of cross-platform libraries for media, PortMedia, and can be downloaded and installed from http://portmedia.sourceforge.net/.

D.1 Preliminaries

What form does the data we are manipulating take? Audio signals can be considered a stream of individual numbers, samples, produced by the soundcard at a rate of sr (sampling rate) samples per seconds (for each audio channel). Each one of these will be a representation of the amplitude of a waveform at a given time and they will be encoded into a certain data type—a single byte, a short, a int, or a floating-point (single- or double-precision) number. Audio samples of more than one channel are grouped into a frame, interleaved, so for multi-channel streams we will have sr frames of samples per second (instead of single samples). Our job will be to take in blocks of frames (or single samples) from the soundcard in an array, do something with them, and send an array of processed frames to the soundcard for output. The size (number of frames) in this buffer will be linked to the IO latency, i.e., the time it takes for the sound to get in and out of the computer. In general, we will try to make this buffer as small as possible, but this will depend on the system. With smaller buffers the program might start to drop samples ("drop-outs"), and we will get clicks and interruptions in the audio stream.

The previous paragraph probably summarizes all we need to know to start programming real-time audio IO with the tools we will study here. We will have to set the parameters for our signal (sampling rate, encoding, number of channels), reserve some memory to place the audio frames (arrays of data), and process the audio sample by sample. Generally speaking, after initialization we will open the soundcard for IO using the parameters described above. PortAudio will then allow us to start a data stream to and/or from the soundcard. When we are done, we just stop the stream, close the device, and terminate the PortAudio session.

D.2   Programming with PortAudio

We will now go through the basic steps of using the PortAudio API. As with other such IO systems, this will take four steps: initialization, device opening, IO operations, and termination.

D.2.1   Initialization

The PortAudio library requires a single header to be placed at the top of the program:

```
#include <portaudio.h>
```

Before its use, the library must be initialized with a call to `Pa_Initialize()`. This returns an error code of the type `PaError`:

```
PaError err;
. . .
err = Pa_Initialize()
```

The error code is equal to the constant `paNoError` if the operation was successful. Otherwise the error string can be retrieved with `Pa_GetErrorText(err)`:

```
printf("%s \n", Pa_GetErrorText(err));
```

D.2.2   Opening the Devices

Before we open a device, we can use a function to discover and list all devices in the system. The following code fragment performs this:

```
ndev = Pa_GetDeviceCount();
for(i=0; i<ndev; i++){
    info = Pa_GetDeviceInfo((PaDeviceIndex) i);
```

```
    if(info->maxOutputChannels > 0) printf("output device: ");
    if (info->maxInputChannels > 0) printf("input device: ");
    printf("%d: %s\n", i, info->name);
}
```

A "logical" device (that is, the one that gets listed) can be either uni-directional or bi-directional. We can open bi-directional devices for input and/or output, but we cannot open a uni-directional input device for output and vice versa. A single hardware device might get listed several times, uni- and bi-directionally, as different logic devices. As PortAudio can sometimes use more than one back-end API, devices can often get listed multiple times (for each of these back ends).

After devices are chosen for input and output, we will proceed to set the parameters for the IO data streams, which will include the selected devices. Filling in some fields in a PaStreamParameters structure, as shown below, does this:

```
PaStreamParameters inparam, outparam;
. . .
memset(&inparam, 0, sizeof(PaStreamParameters));
inparam.device = devin;
inparam.channelCount = 1;
inparam.sampleFormat = paFloat32;

memset(&outparam, 0, sizeof(PaStreamParameters));
outparam.device = devout;
outparam.channelCount = 1;
outparam.sampleFormat = paFloat32;
```

These stream parameters are set separately for input and output. We start by initializing all the structure fields to 0, using memset(). Then we set the chosen device number (devin, devout), the number of channels, and the sample data type. For generality and simplicity, we will use a single-precision floating-point number to hold a sample (paFloat32), and leave PortAudio to select the IO precision depending on the soundcard and platform. This also means that the maximum amplitude of our digital signal will always be 1.0 (0 dB full scale). In addition to the stream parameters used here, there are other fields in the PaStreamParameters data structure. These however are not required for our current purposes (you can check them out in the portaudio.h header file).

Once the stream parameters are decided, we can proceed to open the streams. We can open both input and output streams with a single function call:

```
PaStream *handle;
. . .
err =
Pa_OpenStream(&handle,&inparam,&outparam,SR,BUF,paNoFlag,NULL,NULL);
```

If the call to `Pa_OpenStream` was successful, the open stream is represented by a handle[2] (the first parameter). The second and third parameters are used for the input and output parameter streams, respectively. If one of them is NULL, only one direction is open. Then we have the sampling rate SR and the data buffer size BUF in frames. This is followed by an optional IO flags (paNoFlag for no flags). The last parameters are reserved for one of the two possible modes of IO: asynchronous (or callback-based[3]) and blocking.[4] If the former is used, then we will pass a callback function here and a pointer to some user data as the last parameter. For blocking mode, these parameters are set to NULL. If the streams are successfully opened, we can start streaming with the following call:

```
err = Pa_StartStream(handle);
```

D.2.3   Blocking IO

The blocking mode may be the simplest mode to understand and implement. It works in a very similar form to file IO: two functions are provided, and they will take a buffer and read/write this data from/to a device. The functions will block execution if there is no data to be read or if the writing cannot be performed immediately. In both cases, execution resumes once data is read or written. These functions are used as follows:

```
float buf[BUF];
. . .
err = Pa_ReadStream(handle, buf, BUF);
err = Pa_WriteStream(handle, buf, BUF);
```

For instance, a loop to read data from a soundcard and write it back without modification can be coded as follows (where END is the duration in seconds):

```
while(Pa_GetStreamTime(handle) < END){
    err = Pa_ReadStream(handle, buf, BUF);
    if(err == paNoError){
        err = Pa_WriteStream(handle, buf, BUF);
        if(err != paNoError) printf("%s \n", Pa_GetErrorText(err));
    } else printf("%s \n", Pa_GetErrorText(err));
}
```

The function `Pa_GetSreamTime()` can be used to check the current time of a particular stream. We use it here to keep the processing loop going for the desired duration.

D.2.4   Callback IO

Callback IO requires the programmer to supply a function that will be called by PortAudio whenever data is available for IO. The form of the callback is

```
int audio_callback(const void *input, void *output,
                   unsigned long frameCount,
                   const PaStreamCallbackTimeInfo *timeInfo,
                   PaStreamCallbackFlags statusFlags,
                   void *userData)
```

The callback will be passed the input and output data arrays (of void type, but containing samples in the format set in Pa_OpenStream)) as the first and second parameters, both of which will contain frameCount frames (the next parameter). It will also be passed a time stamp data structure containing the current time, as well as the input/output data references (which are going to depend on the audio latency). The next parameter is a series of stream status flags, which can be checked to ascertain the status of the data stream. The last parameter is the location of the user data[5] passed to the Pa_OpenStream() function. The equivalent code to the blocking IO shown in the previous section would be (note that in this case we do not have any need for user data, so we pass NULL)

```
int audio_callback(const void *input, void *output,unsigned long
                   frameCount, const PaStreamCallbackTimeInfo
                   *timeInfo, PaStreamCallbackFlags statusFlags,
                   void *userData){

    int i;
    float *inp = (float *) input, *outp = (float *) output;
    for(i=0; i < frameCount; i++) outp[i] = inp[i];
    return paContinue;

}
```

with a stream open using this function call:

```
err = Pa_OpenStream(&handle,&inparam,&outparam,SR,BUF,paNoFlag,
                    audio_callback, NULL);
```

The program will also require that we make sure it keeps running for the required duration in seconds. Thus we have to place a time-counting loop that waits until we reach the requested end time (END now is the duration in seconds), calling Pa_GetSreamTime() to check it:

```
while(Pa_GetStreamTime(handle) < END);
```

If we had not included this loop, the program would finish immediately, as there is nothing preventing or blocking the execution. PortAudio calls the callback function, so we do not have direct control of it.

D.2.5   Finalizing

When we are done, we need stop and close the stream. If we are ending our program, we also terminate the PortAudio session:

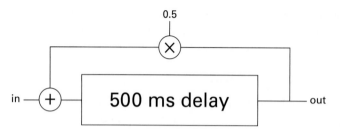

Figure D.1
A conceptual flow chart for the *echo* program.

```
Pa_StopStream(handle);
Pa_CloseStream(handle);
Pa_Terminate();
```

D.3   A Full Example: Echo

We will now present a real-time audio processing example, an echo program using a very common DSP structure, the comb filter (figure D.1). Programming a comb filter is relatively easy; all we need is some memory for the delay (an array) and a read/write pointer that will access it circularly. We place the audio data in the delay and retrieve at the other end, feeding it back into the delay line. This is shown in the following code fragment:

```
float delay[SR/2], out = 0.f;
. . .
    for(j=0; j < BUF; j++) {
        out = delay[rp];
        delay[rp++] = buf[j] + out*0.5;
        if (rp == SR/2) rp = 0;
        buf[j] = out;
    }
```

In the example above, our delay is sr/2 samples long, or half a second. The comb filter algorithm first writes output sample into a temporary variable, then it fills in the delay position vacated by the output sample (with an input sample and the fed-back output) and increments the read/write index. This is wrapped around if it reaches the end of the delay line. Finally, the output buffer (which is the same as the input one) is filled with the current output sample. The feedback gain is 0.5, which means that each echo will be half of the amplitude of the previous one.

Two versions of this example, one using the blocking IO and the other using the callback interface, will be presented. They should work quite similarly, but performance may vary from platform to platform. Also, the buffer size BUF can be adjusted according to the platform/back-end API used. If drop-outs are heard (likely with Windows and MME), BUF can be increased; for lower latency it can be decreased, if your system allows.

The major difference in the code is, of course, the presence of the callback in the second example. Because we will do the processing in the callback, the delay line and the read/write index will have to be passed to it as user data. We will place these two elements in a data structure, which will be dynamically allocated in the main program; then we will pass the pointer to it as the last argument to the `Pa_OpenStream()` function. The callback will then be able to use it in its processing. In the blocking example shown in figure D.1, instead, everything we need is inside the main function.

Compiling these examples is very simple. Assuming PortAudio is installed, as default in `/usr/local/lib`, with headers in `/usr/local/include`, we have the following command (on all systems):

```
gcc -o echo echo.c -I/usr/local/include -L/usr/local/lib -lportaudio
```

D.3.1   Blocking Example

```
#include <stdio.h>
#include <string.h>
#include <portaudio.h>
#define SR 44100.
#define BUF 512 /* increase this if you have drop-outs */
#define END 60

int main(int argc, char** argv){
    PaError err;
    PaDeviceIndex devin,devout, ndev;
    const PaDeviceInfo *info;
    PaStreamParameters inparam, outparam;
    PaStream *handle;
    int i, rp = 0;
    float buf[BUF], out = 0.f;
    float delay[(int)SR/2];

    memset(&delay,0,sizeof(float)*SR/2);
    err = Pa_Initialize();
    if( err == paNoError){
        ndev = Pa_GetDeviceCount();
        for(i=0; i<ndev; i++){
            info = Pa_GetDeviceInfo((PaDeviceIndex) i);
            if(info->maxOutputChannels > 0) printf("output device: ");
            if (info->maxInputChannels > 0) printf("input device: ");
```

```
                printf("%d: %s\n", i, info->name);
        }

        printf("choose device for input: ");
        scanf("%d", &devin);
        printf("choose device for output: ");
        scanf("%d", &devout);

        memset(&inparam, 0, sizeof(PaStreamParameters));
        inparam.device = devin;
        inparam.channelCount = 1;
        inparam.sampleFormat = paFloat32;
        memset(&outparam, 0, sizeof(PaStreamParameters));
        outparam.device = (PaDeviceIndex) devout;
        outparam.channelCount = 1;
        outparam.sampleFormat = paFloat32;

        err = Pa_OpenStream(&handle,&inparam,&outparam,SR,BUF,paNoFlag,
                            NULL, NULL);
        if(err == paNoError){
            err = Pa_StartStream(handle);
            if(err == paNoError){
                while(Pa_GetStreamTime(handle) < 60){
                    err = Pa_ReadStream(handle, buf, BUF);
                    if(err == paNoError){
                        for(i=0; i < BUF; i++) {
                            out = delay[rp];
                            delay[rp++] = buf[i] + out*0.5;
                            if (rp >= SR/2) rp = 0;
                            buf[i] = out;
                        }
                        err = (int) Pa_WriteStream(handle, buf, BUF);
                        if(err != paNoError) printf("%s \n",
                                                    Pa_GetErrorText(err));
                    } else printf("%s \n", Pa_GetErrorText(err));
                }
                Pa_StopStream(handle);
            } else printf("%s \n", Pa_GetErrorText(err));
            Pa_CloseStream(handle);
        } else printf("%s \n", Pa_GetErrorText(err));
        Pa_Terminate();
    } else printf("%s \n", Pa_GetErrorText(err));

    return 0;
}
```

D.3.2 Callback Example

```
#include <stdio.h>
#include <time.h>
#include <string.h>
#include <stdlib.h>
#include <portaudio.h>

#define SR 44100.
#define BUF 512 /* increase this if you have drop-outs */
#define END 60

typedef struct _mydata{
    float delay[(int)SR/2];
    int rp;
} mydata;

int audio_callback(const void *input, void *output,
                   unsigned long frameCount,
                   const PaStreamCallbackTimeInfo *timeInfo,
                   PaStreamCallbackFlags statusFlags,
                   void *userData){

    mydata *p = (mydata *)userData;
    int i, rp = p->rp;
    float out, *delay = p->delay;
    float *inp = (float *) input, *outp = (float *) output;
    for(i=0; i < frameCount; i++){
        out = delay[rp];
        delay[rp++] = inp[i] + out*0.5;
        if(rp >= SR/2) rp = 0;
        outp[i] = out;
    }
    p->rp = rp;
    return paContinue;

}

int main(int argc, char** argv){

    PaError err;
    PaDeviceIndex devin,devout, ndev;
    const PaDeviceInfo *info;
    PaStreamParameters inparam, outparam;
    PaStream *handle;
```

```
        int i;
mydata *data = (mydata *) calloc(sizeof(mydata),1);

err = Pa_Initialize();
if( err == paNoError){
    ndev = Pa_GetDeviceCount();
    for(i=0; i<ndev; i++){
        info = Pa_GetDeviceInfo((PaDeviceIndex) i);
        if(info->maxOutputChannels > 0) printf("output device: ");
        if (info->maxInputChannels > 0) printf("input device: ");
        printf("%d: %s\n", i, info->name);
    }

    printf("choose device for input: ");
    scanf("%d", &devin);
    printf("choose device for output: ");
    scanf("%d", &devout);

    memset(&inparam, 0, sizeof(PaStreamParameters));
    inparam.device = devin;
    inparam.channelCount = 1;
    inparam.sampleFormat = paFloat32;
    memset(&outparam, 0, sizeof(PaStreamParameters));
    outparam.device = (PaDeviceIndex) devout;
    outparam.channelCount = 1;
    outparam.sampleFormat = paFloat32;

    err = Pa_OpenStream(&handle,&inparam,&outparam,SR,BUF,paNoFlag,
                        audio_callback, data);

    if(err == paNoError){
        err = Pa_StartStream(handle);
        if(err == paNoError){
            while(Pa_GetStreamTime(handle) < END);
            Pa_StopStream(handle);
        } else printf("%s \n", Pa_GetErrorText(err));
        Pa_CloseStream(handle);
    } else printf("%s \n", Pa_GetErrorText(err));
    Pa_Terminate();
} else printf("%s \n", Pa_GetErrorText(err));

free(data);
return 0;
}
```

D.4   Final Words

Real-time audio programming with a cross-platform API such as PortAudio can be made simple. The examples shown in this text demonstrate the basic ideas behind the use of that library. However, for more complex systems, other issues may arise, which are beyond the scope of this text. Nevertheless, by offering a plain introduction to real-time audio programming, I hope to have enabled the user to build on the acquired knowledge, so that more involved systems can be tackled. Some further examples are provided with the PortAudio source code. Information on how to download and install this library, and reference documentation, is available at http://portmedia.sourceforge.net/.

Notes

1. Roughly speaking, an API is a set of programming resources (functions, data structures, definitions, etc.) that support a certain development task.

2. A handle is basically a pointer to an open stream. This is actually a pointer to a data structure that is "opaque" (that is, we do not and should not need to know what it holds). We pass the address of the pointer to this data structure (a pointer to a pointer) because the open-stream function will create a variable for this data structure and make the handle point to it. Then this handle can be used as a reference on all operations on the stream, so we know what stream we are manipulating. These operations are for IO, to change and check the stream status, etc.

3. A callback is a function that is given to a system for that system to invoke it at a later time. Setting up callbacks involve writing the code for the function and then passing it as an argument to a function call that "registers" the callback with the system in question.

4. A way to distinguish these two is to consider the concepts of synchronous and asynchronous IO. In the first case, the IO is "in sync" with the rest of the program, so we wait for input, process it and then output, blocking the execution when we come to each one of the stages of IO (in practice, the blocking might only occur at the input), giving the rise to the name "blocking IO." In the latter case, the IO is made independent of the rest of the program, so there is no blocking of execution, and waste of CPU time. Thus, in principle this can be made more efficient. In the case of callback asynchronous IO, the system will issue callbacks when data is ready for either input or output (or both), so the rest of the program is not idle waiting for data. To understand this, we can think that there are two parts of the program running in parallel: the main section, with the code we have written in sequential order, and a secondary one that keeps invoking the callback function whenever it is needed. Although potentially more efficient, this can be more complex to program, as resources (e.g. memory) might need to be shared by the callbacks and the rest of the program. In this case, we might need to protect these resources so that no conflicts arise (such as the different parts of the program trying to assign to a variable at the same time).

5. It is very common for asynchronous systems to have a means of passing some user-allocated data to the callback. The reason is that in many applications, we will need to have some means of passing data

from the main part of the program to the callback and vice versa. The "user-data" argument is designed for that. All we need do is to pass the pointer to any variable we would like to share between the two. Often this variable is a data structure holding several items we need to access in the callback or in the main program. The second example demonstrates this: the callback needs to access some permanent memory for the delay line, so we store it in a data structure, together with the read/write index and pass this as user data.

Appendix E: MIDI Programming with PortMIDI

Victor Lazzarini

MIDI programming is supported by most modern operating systems. They provide libraries for accessing and reading/writing data to MIDI devices. Most modern systems will also provide some means of MIDI playback, either in the form of software, or in hardware (as part of the soundcard). On Windows XP, there is a General MIDI software synthesis device that can be accessed by software. On OSX, it is possible to hook up MIDI to software synthesizers running in a different process (e.g. the Apple-supplied *GarageBand*).

Since the MIDI application programming interfaces (APIs) are different in each system, it is a good idea to use a portable library that implements a cross-platform interface to MIDI. One such library, which is part of the **PortMedia** set of libraries, is **PortMIDI**. It is available for Windows, OS X, and Linux, and allows for programs to be ported more easily from one platform to the next. Programming MIDI with PortMIDI is relatively simple. In this text, we will show how to output MIDI data, listen for MIDI input, and transform a MIDI data stream.

E.1 The Basic Steps

We will start by looking at how to build a PortMIDI program to play some notes to a MIDI device.

E.1.1 Header File and Library Initialization

The PortMIDI headers are

```
#include <portmidi.h>
```

and

```
#include <porttime.h>
```

Before PortMIDI is used, we must initialize it by calling

```
Pm_Initialize();
```

E.1.2   Searching for MIDI Output Devices

First we have to search for any existing MIDI output devices (or ports):

```
int cnt, i;
const PmDeviceInfo *info; /* holds information on devices */

(. . .)

if(cnt = Pm_CountDevices()){
    for(i=0; i < cnt; i++){
        info = Pm_GetDeviceInfo(i); /* gets the device info */
        if(info->output) /* this is 1 if the device is for output */
        printf("%d: %s \n", i, info->name); /* prints the device number
            & name */
    }
} else printf("ERROR: no device found\n");
```

Now we have a list of output devices, which is printed to the terminal. One of the devices can then be chosen from it.

E.1.3   Starting a Timer

Since the duration of MIDI events (notes) is going to be controlled by the program, we need to have a method of counting time. PortMIDI provides one in the form of PortTime, which is a small library included in it, with functions to create and use a software timer. We need to start the timer straight away:

```
Pt_Start(1, NULL, NULL);
```

E.1.4   Opening a Chosen Device

Once we have chosen a device from the list, we can open it:

```
int dev;
PmError retval;
PortMidiStream *mstream;

(. . . .)

/* open the device number 'dev' */
retval = Pm_OpenOutput(&mstream, dev, NULL,512,NULL,NULL,0);
/* check if it is properly open, print a message
    if it is not */
if(retval != pmNoError)
    printf("error: %s \n", Pm_GetErrorText(retval));
```

As can be seen, when we open a device, we pass it the address of a pointer (*mstream). This can be seen as a "handle" for the open device, which we will use whenever we want to do anything with it (e.g., write data to it). More abstractly, this is the "MIDI stream" to which we will be writing. If the device is not properly open, the function will return an error. We can print the error message by looking it up with a PortMIDI function.

E.1.5   Writing MIDI Data

Now we are ready to play. For instance, let's play a series of ascending notes, each one lasting a second, separated by semitones, each one with a different sound. We will have to change the MIDI program for each note, to select a new tone. First some macros to help us out:

```
#define MD_NOTEON 0x90
#define MD_NOTEOFF 0x80
#define MD_PRG 0xC0
#define SBYTE(mess,chan) mess | cha
```

We can use these in the code below. The MIDI data bytes are packed into a long integer and then written to the device, which responds to it immediately:

```
char chan = 0; /* we always use channel 0, for the moment */
long time = 0; /* this will hold the time in milliseconds */
long msg;
int prg = 0;

(. . .)

for(i=60; i <= 72; prg+=4, i++){
   /*
       encode the MIDI message bytes into one single data item
           in this case a PROGRAM message
   */
   msg = Pm_Message(SBYTE(MD_PRG,chan), prg, 0);
   /* write it */
   Pm_WriteShort(mstream, 0, msg);
   /* get the current time */
   time = Pt_Time(NULL);
   /* NOTE ON message */
   msg = Pm_Message(SBYTE(MD_NOTEON,chan), i, 120);

   Pm_WriteShort(mstream, 0, msg);
   /* wait for 1 second */
   while(Pt_Time(NULL) - time < 1000);
   /* NOTEOFF message */
```

```
    msg = Pm_Message(SBYTE(MD_NOTEOFF,chan), i, 120);
    Pm_WriteShort(mstream, 0, msg);
}
```

In fact, we do not need the `msg` variable, as we can plug the `Pm_Message()` code straight into `Pm_WriteShort()`:

```
Pm_WriteShort(mstream, 0, Pm_Message(SBYTE(MD_PRG,chan), prg, 0));
time = Pt_Time(NULL);
Pm_WriteShort(mstream, 0, Pm_Message(SBYTE(MD_NOTEON,chan), i,120));
while(Pt_Time(NULL) - time < 1000);
Pm_WriteShort(mstream, 0, Pm_Message(SBYTE(MD_NOTEOFF,chan),i,120));
```

E.1.6   Finalizing

Once we're done, we just need to clean up the house with a few function calls:

```
Pm_Close(mstream);
Pm_Terminate();
```

E.1.7   Full Program Code: MIDI Playback

```
#include <stdio.h>
#include <portmidi.h>
#include <porttime.h>

#define MD_NOTEON 0x90
#define MD_NOTEOFF 0x80
#define MD_PRG 0xC0
#define SBYTE(mess,chan) mess | chan

int main() {

int cnt,i,dev;
PmError retval;
const PmDeviceInfo *info;
PortMidiStream *mstream;

Pm_Initialize();

if(cnt = Pm_CountDevices()){

    for(i=0; i < cnt; i++){
        info = Pm_GetDeviceInfo(i);
        if(info->output)
            printf("%d: %s \n", i, info->name);
```

```
    }
    printf("choose device: ");
    scanf("%d", &dev);
    Pt_Start(1, NULL, NULL);
    retval = Pm_OpenOutput(&mstream, dev, NULL,512,NULL,NULL,0);

    if(retval != pmNoError)
        printf("error: %s \n", Pm_GetErrorText(retval));
    else {
        char chan = 0;
        int prg = 0;
        long time = 0;
        for(i=60; i < 72; prg+=4, i++){
            Pm_WriteShort(mstream, 0,
                            Pm_Message(SBYTE(MD_PRG,chan), prg, 0));
            time = Pt_Time(NULL);
            Pm_WriteShort(mstream, 0,
                Pm_Message(SBYTE(MD_NOTEON,chan), i, 120));
            while(Pt_Time(NULL) - time < 1000);
            Pm_WriteShort(mstream, 0,
                Pm_Message(SBYTE(MD_NOTEOFF,chan), i, 120));
        }
    }
    Pm_Close(mstream);
} else printf("No available output devices\n");

Pm_Terminate();
return 0;
}
```

E.2   Building and Running a PortMIDI-based Program

E.2.1   Windows (with MinGW/gcc)

Once you have your PortMIDI library installed (say in c:/msys/1.0/local/lib and headers in c:/msys/1.0/local/include), you can build a program with just this:

gcc –o prg source.c -I/usr/local/include –L/usr/local/lib -lportmidi –lwinmm

-lportmidi tells the linker to look for PortMIDI, and –lwinmm tells the linker to look for WINMM (the Windows low-level library on which PortMIDI depends).

Warning: In Windows, using the MinGW terminal, there might be a buffering issue with printf() and scanf() in MIDI programs. Because printf() output is buffered, it will not be displayed until after the program exits; so the program (shown below) will block waiting for input (to `scanf()`), if a device number is entered the program proceeds. When ends, all messages appear on terminal. One solution is to run the program from the Windows command line; another is to double-click on its icon.

E.2.2   On OS X

Similarly, with OS X, once you have PortMIDI installed, the command line is

gcc −o prg `source.c -I/usr/local/include −L/usr/local/lib -lportmidi`

This assumes that the header files are installed in `/usr/local/include` and the PortMIDI library is in `/usr/local/lib`. If the library and headers are installed elsewhere, the `−I` and `−L` options (above) will have to be changed to match the location of these files.

E.2.3   Playing MIDI on OS X

Generally speaking, if there are no MIDI hardware devices in your system, you will have to use a software device. Note also that some hardware devices might be just "output"—that is, you have to connect an external hardware synthesizer to them. So the simplest solution to MIDI playback is to use a software synthesizer. Apple's *GarageBand* can be used as follows:

1. Open the utility program Audio MIDI setup.
2. On 'MIDI DEVICES,' click on IAC device (this is an inter-application MIDI router).
3. Check "the device is online."
4. Open GarageBand.
5. In "Preferences," on the "Audio/MIDI tab," you should see "MIDI status: 1 device connected."
6. Select "IAC Device" from your MIDI output program. GarageBand should now be able to play (and record) whatever your program spills out.

You can use other software synthesizers (e.g., Csound) in the same way, if you have them, by making sure they take their input from IAC.

E.3   MIDI Input

A MIDI input program will generally re-use many of the steps outlined above, except that we will open devices for input instead and read from them . To show how this is done, we will develop a program that monitors MIDI input from a device and prints it out to the terminal.

E.3.1   Searching for MIDI Input Devices

Finding input devices is simple. We need only look for the input flag, as in the following:

```
for(i=0; i < cnt; i++){
    info = Pm_GetDeviceInfo(i);
    if(info->input)
    printf("%d: %s \n", i, info->name);
}
```

E.3.2 Opening an Input Device

Opening an input device follows principles similar to those set forth above, except that now we use the Pm_OpenInput() function:

```
retval = Pm_OpenInput(&mstream,dev,NULL,512,NULL,NULL);
```

E.3.3 Polling the Device and Reading Data

Because we will be reading from the MIDI device, we now need to see if there is data waiting to be read. MIDI data itself is encapsulated in the following structure, holding the MIDI message and a time stamp in milliseconds:

```
typedef long PmTimestamp;
typedef long PmMessage;
typedef struct {
    PmMessage message;
    PmTimestamp timestamp;
} PmEvent;
```

Portmidi offers the Pm_Poll function to check the device for input. If there is data, then we proceed. The code below loops for 1 minute waiting for input; if it finds it, the messages received are printed:

```
while(Pt_Time(NULL) < 60000){
    if(Pm_Poll(mstream)) {
        int count = Pm_Read(mstream, msg, 32);
        for(i=0; i<count; i++) {
            printf("status:%d, byte1=%d, byte2=%d, time=%.3f secs\n",
                Pm_MessageStatus(msg[i].message),
                Pm_MessageData1(msg[i].message),
                Pm_MessageData2(msg[i].message),
                msg[i].timestamp/1000.);
        }
    }
}
```

E.3.4 Full Program Code: MIDI Monitor

```c
#include <stdio.h>
#include <portmidi.h>
#include <porttime.h>

int main() {

    int cnt,i,dev;
    PmError retval;
    const PmDeviceInfo *info;
    PmEvent msg[32];
    PortMidiStream *mstream;
    Pm_Initialize();
    cnt = Pm_CountDevices();
    if(cnt) {
        for(i=0; i < cnt; i++){
            info = Pm_GetDeviceInfo(i);
            if(info->input)
            printf("%d: %s \n", i, info->name);
        }
        printf("choose device: ");
        scanf("%d", &dev);
        Pt_Start(1, NULL, NULL);
        retval = Pm_OpenInput(&mstream, dev, NULL, 512L, NULL,NULL);

        if(retval != pmNoError)
            printf("error: %s \n", Pm_GetErrorText(retval));
        else {
            while(Pt_Time(NULL) < 60000){
                if(Pm_Poll(mstream)) {
                    cnt = Pm_Read(mstream, msg, 32);
                    for(i=0; i<cnt; i++) {
                        printf("status:%d, byte1=%d, "
                                "byte2=%d, time=%.3f\n",
                                Pm_MessageStatus(msg[i].message),
                                Pm_MessageData1(msg[i].message),
                                Pm_MessageData2(msg[i].message)
                                msg[i].timestamp/1000.);
                    }
                }
            }
        }
        Pm_Close(mstream);
```

```
        }
    }
    else printf("No MIDI devices found\n");
    Pm_Terminate();
    return 0;
}
```

E.4   Combining MIDI Input and Output

The final example combines input and output. Triggered by an input NOTEON message, we will play a fast, four-note arpeggio sequence of major thirds.

E.4.1   Searching for and Opening Devices

We will open two devices, one for input and one for output. We will do this in a loop, first displaying and selecting the input and then the output:

```
for(j=0; j<2; j++){
    if(j==0) printf("input devices:\n");
    else printf("output devices:\n");
    for(i=0; i < cnt; i++){
        info = Pm_GetDeviceInfo(i);
        if(j==0 && info->input)
            printf("%d: %s \n", i, info->name);
        if(j==1 && info->output)
    printf("%d: %s \n", i, info->name);
    }
 printf("choose device: ");
 scanf("%d", &dev[j]);
}
```

Once this is done, we can proceed to open the devices, after we start the timer:

```
Pt_Start(1, NULL, NULL);
retval[0] = Pm_OpenInput(&mstream[0], dev[0], NULL, 512L, NULL,NULL);
retval[1] = Pm_OpenOutput(&mstream[1], dev[1], NULL, 512L,
                          NULL,NULL,0L);
```

E.4.2   Polling for Input

The code for detecting input and playing MIDI is similar to the previous examples, except that now it is combined into one big block, which starts by polling and reading input:

```
if(Pm_Poll(mstream[0])) {
    cnt = Pm_Read(mstream[0], msg, 128);
```

E.4.3 Processing MIDI Data

Now we can process the input MIDI data as needed. For each MIDI event, we create a loop that checks if the event is NOTEON and, if it is, fills a buffer with four MIDI events, containing a sequence of notes. This sequence of notes starts at the input note number and goes up by four semitones every tenth of a second (100 ms).

For each NOTEON we also write a NOTEOFF event. The timings of each event are written in the event's time-stamp variable:

```
for(i=0; i<cnt; i++) {
    /* now create the arpeggios in the msgout buffer */
    if((Pm_MessageStatus(msg[i].message) & 0xF0) == MD_NOTEON) {
        for(j=0;j<4; j++){
            /* NOTE ONs with correct timestamp */
            msgout[outcnt].message = Pm_Message(MD_NOTEON | chan,
                    Pm_MessageData1(msg[i].message)+j*4,
                    Pm_MessageData2(msg[i].message));
            msgout[outcnt].timestamp = msg[i].timestamp+100*j;
            if (++outcnt == 1024) outcnt = 0; /* increment count, wrap
                                                around */
            /* NOTE OFFs */
            msgout[outcnt].message = Pm_Message(MD_NOTEOFF | chan,
                    Pm_MessageData1(msg[i].message)+j*4,
                    Pm_MessageData2(msg[i].message));
            msgout[outcnt].timestamp = msg[i].timestamp+100*j+100;
            if (++outcnt == 1024) outcnt = 0;
        }
    }
}
```

E.4.4 Writing to Output

At this stage, when a NOTEON is detected, we will have an output buffer with eight MIDI events: four NOTEONs and four NOTEOFFs in ascending thirds and with correct time stamps. In order to play this buffer, we just loop from the beginning to the end, check whether the events are ready to be played (by looking at their time stamp). Events that have been already played have their time stamp set to –1. We can check for that:

```
/* now msgout might have MIDI events, write them if they are due */
    for(i=0; i < outcnt; i++){
        /* check if they are due by looking at their timestamp */
        if(Pt_Time(NULL) >= msgout[i].timestamp &&
            msgout[i].timestamp >= 0){
```

```
            Pm_WriteShort(mstream[1], 0, msgout[i].message);
            msgout[i].timestamp = -1; /* mark them as played */
        }
    }
```

E.4.5   Full Program Code: A Simple Arpeggiator

```
#include <stdio.h>
#include <portmidi.h>
#include <porttime.h>

#define MD_NOTEON 0x90
#define MD_NOTEOFF 0x80
#define MD_PRG 0xC0

int main() {
    int cnt,i,dev[2], j, outcnt=0, end=60000, chan=0;
    PmError retval[2];
    const PmDeviceInfo *info;
    PmEvent msg[128], msgout[1024];
    PortMidiStream *mstream[2];
    Pm_Initialize();
    cnt = Pm_CountDevices();
    if(cnt) {
        for(j=0; j<2; j++){
            if(j==0) printf("input devices:\n");
            else printf("output devices:\n");
            for(i=0; i < cnt; i++){
                info = Pm_GetDeviceInfo(i);
                if(j==0 && info->input)
                    printf("%d: %s \n", i, info->name);
                if(j==1 && info->output)
                    printf("%d: %s \n", i, info->name);
            }
            printf("choose device: ");
            scanf("%d", &dev[j]);
        }

        Pt_Start(1, NULL, NULL);
        retval[0] = Pm_OpenInput(&mstream[0], dev[0], NULL, 512L,
                                 NULL,NULL);
        retval[1] = Pm_OpenOutput(&mstream[1], dev[1], NULL, 512L,
                                  NULL,NULL,0L);
```

```
if(retval[0] != pmNoError && retval[1] != pmNoError)
    printf("error in input (%s) or in output (%s) \n",
    Pm_GetErrorText(retval[0]), Pm_GetErrorText(retval[1]) );
else {
    while(Pt_Time(NULL) < end){
        /* Poll for inputs */
        if(Pm_Poll(mstream[0])) {
            /* if there are MIDI events waiting, read them */
            cnt = Pm_Read(mstream[0], msg, 32);
            for(i=0; i<cnt; i++) {
            /* now create the arpeggios in the msgout buffer */
                if((Pm_MessageStatus(msg[i].message) & 0xF0) ==
                    MD_NOTEON) {
                    for(j=0;j<4; j++){
                        /* NOTE ONs with correct timestamp */
                        msgout[outcnt].message =
                            Pm_Message(MD_NOTEON | chan,
                                Pm_MessageData1(msg[i].message)+j*4,
                                Pm_MessageData2(msg[i].message));
                        msgout[outcnt].timestamp =
                            msg[i].timestamp+100*j;
                        if (++outcnt == 1024) outcnt = 0; /*
                                increment count, wrap around */
                        /* NOTE OFFs */
                        msgout[outcnt].message =
                          Pm_Message(MD_NOTEOFF | chan,
                                Pm_MessageData1(msg[i].message)+j*4,
                                Pm_MessageData2(msg[i].message));
                        msgout[outcnt].timestamp =
                            msg[i].timestamp+100*j+100;
                        if (++outcnt == 1024) outcnt = 0;
                    }
                }
            }
        }
        /* now msgout might have MIDI events,
            write them if they are due */
        for(i=0; i < outcnt; i++){
            /* check if they are due by looking at their
            timestamp */
            if(Pt_Time(NULL) >= msgout[i].timestamp &&
                msgout[i].timestamp >= 0){
```

```
                        Pm_WriteShort(mstream[1], 0, msgout[i].message);
                        msgout[i].timestamp = -1;/* mark them as played */
                    }
                }
            }
        }
        Pm_Close(mstream[0]);
        Pm_Close(mstream[1]);
    }
    else printf("No MIDI devices found\n");
    Pm_Terminate();
    return 0;
}
```

E.5   Final Words

MIDI programming with a cross-platform API such as PortMIDI is generally straightforward. The examples shown in this text demonstrate the basic tasks that are involved in this work. Although the programs introduced here were mostly simple, they offer all the reader requires to build more complex applications. Some further examples are provided with the PortMIDI source code. Information on how to download and install this library is available at http://portmedia.sourceforge.net/.

Appendix F: Computer Architecture, Structures, and Languages

John ffitch

F.1 Introduction

This appendix introduces the general topic of computer architecture, which is the term usually applied to the overall structural design of a computer. In it I will consider a simple but realistic computer structure and discuss why computer languages came into existence. While for most of the use of a computer it is not necessary to have any concern about what is happening inside, some aspects of programming benefit from this knowledge.

F.2 Some Simple History

The question of who invented the computer is sometimes asked. In fact, despite a number of parochial claims, the current state of the computer has developed from a large number of small suggestions, experiments, and ideas. The ideas of mechanical or automated calculation are certainly old, going back at least to the seventeenth century. Among the inventors and mathematicians who stand a little higher than the rest is the British mathematician Charles Babbage, who in the nineteenth century attempted to build first a mechanical device to print logarithm tables and then a calculating engine. The story of Babbage's life, his raising of money, his spending of even more money, and his dislike of barrel organs and other music is well recorded in his autobiography, *Passages from the Life of a Philosopher* (Longmans, Green, 1864), which is worth a browse at least. His calculating engine never worked, partly due to the problems of mechanical design and partly because Babbage was constantly changing the design. Whatever else, he did identify components that can still be seen in current designs; the processing unit (which Babbage called the "mill"), some memory, and the storing of a program in some coded format. He also proposed that output should be in the form of type. Another feature he identified was input on flat sheets or card with holes in them.

World War II gave a strong boost to the desire for automated calculations. The breaking of the Enigma code involved the use of electro-mechanical devices with many similarities to later computers. One of the minds behind this cryptanalysis was Alan Turing, who in the 1930s had made one of the major advances in the mathematical theory of computation.

(See A. Turing, "On Computable Numbers, with an Application to the Entscheidungsproblem," *Proceedings of the London Mathematical Society* series 2, 42, 1936, no. 2: 230–265.) By the end of the war, with the technical impetus and the availability of army surplus electronics, there was a great flowering of new ideas; among researchers working in the area of computation were John von Neumann in Princeton, Maurice Wilkes in Cambridge, and Frederic Calland Williams in Manchester. Who was first to reach the basic design of the modern computer depends on one's exact definition of it,[1] but it is clear that by the start of the 1950s this design was agreed upon.

F.3   A Basic Computer Design

The common features of all computers are a control unit, a processing unit for data transformation, some memory for data and programs, and some mechanisms for communicating with the outside world. In practice the features may be considered as whole, but conceptually these components have separate functions. Here we will not consider the input and output features; we will concentrate on the others.

It is all too easy to anthropomorphize computers, but at the heart there is very simple mechanism, called the *execution cycle*. There are three stages in the simplest form of this cycle:

1. Fetch an instruction from memory.
2. Arrange to get the next instruction from the following place.
3. Obey the instruction.

To understand the implications of this elementary cycle, we need to consider what we mean by an instruction and how it is represented inside the machine. This requires some understanding of the organization of a computer's memory.

The memory is organized into units called *words*, all of which are the same size in a given system. It is usual to think of words as pigeonholes—i.e., as little cells that can hold data. Each word holds a sequence of binary bits—that is, zeroes and ones. Typically, in most common systems, a word will hold 32 such bits. This collection of bits does not have an intrinsic "meaning," but the computer design will interpret these bits in a variety of ways depending on the circumstances.

The simplest interpretation of a word is as an integer in twos-complement binary notation, and that is the main interpretation for the handling of binary data. We will consider where this interpretation is located after we have considered the other main interpretation: as an instruction.

F.3.1   Instructions

The instructions that are found in a computer are all simple. They can be divided into three groups.

The first group of instructions is generally called arithmetic. Typically it will include addition, subtraction, and negation of integers, usually multiplication,[2] and often division. It may well also include these operations for the floating-point representation of numbers. It will also include a range of Boolean logic operations—and, or, not, and neqv—operating on the word as an array of bits, with 0 as false and 1 as true.

The second group of instructions can be seen as a subset of the first group. It involves the moving of data between different locations. On most machines there are two classes of location. We have already identified the memory as a collection of "pigeonholes," but there will be a number of registers—fast locations residing within the processing unit. The kinds of operation one would expect in this group are loading data from memory to a register, storing a register in memory, and copying data from one register to another.

The third group of instructions are concerned with control. The normal operation of a computer is to obey a sequence of instructions in sequence. The control operations change this normal means of operating by ordering the processor to start a new sequence, and (importantly) doing this conditionally depending on the value of some register.

Some machines add a fourth group of operations to control input and output of data from the computer, but most modern machines do this with special locations in the memory, which when written are automatically printed. For the current purposes we need not concern ourselves with these details.

F.3.2   The Execution Cycle

There is nothing magic about the method of working of computers. All they do is tirelessly perform the execution cycle. We need one more architectural detail to understand this cycle, and that is the idea of a memory address. We have already considered the memory as a collection of pigeonholes. We do need some way of referring to a particular slot, which is called its address. It is usual to ask students to consider houses in a street, and the difference between the house itself and the house number which forms part of the postal address. This analogy works better in some parts of the world than others.[3] In the computer we use integers as addresses. For our simple computer we will assume that the words of memory are numbers from 0 up to whatever is necessary. This allows us to indicate a location by using a number. With this we can examine the execution cycle.

We will have an internal register in the control unit that contains the address of the instruction to be obeyed next. This register is often called the *program counter* (PC). At the start of the execution cycle this register is used to fetch a word value from the memory, the word whose address in held in the program counter (figure F.1). After the instruction has been read from memory into the control unit (figure F.2), the program counter is incremented to address the next memory location and we have the situation shown in figure F.3. The third action in the execution cycle is to decode and execute the instruction that was fetched. Then the cycle starts again, and then again, and. . . .

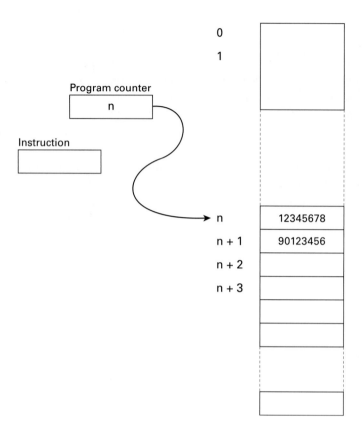

Figure F.1
Execution cycle, start.

The instructions are not magic either. Each instruction is represented in the word as some particular bit pattern. Usually part of the word will represent the operation, and the rest of the work would indicate the arguments. The arithmetic unit may contain a small number of registers in addition to the program counter; let us say there are eight of these registers, which we will name r0 through r7 (figure F.4). Each instruction may refer to two of these registers and/or a constant. A typical instructions sequence may be the following:

```
MOVE    R1, #1234
LOAD    R2, 16(R1)
ADD     R2, R4
STORE   R2, 0(R1)
```

The first instruction sets the value 1234 into the register 1. The next one then loads a value from the memory location 16 beyond the value in register 1 (which we know is 1234, so this loads the value in the location numbered 1250). Then the value of register 4 is added

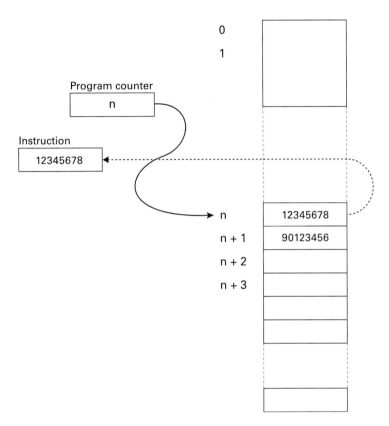

Figure F.2
Execution cycle, step 1.

the value in register 2, and finally stores the value in register 2 in the address held in register 1.

You may be beginning to see that there are problems here, not of deep complexity but of organizational confusion. The programmer of this kind of machine has to keep a close attention as to where values were place, and to what purpose each register is being put.

You will have noticed that in the above description the operation of adding one to the program counter is given as a separate phase of the execution cycle, and before the instruction is obeyed. The reason for this is that it allows the instruction to change the program counter that is to perform a jump. The instruction JUMP #1000 will write the value 1000 to the program counter as part of the obeying of the instruction, and so when the next execution cycle starts the instruction fetched will be that in location 1000 rather than the instruction following the JUMP instruction.

The last component in the construction is the conditional jump, where the program counter is altered only if some condition is true. The kind of conditions that can be tested

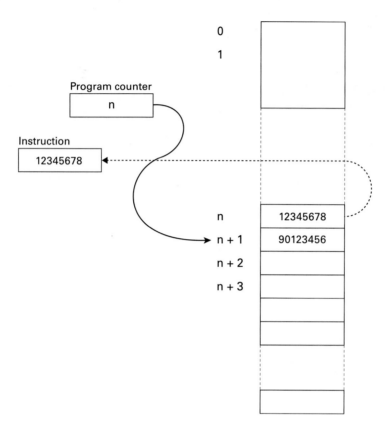

Figure F.3
Execution cycle, step 2.

are the value of a register being zero, or negative, or positive, among a number of other possibilities.

Consider the following instruction sequence at locations 400–404:

```
MOV    R1, #5
MOV    R2, #1
MULT   R2, R1
SUB    R1, #1
JMPNZ  R1, #402
```

Here JMPNZ is an instruction that jumps if the register is not zero. This sequence of instructions will calculate the factorial of 5 (!5=5 x 4 x 3 x 2 x 1 x) in register 2.

Although the examples above are simple, they include all the main features of all computers. To complete this model we have to add operations to read and write to the outside world.

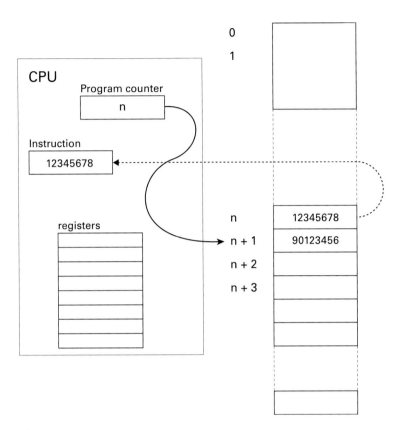

Figure F.4
CPU with registers.

F.4   Features of Modern Computers

The model computer described in section F.3 contains all the salient features of a computer; but you might feel that some trick is being played on you, as present-day computers are more complex. Yes they are, but at the heart of the system are the same ideas: instructions, registers, memory, and an execution cycle. In this section, I will give a brief outline of the ways in which a computer you might purchase now may differ from the model in section F.3.

A slightly frightening feature of the simple computer model above is that it is possible to overwrite the program, which would make debugging programs excessively difficult, as what you see may not be what you have. Most recent machines provide some mechanism to protect the part of the memory being used to store program. Clearly this needs some sophistication so one can store programs in the memory before executing them. It is usual for computers to allow only execution and reading from the program area, and reading and writing (but not execution) from the data area.

Many recent computers will have considerably more registers that the eight in the example. For example, MIPS and Alpha processors have 32, and the SPARC has even more. As register access is faster than memory access this just means that the programmer has the opportunity for writing a faster program if the registers are used well. But this can also be seen as a further problem for the programmer. Some computers may place restrictions on the use of registers, like having one that always contains zero, or making the program counter one of the main collection, or requiring certain operation may only use certain registers. Despite all this complication the overall shape is the same.

A major concern of computer designers is that technology for processor (CPU) construction has been improving very fast, with consequential improvements in processor speed, or clocking rate. Unfortunately the improvements in memory speeds have been much smaller that those in the processor speed, and there is a danger of much of the speed improvement being lost waiting for the slower memory. Consequently most computers use one or more caches. It is possible to make fast memories, but they are considerably more expensive than the other kinds, and they may have size limitations. A cache is a fast memory that sits between the processor and the memory, so that whenever a request is made for a word of memory, a check is made to see if it is in the cache, and if so it is used in preference to waiting for the main memory. When data is written to memory, a copy is retained in the cache in case it is used again. Because of the way we humans tend to write programs, calculating with one collection of data and then going to a different data collection, this caching procedure works remarkably well, with over 80 percent of memory reads being already in the cache in many applications. You will have noticed that if the cache is small the above process must be extended to a strategy for removing values as well.

Many computers also use a three-address architecture rather than the two-address mechanism described above. All this means is that the basic shape of an arithmetic instruction indicates three locations (the two sources and the destination). Then one sees instructions like

```
ADD    R1, R2, R3
```

This instruction is to add the values in registers 2 and 3 together and place the result in register 1. This is not a major conceptual change, but it does increase the opportunity for careful use of registers. Machines of this class also tend to have a larger number of registers.

Since the days of the first electronic computers there has been constant progress in making faster machines. One of the more recent techniques is to use *dual dispatch*, in which two instructions are fetched from memory at the same time and both are obeyed at the same time. This can double the speed, but at the cost of making the programming harder, as instructions are not obeyed in a simple linear fashion.

In this section I have suggested that the model of section F.3 may be refined and developed, but none of these refinements and developments remove the underlying principles of instruction fetch, program counter increment, and instruction execution. Most of the changes introduce problems for the programmer, but bring with them an increase in speed.

Interested readers should look at a standard book on processor design—e.g., J. Hennessy and D. Patterson, *Computer Architecture: A Quantitative Approach*, third edition (Morgan Kaufman 2003), which emphasizes the same message. We need a better way to write programs.

F.5   Organization of Memory

We saw in section F.3 that the standard computer model has "memory," and that memory is just a set of pigeonholes with numeric addresses. This memory structure is often said to be "flat," and it is not very helpful in the writing of programs. Usually it is necessary to impose some additional order on this flat structure. There are many ways in which this can be done, but two common organizations are enshrined in C, in C++, and in other popular programming languages. These two are the *stack* and the *heap*.[4]

F.5.1   A Stack

Formally a stack is a structure that has three operations:

```
push(value)
value = pop()
boolean = isempty()
```

The result of a push of a value followed by a pop is to recover the value. The common physical-world analogy is to a sprung-loaded plate rack such as may still be found in some cafeterias. When a plate is added, the whole pile of plates sinks, and only the top one is accessible. When a plate is removed, the pile floats up to reveal the plate below, but no more. And it is possible to remove all the plates so the pile is empty. This structure is also known as a first-in/last-out structure, as the first value added to the stack is the last removed. Some people prefer the term last-in/first-out, which describes the same process.

Stacks are convenient structures in many parts of computing. There are obviously used in recursive programming, but they have other uses.

Consider how to implement a stack on the flat memory. The simple idea is to start at some location in memory and to maintain a variable that has the address of the top of the stack (initially the start value). Then we can implement *push* by storing the value and incrementing the address of the top of stack (TOS), and *pop* is to decrement the pointer and read the value. We can implement *isempty* by comparing the TOS with the initial value. In simple C, creating a stack of integers, this becomes the following:

```
int *tos;
int *base;

void initialize_stack(int *base_address)
{
    base = tos = base_address;
}
```

```
void push(int value)
{
    *tos = value;
    tos++;
}

int pop(void)
{
    tos--;
    return *tos;
}

int isempty(void)
{
    return (tos==base);
}
```

This code has two problems. First, pop has to check first that the stack is not empty, because then the operation would be an error. This is called underflow, and here is the solution:

```
int pop(void)
{
    tos--;
    if (isempty()) abort();
    return *tos;
}
```

The second problem (much more serious) is overflow. The formal, mathematical definition of a stack has no limit to its maximum size, but in the real world there are limitations. To accept this would require a maximum size for the stack when we initialize, and to make the equivalent check is push for too many values. The revised code is

```
int *tos;
int *base;
int *limit
void initialize_stack(int *base_address, int size)
{
    base = tos = base_address;
    limit = base + size;
}

void push(int value)
{
    if (isfull()) abort();
    *tos = value;
    tos++;
}
```

```
int pop(void)
{
    tos--;
    if (isempty()) abort();
    return *tos;
}

int isempty(void)
{
    return (tos==base);
}

int isfull(void)
{
    return (tos==limit);
}
```

In practice many computers provide hardware assistance to these operations, sometimes in the form of PUSH and POP instructions. Some computers provide a separate memory for a stack, or offer other forms of help.

Use of a falling stack (rather than the rising stack described above) is common. In a falling stack, the pointer is decreased in a push and increased in a pop. With this one can start the stack at the top of memory, and the program at the bottom of memory, and minimize the chance of a collision (although checking is still necessary). The hardware assistance may encourage this form, and there is a rather detailed practical reason for preferring a falling stack in compiler writing, but that is beyond the scope of this chapter.

You may find it helpful to rewrite the simple stack code above to use a falling stack, where the initialization code is presented with a base address and a size. Take care, as it is not quite so simple as you may suspect.

Stack structures are so common in programming languages that one often sees references to "The Stack." But stacks are useful memory organizations beyond the use in programming languages.

F.5.2   The Heap

The second major memory organization is the *heap*. The abstraction is that the user can request an area of memory of a fixed size, and will be passed a pointer to memory at least as large as the requested size. When the user decides that the memory is no longer required, the user passes the area back to the heap so it can be recycled. In C these two operations are characterized by the functions *malloc* and *free*. (In C++ they are the operations *new* and *delete*.) Implementing this is much harder than implementing a stack and has been the subject of much research and experimentation. For the purposes of this chapter we will consider two strategies: first fit and best fit.

F.5.2.1 First Fit

The strategy in first fit is to return the first chunk of memory that is found that is large enough, splitting a chunk if it is too big. The danger of this is that the memory will slowly get split into small chunks and a large request cannot be satisfied. The partial solution to this is to amalgamate adjacent free chunks to reduce the fragmentation.

One way to implement this is to create a header for each block with the size and a flag to say if it is in use. We can scan the memory in address order, looking for a sufficiently large block; the size tells if it is allocatable and also where the next block starts. In C this first implementation, without amalgamation becomes

```c
#define FREE (0)
#define USED (1)
int *heap_start;
int *heap_end;

void initialize_heap(int *base, int size)
{
    *base = size;
    *(base+1) = FREE;
    heap_start = base;
    heap_end = base+size;
}

int *alloc(int size)
{
    int *p = heap_start;
    while (p<heap_end) {
        /* Need two words for the header, so size+2 */
        if (*(p+1)==FREE && *p>=(size+2)) {
            if (*p>=size+5) { /* split block */
                int *ans = p+*p;
                *p -= size+2;
                *ans = size+2; /* construct header */
                *(ans+1) = USED;
                return ans;
            }
            else { /* return entire chunk */
                *(p+1) = USED;
                return p;
            }
        }
        p += *p;
    }
    return NULL; /* Out of memory */
```

```
}
void dealloc(int *p)
{
    int *hdr = p-2;
    *(hdr+1) = FREE;
}
```

This program is not as simple as the stack programs above, and we still need to handle amalgamation.

There are two approaches to rejoining adjacent blocks. One can do it when a memory is freed, by checking the next block (if there is one):

```
void dealloc(int *p)
{
    int *hdr = p-2;
    int *next = hdr+*hdr;
    *(hdr+1) = FREE;
    if (next<heap_end && *(next+1)==FREE)
        *hdr += *next;
}
```

But one would also want to amalgamate with the previous block if it existed and was free. We have to determine whether the previous block requires a scan from the start. But there is a memory scan in the allocation function, so the second and better approach is to amalgamate at allocation time, and do nothing special when freeing. This lazy approach is very efficient, as it amalgamates only if necessary:

```
int *alloc(int size)
{
    int *p = heap_start;
    int *nxt;
    while (p<heap_end) {
        /* Need two words for the header, so size+2 */
        if (*(p+1)==FREE) {
            if (*p>=(size+2)) {
                if (*p>=size+5) { /* split block */
                    int *ans = p+*p;
                    *p -= size+2;
                    *ans = size+2; /* construct header */
                    *(ans+1) = USED;
                    return ans;
                }
                else { /* return entire chunk */
                    *(p+1) = USED;
```

```
                    return p;
                }
            }
            nxt = p+*p;
            if (nxt<heap_end && *(nxt+1)==FREE) {
                *p += *nxt;
            }
            else p += *p;
        }
        else p += *p;
    }
    return NULL; /* Out of memory */
}
void dealloc(int *p)
{
    int *hdr = p-2;
    *(hdr+1) = FREE;
}
```

With first fit there can still be fragmentation of memory, but it is fast and relatively simple.

F.5.2.2 Best Fit

The second memory-allocation structure we will consider is best fit, in which we allocate the chunk on memory that is the closest in size to what is considered acceptable. It may seem that this requires a complete scan of all blocks to find it, but if we maintain a list of free chunks, ordered by increasing size, on allocation we just need to scan this list until we find a chuck large enough, and that will be the best fit. If the fit is not exact then the chunk is split and the additional segment is added back to the list in the correct location. Freeing store is also a matter of adding the chunk back in the correct place. Amalgamation is usually done at freeing time with a complete scan of the list to see if any free chunk is adjacent to the one to be freed.

The header information now must have the size and the address of the next chunk in the chain. Here is the code:

```
int *free_list;

void initialize_heap(int *base, int size)
{
    *base = (int)NULL;
    *(base+1) = size;
    free_list = base;
}
```

```
static void add_to_list(int *old)
{
    int *p = free_list;
    int *last = (int*)&free_list;
    int size = *(old+1);
    while (p!=NULL && *(p+1)<size) {
        last = p; p = (int*)(*p);
    }
    *old = (int)p;
    *last = (int)old;
}

int *alloc(int size)
{
    int *p = free_list;
    int *last = (int*)&free_list;
    while (p!=NULL) {
        if (*(p+1)>=size+2) { /* Found a chunk */
            if (*(p+1)<=size+5) { /* use whole chunk */
                int *ans = p;
                *last = *p;
                return ans;
            }
            else { /* split chunk */
                int *ans = p;
                int *extra = p+size+2;
                *(extra+1) = *(p+1)-size-2;
                add_to_list(extra);
                return ans;
            }
        }
        last = p;
        p = (int *)*p;
    }
    return NULL;
}

void dealloc(int* old)
{
retry:
    {
        int *p = free_list;
        int *last = (int*)&free_list;
        while (p!=NULL) {
```

```
                    if (old + *(old+1) == p) {
                    *last = *p;
                    *(old+1) += *(p+1)+2;
                    goto retry;
            }
            if (old == p+*(p+1)) {
                    *last = *p;
                    *(p+1) += *(old+1)+2;
                    old = p;
                    goto retry;
            }
            last = p;
            p = (int*)(*p);
        }
        add_to_list(old);
    }
}
```

It does not take much effort to see that the freeing process is considerably more complex. There are ways of making it faster, but it is more complex to perform the amalgamations. Usually fragmentation is less with first fit but the additional cost is rarely worthwhile.

The code for both cases can be made clearly with the use of a `struct` to define the header layout, and different casts.

Worst fit is like best fit, except that the largest chunk is always used, with the intention of leaving large chunks. The code is similar, with a free list in decreasing size, but there is less searching, as the first chunk on the free list is always the one to use. There are many other systems and variants; interested readers are referred to D. Knuth, *The Art of Computer Programming*, volume 1, *Fundamental Algorithms*, second edition (Addison-Wesley, 1998).

F.6   Evolution of Computer Languages

Writing programs at the level of sections F.3 and F.4 above is called *assembler programming*. To do it well requires deep concentration and attention to minute detail. If computers are your hobby, there are few aspects of computing that are closer to the real machine. Coding this way has similarities with cryptic crossword puzzles and similar intellectual games. I loved doing this when I young, but the effort took its toll and I rarely do it now. It is still a significant skill in DSP programming, especially in the innermost, most efficiency-critical, sections of code, such as filters, where performance is everything. But for most people this is just another hurdle to creating a solution.

Microprogramming is programming in an even smaller language in order to define what instructions do. Less common now than in the 1980s, micro-programmed machines where implemented using a language that was at a lower level than assembler. In this type of language one would, for instance, define the operations of an addition statement. These languages frequently did many things at the same time, and had obscure restrictions. This form of programming is even harder than dealing with assembler and should be labeled "for geeks only."[5]

What can be done to make programming possible for everyone? The answer is the development of higher-level languages. The problem with the assembler languages outlined above is that they are computer oriented. The way in which the language expresses processes is closely related to what the computer does: moving data, adding registers, or storing data. While humans can work in this way, understanding the actual activity inside the computer,, there is an alternative. This is to devise ways of expressing processes which are closer to our way of thinking, but still can be fairly easily mapped onto the simple execution model. These ways are what are commonly called high-level languages, or programming languages.

The idea is that we prefer to use names for values, rather than the memory address, and that we use symbolic ways of expressing the operations. What kind of symbol really depends on what kind of computation is required. The first programming languages were still close to the actions of the computer, the *autocodes*, but it is usual to credit the first high-level languages: LISP (designed to support mathematical logic), COBOL (for commercial programming), and FORTRAN (for numerical calculation).[6] What can be seen from this is that the programming languages are not just aimed at humans, but at the particular language and ethos of a domain. There have been a large number of these domain-specific languages; there was an attempt to catalogue these some years ago,[7] and there have been some updates,[8] but the list is now very large.

In this book we are concentrating on two languages, C and C++, which are widely used in efficient programming of "systems programming," which is to say these are the commonest languages used to implement other systems, including audio systems and language systems. (See section F.7.) C first came to prominence as the language in which the first UNIX systems were written. C was a direct descendant of B, which was a version of BCPL, which originated in Cambridge, England before migrating to Cambridge, Massachusetts. BCPL has its origins in the language CPL, which has Algol60 and LISP in its heritage. Again we see that computing is a subject that develops internationally, many people having made contributions.

For most people who aspire to write computer programs one of these high-level languages is the sensible approach. That is why this book exists. However to bridge the so-called semantic gap between the simple execution cycle of the computer and the human-oriented programming language we need one more technological component: the compiler.

F.7   Compilers

Compilers are programs designed to translate programs from one language to another, typically from a high-level programming language to assembler or machine language. For most purposes the programmer does not need to know how a compiler works, but there is some advantage to understanding the processes, if only to convince ourselves that it is not magic.

The operations of any compiler can be divided into two major sections: the *front end* and the *back end*. The front end deals with the language, checking the syntax and some semantics of the input in the source language; the back end performs the translation of the program into the target language.

F.7.1   Compiler Front Ends

The front end can be further subdivided into three main components: lexical analysis, syntax analysis, and semantic analysis. The names give the clue to the activity of the front end, which is to analyze the program, eventually removing the way in which the program is expressed and leaving the meaning alone.

F.7.1.1   Lexing

The lexical analysis, or *lexer*, has the task of breaking the stream of characters into tokens, which are the logical equivalent of words and punctuation in natural languages. This is a fairly simple task, but increasingly compilers are using automated processes to create the lexer. The best known of these tools is LEX,[9] but there are many others. The underlying mechanism of these automated lexers is one of the basic methods in computing, the finite-state machine. Finite-state machines (FSMs) are sufficiently important that it is worth considering them. Aside from their use in parsers, they can be used in many ways, including a number of forms of algorithmic composition.

The idea behind the FSM is that there is a concept of the current *state*. By looking at the next object in the input a transition is made to a different state. The only rules are that the number of states is finite and that the transitions are all determined by the pair of values (`current_state`, `input_value`), and after a transition we move to the next input. As a simple example consider recognizing simple words. One starts is an initial state, and looks at the input. If it is white space then change to that same state. On a letter in the input we change to a state we might call "word started." In the word started state, we loop on letters and exit on anything else. This can be succinctly expressed by means of a diagram such as figure F.5. It is not too hard to extend such a diagram to more complex situation (for instance to floating-point numbers) (figure F.6).

When one has created the transition diagram, it is then just a case of simple coding. For example, if the states are numbered, one could have a variable `current_state` and a simple loop like the following (for the first case):

```
#define ERROR_STATE -99
#define END_STATE -1
int FSM_word(void)
```

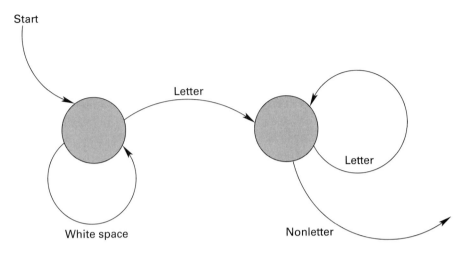

Figure F.5
FSM for words.

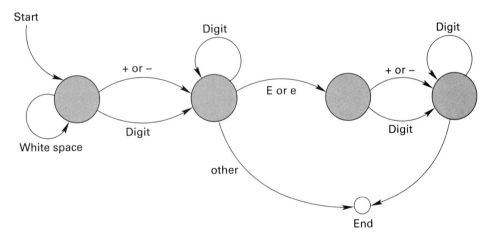

Figure F.6
FSM for floating-point numbers.

```
{
    int current_state = 0;
    int ch;

    while (current_state != END_STATE) {
        ch = getchar();
        switch (current_state) {
        case 0:
            if (isletter(ch)) current_state = 1;
            else if (isspace(ch)) current_state = 0;
            else current_state = ERROR_STATE
            break;
        case 1:
            if (isletter(ch)) current_state = 1;
            else current_state = END_STATE;
            break;
        case ERROR_STATE:
            printf("Syntax error: not a word\n");
            return 0;
    }}
    return 1;
}
```

From this simple example it is not hard to see that the program is very repetitive and follows a simple format. A faster but less clear coding of this FSM would be to construct a table, indexed by the current state and the current character and containing the next state. The code would then become the following:

```
int FSM_word(void)
{
    int current_state = 0;
    int ch;

    while (current_state != END_STATE &&
            current_state != ERROR_STATE) {
        ch = getchar();
        current_state = word_table[current_state][ch];
    }
    if (current_state == ERROR_STATE) {
        printf("Syntax error: not a word\n");
        return 0;
    }
    return 1;
}
```

This would be the same for all FSMs, but with different tables. Constructing these tables can be tedious, but that is what LEX and similar programs do for you.

Finite-state machines such as are used in lexing have been used in algorithmic composition systems. It is fairly easy to see how these processes can be turned into transitions between different note sequences that depend on some input. A FSM can control which transitions are permitted, but can use external control to select the actual progress of the sound. Beginning and ending sections can be controlled, and a structure of climaxes can be imposed on the process.

With a random number generator to get the stream of inputs, one could create a stochastic process reminiscent of the screens used by Iannis Xenakis in his Markovian Stochastic Music. (See Xenakis, *Formalized Music*, revised edition, Pendragon, 1992.) The lexer will usually also remove comments, as these are only for human use.

F.7.1.2 Parsing

The parsing stage of the compiler checks for the grammar of the programming language and builds a representation of the source that is more abstract that the textual form; this representation is usually in the form of a tree. For most designed languages (that is, artificial rather than natural languages) the technology for parser construction is well understood.[10] There are many systems that can be used to generate the necessary code; the commonest are YACC and Bison.[11] These systems take a description of the language and create a program capable of parsing source programs. There are simpler texts covering mainly these aspects; one is J. Bennett, *Compiling Techniques: A First Course Using ANSI C, LEX and YACC*, second edition (Addison-Wesley, 1996).

One would expect the parser to change the sequence

```
a = b + 3 * c + d;
b = fn(e-f);
```

to the tree shown in figure F.7. Notice that this tree is unambiguous. All precedence of the addition and multiplication operator has been resolved and the variables have been identified.

F.7.1.3 Semantics

The last stage of the front end is to check the semantics. This can involve many things, but will certainly include checking that all variables are declared, that the types of variables match, and resolving which variable of a given name is meant. In C++, the semantics will also resolve overloading of operators and methods.

F.7.2 Compiler Back Ends

At the finish of the front end, the source program will have been transformed into an internal representation of its meaning. The syntax, layout, and comments will have been

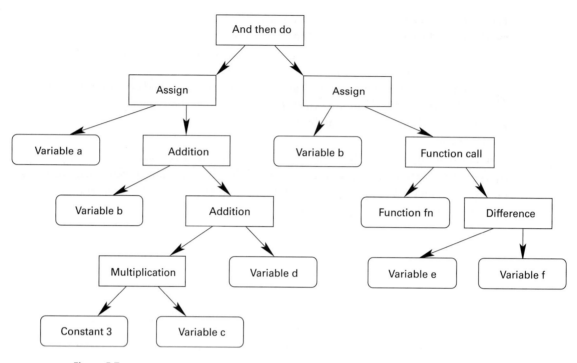

Figure F.7
Parse tree.

removed. The variables will have been associated with their declarations and a variety of similar operations will have been performed. This internal representation usually takes the form of some kind of tree structure and makes up the input to the back end.

There are fewer tools to assist in the back end than in the front end, and the three components are more likely to be intertwined. The following description is therefore lacking in detail. Compiler back-end construction still has many aspects of an art.

F.7.2.1 Machine-Independent Optimization

In addition to generating machine-level code, a compiler will usually attempt to optimize the program. This is a misnomer. What is achieved is to improve the code, without any hope of obtaining the optimal coding. We can expect the machine-independent optimizer to perform a small number of simple tasks, such as recognizing where calculations are performed more than once, calculations that are not used, and constant folding (simplifying simple arithmetic operations which appear in the code). While these all seem small, the overall effect can be quite dramatic. It is also why teachers emphasize to students that clear coding is preferred to hand optimization. Thus,

```
#define ONE (1)
#define ZERO (0)
    a = ONE * b;
    c = ZERO* d;
```

will be treated the same as

```
a = b;
c = 0;
```

The other area in which machine-independent optimizations are concentrated is in the compilation of loops. Programmers often speak of the "90-10 rule"—that 90 percent of the time taken by a program is represented by 10 percent of the code. It is easy to see that these "hot spots" are to be found in loops.

There are a number of ways in which loops can be improved, such as detecting calculations in the body of a loop that are not changed from loop to loop and pre-calculating. For example, a loop written by the user as

```
for (i=0; i<n+100; i++)
    m[i] = k[i+3]*(j+23);
```

will be transformed into

```
TMP1 = n+100;
TMP2 = j+23;
for (i=0; i<TMP1; i++)
    m[i] = k[i+3]*TMP2;
```

Even more interesting is that while the variable i goes from 0 to n+100, the value i+3 will go from 3 to n+103 in step. The loop can be changed to

```
TMP1 = n+100;
TMP2 = j+23;
for (i=0, TMP3=3; i<TMP1; i++, TMP3++)
    m[i] = k[TMP3]*TMP2;
```

This is more efficient than the code we started with, but much less clear.

There are other optimizations that can be performed on this sequence—optimizations that cannot be expressed in the source language.[12]

F.7.2.2 Code Generation

One would expect the compiler to generate code, but in many ways this is the least significant task. As long as the optimizations and semantics have been done clearly, the generation of code is straightforward. The one thing that is not obvious is how to use the registers that any particular machine provides. A good strategy for this will have a real effect on the performance of the resulting code. This subject is too far into computer science for this book, but it is perhaps of interest that that the currently most used technique is based on graph theory and is called the *register coloring* algorithm. It casts the problem of which registers to use into the problem of coloring a graph so no connected node are the same color. This problem can also formulated as that of coloring a map so no adjacent country have the same color, and doing this with a limited number of colors.[13]

F.7.2.3   Machine-Dependent Optimization

The last component of compilation is to use particular knowledge of the target computer to use special features of the machine, odd instructions that can be used only in special cases, replace instruction sequences with ones known to run faster, and similar detailed operations. Naturally these are the hardest to classify, as for each machine they are different.

F.8   Conclusion

This chapter has shown the underlying mechanisms by which computers work, and in particular the fundamental execution cycle. Computers need not be seen as mysterious black (or gray) boxes, but have a simple logical structure. In order to improve programmers' productivity and allow them to think at a raised abstract level, programming languages were introduced. Initially these were fairly *ad hoc* and often specialized to one computer, but we have developed a number of platform-independent general languages. For developing systems, C is currently the most widely available language.

A compiler performs the translation of the high-level (user-oriented) language to the low-level (machine-oriented) language. Much of the internal workings of compilers is complex and follows other technologies. In this chapter references have been make to texts that would allow you to get even deeper knowledge, but realizing the kinds of actions compilers do can assist in writing user programs. Optimizations of code are the responsibility of the compiler, while the user should write with clarity. The part the human plays in creating software is focused on selecting the best representations, data structures, and algorithms.

If you look at your C compiler, you should find that it is possible to select different compiler optimizations. This chapter should assist in understanding what they do.

Notes

1. I was a student of Sir Maurice Wilkes, and I tend to support his claim.

2. But not always, as multiplication is a slower and more difficult operation than addition.

3. In my home town, many houses do not have numbers at all, and where I previously lived in US every house was numbered but most numbers were not housed.

4. Note that the term *heap* has two related meanings. It is used for a general memory system, and also for a particular organization. It is being used in the generic sense here.

5. I have written a great deal of micro code in my time, and it remains to me the most enjoyable style of programming. It is not for everyone!

6. On LISP see J. McCarthy, "Recursive Functions of Symbolic Expressions and Their Computation by Machine, Part I," *Communications of the ACM* 3, 1960, no. 4: 184–195. On COBOL see *Common Business Oriented Language*, technical report, CODASYL, 1959. On FORTRAN see J. Backus et al., "The FORTRAN Automatic Coding System," in Proceedings of the Western Joint Computer Conference, 1957.

7. J. Sammet, *Programming Languages: History and Fundamentals* (Prentice-Hall, 1969).

8. J. Sammet, "Roster of Programming Languages for 1974–75," *Communications of the ACM* 19, 1976, no. 2: 655–669; J. Sammet, "An Overview of High-Level Languages," *Advances in Computers* 20, 1981: 199–259.

9. On LEX, see M. Lesk and E. Schmidt, "LEX—Lexical Analyzer Generator," in *UNIX Research System Programmer's Manual*, tenth edition (Saunders College Publishing, 1990), volume 2, and http://flex.sourceforge.net/.

10. Interested readers are referred to A. Aho, R. Sethi, and J. D. Ullman, *Compilers: Principles, Techniques and Tools* (Addison-Wesley, 1986) (the detailed "Red Dragon Book") and to the less detailed "Green Dragon Book" by the same authors: *Principles of Compiler Design* (Addison-Wesley, 1977).

11. On YACC see S. Johnson, "YACC: Yet Another Compiler-Compiler," in *UNIX Research System Programmer's Manual*, tenth edition (Saunders College Publishing, 1990), volume 2. On BISON see The Bison Manual, available at http//www.gnu.org/manual/bison/index.html.

12. The optimization to which I refer is called *induction variable usage*, and relates in this example to i only being used to address memory and so we could use a TMP variable for &m[0] and add to that to go to the next array element. On a byte-addressed machine, this can not be expressed by the programmer. Again the interested reader is referred to a standard compiler text.

13. Aho et al. explain the algorithm in *Compilers*.

Appendix G: Glossary

John ffitch with Richard Dobson, Victor Lazzarini, and Richard Boulanger

Computing is at the forefront of the creation and use of jargon. In this glossary we bring together short descriptions of key words in computing found in this book. Readers interested in learning more on the subject are referred to the dated but still amusingly accurate Computer Contradictionary *by Stan Kelly-Bootle (MIT Press, 1995).*

0dBFS Standing for "zero decibels full scale," this term is commonly used to define the absolute maximum value for a digital signal ("digital peak") in a number representation; likewise the peak signal level to which analog equipment is calibrated. By convention, maximum level is stated as 0 dB; any signal exceeding 0 dB will be clipped. All other levels are expressed relative to 0 dBFS. For floating-point samples, 0 dBFS is usually 1.0; for 16-bit samples it is 32,768 (corresponding to the maximum negative 16-bit value, 2^{15}). Because of the response of the ear, the decibel is the most appropriate measure of sound level. The term is also widely used to indicate not a peak sample value (or reference voltage) but a peak signal *power* expressed as an RMS (root-mean-square) value. This leads to a subtle but important distinction between 0 dBFS (sine) and 0 dBFS (square). Intuitively we can understand signal power as determined by the area under the curve, when the waveform is drawn. Clearly, this area is less for a sinusoid than for a square wave (the latter indeed giving the maximum theoretical power achievable as the full available area is used). The difference is 3 dB, so if 0 dBFS (square) is 1.0, 0 dBFS (sine) is approximately 0.707. Usually the intended usage will be clear from the context. In Csound, the special name 0 dBFS is used to define the peak sample value; when the term is used by mixing engineers, the full-scale sine power reference is assumed. There is a sound reason for this: a sinusoid reaching digital peak presents the highest power level that can be passed to an ADC without clipping.

Absolute value In mathematics, the magnitude of a number regardless of sign. The absolute value of $+1.5$ is 1.5; the absolute value of -0.7 is $+0.7$. One is said to "take the absolute" of a number. It is represented in C by two library functions: `abs()` for integers and `fabs()` for floating-point values. The latter is a relatively expensive computation. A typical use is in finding the overall or average amplitude of a signal. Audio waveforms are bipolar—samples have both positive and negative values. If these were simply added (and there is no DC offset), the result would simply be zero. This "signedness" should be disregarded in finding the signal level; the absolute value of each sample should be taken.

ADC   Analog-to-digital converter—a device used to convert an electrical current, such as that produced by microphone and amplifier, into a stream of bits that can be manipulated by a computer. A computer soundcard will contain one or more ADCs. In common parlance, the ADC is used as another name for an input soundcard.

Address   A location in computer memory has both its contents and an address. The address is a number that identifies the location uniquely and can be used by a program as identification.

AIFF   See *Audio file formats*.

Algorithm   A finite set of unambiguous rules to solve a problem in a finite time.

Alias   In operating systems and programs, an alternative name for a disk file, a memory location, or a the name of a macro.

Allocate   To identify and acquire a piece of free memory and associate it to a program. This is most often done by means of `malloc`, `calloc`, or `new`.

ALSA   Advanced Linux Sound Architecture, a software layer that includes a collection of device drivers for various soundcards in the Linux OS. It provides the lowest-level audio input and output application programming interface. OSS (Open Sound System) offers similar functionality but is not as commonly found in the most popular Linux distributions.

ALU   Arithmetic and logic unit, the component of the computer hardware that performs the operations on values. The arithmetic component performs addition, subtraction, multiplication, and division. The logic performs bitwise operations from Boolean algebra, such as AND, OR, NEQV, or NOT. (See *CPU*.)

Ambisonics   A way of recording and playing true surround sound, also known as B-Format. Invented in the 1970s by Michael Gerzon of the University of Oxford Mathematical Institute, it is firmly based in the theory of spherical harmonics. The mechanism is complex and still being developed, but it is not the same as 5.1 or a similar discrete speaker format. A special multi-capsule microphone can be used to record an entire three-dimensional sound-field—the principle is that the capsules are as close to coincident as possible, so that they record the exact soundfield at a single point in space, which in turn is reproduced by means of the decoder. The first multi-capsule microphone was the Calrec Soundfield; others have appeared more recently, and some engineers use a set of closely matched discrete micro-phones. The audio signals are not related to speaker positions but rather to the underlying spherical harmonics, and a B-Format decoder is used to render the audio to a particular speaker layout. A special advantage of B-Format is that it is "speaker-agnostic"—a given stream may (in principle) be decoded to as many speakers as are available, including the standard stereo pair.

B-Format supports both two-dimensional and three-dimensional configurations. (All current cinema surround formats, despite being described as three-dimensional, are horizontal-only.) As a rule of thumb, the more speakers used, the better the localization, with a much-reduced tendency for sounds to ''pull'' into the nearest physical speaker. The theory requires that speakers be arranged in a regular geometry, such as a hexagon, a cube, or a dodecahedron. Some small departures from this are possible; for example, there are ways to decode to the popular 5.1 layout, though the quality is compromised. A further special aspect of B-Format is that all the speakers are driven (for example, where speakers are opposite across the array, one will push where the other pulls); thus all the speakers contribute to the overall sound pressure level (SPL).

B-Format is defined as a series of orders. The first order uses four channels, the second order nine channels, and the third order 16. Some channels can be disregarded for playback over a horizontal-only array. Still higher orders are possible, and are a current research topic.

ANSI C   Kernighan and Ritchie originally wrote the C language for their own software development, particularly for the UNIX operating system. A number of confusing parts and potential sources of error were addressed by a committee of the American National Standards Institute, which in 1989 produced a language definition (often called ANSI C or C89). It was quickly adopted by the International Standard Organization (ISO) and by the software community. Very little of the earlier Kernighan-Ritchie C language remains. The ANSI committee continued with a revised standard, producing a new language C99 in 1999. Aspects of this language are common, but the whole language is not so universally adopted.

API   The Application Programming Interface. A programmer need not know everything about a library or a package; all that is necessary is to know how to call it. The API will usually consist of a number of functions with defined arguments and possibly some data structure definitions (in the C language, `struct`). This definition allows the application developer to use the package; at the same time, it allows the developer of a package to modify and improve the system as long as the API does not change.

AquaTerm   A Mac OS X graphics terminal (a plotting front end) written using Objective-C and the Cocoa API.

Argument   A value passed to a function or method, or a space-separated string supplied to a program by means of the command line.

Array   A collection of like-typed data that is accessed by means of a numerical index.

ASCII   Strictly, ASCII is the initials of the phrase American Standard Code for Information Interchange, the commonest mapping of the textual characters of English, together with some pictorial (not alpha-numeric) and other characters. There are a total of 128 characters in this code, including some "control" characters, originally for example for starting a tape, ending transmission, and a number of esoteric operations. It does include the typewriter-like carriage return (CR = 13), line feed (LF = 10), or form feed (more commonly known as page throw) (FF = 12). The actual code is shown in table G.1.

ASIC   An Application-Specific Integrated Circuit—a custom chip that can perform special processing.

Assembler   A program that translates assembly language programs into machine code. Sometimes also used for assembly language.

Assembly code   See *Assembly language*.

Assembly language   A low-level machine-oriented language that reflects, in text, the basic machine instructions. Originally it would have had one line of text for one machine instruction, but today assembly language often contains macros.

Asynchronous   Two processes can be synchronous (that is, both happening at the same rate and time) or asynchronous (where there is no order in which the two processes work).

AU   See *Audio file formats*.

Audio file formats   There are many ways in which plain PCM (pulse code modulation) audio can be stored in a file. They fall into three main categories: uncompressed, lossless compressed, and lossy compressed. Some file formats (tending to be proprietary) are specialized to one or another of these (e.g., the `.mp3` file format for compressed audio). However, the majority of file formats of importance to the musician are, strictly speaking, container formats that can support a wide variety of audio representations, including both plain PCM audio and a variety of compressed formats. Popular container formats include the common RIFF-based formats of WAV and AIFF and more recent introductions such as Apple's new CAF format. These formats include a header and a number of "chunks," all of which have the same general structure of a name, a length, and data. Standard chunks are defined for the audio data itself (whether raw PCM or compressed), metadata (author, album, date, copyright, and so forth), looping information, and much else. The differences between WAV and AIFF lie in the names of the chunks (e.g., "data" for WAV and "SSND" for AIFF) and the byte order of the data.

Lossless compression formats are more specialized and, as the name suggests, give smaller files, but the original data can be reconstructed exactly. Notable in this class are FLAC, Shorten, ALAC, and WMA. These formats use a variety of mathematical and audio processes to reduce the data requirements, and normally achieve about 58 percent compression. The last group (which includes the above-mentioned `.mp3` format) uses psychoacoustic principles to remove parts of the audio that perceptually a human cannot hear, then uses DSP to reduce the data considerably. MP2 and OGG, the best-known algorithms, achieve compressions of about 15 percent of the raw PCM, depending on the type of sounds involved. It is a matter of taste and dispute as to whether lossy compression matters, but it is worth noting

Table G.1

The ASCII codes.

DEC	HEX	CHAR	DEC	HEX	CHAR	DEC	HEX	CHAR
0	00	NULL '\0'	43	2B	+	86	56	V
1	01	SOH	44	2C	,	87	57	W
2	02	STX	45	2D	−	88	58	X
3	03	ETX	46	2E	.	89	59	Y
4	04	EOT	47	2F	/	90	5A	Z
5	05	ENQ	48	30	0	91	5B	[
6	06	ACK	49	31	1	92	5C	\
7	07	BEL '\a'	50	32	2	93	5D	]
8	08	BS '\b'	51	33	3	94	5E	^
9	09	HT 't'	52	34	4	95	5F	_
10	0A	LF '\n'	53	35	5	96	60	`
11	0B	VT '\v'	54	36	6	97	61	a
12	0C	FF '\f'	55	37	7	98	62	b
13	0D	CR '\r'	56	38	8	99	63	c
14	0E	SO	57	39	9	100	64	d
15	0F	SI	58	3A	:	101	65	e
16	10	DLE	59	3B	;	102	66	f
17	11	DC1	60	3C	<	103	67	g
18	12	DC2	61	3D	=	104	68	h
19	13	DC3	62	3E	>	105	69	i
20	14	DC4	63	3F	?	106	6A	j
21	15	NAK	64	40	@	107	6B	k
22	16	SYN	65	41	A	108	6C	l
23	17	ETB	66	42	B	109	6D	m
24	18	CAN	67	43	C	110	6E	n
25	19	EM	68	44	D	111	6F	o
26	1A	SUB	69	45	E	112	70	p
27	1B	ESC	70	46	F	113	71	q
28	1C	FS	71	47	G	114	72	r
29	1D	GS	72	48	H	115	73	s
30	1E	RS	73	49	I	116	74	t
31	1F	US	74	4A	J	117	75	u
32	20	SPACE	75	4B	K	118	76	v
33	21	!	76	4C	L	119	77	w
34	22	"	77	4D	M	120	78	x
35	23	#	78	4E	N	121	79	y
36	24	$	79	4F	O	122	7A	z
37	25	%	80	50	P	123	7B	{
38	26	&	81	51	Q	124	7C		
39	27	'	82	52	R	125	7D	}
40	28	(	83	53	S	126	7E	~
41	29	)	84	54	T	127	7F	DEL
42	2A	*	85	55	U			

that the typical listening environment should factor into this determination. When one is listening to music while traveling on an airplane or a bus, the situation (noise level) is quite different from listening in one's home studio with good monitor speakers.

Audio Units   An audio plug-in architecture developed by Apple for Mac OS X. It provides a common structure for the development of audio applications that support externally provided components (plug-ins). It is a part of the overall *CoreAudio* API. See also *VST* and *LADSPA*.

Backing store   Shortly after the invention of computers, it became clear that there was a need to store data between program runs. The earliest machines used punched tape or punched cards (in particular the Hollerith card, originally used in the US census), but these are inconvenient for larger collections of data. This need gave rise to the development of backing store, first as magnetic tape and later as magnetic drums and disks. The term is used loosely for all data recording mechanisms except main memory.

Bash   The Bourne Again Shell, a command language interpreter closely associated with GCC and the GNU tools. The name is a pun on the surname of Steven Bourne, the original author of the UNIX shell, sh.

Bebugging   Testing can show the presence of bugs but not their absence. How confident can we be that a software package is free of bugs, or at least low in bugs? If (as is common in commercial programming) the testing team is independent of the creating team, we can use bebugging to estimate the bugginess of the code. In bebugging, the writing team deliberately inserts a fixed number of known bugs before passing the code to the testers, then observes how many of these added bugs are detected by the testers. If only half of them are found, it may be assumed that the testers have found only half of the inadvertent bugs. If 90 percent are found, it may be assumed that 90 percent of the real bugs have been found. If all N bugs are detected then one may assume that about $1/(2N)$ of the bugs remain.

B-Format   See *Ambisonics*.

Big-endian   See *Little-endian*.

Binary file   A computer file could be in text format, or it could be in binary, using the bit representation of numbers directly.

Binary format   Most modern computers work in binary; that is, numbers are represented internally in radix 2, where a digit can have one of only two possible values, i.e. 0 and 1. This is considered in more detail in the item on *number representation* below, but one particular implication is that when storing data on a *backing store* it can be maintained in this binary format which uses fewer bits than a representation in ASCII characters. Such binary representations are highly robust in the presence of noise, which makes them ideally suited not only for computer manipulation but also for storage on magnetic media such as tape and disk.

Bit   The smallest unit of information that can be held and processed. This is a single binary digit, which can only have the value 0 or 1. It is sometimes suggested that this 'bit' an abbreviation for binary digit, but this seems unlikely. More complex values and data items can be constructed from a number of bits, using binary arithmetic, vectors of bits, or other arrangements. When worrying about time-critical or space-critical computations, one often counts the number of bits being used to represent something. There is also *bit-twiddling*, a now-deprecated but nevertheless interesting style of computing that cares about the size of a program to such an overarching extent that mathematical games are played with bits. (Exercise for the over-enthusiastic reader: Consider how to swap two values held in variables without using a temporary.)

Blocking IO   A type of IO operation that blocks (stops) program execution while waiting for data to be completely sent or received to or from its source or destination. Conversely, in non-blocking IO the program does not wait for input or output to be completed. (See *Asynchronous*.)

Bluetooth   A short-range wireless communication system for personal area networks (PAN). Its range is about 10 meters. Using the 2.4-gigahertz radio band, it can achieve speeds of up to 1 megabit per second. It is used to attach mouses and keyboards without wires, to facilitate data exchange with mobile (cell) phones, and to enable Nintendo's Wii remote game controller to find applications.

Boolean algebra   Invented by the nineteenth-century Irish mathematician George Boole, Boolean algebra is used to manipulate expressions whose variables are TRUE or FALSE and whose operators are NOT, AND, OR, NEQV, and IMPLIES. This scheme is universally used in binary computers, where each bit has two states (0 and 1, or FALSE and TRUE). It helps in translating logical arguments into mechanical processes.

Buffer   A generic name used for a memory space used to momentarily store data that is going to be subsequently processed in one way or another (for instance, sent to an output). An important use is storing data delivered in bursts (e.g., from a disk drive, or over a computer bus such as PCI), for continuous access under the control of a clock. Buffers are characterized by the order in which data is written and read. By far the most common is the First-In-First-Out (FIFO) buffer. As its name indicates, the order of the data is preserved, experiencing only a delay. The alternative is a FILO buffer (First-In-Last-Out), more commonly referred to as a *stack*.

Bug   An inadvertent error in a computer program or (by transference) in any process.

Bus   An electrical mechanism to communicate binary signals between components of a computer. It is also used for a software mechanism that fulfils a similar role in system design.

Byte   A small collection of bits. The number is usually eight, but not always. It is usually synonymous with the number of bits used to store a character on the particular machine,

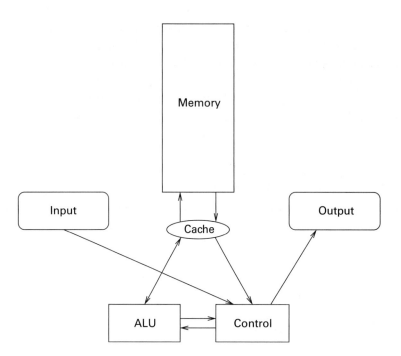

Figure G.1
Cache memory.

and for most architectures that number is eight. Older readers may remember that the PDP10 used seven bits for characters, although this was user-adjustable.

C   A programming language, created by Dennis Ritchie, used in major platforms for systems implementation. It is particularly important for audio programming.

C99   See *ANSI C*.

C++   An object-oriented computer language, originally based on C, that can easily work and integrate with C.

Cache   One of the recurring problems in computer architecture is the mismatch of speed between the central processing unit (CPU) and the main memory. As technology evolves, both of these components are getting faster, but at different rates. Processor speeds are far outstripping affordable memory. The cache is a piece of hardware that seeks to ameliorate this. It is basically a section of fast (and therefore expensive) memory with associated logic (in the case of most modern CPUs, incorporated into the chip itself) so that whenever the processor reads a value or writes a value to memory a copy of the address and value are stored in the cache. If the value is used again, it can be recovered from the cache much faster than from the main memory (figure G.1). Cache works because of two effects: temporal and spatial locality. If we use a value it is likely that we will use it again soon, and we are likely to use values stored close to it in the near future. Surprisingly, this works extremely well, and relatively small amounts of cache give greatly improved performance. Some recent machines use more than one level of cache, which gives rise to terms like L2 ("level-two") cache.

Callbacks   The usual style of programming is imperative; one gives a sequence of operations to perform. An alternative structure is to have a main program that does nothing but wait (in a so-called idle loop); then, when something happens (e.g., a character typed on the console, or a mouse is clicked), a callback function is invoked. When the callback function has done its task, control returns to the idle loop in the main program. This style is frequently used in GUI implementations as an alternative to polling (in which the main program repeatedly asks every component if it needs attention). Callbacks are sometimes called "software interrupts." They are, nevertheless, frequently associated with responses to a hardware-mediated event, such as a notification from a soundcard (or rather, from its driver software) that a new buffer of audio is available. The callback system is central to the operation of an interactive digital audio workstation (DAW), in which all the audio processing (including all inserted plug-ins) is processed inside a single callback function under the control of the audio hardware. Such a callback will typically be run in a high-priority *thread*, so that under high CPU load the GUI elements may become sluggish, but the audio stream will continue without breakup.

cmusic   A music-programming language inspired by the MUSIC-N paradigm, written in the C language by F. Richard Moore. One of its main aspects was the way it took advantage of the UNIX principle of interconnecting programs and shell scripting.

Codec   A conflation of the words 'coder' and 'decoder' that properly describes a system that combines both encoding and decoding functions (e.g., both ADC and DAC) within one device. Nevertheless, it is often used more colloquially to refer to one or the other separately ("output to the codec"). In a second related usage, it refers to any plug-in module required by an application (such as a DAW or a web browser) to decode (or encode to) an otherwise unrecognized file or data format.

Command-line interface   The alternative to a GUI. One types commands to a terminal with arguments and flags, rather than using a mouse and buttons. Though older in style, it has significant advantages for developers.

Compile   Programs written in a textual source form must be translated into a language that can be obeyed by the computer hardware. The process of translation is compilation, and the translated object is called *compiled code* (to distinguish it from *source code*).

Console   When computers were first developed, there was a control desk called a console from which one started programs and stopped the machine. During the transition to multiple users and time sharing, there still remained the operator's console, often as a teletypewriter, overseeing the operation. Personal computers retain this idea of the main controlling input and output, the console, though now it often consists of a screen and a keyboard. By transference, and following the ideas of virtual machines, each program is said to have a controlling console, the (virtual) terminal that started the program, or some even more complex scheme. The console initially provides the main input (*standard in*) and receives the main output (*standard out*).

Controller   A system or device that provides control information for a certain operation, such as a MIDI controller (that sends MIDI information to software) or hardware controllers. A controller thus involves two elements: the physical hardware and the software and/or electrical protocol (e.g., MIDI, OSC, Bluetooth) by which the physical hardware communicates with the receiver.

Core   One of the earliest forms of main memory used the magnetic fields of small doughnut-like rings of ferrite, which were known as *cores*. By passing three wires through the hole in a ring, it was possible to selectively read or write individual bits. This technology, long since superseded, gave rise to the colloquial use of *core* to mean *main memory*. This has largely fallen into disuse, except in the phrase *core dump*. On UNIX-like systems, when a program fails it might produce a dump of the state of the memory in a file called *core*. Modern memories are more likely to be made from electrostatic charge, or from transistor states.

Core Audio   The audio IO software layer on OS X, handling access to devices (soundcards) for which Core Audio device drivers exist. It comprises a collection of APIs for dealing with real-time audio programming, including the management of instrument and effect plug-ins connected in the form of a signal flow graph.

Core MIDI   The MIDI IO software layer on OS X, performing an equivalent function to Core Audio.

CPU   The Central Processing Unit—the component of the computer's hardware that performs all processing and control. It incorporates the arithmetic and logic unit and the mechanisms for getting the next instruction to obey, and performing jumps and similar activities. The name comes from the time when computers had other processing units, usually associated with input and output, and the CPU was the main one, at the center of a ring of devices. With machines having more than one main processor, the name is rather anachronistic.

Crash   A program that fails in an unexpected way is said to have crashed. The cause could be a bug, a memory leak, or some unexpected external event.

Csound   A music-programming language written originally by Barry Vercoe as an update to his *music11* system. As *music11* had been written for a specific machine (the DEC PDP 11), it was due to become obsolete with the advent of new computers. With Csound, we have a system written in the C language and thus portable to any modern platform. The language was adopted by a large user and developer community, underwent a lot of development, and is currently on its fifth version.

CVS   Concurrent Versions System, a suite of programs for managing source control. It allows a number of programmers to cooperate on a single multi-file program. Each user has a copy of the code, and there are extensive mechanisms for checking code into the system, dealing with merging changes, and maintaining records of activity, both for documentation and to allow undoing of changes.

DAC   Digital-to-analog converter—a device used to convert a stream of bits, as produced by a computer, into electrical current that can be amplified and transduced by a loudspeaker. A computer soundcard will contain one or more DACs. In common parlance, the DAC is used as another name for an output soundcard.

Data structure   Any construction to organize data; often associated with the `struct` in C, it can also involve arrays, pointers, and tables.

Debugging strategies   There is only one real way to debug a program, and that is to think. As an aid to this thinking process there are symbolic debuggers like `gdb`, or one could add print statements at intervals in the code to help determine the sequence of operations, or one could obey the program by hand (i.e. without a computer) to see what happens. But ultimately what is needed is thought.

Denormal   In IEEE floating-point arithmetic there is a normalization process performed by the hardware to ensure maximal precision. There are, however, bit patterns that are not valid as normalized IEEE numbers, and these are said to be denormalized. This can indicate underflow (numbers too small to represent) or overflow (numbers too large to represent).

Decrement   To subtract by a fixed amount, usually 1.

Directory   A non-terminal node in the tree of computer files. This is a special type of file that contains references to files and directories.

Direct Memory Access, Buffers, and FIFO   When sending data to or from a peripheral device, such as a disk, the obvious program of a loop sending the words of data to the device is slow and wasteful, as the processor runs much faster that the disk can receive data. This bottleneck can be alleviated by the use of Direct Memory Access (DMA), in which additional hardware allows data to be transferred between memory and disk without the use of the CPU other than to initiate the transfer. This can be combined with a FIFO buffer (or queue) of data blocks so the processor is only used occasionally and could continue with other work. Buffering is a similar concept to smooth the rates of creation and consumption of data.

Disk   One of the main physical methods of bulk storage is a rotating disk covered in some magnetic material. Data can be written onto this surface in a number of concentric tracks by magnetizing the surface. Large disks use a number of these disks, called platters, on the same spindle. Having a reading head for each surface makes it possible to read data in parallel. On fast disks the heads do not actually touch the platter; they "float" just above it, close enough to sense the magnetic field. A "head crash," in which the head touches the rotating platter, usually leads to scratching of the magnetic surface and subsequent loss of information. In order to allow the heads to get very close to the disk, it is important to ensure that the air is very clean (the heads are much closer to the surface than the width of a human hair); for this reason, disk enclosures are usually sealed, and efficient air filters are used.

Disk, floppy   Similar technology to a hard disk, but there is usually one platter, it is floppy rather than rigid, and the head does touch the surface. This limits the speed of rotation, and the density of data that can be reliably written.

Distributed Systems, clusters, and grids   Computers are still getting faster, but there are problems which require more computing power than a single processor can provide. It is possible to have a small number of processors sharing the same memory, disks, and console, to form a shared-memory multiprocessor system. Dual-processor systems are now fairly common, and Linux for one is distributed in a symmetric multiprocessor version; this provides a multi-processing system in a direct fashion. There is, however, a limit to how many processors can share memory, and to go beyond a few it is necessary to consider a distributed system or cluster—e.g., a network of machines, each with its own memory.

Double   See *Number representation.*

Double-buffering   Using two buffers. While one is being emptied, the other is being filled. When the ends of both buffers are reached, their roles are exchanged.

Driver   A software package that mediates operating system requirements with a device, usually a disk or a mouse.

Drum   An alternative to a disk: a rotating cylinder with a magnetic surface. Otherwise similar in operation to a disk, a drum was capably of faster rotation than early disks. For that reason, drums were used for the highest-performance applications. They have fallen out of fashion, as large ones are hard to make. Also, the moment of inertia of a cylinder is larger than for a disk, and so they take longer to reach full speed after start-up. The term 'drum' is still sometimes found in descriptions of some ultra-fast disks and some virtual memory applications.

Emacs   An extensive and extensible screen editor, originally a set of macros for the `teco` editor. It is programmable in a Lisp scripting language, and a large number of plug-ins support different computer languages and systems.

Encapsulation   Hiding details of a data structure, and providing just operations that act on it, in effect making an API for the data.

Endless loop   See *Loop, endless.*

Environment variable   In most operating systems, programs are run not only with arguments (see Command line) but also with an environment. This environment is expressed as a set of string values associated with names. A program can interrogate this environment, and sometimes can add to it or change it. The names are called *environment variables*. In each system a number of standard names are defined (the most common being PATH, which lists directories to be searched for programs); the user may freely add more names.

When one program launches another, the latter normally inherits the environment of the caller; however, it is common (not least for security reasons) to limit the variables that are made available in this way. When working from the command line (i.e. within a command shell program), it is possible to define new temporary environment variables (which may then be passed to any invoked program); when the session is closed, the new variables are lost. To be persistent, an environment variable, has to be placed in a special text file, according to the conventions of the operating system. When a new command session is launched, it reads this file (which may also contain executable instructions) as part of its startup procedure.

FIFO   First-In-First-Out. See *Buffer*.

Filing system   A way of organizing data on a disk or a similar backing store, usually supported by software embedded in the operating system. Most filing systems provide a name for a file of data, and usually files can be collected in folders or directories. There are many additional features, including shortcuts, links, and multiple names. The term *filing system* is also applied more narrowly to low-level organization and software design. On Windows the major filing systems used are VFAT, FAT32, and NFTS; Linux uses ext3, Reiser, XFS, and JFS; Apple uses HFS. There are many other filing systems, all with advantages and disadvantages.

Firewire (IEEE 1394)   IEEE 1394 is a serial communication system, similar to USB, but without a rigid computer-device division, thus supporting peer-to-peer communication. Also hot-pluggable, it is widely used in video cameras. It was initially faster than USB, but recently faster versions of both interfaces have been appearing. Although the name Firewire is owned by Apple, IEEE 1394 identifies it as an independent standard protocol.

Firmware   A computer is physically made from hardware, and runs software. However, there is an intermediate component—programs that are fixed and then installed in a hardware format, permanently in a ROM or a PROM. They may alternatively be stored in an EPROM, which permits multiple burn/erase/rewrite cycles, enabling the firmware to be updated *in situ*. These programs are used to control disks, and in some machines to implement some of the logic of the processor. Once written and debugged, they are changed only rarely, when bugs or improvements are found. This not-completely-soft ware is called *firmware*. The best-known example is the BIOS of an IBM-compatible PC, stored in a PROM. Many early personal computers (including the original Apple Macintosh) had full operating systems (and even programming languages such as BASIC) not loaded into volatile memory but permanently stored in a large PROM chip. This remains the case with many "embedded" systems, such as mobile phones and similar small-scale devices.

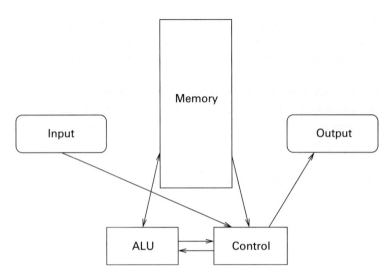

Figure G.2
The five-box model of computer architecture.

Five-box model   A simple model of the architecture of computing systems. The five boxes are memory, arithmetic/logic unit, control unit, input, and output (IO), connected as shown in figure G.2. The memory is connected to the arithmetic and logic unit for data and to the control unit for instructions.

Flags   In the command-line interface, and by transference in graphical interfaces, there is a distinction made between arguments (user parameters) to an operation and flags that control how the operation is to be styled or achieved. By long tradition, a flag is preceded by a hyphen (except on Windows, where a slash is used). Initially, flags were single letters, but now they may be words preceded by pairs of hyphens (−−).

Flash Memory   A low-volume mass storage system on non-volatile memory. Similar to RAM, it is slower to read and much slower to write. But the data remains when removed from power, in contrast with RAM. Flash memory has become common in memory for digital cameras and audio players, and in so-called data keys.

Floating-point data   See *Number representation*.

FLTK   Pronounced "Fulltick," this is a graphics toolbox written for use in C++. It is very easy to use to create simple user interfaces with windows, buttons, and text input. It comes with a window design tool, *Fluid*, that writes most of the C++ code for you. FLTK (which stands for Fast and Light ToolKit) is not very fast when it runs, but is quick to write.

Fluid   Fast Light User Interface Designer, a graphical editor used to produce FLTK source code. It is the quick and easy UI builder for FLTK.

Fork   Each time you run a program on the computer, it is run in a protected environment, rather like a virtual computer, with input and output streams to communicate and system calls. The process of creating such a virtual computer is called *forking*. Initially it is created as a clone of the parent. In most operating systems there is an operation to perform this forking (the function `fork`). The term 'fork' is also used to describe variations of software packages, where a clone with some unique features is made in order to try some experimental ideas, or where there is disagreement on the development of the core system.

FPGA   Field-Programmable Gate Array. This device represents several steps of advance from the custom ROM chip. The latter is created in a chip-fabrication facility from data supplied by the customer. The FPGA, in contrast, is a chip containing a very large number of rudimentary semiconductor building blocks (gates) and interconnections that as supplied do nothing. Instead, computational elements such as adders and multipliers, and interconnections such as data and address busses, can be created by the application programmer using a combination of hardware and software to program the device. In such a way, the device may become a bespoke processor of any kind—e.g., a CPU, a DSP, or a codec. FPGAs are now established and increasingly popular as alternatives to a standard DSP chip. Early devices were limited in speed compared to standard hardware, but this limitation is fast disappearing. Many commercial audio products are now based not on off-the-shelf CPU or DSP chips but on one or more custom-programmed FPGAs.

Full duplex   This term generally refers to devices that can send and receive data concurrently (i.e., a full-duplex soundcard, from which audio can be recorded and to where it can be played at the same time).

Function   In mathematics, a function is a mapping from an ordered set of arguments to a value. Strictly it must be such that the same arguments always give the same answer. This idea is incorporated into computing with less formality. A function should return a value, and a *subroutine* does not, but this usage is not observed as much as it once was.

GCC   The Gnu C Compiler, an implementation of a C compiler that is used in the open-source community and increasingly elsewhere. It conforms largely to the ANSI standards, and it comes with POSIX libraries. An important component of the GNU project, it continues to develop new compilation techniques. It has been implemented on a large number of processors and operating systems, and for that reason it has been the preferred C compiler in this book. Lately the acronym stands for GNU Compiler Collection, as it works as a front-end that supports various languages. The same code base is used for g++, the GNU C++ compiler, and there are variants for Fortran, Pascal, Objective-C, Java, and Ada.

Gnuplot   An interactive, command-line-driven, two- or three-dimensional plotting program.

GUI   A Graphical User Interface—a part of a computer program, often clearly separate from the calculating component, whereby the users select and configure their requirements for the program, e.g. using check boxes, buttons, and pull-down menus. Older (and more sane) programs used a command-line interface.

In a GUI the connection between the user and a piece of software is entirely by means of pictures, buttons, and other visual metaphors. The user is expected to use a mouse or some other pointing device to select options or controls, or to scroll through large amounts of data. In turn, the processing component of the software presents its information graphically, typically only archiving to disk in response to a user request.

The principal elements on which a GUI is based are described by the acronym WIMP (Window-Icon-Menu-Pointer). The GUI is often seen as the antithesis of the command-line interface (CLI).

Hacker   Originally, and still in computer circles, a hacker was a good programmer who could deploy "hacks"—modifications to programs or systems—in a timely and clever way. Many older programmers would be proud to be called hackers. It later was misapplied to programmers who broke the security of computer systems (although the first such were indeed hackers).

Hardware   A term used collectively for the physical parts of a computer system. See *Software* and *Firmware*.

Harvard architecture   The simple five-box model of a computer attaches the memory directly to the central processing unit. In practice, for efficiency reasons a caching system is used in this data part so that the slow speed of memory is not a hindrance to the faster CPU. This architecture was originally called the Princeton architecture in recognition of its adoption by the pioneers at that university. An alternative is to have two data paths between memory and processor, one for data and one for instructions. This is close to the original computer design from Harvard, and so this memory design is called the Harvard Architecture. The idea has been extended by ADI's Super Harvard Architecture (SHARC).

Heap   This term has two almost independent meanings. The more common meaning is in contradistinction to a stack. When a program requires memory, this memory must be allocated somewhere. If the memory is a local variable in C, it is allocated on a stack. If the memory has to persist beyond the function in which it is created, it must be allocated from the heap. This is a (usually) large amount of memory that is reserved for heap allocation, using the functions `malloc`, `calloc`, and `realloc`. The other meaning applies to a special memory organization—a type of binary tree in which both the left and the right descendants of any node are less than or equal to it. A consequence of this structure is that the largest element is always the root of the tree. Heaps are used for organizing queues with priority and for the non-recursive Heap Sort algorithm. For the details of how this structure can be implemented efficiently, see any recent standard textbook on algorithms and data structures.

HID Human Interface Device, a device that connects a human to a computer system. It is often used as part of the USB-HID interface for low-speed devices such as a mouse or a keyboard.

Host The computer that is host to a program.

Hung A program or component is "hung" if it does not respond to a message, and does not produce any output. This state is sometimes described as "catatonic."

IC An integrated circuit or chip is a miniaturized microcircuit consisting of semiconductor devices and some passive components usually manufactured in a thin layer of silicon material.

IDE Integrated Development Environment. There are two primary styles. The first (exemplified by Microsoft's *Visual Studio*) presents a single "parent" window containing multiple "child" windows or panes internally aligned, which can be resized relative to one another. In the second style, a number of visually independent windows are created (e.g., for source code editing, debugging, and compiling) and may be freely moved and overlapped. The best-known example of this style is the original *Metrowerks* compiler for the Macintosh; some elements of this IDE are retained in Apple's *Xcode* environment.

Increment To add a fixed amount, usually 1.

Index See *Array*.

Initialization Setting up the initial values and states in a program or a process.

Instance There is a distinction between a type or an object and a particular example of that type or object. This is akin to the relationship between an `int` and the number 42. We say that 42 is an instance of the type `int`. This term is most often used in object programming to distinguish the definition of an object (which is abstract) from the instance of an object. An instance is, by definition, associated with a location in physical memory, whether on the stack (as a local variable) or on the heap (by means of static or dynamic memory allocation).

Instantiate To create an instance of an object. See *Instance*.

Integer See *Number representation*.

Interactive Allowing interaction with a user (as distinct from *batch*, where the calculation does not involve human intervention).

Interpreter An interpreter evaluates a program directly, rather than translating the program into a binary form (compiling) and then running the binary executable.

Interrupt The simple model of computation, as demonstrated in the classic five-box model of computing, is one of obeying instructions, and then getting the next instruction. The problem with this form is that the computer program either does not react to the external world, or it has to take time to look at all the external activities to see if they require attention ("polling"). Instead, most computers use a hardware process called an *interrupt*. When an external device wants attention—say a character is typed on the keyboard—the main processing loop is interrupted, and the computer is forced to obey code from a location fixed for each device. The original program is suspended in such a way that the program can resume when the external event has been handled. It is important that while the system is actually dealing with the interruption the calculation is not too lengthy, as the system cannot handle a further interrupt from that device. Most computers have a hierarchy of interrupts, with a number of levels or priorities, so some interrupts can be interrupted by higher priority interrupts. In practice, the handling of interrupts is largely tied into the way in which the operating system works. To gain a deeper understanding of interrupts, see a book on operating systems (e.g., H. Deitel, *An Introduction to Operating Systems*, Addison-Wesley, 1984, or W. Stallings, *Operating Systems: Internals and Design Principles*, sixth edition, Prentice-Hall, 2008) or a processor handbook. Interrupts are used on nearly all operating systems, but in time-critical computations interrupts can lead to uncertainty as to how long processes take, and so such systems may rely on polling rather than interrupts, as it is easier to make such a system have a guaranteed response.

IO   Standing for Input and Output, this term generally refers to either the operation of sending or receiving data to/from somewhere or the place where the data emanates from or is sent to (e.g., IO ports). Sometimes written as i/o.

Iteration   From the Latin *iterare*, to repeat; used to describe repeated actions, usually in a loop.

Jack   Short for the *Jack Connection Kit*, this refers to a software layer that runs as a server (or a system service) and is designed to allow audio and MIDI interconnection in a system. Jack allows programs to seamlessly connect to other programs and/or to input and output devices. Originally designed for Linux, it is now fully supported on OS X, and to a lesser extent on Windows. From a program perspective, Jack works as an alternative to a direct IO to a soundcard. The software will take its input from and send its output to a Jack server running on the system. This will then allow signals to be patched in a variety of ways. In general, software needs to be Jack-enabled to talk directly to the server, but there are generic connections that can be used for programs that have not been designed to use it (such as a Core Audio plug-in on OS X).

Java   A programming language that is object oriented, similar to C++, but compiles to virtual instructions, which can be interpreted on (almost) any computer. This is a "write once, run anywhere" language.

Keyword   A keyword is like a "reserved word," but it may be positional and therefore not reserved. Where keywords are not reserved, they can be used as variable names, which leads to legal (if unlikely) statements such as `if if > then then then = if`. This can sometimes cause problems even for the C/C++ programmer. In C 'this' and 'class' are not keywords and can therefore be used as variable names. Indeed both have frequently been found in older C programs. If such code is later compiled as C++, the compiler will report errors. Programmers writing in C but with such usage in mind should consider avoiding these and other C++ keywords.

LADSPA   Linux Audio Developer's Simple Plug-in Architecture, a plug-in and host architecture and an API for audio effects that is free software and is supported by many FOSS programs, including Audacity and Ardour. It provides a common structure for the development of audio applications that support externally provided components (plug-ins). LADSPA was developed by a group of Linux audio developers, but is not restricted to that OS, as plug-ins and hosts exist in other platforms. See *VST* and *Audio Unit*.

Library   Writing programs can be fun, but writing big programs becomes tedious if one has to write all the code oneself. One of the main ways in which we can make use of others' work is to use libraries. A library is a collection of functions that we can use easily with our own program. C comes with a standard library, which every C system must provide. This includes basic operations such as input and output, mathematical functions, and some basic algorithms (e.g. qsort). To use the library routines, we must know the arguments, the types and number of the function, and the result type. The actual implementation of the function is of no concern to the user.

Various programmers publish additional libraries, usually providing a collection of operations for a class of calculations. In this book, some programs have used the *portsf* library for writing soundfiles, and there are other useful libraries. Of course one must take account of their provenance, but overall they provide a significant resource.

There are two classes of library: those that are linked into the running binary (a *static* library), and those that are shared between all programs on a machine. This second class of libraries appears as *shared* or *dynamic* libraries—.dll files in Windows (DLLs); .dylib files in OS X; and .so files in Linux. They are often referred to as *plug-ins*.

A library is a collection of functions and subroutines, usually provided as a precompiled binary with a defined API (q.v.). Most often a library is dedicated to providing one kind of service, such as real time audio, graphics, or reading the state of a game's controller.

Link   Either an alternative name or the process of resolving external and library names in the compilation process.

Linker   The program that performs linking of different binary modules, resolving names to locations.

LINUX   An operating system kernel, largely compatible with UNIX. In 1991, it was a private project of a Finnish student, Linus Torvalds. As it was open-source and did not have direct commercial protection, it became widely accepted as the basis for free and open-source software, and an operating system that should properly be called GNU/Linux. There are a number of distributors, all of whom add individual aspects, but the compatibility across the distributions remains high, and this assists in its development. Because it is well documented, comes with a wealth of development tools, and is very productive, it is largely favored by dedicated software developers (geeks). It is less popular in the community of pure users, as it is perceived as harder to use in desktop mode than Windows or OS X. This is a contentious issue.

Little-endian   On the island of Lilliput, in Jonathan Swift's novel *Gulliver's Travels*, there were two political parties: the Little-endians, who open their boiled eggs at the little end, and the Big-endians, who open them at the big end. In computing, this question is applied to whether the bits and bytes in a word are ordered from top to bottom or from bottom to top. Which is preferable is similar to Lilliputian politics. Intel has espoused little-endian processors, IBM and Motorola processors were big-endian, and some processors (including MIPS and NS) attempted to be neutral.

Loop, endless   See *Endless loop*.

lvalue, rvalue   Two somewhat esoteric terms associated with the design and implementation of languages, but which can occasionally appear as part of a compiler error message. An lvalue is a symbol that can be used on the left-hand side of an assignment, e.g. the name of a variable. Similarly, an rvalue is a symbol that can be used on the right-hand side of an assignment. Errors arise when lvalues and rvalues are mixed up. An explicit number (constant) can only be an rvalue, so the statement 1234 = samp; issues an error. Why are such errors more likely to arise in C++ programs than in C programs? C++ enables arcane type definitions and constructions (through the use of templates and other mechanisms), so that, on occasion, it is not obvious whether a certain symbol or name is an lvalue or an rvalue.

Machine code   The native language, in binary, of the underlying hardware. Not usually seen directly by programmers, it sometimes is seen reflected in an assembler or a debugger.

Macro   An abbreviation; a word that is to be replaced by ("expanded into") some other text. Macros can have arguments, and an expansion can include other macros. There are a number of macro systems; notable among them is the C Pre-Processor (cpp). Also widely used for this purpose is the language m4.

Make   Writing complex software usually requires many separate source files, header files, and private libraries, and it is hard to keep track of what needs to be rebuilt when source code changes. The simple option is to remake everything every time something is changed, but that is very inefficient for large systems. (It takes a significant number of minutes to remake all of Csound, for example.) The alternative is some kind of *make* system. The original system uses the time stamps of files and a *Makefile* that records the dependencies. Recently, tools have been added to help create makefiles, using compiler options (-M in gcc) or other more advanced configuration tools. Use of *make* is highly recommended for all but the most trivial throwaway program.

Member   A particular data item or method is said to be a member of an object if it belongs to that object alone.

Memory leak   A memory leak is said to occur when a program obtains some memory, then loses all references to its address. Repeated memory leaks can lead to very large programs and to memory exhaustion.

Method   A kind of *function* thas is attached to an *object* and can be invoked only on that object. It is the *encapsulation mechanism* used in C++, in Java, and in many object-oriented languages.

Microcode   The concept of assembly-language and machine-language programming is described in appendix F. But how is the low-level machine language itself implemented? It can be made directly out of hardware, using physical implementations of the Boolean logic operations. Alternatively, writing programs in an even simpler lower-level language could do it. This language is likely to control the flow of data inside the processor, or to provide step-by-step control of the simplest operations. The code that does this is called microcode.

Microcode may be similar in style to assembler, but more usually it is horizontal, meaning that a number of operations are initiated at the same time. Writing microcode is akin to writing very short functions, but with many opportunities for optimizations and "clever" ways of achieving the result. Each function can implement one of the machine instructions, so any small improvement in microcode has a significant impact on user programs. Writing microcode has great similarities to cryptic crossword puzzles and mathematical games. It is difficult and slow. The method of microcode comes into fashion and goes out of fashion according to the inventions of electrical engineers. At this writing, it is just coming back from a decade of eclipse.

Microcontroller   A very simple processor that is used to control electrical objects.

MIDI   The Musical Instrument Digital Interface, introduced in 1983. It is a particularly simple and restricted encoding of note-based music with a bias toward modern Western scales. Its primary purpose—to enable control of one keyboard-based synthesizer by another—was soon extended to include computer-based control, recording, and playback. The specification, published by the MIDI Manufacturers Association, defines an electrical connection, a wire allocation, and the transmission speed for communicating MIDI data. The transmission time for a typical three-word MIDI message is approximately 1 millisecond. Despite its ineluctable association with music keyboards (through the use of messages such as NOTE ON and ALL NOTES OFF), the protocol in essence describes little more than the changing state of a number of switches and incremental controllers. This has enabled MIDI to be used for activities almost entirely unrelated to music, such as controlling stage lighting.

Monitor This term usually refers to the physical screen used on a computer, but it is also used for a virtual screen. It also refers to a particular synchronization method.

Multi-tasking In the early days of computing, one way to use a rare and expensive computer was to book time during which the programmer had complete access to the machine. An early development was to allow more than one programmer to use the computer at the same time by means of multi-tasking, in which the computer had two or more programs in executable state at the same time and while one program was waiting for data another program could be processing. Now all major operating systems use multi-tasking. It is sometimes useful for a single problem to be divided into a number of tasks, but the mechanism for communications between these tasks is usually complex unless it is just by means of files. A related method—easier for the programmer—is to use multiple threads. See *Multi-threading*.

Multi-threading Multi-threading is like multi-tasking, but the tasks share the same memory. This means that the threads can communicate by writing and reading variables. There are still problems when two threads both expect to write to the same variable as one cannot be sure in which order they will run, and this is even more unpredictable if the two threads both expect to update the same variable, as the read and write may interleave with the other process.

In POSIX-compliant systems there is a standard set of functions for creating threads, often called the `pthreads` library. One might assume that this kind of programming is just for geeks, but there are a number of occasions in audio processing where threads make for a simple design. A complete example can be found in appendix I.

Music V A music-programming language written by "the father of computer music," Max Mathews, in the FORTRAN language. It can be seen as the culmination of the Bell Laboratories *Music I–Music IV* family of software. It was the first music-programming language to be written in a portable language, although versions of Music IV had been ported to FORTRAN. Thanks to its portability, Music was implemented and customized in computer music centers around the world in the 1970s and the 1980s. The so-called Music-N languages established the Unit Generator model of audio programming, which is now ubiquitous. It is seen in text form in languages such as *Csound* (in which each *opcode* is an Unit Generator), and graphically in applications such as *PD* and *Max/MSP*.

Number representation—integers Most computers represent integers in radix 2, also known as binary. A number N can be represented uniquely by a string of digits d_n in any radix $r > 1$ by means of the formula $N = d_0 r^0 + d_1 r^1 + d_2 r^2 + \cdots + d_n r^n$, where each d_n is in the range from 0 to $r - 1$. If we consider the radix 2, then each digit must be either 0 or 1, which is convenient for representation in a computer. A number is converted into binary by repeatedly outputting a 0 if the number is even, or 1 if odd, then replacing the number by dividing it by 2. For example, if we have a 32-bit basic word, we can represent 2^{32} different values, from 0 to 4,294,967,295. However, this makes no allowance for negative

Table G.2
Examples of eight-bit integer representations.

Decimal	Sign-magnitude	Ones-complement	Twos-complement
42	00101010	00101010	00101010
−42	10101010	11010101	11010110
0	00000000	00000000	00000000
−0	10000000	11111111	00000000
127	01111111	01111111	01111111
−127	11111111	10000000	10000001
−128	error	error	10000000
−1	10000001	11111110	11111111

numbers. There are three ways to extend this representation to signed integers: a sign bit, ones complement, and twos-complement. The last of these is the commonest. It represents a negative N by creating the representation of $-N$; then each bit is inverted (a 0 is replaced by a 1 and a 1 by a 0); finally the number 1 is added. This may seem rather complex, but it has two advantages over other methods. First let us represent -42. We start by considering an eight-bit representation of 42:

$$42 = 0 + 1 \times 2 + 0 \times 2^2 + 1 \times 2^3 + 0 \times 2^4 + 1 \times 2^5 + 0 \times 2^6 + 0 \times 2^7.$$

In the more usual order of digits, $42_{10} = 00101010_2$. To negate this, we flip the bits and add 1,

$$00101010 \rightarrow 11010101 \rightarrow 11010110,$$

so the answer is 11010110.

The two advantages of twos-complement representation are that the top bit acts like a sign bit (a 0 indicating a positive number and a 1 a negative number) and that there is only one representation of zero. The simpler ones-complement representation that is like the method above, but without adding it suffers from having a positive and a negative value for zero. There are simplifications in the arithmetic operation over the sign-magnitude representation that takes the top bit as a sign and uses the simple positive representation. In table G.2 this is summarized with some eight-bit representations of integers.

Number representation—floating-point The format described above does not give a representation of the numbers between 0 and 1. Early computer programmers used a representation called fixed-point, but the usual way of representing these fractional values is as floating-point numbers. A floating-point number is really a fraction, but in a fashion unlike traditional fractions. One bit is assigned to the sign, as it is a sign-modulus representation. The interesting part is the modulus. It is made from two numbers, e (the exponent) and m (the mantissa), and it represents $m \times R^{e-M}$. The conditions on the positive unsigned number

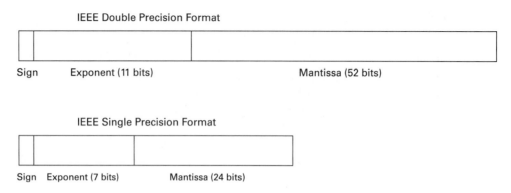

Figure G.3
IEEE floating-point number formats.

m are that $m \times R^{-M}$ is less than or equal to R but greater than R^{-1}, and the constant M is designed to make this possible—essentially, to turn the integer into a fraction. At various times different values of R have been used (16, 8, 10), but the commonest value is 2, which has a number of advantages. The Institute of Electrical and Electronics Engineers refined the representation when using 2, and that structure is used almost everywhere. As can be seen in figure G.3, IEEE floating-point representation comes in two sizes, corresponding to floats and doubles. In both cases the radix is 2, but the number of digits given to the (signed) exponent differs, and the mantissa is significantly different. The additional saving that the IEEE format introduces is that, as m has a size constraint of being between 1 and 1/2 after scaling with M, it follows that the top bit is always set and so does not have to be stored in the word, in effect adding one hidden bit to m.

Object   A unification of a data structure and the actions that operate on that data.

Objective-C   An object-oriented computer language, originally based on C. It differs from C++, and it is rarely found outside Macintosh computers.

Object-oriented programming   A style of programming that emphasizes the object as a fundamental structure of the program. Some languages (C++, Java, Objective-C, Smalltalk) enforce this style rather than just recommending it. (Readers may sometimes encounter references to "object-orientated programming." The extra syllable in the ugly word 'orientated' is unnecessary and has nothing to commend it.)

OGG   A *lossy* compression format that is open-source and patent-free. See *Audio file formats*.

Opcode   An Operation code, originally meaning a computer instruction; also used for virtual instructions in higher-level operations, such as in Csound.

Operand An argument to an operator.

Operator A function, but usually written in an infix notation with the characters +, −, and /. In computing, operators tend to be distinguished from functions only by syntax.

Parameter See *Argument*.

Path A file usually resides in a directory, and that directory resides in another directory—to some depth. The path to the file is the list of directories that are used and ending in the file name. In normal usage the components of the path are separated by a / (or, on Windows, a \). If one takes the path from the current directory, this is a *relative path*; if one takes the path from the root of the files, this is the *full path*. The expression of relative paths is supported by two standard shorthand notations: ./ (for the current directory) and ../ (for the parent directory, or "up one level"); the latter can be concatenated multiple times to ascend the directory hierarchy level by level, possibly all the way back to the root directory. To simplify running programs from multiple directories, an *environment* variable, PATH, is used to specify in which directories to search for the command that a user types on the command line.

PCM Pulse code modulation. There are a number of ways in which audio can be encoded inside a computer. The commonest is PCM, in which the continuous value of the air pressure whose fluctuations cause sound are sampled at regular time intervals (hence the *sampling rate*). These values form a regular data *stream* that can be routed directly to a soundcard or to a file. WAV and AIFF are examples of standard *audio file formats* (q.v.) supporting particular cases of PCM audio data.

Pipe A software pipe is a mechanism for passing the results of one program to another program, usually by directing the standard out (see *Standard input and output*) of the first program and the standard in of the second. This is a very convenient way to do many things without having to invent file names for the intermediate data. In the UNIX command-line systems this is indicated by the character |. (For example, to search for all lines starting with 'Author', sort them into alphabetical order, and remove duplicates in UNIX, one would type grep Author datafile | sort | uniq.) There are many creative uses for pipes in a command-line interface that would be quite difficult with a GUI.

Plug-in A program might allow additional code, not from the original authors, to be incorporated into a program. Such external incorporations are called *plug-ins*, as they plug into the existing framework. Having a plug-in system allows third-party extensions and improvements to a basic system.

Pointer A value that is the address of a location, rather than simply a number.

Port Any (virtual) plug into which something can be connected. More often, it is used to describe a virtual plug or location for connecting computers by means of a network. All communications are multiplexed over the transport system, then associated at each end with a port.

PortAudio   A cross-platform API for audio IO. It supports various operating systems (e.g., Linux, OS X, Windows) and, in these systems, various lower-level audio APIs (ALSA, OSS, Jack, Core Audio, MME, DirectX, ASIO).

PortMIDI   A cross-platform API for MIDI IO.

Precedence   The order of operations, by importance. In particular, it pertains to operators, including addition and multiplication. The operator $*$ has a higher precedence and thus must be performed before the $+$. Precedence is what makes $2 + 3 * 4$ result in the value 14 rather than 20.

Preprocessor   Many computer languages incorporate a preprocessor that transforms the text of a program (usually) into a textual form with modifications—expanded macros, conditional compilation enforced, and so on. In C, the `cpp` program is just that, the C PreProcessor. By transference it can mean any textual changes to a program made by another program before compilation.

Processor   The component of a computing system that obeys instructions or processes instructions and data.

Pseudocode   It is sometimes useful to describe an algorithm in a language not intended for computer evaluation, but in a similar style. Such descriptions are called *pseudocode*.

Python   A scripting language, syntactically similar to C. It supports multiple programming paradigms (e.g., object-oriented and functional), and it features a fully dynamic type system and automatic memory management. Its use of indentation to delimit blocks is unusual, but it is considered easy to write, and its popularity is increasing.

Qt   A cross-platform graphics toolkit that can produce high-performance graphics, widgets, and interfaces.

Random number   A number that cannot be predicted *a priori*. It may have a range or a distribution (frequency of a particular number being presented). On a computer, true random numbers are hard to calculate without some external input from a human or some other unpredictable entity. Instead pseudo-random numbers are often used; such numbers are not truly random, because if you know the algorithm you can predict its value, but it is not easy to break the code.

Raw soundfile   A soundfile without any header information such as sample rate or number of channels. Such a soundfile is usually in PCM format, but the user has to know the details. See *Audio file formats*.

Recursion   Using a function inside itself. A function that calls itself is said to be recursive. Mathematically, this is the correct way to model computation (as in Recursive Function Theory—the solution to a problem depends on solutions to smaller instances of the same problem). It also relates to mathematical induction and is very useful in proving programs to be correct. A classic example is factorial: `factorial(n) = (n==1 ? 1 : n * factorial(n-1));`

Register   Fast memory is expensive memory, but it is possible to create a small number of extremely fast memory locations inside the arithmetic and logic unit or the central processing unit. These memories are called registers, and their correct use is a major factor in the efficiency of a program. Using them for the most commonly used values makes a real difference. The responsibility to use them rests with the compiler, but as a user in C one can give hints to the compiler by declaring variables as `register` as well as their type. Only rarely is this worthwhile; most compilers can make better deductions than programmers, but there are rare occasions when the programmer knows, for example, that a particular function is called a very large number of times.

Reserved words   In a computer language, certain words are reserved to the system and cannot be used as variable names—for example, in C, the words `int`, `for`, `while`, and `double`.

RMS   Root-mean-square, a measure of the power of a signal (rather than its amplitude). The name directly describes the computations required for its calculation. For a given block of samples (which could be a whole soundfile), each sample is squared (negative values thus becoming positive), the average (or mean) is found by summing the squared values and dividing by the number of samples, and the RMS value is found by taking the square root of this sum. This can then be converted to a dB value using the computation dBval = 20 * log10(RMSval). The RMS value is relative to digital peak (0dBFS, q.v.); thus if the RMS of a single cycle of a full-scale sinusoid is taken, the result will be −3 dBFS.

Rvalue   See *Lvalue*.

Scons   A system configuration and building system written in Python that incorporates the concepts of `makefiles` together with fitting the build to the details of the operating system. It is used in the building of Csound and maintains the cross-platform structure.

SConstruct   The configuration file for Scons. It is equivalent to a Makefile. See *Make*.

Script (shell script)   A script is a list of commands stored in a file so they can be performed rapidly in the specified sequence. A particular case is the shell script, a sequence of any commands supported by a given shell. This might be *Bash* in UNIX or OS X (where the script file typically has a `.sh` extension) or the standard DOS console on Windows (where the script file will have the extension `.bat`—hence the usual term in Windows, "batch file"). It goes without saying (almost) that UNIX-style shells such as *Bash* are considerably more powerful than the DOS shell, with a range of control constructs and variable definitions rivaling C itself; many shell scripts are in effect substantial programs in their own right.

Shared libraries, plug-ins, `.dylibs`, DLLs, and `.so` files   One objection to the simple C model of programs is that every program would contain a copy of the basic libraries (`stdio`, `stdlib`, etc.) and so memory use in a multiprogramming computer would increase. The solution is to have shared libraries; that is, libraries that only require one copy that can be used by all active programs. This does impose some restrictions in the design, such as no library-static data, but the gain in memory utilization is significant. Each operating system implements shared libraries in a slightly different fashion. On Linux they are `.so` files (shared versions of `.o` files); on Windows they are called Dynamic-linked Libraries (DLLs) `.dll` files; on Mac OS X they are referred to as plug-ins and are `.dylib` files.

Shell   A command program, especially an interactive command-line program. Examples of shells include the DOS console in Windows (the program itself being `cmd.exe`) and the *Bash* and *tcsh* shells in Linux and OS X. See *Script*.

Software   A term used collectively for the non-physical parts of a computer system. It refers generally to programs in the wide sense.

Stack   An abstract computer structure that has two basic operations, `push` and `pop`. `Push` gives an object to the stack, and `pop` removes an object from the stack and gives it to the caller. The important feature is that `pop` always gives the last object pushed, and thus the structure is a First-In-Last-Out entity (this is the same as a Last-In-First-Out entity). Formally the stack obeys the identity `pop(push(S))= S`. It is also useful to have a way of peeking at the top of the stack, and a way of checking if the stack is empty (in which case a `pop` would give an error).

Stacks can be implemented inside C inside an array, with the additional checking for stack overflow, attempting to push a value onto the stack when there is insufficient room, or by a linked list structure. But the particular stack that has the largest implications for the user is the system stack.

In an implementation of C, there is a need for a stack to record the nesting of function calls. (One expects to have the abstract stack behavior, such that calling a function pushes the current location, and returning pops the location so then the program continues from the call.) This same stack is also used for local variables; so when a function is called, new variables are allocated on the stack, and once the function exits, these locations are removed. This explains why it is a serious programming error to take the address of a local variable and then return it after the function has exited, as the location is no longer valid, and will be reused for other values.

Standard C Libraries   ANSI C requires that certain functions be available from a C program as libraries. These are supposed to be reliable and ubiquitous. They include functions of input and output (`stdio`), mathematical operations (`math`), strings operations (`string`), and character types (`ctype`). These are in effect an API for all C programs, for all platforms used in the same way.

Standard input and output   The ANSI C standard specifies that every program should be started with one input stream and two output streams attached. These are called *standard in* (`stdin`), *standard out* (`stdout`), and *standard error* (`stderr`). A simple program can read from stdin and write to stdout knowing that they exist. The default for most systems is that these two are connected to the keyboard and the screen, respectively, and can be used together with *pipes* (q.v.). stderr is used for error messages and it also defaults to the screen. It is initialized to be unbuffered, so any message written to stderr will appear immediately and not when a line is complete. It is good practice to use stderr for errors and stdout for results. Note that, although they both use the terminal, they are conceptually separate, and one can pipe stdout without changing stderr.

Stderr   See *Standard input and output.*

String   An ordered set of characters. In C, a special character, the NUL character (notated as \0), terminates a string.

Structured programming   A term for some early-1970s ideas on how to make complex software systems. The original ideas focused on top-down programming and flow diagrams, and this principle developed in the early 1980s into Software Engineering.

SVN   Subversion, an alternative "source control system" that allows a number of programmers to cooperate on a single multi-file program. Subversion is more recent than cvs and is usually preferred. (See *CVS.*)

Synchronous   See *Asynchronous.*

Terminal   Every interactive program has a controlling terminal (similar to a console). It may consist of the keyboard and the screen, or it may be a virtual terminal. The keyboard-screen combination is also called the terminal. The term originates from the terminal traditionally being the end point of the results.

Text editor   A program that allows editing, changing, insertion, and deletion of textual information, including programs. The alternatives include binary editors (which edit binary data) and link editors (which create working programs from binary and libraries).

Thread   Simple programs have a concept of program location (often kept in an internal register called the *program counter*). If a program wishes to have the illusion of running two functions simultaneously, a thread system can be used. Each thread has its own program counter, and the operating system chooses which thread to run on the basis of its own planning. If the two threads are completely independent, having independent programs and data, they are usually called *processes*, and in multi-processing systems (such as UNIX and later Windows systems) it is these processes that constitute programs apparently running at the same time. Unless there is more than one central processing unit, in reality only one thread can be running, but if the processor is shared between them (switching between them at high speed) the illusion is very good. If two or more threads share both program and data, they are often called *lightweight* threads. This becomes a useful programming tool—for example, one thread can be checking the user interface while the other synthesizes some sound.

Transcendental number A real number that cannot be defined as the root of a polynomial equation. Notable examples are π and e. There are in fact more transcendental numbers than algebraic numbers, but they do not often occur in normal use, apart from those two.

UI   User interface. See *GUI*.

UNIX   A seminal software system in the history of software was the MIT *Multics* operating system. It was designed from the outset to support many users with a high degree of security of programs and data, and a high degree of user privacy. It was a complex system, and it ran on what was at the time a large computer. A desire for an operating environment on a simpler minicomputer led Brian Kernighan and Dennis Ritchie to conceive of a single user operating system that still provided a secure filing system and protections. This system became UNIX. It was developed largely at Bell Laboratories and was proprietary to AT&T. Popular among computer researchers, it was further developed with additional software, especially at the University of California at Berkeley. It was the inspiration for much of Linux and indeed other operating systems. Although proprietary rights mean that much is no longer common, the underlying principles it introduced remain, and can be seen in Windows, OS X, and (overwhelmingly) in Linux.

Usage message   A statement that lists the required arguments that are expected, and the optional arguments that are accepted. It is often the case that when a program is provided with incorrect arguments, it responds with a usage message.

USB   Universal Serial Bus, a standard for attaching electronic objects to computers. Various versions provide various data speeds. Many desktop and laptop computers provide USB sockets, which make it easy to add hardware to a computer. It is important that USB is a "hot-plug" system—that is, devices can be plugged in or unplugged without the need to restart the computer. The specification also provides for power to be distributed from the computer to the device over the same connection. The power available is small, but it is sufficient to power Bluetooth, Ethernet, ASCII keyboards, mouses, and flash memory devices. All modern operating systems have the necessary code to recognize and communicate with USB devices.

Variable   In the words of an old joke, a variable does not. It is a named location in machine memory in which values are stored, read, or modified under user control.

Vector   A one-dimensional array.

Vi   A screen editor descended from the original UNIX `ed` command and from Steven Bourne's E3 editor. It has acquired extensibility, but not so much as `emacs`.

Virtual memory   Some programs require a very large amount of memory, more than can be afforded. One solution to this problem is to use virtual memory. Because of spatial locality, one usually only needs part of the memory in any small period of time, so the data not currently being used can reside on a much cheaper drum or disk. (See *Cache*.) In hardware virtual memory, when the program attempts to access memory that is not actually present an interrupt routine arranges that a new part of the memory is loaded from the disk, saving some unused part if necessary. This *swapping* is usually arranged in fixed-size chunks called *pages*. If there is sufficient real memory and a good implementation of the virtual memory system, the time spent swapping is small relative to the total run time. But if things go wrong, the system is said to be *thrashing*, as pages are read and written more frequently than is desirable.

Virtual memory ideas can also be implemented in software, but it takes much more programming and design to make it work well.

A similar concept to *virtual* is *transparent*. If you can see the memory and it is there, it is called real. If you can see it but it is not there, it is called virtual. If you cannot see it but it is there, it is said to be transparent. If you cannot see it and it is not there, it is vaporware (or a salesman's press release).

VST   Virtual Studio Technology, a plug-in, host architecture, and API for digital audio effects and software synthesizers. It provides a common structure for the development of audio applications that support externally provided components (*plug-ins*). Steinberg Media Technologies Gmbh developed VST, and its license does not allow the redistribution of the API header and source files; developers must obtain these from the vendor directly. For similar APIs, see *LADSPA* and *Audio Units*.

Waterfall model   The waterfall model of software development postulates five stages: Requirements, Specification, Design, Programming, and Maintaining. Each stage should be completed before the next one starts, and if problems are found one returns to the previous stage where the problem lies, fixes it, and then works through the stages. The name comes from the diagram that is usually used to explain this.

WAV   See *Audio file formats*.

Wrapper   A piece of software that provides elements of one language (e.g. functions, classes, or constant definitions) in the form and syntax of another language. One common example is a C-language API "wrapped" as a scripting language module (e.g. an extension to Python or Tcl). Wrapping gives programmers access to the API directly from these languages instead of having to write their software in C. The most commonly wrapped languages are C and C++. There are also systems that can automatically generate wrappers, such as SWIG.

White space   The collective name for characters that do not cause a mark, such as a space, a tab and a newline, or a line break. In C and C++, most white space has no semantic meaning, and it is removed by the *pre-processor* before compilation starts. However, white space has one important use: as a delimiter (or separator) for command-line arguments. Contemporary operating systems have popularized the use of file and directory names incorporating white space (e.g., "Program Files"). Not all programmers (or all users) regard this as a positive step. When one is supplying such names to a command-line program, one must enclose them in quotation marks. Alternatively, the offending space character has to be *escaped*, as this example: `cd my\ music\ folder`.

Xcode   A suite of free software-development tools, provided by Apple, that includes a modified version of the GNU Compiler Collection (GCC) and uses GDB as the backend for its debugger. Also the name of Apple's Integrated Development Environment.

X11   A system for using bit-mapped screens. It is the basis of a number of screen systems, including KDE and Gnome. The default system in UNIX and Linux, it is also used on OS X.

Appendix H: An Audio Programmer's Guide to Mathematical Expressions

John ffitch

This appendix will provide a basic reference to the mathematical expressions used throughout this book. It is by no means is an exhaustive discussion of the subject.

H.1 Algebraic Expressions

H.1.1 Exponents

The following are the basic rules for exponents (with a and b positive):

$$a^p a^q = a^{p+q},$$

$$\frac{a^p}{a^q} = a^{p-q},$$

$$(a^p)^q = a^{pq},$$

$$a^{-p} = \frac{1}{a^p},$$

$$a^0 = 1 \quad (\text{if } a \neq 0),$$

$$(a^m)^{1/n} = a^{m/n} \quad (m \text{ and } n \text{ positive integers}),$$

$$\left(\frac{a}{b}\right)^{1/n} = \frac{a^{1/n}}{b^{1/n}} \quad (n \text{ a positive integer}),$$

$$(ab)^q = a^q b^q.$$

H.1.2 Logarithms

The definition of a logarithm p to the base a of x is

$$\log_a x = p \quad \text{so that} \quad a^p = x \quad (a \text{ not } 0 \text{ or } 1).$$

With that in mind, the following expressions are defined:

$$\log_a xy = \log_a x + \log_a y,$$

$$\log_a \frac{x}{y} = \log_a x - \log_a y,$$

$$\log_a x^y = y \log_a x.$$

The bases commonly used in logarithms are normally limited to 2, 10, and $e\,(= 2.7182818\ldots,$ the natural base of logarithms). To change the base we can use

$$\log_a x = \frac{\log_b x}{\log_b a}$$

or

$$\log_a x = C(a, b) \log_b x, \quad \text{where} \quad C(a, b) = \frac{1}{\log_b a}.$$

Now we can find the different values of the constant $C(a, b)$ for converting between the three common bases:

$$C(2, 10) = 3.321928 \; C(2, e) = 1.442695,$$

$$C(e, 10) = 2.302585 \; C(e, 2) = 0.693147,$$

$$C(10, 2) = 0.301029 \; C(10, e) = 0.434294.$$

For example:

$$\log_{10} x = C(10, 2) \log_2 x = 0.301029 \log_2 x.$$

H.1.3   Sum and Series Expressions

The notation of sums in series uses the Greek capital letter *sigma* (Σ) to indicate, in a compact form, addition of terms (which may be infinite):

$$\sum_{k=1}^{n} k = 1 + 2 + 3 + \cdots + n.$$

The left-hand side of this equation reads, in English, "the sum from k equals 1 to n of k." In mathematical terminology, k is the *index of summation* and the right-hand side is the *expansion*. Such expressions will usually be more complicated, but the principles are the same: there will be a certain number of terms (which will be, for instance, equal to n, if we started at 1, and this number might be infinite), and the summation index is incremented by 1 in each term of the expansion. For instance, the following expression has k as a subscript to A (indicating several different values for A) and as a multiplier inside the cos() function:

$$\sum_{k=1}^{n} A_k \cos(k\omega) = A_1 \cos(\omega) + A_2 \cos(2\omega) + \cdots + A_n \cos(n\omega).$$

H.1.4   Product Expressions

Similar to sums, we have an expression that combines several factors in a product, using a capital pi (Π) and following the same principles outlined in subsubsection H.1.3:

$$\prod_{k=1}^{n} k = 1 \times 2 \times 3 \times \cdots \times n$$

H.1.5   Polynomials

Generalizing the principles presented above, we call an expression that involves only integer powers of any unknown a *polynomial in x*. The following is a polynomial in one unknown, x:

$$f(x) = a_n x^n + a_{n-1} x^{n-1} + \cdots + a_2 x^2 + a_1 x^1 + a_0.$$

In mathematical terms, n is the *degree of the polynomial*, a_n is a coefficient of x^n, and a_0 is the *constant term* (because this coefficient is not multiplying any variable).

H.1.6   Functions

A function is a mathematical expression that maps one or more arguments into a value or a result. Essentially, given an input, a function produces a unique output. For instance, the trivial function $f(x) = x$ maps the argument x on itself, $f(x) = 2x$ doubles x, and $f(x) = x^2$ squares the function's argument. A polynomial function of one argument can be classified depending on the maximum exponent of the variables found in its definition. In the above examples, the first two functions are called *functions of the first degree*, or *linear* (their plots produce straight lines), and the third is a *quadratic* or *second-degree* function. Other higher-order polynomial functions are called *cubic*, *quartic*, and so on. There are also non-polynomial functions in which f involves more complicated expressions, such as sines or cosines.

H.1.7   Equations

When a function $f(x)$ is equated with 0, as in $f(x) = 0$, we have an *equation*, which may have one or more *roots*. A *root* is a number that, when assigned to the argument of a function $f(x)$, produces zero as a result, i.e., makes the equation $f(x) = 0$ valid. An equation can have more than one root, depending on its type. Polynomial equations in one unknown have a particularly simple rule: the number of roots is the same as the degree. A linear equation will have

Table H.1
Right-angled triangle definitions.

Sine	$\dfrac{\text{Opposite side to } \theta}{\text{Hypotenuse}}$	or $\sin\theta = \dfrac{O}{H}$	Measured on y axis
Cosine	$\dfrac{\text{Adjacent side to } \theta}{\text{Hypotenuse}}$	or $\cos\theta = \dfrac{A}{H}$	Measured on x axis
Tangent	$\dfrac{\text{Opposite side to } \theta}{\text{Adjacent side to } \theta}$	or $\tan\theta = \dfrac{O}{A}$	Equivalent to the line BC

one root, a quadratic equation will have two; a cubic equation will have three, and so on. In order for this to be true, we must distinguish equal roots (as in the equation $x^2 - 2x + 1 = 0$, whose roots are $x = 1$ and $x = 1$. We also need complex numbers to make this work (see section 3.7). This rule is called the Fundamental Theory of Algebra. For non-polynomial functions there is no equivalent simple rule. Indeed, the equation $\sin(1/x) = 0$ has on infinite number of roots between 0 and 1.

H.2   Trigonometry

H.2.1   Angle Units

Angles are subdivisions of a circle and are typically measured in degrees or radians. When degrees are used, the circle is divided into 360 "slices." One of these "slices" can be subdivided into 60 minutes, and one minute into 60 seconds). When radians are used, angle values are related to the diameter and the circumference of a circle. (Radians are preferred in this book.) The ratio of the circumference to the diameter of a circle, the irrational number π ($= 3.14159\ldots$), is the basis for the radian:

$c = \pi \times d,$

$d = 2r,$

$c = 2\pi$ radians,

where c is the circumference, d is the diameter, and r is the radius. The radian is a natural measure for angles. There are 2π radians in a full circle (360°), so half a circle is π radians (180°), one-fourth of a circle is $\pi/2$ (90°), and so on.

H.2.2   Basic Trigonometric Functions

Using table H.1 and figure H.1, we can define the basic trigonometric functions: $\sin(\theta)$, $\cos(\theta)$, and $\tan(\theta)$. If the radius of the circle in figure H.1, which is the same as the hypotenuse (H), is set to 1, these functions are more easily identified as the line O, the line A, and the ratio O/A, respectively. Notice that the values of $\sin(\theta)$ are obtained by reading the *projec-*

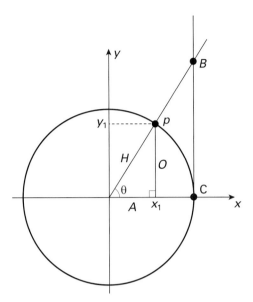

Figure H.1
Right-angled triangle and trigonometric circle.

tion of the point p on the y axis. This means that if we trace a line from p, parallel to the x axis, the point at which it intersects the y axis will be equivalent to the sine of θ. That is the mathematical meaning of *projection*. In its turn, $\cos(\theta)$ is taken similarly from the x axis. The tangent can then be defined as the ratio of the sine and the cosine of an angle. Cosine and sine functions provide the basis for the most fundamental types of audio signals.

H.2.3 Trigonometric Identities

To facilitate the change of some formulas and derivation of expressions, a number of trigonometric identities are given, here is a collection of some of these:

$\sin^2 A + \cos^2 A = 1,$

$\sin(-A) = -\sin A,$

$\cos(-A) = \cos A,$

$\tan(-A) = -\tan A,$

$\cos(A) = \sin(A + \pi/2),$

$\sin(A) = \cos(A - \pi/2),$

$\sin(A \pm B) = \sin(A)\cos(B) \pm \cos(A)\sin(B),$

$$\cos(A \pm B) = \cos(A)\cos(B) \mp \sin(A)\sin(B),$$

$$\sin 2A = 2\sin A \cos A,$$

$$\cos 2A = \cos^2 A - \sin^2 A,$$

$$\sin^2 A = \frac{1 - \cos 2A}{2},$$

$$\cos^2 A = \frac{1 + \cos 2A}{2},$$

$$\cos A \cos B = \frac{\cos(A - B) + \cos(A + B)}{2},$$

$$\sin A \sin B = \frac{\cos(A - B) - \cos(A + B)}{2},$$

$$\sin A \cos B = \frac{\sin(A + B) + \sin(A - B)}{2},$$

$$\cos A \sin B = \frac{\sin(A + B) - \sin(A - B)}{2},$$

$$\sin A \pm \sin B = 2\sin\left(\frac{A \pm B}{2}\right)\cos\left(\frac{A \mp B}{2}\right),$$

$$\cos A + \cos B = 2\cos\left(\frac{A + B}{2}\right)\cos\left(\frac{A - B}{2}\right),$$

$$\cos A - \cos B = -2\sin\left(\frac{A + B}{2}\right)\sin\left(\frac{A - B}{2}\right).$$

In the expressions above, $a \pm b = c \mp d$ means $a + b = c - d$ and $a - b = c + d$. Some of these identities are very significant in audio programming. For instance,

$$\cos A \cos B = \frac{\cos(A - B) + \cos(A + B)}{2}$$

indicates that if you multiply two sinusoid signals of two different frequencies (A and B), you will get a mix (sum) of two components as the sum ($A + B$) and difference ($A - B$) of the two frequencies. Furthermore, each of these two components will have half the original amplitude. This is known as *ring modulation*.

H.3   Differential Calculus

An important development of the algebraic operations described above is found in the differential calculus. The main interest is in describing the rate of change of expressions. Originally the calculus was developed to understand velocity and acceleration of celestial bodies.

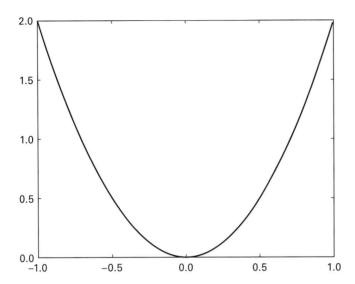

Figure H.2
A plot of $f(x) = 2x^2$.

H.3.1   Differentiation

We seek to provide a mathematical description of the instantaneous change in an expression. For instance, if we have the expression $f(x) = ax^2$ then the curve is as shown in figure H.2. The change in the expression can be characterized by the tangent to the curve at a point. The differential calculus is a way to give an algebraic expression to this tangent as a function of the point where it happens.

We consider a point x and a close point $x + \partial x$, and draw a line between $f(x)$ and $f(x + \partial x)$ to produce a chord. The growth is then $(f(x + \partial x) - f(x))/\partial x$. As ∂x gets smaller, the chord gets closer to the tangent to the curve at x. The intention of the calculus was to consider the limit of the expression $(f(x + \partial x) - f(x))/\partial x$ as ∂x tends to zero. In the case of our example this limit is

$$lim(\partial x \to 0)(a(x + \partial x)^2 - ax^2)/\partial x = lim(\partial x \to 0)(ax^2 + 2ax\partial x + \partial x^2 - ax^2)/\partial x$$

$$= lim(\partial x \to 0)(2ax + \partial x)$$

$$= 2ax,$$

and so we have determined the expression for the tangent of a quadratic form, which is called the *derivative* of the form. This is usually written as $df(x)/dx$ or sometimes, when unambiguous, $f'(x)$.

In general, the derivative of a polynomial term x^n can be easily shown[1] to be nx^{n-1}, and the rules for the derivatives of sums and differences are

$$\frac{d(A+b)}{dx} = \frac{dA}{dx} + \frac{dB}{dx}$$

and

$$\frac{d(A-b)}{dx} = \frac{dA}{dx} + \frac{dB}{dx}.$$

The equivalent rules for derivatives of products are

$$\frac{d(Ab)}{dx} = \frac{BdA}{dx} + \frac{AdB}{dx}$$

and

$$\frac{d(A/b)}{dx} = \frac{BdA/dx - AdB/dx}{B^2}.$$

These allow us to calculate derivatives of any polynomial form.

Other Derivative Functions

The derivatives of other functions can also be calculated. The proofs are mainly beyond this text, but we will consider one of these, $d\sin(x)/dx$. The definition is

$\mathrm{limit}(\partial x \rightarrow 0)(\sin(x + \partial x) - \sin(x))/\partial x.$

Using the formula above for $\sin(A + B)$, we see that this is the same as

$\mathrm{limit}(\partial x \rightarrow 0)(\sin(x)\cos(\partial x) + \cos(x)\sin(\partial x) - \sin(x))/\partial x.$

For small values of ∂x, $\cos(\partial x)$ is approximately 1 and $\sin(\partial x)$ is approximately ∂x, so we can simplify this to

$\mathrm{limit}(\partial x \rightarrow 0)(\sin(x) + \cos(x)\partial x - \sin(x))/\partial x = \cos(x).$

The other results are proved in similar ways. These are

$d\sin(x)/dx = \cos(x)$ (with x expressed in radians),

$d\cos(x)/dx = -\sin(x)$,

$d\tan(x)/dx = \tan^2(x) + 1$,

$da^x/dx = a^x\,log(a)$ (using the natural logarithm, base e),

$dlog(x)/dx = 1/x$,

$df(g(x))/dx = dg(x)/dx\ df(g(x))/dg(x)$.

H.3.2   Anti-Differentiation

The opposite of differentiation can be seen in two ways. The first is as anti-differentiation; that is to answer the question "What function has $f(x)$ as its derivative?" In simple polynomial cases this can easily be achieved by the inverse of the rules in section 3.1:

antideriv$(x^n) = x^{n+1}/(n+1)$ (with n not equal to -1),

antideriv$(1/x) = \log(x)$,

antideriv$(a^x) = a^x/\log(a)$.

In general this operation is a great deal harder than calculating the derivative. It is an example of an *inverse problem*. There is also a small matter of ambiguity. As da/dx is zero for any constant a, it follows that the anti-derivative of x^n can have any constant added without breaking the relationship. This is called the *arbitrary constant*, and the operation is ambiguous regarding this constant.

H.3.3   Integration

The other aspect of the differential calculus is *integration*. That is the operation of calculating the area under a curve. The area under the curve $f(x)$ and above the x axis between the points a and b is written

$$\int_a^b f(x)\,dx.$$

It is easy to see that the integral is closely related to the anti-derivative. Suppose that

$$F(x) = \int_a^x f(y)\,dy$$

and we consider the derivative of $F(x)$. The definition gives it as

$\lim(\partial x \to 0)(F(x + \partial x) - F(x))/\partial x,$

which is like adding a thin strip to F of width ∂x and height $f(x)$. So we can see that $dF(x)/dx$ is $f(x)$ and so integration and derivatives are inverses of each other. Strictly this remark is true only for functions that do not have infinite values at any point.

H.4   Numeric Systems

H.4.1   Natural numbers

The simplest numeric system is based on the set of positive integers: 1, 2, 3, 4, ... These are called *natural numbers*, whose set is denoted by $\mathbb{N}$. Some people include 0 in this set, but it is known that early mathematics did not include the concept of null.

H.4.2   Integers

If this is not enough for our use, then we can include 0 and *negative quantities* (... −2, −1, 0, 1, 2, ...), which make up the *integer numbers* (the "whole" numbers, whose set is denoted by $\mathbb{Z}$). The use of positive and negative quantities is fundamental for certain areas of mathematics, including algebra. The concept of negative numbers is more abstract than the idea of natural numbers, and it came later in the evolution of mathematics.

H.4.3   Rationals

Whole numbers do not include numbers that have fractional parts, such as 1.25 or 3/2. *Rational numbers*, whose set is denoted by $\mathbb{Q}$ are numbers that can be expressed as a ratio a/b, with $b \neq 0$. (This includes all integers, because they can be expressed as $n/1$.) Every number has a decimal expansion, in which the number is represented by the sequence $\{a_n \ldots a_1, a_0, a_{-1}, a_{-2}, \ldots, a_{-m}\}$, where $n = \sum a_k 10^k$. If the sequence is finite (that is, for integers less than some m all the a's are zero), the number is rational. The proof of this is easy to create. If the a's start repeating a pattern indefinitely after some point, then the number is also rational. The proof of that involves formulas for summing series.

H.4.4   Algebraic Numbers

Numbers that are the roots of polynomial equations are called *algebraic*. All rational numbers are algebraic, and a/b is the root of the equation $bx = a$, but not all algebraic numbers are rational. The simplest example is $\sqrt{2}$. It has been known since the time of Pythagoras that there is no a/b that is equal to $\sqrt{2}$. The proof is fairly simple: Suppose that $\sqrt{2} = a/b$ and this fraction is in its simplest form. Then squaring both sides and multiplying by b^2 we see that $2b^2 = a^2$, from which it follows that a^2 is even and so a is even. Let $2c = a$. Now we have $2b^2 = 4c^2$, and so b^2 is even and so is b. As a and b are both even, the fraction a/b can be simplified, contrary to our assumption, and so there is no rational answer.

H.4.5   Transcendental Numbers

Somewhat surprisingly, there are numbers that are not even algebraic. The proofs of this are deep, but examples include π and the base of the natural logarithms, e. In fact, mathematically there are more transcendental numbers that algebraic ones, but somehow one does not come across many.

H.4.6   Reals

The set of Real Numbers includes all rational and algebraic and transcendental numbers. Their *geometric* interpretation is as *unidimensional* quantities, points in an infinite line, with integers equally spaced along it, and a real number a to the left of a real number b if $a < b$. The set of real numbers, denoted by $\mathbb{R}$, is used in many places for a in this book, but it has some limitations. For instance, it cannot solve equations whose solution includes taking the square root of a negative number. The square root of negative quantities is simply not defined in the $\mathbb{R}$ set. You can think of these limitations as a consequence of the numbers having to be on a single line—of their being unidimensional. Some numbers will not fit that property and will lie elsewhere.

H.4.7   Complex Numbers

The complex number set, denoted by $\mathbb{C}$, is a set that includes a definition for square roots of negative numbers. A complex number can be represented as made up of a real part and an imaginary part, as in $a + ib$, where a is the real part and ib is the imaginary part. (The $+$ sign can be interpreted as usual, because its arithmetic properties are intact, but can also be seen as *binding* the two parts.) The i in the imaginary part is equal to the square root of -1, so $i = \sqrt{-1}$ and $i^2 = -1$.

With this definition, we are able to represent any negative square root, for instance

$$\sqrt{-4} = 2\sqrt{-1} = 2i,$$

and even square roots of complex numbers, for example

$$\sqrt{i} = \frac{\sqrt{2}(i + 1)}{2}.$$

The imaginary unit i is also sometimes notated as j, depending on the other variables used in a given expression (so that it is not confused with them). Just as any real number can be thought of as a point on an infinite line, a complex number can be thought of as a point on an infinite plane, i.e. a bi-dimensional quantity. The complex number plane (figure H.3) is made by adding an axis at a right angle to the real axis (the line on which real numbers lie). This axis is called the *imaginary axis*. Now we can interpret the complex number $a + ib$ as the intersection point of a line from the real axis at a with a line from the imaginary axis at b. In this case, the i quantity identifies the part of the number that will be reflected on the imaginary axis.

Complex numbers can have many representations, but two are particularly important. The first is its rectangular form, as we see in figure H.3. In this form, the complex number z can be represented as $z = a + ib$, with $\mathrm{Re}[z] = a$ the real part and $\mathrm{Im}[z] = b$ the imaginary part. The quantities a and b are just points on the two axes. The second representation of complex numbers is the polar form, which in figure H.3 is the representation of the number r at an angle θ or, using a common notation, $r \angle \theta$. The magnitude (or modulus) r of the number is the distance from the origin to the point and θ, the argument, is the angle this line makes with the real axis (figure H.2). The formulas for these are

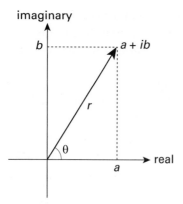

Figure H.3
The complex plane.

Modulus $|z| = \text{sqrt}(x^2 + y^2)$

and

argument$(x) = \arctan(y/x)$.

Addition or subtraction of complex numbers: In rectangular form, the real and imaginary parts are added or subtracted separately:

$(a + ib) + (c + id) = (a + c) + i(b + d)$.

Multiplication: The ordinary algebraic rules are still valid here (remember that i^2 is -1):

$(a + ib)(c + id) = ac + iad + ibc + i^2 bd$

$$= (ac - bd) + i(ad + bc).$$

For example,

$(2 + 3i) * (4 + i) = 8 + (3i * i) + 2i + 12i$

$$= 8 - 3 + 14i$$

$$= 5 + 14i.$$

(Division will be discussed a little later.)

In polar form the operations of multiplication and division are easier than in rectangular form; we multiply/divide the magnitudes and add/subtract the angles, as in

$(r_1 \angle \theta_1) \times (r_2 \angle \theta_2) = (r_1 \times r_2) \angle (\theta_1 + \theta_2)$.

A means of linking the two representations above is given by the extremely important *Euler's formula*. Consider a point on the complex plane with magnitude 1 and argument θ.

From figure H.1 we can see that the real part is $\cos(\theta)$ and the imaginary part is $\sin(\theta)$. From this remark we define a new expression $E(\theta) = \cos(\theta) + i\sin(\theta)$ as the complex number on the unit circle whose argument is θ. Some algebra, and the formulae given in subsection H.2.3, shows that $E(\theta)E(\phi)$ is

$$(\cos(\theta) + i\sin(\theta))(\cos(\phi) + i\sin(\phi)) = \cos(\theta + \phi) + i\sin(\theta + \phi)$$

$$= E(\theta + \phi).$$

This is the result we expect from the polar multiplication rule, but it should be noted that this is the same formula that was give in subsection H.1.1 for multiplications of two exponentials. Borrowing from the differential calculus, we know that the derivative of $E(\theta)$ is

$$-\sin(\theta) + i\cos(\theta),$$

or

$$i(\cos(\theta) + i\sin(\theta)) = iE(\theta).$$

As we know that the derivative of e^{ax} is ae^{ax}, we can identify the E function as just $e^{i\theta}$, and so we arrive at Euler's formula:

$$e^{i\theta} = \cos\theta + i\sin\theta.$$

There are other ways of deriving this formula, including from the Taylor series, but this derivation is sufficient for our purposes. The numerical value of e is not important (it is between 2 and 3); it is just a fixed transcendental number (the "natural base of logarithms"). However, the concept of the formula is important. Any complex number can be represented by this formula, and so it is effectively another form that connects the two previous representations:

$$R \angle \theta = Re^{i\theta} = R[\cos\theta + i\sin\theta] = R[a + ib],$$

with

$$a = \cos(\theta)$$

and

$$b = \sin(\theta).$$

A special case of Euler's formula is when θ is π, when it becomes $e^{i\pi} = -1$, neatly connecting e, π, and 1. Also interesting is that $e^{2i\pi} = 1$.

Finally, complex numbers can have an operation called *complex conjugation*, normally defined as follows:

$z^* = a - ib$ is the complex conjugate of $z = a + ib$ and vice versa.

If $z = r \angle \theta$ then $z^* = r \angle -\theta$.

$$z = Re^{i\theta}, z^* = Re^{-i\theta}.$$

The following are relations obtained by adding, subtracting, and multiplying a number and its complex conjugate:

$$z + z^* = 2x = 2\text{Re}[z],$$

$$z - z^* = 2jy = 2\text{Im}[z],$$

$$z \times z^* = \text{Re}^{j\theta}\text{Re}^{-\theta j} = R^2 e^{j\theta - j\theta} = R^2 = |z|^2.$$

Division of complex numbers in rectangular format can now be defined as

$$(a + ib)/(c + id) = ((c - id)(a + ib))/((c - id)(c + id))$$

$$= (c - id)(a + ib)/(c^2 + d^2),$$

and the rule for multiplication completes the calculation.

H.4.8   Complex Multiplication as Rotation

An interesting consequence of the multiplication rule in polar form,

$$(r_1 \angle \theta_1) \times (r_2 \angle \theta_2) = (r_1 \times r_2) \angle (\theta_1 + \theta_2),$$

is that if r_2 is 1 then multiplying by $e^{i\theta}$ just adds θ to the argument of the other number, and so rotates the number by the angle θ about the origin. Special cases of this include $i = e^{i\pi/2}$, so multiplying by i is rotation by 90°.

H.5   Final Words

Many of the concepts introduced here are explored in more detail in some of the chapters where they feature more prominently. For an extensive compilation of mathematical expressions and formulas, we recommend *Handbook of Mathematical Functions with Formulas, Graphs, and Mathematical Tables*, edited by M. Abramowitz and I. Stegun (Dover, 1965). For the reader with further interest in mathematics, we suggest the following books: R. Penrose, *The Road to Reality* (Vintage, 2005); S. Hawking, *God Created the Integers* (Running Press, 2005).

Note

1. The calculation is to perform the same calculation:

$$\lim(\partial x \to 0)((x + \partial x)^n - x^n)/\partial x = \lim(\partial x \to 0)(x^n + (n - 1)x^{n-1}\partial x + (n - 1)(n - 2)x^{n-2}\partial x^2/2 + \cdots - x^n)/\partial x$$

$$= \lim(\partial x \to 0)((-n1)x^{n-1} + (n - 1)(n - 2)x^{n-2}\partial x + \cdots)$$

$$= (-n1)x^{n-1}.$$

Contents of the DVD

Continuations of Chapters

Delay Lines and Noise Generation
Richard Dobson

Digital Filters
Richard Dobson

From C to C++
Richard Dobson

Audio Processing in C++
Richard Dobson

Audio Plug-ins in C++
Richard Dobson

APB and DVD Chapter Summaries: An Annotated Outline
Richard Dobson

Continuing Down the Audio Stream
Gabriel Maldonado

Working with Control Signals to Build a SoftSynth with a Cross-Platform GUI
Gabriel Maldonado

More VST Plug-ins
Victor Lazzarini

Algorithmic Patch Design for *Synmod*
Eric Lyon

Algorithmic Sound Design
Eric Lyon

Foundations

Compiling Software in the OS X Terminal—UNIX-style
Joo Won Park

Building Linux Audio Applications from Source: A User's Guide
David L. Phillips

A Guide to Linux Audio Applications
David L. Phillips

MIDI Programming

The MIDI Spec and Programming with PortMIDI
Tim Lukens

A MIDI-Based Algorithmic Composition Library
John ffitch

Synthesis and Signal Processing Techniques

Dynamic Range Processing
Andrés Cabrera

Binaural Audio Processing: A Sample Application
Brian Carty

Sound Manipulation Using Spectral Modeling Synthesis
John Glover

Composing Noise
Jaeho Chang

Graphical User Interfaces for Audio Programs

Developing Music Software Interfaces
Steven Yi

Graphical User Interfaces for Audio Programs Using the Qt Toolkit
Andrés Cabrera

The *FilterResponse* Graphical Filter Utility
John ffitch

Xcode-Based Audio Application Tutorials

Converting Command Line Applications to Xcode Projects
Jaeho Chang

Carbon Audio Programming for Mac OS X
Allan Seago

Getting Started with Cocoa-Based Application Programming
Barry Threw

Objective-C and Cocoa Programming with Xcode
Chen Sokolovsky

Audio Programming Basics in Xcode
Taemin Cho

Xcode-Based Alternate Controller Programming

Alternate Controllers: Connecting to HID Devices in Cocoa
Andrew Beck

Programming the Sudden Motion Sensor to Control Audio on the Mac
Taemin Cho

A Video Controller of Audio in Xcode
Taemin Cho

Apple iPhone Audio Programming

A Real-time Spectral Processor for the iPhone
Johannes Bochmann

Apple Audio Unit Plug-ins from Csound Opcodes

Converting Csound Opcodes into Apple Audio Unit Plug-ins
Jonathan Bailey

Waveshaping: From Csound to Cocoa
Federico G. Saldarini

The Csound5 API

Developing Audio Software with the Csound Host API
Rory Walsh

Microcontrollers

Embedded One-Bit Audio: Making a Microcontroller Sing
Andrew Beck

An Audio Programming Course for Electronic Musicians

Learning C with Csound
Richard Boulanger and Jonathan Bailey

From Csound to Sound in C
Richard Boulanger, Jonathan Bailey, and Tim Lukens

Real-Time MIDI Control and Audio Processing in C
Richard Boulanger, Max Mathews, and Tim Lukens

From the Command Line to the IDE: Audio Programming in Xcode
Richard Boulanger

The Audio Programming Glossary

Author Bios, Photos, Audio, Links and Favorites

Special Content

The Audio Programming Book and DVD Source Code

Selections from The OLPC Sound Sample Archive

Classic Computer Music Software and Source Code: Music V, cmusic, Csound

Current Computer Music Software and Source Code: Csound5, csound~, WinXound, Ounk, pyo, and the SndObj Library

References

Abadi, M., and L. Cardelli. 1996. *A Theory of Objects*. Springer-Verlag.

Abe, T. 1997. The IF spectrogram: A new spectral representation. In Proceedings of the International Symposium on Simulation, Visualization and Auralization for Acoustic Research and Education, Tokyo.

Abramowitz, M., and I. Stegun, eds. 1965. *Handbook of Mathematical Functions with Formulas, Graphs, and Mathematical Tables*. Dover.

Aho, A., R. Sethi, and J. Ullman. 1977. *Principles of Compiler Design*. Addison-Wesley.

Aho, A., R. Sethi, and J. Ullman. 1986. *Compilers: Principles, Techniques and Tools*. Addison-Wesley.

Aho, A., J. Ullman, and J. Hopcroft. 1983. *Data Structures and Algorithms*. Addison-Wesley.

Babbage, C. 1864. *Passages from the Life of a Philosopher*. Longman.

Backus, J. 1977. *The Acoustical Foundations of Music*, second edition. Norton.

Backus, J. W., R. Beer, S. Best, R. Goldberg, L. Haibt, H. Herrick, R. Nelson, D. Sayre, P. Sheridan, H. Stern, I. Ziller, R. Hughes, and R. Nutt. 1957. The FORTRAN automatic coding system. In Proceedings of the Western Joint Computer Conference, Los Angeles.

Barton, D., and J. Fitch. 1972. The application of symbolic algebra systems to physics. *Reports on Progress in Physics* 35: 235–314.

Bennett, J. 1996. *Compiling Techniques: A First Course Using ANSI C, LEX and YACC*, second edition. Addison-Wesley.

Bidlack, R. 1992. Chaotic systems as simple (but complex) compositional algorithms. *Computer Music Journal* 16 (3): 33–47.

Boulanger, R., ed. 2000. *The Csound Book*. MIT Press.

Boulanger, R., and J. ffitch. 2003. Teaching software synthesis: From hardware to software synthesis.'' In *Global Village—Global Brain—Global Music: KlangArt-Kongress 1999*, ed. B. Enders and J. Strange-Elbe. Electronic Publishing.

Bracewell, R. 1968. *The Fourier Transform and Its Applications*. McGraw-Hill.

Bryant, R., and D. O'Hallaron. 2003. *Computer Systems: A Programmer's Perspective*. Prentice-Hall.

Burtch, K. 2004. *Linux Shell Scripting with Bash*. Sams.

Cameron, D., J. Elliott, M. Loy, E. Raymond, and B. Rosenblatt. 2004. *Learning GNU Emacs*, third edition. O'Reilly Media.

Chowning, J. 1973. The synthesis of complex audio spectra by means of frequency modulation. *Journal of the Audio Engineering Society* (21): 526–534.

Chowning, J., and R. Bristow. 1986. *FM Theory and Applications by Musicians for Musicians*. Yamaha Music Foundation.

CODASYL. 1959. *Common Business Oriented Language*. Technical report.

Cody, W., and W. Waite. 1980. *Software Manual for the Elementary Functions*. Prentice-Hall.

Cook, P. 2002. *Real Sound Synthesis for Interactive Applications*. A. K. Peters.

Davenport, J., Y. Siret, and E. Tournier. 1993. *Computer Algebra, Systems and Algorithms for Algebraic Computation*, second edition. Academic Press.

De Furia, S., and J. Sciacciaferro. 1989. *MIDI Programmers Handbook*. M & T Publishing.

Deitel, H. 1984. *An Introduction to Operating Systems*. Addison-Wesley.

Deitel, H. 2006. *C: How to Program*, fifth edition. Prentice-Hall.

Deitel, H., and P. Deitel. 2007. *C++: How to Program*, sixth edition. Prentice-Hall.

Deitel, H., P. Deitel, and D. Choffnes. 2003. *Operating Systems*, third edition. Prentice-Hall.

Disch, S., and U. Zölzer. 1999. Modulation and delay line based digital audio effects. In Proceedings of the Second COST-G6 Workshop on Digital Audio Effects, Trondheim.

Dodge, C., and T. Jerse. 1985. *Computer Music*. Schirmer Books.

Dolson, M. 1986. The phase vocoder tutorial. *Computer Music Journal* 10 (4): 14–27.

ffitch, J. 2005. On the design of Csound5. In Proceedings of the Third International Linux Audio Conference, Karlsruhe.

Flanagan, J., and R. Golden. 1966. Phase vocoder. *Bell System Technical Journal* 45: 1493–1509.

Ford, W., and W. Topp. 2001. *Data Structures with C++ Using STL*, second edition. Prentice-Hall.

Forman, S. 1990. *Numerical Algorithms That (Usually) Work*. Mathematical Association of America.

Friedman, D. 1985. Instantaneous-frequency distribution vs. time: An interpretation of the phase structure of speech. In Proceedings of the International Conference on Audio and Speech Signal Processing, Tampa.

Ghezi, C., and M. Javayeri. 1987. *Programming Language Concepts*, second edition. Wiley.

Graham, R., D. Knuth, and O. Patashnik. 1994. *Concrete Mathematics*. Addison-Wesley.

Hawking, S. 2005. *God Created the Integers*. Running Press.

Hennessy, J., and D. Patterson. 2003. *Computer Architecture: A Quantitative Approach*, third edition. Morgan Kaufman.

Howard, D., and J. Angus. 2006. *Acoustics and Psychoacoustics*, third edition. Focal Press.

Howe, H. 1975. *Electronic Music Synthesis*. Norton.

Jaffe, D. 1987. Spectrum analysis tutorial, part 1: The discrete Fourier transform. *Computer Music Journal* 11 (2): 9–24.

Jaffe, D. 1987. Spectrum analysis tutorial, part 2: Properties and applications of the discrete Fourier transform. *Computer Music Journal* 11 (3): 17–35.

Johnson, S. 1990. Yacc: Yet another compiler-compiler. In *UNIX Research System Programmer's Manual*, volume 2, tenth edition. Saunders College Publishing.

Kaiser, J. 1963. Design methods for sampled data filters. In Proceedings of the First Allerton Conference on Circuit and System Theory, Urbana.

Kelly, J., C. Lochbaum, and V. Vyssotsky. 1961. A block diagram compiler. *Bell System Technical Journal* 40: 669–676.

Kelly-Bootle, S. 1995. *The Computer Contradictionary*, second edition. MIT Press.

Kerninghan, B., and D. Ritchie. 1988. *The ANSI C Programming Language*. Prentice-Hall.

Knuth, D. 1998. *The Art of Computer Programming*, volume 1: *Fundamental Algorithms*, second edition. Addison-Wesley.

Knuth, D. 1998. *The Art of Computer Programming*, volume 2: *Seminumerical Algorithms*, second edition. Addison-Wesley.

Knuth, D. 1998. *The Art of Computer Programming*, volume 3: *Sorting and Searching*, second edition. Addison-Wesley.

Laakso, T., V. Valimaki, M. Karjalainen, and U. Laine. 1996. Splitting the unit delay. *IEEE Signal Processing Magazine* 13 (1): 30–60.

Lazzarini, V. 1998. A proposed design for an audio processing system. *Organised Sound* 3 (1): 77–84.

Lazzarini, V. 2000. The sound object library. *Organised Sound* 5 (1): 35–49.

Lazzarini, V. 2002. Audio signal processing and object oriented systems. In Proceedings of the Fifth International Conference on Digital Audio Effects, Hamburg.

Lazzarini, V. 2005. Extensions to the Csound language: From user-defined to plugin opcodes and beyond. In Proceedings of the Third Linux Audio Developer's Conference, Karlsruhe.

Lazzarini, V., J. Timoney, and T. Lysaght. 2006. Spectral signal processing in Csound 5. In Proceedings of the International Conference on Computer Music, New Orleans.

Lesk, M., and E. Schmidt. 1990. Lex—A lexical analyzer generator. In *UNIX Research System Programmer's Manual*, volume 2, tenth edition. Saunders College Publishing.

Loukides, M., T. O'Reilly, and S. Powers. 2002. *UNIX Power Tools*, third edition. O'Reilly Media.

Loy, G. 2006. *Musimathics: The Mathematical Foundations of Music*, volume 1. MIT Press.

Loy, G. 2007. *Musimathics: The Mathematical Foundations of Music*, volume 2. MIT Press.

Mathews, M. 1961. An acoustic compiler for music and psychological stimuli. *Bell System Technical Journal* 40: 677–694.

Mathews, M. 1969. *The Technology of Computer Music*. MIT Press.

Mathews, M., and J. Pierce, eds. 1989. *Current Directions in Computer Music Research*. MIT Press.

Matloff, N., and P. Salzman. 2008. *The Art of Debugging with GDB, DDD, and Eclipse*. No Starch Press.

McCarthy, J. 1960. Recursive functions of symbolic expressions and their computation by machine, part I. *Communications of ACM* 3 (4): 184–195.

Meyer, B. 1990. *Introduction to the Theory of Programming Languages*. Prentice-Hall.

Miranda, E., and M. Wanderley. 2006. *New Digital Musical Instruments*. A-R Editions.

Moore, F. 1977. Table lookup noise for sinusoidal digital oscillators. *Computer Music Journal* 1 (2): 26–29.

Moore, F. 1990. *Elements of Computer Music*. Prentice-Hall.

Moorer, J. 1978. The use of the phase vocoder in computer music applications. *Journal of the Audio Engineering Society* 24: 717–727.

Moorer, J. 1979. About this reverberation business. *Computer Music Journal* 3 (2): 13–18.

Newham, C. 2005. *Learning the bash Shell (In a Nutshell)*. O'Reilly Media.

Openheim, A., and R. Schafer. 1975. *Digital Signal Processing*. Prentice-Hall.

Ousterhout, J. 1994. *Tcl and the Tk Toolkit*. Addison-Wesley.

Penrose, R. 2005. *The Road to Reality*. Vintage.

Pesch, R., S. Shebs, and R. Stallman. 2002. *Debugging with GDB: The GNU Source-Level Debugger*. Free Software Foundation.

Pierce, J. R. 1983. *The Science of Musical Sound*. Freeman.

Pope, S. 1991. Machine tongues XI: Object oriented design. In *The Well Tempered Object*, ed. S. Pope. MIT Press.

Pope, S., and G. Van Rossum. 1995. Machine tongues XVIII: A child's garden of soundfile formats. *Computer Music Journal* 19 (1): 25–63.

Press, W., S. Teukolsky, W. Vetterling, and B. Flannery. 2007. *Numerical Recipes*, third edition. Cambridge University Press.

Puckette, M. 2007. *The Theory and Techniques of Electronic Music*. World Scientific Press.

Roads, C. 1996. *Computer Music Tutorial*. MIT Press.

Roads, C., S. Pope, A. Picialli, and G. Poli, eds. 1997. *Musical Signal Processing*. Swets & Zeitlinger.

Robbins, A. 2005. *GDB Pocket Reference*. O'Reilly Media.

Risset, J. C. 1969. *An Introductory Catalogue of Computer Synthesized Sounds*. Bell Laboratories.

Sammet, J. 1969. *Programming Languages: History and Fundamentals*. Prentice-Hall.

Sammet, J. 1976. Roster of programming languages for 1974–75. *Communications of the ACM* 19 (2): 655–669.

Sammet, J. 1981. An overview of high-level languages. *Advances in Computers* 20: 199–259.

Sandige, R. 2001. *Digital Design Essentials*. Prentice-Hall.

Schafer, R., and L. Rabiner. 1973. A digital signal processing approach to interpolation. *Proceedings of the IEEE* 61 (6): 692–702.

Schroeder, R. M. 1962. Natural sounding artificial reverberation. *Journal of the Audio Engineering Society* 10: 219–223.

Smith, J., and J. Angell. 1982. A constant-gain digital resonator tuned by a single coefficient. *Computer Music Journal* 6 (4): 36–40.

Stallings, W. 2008. *Operating Systems: Internals and Design Principles*, sixth edition. Prentice-Hall.

Steiglitz, K. 1963. The General Theory of Digital Filters with Applications to Spectral Analysis. Sc.D. dissertation, New York University.

Steiglitz, K. 1994. A note on constant-gain digital resonators. *Computer Music Journal* 18 (4): 8–10.

Steiglitz, K. 1996. *A Digital Signal Processing Primer*. Prentice-Hall.

Stones, R., and N. Matthew. 2000. *Beginning Linux Programming*. Wrox.

Stroustrop, B. 1991. *The C++ Programming Language*, second edition. Addison-Wesley.

Taube, H. 2004. *Notes from the Metalevel*. Taylor & Francis.

Tennenbaum, A. 1989. *Data Structures Using C*. Prentice-Hall.

Turing, A. 1936. On computable numbers, with an application to the Entscheidungsproblem. *Proceedings of the London Mathematical Society* 42 (2): 230–265.

Verfaille, V., and D. Arfib. 2002. Implementation Strategies for Adaptive Digital Effects. In Proceedings of the Fifth Conference on Digital Audio Effects, Hamburg.

Verfaille, V., U. Zolzer, and D. Arfib. 2006. Adaptive digital audio effects (a-DAFx): A new class of sound transformations. *IEEE Transactions on Audio, Speech and Language Processing* 14 (5): 1817–1831.

Warren, H. 2002. *Hacker's Delight*. Addison-Wesley.

Watson, G. 1944. *A Treatise on the Theory of Bessel Functions*, second edition. Cambridge University Press.

Wishart, T. 1995. *Audible Design*. Orpheus the Pantomime.

Xenakis, I. 1992. *Formalized Music*, revised edition. Pendragon.

Zölzer, U., ed. 2002. *DAFX—Digital Audio Effects*. Wiley.

About the Authors

Jonathan Bailey is a software developer and a drummer.

Andrew Beck is an audio programmer who has studied at the Berklee College of Music and the Georgia Institute of Technology.

Johannes Bochmann is a freelance electronic artist and a computer scientist.

Richard Boulanger is a professor of electronic production and design at the Berklee College of Music.

Andrés Cabrera is a lecturer in music technology at Pontificia Universidad Javeriana. He is the author of the Csound front end *QuteCsound*.

Brian Carty is a PhD student and a lecturer in the music department at the National University of Ireland at Maynooth.

Jaeho Chang is an associate professor of music technology at the Korea National University of Arts.

Taemin Cho is a guitarist, a composer, and a music technologist. He is pursuing a PhD in music technology at New York University.

Richard Dobson is a freelance software developer, a core developer for the Composers Desktop Project, and a virtuoso flautist. He teaches at Bath Spa University.

John ffitch is a professor of software engineering at the University of Bath and the director of Codemist Ltd.

John Glover is a computer scientist, a musician, and a composer. He is a researcher and a PhD student in the Music Department at the National University of Ireland at Maynooth.

Victor Lazzarini is a senior lecturer in music at the National University of Ireland at Maynooth.

Tim Lukens is a software developer. He is a graduate of the Berklee College of Music, where he majored in electronic production and design.

Eric Lyon is a composer, a computer music researcher, and an educator at the Sonic Arts Research Centre at Queen's University in Belfast.

Gabriel Maldonado is a composer, a guitarist, a researcher, a video artist, and a VJ. He is president of the Ecuadorian Estuardo Maldonado Art Foundation.

Joo Won Park is a composer, a researcher, and an assistant professor of music at the Community College of Philadelphia.

David L. Phillips is a music teacher, a performer, and an author.

Robert Gerard Pietrusko is a designer and an engineer. He prepared most of the figures for this book.

Federico G. Saldarini is a digital artist, a sound designer, and a computer scientist. He attends Portland State University in Oregon.

Allan Seago is a senior lecturer in the Department of Art Media and Design at London Metropolitan University.

Chen Sokolovsky is a musician and a programmer.

Barry Threw is an electronic musician and a media technologist.

Rory Walsh is Director of Music Technology at the Dundalk Institute of Technology.

Steven Yi is a composer and programmer. He is an editor of *The Csound Journal* and the author of the *blue* music composition environment.

Index

Absolute value, 214

Access violation, 325

Accumulating sum (+=), 310

Additive synthesis, 450, 573, 574

Address
  aligning, 139
  of data in memory, 78, 79, 81, 110–114, 118,
    143, 168, 169, 307, 341, 347, 351–352, 357,
    359, 368–374
  of function, 368, 369, 374, 375

ADSR, 478–480

AIFF-C, 192

Algorithm, 95, 220, 237, 249, 385

Algorithmic composition, 655

Aliasing, 261, 270, 292, 299, 434, 439, 440

Allpass filter, 494

ALSA, 364, 365, 372

Ambisonics, 193

Amplitude response, 453, 454

Analog signals, 431

ANSI, 137, 138, 160, 221, 263, 297, 324

API (application programming interface), 190,
  194, 280

Arguments to programs, 40, 350, 351

Arithmetic
  inverse, 236
  logarithm, 75, 76
  raising to power, 68, 69
  ratio, 230, 231, 259
  reciprocal, 232
  square, square root, 234

Arrays, 27–29, 79–81, 90, 94, 115, 338–345,
  349–353, 363, 370, 377–380
  allocation, 132, 139
  as container, 90, 106
  errors, 81, 82, 113, 124, 177
  index, 80, 81, 115, 177, 298
  initialization, 80–82, 268
  name as pointer, 111, 112
  of arrays, 90, 117–119, 135
  of objects, 287
  sequential access, 113, 249
  size, 103, 106, 132
  subscript, 80

ASIO, 364, 365

Audacity, 157, 173, 206, 253

Audio file formats
  AIFF, 337, 351, 353
  raw binary, 338, 344–348
  WAV, 337, 338, 345–353

Audio frames, 350

Audio IO, 771

Audio channels, 744

Audio signal, 329, 332, 365

Automation, 130, 239

Bessel functions, 458

Binary files, 741

Black box, 332, 333, 357, 359

Block diagram, 333, 335

Blocking I/O, 363, 364, 378, 774

BLODI, 629

Breakpoint, 721

Breakpoints file, 130, 132, 220, 223, 226–228, 292

array of, 135

overhead, 237

span, 230

stream object, 277

Buffering, 348, 359, 360, 377, 378

Buffers, 349–354, 359–361

circular, 491, 492

FIFO, 360

input, 360

memory, 95, 113, 114, 180

output, 360

underrun, 361

Bugs, 57, 81, 107, 142, 177

Butterworth filters, 484

Byte ordering, 749

Byte reversal, 169, 320, 749, 759–762

C language, 329–332, 337, 350, 352

argc, 40, 349–351, 354–357

argv, 40, 349–357

atof, atoi, atol, 41, 82, 83, 91, 105, 354, 355, 358

bitwise operators, 22–24

break, 16, 101–103, 118, 125, 141, 197, 339–342, 354, 355

building programs, 5

case, 16, 339–342

cast operator, 8, 343, 345, 347, 370, 379

char, 8

character set, 6

compiling programs, 4, 709

const, 82–84, 124, 236

data types, 7, 8

do . . . while loop, 20, 100, 101, 114, 115, 177, 350, 352, 356, 359

else, 15, 119–121, 125

enum, 161, 162, 189, 268, 273, 315

for loop, 20, 21, 99, 100, 106, 107, 113, 177, 331, 343–345, 366, 370, 380

functions, 24, 25, 60, 61

goto, 201, 339–342, 350, 352, 355, 356

if, 14, 15, 84

linking, 5, 711

long, 7, 339, 343, 349–357, 366, 369–372, 377–381

order of operations, 9, 73–75

return, 24, 25, 138, 339, 349, 354, 355

short, 7, 344, 347, 381

standard library, 28, 330, 365

static, 286, 313

stdio, 10–13, 330, 338, 341, 346–349, 354, 359, 366, 377

structures, 35–39, 133, 225

switch/case/default, 16, 194, 196, 197, 276, 339–342, 354, 358

typedef, 36, 134–136, 179, 189, 276

while loop, 20, 95, 96, 101, 108, 319

C++ language, 324, 327, 329, 331

access control, 48

classes, 48, 49

plug-ins, 513–516

structures, 44

virtual functions, 52

CAF, 193

Calculus, 860–863

Callback function, 363, 366

Callbacks, 34, 35, 363–371, 774, 775

Cancellation effects, 293

Casting, 392

Code

analysis, 248

bloat, 312

block, 59, 85, 95–99, 115, 120, 122

data hiding, 188

dependent block, 86, 96, 97, 100, 101

design, 57, 89, 99, 103, 136, 157, 255

encapsulation, 188, 255, 264, 280, 311

error handling, 201, 221, 228

generation, 56

implementation file, 264

incremental development, 86, 241

inline, 219

label, 202

low-level, 56, 157, 255
optimization, 55, 56, 83, 116
robustness, 237, 311
self-documenting, 63, 88, 162, 177, 263, 270, 316, 321, 327
structure, 60, 69, 124, 213
Code layout, 69, 121, 176
duplication, 201
`else` block, 120, 123
indentation, 85, 86, 121, 176
white space, 58, 70, 131, 168, 176
Comb filter, 493, 494, 552
Command line, 58, 89, 78, 89, 143, 151, 176, 179
`argc`, `argv`, 40, 90–93
argument, 96, 104, 110, 116, 121, 123, 129, 244, 317
and GUI programs, 93
input, 89, 90
Command-line interface, 633
Comments (source code), 58, 59, 62, 70, 72, 82, 104, 125, 194, 195, 251
Compiled languages, 3
Compilers, 813, 814
Complex numbers, 865–868
Complex signals, 441–444
Compressed files, 703
Computation overhead, 229, 237
Computation speed, 55–57, 115, 116
Computer languages, 812, 813
Concert pitch, 161
Conditional compilation, 159, 160, 187
Conditional debugging, 726
Continue, 142
Continuous-time signals, 431
Control rate, 468, 469
Control signal, 270, 293
Convolution, 498, 529–531, 597
fast, 531–535
graphic, 541
spectral, 540
Cook, Perry, 326
Core dumps, 736

Creation, vs. initialization, 266
Creation function (object), 265, 306, 308
Cross-synthesis, 546
Cubic interpolation, 472
Csound, 109, 114, 320, 327, 582, 682–684

DAC (digital-analog converter), 329, 337, 338, 346–348, 353, 360, 361, 377
Data plotting, 147
Dataspace, 45
Debugger, 719
Debugging, 57, 129, 146, 147, 151, 162, 720
Decibel, 154, 208, 210, 211, 234
Declaration function, 62, 137
Declaration variable, 65, 70–72, 83, 133, 135
Declarative programming, 332
Decrement, 97
Default values, 117, 124, 244
Defensive programming, 57, 82, 83, 146, 162, 236
Definition, vs. declaration, 264
Delay, 451, 452
Delay line, 490–493
Denormal number, 180
Dependency, 185, 226
Destruction function, 306
Destructive, vs. non-destructive, 194, 200, 202
Digital audio signal, 329, 431
Discrete Fourier transform, 521–525
Discrete-time signal, 431
Distortion, 195, 286, 302, 319
Division by zero, 217, 231, 322
Documentation, 57, 89, 136, 190, 236, 238, 266, 323, 325
Doppler shift, 323
DOS, 60, 67, 89, 93, 131, 147
Drop-out, 360, 361, 377
DSP (digital signal processing), 341
Dynamic range, 211

Efficiency, 220, 237, 267, 297
Emacs, 714
Encapsulation, 48, 333

Endianness, 169, 170, 174, 185, 320

Entry point, 5

Envelope

ADSR, 253

amplitude, 110, 130–132, 155, 212, 239, 241

breakpoint file, 237

on dB scale, 212

exponential, 475, 476

extraction, 239, 244

following, 242

generators, 477–481

linear, 474, 475, 478

stereo pan, 132

tables, 474–477

Environment variable, 704

Escape character, 61

Euler, Leonhard, 180

Euler's formula, 867

Execution cycle, 798–802

Exponential attack, 151, 152

Exponential decay, 149, 150, 154, 158, 160, 164, 166, 167

Fall-through, 291

Fast Fourier transform, 529

Feedback, oscillator, 642

Fencepost problem, 420, 421

File permissions, 700

File extension, 190, 199, 320, 321

Filter, 55, 114, 160, 327

and aliasing, 270

direct forms I, II, 485

equation, 453

FIR, feedforward, 452–456

high-pass, 486

IIR, feedback, 452, 456, 457, 483–488

linear-phase, 455

low-pass, 242, 486, 581

module, 651

pole, 457

Flag, 352–359, 366, 369, 370, 374, 375, 379–381

Flanger, 495, 496

Floating point, 65, 66, 71, 72, 75–77, 98, 142, 168, 173, 178, 192, 195, 198, 203, 211, 214, 297, 301, 325, 762

Flow chart, 332–334

Flow control, 14–16

initializer statement, 99, 134, 226, 322

update statement, 322

Formatted output, 60, 72, 94, 117–119,123, 124, 168, 247

Fourier series, 448–451

Fourier transform, 521

Frequency

fundamental, 287

of MIDI note, 68, 69

modulation, 317, 264

negative, 264, 267

as phase increment, 263

Frequency modulation (FM), 264, 459, 460

Frequency response, 456

Function

address, 275

arguments, 61

body, 60

creation, 265, 277, 278, 294, 296, 305, 306, 308, 312, 319

declaration (prototype), 62, 71, 83, 137, 168, 264

in expression, 88

`main`, 5, 58–60, 90, 203

overloading, 46, 266

signature, 387

static, 313

user-defined, 137, 138

wrapper, 180

Function generator, 254

Functions, mathematical, 857

Function tables, 335–337, 432

Fundamental frequency of analysis, 523

Gain, 209

Gardner, Bill, 187

Generality, 220, 255, 327

Geometric series, 149

Gnuplot, 147, 154, 160, 163, 241

Guard point, 297, 304, 312

Hamming window, 542, 543

Hanning window, 542, 543

Hardware, 56, 57, 67, 113, 125, 180, 297

Harmonic (component), 287, 288, 292, 318

Header files, 4, 62, 69, 70, 135, 137, 160

Headphones, 234

Heap, 807

Henon map, 657

High-level language, 56, 110

Host-APIs, 364–374

Host-driven mechanism, 363

Imaginary number, 441, 442, 865

Imperative programming, 333

Increment, 97

Incremental development, 86, 223

Indirection, 92, 110, 111, 119

Inharmonicity, 317, 320

Inheritance, 52, 503, 504

Instantaneous frequency distribution, 568

Instructions, 798

Interleaving (samples), 163

Interpolation, 398–402

    cubic, 400

    exponential, 475, 564

    linear, 398, 472, 475, 596, 564

    quadratic, 400

Interpreted languages, 4

Interpreter, 147

Inverse DFT, 525–527

Iteration, 95

Keyword, 6, 58, 60, 64, 67, 84, 101, 133, 134, 142, 161, 194, 201, 236, 286, 313

Latency, 361–364, 367–369, 372–374, 378

Lexer, 814–817

Library, 4, 5, 57, 61, 62, 82, 84, 124, 125, 137, 162, 176, 186, 206, 220, 227, 287, 330, 332, 341, 345–350, 353–359, 363–365, 369, 371, 376–380

Libsndfile, 187, 763–769,

Linear interpolation, 230, 241, 242, 286, 302, 327

Linear pan, 221, 234

Linking, 185

Listening test, 226, 233, 270, 305

Logarithms, 855, 856

Logical expressions, 14

Lookup tables, 335–337, 465

Loop, 19–21, 91, 95–99, 102, 106, 112, 118, 124, 125, 142, 201, 202, 233, 251, 290

Macintosh, 56, 89, 93, 147, 148, 173, 175, 199, 321

Macro, 179, 219, 333, 335, 338, 341, 342, 346, 347, 350, 358, 359, 365, 379

Maintenance, 422

Makefile and *make*, 185, 188, 206, 208, 226, 320, 418, 712

Mapping

    of ideas to performance instructions, 680

    of instructions to performers, 679, 680

Mathematics, 855–868

    approximations, 261

    C definitions, 261

    computation, 298

    e (Euler's number), 75, 180, 867

    exponential, 154, 180, 212, 239, 855

    irrational number, 261, 864

    logarithm, 75, 154, 180, 210, 212, 855, 856

    orthogonal, 324

    π (pi), 180, 236, 259, 324, 858

    radian, 236, 259, 260, 858

    right angle, 324, 858

    sine, cosine, 235, 256, 258, 286, 293, 299, 437, 858, 859

    transcendental number, 261, 864

    trigonometry, 236, 256, 437, 858

Mathews, Max, 335, 629

Max/MSP, 332

Member variables, 45

Memory
  allocation, 39, 40, 139, 807
  error testing, 201
  freeing, 40, 141
  heap, 325,
  leak, 279
  for objects, 266
  on/off chip, 297
  organization, 805
  and `printf`, 140
  and `realloc`, 140, 143
  stressing, 180
  virtual, 180
Methods (functions), 264
Methodspace, 45
MIDI, 56, 68, 69, 75, 76, 80, 86, 92, 103, 110, 117, 783
Mixing, 445
MME, 364, 365, 372, 373
Modular synthesizer, 629
Modulus operation, 465
Morphing, 564
MUSIC I–MUSIC V languages, 335

Noise, 270
  generation, 645, 646
  quantization, 322
  truncation, 302, 305
Normalization, 212–217, 310
Normalize (samples), 154, 208, 242
Numeric systems, 863–868
Nyquist limit, 261, 299

Object, 75, 78, 79, 94, 112, 130–134, 168, 255, 264, 265, 305, 316, 325, 327
  behavior, 264
  in C, 132
  derivation and inheritance, 307, 308
  initialization, 265
  lifetime, 325
  state, 57, 264
  stream, 264, 277
Objected-oriented design, 383

Objected-oriented programming, 3, 49, 332–343
Offset, 446, 447
Open-source, 357, 364
Operator, 64, 323
  += (accumulator), 20, 290
  ++, −, 20, 97
  % (modulus), 98, 319
  and ?: test, 15, 218, 219, 284
  AND, OR (||, &&), 222–224, 307
  assignment, 65, 71, 74
  association, 9, 73, 74, 275
  comma, 284, 322, 323
  comparison, 84, 97, 264
  conditional, 229, 251, 280, 323
  contents-of, address-of (*, &), 110
  indirection, 92, 110, 111, 119
  logical, 14, 99
  NOT (!), 229
  overload, 134
  precedence, 9, 73–75, 88, 113, 115, 143, 179
  `sizeof`, 67, 139
  `struct`, 35, 265, 308
  true, false, 84, 85, 97, 101, 176, 218,
  unary, binary, 64
Orchestral composition, 677–679
Oscillator, 95, 259, 464, 630
  bank, 255, 287
  feedback, 642
  low-frequency, 270
  sine wave, 263
OS X, 56, 89, 160, 178, 321
Overlap-add, 531, 532
Overloading, 46, 53

Pan, 219, 221, 323
  constant power, 235
  pairwise, 323
Parentheses, 74, 275
Parser, 817
Pascal, 175, 323
Path, relative, 206
PD, 332

PEAK chunk, 195, 200, 269

Performer groups, 678, 687

Performers, 678, 686

Periodic signal, periodicity, 259, 287, 299

P-fields, 682

Phase, 258, 259, 261, 286, 293, 296, 298, 301

Phase derivative, 568

Phase difference, 261

Phase modulation, 457–459

Phase pointer, 337–343, 366, 367, 370, 371, 376, 379, 380

Phase response, 454, 455

Phase unwrapping, 558

Phase vocoder, 557, 617

Phase wrapping, 263, 304

Pipe, 176, 178, 705

Pitch shifting, 505, 506, 621

Pointer manipulation, 112, 113, 306
  cast, 140
  increment, 115, 177, 178
  temporary, 143

Pointers, 30–32, 77, 78, 337, 341, 347–351, 357–360, 365, 369–380
  arithmetic, 110, 112, 113, 116, 117, 124
  to functions, 34, 274, 275, 308
  NULL, 80, 86, 90, 132, 140, 280
  tests in expressions, 224

Polar format, 443, 527, 865

Polynomials, 857

Portaudio, 346, 364–375, 378–381, 771

Portmidi, 783

Portsf, 344, 355, 358, 359, 377, 400

Precision, numeric, 65, 66, 106, 151, 157, 168, 177, 180

Preprocessor, 5, 62, 70, 136, 159, 321
  #define, 136, 321
  #elif, 344–346
  #else, 344–346
  #endif, 344–346
  #ifdef, 344–346
  #include, 187, 330, 338, 344–346, 349, 354, 366
  macro, 179, 219, 326

Processes, 706

Processing time, 296, 299

Products, 857

Programming
  modular, 165
  testing, 206, 233

Progress message, 207

Pseudo-code, 101, 119, 141

Public and private, 48, 286, 305, 313, 316

Pulse-code modulation, 434, 435

Quantization, 434

Quantization noise, 436

Queue, 360

Random-access memory (RAM), 329

Read and update, 267

Reaktor, 332

Real numbers, 441, 864

Rectangular format, 443, 527, 865

Redirection (stream), 178, 705

Rescaling, 347, 352

Reserved word, 60

Resonators, 487, 488, 551

Resources (machine), 201, 225

Return values and variables, 345, 348, 351, 352, 358–360, 367–374, 378–381

Ring modulation, 447, 448

RMS (root mean square), 488, 590

Robustness, 82, 101, 220

Rounding, 76

Sample, 160, 432, 744
  format, 173, 191, 195
  frame, 200
  rate (frequency), 161, 191, 259, 263
  precision, 743
  window, 244

Sample-and-hold, 649

Samples, 329–352, 359–381

Sampling increment, 333–343, 358, 359, 365–371, 376, 464

Sampling period, 432

Sampling, regular vs. irregular, 239, 241
Sampling theorem, 433
Sawtooth wave, 449, 467
Scaling, 445, 446
Scope, 121, 122
Scripts, 708
Series, 856
Shell, 697
Shell command, 60, 88, 89, 131
Short-time Fourier transform (STFT), 539–544
Signal processing, 201, 320, 341
Signal-to-noise ratio, 436
Sign bit, 66
Sine wave (sinusoid), 158, 185, 233, 236, 256, 437–439, 464
Skeleton code, 104, 202
SNDAN, 170
Software engineering, 383, 385
Soundfield, 193
Soundfile
  AIFF, 754–762
  and byte-swapping, 320
  digital peak, 211
  find maximum, 214
  formats, 163, 185
  header, 167, 173, 185, 198, 320
  libraries, 186
  multi-channel, 187, 191
  raw binary, 157, 168, 185, 742
  RIFF-Wave, 746–754
  self-describing, 185, 320, 746
  skeleton program, 202, 221
Source files, 4
Space-time trade-off, 395
Spatialization, 323
Specialization, 52, 53
Spectral coefficient, 523
Spectral interpolation, 564–568
Spectral signals, 617, 618
Spectrum, 286, 287, 292, 521–538
Square wave, 449, 467
Stack, 805,
Standard I/O, 10–13, 341

Standard I/O streams (stdin, stdout, stderr), 151, 154, 178
Standard output, 329–333, 337, 338, 344–348, 377
Standard torus map, 669
Statements, 60, 63–65, 70, 72, 74, 80, 85, 96, 99, 113, 120, 122, 133, 177
Stepping, 724
Stereo, 132, 163, 191, 192, 195, 219, 221, 224, 226, 233–235, 323
Streams, 329–381, 705
String, 61, 71, 72, 78–83, 89–94, 117–119, 142, 175
Structured programming, 332
Surround, 192, 193, 322
Syntactic sugar, 100
Synthesis, 155, 161, 241, 264
  additive, 158, 255, 286, 287
  subtractive, 270
  waveforms, 254–256, 299

Table
  implemented as C array, 330, 338
  index, 336, 465
Table lookup, 335–337
Table lookup oscillator, 286, 297, 299
  interpolating, 302
  truncated, 286, 301
Taylor series, 297
Tcl/Tk, 408
Template program, 209, 221
Terminal (OS X), 89, 93, 148
Testing, 129, 299, 317, 419, 420
  bebugging, 420
  black-box, 420
  reversion, 423
  white-box, 420
Test signal, 226, 253, 254, 268, 270
Text files, 740
Tick function, 270, 271, 276, 277, 308, 309, 326
Time constant, 150, 154
TinyAudioLib, 344–349, 352–354, 359, 363, 377, 378

Trapped in Convert, 655
Triangle wave, 185, 449, 467
Trigonometry, 236, 256, 858–860
Truncating oscillator, 466, 467
Tuning, 68, 94, 175
Tuning fork, 158, 164, 164
Types, 7, 65
 abstract, 136, 264
 `bool`, 323,
 casting, 8, 74–76, 139, 140, 301
 `clock_t`, 297
 collection, 110, 133
 conversion, 8, 71
 float, 7, 8, 331, 338–358, 366–370,
 integer, 7, 66, 67, 374, 377–381
 numeric, 7, 8, 65, 66
 promotion/demotion, 8, 75, 76
 signed/unsigned, 7, 66–68, 134, 139, 168,
  173
 `size_t`, 139, 168, 175, 180
 string, 29, 61, 71, 78–83, 89, 90, 117, 118, 124,
  142, 175,
 `struct`, 35, 44, 133–135, 138, 178, 179, 225
 `void`, 139, 140, 168

UNIX, 56, 60, 89, 93, 116, 131, 147, 160, 168,
 176, 178, 188, 197, 236, 321, 322
Usage message, 92, 104, 117, 162, 176, 206,
 245
User interface,
 command line, 403
 graphical, 408
 positional and tagged, 405

Variable delay line, 494, 495
Variables, 7, 63–65, 107, 175
 Boolean, 315, 323
 constant, 83, 265
 counter, 115, 249, 269
 declaration, 65, 70, 72, 104
 flag, 124, 251, 317
 initialization, 72, 80, 81, 110, 247
 left-hand/right-hand side, 65, 175

local/global scope, 9, 70, 121–125, 138, 250,
 325
 pointer, 77–85, 92, 110–112
Vector, 90, 467
Von Hann window, 542, 543
VST, 180, 502, 503

Watchpoint, 728
WaveArts, 187
Waveform, 211
 geometric, 270, 286
 (non)band-limited, 270, 286
 pulse, 318
 sawtooth, 288, 315
 square, 288
 triangle, 288, 296, 310
WAVEFORMATEXTENSIBLE, 192
Wavetable synthesis, 335–337, 464–469
Wavetable playback, 383, 384
White space, 58, 131, 168, 176
Windowing, 539–543
Windows, 67, 82, 89, 93, 134, 168, 169, 201
Wraparound, 177, 298, 301